Instructor's Edition

DESTINOS

SECOND EDITION OF THE ALTERNATE EDITION

A Telecourse Designed by

Bill VanPatten
University of Illinois at Chicago

Martha Alford Marks

Richard V. Teschner
University of Texas, El Paso

Thalia Dorwick
Coordinator of Print Material for The McGraw-Hill Companies, Inc.

Instructor's Edition Notes by

Rodney Bransdorfer
Central Washington University

Natalie Lefkowitz
Central Washington University

Boston   Burr Ridge, IL   Dubuque, IA   Madison, WI   New York   San Francisco   St. Louis
Bangkok   Bogotá   Caracas   Kuala Lumpur   Lisbon   London   Madrid   Mexico City
Milan   Montreal   New Delhi   Santiago   Seoul   Singapore   Sydney   Taipei   Toronto

McGraw-Hill Higher Education

A Division of The **McGraw-Hill** *Companies*

This is an book.

Destinos
Second Edition of the Alternate Edition

This book is printed on acid-free paper.

1 2 3 4 5 6 7 8 9 0   KPH KPH   0 9 8 7 6 5 4 3 2

ISBN 0-07-249708-4 (Student Edition)
ISBN 0-07-249717-3 (Instructor's Edition)

Editor-in-chief: Thalia Dorwick
Publisher: William R. Glass
Director of development: Scott Tinetti
Senior marketing manager: Nick Agnew
Senior project manager: Christina Gimlin
Senior production supervisor: Pam Augspurger
Designer: Matthew Baldwin
Cover designer: Matthew Baldwin
Illustrators: Lori Heckelman and Alan Eitzen
Senior photo research coordinator: Nora Agbayani
Editorial assistant: Fionnuala McEvoy
Compositor: TechBooks
Printer: Quebecor, Kingsport Hawkins
Typeface: 10/12 Garamond

The Library of Congress catalogues an earlier edition of this work in the following manner:

Van Patten, Bill.
   Destinos: An Introduction to Spanish / Bill VanPatten, Martha Alford Marks, Richard V. Teschner.
      p. cm.
   Includes index.
   -ISBN 0-07-002069-8
   1. Spanish language—Textbooks for foreign speakers—English.   I. Marks, Martha.
II. Teschner, Richard V.   III. Title.
PC4128.V36   1991   91-32511
468.2'421—dc20   CIP

Grateful acknowledgment is made for use of the following:

Realia: *Page 169* © Librerías Fausto; *209* © Diario las Américas; *220* © Quino/Quipos; *229* © *Casas y Jardines,* Editorial Contémpora; *281* Reprinted with permission of Gary G. Wiesman, M.D., F.A.C.S.

All photographs except those listed on page A58 are supplied courtesy of Olivia Tappan and Creative Television Associates (Boston).
(Continued on page A58)

HIGHLIGHTS OF THE VOCABULARY AND GRAMMAR TOPICS IN THE TEXTBOOK AND WORKBOOK/STUDY GUIDES

Note: Grammar topics are grouped by unit, not by the order of their introduction. Not all topics are included here.

	Vocabulario	*Gramática*
Lecciones 1–2 *pages 4–21*	cognates; family members	**ser**; articles and gender; possession

UN VIAJE A SEVILLA (ESPAÑA)
page 23

Lecciones 3–6 *pages 24–25*	numbers (0–21); academic subjects; animals; days of the week; telling time	**hay**; **estar**; **ir**; present tense (regular verbs); subject pronouns; personal **a**; interrogatives; adjective agreement

UN VIAJE A MADRID (ESPAÑA)
page 65

Lecciones 7–11 *pages 66–112*	clothing; numbers (21–99); interrogatives; months; seasons; colors; descriptive adjectives	**saber**; **conocer**; present tense (irregular verbs, stem-changing verbs); reflexive pronouns; more on possession and adjectives; demonstratives; **ser** and **estar**

UN VIAJE A LA ARGENTINA
page 113

Lecciones 12–18 *pages 114–179*	numbers (100–1000); food groups; writing and written materials	preterite tense; object pronouns; more on using adjectives; verbs used reflexively and nonreflexively; **gustar** and verbs like it

---

Note: Because of the repeating lesson structure in the textbook, only certain sections of the lessons are listed in the Contents. This is the repeating lesson structure for all except review lessons:

Preparación	**Un poco de gramática**
¿Tienes buena memoria?	**Lectura cultural**
Vocabulario del tema	**Vocabulario**

Additional **Notas culturales** appear as appropriate.

Contents

Contents   **vii**

Vocabulario del tema	Un poco de gramática	Nota cultural/ Lectura cultural

Contents

Vocabulario del tema	Un poco de gramática	Nota cultural/ Lectura cultural

UN VIAJE A MÉXICO: LA CAPITAL

Contents

Vocabulario del tema	Un poco de gramática

Preface

Destinos: What Is It?

An old man has retired to his hacienda outside a small town close to Mexico City. With the wealth he has accumulated since leaving Spain at the end of its bloody Civil War, he is restoring the hacienda to its original sixteenth-century splendor. But his health has begun to fail, and now he hopes to live out the remainder of his years peacefully, in the tranquility of the Mexican countryside.

Then a letter arrives—a letter in which a woman from Spain makes claims about the old man's past. Gathering his family around him, he reveals a secret, then announces that he must send someone to Spain to speak with the writer of the letter.

Enter Raquel Rodríguez, an attorney from Los Angeles, who accepts the task of locating the letter writer and investigating her claims. What *is* the old man's secret? And what will Raquel discover on her unforgettable journey?

If all this sounds like a Friday night television show, you are only half right! This story is the premise for *Destinos*. Consisting of fifty-two half-hour video episodes, *Destinos* is a television and video course that allows beginning language learners to hear Spanish and experience its cultural diversity while following a compelling story full of human emotions, the surprises that real life often offers, and the force of the human spirit.

Understanding Spanish

Adapting the format of the highly popular Hispanic *telenovela* (soap opera), *Destinos* is innovative in adopting a comprehension-based approach for the teaching of Spanish. The series, of course, allows students to develop speaking and writing skills, and abundant reading materials are also provided. But *Destinos* is especially suited to help learners develop good *listening comprehension skills*.

In each episode there are three kinds of Spanish. Two of them are specifically designed to be comprehensible to the beginner: the Spanish spoken by an off-screen narrator and that spoken by Raquel Rodríguez as she reviews the major highlights at the end of each episode. The purpose of this type of Spanish is to provide appropriate language for acquisition, that is, language that students can understand and from which they can learn.

In addition to this purposefully comprehensible Spanish, each episode also contains segments of more rapid conversational Spanish, that is, when the characters are speaking to each other. In most cases, actions and context will allow student viewers to follow this type of Spanish. Students are encouraged to follow along, get the general idea, and let comprehension develop over time. They are not asked to study and learn this type of Spanish, although they will often "pick up" words and phrases repeated in conversation (or emphasized in particular scenes). After watching the whole series, students should have achieved a level of comprehension far beyond that of most beginning students.

Another important feature of the Spanish of *Destinos* is captured in the review segments that Raquel usually provides toward the end of each show. Raquel's review is accompanied by sentences on-screen that allow students to see how major grammatical features work. Thus, students not only *hear* Spanish that they can understand: they also *see* Spanish that they can understand, which further promotes language learning.

The Goals of *Destinos*

If, in addition to watching the series, the student uses the Textbook along with the Workbook/Study Guides and the audio program, he or she can expect to accomplish a great deal with *Destinos*.

- By the end of one year a student-viewer should be able to understand most Spanish spoken slower than normal pace, understand some Spanish spoken at normal pace, and develop skills and coping strategies for filling in the gaps of imperfect comprehension.
- In terms of speaking, students should be able to ask and answer questions on a variety of everyday topics, describe people and places, narrate recurring (present) events, and achieve some ability in narrating past events.

- Students should be able to perform many daily routines, such as making phone calls, greeting and departing, and so on.
- Students should be able to read almost any simple material, and will have gained some experience in reading materials written for the native-speaking reader.
- The writing skills that students develop will often be the same as the speaking skills, that is, the ability to describe and narrate in the present, and to some extent in the past, and so on.

In addition to gaining these language skills, students who use the *Destinos* materials will gain a wealth of cultural knowledge and awareness about the areas of the world in which Spanish is spoken.

What's New in the Second Edition of *Destinos*?

Destinos was originally developed both to serve students enrolled in distance learning courses and those in the standard classroom environment.

In 1997, McGraw-Hill published *Destinos: Alternate Edition*, which kept the framework and content of the First Edition but added interactive materials throughout that were best suited for classroom instruction. The Second Edition of *Destinos: Alternate Edition* maintains that classroom-friendly interaction but has expanded upon it, including even more student interaction.

The Second Edition also contains:

- a new Listening Comprehension CD program (packaged free with every new copy of the Textbook) that contains over *seven hours* of audio
- new lesson-ending **Intercambio** activities that provide students the opportunity to talk about the storyline and themselves in pairs and small groups
- new **Lectura cultural** features, providing extended reading passages and follow-up questions
- newly colorized drawings that make the Textbook activities more engaging and appealing

- new **Para escribir** setup activities that students will then complete in the Workbook/Study Guides

In addition, the Second Edition of *Destinos* is accompanied by an unparalleled supplements package with a strong focus on multimedia, in particular:

- a new interactive CD-ROM that contains work with the video storyline as well as vocabulary and grammar practice
- a new content-rich website with a wealth of resources for students and instructors alike.

The Student Textbook and Other Student Materials

THE TEXTBOOK

The Textbook that accompanies the *Destinos* series contains fifty-two lessons, each corresponding to one episode of the series. Episodes 6, 11, 18, 25, 26, 36, and 48–51 are review shows in which characters in the series take stock of what has happened up to that point. In these lessons in the Textbook, students review the story line and other material presented thus far.

With the exception of these review lessons and of Lesson 52 (atypical because it is the last in the series), a typical lesson in the Textbook is divided into the following main sections: **Preparación**, **¿Tienes buena memoria?**, **Vocabulario del tema**, **Un poco de gramática**, and the new **Intercambio** sections, as well as a chapter opener. Each of the main title sections is numbered to help instructors write class syllabi (**Preparación** is labeled 1, **¿Tienes buena memoria?** is labeled 2, and so on). In this way, instructors may refer to activities in these sections as 1B (*Actividad B* in **Preparación**), 3C (*Actividad C* in **Vocabulario del tema**), and so on.

On the following pages, you will find a Visual Tour of *Destinos* that will help you to understand the features of the main sections of the Textbook.

Visual Tour of *Destinos*

Each lesson begins with an image from the video that captures a key moment from that episode. The lesson-opening pages also contain **Objetivos**, which outline the vocabulary, grammar, and cultural themes of the lesson. A CD-ROM icon also indicates that students can further practice material from this lesson in an interactive format.

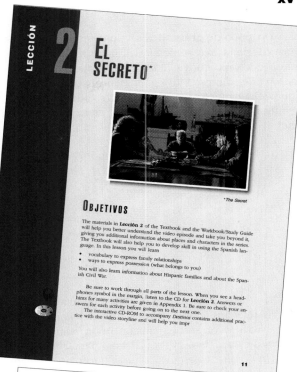

The purpose of **Preparación** is to refresh students' memory about where the story left off in the last episode and to preview story elements and conversations from the upcoming episode. In this section, students make guesses about what might happen, listen to and read some of the conversations that they will see in the upcoming episode, and generally prepare themselves for watching it.

In **¿Tienes buena memoria?** students are "tested" on what they understand about events and characters from the current episode, and they are encouraged to think about those characters and the situations in which they find themselves. For those using *Destinos* in a classroom setting, the activities in this section may serve as a springboard for continued discussion about the story and characters.

Vocabulario del tema sections usually review and offer opportunities for using vocabulary presented during the episode. At times, these sections also present new vocabulary that ties in with some situation in which the characters are involved. As students work through these sections, they first use the vocabulary to refer to the episode or other people, and they work toward using the vocabulary to talk about themselves and their own lives.

Un poco de gramática sections preview a grammatical point that students will learn more about in the Workbook/Study Guides. Each preview usually offers a brief glimpse into a grammatical point, followed immediately by an activity in which students are generally not asked to reproduce the grammatical point but instead to see and understand it in context.

Each lesson continues with a **Lectura cultural** that is relevant to the current episode. This is usually a review of and expansion upon some aspect of culture (art, history, social commentary, and so on). In some cases new cultural information is introduced that was not featured in the episode.

Everyday cultural information (that is, habits and customs) is featured in briefer **Notas culturales** that appear as needed in each lesson.

New to the Second Edition are **Intercambio** sections, which provide students with the opportunity to complete a lesson-ending task in pairs or small groups. Many **Intercambio** activities are video-based, allowing students to speculate on the characters or storyline or to put themselves in situations similar to those presented in the episode.

Icons

 The headphones icon indicates that material for the corresponding section of the Textbook can be found on the Listening Comprehension CD program that is packaged free with each new copy of the text.

 This icon indicates work to be done in pairs or small groups.

 The CD-ROM icon reminds students that the CD-ROM to accompany *Destinos* provides more practice with the video episode and with the Spanish language.

The following materials appear at the end of the Textbook:

- an answer section for students to check their answers to many textbook activities (Appendix 1)
- charts featuring the Spanish verb system (Appendix 2)
- a complete Spanish-English end vocabulary
- a brief reference index of the major characters in the series
- an index of the content of the Textbook.

THE WORKBOOK/STUDY GUIDES

There are two Workbook/Study Guides for students in the *Destinos* program: Workbook I (Lessons 1–26) and II (Lessons 27–52).

- Most lessons begin with a short reading or listening selection called **Más allá del episodio**. This contains information about characters and situations that goes beyond what appears in the episodes; for example, why some characters act the way they do. In some cases, background information about the story line is presented; for example, how a particular character came to live in a particular place or what was going on at the time another character did something.
- **Vocabulario del tema** provides additional writing and listening practice with the vocabulary theme presented in the Textbook. Many of the audio portions used to practice the vocabulary are taken directly from the video episodes.
- In many lessons **Conversaciones** sections allow students to listen to and work with everyday con-

versational tools—for example, how to answer the phone, how to indicate that you don't understand, how to express gratitude, and so on.

- In **Gramática** the Workbook/Study Guides expand on the grammatical and structural features of Spanish previewed in the Textbook, allowing for more in-depth study of Spanish.
- Cognate study (**¡Aumenta tu vocabulario!**) and pronunciation sections (**Pronunciación**) are included in Workbook/Study Guide I. Workbook/Study Guide II features sections on reading authentic materials, called **¡A leer!**, and review sections called **Repaso**.
- Both Workbook/Study Guides have composition sections called **Para escribir**.
- Students may monitor their progress by taking a Self-Test at the end of most lessons.

Some lessons contain **Notas culturales**, as needed, and most lessons end with a **Vocabulario** list of additional active vocabulary that supplements that of the Textbook.

As happens in the Textbook, the Workbook/Study Guide lessons that correspond to review episodes do not follow this repeating format. Rather, they consist of summary and review sections on grammar structures and of review activities that focus on vocabulary, knowledge of the story line, and self-expression.

Students will find the following materials at the end of the Workbook/Study Guides:

- an answer section for students to check their answers to many Workbook/Study Guide activities (Appendix 1)
- charts featuring the Spanish verb system (Appendix 2)
- an index of the content of the Workbook/Study Guides, integrated with that of the Textbook.

A COMMENT ABOUT METHODOLOGY

Instructors and students alike will want to take special note of the input-to-output nature of the Textbook and Workbook/Study Guide materials. Students see and hear language used before being asked to produce it. The **Preparación** and **¿Tienes buena memoria?** sections use written and spoken language that students respond to first by checking, marking true/false, selecting the best guess, supplying the name of a character, and so on. Only later in the course are they explicitly asked to talk or write about the episodes and characters in these sections. In the sections that deal with vocabulary and grammar, students first encounter input activities, ones in which the target item is seen or heard in a simple context. After several input activities, they engage in more productive use of the items.

Other Components of the Series

The following materials accompany the television series, student Textbook, and Workbook/Study Guides:

For Students:

- a new Listening Comprehension CD program that contains over *seven hours* of audio material designed to be used with the Textbook; this audio CD program is packaged *free* with every new book purchased
- an audiocassette or audio CD laboratory program (Part I: Lessons 1–26; Part II: Lessons 27–52) designed to be used with the Textbook and Workbook/Study Guides
- an optional software program (for IBM and Macintosh) by John Underwood (Western Washington University), featuring some comprehension, vocabulary, and grammar activities that supplement those in the Textbook and Workbook/Study Guides
- an interactive CD-ROM that offers creative practice with the plot of the video series, vocabulary, grammar, culture, as well as other resources designed to help students improve their comprehension of the series and their Spanish language skills
- a text-specific website that contains a host of resources for students, including episode summaries, practice quizzes, cultural activities and links, and much more
- professional supplements (medical, legal, education, social services, business, tourism) by Ralph Kite and Deni Heyck (Loyola University of Chicago), with accompanying cassette programs, for those wishing to learn Spanish for use in professional settings
- Student Viewer Handbooks I (Lessons 1–26) and II (Lessons 27–52), appropriate for using *Destinos* as a supplement only, rather than as a full Spanish course.

For Faculty:

- an Instructor's Edition, created by Rodney Bransdorfer and Natalie Lefkowitz (both of Central Washington University), with on-page suggestions for stimulating classroom discussion, using existing activities in interactive formats, and checking for comprehension
- a Faculty Guide that offers, among other things, general suggestions for using the series, lesson-by-lesson suggestions and supplementary activities, additional Self-Tests, and sample examinations
- a Testing Program that offers a variety of testing vehicles developed by instructors across the country who use *Destinos* (also available in electronic format)
- a videoscript (of the series episodes) and an audioscript (of the materials in the audio program)
- video modules (with an accompanying Instructor's Guide) that highlight functional language, vocabulary presentations, and cultural information. (These may be used independently of the series.)
- a music CD that contains all of the series music created specifically for *Destinos*
- a text-specific website that contains a host of resources for instructors, including episode summaries, a character picture file, portions of the Faculty Guide, links to professional resources, and much more

Additional materials may become available throughout the life of the series.

How to Use *Destinos*

In a traditional classroom setting *Destinos* may be used in a number of ways:

- The Textbook and video episodes may both be used in the class. For example, the **Preparación** section could be an activity for the whole class, after which the class could view the episode together. On subsequent days the rest of the Textbook could be completed in class. Most of the material in the Workbook/Study Guides could be assigned for homework, with follow-up discussions and selected activities done in class.
- The Textbook only could be used in class. Students could view the episodes at home, in the media center, or in the language laboratory.
- The First Edition of *Destinos* is especially appropriate as a complete telecourse for the distance ("at-home") learner. Students watch each episode and complete all sections of the Textbook and Workbook/Study Guide. The Second Edition of the Alternate Edition of *Destinos* is better suited to the regular classroom environment.

In all cases it is recommended that students watch each episode from beginning to end, without interruption. Students can replay and review selected segments (for pedagogical purposes, for enjoyment, and so on) once they are familiar with the content of an episode. The Faculty Guide provides more detailed suggestions for using the *Destinos* materials.

Where Else Can *Destinos* Be Used?

The *Destinos* materials can also be used:

- as a complete college-credit television course
- as the foundation for a classroom-based beginning Spanish course at the college level
- as an offering for adult or continuing education students
- as the foundation for a classroom-based first- and second-year Spanish course at the high-school level
- as a supplement to beginning, intermediate, or advanced courses, at all levels of instruction
- as a resource for informal learning
- as training materials for Spanish-language classes in business and industry
- as an important addition to library video collections.

Acknowledgments

A project of this magnitude has a life of its own. So many people have helped with the television series and print materials that it is impossible to acknowledge the work and contributions of all of them in detail. Here are some of the highlights.

Members of the Advisory Board, The Annenberg/CPB Project and WGBH

Bill VanPatten
Series Designer, Professor of Spanish and Second Language Acquisition, University of Illinois at Chicago

Thalia Dorwick
Publisher, Foreign Languages and ESOL
The McGraw-Hill Companies, Inc.

Trisha R. Dvorak
Continuing Education Specialist, University of Washington

Rose Lee Hayden
Senior Vice President, Institute for Corporate and Government Strategy

Martha Alford Marks
Language Proficiency Testing Expert

Douglas M. Morgenstern
Senior Lecturer in Spanish, MIT and Harvard University Extension School

Eduardo Alberto Peniche
Associate Professor of Foreign Languages, Central Virginia Community College

Joy Renjilian-Burgy
Coordinator of Language and Literature Instruction, Wellesley College

Harry L. Rosser
Professor of Spanish
Boston College

Carmen Salazar
Chairperson, Department of Foreign Languages
Los Angeles Valley College

Richard V. Teschner
Professor of Spanish
University of Texas at El Paso

Thomas C. Wilson
Director, Open University of South Florida

Cultural and Linguistic Consultants, The Annenberg/CPB Project and WGBH

Alejandro Benes
Series Executive Editor

Efraín Barradas
Associate Professor of Spanish
University of Massachusetts

Teresa Almendros Cook
Associate Professor of Spanish
Piedmont Virginia Community College

Ester Gimbernat de González
Associate Professor of Hispanic Studies
University of Northern Colorado

Samuel Saldívar
Professor of Spanish
United States Military Academy

Cultural and Linguistic Consultants, The McGraw-Hill Companies, Inc.

Eduardo Cabrera

Laura Chastain

María José Ruiz Morcillo

Instructors

Catalina Aguilar, Fort Lewis College

Warren Ashby, Bethune-Cookman College

Patrick Brady, Tidewater Community College

Daniel Briere, University of Indianapolis

Marichu Bucelli, George Mason University

Racquel Caytan, Rice University

Linda Fader, Holy Family College

María Goddard, Xavier University

Lola Herez-Moya, Monterey Peninsula College

Christina Lambert, County College of Morris

Robin Martínez, Colorado State University

Norma River, Millersville University

Stewart Siegelman, County College of Morris

Miguel Verano, United States Air Force Academy

Rita Wirkala, Bellevue Community College

The authors of *Destinos* would also like to extend special thanks to the following individuals and organizations:

- The Annenberg/CPB Project (Washington, D.C.), especially to Lin Foa and Lynn Smith, for financial and creative support of the television series on which this Textbook is based.
- WGBH Boston and to Michele Korf, Beth Kirsch, and Betsy Ryles, for their guidance and support at different stages of the project's development, and especially to Michele, for always being there.
- The staff at Creative Television Associates (Boston), especially Fred Barzyk, Al Potter, Olivia Tappan, and Erin Delaney, as well as the film and sound editors (Ricardo Camacho, Christian Picker, Miguel Picker, and Jean Boucicaut), for the role they all played in bringing the series to you; special thanks to Olivia, for being our on-location photographer, and to Erin, for providing living proof that an input-based approach really does work!
- The many instructors who reviewed the original edition and provided enlightening feedback that helped to shape the Second Edition.
- Rodney Bransdorfer and Natalie Lefkowitz (both of Central Washington University), for their work on the Instructor's Edition.
- Trisha R. Dvorak, Alex Binkowski, Michèle Sarner, Ralph Kite, and María José Ruiz Morcillo, for their help with various aspects of the creation of the First Edition.
- The development, editorial, and production staff at McGraw-Hill, especially William Glass, Scott Tinetti, Christina Gimlin, Matthew Baldwin, and Diane Renda.

Last but not least, a very special thank you to Liliana Abud ("Raquel"), whose professional skill as an actress and generosity as a human being helped to keep us going during long working days on the set and at the computer.

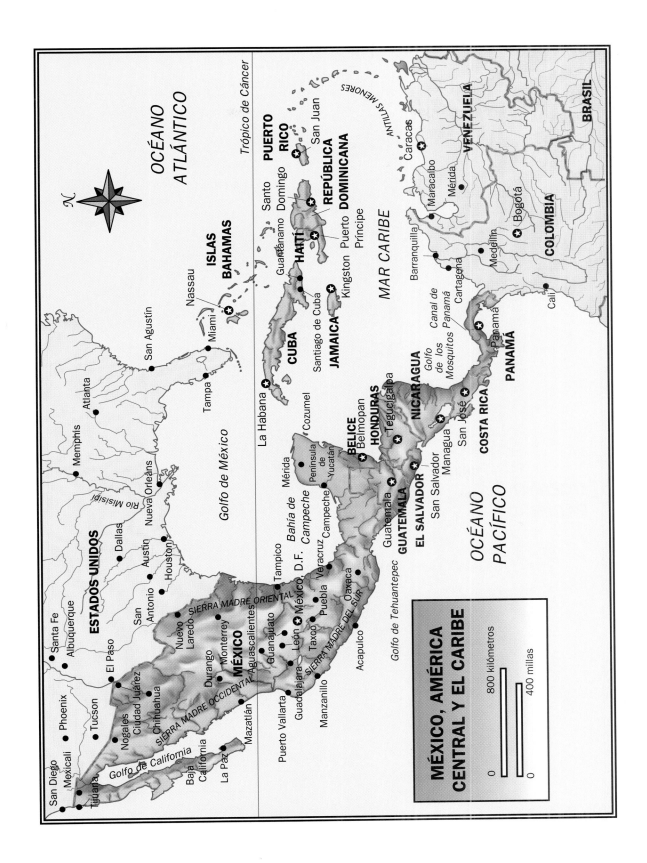

MÉXICO, AMÉRICA
CENTRAL Y EL CARIBE

MAR CARIBE

OCÉANO ATLÁNTICO

Maracaibo
Barranquilla
Caracas
PANAMÁ
VENEZUELA
GUYANA
Medellín
Georgetown
Paramaribo
Panamá
Georgetown
Bogotá
SURINAME
Cayena
Cali
COLOMBIA
GUYANA FRANCESA
Río Orinoco
Quito
Ecuador
ECUADOR
Río Amazonas
Belém
Guayaquil
Manaus
PERÚ
CORDILLERA DE LOS ANDES
BRASIL
Recife
Cuzco
Lima
La Paz
Arequipa
Brasília
BOLIVIA
Sucre
Antofagasta
PARAGUAY
Río de Janeiro
CHILE
Asunción
Trópico de Capricornio
San Miguel de Tucumán
São Paulo
OCÉANO PACÍFICO
La Serena
OCÉANO ATLÁNTICO
Córdoba
Rosario
Valparaíso
URUGUAY
Santiago
ARGENTINA
N
Concepción
Buenos Aires
Montevideo
Río de la Plata
Bahía Blanca
Puerto Montt
Bariloche
Chiloé

Islas Malvinas
Estrecho de Magallanes
Punta Arenas
Tierra del Fuego
Cabo de Hornos

AMÉRICA DEL SUR

0   1500 kilómetros

0   1000 millas

xxii

E S P A Ñ A

200 kilómetros

100 millas

0

0

FRANCIA

ANDORRA

Golfo de León

Costa Brava

CATALUÑA

Barcelona

Lérida

Tarragona

Castellón

Menorca

Mallorca

Palma

ISLAS BALEARES

Ibiza

Formentera

MAR MEDITERRÁNEO

ISLAS CANARIAS

Lanzarote

Fuerte-
ventura

Santa Cruz
de Tenerife

Las Palmas

Las Palmas
de Gran
Canaria

Tenerife

La
Palma

Gomera

Hierro

200 kilómetros

100 millas

0

0

MAR CANTÁBRICO

*Bahía de
Vizcaya*

San Sebastián

Santander

CANTABRIA

LOS PIRINEOS

Pamplona

NAVARRA

Bilbao

PAÍS
VASCO

Logroño

LA RIOJA

Zaragoza

Río Ebro

ARAGÓN

Valencia

COMUNIDAD
VALENCIANA

Alicante

Costa Blanca

Cartagena

Orán

ASTURIAS

Oviedo

Santiago de
Compostela

La Coruña

GALICIA

Vigo

Burgos

CASTILLA-LEÓN

León

Valladolid

Zamora

Salamanca

E S P A Ñ A

Río Duero

Segovia

Ávila

El Escorial

SIERRA DE GUADARRAMA

Guadalajara

MADRID

Madrid

Toledo

CASTILLA-
LA MANCHA

Ciudad Real

Albacete

Almadén

SIERRA MORENA

Linares

Jaén

MURCIA

Murcia

Lorca

Almería

Granada

SIERRA NEVADA

Málaga

Costa del Sol

Gibraltar (R.U.)

Ceuta (Esp.)

ANDALUCÍA

Río Guadalquivir

Córdoba

Jerez de la Frontera

Cádiz

Sevilla

Huelva

*Golfo de
Cádiz*

Tánger

EXTREMADURA

Cáceres

Mérida

Badajoz

PORTUGAL

Río Tajo

Río Guadiana

Lisboa

Oporto

OCÉANO
ATLÁNTICO

N

DESTINOS

Episodes 1–26

The story begins at La Gavia, a historic estate near Toluca, Mexico . . .

Entremeses* 1

Here are some phrases and expressions you can use to greet your classmates and to exchange information with them.

SALUDOS Y DESPEDIDAS

Greetings and Leave-takings

Hola.	Hello.
Buenos días.	Good morning.
Buenas tardes.	Good afternoon (*used until 8:00 or 9:00 P.M.*).
Buenas noches.	Good evening (*used after 9:00 P.M.*).
¿Cómo estás?	How are you?
¿Qué tal? **¿Cómo te va?**	How's it going?
Muy bien, gracias. ¿Y tú?	Very well, thanks. And you?
Estoy bien, gracias.	I'm well, thank you.
Adiós.	Good-bye.
Hasta mañana.	See you tomorrow.
Nos vemos.	We'll be seeing each other.

PRESENTACIONES

Introductions

¿Cómo te llamas?	What's your name?
Me llamo...	My name is . . . (*lit.* I call myself)
Mi nombre es...	My name is . . .
Soy...	I'm . . .
Y tú, ¿cómo te llamas?	And you, what's your name?
Mucho gusto.	It's a pleasure to meet you.
¿De dóndes eres?	Where are you from?
(Soy) De...	(I'm) From . . .

*Interludes

Suggestions:
- Go over the expressions listed and have students pronounce them after you. Practice pronunciation with choral and individual repetition.
- Model a few exchanges with individual students, varying your vocabulary to include the different ways of greeting and leave-taking. You may want to shake hands as most people would in Spanish-speaking countries. To one student, say *Hola. ¿Cómo estás?* (If student appears unsure of how to respond, prompt by whispering *Muy bien, gracias, ¿y tú?*) *Estoy bien, gracias. Adiós.* Move on to another student and repeat the exchange, opening with *Buenos días, Buenas tardes,* or *Buenas noches* and varying the other possible expressions during the exchange.

Note: Informal (*tú*) speech is used here and throughout the text. You may wish to tell students that they will learn other, more formal ways to greet and say good-bye to people at a later time.

Suggestion: Go over the expressions listed and have students pronounce them after you. Practice pronunciation with choral and individual repetition.

¡OJO! Students frequently confuse *Me llamo* with *Mi nombre es* and say «*Me llamo es*». Call attention to the literal translation of *Me llamo* (*I call myself*) and make sure they understand that *llamo* does not mean *name*.

Suggestion: Model a few exchanges with individual students, shaking hands and varying your vocabulary to include the different ways of introducing yourself. To one student, say *Me llamo profesor(a) _____. ¿Cómo te llamas?* (If student appears

2

Actividad A. ¡Hola!

Fill in each blank logically with a phrase from the options given.

1. —Hola. ¿Cómo estás?
    —_____ ¿Y tú?
    a. ¿Cómo te llamas?   b. Me llamo Elena.   c. Muy bien, gracias.

2. —¿Cómo te llamas?
    —_____ ¿Y tú?
    a. Soy Jorge.   b. Hasta mañana.   c. Hola. ¿Cómo estás?

3. —Adiós. Buenas tardes.
    —_____
    a. Me llamo José.   b. Hasta mañana.   c. Hola. ¿Cómo estás?

4. —Hola. Me llamo Patricia. ¿Y tú?
    —_____ Mucho gusto.
    a. Nos vemos.   b. Soy Carlos.   c. Estoy bien.

5. —Hola. Buenos días. ¿Cómo estás?
    —_____ ¿Y tú?
    a. Estoy bien, gracias.   b. Adiós. Hasta mañana.   c. Me llamo Juan.

Actividad B. Encuentros (*Meetings*)

Rearrange the lines in each group to create a logical dialogue. Put the lines in numerical order, beginning with number 1.

A. _____ ¿Cómo estás, Esteban?
    _____ Estoy bien, gracias.
    _____ Hola. Soy Elena. ¿Y tú?
    _____ Mucho gusto. Me llamo Esteban.
    _____ Muy bien, gracias. ¿Y tú?

B. _____ Mi nombre es Pablo.
    _____ ¿Cómo te llamas tú?
    _____ Muy bien, gracias.
    _____ Hola. ¿Cómo te llamas?
    _____ ¿Cómo estás, Julia?
    _____ Me llamo Julia.

Actividad C. Más (*More*) encuentros

Paso (*Step*) 1

Now that you are familiar with several expressions used to introduce yourself and meet others, get up and circulate through the classroom and meet as many people as you can. You should greet them first and say good-bye when you have finished speaking. Be sure to write down their names.

Paso 2

Now report to the class the names of the people you just met. Use the following phrases.

Se llama…	His/Her name is . . . (*lit.* He/She calls him/herself . . .)
Su nombre es…	His/Her name is . . .

Left margin notes:

unsure of how to respond, offer possibilities: *¿Te llamas Roberto, Juan, Jaime...?*) *Ah, te llamas _____. Mucho gusto* (shake hands). *Soy de _____. ¿De dónde eres?* (Again, if student appears unsure of how to respond, offer possibilities: *¿Eres de _____?*) *Ah, de _____. Una ciudad muy bonita.* Then move on to another student and repeat the exchange, but start with *Mi nombre es* or *Soy.*

Act. A, Suggestion: If you have already practiced the pronunciation of the expressions, have students work in pairs. Partners take turns reading aloud the first part of the exchange and responding with the appropriate option.

Act. A, Follow-up: Check answers by calling on student pairs to present the exchanges aloud for the class. If they complete the exchange correctly, say: *Muy bien.* If not, say: *No es cierto.* Have them try again, saying: *No es* a (b/c), *es* b (a/c). *Repitan, por favor.*

Act. B, Suggestion: Give students about 3 minutes to complete the activity individually or in pairs. Then go over the answers as whole class.

Act. C, Paso 1, Suggestion: Circulate with your students, introducing yourself, and providing a model for them to emulate.

Act. B, Follow-up: Call on pairs or have volunteers present the dialogues aloud to the class.

Act. C, Optional: *El juego de nombres.* Emphasize before Part 1 that the object is to *memorizar los nombres.* You can explain each step in Spanish using mime, gestures, and lots of repetition. *Part 1:* Students form a circle with their chairs. One student throws a small soft ball or throw toy to another student. The person who catches the ball simply calls out his/her own name. He or she then throws the ball to another person who calls out his/her own name. Continue for 5–10 minutes until everyone has caught the ball several times. *Part 2:* One student says the name of another student and throws the ball to him/her. That person names another student and throws the ball to him/her. Continue for 5–10 minutes until everyone has caught the ball several times. *Follow-up:* Call on individual students to see how many names they can remember around the circle. If they forget a name, have them ask: *¿Cómo te llamas?*

1

LA CARTA*

Note: In future episodes, you will be able to ask simple guiding questions in Spanish about the photos before viewing the video. As this is the first episode, no questions in Spanish are given here.

The Letter

OBJETIVOS

The materials in **Lección 1** of the Textbook and the Workbook/Study Guide will help you better understand the video episode and take you beyond it, giving you additional information about places and characters in the series. The Textbook will also help you to develop skill in using the Spanish language. In this lesson you will learn

- about cognates (words that look alike in English and Spanish and mean the same thing)
- about some simple Spanish verb forms

Be sure to work through all parts of the lesson. When you see a headphones symbol in the margin, listen to the CD for **Lección 1**. Answers or hints for many activities are given in Appendix 1. Be sure to check your answers for each activity before going on to the next one.

The interactive CD-ROM to accompany *Destinos* contains additional practice with the video storyline and will help you improve your skills in Spanish.

Preliminary: See Faculty Guide for additional information and activities for this lesson.

- **Variation:** For activities marked with the headphones icon, you may wish to read from the Audioscript instead of playing the CD.
- **Suggestion:** Make sure students are familiar with the activities before you read from the Audioscript or play the CD.

BEFORE VIEWING . . .

Be sure to complete the preview section (called **Preparación**) in **Lección 1** before viewing **Episodio 1** (the video segment that corresponds to **Lección 1**).

1

PREPARACIÓN

Suggestions:

- For the first episode, you may wish to do the *Preparación* section in class, walking students through the activities, emphasizing that this section is designed to get them thinking about what they will see and hear in the upcoming episode. As a prediction exercise, it has no (in)correct answers, although the information in the photos should help the students make logical choices. Make sure that students read the entire introduction to the section before beginning the activities.
- Before watching the video, go over the vocabulary list at the end of the chapter and have students pronounce the words after you.
- Assign *Preparación* activities as homework and then go over them quickly in class before viewing the video.

Act. A, Variation: To acclimate the students to hearing Spanish, ask the question in Spanish as they follow the text in English: *¿Dónde creen que la acción del primer episodio pasará?* Then offer all the options in Spanish before repeating them, one at a time: *¿Pasará en los EEUU, en la Argentina, en México o en España? Número uno, en los EEUU. ¿Sí o no? Número dos, en la Argentina,* etc.

You are about to watch **Episodio 1** from *Destinos*. At times you will hear narration in English that will explain things and help you follow along, and you will also hear a lot of Spanish. Even though you probably have never studied Spanish before, you will be able to understand much of what you hear because several kinds of Spanish are used. There is

- Spanish spoken directly to you by the narrator, which you will learn to understand with relative ease
- Spanish spoken directly to you by a special character, who will review the highlights of the video episode for you at the end of each show
- Spanish spoken by the characters to one another, which at first will be more difficult for you to understand.

As you watch the video episodes, especially at the beginning of the series, you should focus in particular on the Spanish spoken to you by the narrator and the special character. Just relax and listen, and you'll be surprised by how much you can understand. As for the Spanish spoken by the characters to each other, just try to get the gist (general idea) of it. As you continue with the series, you will find yourself understanding more and more of that type of Spanish.

Throughout the Textbook, the **Preparación** section is intended to start you thinking about the program and speculating about what may happen in the next video episode. So now, even before you watch the first episode, take a few moments to speculate about what it may be about. Look at the cover of this Textbook, at the opening page of the main text (on page 1), and at the **Lección 1** opening page (with its titles and visual material). Think about what the series title, *Destinos*, might mean. If you guessed either *destinies* or *destinations*, you were right. The title of the series is a play on both words. Now complete the following activities.

Actividad A.

Where do you think the first episode of *Destinos* will take place?

1. _____ in the United States
2. _____ in Argentina
3. _____ in Mexico
4. _____ in Spain

Actividad B.

What do you think the principal setting will be?

1. _____ a restaurant
2. _____ a hacienda (an estate)
3. _____ a university campus
4. _____ a hotel

Actividad C.

What do you think will set the story in motion?

1. _____ a letter
2. _____ a telephone call
3. _____ a telegram
4. _____ a crime

When you have finished watching **Episodio 1,** come back and see how accurate your first guesses were. Read through the activities again at that time and change your answers if you wish. Then check your answers in Appendix 1.

. . . AFTER VIEWING

2

¿TIENES BUENA MEMORIA?

In this repeating section of the Textbook you will review important information from the episode that you have just watched.

Actividad A. ¿Quiénes son? (*Who are they?*)

Now that you have watched **Episodio 1** of *Destinos,* look at the following photos and match them with the brief descriptions. As you do this activity, you will be reading brief, relatively easy sentences in Spanish. You should guess at the meaning of words you don't immediately understand.

1. _____ Raquel es abogada. Vive (*She lives*) en Los Ángeles.
2. _____ Fernando es el paciente de Julio, el médico.
3. _____ Es una persona muy misteriosa.

a.   b.   c.

Act. B, Suggestions:
- Students will often work in pairs throughout the course. To add variety and help students get to know each other, assign different pairs as often as possible. For this activity, you may wish to have students change partners between *Paso 1* and *Paso 2*. Make sure to circulate during pair and group work, not only to evaluate student progress, but also to offer any help needed during the activity.
- Practice pronouncing the identifications before students begin the activity. Make sure they are not pronouncing the *h* in *hacienda, hijo,* and *hija*.
- Model the exchange in *Paso 2* before students begin.

Act. C, Answers:
1. b 2. b 3. a

Actividad B.   ¿Cómo se llaman? (*What are their names?*)
Paso 1

Take turns with a classmate asking and answering these questions about **Episodio 1.** When your partner answers, indicate "Sí, es cierto" (*Yes, that's right*) or "No, no es cierto (*No, that's not right*). Su nombre es...," as appropriate.

¿Cómo se llama...

1. el doctor de don Fernando?
2. el profesor de literatura (es hijo [*son*] de don Fernando)?
3. la hacienda de don Fernando?
4. la abogada de Los Ángeles?
5. la hija (*daughter*) que vive en la hacienda?
6. el hijo que vive en la hacienda?
7. el hijo que vive en Miami?

Paso 2

Working in pairs, play the role of a character from **Episodio 1.** See whether your partner can guess who you are.

> MODELO: TÚ: Soy el doctor de don Fernando.
> COMPAÑERO/A: Eres (*You are*) Julio. / Te llamas Julio.
>   TÚ: Sí, es cierto.

Actividad C.   ¡Un desafío! (*A challenge!*)
Paso 1

Raquel's story review at the end of **Episodio 1** contains a lot of information about the characters in *Destinos.* You will have the opportunity to hear and review this information again in upcoming episodes. For now, just focus on Raquel.

Listen again as Raquel describes herself. Then complete the sentences based on what you know about her.

1. _____ El nombre (*name*) completo de Raquel es
   a. Raquel Gómez.
   b. Raquel Rodríguez.

2. _____ Raquel es
   a. cubanoamericana.
   b. mexicoamericana.

3. _____ Raquel vive en
   a. Los Ángeles.
   b. Miami.

Paso 2
Check your answers by listening to the CD.

3

VOCABULARIO DEL TEMA

This repeating section of the Textbook generally focuses on families of words explicitly presented in the video episode. However, since the concept of cognates is so important for your success in working with the *Destinos* materials, it is the topic of this first **Vocabulario del tema** section.

Emphasis: Point out that cognates might not be identical in spelling and that pronunciation of the English and Spanish versions might be very different.

Los cognados

As you have already noticed from both the video episode and the Text-book, you can understand much of the Spanish language you have heard because there are many words that are similar in Spanish and English. These words, called *cognates,* look—and often sound—alike in both languages.

Sometimes cognates exist because one language has "borrowed" words from the other. English has acquired many words from Spanish, such as *patio, rodeo, canyon,* and so on. Likewise, Spanish has acquired words from English: **automóvil, computadora, radio,** . . .

Other cognates exist because English and Spanish are both Indo-European languages. You have already guessed the meaning of **destinos,** the Spanish cognate of English *destinies* or *destinations.* You will practice this type of guessing constantly as you work with the video and text materials for *Destinos.* This strategy involves *inferring* the meaning of words from context (the words that surround the "guess" word). Another useful strategy is to simply *skip* over words you do not understand.

Act., Suggestion: Assign as homework and then go over answers quickly in class.

Actividad. Más cognados

Some of the important words you have heard and used so far in **Lección 1** are cognates, and some are not. This activity will give you practice using both cognates and noncognate words.

Read the following sentences about **Episodio 1.** Then indicate which cat-egory the highlighted words belong to.

a. Es un lugar (*place*).
b. Es un concepto.
c. Es una cosa (*thing*).
d. Es una persona.

Act., Answers: 1. b 2. d 3. d 4. d 5. d 6. c 7. b

MODELO: La Gavia es **una hacienda.** →
a. **(una hacienda)** Es un lugar.

Act., Follow-up: Write a list of simple Spanish words on the board. Have students determine whether or not they are cognates. For example: *libro* (no), *clase* (sí), *profesor* (sí), *hijo* (no), *estudiante* (sí), *casa* (no), *universidad* (sí), *fotografía* (sí), *pequeño* (no), *histórico* (sí), *importante* (sí).

1. _____ La Gavia tiene **una historia** muy importante.
2. _____ Don Fernando es **el patriarca** de la familia Castillo Saavedra.
3. _____ Raquel es **abogada**.
4. _____ Raquel es **mujer**. Mercedes es **mujer** también.
5. _____ Don Fernando es **hombre**. Ramón es **hombre** también.
6. _____ Don Fernando tiene **una carta**.
7. _____ En la carta hay (*there is*) **un secreto**.

4

UN POCO DE GRAMÁTICA

This repeating section of the Textbook presents information about Spanish grammar in an easy-to-understand fashion that you can put to use immediately to talk about the video episode, yourself, and others.

Expressing *is* and *are*

In this lesson you have heard and seen the Spanish equivalents of English *is* and *are*: **es** and **son**. Here are some examples of their use in context.

Mi historia **es** muy importante para la familia Castillo.

Juan **es** profesor de literatura.

Dos personas en esta historia **son** importantes.

My story is very important for the Castillo family.

Juan is a literature professor.

Two people in this story are important.

Actividad. ¿Cómo son? (*What are they like?*)

Identify the following persons, places, and things in as many ways as you can, using **es** or **son** and the phrases below. Several answers are possible for each item. Be alert to **-s** endings, which often signal plurality (more than one) in Spanish, just as they do in English. The word **no** will make your answers negative.

MODELOS: Mi universidad (muy grande) → Mi universidad (no) **es** muy grande.

Mis clases (interesantes) → Mis clases (no) **son** interesantes.

Personas, cosas y lugares

1. mis padres (*parents*)
2. el profesor/la profesora de español
3. mi universidad
4. mis amigos (*friends*)
5. mis actores favoritos
6. mis clases
7. mi perro/gato (*dog/cat*)
8. mis políticos (*politicians*) favoritos
9. ¿ ?

Adjetivos

inteligente/inteligentes
muy grande/muy grandes
interesante/interesantes
joven/jóvenes (*young*)
especial/especiales
difícil/difíciles (*hard, difficult*)

liberal/liberales
conservador/conservadores
bilingüe/bilingües
amable/amables
imposible/imposibles de entender (*to understand*)

VOCABULARIO

This is a reference list of some words that appear frequently in **Lección 1** in the Textbook, and that are important for understanding and discussing the lesson. Be sure that you understand the meaning of most of them. Don't feel that you have to be able to use all of them right now. You will continue to work with them in upcoming lessons.

Las personas   (People)

la abogada	lawyer
el doctor	doctor
el hombre	man
la mujer	woman
el patriarca	patriarch, male head of the family

Los lugares   (Places)

la hacienda	estate, hacienda

Las cosas   (Things)

la carta	letter

Los conceptos   (Concepts)

la historia	story; history

Los verbos   (Verbs)

es	is
son	are
tiene	he/she has
vive	he/she lives

Las palabras adicionales (Additional Words)

¿quién?	who?
de	of; from
en	in
muy	very
no	no
para	for
sí	yes
también	also
y	and

Palabras del texto

Note: These words are used in headings in the Textbook and in the structure of the *Destinos* materials. Be sure that you understand their meaning.

la actividad	activity	**la lección**	lesson	**el vocabulario**	vocabulary
el desafío	challenge	**el modelo**	model	**buena**	a good memory
el episodio	episode	**el objetivo**	objective	** memoria**	
la gramática	grammar	**el paso**	step	**cierto/falso**	true/false
el idioma	(Spanish)	**la preparación**	preparation	**¿tienes... ?**	do you have . . . ?
** (español)**	language	**el tema**	theme, topic	**un poco de...**	a bit of . . .

2

EL SECRETO*

*The Secret

OBJETIVOS

The materials in **Lección 2** of the Textbook and the Workbook/Study Guide will help you better understand the video episode and take you beyond it, giving you additional information about places and characters in the series. The Textbook will also help you to develop skill in using the Spanish language. In this lesson you will learn

- vocabulary to express family relationships
- ways to express possession (what belongs to you)

You will also learn information about Hispanic families and about the Spanish Civil War.

Be sure to work through all parts of the lesson. When you see a head-phones symbol in the margin, listen to the CD for **Lección 2**. Answers or hints for many activities are given in Appendix 1. Be sure to check your answers for each activity before going on to the next one.

The interactive CD-ROM to accompany *Destinos* contains additional practice with the video storyline and will help you improve your skills in Spanish.

BEFORE VIEWING . . .

Be sure to complete the preview section (called **Preparación**) in **Lección 2** before viewing **Episodio 2** (the video segment that corresponds to **Lección 2**).

1 PREPARACIÓN

Preliminary: See Faculty Guide for additional information and activities for this lesson.
• **Variation:** For activities marked with the head-phones icon, you may wish to read from the Audioscript instead of playing the CD.
• **Suggestion:** Make sure students are familiar with the activities before you read from the Audio-script or play the CD.

Suggestions:
• Before watching the video, go over the vo-cabulary list at the end of the chapter and have students pronounce the words after you.
• Assign *Preparación* ac-tivities as homework and then go over them quickly in class before viewing the video.

Act. A, Answers: 1. *de España* 2. *El secreto tiene que ver con la vida pri-vada de don Fernando.*

As you prepare to watch **Episodio 2** from *Destinos*, remember the three kinds of Spanish you will hear: Spanish spoken directly to you by the narrator, Spanish spoken to you by Raquel, and the Spanish that the charac-ters speak to each other. As you continue with the program, you will find that you understand more and more of all three kinds of Spanish.

Actividad A.

At the end of **Episodio 1**, you saw don Fernando crush a letter in his hand. Answer the following questions about the letter. As you read the questions, remember what you know about don Fernando and try to make logical guesses. There are no right or wrong answers so far.

1. ¿De dónde (*From where*) es la carta?
   _____ de España
   _____ de los Estados Unidos
   _____ de la Argentina
   _____ de otra (*another*) parte de México

2. El narrador dice (*says*): «Don Fernando tiene un secreto importante. El secreto está en una carta… una carta importante.» ¿Cuál (*What*) es el se-creto de la carta? (¡OJO!* tiene que ver con = *has to do with*)

   _____ El secreto tiene que ver con la vida privada (*personal life*) de don Fernando.
   _____ El secreto tiene que ver con asuntos legales (*legal matters*).
   _____ El secreto tiene que ver con la compañía de don Fernando.

Actividad B.

During **Episodio 1**, don Fernando says to Ramón, "Llama a tus hermanos. Y a tu tío Pedro." If **llamar** means *to call*, can you guess who Ramón will be calling in this episode?

Act. B, Answer: *Ramón va a llamar a otras per-sonas de la familia.*

Ramón va a llamar (*is going to call*)
_____ a otros médicos.   _____ a una abogada.
_____ a unos amigos.   _____ a otras personas de la familia.

---

* ¡OJO! = *Watch out!*

When you have finished watching **Episodio 2**, come back and see how accurate your first guesses were. Read through Activities A and B again at that time and change your answers if you wish. Then check your answers in Appendix 1.

Actividad C.

Listen to the following phone call that Ramón will make to his brother Carlos during **Episodio 2**. Knowing that **Hoy vino**… means that someone *came today*, can you guess what Ramón is telling Carlos? (*Hint*: Remember what you saw in **Episodio 1**.)

Ramón le dice a Carlos que (*that*)

Act. C, Answers: b, b; sí

a. _____ hoy vino una abogada.
b. _____ hoy vino el médico para ver (*to see*) a don Fernando.
c. _____ hoy vino Juan.

Listen to the conversation again. Knowing that **¿Puedes… ?** means *Can you . . . ?*, what do you think that Ramón is asking Carlos to do? What does Carlos answer?

Ramón desea que Carlos venga a (*come to*)

a. _____ un hospital.
b. _____ la hacienda.
c. _____ Los Ángeles.

Carlos dice que _____ sí _____ no.

 . . . AFTER VIEWING

2

¿TIENES BUENA MEMORIA?

Actividad A. **La familia de don Fernando**
Paso 1

Today you met all of the known relatives in don Fernando's immediate family, plus a few other people. Review what you know about them by matching the people on the left with their descriptions on the right. Don't be discouraged if you can't get all of the items correct this time. You will be working with the same characters throughout the whole series. This is only your first chance to practice their names.

1. _____ Ramón
2. _____ Pedro
3. _____ Juan
4. _____ Carlos
5. _____ Mercedes
6. _____ Rosario
7. _____ Carmen

a. hijo de don Fernando; director de una compañía
b. esposa de don Fernando y madre de sus cuatro (4) hijos
c. hija de don Fernando; vive en La Gavia
d. la esposa secreta de don Fernando
e. hijo de don Fernando; vive en La Gavia
f. hermano de don Fernando; profesor en México
g. hijo de don Fernando; profesor en Nueva York

¡Un desafío! ¿Tienes una memoria muy buena?

1. _____ Gloria
2. _____ Pati
3. _____ Consuelo
4. _____ Lupe
5. _____ Maricarmen
6. _____ Julio
7. _____ Ofelia
8. _____ Raquel

a. médico de la familia
b. esposa de Carlos
c. esposa de Juan
d. cocinera (*cook*)
e. hija de Consuelo y Ramón
f. secretaria de Carlos
g. antigua (*former*) estudiante de Pedro
h. esposa de Ramón

Paso 2
Check your answers by listening to the audio CD.

Actividad B. ¿Quién es?
Paso 1
Quiz a partner on the video characters by asking about where each one lives. Does your partner know all of them?

> MODELO: TÚ: ¿Dónde vive Carlos?
> COMPAÑERO/A: Vive en Miami.

Personajes (*Characters*)

1. Pedro 2. Lupe 3. Juan 4. Julio 5. Raquel 6. Pati 7. Ramón
8. Carlos

Lugares

la Ciudad de México, La Gavia, Los Ángeles, Miami, Nueva York

Paso 2
Turn the tables! The person who answered in **Paso 1** will now ask other questions about the characters. The person answering the questions should close his or her book.

> MODELO: COMPAÑERO/A: ¿Quién es abogada?
> TÚ: Raquel.
> COMPAÑERO/A: ¡Sí!

Profesiones

director de la Compañía Castillo Saavedra, S.A.*, administrador de la hacienda, profesor de literatura en la universidad, profesora de teatro en la universidad, abogado, abogada, cocinera en La Gavia, médico de la familia

Actividad C. **El secreto**

At the family conference called by don Fernando, the patriarch revealed the information contained in the letter he received from Spain. Which of these possibilities does he suggest? ¡OJO! There may be more than one right answer.

Act. C, Answers: *Don Fernando tiene otra esposa. Don Fernando tiene otro hijo.*

_____ Don Fernando tiene otra hacienda.
_____ Don Fernando tiene otra esposa.
_____ Don Fernando tiene otro hermano.
_____ Don Fernando tiene otro hijo.

Nota cultural, Optional: Briefly discuss some common family units in the U.S. and how the living arrangements differ from those of Hispanic families.

Nota cultural Las familias hispánicas

It is more typical of Hispanic families for many members of the extended family (all of the relatives, not just the immediate family) to live under the same roof. Widowed grandparents and unmarried aunts and uncles, in particular, may stay in the family home. Unmarried children tend to live with their parents much longer, in some cases for their whole lives. As is the case with Ramón, even married family members may still live under the same roof as their parents. This custom is changing somewhat in modern Hispanic society, especially in urban areas.

Regardless of whether it is a cause or a result of these living arrangements, there is a certain closeness in Hispanic families. How does this compare with *your* own experience?

3

VOCABULARIO DEL TEMA

This repeating section of the Textbook presents groups of vocabulary words presented in the video episode. Sometimes additional words—vocabulary

---

* Castillo Saavedra, S.A. es la compañía de don Fernando. S.A. (Sociedad Anónima) significa *Inc.* en inglés.

from the same family or a new group of words—are presented only in the Textbook. Vocabulary lists presented in this section are always included on the CD.

Los miembros de la familia

los padres	parents
el padre/la madre	father/mother
los hijos	children
el hijo/la hija	son/daughter
los hermanos	brothers and sisters
el hermano/la hermana	brother/sister
los tíos	uncles and aunts
el tío/la tía	uncle/aunt
los esposos	husband and wife, spouses
el esposo/la esposa	husband/wife

Actividad A. ¿Cuál (*Which*) es mi familia?

Listen as the speakers on the CD describe their family tree. Then select the drawing that best matches the description you heard. Look at the drawings in each group before you listen to the description.

GRUPO 1   GRUPO 2

Actividad B. La familia de mi compañero/a
Paso 1

Interview someone in the class about members of his or her family. Select three of the following relatives listed and ask your partner questions about them. Find out at least three things about each person.

---

* Q.E.P.D. = Que en paz descanse (*May he/she rest in peace*)

a. un hermano
b. una hermana
c. el padre
d. la madre
e. un tío
f. una tía
g. un primo
h. una prima

Paso 2 (Optativo)

Using the information you obtained in **Paso 1,** write a brief paragraph (no more than 50 words) about your partner's family. Here are some phrases you can use to help you write your paragraph:

MODELO: Mi compañero/compañera (*nombre*) tiene una hermana / cuatro hermanos / … . Se llama(n)… Vive(n) en…

Actividad C.   ¿Quién es?

Look at the following photographs. The speaker on the CD will ask you to identify each person by number. State that person's relationship to someone else, referring back to the preceding photogaphs if necessary. You will then hear a factually correct statement on the CD. In some cases, more than one relationship is possible.

MODELO: (*you hear*) —¿Quién es la persona de la foto número uno?
(*you say*) —Es Juan, hijo de don Fernando.
(*you hear*) —Es Juan, hijo de don Fernando y hermano de Mercedes, Ramón y Carlos.

1. (uno)

2. (dos)

3. (tres)

4. (cuatro)

4

UN POCO DE GRAMÁTICA

The Workbook/Study Guide contains more detailed explanation and practice of this grammar point.

Emphasis: Spanish does not use the apostrophe for expressing possession.

Expressing Possession

In this lesson, you have heard and seen the possessive construction **de** + name.

la familia **de** Fernando	*Fernando's family*
la esposa **de** Ramón	*Ramón's wife*

You have also seen and heard the possessive adjectives **su** and **sus**. Note their multiple meanings in these phrases.

su padre	*his / her / their father*
sus hermanos	*his / her / their brothers*

Don't worry if you're confused about how to distinguish the meanings of these words. As with cognates, the context (surrounding information) will make the meaning of **su** and **sus** (and words like them) clear.

Act., Optional: You may want to provide pictures of the famous people in the activity.

Act., Answers: 1. *Sus hijos fueron John F. (Jack) Kennedy y Robert F. (Bobby) Kennedy.* 2. *Su padre fue Pablo Picasso.* 3. *Su madre fue Eva (Eve) (y su padre fue Adán [Adam]).* 4. *Su esposa fue Eleanor Roosevelt.* 5. *Su hermana fue Gretel.* 6. *Su hermano es Michael Jackson.*

Actividad. **Parentescos (*Relationships*) famosos**
Paso 1

How much do you know about the following famous relationships? With a classmate, ask and answer questions to test your knowledge of the lives of these famous people.

¡OJO! Unos son fáciles (*easy*), otros son muy difíciles…

Before you begin, note the following information: **¿Quiénes?** is the plural form of **¿Quién? Fue** and **fueron** are the past-tense forms of **es** and **son**, respectively.

Fáciles

1. Rose Kennedy. ¿Quiénes fueron sus hijos? Fueron dos políticos muy importantes en la década de los 60 (sesenta).
2. Paloma Picasso. ¿Quién fue su padre, pintor muy famoso?
3. Caín y Abel. ¿Quién fue su madre?
4. Franklin D. Roosevelt. ¿Quién fue su esposa, también muy activa en causas sociales?
5. Hansel. ¿Quién fue su hermana?
6. LaToya y Janet Jackson. ¿Quién es su hermano, cantante muy famoso?

Un poco difíciles

7. Jane Fonda. ¿Quién es su hermano, también actor? ¿Quién fue su padre, actor muy famoso?
8. Penélope. ¿Quién fue su esposo, héroe de la Guerra de Troya?
9. Rómulo. ¿Quién fue su hermano gemelo (*twin*), fundador de Roma?
10. Enrique VIII (octavo) de Inglaterra. ¿Quién fue su hija, una de las monarcas más importantes de Inglaterra?
11. Elizabeth Taylor. ¿Quién fue su quinto (*fifth*) esposo, actor ya muerto?
12. Martin Sheen. ¿Quiénes son sus dos hijos, también actores?

Paso 2

Using **su** or **sus** and family members as clues, see if your partner can guess what famous person you are talking about. Then switch roles.

MODELO: TÚ: Su hermana es Shirley MacLaine. Su esposa se llama Annette Bening.

COMPAÑERO/A: ¿Warren Beatty?

TÚ: ¡Sí!

5

LECTURA CULTURAL

La Guerra Civil española

This repeating section of the Textbook presents a cultural reading that presents various aspects of Hispanic cultures. These readings are always accompanied by a brief activity.

As you know, don Fernando fought in the Spanish Civil War and left Spain soon after it ended. Look over the following information about this violent period in Spanish history. Remember to guess the meaning of as many words as possible.

La Guerra Civil española

¿Cuándo ocurre?
de 1936 a 1939

¿Quiénes son los adversarios?
Los republicanos contra los nacionales. La mayoría[1] de los republicanos eran[2] demócratas y los nacionales eran aliados de Hitler y Mussolini. El general Francisco Franco

[1]*majority*   [2]*were*

era el líder de los nacionales. Se convirtió en[3] dictador de España después del[4] triunfo de los nacionales en 1939.

Acontecimientos[5] importantes

La Segunda República (1931–1936)
La rebelión de Franco (el 18 de julio de 1936)
El asesinato en Granada del poeta y dramaturgo Federico García Lorca (1936)
El bombardeo de Guernica (1937)
Fin de la Guerra Civil (el 1° de abril de 1939)

[3]*Se…He became*   [4]*después…after the*   [5]*Events*

Guernica de Pablo Picasso (en el Museo Nacional Centro de Arte Reina Sofía, Madrid)

Act., Point out: Point out that, as a prediction exercise, this has no (in)correct responses.

Actividad. ¿Y don Fernando?

Make predictions about don Fernando's life based on the information in the **Lectura cultural**.

1. On which side in the Spanish Civil War did Fernando probably fight?
2. In what year did Fernando and Rosario probably become separated?
3. When did Fernando probably leave Spain?

6

INTERCAMBIO

This repeating section of the Textbook is a lesson-culminating activity that will allow you to speak more in depth about the video storyline, its characters, your classmates, and yourself.

    In this activity you will try to get members of the class to guess which *Destinos* characters you are talking about. Try to stump your classmates!

Paso 1

Think of two characters and prepare two statements that describe each one. Ask your instructor for help with new vocabulary items if you need them.

> MODELO: Esta persona no vive en La Gavia. Tiene esposa pero no tiene hijos. ¿Quién es?

Paso 2

Your instructor will call on students to read their statements. The student whose character description is identified by the *least* number of people wins!

Intercambio, **Suggestions, *Paso 1:*** Encourage students to write clever descriptions (i.e., ones that haven't been mentioned before) about their characters. Walk around the room and ask students if they need help with vocabulary items. ***Paso 2:*** After each student reads his or her statements, have the rest of the class write down who they think the character is. Then call on individual students and ask them *¿Quién es?* When a student gets the correct answer, ask for a show of hands and tally the number of people who guessed that character.

VOCABULARIO

Los miembros de la familia (Members of the Family)

los esposos	husband and wife, spouses
el esposo/la esposa	husband/wife
los hermanos	brothers and sisters
el hermano/la hermana	brother/sister
los hijos	children
el hijo/la hija	son/daughter
los padres	parents
el padre/la madre	father/mother
los tíos	uncles and aunts
el tío/la tía	uncle/aunt

Las personas (People)

el director	head, leader; director
el estudiante	student
el profesor	professor

Los conceptos (Concepts)

la compañía	company (*business*)
el matrimonio	marriage
el secreto	secret

Las palabras adicionales (Additional Words)

¿cuál?	which? what?
otro	other, another
pero	but
que	that
su/sus	his/her/their
ya	already
ya no	no longer
está muerto/muerta	is dead
ya murió	already died

Palabra del texto

la conversación	conversation

Un viaje a Sevilla (España)

La Catedral de Sevilla

3

EL COMIENZO*

Suggestion: Have students look at the photo, describe what they see, and talk about what they think might happen. Ask questions about the photo to prompt student discussion: *¿Quiénes son estas mujeres? ¿Es posible que esta persona sea Rosario? ¿Es posible que esta persona escribió la carta a don Fernando? ¿Quiénes son los chicos?* etc.

*The Beginning

OBJETIVOS

The materials in **Lección 3** of the Textbook and the Workbook/Study Guide will help you better understand the video episode and take you beyond it, giving you additional information about places and characters in the series. The Textbook will also help you to develop skill in using the Spanish language. In this lesson you will learn

- how to express the Spanish numbers from 0 to 21
- how to talk about what other people are doing

You will also learn about the country of Spain and about Hispanic last names.

Be sure to work through all parts of the lesson. When you see a headphones symbol in the margin, listen to the CD for **Lección 3**. Answers or hints for many activities are given in Appendix 1. Be sure to check your answers for each activity before going on to the next one.

The interactive CD-ROM to accompany *Destinos* contains additional practice with the video storyline and will help you improve your skills in Spanish.

BEFORE VIEWING . . .

1

PREPARACIÓN

Preliminary: See Faculty Guide for additional information and activities for this lesson.
• **Variation:** For activities marked with the headphones icon, you may wish to read from the Audioscript instead of playing the CD.
• **Suggestion:** Make sure students are familiar with the activities before you read from the Audioscript or play the CD.

Suggestions:
• Before watching the video, go over the vocabulary list at the end of the chapter and have students pronounce the words after you.
• Assign *Preparación* activities as homework and then go over them quickly in class before viewing the video.

Optional: Brainstorm as a whole class or in small groups what students already know about Spain and what they think it is like. List the ideas on the board and have students copy them. If they express their ideas in English, write down the Spanish equivalents. As the unit in Spain unfolds over the next several episodes, have students refer to this list to see whether or not their ideas were accurate. Which ideas would they change? What did they see or hear that made them change their minds?

Actividad A.

In **Episodio 1** of *Destinos* you met Raquel Rodríguez. Indicate whether the following statements about Raquel are **Cierto (C)** or **Falso (F)**.

C F 1. Raquel es hija de don Fernando.
C F 2. Es abogada.
C F 3. Vive y trabaja (*works*) en Los Ángeles.
C F 4. Es mexicoamericana.
C F 5. Cree (*She believes*) que Rosario vive en España.

Act. A, Answers: 1. F 2. C 3. C 4. C 5. C

Actividad B.

In **Episodio 2** you learned information about a trip Raquel will take. Because this episode is called **El comienzo**, it is a safe bet that her trip will start in this episode.

Where will Raquel go and for what reason? What information does she already have? ¡OJO! There may be more than one appropriate answer.

1. Raquel va a viajar a (*is going to travel to*)
   _____ España.
   _____ la Argentina.
   _____ Puerto Rico.

Act. B, Answers: 1. *España* 2. *Rosario; la persona que escribió la carta; otro hijo de don Fernando* 3. *el nombre de la persona que escribió la carta; el nombre de la calle donde la persona vive* (See Appendix 1 for expanded answers.)

2. Raquel va a buscar a (*is going to look for*)
   _____ Rosario, la primera (*first*) esposa de don Fernando.
   _____ Carmen, la segunda (*second*) esposa de don Fernando.
   _____ la persona que escribió (*wrote*) la carta.
   _____ otro hijo de don Fernando.

3. Raquel probablemente sabe (*knows*)
   _____ el nombre del hijo de Rosario y don Fernando.
   _____ el nombre de la persona que escribió la carta.
   _____ el nombre de la calle (*street*) donde la persona vive.

Actividad C.
Paso 1

Listen to the following conversation that Raquel will have with the receptionist at her hotel in Spain. **¿Dónde está... ?** means *Where is . . . ?* Now that you know that, what does Raquel ask about?

Raquel pregunta (*asks*) dónde está

a. _____ Rosario.
b. _____ la calle Pureza.
c. _____ el hijo de Rosario y don Fernando.

Paso 2

Listen to the conversation again. **¿Está lejos?** means *Is it far away?*
Now that you know that, what information does the receptionist give to Raquel?

El recepcionista dice que la calle Pureza

Act. C, Answers: Paso 1: b; Paso 2: a, c

a. _____ está lejos, un poco lejos.
b. _____ no está lejos.
c. _____ está en el barrio de Triana (*Triana district*).
d. _____ no está en la ciudad.

. . . AFTER VIEWING

2 ¿TIENES BUENA MEMORIA?

Actividad A. Los nuevos personajes (*New characters*)

Paso 1

In **Episodios 1** and **2** you met the members of the Castillo family. Now you have gotten to know a few more characters. Can you match the names of some of the new characters with their photos?

1.

3.

a. Teresa Suárez
b. Elena Ramírez
c. Miguel Ruiz
d. Roberto, el taxista
e. Raquel Rodríguez

Paso 2

Now match the characters with the statements that describe them or what they do in the video episode. ¡OJO! More than one name may be possible for each statement.

1. _____ Busca a la señora Teresa Suárez.
2. _____ Entra en el barrio de Triana con Raquel.

3. _____ Entra en la iglesia (*church*) de Santa Ana.
4. _____ Habla (_?_ *talks*) con dos chicos en la calle.
5. _____ Ya no vive en Sevilla.
6. _____ Su madre está en el mercado (*market*).
7. _____ Habla con Raquel en el mercado.
8. _____ Explica la historia de la carta.

Actividad B. Descripciones

Make up two or three true sentences about one of the characters that appear in **Episodio 3**. Work with a partner and take turns guessing the person that each of you describes.

MODELO: TÚ: Es madre de dos hijos. Sus hijos se llaman
Miguel y Jaime. Vive en Sevilla.
COMPAÑERO/A: ¿Es Elena Ramírez?
TÚ: ¡Sí!

Actividad C. ¿Cuánto saben? (*How much do they know?*)
Paso 1

Don Fernando's family knew nothing about the existence of Rosario. Based on what you have seen and heard in **Episodio 3**, do the following new characters have any information to give Raquel about the case?

a. Es posible.
b. No sabe nada. (*He/She doesn't know anything.*)
c. Probablemente no sabe nada.

1. _____ Miguel Ruiz
2. _____ Elena Ramírez
3. _____ el esposo de Elena
4. _____ el taxista

Paso 2

Now listen to a brief excerpt from Raquel's conversation with Elena Ramírez and change any answers if necessary.

Nota cultural   Los apellidos hispanos

You have probably noticed in previous lessons that the Castillo family is sometimes called **la familia Castillo Saavedra** and sometimes just **la familia Castillo**. In most Hispanic countries people use two last names (**apellidos**). The first is the name of the father, the second that of the mother. It is correct to call a person by the first of the two names (the name of one's father) or by both names. Thus, both **la familia Castillo** and **la familia Castillo Saavedra** are authentic usages.

Miguel and Jaime, who are the sons of Miguel Ruiz and Elena Ramírez, have the last names **Ruiz Ramírez**. Elena's son, Miguel, is known either as **Miguel Ruiz** or as **Miguel Ruiz Ramírez**. It would not be correct to call him **Miguel Ramírez**.

A married woman can add the preposition **de** before her husband's last name. So **Teresa Suárez** could also be called **Teresa Suárez de Ruiz**. However, in Spain it is very common for a woman to use only her maiden name: **Teresa Suárez**, **Elena Ramírez**. Elena's full married name is **Elena Ramírez de Ruiz**.

3

VOCABULARIO DEL TEMA

Los números del 0 al 21*

0 cero		
1 uno	11 once	21 veintiuno
2 dos	12 doce	
3 tres	13 trece	
4 cuatro	14 catorce	
5 cinco	15 quince	
6 seis	16 dieciséis†	
7 siete	17 diecisiete	
8 ocho	18 dieciocho	
9 nueve	19 diecinueve	
10 diez	20 veinte	

Suggestion: Practice pronunciation of the numbers with choral and individual repetition.

Point out:
- The *z* of *diez* changes to a *c* when the numbers 16–19 are written as one word but not when written as 3 words.
- There is a written accent on *dieciséis.*

Uno is the number used in counting. As you know, **un** is used before masculine nouns, **una** before feminine ones. Note how **vientiuno** is used before nouns: **veintiún clientes**, **veintiuna oficinas**.

---

* The speaker on the audio CD pronounces the Spanish letters *c* (before **e** or **i**) and *z* in these numbers the way they are pronounced in most of the Spanish-speaking world. Some of the speakers you have heard in the video episode—Jaime and the hotel clerk, for example—said the numbers with the pronunciation heard in most of Spain.

† The numbers 16 through 19 and 21 can be written as one word (as in the list) or as three: **diez y seis, diez y siete, diez y ocho, diez y nueve, veinte y uno**.

Actividad A. ¿Cuál es el número?

You will hear the street numbers of five of the houses on **la calle Pureza**, but you will hear them out of order. Listen and indicate the order in which you hear them by writing the letters **a** through **e** next to the addresses.

——— 16A   ——— 19A
——— 17A   ——— 20A
——— 18A

Actividad B.

Listen as your instructor describes different people's class schedules. How many hours/credits is each person taking this semester?

1. . . .   2. . . .   3. . . .   4. . . .   5. . . .

4

UN POCO DE GRAMÁTICA

Using Verbs to Talk About Others

In this episode you have heard many verb forms used to tell what characters are doing at the moment. Most present-tense Spanish verbs used to talk about someone other than the speaker end either in **-a** or in **-e**. Note the verbs in this brief description of Raquel.

Raquel viv**e** en Los Ángeles.   *Raquel lives in Los Angeles.*
Viaj**a** a España.   *She is traveling to Spain.*

When talking about two or more people, an **-n** is added.

Raquel y el taxista pregunta**n** a   *Raquel and the taxi driver ask*
dos chicos dónde vive**n** la   *two boys where Mrs. Suárez*
señora Suárez y su familia.   *and her family live.*

These forms are called *third-person* verbs. You will learn more about them in the Workbook/Study Guide. (Did you notice in the sentence **Viaja a España** that the subject of the verb does not have to be used?)

Actividad. Fotografías

Work with a partner or in small groups. Using the list of verbs and other useful vocabulary, take turns making up sentences about each photo. How many sentences can your group come up with?

Verbos

habla(n)   tiene(n)   llega(n)
trabaja(n)   escribe(n)   pregunta(n)
lee(n)   busca(n)

Vocabulario útil: la barbería, el barrio de Triana, el mensaje (*message*), el peluquero (*barber*), el taxista, la tienda (*store*)

1.

2.

3.

4.

5.

5

LECTURA CULTURAL

España, un país[1] de contrastes

🎧 Refresh your memory about the geography of Spain by listening to what the narrator told you at the beginning of **Episodio 3.** Try to associate the place names you hear with this map. Then, when the recorded portion is over, continue on with the reading in the Textbook.

[1]nación

España es un país de contrastes. Entre el norte y el sur hay una enorme diferencia. En el norte hay muchas montañas, bosques[2] y centros industriales. En el sur el terreno es más seco[3] y hay menos industria. También hay mucha influencia árabe en el sur, en Andalucía.

Datos[4] importantes

la capital: Madrid

el gobierno:[5] una monarquía constitucional, que preside el rey Juan Carlos I (primero)

la organización política: 17 comunidades autónomas[6]

el idioma[7] oficial: el español (el castellano)

otros idiomas: el catalán (Cataluña), el gallego (Galicia), el vascuence (el País Vasco)

la población: 39.000.000 (treinta y nueve millones) de habitantes

[2] *forests*   [3]más... *drier*   [4]Información
[5]*government*   [6]comunidades... regiones
[7]*language*

Los Pirineos, montañas entre Francia y España

Una zona agrícola, cerca de Córdoba

Actividad.   ¿Cuánto sabes (*How much do you know*) de España?

Based on the information provided in the preceding **Lectura cultural**, are the following statements **Cierto (C)** or **Falso (F)**?

C   F   1. España es un país uniforme.
C   F   2. Hay mucha influencia árabe en el sur.
C   F   3. En España se habla sólo español.
C   F   4. Madrid está en el centro de la península.
C   F   5. España es una dictadura.

6

INTERCAMBIO

In this activity you will interview a classmate and ask some basic questions about someone in his or her family, then compare that person with a character from *Destinos*.

Intercambio, Suggestions, Paso 1: Allow 4–5 minutes for students to write down a family member or to write questions. **Paso 2:** Allow 5–6 minutes for the comparisons. **Paso 3:** After all descriptions have been read, indicate that the student whose relative has the most in common with Raquel wins.

Intercambio, Optional: You may wish to have those interviewed become the interviewers and vice versa so that all students have a chance to make comparisons.

Paso 1

The class should be divided into two groups: those who will interview and those who will be interviewed. For those who will be interviewed, think of a member in your own extended family who has the most in common with Raquel Rodríguez. Write that person's name and family relation down on a sheet of paper. For those who interview, prepare a series of questions you could ask to compare that person to Raquel. Ask your instructor for help if you need it. You should prepare at least eight questions!

> MODELOS: Esta (*This*) persona, ¿dónde vive?
> ¿Tiene un trabajo? ¿Dónde?
> ¿Tiene esposo o esposa? ¿Cómo se llama?

Paso 2

For those who interview, write up a brief comparison of your classmate's relative and Raquel. You must make at least five comparisons.

> MODELO: El pariente* de Cathy vive en San Francisco. No vive en Los Ángeles, como Raquel. Es profesora, no es abogada. Como Raquel, no tiene esposo...

Paso 3

Read your description to the class. Then listen to your instructor's comments.

---

* ¡OJO! The word **pariente** is a false cognate. It means *relative*, not *parent*.

VOCABULARIO

Los verbos

busca	he/she looks for
cree	he/she believes
entra (en)	he/she enters
escribe	he/she writes
está	he/she is (*located*)
explica	he/she explains
habla	he/she speaks, talks
llega	he/she arrives
necesita	he/she needs
pregunta	he/she asks
tiene	he/she has
toma	he/she takes
trabaja	he/she works
viaja	he/she travels
visita	he/she visits

Las personas

los abuelos	grandparents
el abuelo/	grandfather/
la abuela	grandmother
el amigo/la amiga	friend
el chico/la chica	boy/girl, young kid
el señor (Sr.)*	gentleman, man; Mr.
la señora (Sra.)[†]	lady, woman; Mrs.
la señorita (Srta.)	young(er) lady, single woman; Miss[‡]

Los conceptos

el apellido	last name
el comienzo	beginning
el nombre	(first) name

Los números

cero, uno, dos, tres, cuatro, cinco, seis, siete, ocho, nueve, diez, once, doce, trece, catorce, quince, dieciséis, diecisiete, dieciocho, diecinueve, veinte, veintiuno

Las palabras adicionales

ahora	now
con	with
a	to
al	to the (**a + el**)[§]
del	of the (**de + el**)[§]

---

[*] Note that the abbreviations for these words are capitalized but that the words themselves are not: **el señor Castillo, el Sr. Castillo.**

[†] **La señora** is used to refer to a married woman of any age and often to a middle-aged woman (whether or not her marital status is known).

[‡] Note that there is no Spanish equivalent for English *Ms.*

[§] Only the article **el** contracts with the words **a** and **de** to form the contractions **al** and **del.** Other articles do not contract: **a la iglesia, de los abuelos.**

4

Suggestion: Have students look at the photo, describe what they see, and talk about what they think might happen. Ask questions about the photo to prompt student discussion. *¿Qué hace Raquel? ¿Por qué?*, etc.

PERDIDO*

*Lost

OBJETIVOS

The materials in **Lección 4** of the Textbook and the Workbook/Study Guide will help you better understand the video episode and take you beyond it, giving you additional information about places and characters in the series. The Textbook will also help you to develop skill in using the Spanish language. In this lesson you will learn

- names of courses that you may be taking
- names for common household pets
- ways to describe in Spanish

You will also learn about Sevilla and about the educational system in Hispanic countries.

Be sure to work through all parts of the lesson. When you see a headphones symbol in the margin, listen to the CD for Lección 4. Answers or hints for many activities are given in Appendix 1. Be sure to check your answers for each activity before going on to the next one.

The interactive CD-ROM to accompany *Destinos* contains additional practice with the video storyline and will help you improve your skills in Spanish.

▣ BEFORE VIEWING . . .

1

PREPARACIÓN

Actividad A.

In the last episode of *Destinos* you followed Raquel to Spain. What do you remember about her trip? Complete the following statements.

1. Raquel está ahora en… Barcelona / Sevilla / Madrid.
2. Tiene una carta escrita por (*written by*)… Teresa Suárez / Pedro Castillo / don Fernando.
3. Busca a… Miguel Ruiz / Elena Ramírez / Teresa Suárez.
4. En la calle, habla primero (*first*) con… dos chicos / dos esposos / dos taxistas.
5. Dicen (*They say*) que la señora Suárez vive ahora en… Barcelona / Málaga / Madrid.
6. Caminan (*They walk*) al mercado y Raquel habla con… Teresa Suárez / Elena Ramírez / Mercedes.
7. Elena es… la madre / la abuela / la hermana …de los chicos.
8. Elena… tiene / no tiene / también desea …información sobre (*about*) Rosario.

Actividad B.

What do you think will happen in this episode? Try to predict what will happen by answering the following questions.

1. In **Episodio 3** you learned that Teresa Suárez is currently living in Madrid. Do you think that Raquel will be able to make contact with her? If so, how?

   a. _____ Teresa Suárez no desea hablar con Raquel.
   b. _____ Raquel no habla con Teresa Suárez en este (*this*) episodio.
   c. _____ Raquel habla con Teresa por teléfono.

2. You also learned that Elena Ramírez knows nothing about the letter that señora Suárez wrote to don Fernando. Do you think her husband knows something?

   a. _____ El esposo de Elena no sabe nada (*knows nothing*).
   b. _____ El esposo sabe algo (*knows something*).

Actividad C.
Paso 1

Listen to the following conversation that Raquel will have with Miguel Ruiz, Elena's husband. **Ya hablé** means *I already spoke*. Now that you know that, with whom did Miguel speak and what did he learn?

a. _____ Miguel habló (*spoke*) con Teresa Suárez.

b. _____ Miguel habló con Rosario.

c. _____ Miguel no sabe nada.

d. _____ Miguel sabe algo interesante.

Paso 2

Listen to the conversation again. **Vaya** means *go*. Now that you know that, how will Raquel and Teresa Suárez make contact?

a. _____ La señora Suárez desea hablar con Raquel por teléfono.

b. _____ La señora Suárez desea hablar con Raquel en Sevilla.

c. _____ La señora Suárez desea hablar con Raquel en Madrid.

 . . . AFTER VIEWING

---

2 # ¿TIENES BUENA MEMORIA?

Actividad A. **En este episodio**

All of the following events took place during the two days shown in **Episodio 4**, but . . . in what order did they occur? Put them in order, from 1 to 3 or 4 in each group.

Por la noche (*In the evening*)

a. _____ Miguel revela su conversación con su madre.

b. _____ Raquel llama (*calls*) a Pedro Castillo por teléfono y habla con él.

c. _____ Raquel decide viajar a Madrid en tren.

Al día siguiente (*The next day*)

a. _____ La familia entra en una pastelería.

b. _____ Miguel padre compra un perro.

c. _____ Osito se escapa y se pierde (*he gets lost*).

d. _____ La familia lleva (*takes*) a Raquel al mercado de los animales.

Actividad B. **Los nuevos personajes**

Paso 1

Can you match the following new characters with their photos?

1.　　　　2.　　　　3.　　　　4.

a. Osito
b. Miguel hijo
c. Jaime
d. Miguel padre

Paso 2

Now, working with a partner, take turns reading the true/false statements about the characters from **Episodio 4**. The person who answers **Cierto** or **Falso** must have his or her book closed.

Miguel padre

C F 1. Trabaja en turismo, como guía.
C F 2. Revela parte del secreto de Rosario.
C F 3. Compra un animal para su hijo.

Jaime

C F 4. Toma un fino (*sherry*) con Raquel y sus padres.
C F 5. Acepta la responsabilidad de tener (*having*) un perro.
C F 6. No le gusta (*He doesn't like*) la escuela.

Miguel hijo

C F 7. Está en octavo (*8th*) grado.
C F 8. Su materia favorita es ciencias naturales.
C F 9. No le gusta estudiar.

3

VOCABULARIO DEL TEMA

Optional: Hold up items that represent each school subject (e.g., math equation, important historical date, sports pictures, textbooks) as you go over the vocabulary.

En el Colegio de San Francisco de Paula

LAS ASIGNATURAS DE MIGUEL

la historia
las matemáticas
las ciencias naturales
la religión
el español
el inglés
la educación física

LAS ASIGNATURAS DE JAIME

el español
la religión
las ciencias naturales
las matemáticas
las ciencias sociales
la educación física

Remember that the word **colegio** is a false cognate. It means *grade school* or *high school.* This **Colegio,** like many in Spain, is affiliated with a religious order.

Actividad A.   ¿Qué estudian los hermanos Ruiz?

What do you remember about the courses that Miguel and Jaime are taking? Indicate whether the following statements refer only to Miguel (**M**), only to Jaime (**J**), or to both boys (**2**). Try this without looking at the preceding list.

Act. A, Answers: 1. 2 2. J 3. 2 4. M 5. J

M   J   2   1.   Estudia ciencias naturales.
M   J   2   2.   Tiene un curso de ciencias sociales.
M   J   2   3.   Estudia en un colegio religioso.
M   J   2   4.   Toma inglés.
M   J   2   5.   No estudia historia.

Actividad B.

You will hear a series of descriptions of what happens in different classes that Miguel and Jaime are taking. Match the descriptions with the following courses.

Act. B, Answers: a. 3 b. 2 c. 4 d. 1

a. _____ las matemáticas   c. _____ la religión
b. _____ la educación física   d. _____ el inglés

Actividad C.   ¿Y tú?

Act. C, Suggestion: Assign for homework as a mini-composition.

What do grade school students typically study in your area? Imagine that you are describing to Miguel and Jaime what students study where you live by completing the following sentences.

Donde yo vivo, los chicos estudian _____, _____ y

_____. No estudian _____.

Otras materias

LAS ARTES LIBERALES*	LAS CIENCIAS NATURALES	LAS MATEMÁTICAS	OTRAS MATERIAS
el arte	la biología	el cálculo	el comercio
la filosofía	la química		las comunicaciones
las lenguas extranjeras			la contabilidad
la literatura	LAS CIENCIAS SOCIALES		los estudios agrícolas
	la psicología		la informática
	la sociología		

Vocabulary, Suggestion: As you go over the vocabulary, ask students to raise their hands in answer to the question, *¿Quién estudia _____?* (Fill in the blank with each of the subjects.)

This list of subjects includes a number usually studied only at the college level. Most of them are easily recognizable cognates. Can you find the Spanish equivalents of *business* (Hint: *commerce*), *foreign languages, accounting* (Hint: *counting*), *chemistry?*

Many subjects have been listed here. You should learn primarily those that you are taking or that are of interest to you. If your major is not included in the list of courses, look it up in a dictionary or ask your instructor.

---

* *Note:* **el arte** (*sing.*), but **las artes** (*pl.*). Other terms for *liberal arts* heard in the Hispanic world are **Filosofía y letras, Las letras, Las humanidades**. Ask your instructor which term to use.

Actividad D.

You will hear three Hispanic college students talk about what they are studying this term.

Paso 1

Listen and take notes on what they are studying.

ANITA   RAÚL   CELIA

_____   _____   _____

_____   _____   _____

_____   _____   _____

_____   _____   _____

Paso 2

Now report to the class how your schedule is similar to or different from that of the three people in **Paso 1**.

MODELO: Raúl tiene una clase de _____, pero yo no.

Yo estudio _____ y Raúl también…

Nota cultural   En las universidades hispánicas

After completing their high-school degree (called **el bachillerato**), students in most Hispanic countries who enter the university must immediately select a major and follow a prescribed series of courses (with few electives). Courses tend to last for a full year, with obligatory examinations at the end of the course.

Follow-up: If you have ever attended a university in a Hispanic country, briefly relate your own experiences and compare them with information in the *Nota*.

Observaciones_____
del Profesor

Alumno _____

Asignatura_____ NATURALEZA

Curso _5º , Un. 4ª , Obj. 1.2.2.

Fecha_____ – Noviembre

Calificación

1.- ¿ Qué órganos forman el aparato circulatorio ?

2.- ¿ Qué elementos forman la sangre ?

3.- Las _____ son los vasos sanguíneos que conducen la sangre desde los órganos hasta el corazón.

Las _____ son los vasos sanguíneos que conducen la sangre desde el corazón a todos los órganos del cuerpo.

Actividad E. **Nuestras (*Our*) clases**

What courses are you and your friends taking this semester/quarter (**este se-mestre/trimestre**)? Answer by completing as many of the following sentences as necessary.

> Yo tomo...
> Mi amigo ____(*nombre*)____ toma...
> Mi amiga ____(*nombre*)____ toma...
> Otros amigos toman...

Act. E, Extension: Do a *Firma aquí* activity about school subjects. Say *Hay que buscar a una persona que estudia cada materia.* Have students make a list of the different subjects. Students take their lists, circulate in the class, and ask, for example, *¿Estudias francés?* If the response is *Sí,* the student has the person sign his/her name. If it is *No,* they must continue asking. Limit the search to 5–10 minutes. Go over as a group, asking *¿Quiénes estudian francés?,* etc. Students answer using names they have gathered.

Actividad F. **Típicamente...**

Now give the courses that are typically taken by certain groups of students at your school.

> Los estudiantes de primer año (*freshmen*) toman...
> Los estudiantes de ciencias toman...
> Los estudiantes de artes liberales toman...
> Los atletas toman...

Vocabulary, Suggestion: Show toy animals or pictures while going over the vocabulary. Ask students *¿Quién tiene un _____ ? ¿Cómo se llama? ¿Cuántos años tiene?* etc.

Los animales domésticos

el perro	dog
el gato	cat
el pájaro	bird
el pez*	fish

Vocabulary, Extension: Compare Spanish animal sounds to English equivalents, e.g., cow = *muuu,* horse = *ahiii,* dog = *guau guau,* cat = *miau,* duck = *cua cua,* chick = *pío pío,* hen = *cloc cloc,* rooster = *qui-qui-ri-quí,* lion = *grrr.* The song *"De colores"* includes some of these sounds.

Actividad G. **Animales de todo tipo**

You will hear the narrator from **Episodio 4** describe **el mercadillo de animales** visited by Raquel and the Ruiz family. Listen specifically for the following information.

Act. G, Answers: Fish: (*peces*) *tropicales* Birds: *canarios, loros* (parrots), *patitos* (ducklings)

> One type of fish that is sold there: _____
>
> One type of bird that is sold there: _____

---

* The **-z** at the end of a word changes to **-c** when the plural is formed: **pez** → **peces**. This spelling change does not affect pronunciation.

Act. H, Follow-up: Assign for homework as mini-composition.

Actividad H.   Más animales

Are animals part of your life in any way? Choose the sentences that best describe you, and complete them if necessary.

Tengo _____. Se llama (*Its name is*) _____.

No tengo ningún animal.

Los estudiantes de mi residencia (*dorm*) tienen _____.

En la casa (*house*) donde yo vivo, hay _____.

En la casa de mis padres (hijos), hay _____.

Mi hijo/a (esposo/a, amigo/a) desea tener (*to have*) _____.

4

UN POCO DE GRAMÁTICA

The Workbook/Study Guide contains more detailed explanation and practice of this grammar point.

Suggestion: Have students go through the description of Osito and change all singular forms to plurals and plurals to singulars.

Variation: Have students close books and write the description as you read it aloud. Then have them underline all the adjectives in the paragraph and draw arrows to the nouns they modify.

Note: Adjectives and nouns agree in grammatical gender, regardless of the subject being discussed. Adjectives that modify *la persona* will always be feminine, no matter what the sex of the referent is. The same is true of *el individuo. Jaime es una persona pequeña. Raquel es un individuo simpático.*

Describing

You have already learned that Spanish articles must reflect the gender and number of the nouns they accompany: **el perro, los perros**. Adjectives (words that describe nouns) are like articles in that they too must agree in gender and number with the noun they modify. Notice how adjectives are used in the following description of Osito, the lost dog from **Episodio 4**.

El perro de Jaime se llama Osito porque es pequeñ**o** y negr**o**. Osito es un perro muy inteligent**e** y cariños**o**. En general, los perros son animales muy inteligent**es**. También son muy fiel**es**. Algunas personas creen que los gatos son más list**os**, pero Jaime no está de acuerdo.

Jaime's dog is called Osito because he is small and black. Osito is a very intelligent and affectionate dog. In general, dogs are very intelligent animals. They are also very loyal. Some people think that cats are brighter, but Jaime doesn't agree.

Note the following patterns of adjective agreement:

inteligente → inteligentes (+ **s**)
fiel → fieles (+ **es**)

You will learn more about adjectives in the Workbook/Study Guide.

Actividad.   Los animales domésticos

Pets—and the pet industry supporting them—play an important role in this country. This is one of the aspects of our culture that strikes some Hispanics as unusual, because less importance is given to animals in many Hispanic settings. Here, however, animals tend to be treated like family members, and people often have strong opinions about their pets and animals in general.

Paso 1

Describe an animal you know or know about, forming complete sentences with elements from each column. (You can listen to the list of **Otros animales** and the adjectives on the CD.)

Otros animales: el caballo (*horse*), el canario, el *hámster,* el loro (*parrot*), el lagarto (*lizard*), la serpiente, la tortuga

> MODELO: El perro de mi hijo es cariñoso y fiel.

Mi _____	es
El _____ de mi	
(amigo, hijo…)	
Garfield	
Snoopy, Lassie, Benji	
el señor Ed	

inteligente/tonto (*dumb*)
cariñoso/indiferente
fiel (*faithful*)
(in)dependiente
perezoso (*lazy*)
cruel, egoísta
bonito (*pretty*)/feo (*ugly*)
(im)paciente
hablador (*talkative*)
furtivo (*sneaky*)
pequeño/grande (*large*)
lento (*slow*)/rápido

Lectura cultural, **Suggestion:** Have students look at maps and text together in class before assigning listening activity as homework, It is helpful to have a large map of Sevilla in front of the room or on an overhead.

Lectura cultural, **Point out:** Mention the *ceceo* (pronunciation of *c* as unvoiced *th*) in Castilian Spanish and have students listen for it in specific words.

Paso 2

Now make generalizations about some of the following animals. Feel free to compare characteristics, as in the model. Use adjectives from **Paso 1**.

> MODELO: En general, los perros son dependientes. Pero los gatos son independientes.

Animales: los perros, los gatos, los pájaros, los peces, los caballos, los lagartos, las serpientes, las tortugas

---

5

LECTURA CULTURAL

Sevilla

In **Episodios 3** and **4**, many of the scenes you saw took place in Sevilla. Refresh your memory about Sevilla by listening to what the narrator told you at the beginning of **Episodio 3**. Try to associate the place names you hear with scenes you remember from the video episodes. Then complete the following activity.

Which of the following statements accurately describe Sevilla, based on what you now know?

C   F   1. Hay muchas iglesias en Sevilla.

C   F   2. No hay muchas tradiciones religiosas en la ciudad.

C   F   3. Es una ciudad de patios y jardines (*gardens*).

C   F   4. La ciudad tiene muchos monumentos históricos.

C   F   5. Sevilla no tiene barrios modernos.

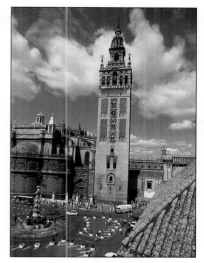

La Torre de la Giralda tiene 97 (noventa y siete) metros de alto.

After you have read the following passage about Sevilla, review this activity to see whether you wish to change any answers.

Sevilla es una típica ciudad de Andalucía. Está situada a orillas del[1] río Guadalquivir. Tiene barrios modernos, pero muchas personas creen que las partes más interesantes de Sevilla son sus zonas históricas.

El barrio de Santa Cruz es la parte más antigua[2] de la ciudad. Es famoso por sus calles estrechas[3] y por los hermosos patios en el interior de las casas. En el pasado muchos judíos vivían[4] en este barrio.

Los monumentos más famosos de Sevilla son éstos:

- la antigua Catedral, de estilo gótico
- la tumba de Cristóbal Colón, que está en la Catedral
- la Giralda, una torre de la Catedral
- El Alcázar,[5] con su arquitectura de estilo árabe y sus bonitos jardines.

Sevilla es también muy famosa por sus procesiones de Semana Santa.[6] Muchas personas participan en estas procesiones. Las diferentes cofradías[7] desfilan[8] por las calles de la ciudad. Cargan[9] enormes pasos[10] que representan escenas de la vida[11] de Jesucristo. Algunos pasos tienen cruces o estatuas de la Virgen María o de Jesús.

En estas descripciones, se ve[12] la influencia de las tres culturas que convivían[13] en Sevilla en siglos anteriores: la cultura judía, la árabe y la cristiana.

[1]*a... on the banks of the* [2]*más... oldest* [3]*narrow* [4]*muchos... many Jewish people lived*
[5]*El... Royal Palace* [6]*Semana... Holy Week* [7]*brotherhoods* [8]*caminan* [9]*They carry* [10]*floats*
[11]*life* [12]*se... one can see* [13]*coexisted, lived together*

Actividad. **Un viaje a Sevilla**

Based on the information provided in the preceding text, indicate what you would like to see if you went to Sevilla. Use the expression **Me gustaría** (*I would like*) plus an infinitive.

MODELO: Me gustaría visitar la Catedral y la Giralda.

Verbos útiles: visitar, caminar (en), entrar (en), fotografiar

---

6

INTERCAMBIO

Paso 1

In pairs, use the following questions to interview each other. You may add questions if you like and may consult your instructor for help. Jot down all information you get from your partner because you will need it later.

1. ¿Cuál es tu especialización (*major*)?
2. ¿Qué clases tienes este semestre (trimestre)?
3. ¿Cuál es tu clase favorita?
4. ¿Quién es tu profesor favorito (profesora favorita)?

Paso 2

With the notes you took in **Paso 1,** write a short paragraph in which you talk about your partner's college experience. Be prepared! Your instructor may call on you to read the information out loud.

VOCABULARIO

Los verbos

aceptar	to accept
caminar	to walk
comprar	to buy
decidir	to decide
estudiar	to study
llamar	to call
llevar	to take (*something somewhere*)
sabe (algo)	he/she knows (something)
no sabe nada	he/she doesn't know anything

Los animales domésticos

el gato	cat
el pájaro	bird
el perro	dog
el pez (*pl.* **peces**)	fish

Los lugares

la casa	house, home
el colegio	grade/high school

Las materias (Courses)

la asignatura*	subject
el curso	course; class

---

* As you saw in the video episode, this word is used in Spain to mean *school subjects*. **La materia** is also widely used in the Spanish-speaking world to mean *course* or *subject*.

el arte (*pl.* **las artes**)	art
la biología	biology
el cálculo	calculus
las ciencias (**naturales, sociales**)	(natural, social) science
el comercio	business
la comunicación	communications
la contabilidad	accounting
la educación física	physical education
el español	Spanish
los estudios agrícolas	agriculture
la filosofía	philosophy
la informática	data processing
el inglés	English
la lengua (**extranjera**)	(foreign) language
la literatura	literature
las matemáticas	mathematics
la psicología	psychology
la química	chemistry
la religión	religion
la sociología	sociology

Repaso: la historia

Los adjetivos (Adjectives)

bueno/buenos	good
cariñoso/cariñosos	affectionate
negro/negros	black
perdido/perdidos	lost
primero/primeros	first

Las palabras adicionales

al día siguiente	the next day
donde yo vivo	where I live
por teléfono	by telephone
porque	because
todavía	still, yet
(a Jaime) le gusta* + *inf.*	(Jaime) likes (*to do something*)
no le gusta + *inf.*	he doesn't like (*to do something*)

Palabras del texto

el repaso review

In the **Vocabulario** section, this word introduces thematic vocabulary that has been listed in previous lessons of the Textbook or Workbook/Study Guide.

---

*Whenever you see or hear a form of the verb **gustar**, remember that the topic is someone's likes or dislikes. You will learn more about using **gustar** in upcoming lessons.

5

LA DESPEDIDA*

Suggestion: Have students look at the photo, describe what they see, and talk about what they think might happen. Ask questions about the photo to prompt student discussion. Use of the present tense to talk about the future is OK at this point. Focus here is on content, not grammatical accuracy.

*The Farewell

OBJETIVOS

The materials in **Lección 5** of the Textbook and the Workbook/Study Guide will help you better understand the video episode and take you beyond it, giving you additional information about places and characters in the series. The Textbook will also help you to develop skill in using the Spanish language. In this lesson you will learn

- how to express the days of the week in Spanish
- how to tell time
- how to talk about your activities with others

You will also learn about Arabic influence in southern Spain.

Be sure to work through all parts of the lesson. When you see a headphones symbol in the margin, listen to the CD for **Lección 5**. Answers or hints for many activities are given in Appendix 1. Be sure to check your answers for each activity before going on to the next one.

The interactive CD-ROM to accompany *Destinos* contains additional practice with the video storyline and will help you improve your skills in Spanish.

BEFORE VIEWING . . .

1

PREPARACIÓN

Preliminary: See Faculty Guide for additional information and activities for this lesson.
- **Variation:** For activities marked with the headphones icon, you may wish to read from the Audioscript instead of playing the CD.
- **Suggestion:** Make sure students are familiar with the activities before you read from the Audioscript or play the CD.

Suggestions:
- Before watching the video, go over the vocabulary list at the end of the chapter and have students pronounce the words after you.
- Assign *Preparación* activities as homework and then go over them quickly in class before viewing the video.

Actividad A.

Although Raquel has not yet unraveled the secret of the letter, she has accumulated some information and, being a lawyer, has kept careful records of it. How much do you remember about the details of the case?

Paso 1

In simple sentences, answer the following questions about Raquel's investigation.

1. ¿Cómo se llama la persona que escribió la carta?
2. ¿Dónde vive esa (*that*) persona?
3. ¿Desea hablar con Raquel?
4. ¿Adónde necesita ir (*to go*) Raquel para hablar con ella?
5. ¿Sabe algo de Rosario la familia Ruiz?
6. ¿Cómo debe ir Raquel a Madrid?

Act. A, Answers: *Paso 1: 1. Se llama Teresa Suárez. 2. La señora Suárez vive en Madrid. 3. Sí, desea hablar con Raquel. 4. Raquel necesita ir a Madrid. 5. La familia Ruiz no sabe nada de Rosario. 6. Debe ir en tren. Paso 3: 1. No saben nada 2. por teléfono 3. con otro hijo 4. compra un perro 5. se pierde en*

Paso 2

Now listen to the questions and answers on the CD.

Paso 3

Now choose the appropriate words and phrases to complete the following paragraph.

1. No saben nada / Saben algo
2. personalmente / por teléfono
3. con otro hijo / con Rosario
4. compra un gato / compra un perro
5. camina por (*through*) / se pierde en (*gets lost in*)

En Sevilla, Raquel conoce a[a] los miembros de la familia Ruiz.

_____[1] de Rosario, pero Miguel Ruiz habla con su madre

_____[2] Por eso[b] Raquel sabe que debe ir a Madrid para hablar con

ella. Raquel no debe ir mañana,[c] porque la señora Suárez está en Barcelona,

_____[3] Por eso Raquel tiene un día libre[d] y pasa el tiempo con la

familia. En la mañana,[e] todos visitan el mercadillo de los animales, donde

Miguel padre _____[4] para su hijo Jaime. Pero Jaime no es muy

responsable y el perro, que se llama Osito, _____[5] las calles del

barrio de Santa Cruz.

[a]conoce... *meets*   [b]Por... *For that reason*   [c]*tomorrow*   [d]un... *a free day*   [e]*morning*

Paso 4
Now listen to the completed paragraph on the CD.

Act. B, Point out: As a prediction exercise, this has no (in)correct responses.

Actividad B.

At the end of **Episodio 4**, the entire Ruiz family disappeared along with Raquel into the narrow streets of el barrio de Santa Cruz. What do you think will happen in this video episode? In each group, choose the statement that best expresses what you expect to see.

1. _____ Jaime encuentra (*finds*) a su perro.
_____ Hay un accidente y Osito está muerto.
2. _____ Jaime se pierde también en el barrio de Santa Cruz.
_____ Raquel se pierde también.
3. _____ Raquel sale (*leaves*) para Madrid hoy (*today*).
_____ Raquel decide quedarse (*to stay*) en Sevilla otro día.

Actividad C.

Listen to the following conversation between Raquel and Elena Ramírez in the barrio de Santa Cruz. **¿Dónde nos encontramos?** means *Where shall we meet?* Now that you know that, try to listen for the name of their meeting place.

1. Elena dice que van a encontrarse (*they are going to meet*) en

a. _____ otra calle.
b. _____ un café.
c. _____ La Giralda.

Listen to the conversation again. Knowing that Raquel and Elena have arranged to meet, can you determine approximately at what time they will meet? *Hint*: Listen for a number.

2. Elena y Raquel van a encontrarse aproximadamente

a. _____ a las dos. | Act. C, Answers: 1. c 2. b
b. _____ a las once.

 . . . AFTER VIEWING

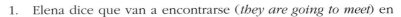

2

¿TIENES BUENA MEMORIA?

Act. A, Suggestion: Give students about 3 minutes to complete the activity individually or in pairs and then compare answers as whole class.

Actividad A. Por la mañana (*In the morning*)

The events of the morning in Sevilla involve primarily three characters: Raquel, Jaime, and a new character, **el ciego**. Match those characters with the statements that describe them or indicate what they do in the video episode. ¡OJO! More than one name may be possible for each statement.

1. _____ Corre (¿_____? *runs*) por las calles del barrio.

2. _____ Habla con un niño (*boy*) en la calle.

3. _____ Encuentra al perro en la Plaza de las Tres Cruces.

4. _____ Habla con el ciego.

5. _____ Vende (¿_____? *sells*) cupones de la lotería.

6. _____ Necesita estar en la Giralda a las once y media.

7. _____ Dice que tener un perro es una gran responsabilidad.

8. _____ Compra caramelos.

9. _____ Se pierde.

10. _____ Entra en la Catedral.

Act. A, Answers: 1. *Jaime, Raquel* 2. *Jaime, Raquel* 3. *el ciego, Jaime* 4. *Raquel, Jaime* 5. *el ciego* 6. *Raquel* 7. *el ciego* 8. *Raquel* 9. *Jaime, Raquel* 10. *Raquel* (See Appendix 1 for expanded answers.)

Actividad B. **Por la tarde y al día siguiente (*the next day*)**

Using the cues given below, write seven sentences, each describing a significant event in **Episodio 5**. ¡OJO! *Do not* write the sentences in the order in which they happened. Then exchange sentences with a partner and read them aloud in the correct order.

Act. B, Suggestion: Tell students that they only need to match the subjects with the appropriate actions in order to write complete sentences. The verbs are already conjugated for them.

Sujetos	**Acciones**
Raquel	compra un billete (*ticket*)
el Alcázar	desean visitar el Alcázar
el tren	llegan a la estación del tren
todos	está cerrado (*closed*)
	cenan (*they have dinner*) en un restaurante elegante
	sale de (*leaves*) la estación
	dicen adiós

Act. B, Answers: 1. *Todos desean visitar el Alcázar.* 2. *El Alcázar está cerrado.* 3. *Todos cenan en un restaurante elegante.* 4. *Todos llegan a la estación de tren.* 5. *Raquel compra un billete.* 6. *Todos dicen adiós.* 7. *El tren sale de la estación.*

Actividad C. **¡Un desafío!**

Act. C, Suggestion: Give students about 2 minutes to complete the activity individually or in pairs and then compare answers as whole class.

Some of the events of **Episodio 5** have to do with a specific time. It is possible to understand the video episode without catching the specific hours mentioned, but . . . perhaps you did! Do you remember at what time the following events took place or were supposed to take place?

¿A qué hora...

Act. C, Answers: 1. d 2. c 3. d (See Appendix 1 for expanded answers.)

1. _____ deben encontrarse en la Giralda Raquel y Elena?

2. _____ llegan al Alcázar?

3. _____ sale Raquel para Madrid?

a. A las doce.
b. A las once.
c. A la una.
d. A las once y media.
e. A las doce y media.
f. A la una y media.

VOCABULARIO DEL TEMA

3

Suggestion: Practice pronunciation of the days of the week with choral and individual repetition.

Note: Tell students to use *los* with the days of the week to express *on* when referring to habitual or repeated actions or events: *los lunes* = on Mondays.

Los días de la semana

lunes	Monday	**viernes**	Friday
martes	Tuesday	**sábado**	Saturday
miércoles	Wednesday	**domingo**	Sunday
jueves	Thursday		

Did you notice that the days of the week are not capitalized and that the week starts with Monday? Use the article **el** before the days of the week to express *on*: **el lunes** = *on Monday*.

lunes 14	*martes 15*	*miércoles 16*	*jueves 17*	*viernes 18*	*sábado 19*
8	8	8	8	8	
9	9	9	9	9	
10	10	10	10	10	
11	11	11	11	11	
12	12	12	12	12	
13	13	13	13	13	
14	14	14	14	14	*domingo 20*
15	15	15	15	15	
16	16	16	16	16	
17	17	17	17	17	

Actividad A. Una semana decisiva

The video episodes of *Destinos* that you have seen thus far take place during a decisive week in the lives of don Fernando's family. Listen as the narrator relates the events of that week. Then identify the following actions by the day of the week on which each occurs, beginning with **el lunes**.

Act. A, Answers: 1. *el domingo* 2. *el viernes* 3. *el jueves* 4. *el sábado* 5. *el martes* 6. *el miércoles* 7. *el lunes*

1. _____ Raquel va con la familia Ruiz al mercadillo de los animales.

2. _____ Raquel sale de México para Sevilla.

3. _____ Pedro habla con Raquel y Raquel acepta el caso.

4. _____ Raquel comienza su investigación en Sevilla.

5. _____ Los miembros de la familia llegan a La Gavia.

6. _____ Don Fernando habla con su familia. Revela el secreto.

7. _____ El doctor habla con don Fernando, en La Gavia.

Actividad B. La semana de Miguel

The speaker on the audio CD will tell you one special thing that Miguel typically does each day of the week. The days are mentioned out of sequence. Listen carefully and indicate where Miguel is on each day.

Miguel está

a. _____ en casa.

b. _____ en la iglesia.

c. _____ con su padre.

d. _____ en el mercado.

e. _____ en casa de su abuela.

f. _____ en casa de un amigo.

g. _____ con su madre.

Now listen as Miguel's week is described in sequence, with some additional information. How much more can you understand?

lunes	martes	miércoles	jueves	viernes	sábado	domingo

Actividad C. ¡Firma (*Sign*) aquí, por favor!

Write down your class schedule for an entire week. Then survey your classmates to find people who have similar schedules. When you find someone whose schedule is similar to yours, have that person sign his or her name next to that day of the week.

MODELO:
TÚ: Tengo tres clases los lunes. / No tengo clases los viernes, …
COMPAÑERO/A: Yo también. / Yo tampoco (*Neither do I*).
TÚ: ¡Firma aquí, por favor!

If someone answers that his or her schedule is different from yours (**No, sólo** [*only*] **tengo una clase los lunes**, …), be sure to thank him or her before moving on to the next person.

¿Qué hora es?

Use the question **¿Qué hora es?*** to ask *What time is it?* Here are ways to answer.

Es la una.

Son las dos y veinte.

Son las tres.

Son las seis.

Son las nueve y diez.

---

* The question you have heard in the episode, **¿Qué horas son?**, is a variation used primarily in Mexico and by those of Mexican descent in the United States.

Es la una menos diez.   Son las ocho y cuarto.   Son las diez y media.   Son las cinco menos cuarto.

Use **y** to express minutes between the hour and the half hour. Use **menos** to express minutes between the half hour and the next hour. The phrase **y cuarto** expresses the quarter hour and **y media** the half hour.

The time of day is indicated more precisely by adding the following phrases.

de la mañana	*in the morning*
de la tarde	*in the afternoon/evening*
de la noche	*in the evening/at night*
Son las ocho y media **de la mañana**.	*It's eight-thirty in the morning.*
Son las tres menos cuarto **de la tarde**.	*It's a quarter to three in the afternoon.*

To indicate that something happens at a particular hour, use the phrases **a la...** or **a las...** .

Raquel y Jaime llegan tarde a la Giralda, **a las doce**.	*Raquel and Jaime get to the Giralda late, at 12:00.*

Nota cultural   Hablando de la hora...
(Talking about time . . .)

Although phrases in two languages may be roughly equivalent, cultural differences often make that correspondence less exact. For example, the Spanish phrase **de la tarde** does not exactly correspond to *in the afternoon,* the English equivalent offered above. Because lunch in Hispanic countries is generally served at 2:00 (or later) and dinner at 10:00 (or later), **la tarde** is often viewed as lasting until the dinner hour. Thus, in Spanish one speaks of **las ocho de la tarde**, which would be *8:00 in the evening* in English.

Another difference between English and Spanish time-telling systems is the more frequent use of the 24-hour clock in Hispanic countries. Note in the photo how the visiting hours for **La Giralda** are indicated. (When the time given is after 12:00 noon, simply subtract 12 to get the hour: 15:00 → 3:00 P.M.) Times in transportation schedules and TV listings are generally given using the 24-hour system.

Actividad D.   ¿Qué hora es?

You will hear a series of segments from **Episodio 5**. Listen carefully to them and try to catch the times of day you hear.

1. Raquel dice…
2. El ciego dice…
3. Los niños dicen…

Actividad E.   ¿Qué hora es?

Now it's your turn to answer the question. When you hear the number for each item, tell what time it is on the clockface shown. The speaker on the CD will give you the correct answer.

MODELO: (*you see*)
          (*you say*)   —Son las cinco.
          (*you hear*) —Son las cinco.

1. 1.00   2. 1.30   3. 2.00   4. 2.15

5. 9.00   6. 8.45   7. 6.10   8. 8.50

Actividad F.   Un día típico de Susan

Here are some of the things that Susan, a colleague of Raquel, does on a typical day. Look at the drawings and match them with the appropriate statements. Then complete the statements with the times of day.

1. _____ Toma algo en la cafetería a…
2. _____ Sale de la oficina a…
3. _____ Susan llega a la oficina a…
4. _____ Trabaja hasta (*until*) muy tarde, hasta…
5. _____ Susan habla con un cliente a…
6. _____ Entra en su apartamento a…
7. _____ Escribe un reporte a…
8. _____ Cena con una amiga a…

a.   b.   c.   d.

e.   f.   g.   h.

Actividad G. Mi horario (*schedule*)

How does your schedule compare to Susan's? Using the preceding sentences as a guide, form as many sentences as you can about your own schedule, changing details as needed. **Act. G, Suggestion:** Have students take turns reading their sentences to each other in pairs or small groups.

MODELO: Llego a la universidad a la(s)...

Act. G, Optional: Have students compare schedules in pairs, taking turns reading sentences. Make sure they pay close attention and take notes on their partner's schedule. Encourage them to exchange the information orally, not to simply show each other their written sentences. Tell them to keep the information they gather for the next section.

4

UN POCO DE GRAMÁTICA

The Workbook/Study Guide contains more detailed explanation and practice of this grammar point.

Using Verbs to Talk About Group Activities

You have already learned to use verbs to talk about what *you* and *I* are doing individually. To indicate what *we* are doing together, use the endings **-amos**, **-emos**, or **-imos**.

MIGUEL: Jaime y yo viv**imos** en el barrio de Triana. Estudi**amos** en la escuela San Francisco de Paula. Mamá dice que deb**emos** estudiar más...y yo no comprendo. ¡Creo que Jaime necesita estudiar mucho más que yo!

MIGUEL: *Jaime and I live in the Triana District. We study at the St. Francis de Paula school. Mom says that we should study more . . . and I don't understand. I think that Jaime needs to study a lot more than I do!*

Note: You may wish to review the verb paradigms for regular *-ar, -er,* and *-ir* verbs.

Optional: Have students use the information they gathered from the optional Actividad G (annotation, above) to prepare a report for the

Actividad. ¿Qué hacemos? (*What do we do?*)

What do we do as adults that children (**los niños**) don't? What do we do that's the same? Using the following list of phrases (and any others you can think of), make statements according to the model.

MODELO: beber cerveza (*to drink beer*) → Nosotros los adultos **bebemos** cerveza. Los dos (adultos y niños) **bebemos** leche (*milk*).

manejar (*to drive*) un auto
votar en las elecciones
asistir a la escuela
comer pizza
hablar por teléfono
escribir cartas
decir la hora (*to tell time*)

LECTURA CULTURAL

La España árabe

In previous episodes, you have learned a good deal about Sevilla and its cultural heritage. Do the following statements accurately describe Sevilla and the history of the region, based on what you now know?

C F 1. Andalucía es una región donde predomina la influencia árabe.
C F 2. Los árabes vivieron (*lived*) en España por mucho tiempo.
C F 3. En el arte árabe no se reproduce la figura humana.
C F 4. La Alhambra era (*was*) la residencia de los monarcas árabes. (¿Recuerdas *Tales of the Alhambra*, de Washington Irving?)

After you have read the following passage about the general cultural history of southern Spain, review this activity to see whether you wish to change any answers. The passage is included in the audio CD as well. You may wish to listen to it on the CD the first time you read it.

Es en Andalucía donde hay más influencia del arte árabe. Fiel al dogma del Corán, el arte árabe no reproduce nunca la figura humana. Se caracteriza por sus líneas curvas y sus complicados motivos geométricos.

En estas fotografías se ven algunos[1] de los monumentos más famosos de la cultura árabe en España. Identifica la foto que corresponda a cada descripción.

[1]*some*

1.

2.

_____ La Alhambra, de Granada, era residencia de los reyes[2] moros y un verdadero palacio del placer.[3] El Patio de los Leones es el sitio que los turistas visitan con más frecuencia.

_____ El Alcázar de Sevilla es un palacio árabe, construido en el siglo[4] XIV. Esta residencia de los monarcas es de estilo mudéjar. El arte mudéjar combina la ornamentación árabe y la arquitectura del arte cristiano.

_____ La Mezquita[5] de Córdoba es hoy una catedral cristiana. Este antiguo[6] templo del Islam tiene una infinidad de columnas de mármol[7] de formas diferentes.

¿Por qué[8] hay tanta influencia árabe en esta parte de España?

Datos importantes sobre los siglos VIII–XV

● 711 (setecientos once): Los árabes invaden la Península Ibérica. Encuentran mucha oposición, pero después de[9] siete

3.

Lectura cultural, Preguntas: 1. *¿Dónde se encuentra la Alhambra? (Granada)* 2. *¿Dónde se encuentra el Alcázar? (Sevilla)* 3. *¿Dónde se encuentra la Mezquita? (Córdoba)* 4. *¿Cómo se llaman los Reyes Católicos? (Isabel y Fernando)*

[2]*kings* [3]*pleasure* [4]*century* [5]*Mosque* [6]*former* [7]*marble* [8]*¿Por... Why* [9]*después... after*

años, dominan toda la Península, con excepción del País Vasco y parte de Asturias.

- 1492 (mil cuatrocientos noventa y dos): Isabel de Castilla y Fernando de Aragón, los Reyes Católicos, conquistan Granada, el último reino[10] moro en territorio español. Es el fin de la dominación árabe en España… y el comienzo de la dominación española del Nuevo Mundo, con el primer viaje de Cristóbal Colón.

Una de las principales características de la dominación árabe en España es la tolerancia religiosa. Con unas excepciones, hay largos períodos de convivencia[11] pacífica. Cristianos, árabes y judíos viven y trabajan juntos.[12] En contraste, en 1492 los Reyes Católicos expulsan a los judíos. Los que[13] no desean convertirse al catolicismo están obligados a salir de España.

[10]último… *last kingdom*   [11]*living together*   [12]*together*   [13]Los… *Those who*

Actividad.   ¿Árabe, cristiano o judío?

Based on the passage you have just read, who would have made the following statements, **los árabes**, **los cristianos**, or **los judíos**?

1. No debemos reproducir la figura humana en el arte.
2. Vivimos juntos con árabes y cristianos… y sin problemas.
3. Expulsamos a los judíos en 1492.

6

INTERCAMBIO

In this activity, you will compare your class schedule with those of your classmates.

Paso 1
Using the chart below, write out your class schedule.

	lunes	martes	miércoles	jueves	viernes
8.00					
9.00					
10.00					
11.00					
12.00					
1.00					
2.00					
3.00					
4.00					
5.00					

Paso 2

Walking about the room, try to find at least three people who each have at least one class subject that you have. Also find out at what time your classmates have those classes. Keep track of the information in the chart from **Paso 1**.

> MODELO: TÚ: ¿Tienes una clase de biología? ¿Sí? ¿A qué hora?
> ¿Tienes una clase de arte? ¿No? Gracias.

Paso 3

Write out three statements about what you discovered.

> MODELO: TÚ: Mary y yo tenemos una clase de biología. Ella va a la clase a las 9.00 los martes y jueves pero yo voy a las 11.00 los lunes y miércoles...

VOCABULARIO

Los verbos

cenar	to have dinner
comprender	to understand
correr	to run
vender	to sell
dice(n)	he/she says (they say)
encuentra(n)	he/she finds (they find)
se pierde	he/she gets lost
sale(n)	he/she leaves (they leave)
va(n)	he/she goes (they go)
vamos	we go

Las personas

el ciego	blind man
el niño/la niña	young boy/young girl

¿Qué hora es? (What Time Is It?)

Es la una.	It's one o'clock.

Son las dos (tres...)	It's two (three . . .) o'clock.
...y cuarto	. . . fifteen (quarter past . . .)
...y media	. . . thirty (half past . . .)
...de la mañana	A.M., in the morning
...de la tarde	P.M., in the afternoon
...de la noche	P.M., in the evening/at night
¿A qué hora... ?	At what time . . . ?
a la.../a las...	at . . .

Los días de la semana (Days of the Week)

lunes, martes, miércoles, jueves, viernes, sábado, domingo

Las palabras adicionales

hoy	today
más	most

¿MAESTRA?*

Teacher?

OBJETIVOS

Part of this episode is a review. Be sure to work through all parts of the lesson. When you see a headphones symbol in the margin, listen to the CD for **Lección 6**. Answers or hints for many activities are given in Appendix 1. Be sure to check your answers for each activity before going on to the next one.

The interactive CD-ROM to accompany *Destinos* contains additional practice with the video storyline and will help you improve your skills in Spanish.

BEFORE VIEWING . . .

Preliminary: See Faculty Guide for additional information and activities for this lesson.
• **Variation:** For activities marked with the headphones icon, you may wish to read from the Audioscript instead of playing the CD.

1

PREPARACIÓN

• **Suggestion:** Make sure students are familiar with the activities before you read from the Audioscript or play the CD.

Suggestions:
• Before watching the video, go over the vocabulary list at the end of the chapter and have students pronounce the words after you.
• Assign *Preparación* activities as homework and then go over them quickly in class before viewing the video.

The Workbook/Study Guide contains additional practice and review.

Actividad A.

In previous episodes of *Destinos* you have followed Raquel's investigation to Spain. What do you remember about her investigation and trip? Select the correct statement in each group. **Act. A, Answers:** 1. a 2. a 3. b

1. _____ a. En Sevilla, Raquel habla con uno de los hijos de Teresa Suárez.
   _____ b. En Sevilla, Raquel habla con Teresa Suárez.
2. _____ a. Raquel sale de Sevilla para Madrid.
   _____ b. Raquel sale de Madrid para Sevilla.
3. _____ a. Raquel va en avión.
   _____ b. Raquel va en tren.

Act. B, Suggestion: You may want to have students work in pairs for this exercise to brainstorm what they remember.

Act. B, Point out: As a prediction exercise, this has no (in)correct responses.

Actividad B.

What do you think will happen in this video episode? Try to predict what will happen by answering the following questions.

1. Raquel will speak to this person on the train. Who do you think he is?
   _____ Es reportero.
   _____ Es el conductor del tren.

2. What do you think this person wants?
   _____ Desea entrevistar (*to interview*) a Raquel.
   _____ Desea viajar con Raquel en su compartimiento.

Act. B, Answers: 1. *Es un reportero.* 2. *Desea entrevistar a Raquel.*

Actividad C.
Paso 1

Here is part of a conversation that Raquel will have with someone on the train. Read through the conversation to get a general idea of what it is about.

Act. C, Answers: 1. b 2. b 3. a

—Aquí estoy en el rápido de Sevilla a Madrid. Conmigo está la ganadora del premio especial de la Organización Nacional de Ciegos.
—¿La lotería?
—Ud. estará muy contenta de su buena suerte.
—Perdone, pero no sé de qué habla.
—Esta maestra de primaria es la señora Díaz. Su clase de sexto grado le compró un cupón y...

 ### Paso 2

Now listen to the conversation on the audio CD. **Su buena suerte** means *your good luck.* Now that you know that, can you guess the meaning of the words **ganadora** and **premio**?

1. La palabra **ganadora** significa
   a. _____ a person who lives in Granada.
   b. _____ winner.

2. La palabra **premio** significa
   a. _____ primary.
   b. _____ prize.

3. Based on your guesses so far, on the title of this video episode (called **¿Maestra?**), and on what you have learned in **Actividad C**, what do you think is happening?
   a. _____ El hombre cree que Raquel es otra persona.
   b. _____ El hombre sabe algo de don Fernando y busca más información, como Raquel.

 . . . AFTER VIEWING

2

¿TIENES BUENA MEMORIA?

Actividad A. Los nuevos personajes

The most important new character in this video episode appears to be the reporter. What do you remember about the interaction between him and Raquel? Complete the following statements. ¡OJO! There may be more than one right answer in some cases.

1. El reportero se llama… Federico Suárez / Afredo Sánchez.
2. Alfredo cree que Raquel es… la ganadora de un premio / una reportera para la televisión / una maestra de primaria.
3. Alfredo… encuentra / no encuentra …a la maestra de primaria durante este episodio.
4. Raquel… acepta / rechaza (*rejects*) …el interés que tiene el reportero en el caso de don Fernando.
5. El reportero… desea investigar más / acepta la negativa de Raquel.

Actividad B. En este episodio

All of the following events took place during the trip shown in **Episodio 6**, but . . . in what order did they occur? Put them in order, from 1 to 4 in each group.

En el compartimiento de Raquel

a. _____ Raquel dice que no es la ganadora del premio.
b. _____ Un reportero desea entrevistar a Raquel.
c. _____ Raquel escribe en su computadora. Está sola.
d. _____ Otro señor entra en el compartimiento.

Luego

a. _____ Raquel dice que el caso es un secreto.
b. _____ El tren llega a la estación.
c. _____ El reportero pregunta mucho sobre el caso de Raquel.
d. _____ Raquel y el reportero comen (*eat*) algo.

En la estación del tren

a. _____ Raquel sale en taxi.
b. _____ Ve el sobre (*envelope*) de la carta.
c. _____ El reportero acompaña a Raquel a un taxi.
d. _____ El reportero llama a su oficina.

3

REPASO DE LOS EPISODIOS 1–5

Actividad A. Resumen

Complete the following summary of the first five video episodes of *Destinos* with words from the following lists. ¡OJO! Not all of the words will be used.

Nombres: Jaime, don Fernando, Teresa Suárez, Miguel, Rosario, Ramón

Miembros de la familia: el esposo, el hijo, el hermano, el tío

Lugares: México, España, La Gavia, Sevilla, Madrid

Verbos: toma, investiga, vende, vive, compra, encuentra, saben

Otras palabras: algo, nada, siempre

En México, un hombre muy viejo está gravemente enfermo. Se llama

_____.[1] Este señor recibe una carta y la carta tiene un gran secreto.
El señor revela el secreto a su familia: que su primera esposa,

_____,[2] no murió en la Guerra Civil española.

Pedro, el _____[3] de don Fernando, llama a Raquel Rodríguez.

Raquel va a viajar a _____,[4] a la ciudad de _____,[5] para

buscar a _____,[6] la persona que escribió la carta. Pero la señora ya

no _____[7] allí.[a] Raquel habla con Elena Ramírez y con su

_____[8] Miguel Ruiz, quien es también un _____[9] de

Teresa Suárez. Ellos no _____[10] nada de la historia de Rosario.

El domingo Raquel acompaña a la familia al mercadillo de los animales.

Los hijos de Miguel y Elena quieren un perro y su padre _____[11]

uno. ¿Y qué pasa? El perro se escapa y _____[12] se pierde en las

calles de Sevilla buscándolo.[b] Raquel corre por las calles también y finalmente

_____[13] a Jaime. Los dos hablan un poco con un hombre ciego

que _____[14] cupones de la lotería.

[a]*there* [b]*looking for him*

Por fin Raquel y Jaime se reúnen con el resto de la familia. Al día

siguiente Raquel _____¹⁵ un tren para Madrid. Allí vive la

señora Suárez con otro hijo. Raquel todavía no sabe _____¹⁶

de Rosario.

Act. B, Suggestion: Have students practice conversations several ways: teacher to student, half the class to the other half, in pairs.

Actividad B.   Una fiesta

Your instructor will assign everyone in the class the identity of a character from the first five episodes of *Destinos*. The class will then have a party, at which everyone mingles and greets each other. ¡OJO! You must not give your identity to anyone until they guess it. Can you find out who everyone is?

VOCABULARIO

Las personas

el ganador/la ganadora	winner
el maestro/la maestra	grade-school teacher
el reportero/la reportera	reporter, journalist

Las cosas

el premio	prize

Un viaje a Madrid (España)

La Plaza Mayor de Madrid

LA CARTERA*

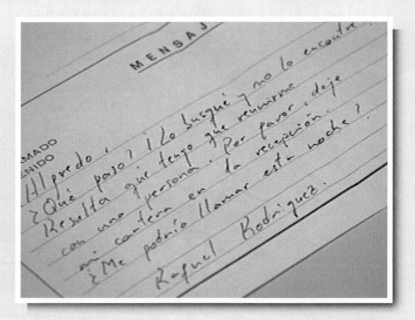

*The Wallet

OBJETIVOS

The materials in **Lección 7** of the Textbook and the Workbook/Study Guide will help you better understand the video episode and take you beyond it, giving you additional information about places and characters in the series. The Textbook will also help you to develop skill in using the Spanish language. In this lesson you will learn

- Spanish numbers from 21 to 99
- names for many articles of clothing
- ways to talk about who and what you know

You will also learn about the transition from dictatorship to democracy in today's Spain.

Be sure to work through all parts of the lesson. When you see a headphones symbol in the margin, listen to the CD for **Lección 7**. Answers or hints for many activities are given in Appendix 1. Be sure to check your answers for each activity before going on to the next one.

The interactive CD-ROM to accompany *Destinos* contains additional practice with the video storyline and will help you improve your skills in Spanish.

BEFORE VIEWING . . .

Preliminary: See Faculty Guide for additional information and activities for this lesson.
• **Variation:** For activities marked with the headphones icon, you may wish to read from the Audioscript instead of playing the CD.
• **Suggestion:** Make sure students are familiar with the activities before you read from the Audioscript or play the CD.

1

PREPARACIÓN

Suggestions:
• Before watching the video, go over the vocabulary list at the end of the chapter and have students pronounce the words after you.
• Assign *Preparación* activities as homework and then go over them quickly in class before viewing the video.

a.

b.

Actividad A.
Paso 1
In the last episode of *Destinos* Raquel left Sevilla by train, on her way to Madrid to meet Sra. Suárez. What happened on the train? Indicate what you remember by identifying these two men.

1. _____ Viaja con Raquel en su compartimiento.
2. _____ Es reportero de la televisión.

Paso 2
Now indicate whether the following statements about **Episodio 6** are **Cierto (C)** or **Falso (F)**.

Act. A, Answers: *Paso 1:*
1. b   2. a; ***Paso 2:*** 1. C
2. F   3. F   4. F (See Appendix 1 for expanded answers.)

C F 1. El reportero cree que Raquel es otra persona.
C F 2. El reportero no sabe por qué (*why*) Raquel está en España.
C F 3. El señor que viaja en el compartimiento con Raquel se llama Alfredo Sánchez.
C F 4. El reportero no tiene ningún (*any*) interés en el caso que investiga Raquel.

Act. B, Point out: As a prediction exercise, this has no (in)correct responses.

Actividad B.
What do you think will happen in this episode of *Destinos*? Indicate whether the following events are likely (**Probable**) or unlikely (**Improbable**) to happen.

P IMP 1. Raquel finalmente conoce a la Sra. Suárez.
P IMP 2. El reportero sigue (*follows*) a Raquel porque quiere saber algo más del caso.
P IMP 3. El reportero encuentra a la maestra que ganó (*won*) el premio de la lotería.
P IMP 4. El reportero es persistente. Por fin Raquel le dice algo del caso que investiga.

Act. C, Answer: 3

Actividad C.
Here is one of the new characters you will meet in **Episodio 7**. As you look at the photo, listen to the brief description on the CD. Then indicate who you think the man might be.

1. _____ Es el asistente que trabaja con el reportero.
2. _____ Es el recepcionista del hotel donde se aloja (*stays*) Raquel en Madrid.
3. _____ Es un hijo de la Sra. Suárez; vive en Madrid con ella.
4. _____ Es el hijo de don Fernando y Rosario.

Actividad D.
Paso 1

Here is part of a conversation that Raquel will have with a bellhop (**un botones**) at her Madrid hotel. Read through the conversation to get a general idea of what it is about.

> BOTONES: ¡Qué pena lo de la cartera! Ojalá la encuentre pronto.
> RAQUEL: Gracias. Un amigo está buscando el taxi ahora mismo. ¿Me puede hacer el favor de dejar un mensaje con el recepcionista?
> BOTONES: Con mucho gusto, señorita.
> RAQUEL: Cuando vuelva mi amigo, que me llame por teléfono.
> BOTONES: ¿Y cómo se llama su amigo?
> RAQUEL: Alfredo Sánchez. Bueno, realmente no es mi amigo. Es un reportero que conocí en el tren.

Paso 2

Now listen to the conversation on the CD. **Dejar** means *to leave*. Now that you know that, can you guess the meaning of the word **mensaje**?

La palabra *mensaje* significa

a. _____ messenger
b. _____ message

Based on your guesses so far, on the title of this video episode, and on what you have learned in **Actividad D**, what do you think will happen to Raquel?

a. _____ Raquel pierde (*loses*) su cartera.
b. _____ Raquel encuentra la cartera de otra persona, una persona muy importante para el caso.

 . . . AFTER VIEWING

2

¿TIENES BUENA MEMORIA?

Actividad A. ¿Quién... ?
Paso 1

In **Episodio 7** you met some new characters and there is some confusion about who is who! Show that you know the characters by matching the following characters with their brief description.

1. _____ Federico Ruiz
2. _____ Alfredo Sánchez
3. _____ el Sr. Díaz

a. un reportero
b. otro hijo de la Sra. Teresa Suárez
c. el botones que toma el mensaje de Raquel
d. un maestro de primaria

Paso 2

Working with a partner, one of you should cover the following sentences while the other reads them aloud. The first student tries to match the characters with the statements that describe them and must also *make one other statement* about that person. ¡OJO! More than one name may be possible for some statements.

a. Federico Ruiz   d. Raquel Rodríguez
b. Alfredo Sánchez   e. Teresa Suárez
c. el Sr. Díaz

1. _____ Pierde su cartera.
2. _____ Encuentra la cartera perdida.
3. _____ Busca a Raquel en el hotel.
4. _____ Quiere conocer (*meet*) a Raquel.
5. _____ Está alojado/a (*staying*) en el Hotel Príncipe de Vergara.
6. _____ Espera (*Waits for*) a una persona en el hotel.

Actividad B.   ¿Qué pasa?
Paso 1

At this point, you know more about what happened this evening at the Hotel Príncipe de Vergara than some of the characters do! Answer the following questions about the slightly confusing events that happened in **Episodio 7**.

1. ¿Por qué no recibe Raquel su cartera en este episodio?
    a. _____ Porque Alfredo dice que no puede (*he can't*) llegar al hotel hasta mañana.
    b. _____ Porque Raquel no puede encontrar a Alfredo y decide irse con Federico.

2. ¿A quiénes confunde el botones cuando escribe la nota?
    a. _____ Confunde a Alfredo Sánchez con Federico Ruiz.
    b. _____ Confunde al Sr. Díaz con Alfredo Sánchez.

3. ¿Qué confusión hay con el Sr. Díaz en la recepción?
    a. _____ Creen que es una *señora*.
    b. _____ No tienen su reservación.

Paso 2
Now listen to the answers on the CD.

Actividad C.   ¡Un desafío!

Spain has a long and proud tradition of government by monarchy. You saw a number of famous Spanish monarchs in this video episode and you will learn more about the current Spanish monarchy later on in this lesson. Here are some of the names of the rulers from the video episode, in chronological order. Given what you know about Spanish history, can you match the names with the brief descriptions of them? ¡OJO! More than one name may be possible for each statement.

a. Alfonso X, el Sabio (*The Wise*)   c. Isabel de Castilla
b. Fernando de Aragón   d. Carlos I

1. _____ Es esposo de una reina católica.
2. _____ Cristóbal Colón habla con esta persona acerca de un proyecto especial.
3. _____ Es un monarca español durante la época de la grandeza del Imperio español.
4. _____ Conquistan a los árabes.
5. _____ Es monarca cuando todavía hay muchos árabes en España.

3

VOCABULARIO DEL TEMA

La ropa

la blusa	blouse	**la falda**	skirt
la bufanda	scarf	**el jersey**	sweater (*Spain*)
la camisa	shirt	**las medias**	stockings
la camiseta	T-shirt	**los pantalones**	pants
los calcetines	socks	**el suéter**	sweater
la chaqueta	jacket	**el vestido**	dress; woman's suit
la corbata	necktie	**el zapato**	shoe
unas medias	a few pairs of stockings	**un par de...** zapatos pantalones	a pair of . . . shoes pants
unos calcetines	a few pairs of socks		

Of the two words that express *sweater,* **el suéter** is more widely used in the Spanish-speaking world. **El jersey** is used primarily in Spain.
   Note the use of **unos/unas** to mean *a few.*

ROPA DE CABALLERO	LINGE DE MESSIEURS	GENTLEMEN'S LINEN	PTAS.
Camisa	Chemise	Shirt	450
Camiseta	Chemisette	Undershirt	250
Calzoncillo . . .	Caleçon	Underpants	250
Calcetines . . .	Chaussettes . . .	Socks	225
Pañuelo	Mouchoir	Handkerchief . . .	275

Actividad A. ¿Qué ropa tiene Raquel?

Listen as Raquel lists the articles of clothing that she has brought with her on this trip. As she mentions each item, check it off in the following drawing and note how many of each item she has. ¡OJO! Some of the items depicted are not in Raquel's luggage. Look at the items before Raquel begins.

Act. A, Answers:
2 blusas, 2 suéteres, una falda, un vestido, 2 pares de zapatos, unas medias, un par de pantalones. Raquel decide que no tiene suficiente ropa.

Act. A, Follow-up: Ask students: *¿Qué ropa necesita Raquel? ¿Necesita otro vestido? ¿más zapatos?*, etc.

What does Raquel finally say about the amount of clothing she has with her?

_____ Tengo suficiente ropa.

_____ No tengo suficiente ropa.

Actividad B. ¿Dónde está la ropa de Federico?

Listen as Teresa Suárez comments on the way her son takes care of his clothing. As she mentions each item, check it off in the following drawing. ¡OJO! Some of the items depicted are not in Federico's room. Look at the items before Sra. Suárez begins.

Act. B, Answers: *camisa, camiseta, calcetines, corbata, chaqueta, pantalones, bufanda, jersey. La Sra. Suárez no está muy contenta con su hijo.*

Act. B, Follow-up: Ask students: *¿Tienes la ropa muy ordenada como Raquel o muy desordenada como Federico? ¿Les importa mucho la ropa? ¿Les gusta comprar ropa?*

How do you think Sra. Suárez feels about the way her son takes care of things?

_____ Cree que Federico es muy ordenado (*neat*). Está muy contenta con él.

_____ No está muy contenta con él. Federico no es muy ordenado.

Actividad C. ¿Qué llevan?

What was Raquel wearing when she arrived at the hotel? What is Alfredo wearing in this photo? Describe their clothing as completely as you can.

Raquel lleva…

Alfredo lleva…

Act. C, Follow-up: Bring in about 6 pictures of a variety of people wearing different types of clothing. Have the students form pairs with one partner facing the front of the class and the other facing the rear. Line up the pictures in the front of the class so that one partner can see them but the other cannot. Then, the front-facing partner describes one of the pictures. Encourage students to negotiate misunderstandings by using expressions such as *No entiendo. Repite, por favor. ¿Cómo?*, etc. When they finish, the other person looks at the pictures and tries to determine which one his/her partner has described.

Act. D, Optional vocabulary: *la gorra, los guantes, los pantalones cortos, la sudadera, el traje.* Be prepared to supply additional vocabulary if requested.

Actividad D. La ropa de mi compañero/a
Paso 1

Act. D, Follow-up: Poll students to find out what clothing people need most. Have a student come to the board and keep track of the articles of clothing. Ask *¿Qué ropa necesita tu compañero/a?* Then, *¿Quién más necesita _____?* After determining the most-often mentioned clothing, ask *¿En esta ciudad, qué tienda tiene buen(a/os/as) _____?*

Asking at least ten questions, find out what a classmate's wardrobe is like. Jot down his or her answers.

> MODELO: TÚ: ¿Cuántos pares de zapatos tienes? ¿Tienes zapatos formales o sólo (*only*) tienes zapatos de tenis?…

Paso 2

Based on the information you have obtained, decide what articles of clothing your partner could use to augment his or her wardrobe. Ask your instructor for help with vocabulary if necessary.

Vocabulary, Suggestion: Practice pronunciation with choral and individual repetition.

Los números del 21 al 99

21 veintiuno*	30 treinta	70 setenta
22 veintidós	31 treinta y uno*	80 ochenta
23 veintitrés	32 treinta y dos	90 noventa
24 veinticuatro	33 treinta y tres	
25 veinticinco	…	
26 veintiséis	40 cuarenta	
27 veintisiete	50 cincuenta	
28 veintiocho	60 sesenta	
29 veintinueve		

Express a year in the twentieth century by using the phrase **mil novecientos** (19–) followed by the appropriate numbers. Express a year in this century by using **dos mil** followed by the appropriate numbers.

1993	mil novecientos noventa y tres
2003	dos mil tres

---

* The numbers 21–29 can be written as one word (as in the list) or as three: **veinte y uno, veinte y dos.** From 31 to 99, compound numbers are written as three words only.

Actividad E.   ¿Cuál es el número?

The speaker on the CD will say a number. Circle the number you hear in each group.

1.   63   73   53   3.   76   66   36
2.   41   81   91   4.   55   45   95

Actividad F.   ¿Cuál es el teléfono?

Now the speaker will give a series of telephone numbers. As you listen, supply the missing numbers.

1.   3–_____–33–_____   3.   7–36–_____–_____   5.   5–_____–25–_____
2.   _____–99–_____–68   4.   _____–75–_____–91   6.   7–15–_____–_____

Actividad G.   Números... y más números

You may not have to deal with as many numbers as does the hotel receptionist in Sevilla, but there are still many numbers that are personally important to you. Give the following numbers in Spanish.

1.   tu número de teléfono: el... (¡OJO! Follow the pattern for telephone numbers shown in **Actividad F**.)
2.   el número de teléfono de tu mejor amigo/a (*best friend*)
3.   el número de teléfono de tus padres/tus hijos
4.   la edad (*age*) de uno de tus padres: Mi padre/madre tiene _____ años.
5.   ¿tu número de la suerte (*lucky*)?

Actividad H.   En el año 2050...

Have you ever thought about how old you will be in certain years? See whether you can give your age for each year below.

MODELO: En el año _____, tendré

_____ años (*I*

will be _____ *years old*).*

1. 2005   2. 2015   3. 2022   4. 2041   5. 2050

---

*The phrase **tener... años** means *to be . . . years old*. **Tendré** is a future form of **tener**.

4

UN POCO DE GRAMÁTICA

The Workbook/Study Guide contains more detailed explanation and practice of this grammar point.

Note: You may wish to present the complete present-tense paradigms of *saber* and *conocer*.

Expressing *knowing*

Spanish speakers use **saber** to indicate that someone knows something and **conocer** to indicate knowing a person, meeting someone for the first time, or being familiar with a place.

Raquel no **sabe** dónde vive Rosario.	*Raquel doesn't know where Rosario lives.*
Sólo Teresa Suárez **conoce** a Rosario.	*Only Teresa Suárez knows Rosario.*

You will learn the irregular **yo** forms (**sé**, **conozco**) in the Workbook/Study Guide.

Actividad. ¿Qué sabes? ¿A quién conoces?

Indicate whether you think these statements are **Cierto** (**C**) or **Falso** (**F**) for anyone in the class.

Act., Point out: *saber* + *infinitive* = to know how to do something.
Act., Follow-Up: Verify answers by asking questions of the class in general. Ask for a show of hands if statements are true for any of the students.

Alguien (*Someone*) en esta clase…

Act., Variation: Do as a *Firma aquí* activity. Model question formation in *tú* form with *saber* and *conocer*. Give students about 5 minutes to go around the class asking the questions. If possible, they should find a different person to sign for each question. Follow up by asking the class ¿*Quién conoce personalmente al presidente / a la presidenta de la universidad?*, etc. Students respond with the name of a classmate who signed their paper.

C F 1. conoce personalmente al presidente / a la presidenta de la universidad.
C F 2. sabe tocar el violín.
C F 3. conoce la ciudad de Montreal.
C F 4. sabe bailar la salsa.
C F 5. conoce a un actor famoso / una actriz famosa.
C F 6. conoce un buen lugar en esta ciudad para comer *sushi.*
C F 7. sabe patinar sobre hielo (*ice-skate*).
C F 8. sabe mucha información acerca de (*about*) la civilización azteca.

Lectura cultural, **Sugestion:** Assign as homework and go over answers quickly in class. Remind students that they should not expect to understand every word of the reading, but rather to get the main ideas.

5

LECTURA CULTURAL

De la dictadura a la democracia

Refresh your memory about modern Spain by listening to what the narrator told you about the Spanish government in this video episode. Then reread the **Lectura cultural** about **la Guerra Civil española** in **Lección 2**. Reviewing information you already know about a topic makes reading about it easier. Before reading, you may also want to take a quick look at the questions in the **Actividad** that follows this **Lectura cultural.**

Lectura cultural, **Preguntas:** 1. ¿*Cuántos años duró la dictadura de Franco?* (36 años) 2. ¿*En qué año murió Franco?* (en 1975) 3. ¿*En qué año ocurrieron las primeras elecciones democráticas después de la muerte de Franco?* (en 1977); ¿*Cierto o Falso?* 4. *Los reyes Juan Carlos y Sofía no son populares en España.* (F) 5. *El papel político de los reyes españoles es semejante al papel de los reyes ingleses.* (C) 6. *España no tiene ninguna relación con el resto de Europa.* (F)

Desde 1939 hasta 1975 España es gobernada por[1] el régimen dictatorial del general Francisco Franco. La muerte[2] del general Franco en 1975 abre las puertas[3] a la democracia. Dos días después de[4] su muerte, el 22 de noviembre, don Juan Carlos I (nombrado por Franco su sucesor) es proclamado Rey de España. Son días difíciles para todos, pero el deseo de libertad y democracia permite una transición política pacífica.

En 1977 se celebran las primeras elecciones democráticas desde[5] 1936. La principal tarea[6] del nuevo gobierno es redactar[7] una nueva Constitución, con la colaboración de todos los partidos[8] políticos. La Constitución se aprueba[9] popularmente en diciembre del 78. Adolfo Suárez es elegido el primer presidente de gobierno

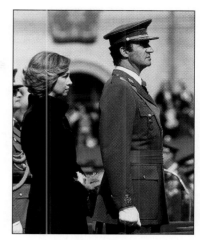

El rey don Juan Carlos y la reina doña Sofía

bajo la nueva Constitución. En 1982 los españoles votaron un gobierno socialista presidido por Felipe González, líder de su partido hasta 1995.

Así como en Inglaterra, el rey de España no tiene mucho poder[10] político. Más bien[11] es un símbolo de la larga historia política del país.[12] Pero, además de su papel[13] simbólico, el rey tiene algunos deberes. Por ejemplo, representa a España en muchas funciones nacionales e[14] internacionales.

Don Juan Carlos de Borbón y doña Sofía reinan en España con el respeto y la admiración de todo el pueblo.[15] En pocos años España se ha transformado de un país aislado[16] a un país europeo moderno. En el año 1986 entra en la Comunidad Económica Europea (que ahora se llama la Unión Europea), afirmando así su nueva posición en el continente.

---

[1]gobernada... *governed by* [2]*death* [3]abre... *opens the doors* [4]después... *after* [5]*since* [6]*task*
[7]escribir [8]*parties* [9]se... *is approved* [10]*power* [11]Más... *Rather* [12]*nación* [13]*role* [14]y [15]todo...
all the people [16]se... *has transformed herself from an isolated country*

Actividad.   ¿Cuánto sabes?

Match the names on the left with the descriptions on the right.

1. _____ el régimen de Franco
2. _____ el gobierno actual de España
3. _____ don Juan Carlos
4. _____ Adolfo Suárez
5. _____ Felipe González
6. _____ doña Sofía
7. _____ el rey español

a. Reina de España y esposa de Juan Carlos
b. una monarquía constitucional
c. el primer presidente del gobierno bajo la Constitución del 78
d. una dictadura
e. Rey de España; nombrado por Franco su sucesor
f. papel político más simbólico que verdadero
g. presidente socialista de España

6

INTERCAMBIO

In this activity you will practice talking about clothing that you and your classmates wear.

Paso 1
Observe your classmates and their clothes. In the chart below, jot down the number of items of clothing you see in class today.

La ropa que llevamos hoy			
bluejeans	otros tipos de pantalones	faldas	vestidos
jerseys	sudaderas (sweatshirts)	camisas	camisetas
blusas	zapatos de cuero (leather)	zapatos de tenis	zapatos para correr (running)
zapatos de otro tipo	¿ ?	¿ ?	¿ ?

Paso 2
Write down the three most popular articles of clothing you have noticed. Then using the following phrases or others you can think of, prepare a statement about each to explain why they are so popular.

1. _____   2. _____   3. _____

ser cómodo/a (*comfortable*)   durar (*to last*) mucho
ser barato/a (*inexpensive*)   ir bien con cualquier tipo de ropa
ser fácil de lavar (*wash*)   estar de moda (*in style*)

Intercambio, Paso 3,
Suggestion: Ask students to name the least popular item of clothing worn in class today. Using the phrases from *Paso 2*, why do they think students don't wear that article of clothing so much to class?

Follow-up: Ask students to identify the type of clothing that they think Raquel *never* wears and why.

Paso 3
Read your statements to the class. How many of your classmates say the same thing as you?

VOCABULARIO

Los verbos

dejar	to leave (*something*) behind
esperar*	to wait (for)
llevar	to wear
conoce	he/she knows, meets (*a person*)
pierde	he/she loses
puede	he/she can

Repaso: **sabe**

La ropa (Clothing)

la blusa	blouse
la bufanda	scarf
los calcetines	socks
la camisa	shirt
la camiseta	T-shirt
la cartera	wallet
la chaqueta	jacket
la corbata	necktie
la falda	skirt
el jersey (*Spain*)	sweater
las medias	stockings
los pantalones	pants
el suéter	sweater
el vestido	dress; woman's suit
el zapato	shoe

un par de...	a pair of . . .

Las personas

el botones	bellhop
el recepcionista	receptionist

Las cosas

el mensaje	message

Los números

treinta, cuarenta, cincuenta, sesenta, setenta, ochenta, noventa

mil novecientos...
dos mil...

Las palabras adicionales

acerca de	about
después de	after
¿por qué?	why?

---

*Note that *for* is included in the meaning of the verb **esperar** (just as **buscar** means *to look for*) Remember to use the personal **a** after this verb with specific persons. *Compare:* **Raquel espera el tren, Raquel espera a Jaime.**

8

EL ENCUENTRO*

Suggestion: Have students look at the photo, describe what they see, and talk about what they think might happen. Ask questions about the photo to prompt student discussion.

*The Encounter

OBJETIVOS

The materials in **Lección 8** of the Textbook and the Workbook/Study Guide will help you better understand the video episode and take you beyond it, giving you additional information about places and characters in the series. The Textbook will also help you to develop skill in using the Spanish language. In this lesson you will learn

- more about asking questions in Spanish
- more about the system of Spanish verbs

You will also learn about the differences between various areas of Spain.

Be sure to work through all parts of the lesson. When you see a headphones symbol in the margin, listen to the CD for **Lección 8**. Answers or hints for many activities are given in Appendix 1. Be sure to check your answers for each activity before going on to the next one.

The interactive CD-ROM to accompany *Destinos* contains additional practice with the video storyline and will help you improve your skills in Spanish.

BEFORE VIEWING . . .

Preliminary: See Faculty Guide for additional information and activities for this lesson.
• **Variation:** For activities marked with the headphones icon, you may wish to read from the Audioscript instead of playing the CD.
• **Suggestion:** Make sure students are familiar with the activities before you read from the Audioscript or play the CD.

1

PREPARACIÓN

Suggestions:
• Before watching the video, go over the vocabulary list at the end of the chapter and have students pronounce the words after you.
• Assign *Preparación* activities as homework and then go over them quickly in class before viewing the video.

Actividad A.

Act. A, Answers:
1. a. *Raquel Rodríguez (con el recepcionista)* 2. d. *Alfredo Sánchez (con Raquel)* 3. c. *el recepcionista (con el Sr. Díaz)* 4. d. *Alfredo Sánchez (con Raquel)* 5. a. *Raquel Rodríguez (con Alfredo)* 6. b. *Federico Ruiz (con Raquel)*

In the last video episode of *Destinos*, you watched a "comedy of errors" that occurred at Raquel's hotel. Things were lost, everyone was looking or waiting for someone else, and identities were confused. To be sure that you have understood the details, match these statements with the characters who made them.

a. Raquel Rodríguez   b. Federico Ruiz   c. el Sr. Díaz   d. Alfredo Sánchez

1. «¡Huy! No encuentro mi cartera.»
2. «No se preocupe. José María y yo se la vamos a buscar.»
3. «Perdón. Hay un error. La tarjeta está a nombre de la Sra. Díaz.»
4. «Ya he conseguido (*managed to get*) su cartera.»
5. «Por ser tan amable, lo invito a tomar algo.»
6. «Mi madre está muy agradecida y quiere invitarla a cenar con nosotros en casa esta noche.»

¡Un desafío! Can you also indicate with whom each character is speaking?

Actividad B.

The title of this episode, **El encuentro**, refers to the fact that Raquel will finally talk to Teresa Suárez. What questions is Raquel likely to ask her? Indicate whether it is **Probable (P)** or **Improbable (IMP)** that Raquel will ask these questions.

Act. B, Answers: 1. IMP 2. P 3. IMP 4. P 5. P (See Appendix 1 for expanded answers.)

P   IMP   1. ¿Por qué vive Ud. ahora en Madrid?
P   IMP   2. ¿Dónde está Rosario ahora?
P   IMP   3. ¿Cuándo murió el Sr. Ruiz, su esposo?
P   IMP   4. ¿Cómo sabe Ud. que don Fernando fue el esposo de Rosario?
P   IMP   5. ¿Cómo se llama el hijo de Rosario y don Fernando?

   Now formulate two more questions that Raquel might ask Sra. Suárez. How do you think Sra. Suárez will answer all of these questions?

Actividad C.

Act. C, Suggestion: Have students role-play the dialogue in *Paso 3*, first between teacher and student, then between one half of the class and the other, and finally in pairs.

In this activity you will learn about some key words and phrases that will enhance your understanding of **Episodio 8**.

Paso 1

Listen to the following excerpt from Raquel's conversation with Teresa Suárez. Now read the following sentences as you listen to them on the CD.

Don Fernando se casó con Rosario en 1935.
Don Fernando se casó con Carmen en 1942.
Teresa Suárez se casó con Juan Ruiz en 1941.

What do you think the phrase **se casó** means? If you guessed *got married*, you were right.

Paso 2

Look at this document, then answer the questions that follow.

This document is called **un certificado de nacimiento**. What kind of document do you think it is?

a. _____ an invitation to a function of some kind
b. _____ a letter
c. _____ a birth certificate
d. _____ a marriage license

Paso 3

As you know, Sra. Suárez is much older than Raquel. After Raquel has asked her questions, Teresa has a few of her own. Read this excerpt from their continuing conversation, and pay particular attention to the phrase **Cuando yo tenía su edad...**

SUÁREZ: ¿Es Ud. pariente de Fernando?
RAQUEL: No. Soy abogada. La familia de él me pidió que investigara el paradero de Rosario.
SUÁREZ: Así que tampoco es amiga cercana de la familia...
RAQUEL: Realmente no. Conozco bien a Pedro, el hermano de don Fernando.
SUÁREZ: Una señorita como Ud. tan atractiva, bien educada... ¡Y abogada! Eso era casi imposible cuando yo tenía su edad. Y ahora es tan corriente.

Paso 4

Now listen to the excerpt on the CD. Then answer the following question.

What do you think Teresa means when she says **cuando yo tenía su edad**?

a. _____ When I met my husband . . .
b. _____ When I was your age . . .
c. _____ When I left my home . . .

. . . AFTER VIEWING

2

¿TIENES BUENA MEMORIA?

Actividad A. ¿Quién lo hizo?

The following statements summarize the main events of **Episodio 8**. Who
carried out each one? ¡OJO! More than one name may be possible for each
statement.

¿Quién... ?

a.   Raquel
b.   Teresa
c.   Federico

1. _____ Finalmente conoce a la Sra. Suárez.
2. _____ Hace varias preguntas.
3. _____ Dice que Rosario vive en la Argentina.
4. _____ Dice que don Fernando está en el hospital.
5. _____ Tiene una carta de Rosario.
6. _____ Toma un fino (*sherry*) y cena.
7. _____ Cuenta (*tells*) la historia del perro perdido.
8. _____ Lleva a Raquel a su hotel.
9. _____ Llama a Elena Ramírez.
10. _____ Recibe un TELEX.

 ### Actividad B. ¿Quién lo va a hacer?

Work with a classmate to review the plans that people made in **Episodio 8**.
One of you will close the book while the other reads aloud the things that
the characters planned to do. Try to match each activity with the appropriate
character.

1.   Va a conseguir (*obtain*) un certificado de nacimiento.
2.   Va a darle una foto a la Sra. Suárez.
3.   Va a visitar un taller de guitarras.
4.   Va a tener que viajar a la Argentina.
5.   Va a visitar un museo famoso.
6.   Va a darle una cartera a Raquel.

Nota cultural La comida española

Tapas (Spanish *hors d'oeuvres*) have recently become popular in the United States. Consequently, you probably weren't surprised to see a number of the characters in *Destinos* having **tapas**. Olives (**las aceitunas**) and portions of **tortilla española** are typical Spanish snacks; others include **jamón serrano** (cured Spanish ham, similar to prosciutto) and **calamares fritos** (fried squid rings).

Having a snack and a drink of some kind in the late afternoon—a soft drink or mineral water, hot tea, an alcoholic beverage—is a popular Hispanic custom. In this video episode and in a previous episode you have seen some of the characters having **un fino** (a dry Spanish sherry), accompanied by the toast **¡Salud!** (*To your health!*). As you will see, the specific food items and beverages for the afternoon snack vary from country to country.

Finally, note that places like the bar (visited by Sr. Díaz and the reporter) and variations on them (**la Cervecería Giralda** from **Episodio 4**) do not have the negative connotations they can have in other cultures. You may recall that Miguel and Elena's children accompanied their parents into the pub.

Actividad C. ¿Qué más sabes ahora?

Raquel is finally finding out something about Rosario.

Paso 1

Indicate which of the following pieces of information Teresa Suárez gives Raquel.

1. _____ el nombre del segundo esposo de Rosario
2. _____ el número de teléfono de Rosario
3. _____ la fecha (*date*) en que Rosario se casó con Fernando
4. _____ la dirección (*address*) de Rosario en la Argentina
5. _____ el cumpleaños (*birthday*) de Rosario
6. _____ el nombre del hijo de Rosario y don Fernando

Paso 2

Now listen to Raquel's review of the essential information she has learned. She will repeat some of the details, so you have two chances to catch them. Because Raquel is talking about the past, remember that she will use many past-tense forms.

Paso 3

Now complete the following version of Raquel's review. Choose words and phrases from this list.

murió	la Argentina	un hijo	se casó
no murió	México	una hija	no se casó

La Sra. Suárez me cuenta la historia de Rosario. Rosario _____[1] durante la Guerra Civil española. Tampoco[a] murió don Fernando. Pero los dos creían que el otro había muerto.[b] Rosario sí tuvo _____[2] llamado[c] Ángel. Rosario y su hijo fueron a vivir a _____.[3] Allí[d] Rosario _____[4] de nuevo.[e] Su segundo esposo se llama Martín Iglesias.

[a]*Neither*   [b]había... *had died*   [c]*named*   [d]*There*   [e]de... *again*

3

VOCABULARIO DEL TEMA

Suggestion: Practice pronunciation with choral and individual repetition.

Las palabras interrogativas

¿cómo?	how?	**¿dónde?**	where?
¿cuál(es)?	which?	**¿por qué?**	why?
¿cuándo?	when?	**¿qué?**	what?
¿cuánto(s)?	how much? how many?	**¿quién(es)?**	who?

Most of these interrogative words should be familiar to you by now.

Note that interrogative words have an accent mark and that they are used with the inverted question mark (¿). You will learn more about using interrogatives in the Workbook/Study Guide.

Act., Variation: Practice interrogatives by playing Jeopardy with your students. Write answers on index cards and distribute them to each student. Divide the class into teams. One team member states the answer, and another team member asks the appropriate question. Models: *En Madrid.* (*¿Dónde está Raquel ahora?*); *Se llama Alfredo Sánchez.* (*¿Cómo se llama el reportero?*); *Tiene dos esposas.* (*¿Cuántas esposas tiene don Fernando?*), etc.

Actividad.   El profesor / La profesora

Paso 1

The class should divide into eight groups. Your instructor will assign one interrogative word (**¿cómo?**, **¿dónde?**, ...) to each group. Each group then creates a list of at least three questions to ask your instructor, such as where he or she lives, how he or she gets to school, and so on.

MODELO: ¿Dónde vive Ud.? (¿Dónde vives?)* ¿Dónde... ?

Paso 2

Each group then asks their questions from **Paso 1** until all questions have been asked. Be sure to jot down your instructor's responses to all questions.

---

* Depending on how you generally address your professor, you should use either **tú** or **usted** forms. See the **Nota cultural** on the next page for more information.

Paso 3 (Optativo)

Using the information obtained during **Paso 2**, write a paragraph of no more than 50 words about your instructor. While organizing your paragraph, feel free to edit and reorganize information so that your writing flows smoothly.

Nota cultural, **Extension:** Ask students whether they would use *tú* or *usted* with the following people: *un profesor, un niño, unas amigas, papá, el presidente de la universidad, la policía, una hermana.*

Nota cultural   Nos podemos tutear

As you know, Raquel uses **usted** with people she does not know well. In this video episode of *Destinos,* however, you heard one speaker "negotiate" for a less formal way of speaking. Do you remember who that was? As you listen, try to determine the word the speaker uses to describe informal use.

The words Federico used to express *using* **tú** *with each other* were **tutearse** or **tratarse de tú.** If someone asks you to do that, you will want to begin addressing him or her by using the second-person singular verb forms, just as Raquel shifts from **trabaja** to **trabajas**.

When everyone was in Teresa's kitchen, Federico tried to make Raquel feel at home with a frequently used phrase: **Está en su casa.** Now that Federico and Raquel address each other with **tú**, he would say: **Estás en tu casa.**

4

The Workbook/Study Guide contains more detailed explanation and practice of this grammar point.

Emphasis: Go over the paradigms for stem changing *-ar* and *-er* verbs on an overhead transparency. Stress the importance of learning these forms and note that the *yo* form is often different. **Suggestion:** Have students write out conjugations for these verbs for homework after going over them. **Follow-up:** In class the following day have the students put the verb paradigms on the board at the beginning of the class.

Optional:
• Have competition using first- and third-person forms in present tense. Divide the class in half.

Un poco de gramática

More About Verbs

You are already familiar with stem-changing verbs in Spanish.

> Raquel **encuentra** a Jaime en el barrio de Santa Cruz.
> Fernando **tiene** un hijo con Rosario.

These verbs are called stem-changing because four forms have a vowel change in the stem. Note the infinitives of the previous verbs in the following sentences.

> Raquel desea **encontrar** a Rosario.
> Fernando quiere **tener** noticias de Rosario.

Querer (**quiere**), another stem-changing verb, is a synonym of **desear**.
    You will learn more about stem-changing verbs in the Workbook/Study Guide.

You give the infinitive and a subject pronoun and one student from each team writes the appropriate form of the verb. For instance, you say *hacer, yo,* or *tener, ella,* and one student from each team quickly writes *hago* or *tiene* on the board. The first one to write the correct form wins a point for the team.
• Make a cube with a different subject pronoun appearing on each side. Have students toss the cube to each other, calling out infinitives. The person who catches the cube must conjugate the verb according to the subject pronoun facing him/her.

Actividad. ¿Quién en la clase?

How well do you know your classmates? Decide which member of the class is best described by the following statements. If no one fits the description, say **Nadie** (*No one*). As you read the statements, note the stem changes (for example, **viene** from **venir**).

> MODELO: Con frecuencia viene tarde a clase. → Con frecuencia Ken viene tarde a clase. (Nadie viene tarde a clase.)

Act., Suggestion: Do as a whole-class activity.

Act., Follow-up: Give names of individual students and ask the class what they do. Model: *Ken. ¿Qué hace Ken?* (*Viene tarde a clase.*)

1. Con frecuencia viene tarde a clase.
2. Duerme (*Sleeps*) en clase.
3. Tiene un auto nuevo.
4. Prefiere tener las clases por la tarde.
5. Prefiere tener las clases por la mañana.
6. Puede graduarse al final del semestre.
7. Pierde objetos frecuentemente.
8. Quiere tener muchos niños.
9. No quiere tener niños.
10. Sueña despierto/a (*Daydreams*) mucho.

Lectura cultural, **Suggestions:** Have students look at maps and text together in class before assigning listening activity for homework. It is helpful to have a large map of Spain in front of the room or on an overhead.

5

Lectura cultural

Las diferencias regionales en España

Before reading this **Lectura cultural**, refresh your memory about modern Spain by listening to what the narrator told you about the cities of Madrid and Sevilla in this video episode. Then reread the **Lectura cultural** in **Lección 3** about the contrasts that Spain presents, and the one in **Lección 5** about the Arab influence in Spain.

España se divide políticamente en 17 comunidades autónomas. Cada[1] autonomía tiene sus propias características geográficas y culturales.

Cataluña: en el norte

Cataluña es una de las zonas más prósperas de España. Es un centro industrial, agrícola y comercial muy importante. En Cataluña se habla otra lengua romance además del español: el catalán.

Barcelona es la ciudad catalana más grande y la segunda ciudad de España. La huella[2] del gran arquitecto Antoni Gaudí da un sabor[3] muy especial a esta ciudad cosmopolita.

[1]*Each*   [2]*influence*   [3]*flavor*

La Catedral de la Sagrada Familia, una iglesia excepcional de Barcelona: obra de Gaudí

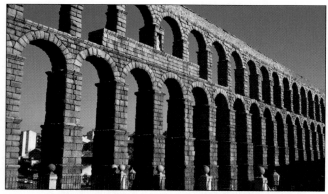

El acueducto de Segovia: un monumento de la civilización romana.

Castilla: el centro de la Península

En realidad hay dos comunidades con este nombre. Castilla-La Mancha es la zona más central del país. Tiene grandes extensiones de cereales[4] y molinos de viento.[5]

Castilla-León está llena de monumentos de gran interés histórico: la universidad de Salamanca (una de las más antiguas[6] de Europa), el acueducto romano de Segovia y otros.

[4]*grains*   [5]molinos... *windmills*   [6]más... *oldest*

Andalucía: en el sur

La variedad geográfica de Andalucía es impresionante. Hay dunas de arena[7] blanca, pueblecitos blancos. Tiene también las playas de la Costa del Sol, la Sierra Nevada y los mayores[8] desiertos del continente europeo (escenario de las famosas películas[9] del oeste de Clint Eastwood). ¿Y andaluces famosos? Entre ellos, Pablo Picasso, Diego Velázquez, el compositor Manuel de Falla y el poeta y dramaturgo Federico García Lorca.

Algunas autonomías en breve

- Valencia: Una zona agrícola muy rica, produce las famosas naranjas[10] valencianas.
- Asturias: Con sus montañas, valles y lagos, es la Suiza española.
- el País Vasco: La comunidad más industrializada y rica de España también atrae a los turistas a San Sebastián. Aquí se habla un idioma de origen desconocido.[11]
- Extremadura: En esta tierra de ganado[12] nacieron muchos de los exploradores del continente americano: Cortés, Pizarro, Balboa.
- las islas Canarias: Con su antiguo volcán, el Teide, son las islas Hawai del Océano Atlántico.

[7]*sand*   [8]*biggest*   [9]*movies*   [10]*oranges*   [11]*unknown*   [12]*cattle*

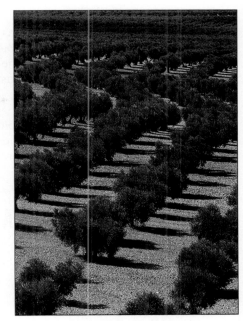

Olivares en una meseta de Andalucía

Actividad.   ¿Dónde?

Where would you expect to find the following people and things in Spain?

1. personas bilingües
2. casas muy antiguas
3. monumentos romanos
4. granjas (*farms*)
5. playas con hoteles
6. un paisaje (*landscape*) impresionante
7. muchas fábricas (*factories*)
8. ranchos

6

INTERCAMBIO

Paso 1

By now you have some ideas about Raquel. Using the interrogative words you know, make up five questions you would like to ask Raquel to find out more information about her. Use at least three different question words.

MODELO: TÚ: ¿Por qué no tienes marido?

Paso 2
Pass the questions to the person on your right. That person will try to answer those questions based on what he or she thinks of Raquel. You will answer questions from the person on your left. When you are finished, return the questions with answers to the person on your left.

Paso 3
One or two people will read their questions and answers out loud. If you have a similar question, raise your hand and tell the class how the person to your right answered. Are you all in agreement about Raquel and her life?

VOCABULARIO

Los verbos
se casó con — he/she married
cuenta — he/she tells
quiere — he/she wants

Los conceptos
la dirección — address
el encuentro — meeting
la guerra — war

Las palabras interrogativas (Interrogative Words)
¿cuándo? — when?
¿cuánto(s)? ¿cuánta(s)? — how much? how many?

Repaso: ¿cómo?, ¿cuál(es)?, ¿dónde?, ¿por qué?, ¿qué?, ¿quién(es)?

Los adjetivos
segundo/a — second

Las palabras adicionales
de nuevo — again
hacer preguntas — to ask questions

9

Estaciones*

*Seasons

Objetivos

The materials in **Lección 9** of the Textbook and the Workbook/Study Guide will help you better understand the video episode and take you beyond it, giving you additional information about places and characters in the series. The Textbook will also help you to develop skill in using the Spanish language. In this lesson you will learn

- names for the months and seasons
- colors
- more ways to talk about what you are doing

You will also learn about different kinds of Spanish music, including a special kind of singing group called **una tuna**.

Be sure to work through all parts of the lesson. When you see a headphones symbol in the margin, listen to the CD for **Lección 9**. Answers or hints for many activities are given in Appendix 1. Be sure to check your answers for each activity before going on to the next one.

The interactive CD-ROM to accompany *Destinos* contains additional practice with the video storyline and will help you improve your skills in Spanish.

BEFORE VIEWING . . .

Preliminary: See Faculty Guide for additional information and activities for this lesson.
● **Variation:** For activities marked with the headphones icon, you may wish to read from the Audioscript instead of playing the CD.
● **Suggestion:** Make sure students are familiar with the activities before you read from the Audioscript or play the CD.

1

PREPARACIÓN

Suggestions:
● Before watching the video, go over the vocabulary list at the end of the chapter and have students pronounce the words after you.
● Assign *Preparación* activities as homework and then go over them quickly in class before viewing the video.

Actividad A.

Episodio 8 was important in terms of the progress of Raquel's investigation. For the first time, Raquel has learned some concrete information about the case she is investigating. How much do you remember about the progress she made? Indicate whether the following statements are **Cierto (C)** or **Falso (F)**. If Raquel still does not know a particular piece of information, indicate **no se sabe todavía (NSS)**.

Act. A, Answers: 1. a. C b. F c. C d. F e. NSS 2. a. C b. F c. C d. F e. F (See Appendix 1 for expanded answers.)

1. Raquel descubre que Rosario
    C   F   NSS   a. no murió en la guerra.
    C   F   NSS   b. no tuvo un hijo.
    C   F   NSS   c. se fue a vivir a la Argentina.
    C   F   NSS   d. nunca se casó de nuevo.
    C   F   NSS   e. murió en la Argentina.
2. Al final del Episodio 8, Raquel
    C   F   NSS   a. llama a Elena Ramírez.
    C   F   NSS   b. necesita saber la dirección de Rosario en Buenos Aires.
    C   F   NSS   c. quiere un certificado de nacimiento.
    C   F   NSS   d. tiene la cartera perdida.
    C   F   NSS   e. recibe una carta.

Act. B, Point out: As a prediction exercise, this has no (in)correct responses.

Actividad B.

At the end of the last video episode Raquel received a TELEX. What do you think the TELEX is about? Choose the description that best expresses your expectations.

```
GA
27063
08111
27063 NHBAM E
*
27063 NHBAM E
27064 NHPVM E

    QUERIDA RAQUEL:
FERNANDO ESTA PEOR. ME URGE COMUNICARME CONTIGO.
  LLAMAME AL HOSPITAL INGLES 3-95-72-83

            SALUDOS, PEDRO
```

1. _____ Es un TELEX de Pedro. Le dice a Raquel que don Fernando está muy mal. Ella debe llamar a la familia Castillo inmediatamente.
2. _____ Es un TELEX de la oficina de Raquel en Los Ángeles. Ella tiene que volver a la oficina lo más pronto posible (*as soon as possible*).
3. _____ Es un TELEX del hotel Doña María, en Sevilla. Tienen algunas cosas que Raquel dejó en el hotel.

. . . AFTER VIEWING

2

¿TIENES BUENA MEMORIA?

Actividad A.   ¿Quién lo hace?

Match the following events or actions from the video episode with the person or persons associated with them. ¡OJO! More than one character may be associated with each item.

a.   Teresa Suárez
b.   Raquel Rodríguez
c.   el Sr. Díaz
d.   Federico Ruiz
e.   Alfredo Sánchez

1. _____ Va a un taller (*shop*) de guitarras para ver a Federico.
2. _____ Le da algo a Raquel.
3. _____ Escucha (*Listens to*) música.
4. _____ Quiere saber más acerca de un caso interesante.
5. _____ Revela la información correcta acerca de un caso.
6. _____ Compra ropa.
7. _____ Aprende (*Learns*) algo acerca de un caso.
8. _____ Va a una agencia de viajes.

Nota cultural, Note: In most parts of Spain, *un café solo* is served as a plain shot of espresso in a demitasse with sugar on the side. *Un cortado* is an espresso "cut" with just a bit of steamed milk, about half as much as for *un café con leche*. In Spain, *café con leche* is generally considered a breakfast drink while *un café solo* or *un cortado* is served after lunch or dinner. In the Spanish-speaking world, coffee is almost never served during meals other than breakfast, but rather as an after-meal drink.

Nota cultural   Un café, por favor

When Raquel ordered coffee (**un café, nada más**), the waiter poured it immediately from the pot that he had in his hand. Raquel could also have ordered her coffee by saying **un café solo**.

The waiter had to return with Alfredo's order, which was somewhat different: **Y un café con leche, por favor**. In many parts of the Spanish-speaking world, very strong coffee (almost like *espresso*) is mixed with warm or hot milk (**leche**). Sometimes the milk is served on the side and added by the customer, to his or her taste.

Actividad B.   Preguntas

With a partner, ask and answer the following questions about the characters listed. Try to combine your answers to form a brief description of events that took place in **Episodio 9**.

1.   don Fernando
     ¿Ya murió don Fernando?   ¿Dónde está ahora?   ¿Sabe esto Raquel?   ¿Cómo?

2. el Sr. Díaz

¿Por qué está el Sr. Díaz de viaje (*on a trip*)?   ¿Qué ganó?

3. Raquel

¿Adónde tiene que ir Raquel ahora?   ¿Qué necesita hacer antes de salir de Madrid?

3

VOCABULARIO DEL TEMA

Los meses y las estaciones del año

el invierno winter	**la primavera** spring	**el verano** summer	**el otoño** autumn
diciembre	marzo	junio	septiembre
enero	abril	julio	octubre
febrero	mayo	agosto	noviembre

Note that many Spanish speakers prefer the form **setiembre** (without the **p**). As you saw in **Episodio 9**, the seasons are reversed in the southern hemisphere.

ENERO						MARZO
L		7	14	21	28	
M	1	8	15	22	29	
M	②	9	16	㉓	30	
J	3	10	17	24	31	
V	4	11	18	25		
S	5	12	19	26		
D	6	13	20	27		

FEBRERO
L   4 11 18 25
M   5 12 19 26
M   6 13 20 27
J   7 14 21 ㉘
V ① 8 15 22
S 2 9 16 23
D 3 10 17 24

MARZO
L   4 11 18 25
M   5 12 19 26
M   6 13 20 27
J   7 14 21 28
V 1 8 ⑮ 22 29
S 2 9 16 23 30
D 3 10 17 24 31

Actividad A.   ¿México o Chile?

As you watched **Episodio 9**, you answered questions about the seasons in Spain and Argentina. Now do the same for Mexico and Chile. First listen to a description of the seasons in the different hemispheres. Then answer the questions you hear.

¿Se refiere a México o a Chile?

1. …   2. …   3. …   4. …

Actividad B.   ¿En qué mes... ?

Listen as the names of the following holidays are said by the speaker on the CD. Then indicate in Spanish the name of the month in which the following events occur in this country.

1. la celebración de la independencia de los Estados Unidos
2. el aniversario de la llegada (*arrival*) de Cristóbal Colón a América
3. el Día de Dar Gracias

4. el primer día del año
5. el Día del Padre
6. el Día de la Madre
7. el Día de San Valentín (el Día de los Enamorados [*Lovers*])
8. el Día de San Patricio
9. el Día del Trabajo (*Work*)
10. la Navidad y Chanuka

Actividad C.   ¿En qué estación?

Find someone in the class who has a birthday in each season listed below.
Write his or her name in the blank next to the name of the season. Then ask
the person to name the month in which he or she was born.

1. el invierno _____   (mes) _____
2. la primavera _____   (mes) _____
3. el verano _____   (mes) _____
4. el otoño _____   (mes) _____

Los colores

amarillo	yellow	**morado**	purple
anaranjado	orange	**negro**	black
azul	blue	**rojo**	red
blanco	white	**rosado**	pink
gris	gray	**verde**	green
marrón, pardo	brown		

Remember that adjectives must agree in number and gender with the nouns they modify.

- Adjectives that end in **-o** have four forms: **rojo,
  roja, rojos, rojas**.
- Adjectives that end in **-e** or in most consonants have
  only a singular and a plural form: **verde, verdes**; **azul, azules**.

Actividad D.   Asociaciones

What colors do you associate with the following words and phrases?

MODELO: la Navidad → el (color) verde, el (color) rojo…

1. el invierno
2. el verano
3. la primavera
4. el otoño
5. los peces tropicales
6. el perro Osito
7. Rosario
8. los gatos que traen mala suerte (*luck*)
9. el día de San Valentín
10. el día de San Patricio

Actividad E. La ropa más apropiada

Describe the clothing you think is most appropriate for the following occasions or the following places. Specify colors whenever possible.

Palabras útiles: las botas, los guantes (*gloves*), los pantalones cortos (*shorts*), un sombrero, una gorra (*cap*), el pijama

1. un partido (*game*) de fútbol norteamericano en tu universidad, en noviembre
2. un partido de béisbol, en julio
3. una discoteca, en mayo
4. un baile de gala (*formal*), en junio
5. una clase de química, en septiembre
6. un viaje a Colorado en febrero, para esquiar (*ski*)
7. un viaje a Acapulco, en agosto
8. un día en casa, en enero
9. una fiesta de Halloween

Actividad F. ¿Y tú?

Describe four things that you are wearing today, being certain to specify the color(s) of each item. Then select two other people and describe what they are wearing.

1. Hoy llevo… Me gustaría (*I would like*) llevar…
2. Mi amigo/a (profesor[a], esposo/a, hijo/a…) lleva…

4

UN POCO DE GRAMÁTICA

More About Talking About Yourself

When you are talking about someone else, you already know that **se** is used with some verbs.

> Raquel y la Sra. Suárez **se sientan** a hablar.
> El maestro **se llama** el Sr. Díaz.

To talk about yourself, use **me** with these verbs.

RAQUEL: **Me llamo** Raquel Rodríguez y soy una abogada muy dedicada. Nunca **me olvido** de mi cliente en México y siempre **pienso** en los detalles del caso. En este viaje no tengo mucho tiempo para pensar en mí… Y ahora… ¡otro viaje!

Did you notice in the example that stem-changing verbs also have a stem change in the **yo** form (**pienso**)?

Act., Extension: Have students create 2 more statements in the first-person singular. They should be statements that they believe someone in the class, including the professor, might make. Have individual students read a statement to the person they think might make it; the person addressed should respond with *Es cierto* or *No es cierto.*

Act., Optional: Read the following statements and have students identify the *Destinos* character who might say them: 1. *Me siento en el restaurante a hablar con Alfredo.*

Actividad.   ¿Quién habla?

(Raquel); 2. *Recuerdo muy bien a Rosario porque era buena amiga mía. (la Sra. Suárez)*; 3. *Pienso casarme con mi novia* (girlfriend) *pronto. (Federico*

Which of your friends, professors, acquaintances, or family members might make the following statements? If no one would, write **Nadie.**

1. _____ En clase, siempre me siento cerca (*near*) del profesor / de la profesora.

Ruiz); 4. *Vuelvo a Sevilla en unos días. (el Sr. Díaz)*; 5. *Me siento muy triste* (sad) *cuando pienso en la tragedia de don Fernando y Rosario. (la Sra. Suárez,*

2. _____ Pienso viajar a Europa algún (*some*) día.
3. _____ Me siento muy triste (*sad*) cuando pienso en mi madre.
4. _____ Empiezo a trabajar el año que viene (*next year*).
5. _____ Me acuerdo de cuando se casó (*got married*) mi hija.
6. _____ Vuelvo con frecuencia a la ciudad donde nací (*I was born*).
7. _____ Siempre me olvido de algo (*something*) cuando salgo de mi casa.
8. _____ Pienso casarme al final del año.

Raquel); 6. *No puedo comprender qué pasó con la maestra… (Alfredo Sánchez)*; 7. *Quiero comprar esta blusa de color salmón, por favor. (Raquel)*; 8. *Empiezo a contarle la historia al reportero. (el Sr. Díaz)*

5

LECTURA CULTURAL

La música española

Lectura cultural, Suggestions:
• Assign as homework and go over answers quickly in class. Remind students that they should not expect to understand every word of the reading, but rather to get the main ideas.
• Bring cassettes or CDs of your favorite Spanish music to class and play it for students. Explain why you like it and get their opinions. If you don't have any Spanish music in your collection, ask your colleagues or try your university or public media library.

In this video episode you learned about a special kind of Spanish musical group called **una tuna**. Refresh your memory about Spanish **tunas** by listening to an excerpt from **Episodio 9**. Then complete the following activity.

Which of the following statements accurately describe Spanish music, based on what you know now?

Lectura cultural, Answers:
1. F 2. F 3. C 4. C 5. F

C F 1. Toda la música española es folklórica, como las tunas.
C F 2. A los españoles no les gusta la música importada de otras naciones.
C F 3. El flamenco es de origen árabe y gitano (*gypsy*).
C F 4. Existe en España un tipo de «*light opera*» como «*Oklahoma*».
C F 5. La música preferida de los jóvenes es la ópera.

After you read the following passage about Spanish music, review this activity and see whether you wish to change any answers.

Toda la diversidad geográfica y cultural de España se refleja[1] en su música popular y en sus danzas. Probablemente el *folklore* español más conocido[2] en todo el mundo es el andaluz. El flamenco es una variedad de este *folklore*. El flamenco tiene profunda influencia oriental, árabe y gitana. Es una combinación de canciones[3] y bailes[4] que suele[5] acompañarse con palmas[6] y guitarras… y los famosos ¡*olé*!

[1]se… *is reflected*   [2]más… *best known*   [3]*songs*   [4]*dances*   [5]*is usually*   [6]*clapping hands*

Lectura cultural, Preguntas: 1. ¿Cuáles son dos formas de música folklórica en España? (flamenco, tunas) 2. ¿Pueden nombrar un compositor español de música clásica? (Albéniz, de Falla) 3. ¿Pueden nombrar un cantante lírico de España? (Montserrat Caballé, Plácido Domingo, Victoria de los Ángeles, José Carreras) 4. ¿Cómo se llama un grupo de música moderna de España? (Mecano)

Otro tipo de música muy típica de España es la zarzuela. Es un teatro lírico enteramente español de origen. La zarzuela, como una pequeña ópera, combina la declamación, el canto y la danza. Las zarzuelas reflejan las costumbres[7] o tradiciones de las diferentes zonas de España.

¿Te gusta la música clásica? Si dices que sí, probablemente reconoces los nombres de los siguientes grandes compositores de música clásica.

- Isaac Albéniz: la suite «Iberia», viaje musical por toda la Península
- Manuel de Falla: los ballets «El amor brujo»[8] y «El sombrero de tres picos»[9]

Y seguro que conoces los nombres de los siguientes cantantes líricos famosos internacionalmente: Montserrat Caballé, Plácido Domingo, Victoria de los Ángeles, José Carreras…

Pero no toda la música española es folklórica o clásica. El *rock* es la música más popular entre los jóvenes.[10] Y hay sitio para otros estilos. Hay canciones sociales, música melódica,[11] música con raíces[12] tradicionales, canciones románticas… El cantante español romántico de más fama internacional es Julio Iglesias. Un grupo moderno muy famoso desde hace años[13] es Mecano. Y el catalán Joan Manuel Serrat goza de fama mundial. A los jóvenes les gusta también la música importada, y hay para todos: Madonna, R.E.M., Ray Charles…

[7]*customs* [8]*El… Love, the Magician* [9]*El… The Three-Cornered Hat* [10]*young people* [11]*easy-listening* [12]*roots* [13]*desde… for a number of years*

Actividad. La música española y la norteamericana

What U.S. singers, groups, or works do you associate with the following types of Spanish music?

1. el *rock*
2. la canción social
3. la música melódica
4. la música con raíces tradicionales
5. la canción romántica
6. la zarzuela

6

INTERCAMBIO

Paso 1

Using all the Spanish you know now, write six statements about what you do on a typical day.

MODELO: Trabajo por la tarde, después de mis clases.

Paso 2

Using **Paso 1** as your base, interview people until you find someone who shares two or more activities with you. The person who finds someone with the most common activities wins!

MODELO: TÚ: ¿Trabajas por la tarde? ¿Sí? ¡Yo también!

VOCABULARIO

Los verbos

aprender	to learn
escuchar	to listen (to)
recibir	to get, receive

Los lugares

el taller	shop (*for manufacturing or repair*)

Los colores

amarillo/a	yellow
anaranjado/a	orange
azul	blue
blanco/a	white
gris	gray
marrón, **pardo/a**	brown
morado/a	purple
rojo/a	red
rosado/a	pink
verde	green

Repaso: **negro/a**

Las estaciones del año (Seasons of the Year)

la primavera	spring
el verano	summer
el otoño	autumn
el invierno	winter

Los meses del año: enero, febrero, marzo, abril, mayo, junio, julio, agosto, septiembre, octubre, noviembre, diciembre

LECCIÓN 10

CUADROS*

*Paintings

OBJETIVOS

The materials in **Lección 10** of the Textbook and the Workbook/Study Guide will help you better understand the video episode and take you beyond it, giving you additional information about places and characters in the series. The Textbook will also help you to develop skill in using the Spanish language. In this lesson you will learn

* ways to describe physical characteristics
* more ways to talk about what you are going to do with others

You will also learn information about a number of well-known Spanish artists.

Be sure to work through all parts of the lesson. When you see a head-phones symbol in the margin, listen to the CD for **Lección 10**. Answers or hints for many activities are given in Appendix 1. Be sure to check your answers for each activity before going on to the next one.

The interactive CD-ROM to accompany *Destinos* contains additional practice with the video storyline and will help you improve your skills in Spanish.

BEFORE VIEWING . . .

Preliminary: See Faculty Guide for additional information and activities for this lesson.
• **Variation:** For activities marked with the headphones icon, you may wish to read from the Audioscript instead of playing the CD.
• **Suggestion:** Make sure students are familiar with the activities before you read from the Audioscript or play the CD.

1

Preparación

Suggestions:
• Before watching the video, go over the vocabulary list at the end of the chapter and have students pronounce the words after you.
• Assign *Preparación* activities as homework and then go over them quickly in class before viewing the video.

Actividad A.

During the last video episode of *Destinos*, several situations were "wrapped up" and others continued to develop. Indicate whether the following statements about the episode are **Cierto** (**C**) or **Falso** (**F**).

Act. A, Answers: 1. C 2. F 3. F 4. F 5. F (See Appendix 1 for expanded answers.)

C F 1. Don Fernando está muy mal; está ahora en el hospital.

C F 2. Raquel pierde su cartera de nuevo.

C F 3. Raquel necesita comprar ropa porque en la Argentina es otoño.

C F 4. Alfredo convence a Raquel de que el caso de don Fernando debe presentarse en la televisión.

C F 5. Elena llama a Raquel para decirle que no puede obtener el certificado de nacimiento de Ángel Castillo.

Act. B, Point out: As a prediction exercise, this has no (in)correct responses.

Actividad B.

In this video episode you will see Raquel's last night and day in Madrid. Based on what you learned in the last episode and on your intuition, what do you think she will do?

Act. B, Answers: 1. *sí* 2. *sí* 3. *sí* 4. *un museo* (*Pero no puedes saber eso sólo por el título. Todos los lugares son posibles.*)

Sí No 1. ¿Va a ver a Alfredo y al Sr. Díaz una vez más (*once more*)?

Sí No 2. ¿Va a conocer a la novia de Federico?

Sí No 3. ¿Va a despedirse de (*say good-bye to*) la Sra. Suárez?

4. El título de este episodio es «Cuadros». ¿Qué lugar crees que Raquel va a visitar en este episodio?

a. _____ la casa de un artista   c. _____ una galería de arte

b. _____ un museo

Actividad C.

You have seen in other video episodes that Sra. Suárez has a tendency to comment on the actions of others. Listen to the advice she gives Raquel as they say good-bye. **El corazón** means *heart*.

What kind of advice do you think Sra. Suárez is offering?

Act. C, Answers: 1. *su vida personal* 2. *su trabajo* 3. *un novio*

1. La Sra. Suárez le da a Raquel consejos (*advice*) sobre
   _____ su vida profesional.   _____ su vida personal.

2. Parece que la Sra. Suárez cree que Raquel piensa demasiado (*too much*) en
   _____ su trabajo.   _____ sus padres.

3. La Sra. Suárez probablemente cree que Raquel debe buscar
   _____ más clientes.   _____ un novio (*boyfriend*).

Act. D, Suggestion: Have students work in pairs to compare the pictures.

3. con barba/ sin (*without*) barba

4. de pelo corto, no largo/ de pelo largo, no corto

Actividad D.

Look at the painting on the left of San Jerónimo by a Spanish artist and listen as it is described. The description contains some of the words and phrases for describing people that you will learn in this lesson. As you listen, indicate the word or phrase that you hear in each pair.

1. alto/bajo

5. ojos expresivos/ojos tristes

Now compare the painting of San Jerónimo with the painting on the right by another Spanish painter. What physical differences do you notice in the people in each painting? Keep these differences in mind when you listen to the narrator in the video episode describe the people in the painting.

2. delgado/gordito

Act. D, Answers: Students should indicate the following words: *alto; delgado; con barba; del pelo corto, no largo; ojos expresivos*

... AFTER VIEWING

2

¿TIENES BUENA MEMORIA?

Actividad A.   ¿Qué hicieron?

Paso 1

Indicate the statements that are true for each of the following characters you saw in **Episodio 10**.

Raquel
1. _____ Por fin le da la foto de Miguel y Jaime a la Sra. Suárez.
2. _____ No ve al reportero y al Sr. Díaz otra vez (*again*).
3. _____ Todavía no tiene el certificado de nacimiento de Ángel Castillo.

Federico
4. _____ Tiene una novia que es pintora.
5. _____ No tiene la oportunidad de despedirse de Raquel.

Act. A, *Paso 1*, Answers: Statements 1, 6, 7 are true.

La Sra. Suárez
6. _____ Va con Raquel a la escuela de baile donde trabaja la novia de Federico.
7. _____ Se despide de Raquel y le da un consejo.

Paso 2

Now listen as the speaker on the CD gives the answers.

Actividad B. ¡Un desafío!

With a partner, discuss the following details from **Episodio 10**. How much can you both remember?

1. Después de cenar con la Sra. Suárez, Federico y su novia, ¿cómo vuelve Raquel a su hotel?
2. ¿A qué hora debe salir el vuelo (*flight*) de Raquel para Buenos Aires?
3. Hay una maestra de primaria en el Prado. ¿De qué pintor le habla a la clase?
4. ¿A quién le escribe Raquel una tarjeta postal (*postcard*)?

3

VOCABULARIO DEL TEMA

¿Cómo son? Los adjetivos descriptivos

alto/a	tall
bajo/a	short (*in height*)
de mediana estatura	average height

bonito/a	pretty, attractive (*said of women*)
guapo/a	pretty; handsome
feo/a	ugly, unattractive

corto/a	short (*in length*)
largo/a	long

grande	big	**delgado/a**	thin, slender	**joven**	young
pequeño/a	small	**gordito/a**	plump, fat	**nuevo/a**	new
				viejo/a	old

Tiene...	He/She has . . .	**Tiene...**	He/She has . . .
barba	a beard	**pelo largo**	long hair
pelo rubio	blond hair	**corto**	short hair
castaño	brown hair	**ojos claros**	light-colored eyes
negro	black hair	**oscuros**	dark eyes
blanco	white hair	**expresivos**	expressive eyes
canoso	gray hair		

Note that when **grande** comes before a masculine or feminine noun, it shortens to **gran** and means *great*: **El Greco es un gran pintor**.

Actividad A. **Retratos (*Portraits*) de El Greco y Velázquez**

Listen again as the narrator describes these paintings by two famous Spanish painters. Then answer the questions that follow.

San Andrés y San Francisco de El Greco

Las Meninas (Ladies in Waiting) de Velázquez

Identifica en los cuadros a la figura que...

MODELO: es alta* → El pintor es alto.

1. tiene barba
2. tiene pelo rubio
3. es delgada
4. es baja

5. es alta
6. tiene pelo blanco
7. es vieja
8. tiene ojos expresivos

9. es bonita
10. tiene pelo largo

 Actividad B. **¿A quién se describe?**

You will hear a series of descriptions on the CD. Match the description with the following photos. First take a few seconds to scan the photos.

a. _____

b. _____

c. _____

d. _____

---

* As you know, Spanish adjectives agree in number and gender with the nouns they modify. The adjectives in this activity agree with the feminine noun **la figura**; they are feminine for that reason. If you use them to modify a masculine noun (or to modify a plural noun), you will need to change the form of the adjective to make it agree.

e. _____   f. _____   g. _____

Act. B, Answers: a. 4
b. 6 c. 5 d. 1 e. 8 f. 2 g. 3
h. 7

You should recognize all of these people, but you do not need to remember their names to do the activity.

Actividad C. **Más descripciones**

Create a brief description of a classmate. The classmate will do the same of you. Then exchange descriptions and see whether each of you agrees with the description your partner made of you. You may wish to look at Workbook /Study Guide **Actividad E** (Section 27) for additional guidance.

h. _____

Act. C, Variation: Students take turns describing famous people, their classmates, professors, etc. Their partner must try to guess who is being described.   **Act. C, Follow-up:** For homework, have students use a family photo or magazine picture and write 5 sentences, using adjectives to describe the people in the picture.

Nota cultural Kissing Hello and Good-bye

In Spain, as well as in other parts of the Hispanic world, people frequently kiss hello and good-bye. This form of greeting is practiced by women with other women and by men with women, but not usually by men with other men.

As you have probably noticed in the video episode, in Spain the kiss is a double one. Women embrace lightly and touch cheeks, first one side, then the other, as they make a soft kissing sound. The same sequence can be followed by a man with a woman, depending on the closeness of the relationship between them. In this video episode, Raquel and Federico shake hands and embrace as they kiss, even though they do not know each other all that well.

In other parts of the Hispanic world one kiss is more common. The question of whether or not to embrace is an individual one, depending on how comfortable one is with the other person.

4

The Workbook/Study Guide contains more detailed explanation and practice of this grammar point.

Emphasis: Review subject pronouns and their corresponding reflexive pronouns in a chart on the board or on an overhead transparency (*yo: me, tú: te, él/ella/ usted: se, nosotros/as: nos, vosotros/as: os, ellos/ellas/ustedes: se*).

UN POCO DE GRAMÁTICA

More About Talking About Group Activities

You have already learned to use stem-changing verbs and the pronouns **me**, **te**, and **se** with some verbs to talk about what others are doing.

Suggestion: Have students write out full conjugations of these verbs after going over them.

Follow-up: In the following class have students put the verb paradigms on the board at the beginning of the hour.

Optional: Have a relay race using reflexive verbs. Divide the class in half. You give the infinitive and a subject pronoun and one student from each team writes the appropriate form of the verb. For instance, you say, *sentirse, yo,* and one student from each team quickly writes *me siento* on the board. The first one to

write the correct form wins a point for the team.

Don Fernando, ¿**piensa** Ud. mucho en Rosario?

RAQUEL: **Me siento** a hablar con la Sra. Suárez.

Stem-changing verbs do not keep the stem change in the **nosotros** form.

FEDERICO: **Pensamos** ir a Los Ángeles algún día, Raquel. Bueno, si **podemos**, vamos a ir. Todo depende del dinero (*money*), ¿sabes?

Verbs that require reflexive pronouns use **nos** in the **nosotros** form.

MARÍA: Federico y yo vamos a **casarnos** este verano. ¡**Nos sentimos** muy felices!

You will learn more about these forms in the Workbook/Study Guide.

Actividad. ¿Qué hacemos?
Paso 1
Indicate whether the following sentences are **Cierto** (**C**) or **Falso** (**F**) for you and your classmates.

C F 1. Siempre nos acordamos de traer (*to bring*) la tarea a clase.
C F 2. Nos sentamos en el mismo (*same*) lugar todos los días.
C F 3. Queremos sacar (*to get*) una A en esta clase.
C F 4. No nos olvidamos nunca de estudiar para los exámenes.
C F 5. Podemos entender al profesor/a la profesora sin mucha dificultad.

Paso 2
Working with a partner, compare your answers. How many do you agree on? Then, correct the statements you both marked as **Falso**.

LECTURA CULTURAL

Los grandes maestros de la pintura española

The previous activities in this lesson have allowed you to listen again to information from the video episode about El Greco and Velázquez. Before beginning to read this **Lectura cultural**, listen again to what you heard about Goya in the episode. Then go back to **Lección 2** and look at the painting *Guernica* by Pablo Picasso, another famous Spanish painter. In the activity that follows the **Lectura cultural**, you will use all of the information you have to decide which of the four created works you have not seen previously in the *Destinos* materials.

Lectura cultural, **Suggestion:** Have students look at maps and text together in class before assigning listening activity as homework. It is helpful to have a large map of Spain in front of the room or on an overhead.

Los pintores

ESPAÑA

Zaragoza

Madrid

Toledo

Sevilla

Málaga

- ### Doménikos Theotokópoulos, El Greco[1]
  Fechas: 1541 (Creta)–1614 (Toledo)
  Obras[2]/Estilo: Temas religiosos, colores sombríos[3] y oscuros, forma alargada y estilizada de sus figuras.

- ### Diego de Silva y Velázquez
  Fechas: 1599 (Sevilla)–1660 (Madrid)
  Obras/Estilo: Uso de la luz[4] y de la perspectiva, muchos colores vivos, temas de la realidad, retratos de la familia real.[5]

- ### Francisco de Goya y Lucientes
  Fechas: 1746 (Zaragoza)–1828 (Francia)
  Obras/Estilo: Al principio,[6] retratos de la familia real, con espíritu crítico. En su período negro, formas grotescas. Precursor de la pintura moderna.

- ### Pablo Ruiz Picasso
  Fechas: 1881 (Málaga)–1973 (Francia)
  Obras/Estilo: Al principio, cuadros realistas, de las épocas azul y rosa. Luego, padre del «cubismo», estilo que trata de[7] presentar varias facetas del tema al mismo tiempo.[8] Enorme influjo[9] sobre el arte contemporáneo.

Goya y Picasso: ¿Tienen algo en común?

Lectura cultural, **Preguntas:** 1. *¿Cuándo vivió El Greco? (1541–1614), ¿Velázquez? (1599–1660), ¿Goya? (1746–1828) ¿Picasso? (1881–1973). 2. ¿Cuál es el estilo de cada artista?* (see text) 3. *¿Qué tienen en común Goya y Picasso?* (see text) 4. *¿Qué estilo de arte prefieres?*

- Su obra es extensa y muy variada.
- En algunas de sus obras denuncian los abusos políticos y sociales de su época.
- Fueron testigos[10] de la crueldad de la guerra.
- Ofrecen una visión expresionista (no realista) de la realidad.
- Cultivaron el grabado[11] además de la pintura.
- Murieron en Francia.

[1]El... *The Greek* [2]*Works* [3]*somber* [4]*light* [5]*royal* [6]Al... *At the beginning* [7]trata... *tries to* [8]al... *at the same time* [9]*influence* [10]*witnesses* [11]*etching*

Actividad. ¿Quién es el artista?

Based on what you have seen and read (and also on what else you may know about art history), what Spanish artist is the creator of each of these works? Explain why you made your decision.

6

INTERCAMBIO

In this activity, you will discuss physical traits of family members.

Paso 1
Interview someone in the class, asking questions about his or her mother's and father's physical traits. You may ask your instructor for help if you need it. (If your partner is an adopted child [**un hijo adoptivo/una hija adoptiva**] or does not remember his or her parents, ask him or her questions about family members he or she *does* know, even if they are of his or her adoptive family.)

Descripción de la mamá	Descripción del papá	¿Otro miembro de la familia?

Paso 2
Now describe who your partner most closely resembles, the mother or the father (or another family member). Write up your reasons, using the following models. The verb phrase **se parece a** means *he/she resembles.*

MODELOS: _____ se parece más a su papá porque… En ciertas cosas, se parece a su mamá. Por ejemplo, …

            _____ no se parece ni a su mamá ni a su papá porque…

VOCABULARIO

Los verbos

despedirse (i) (de)   to say good-bye (to)

Los adjetivos

alto/a   tall
bajo/a   short (*in height*)
bonito/a   pretty, attractive (*said of a woman*)
corto/a   short (*in length*)
delgado/a   thin, slender

feo/a   ugly, unattractive
gordito/a   plump, fat
grande (gran)   big; great
guapo/a   pretty; handsome
joven   young
largo/a   long
nuevo/a   new
pequeño/a   small
viejo/a   old

Más frases para las descripciones

Es de mediana estatura.	He/She is of average height.
Tiene...	He/She has . . .
barba	a beard
pelo rubio	blond hair
castaño	brown hair
negro	black hair
blanco	white hair
canoso	gray hair
pelo largo	long hair
corto	short hair
ojos claros	light-colored eyes
oscuros	dark eyes
expresivos	expressive eyes

Las personas

el novio/ la novia	boyfriend/ girlfriend
el pintor/la pintora	painter

El arte

el baile	dance
el cuadro	painting
el museo	museum
el retrato	portrait

Las palabras adicionales

otra vez	again
una vez más	one more time

11

LA DEMORA*

Suggestion: Have students look at the image, describe what they see, and talk about what they think might happen. Ask questions about the image to prompt student discussion.

MENSAJE

Sr. D.

..........Sta..........

..........RODRIGUEZ..........

Habitación n.° ......631......

*The Delay

OBJETIVOS

Part of this video episode is a review. Be sure to work through all parts of the lesson. When you see a headphones symbol in the margin, listen to the CD for **Lección 11**. Answers or hints for many activities are given in Appendix 1. Be sure to check your answers for each activity before going on to the next one.

The interactive CD-ROM to accompany *Destinos* contains additional practice with the video storyline and will help you improve your skills in Spanish.

BEFORE VIEWING . . .

Preliminary: See Faculty Guide for additional information and activities for this lesson.
• **Variation:** For activities marked with the headphones icon, you may wish to read from the Audioscript instead of playing the CD.
• **Suggestion:** Make sure students are familiar with the activities before you read from the Audioscript or play the CD.

1

PREPARACIÓN

Suggestions:
• Before watching the video, go over the vocabulary list at the end of the chapter and have students pronounce the words after you.
• Assign *Preparación* activities as homework and then go over them quickly in class before viewing the video.

Actividad A.
Paso 1

As you know, the opening narration of each video episode consists of a summary of what happened in the previous episode. First read the following sentences that are based on the opening review in **Episodio 11**. Then indicate whether they are **Cierto** (**C**) or **Falso** (**F**), based on what you remember about that episode.

Act. A, *Paso 1*, Answers:
1. C 2. F 3. C 4. F 5. C
6. C 7. F 8. C (See Appendix 1 for expanded answers.)

C F   1. Raquel conoce a María, la novia de Federico.

C F   2. Cena con ellos y con la Sra. Suárez, pero no se despide todavía.

C F   3. Antes de salir para Buenos Aires, Raquel va al Museo del Prado.

C F   4. Allí ve algunas obras de artistas españoles muy importantes: El Greco, Murillo y Picasso.

C F   5. Al final de su visita al Museo del Prado, Raquel se encuentra con Alfredo y el Sr. Díaz.

C F   6. Cuando Raquel vuelve a su hotel, hay un mensaje para ella, de la agencia de viajes.

C F   7. Raquel trata de (*tries to*) comunicarse con la agencia de viajes. Por fin puede hablar con ellos.

C F   8. Decide ir a la agencia para preguntar qué pasa con su reservación.

 ### Paso 2

Act. B, Point out: Use of *Estimada* as a formal salutation for letters, messages, etc.

Now listen to the narration on the CD and check your answers.

Act. B, Answers: *La agencia no puede confirmar su reservación.* The second part of this activity has no (in)correct responses.

Actividad B.
Here is a message that the hotel receptionist will give to Raquel in this video episode. What problem is Raquel going to encounter, according to the message?

_____ La agencia perdió su billete (*ticket*).
_____ La agencia no puede confirmar su reservación.

If you were Raquel, what would you do? Keep in mind that Raquel is a bit tired from all of her traveling and from all of the experiences she has had in the last few days.

DIA _____
HORA _____
RECIBIDO POR: _____

COMUNICACION DE

MENSAJE

☐ HA LLAMADO
☐ HA VENIDO

D. *Estimada Sta. Rodriguez:*
Sentimos mucho informarle que hemos tenido problemas en reservar su asiento en el vuelo 897 para Buenos Aires, haga el favor de llamarnos lo más pronto posible 2-52-73-61

Roberto Ruiz
Agencia Águila

Yo creo que

a. _____ Raquel debe ir directamente al aeropuerto. Allí puede tomar un café y esperar su vuelo (*flight*).

b. _____ Raquel debe preguntarle al recepcionista si ella puede subir a (*go up to*) su habitación.

c. _____ Raquel debe visitar otros lugares interesantes o históricos, por ejemplo, otros museos.

 . . . AFTER VIEWING

¿TIENES BUENA MEMORIA?

Act. A, Suggestion: Give students about 3 minutes to complete the activity individually or in pairs and then compare answers as a whole class.

Act. A, Answers: a. 4 b. 2 c. 1 d. 5 e. 6 f. 3

Act. B, Note: Students may still have problems forming questions, particularly with respect to the difference between *¿qué?* and *¿cuál?* and correct word order with prepositions in phrases such as *¿a qué hora?* For now, have them use *¿cuál?* before the verb *ser* and *¿qué?* before things. Remind them that Spanish

does not allow placement of prepositions at the end of a clause as English does.

Actividad A.   **En este episodio**

All of the following events took place during Raquel's last few hours in Madrid, but . . . in what order did they occur? Put them in order, from 1 to 6.

Raquel

a. _____ descansa (*rests*) unas horas.

b. _____ se entera de (*finds out*) que hay una demora.

c. _____ va a la agencia de viajes para resolver el problema.

d. _____ se despierta cuando suena el teléfono.

e. _____ va al aeropuerto y sale para la Argentina.

f. _____ vuelve al hotel y sube a su habitación.

Actividad B.   **¡Un desafío!**

Working with a partner and using the cues below, take turns asking and answering questions about details from this video episode and from previous ones.

Act. B, Suggestion: Before beginning the activity, have students review interrogative words (*Lección 8*). Model question formation for item 1. *¿Cómo se llama el hotel de Raquel en Madrid?* (Príncipe de Vergara).

Act. B, Sample Questions: 2. *¿Cuál es el número de la habitación de Raquel?* (el 631) 3. *¿Qué cosa le da Raquel a la Sra. Suárez?* (una foto de Jaime y Miguel con Osito) 4. *¿Qué cosa le da la señora a Raquel?* (una carta para Rosario) 5. *¿A qué hora sale el vuelo de Raquel para la Argentina?* (a las 9.00) 6. *¿Cuál es el número del vuelo?* (el 897)

1. el hotel de Raquel en Madrid
2. el número de la habitación de Raquel
3. Raquel le da algo a la Sra. Suárez
4. la Sra. Suárez le da algo a Raquel
5. la hora que sale el vuelo de Raquel para la Argentina
6. el número del vuelo
7. ¿ ?

REPASO DE LOS EPISODIOS 7-10

Actividad A.   **El sueño (*dream*) de Raquel: Primera parte**

Complete the following summary of the first part of Raquel's dream with words from the following lists. ¡OJO! Some words will be used more than once. Others may not be used at all.

Verbos: buscar, conocer, creer, dar, deber, decir, empezar, encontrar, ir, llegar, poder, revelar, salir, tomar, volver

Cosas: la cartera, la corbata, el mensaje

Personas: el botones, el cliente, el recepcionista, el reportero

Otras palabras: pero, porque, pronto

Después de volver al hotel, Raquel sube a su habitación y toma una siesta. Mientras duerme,[a] _____[1] a soñar con lo que ha pasado desde que salió de Sevilla.[b]

Primero, toma el tren de Sevilla a Madrid. En el tren, _____[2] a dos señores. Uno se llama Alfredo Sánchez y es _____[3] de televisión. Alfredo _____[4] a una maestra para entrevistarla.[c] Alfredo _____[5] que Raquel es la maestra, pero Raquel le _____[6] que no, que está equivocado.[d] En el coche-comedor[e] del tren, Alfredo _____[7] a hacerle preguntas a Raquel acerca de su investigación, pero Raquel no _____[8] nada del caso.

Cuando por fin llega a su hotel en Madrid, Raquel descubre que ha dejado[f] su _____[9] en el taxi. Alfredo y su asistente _____[10] a buscarla. Por fin (ellos) la _____,[11] pero Raquel no está cuando ellos _____[12] al hotel.

Al día siguiente, Raquel y Alfredo se encuentran[g] en el hotel y Alfredo le _____[13] a Raquel el objeto perdido. Mientras _____[14] un café, Alfredo intenta convencer a Raquel una vez más de que el caso de don Fernando _____[15] ser muy interesante para un reportaje de televisión. _____[16] Raquel le dice que no, que ella _____[17] respetar el secreto profesional de su _____.[18]

[a]Mientras... *While she sleeps*   [b]soñar... *to dream about what has happened since she left Sevilla* [c]*interview her*   [d]*mistaken*   [e]*dining car*   [f]ha... *has left*   [g]se... *meet*

Actividad B.   El sueño de Raquel: Segunda parte
Paso 1

Choose the appropriate completion for each sentence.

Raquel también sueña con la Sra. Suárez.

1. Raquel va a la casa de la Sra. Suárez porque
   a. _____ la Sra. Suárez la llama por teléfono y la invita.
   b. _____ el hijo de la Sra. Suárez va al hotel y la invita.

2. Durante la conversación con la Sra. Suárez, Raquel se entera de (*learns*) que, después de la guerra, Rosario se fue a vivir a
    a. _____ Sevilla.   c. _____ México.
    b. _____ la Argentina.

3. La Sra. Suárez también le dice a Raquel que Rosario
    a. _____ se casó de nuevo con un rico hacendado.
    b. _____ se casó de nuevo con un político importante.

4. Según (*According to*) Teresa Suárez, don Fernando y Rosario tuvieron (*had*)
    a. _____ un hijo.   b. _____ una hija.

5. Según la dirección que tiene Raquel, Rosario vive
    a. _____ cerca de Buenos Aires.
    b. _____ cerca de Bariloche.

 Paso 2
Now check your answers on the CD.

4

PARA ESCRIBIR

In this section of the Textbook, found in future *Repaso* lessons, you will be introduced to a longer writing assignment found in the Workbook/Study Guide. In each writing assignment, you will narrate events (in the present tense at first and then, eventually, in the past), describe people and events, and express opinions about many things.

In this lesson, you will write a short narration in which you describe your daily routine to someone who is not familiar with it. You want to tell the reader as much as you can about what you do and also include some interesting information about yourself. Your narration should be no fewer than 150 and no more than 250 words long.

Go to the Workbook/Study Guide to begin this writing activity.

VOCABULARIO

Los verbos
subir (**a**)   to go up to (*a place*)

Los sustantivos
la demora   delay
el vuelo   flight

Las palabras adicionales
por fin   finally

Un viaje a la Argentina

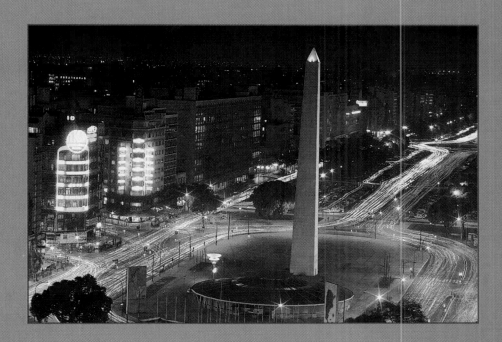

El Obelisco de Buenos Aires conmemora la fundación de la ciudad.

REVELACIONES*

*Revelations

OBJETIVOS

The materials in **Lección 12** of the Textbook and the Workbook/Study Guide will help you better understand the video episode and take you beyond it, giving you additional information about places and characters in the series. The Textbook will also help you to develop skill in using the Spanish language. In his lesson you will learn

• how to express the Spanish numbers from 100 to 1000
• how to talk about what other people did in the past

You will also learn about Argentina, both past and present.

Be sure to work through all parts of the lesson. When you see a headphones symbol in the margin, listen to the CD for **Lección 12**. Answers or hints for many activities are given in Appendix 1. Be sure to check your answers for each activity before going on to the next one.

The interactive CD-ROM to accompany *Destinos* contains additional practice with the video storyline and will help you improve your skills in Spanish.

BEFORE VIEWING . . .

Preliminary: See Faculty Guide for additional information and activities for this lesson.
• **Variation:** For activities marked with the headphones icon, you may wish to read from the Audioscript instead of playing the CD.
• **Suggestion:** Make sure students are familiar with the activities before you read from the Audioscript or play the CD.

1

PREPARACIÓN

Suggestions:
• Before watching the video, go over the vocabulary list at the end of the chapter and have students pronounce the words after you.
• Assign *Preparación* activities as homework and then go over them quickly in class before viewing the video.

Optional: Brainstorm as a whole class or in small groups what students already know about Argentina and what they think it is like. List the ideas on the board and have students copy them. As the unit in Argentina unfolds over the next several episodes, have students refer to this list to see whether or not their ideas were accurate. Which ideas would they change? What did they see or hear that made them change their minds?

Actividad A.

In the last video episode of *Destinos* Raquel left Madrid by plane, on her way to Buenos Aires to continue her search for Rosario. Indicate whether the following statements about the events immediately preceding her departure are **Cierto** (**C**) or **Falso** (**F**).

C F 1. Raquel pierde su vuelo.
C F 2. Hay una demora y el vuelo no sale cuando debe.
C F 3. Raquel habla con don Fernando por teléfono.
C F 4. Raquel se duerme en su habitación.
C F 5. Piensa en el consejo (*advice*) de la Sra. Suárez.
C F 6. Sabe dónde Rosario vive en la Argentina.

Act. A, Answers: 1. F 2. C 3. F 4. C 5. C 6. C 7. *Es el consejo de la Sra. Suárez.* (See Appendix 1 for expanded answers.)

¡Un desafío! ¿Tienes una memoria excelente? You have heard the following phrase in a previous video episode of *Destinos*. Identify it briefly by telling who said it and in what context.

7.   «Hay que dedicarle tiempo al corazón.»

Act B, Point out: As a prediction exercise, there are no (in)correct responses.

Actividad B.

Here are photographs of some of the places and events you will see in **Episodio 12**. What do you think is happening in each?

1. Raquel está en
   a. _____ un parque.
   b. _____ un cementerio.
   c. _____ una estancia.

Act. B, Suggestion: Assign as homework the day before viewing the video. Then, before showing the video, find out by a show of hands how many students marked each answer. Then ask ¿*Por qué creen que Raquel está en un parque? ¿un cementerio? ¿una estancia?* Continue in the same manner, encouraging students to respond in Spanish as best they can.

2. Toma una fotografía de
   a. _____ Rosario.
   b. _____ un monumento
   c. _____ una tumba.

3. Raquel toca a la puerta (*knocks on the door*) en
   a. _____ una estancia.
   b. _____ una casa en Buenos Aires.

4. La persona que contesta (*answers*) es
   a. _____ Martín Iglesias.
   b. _____ Rosario.
   c. _____ una persona desconocida (*unknown*).

. . . AFTER VIEWING

2

¿TIENES BUENA MEMORIA?

Actividad A. ¿Quién es?

In **Episodio 12** you met these new characters. Identify them and tell where they work, then indicate why they are important to Raquel's investigation.

1. Este hombre se llama
   a. _____ Cirilo.   b. _____ Francisco.   c. _____ Esteban.

2. Es
   a. _____ botones.   b. _____ chofer.   c. _____ gaucho.

3. Trabaja en
   a. _____ el hotel.   c. _____ la estancia.
   b. _____ Buenos Aires.   Santa Susana.

4. Es un personaje importante porque
   a. _____ le dice a Raquel que Rosario se mudó (*moved*) a la capital y le
      da su dirección.
   b. _____ le dice a Raquel que Rosario ya murió.

5. Este hombre se llama
   a. _____ Enrique Casas.   c. _____ Arturo Iglesias.
   b. _____ Ángel Castillo.

6. Es
   a. _____ profesor.   c. _____ abogado.
   b. _____ médico (psiquiatra).

7. Trabaja en
   a. _____ su casa.   b. _____ el hotel.   c. _____ la universidad.

8. Es un personaje importante porque
   a. _____ quiere ayudar (*help*) a Raquel a buscar a Rosario.
   b. _____ es hijo de Rosario y medio hermano de Ángel Castillo.

Actividad B. ¿Qué pasó?

With a partner, take turns indicating whether the following events happen (**Sí**) or not (**No**) in **Episodio 12**. If you answer **No**, correct the statement.

Sí No 1. En el hotel no hay habitación reservada para Raquel.

Sí No 2. Raquel tiene mucha energía cuando llega. Va directamente a la estancia para buscar a Rosario.

Sí No 3. Cuando Raquel llega a la estancia Cirilo contesta la puerta.

Sí No 4. Raquel sabe que Rosario ya murió.

Sí No 5. Arturo le cuenta a Raquel la triste (*sad*) historia de Martín, su padre y padrastro (*stepfather*) de Ángel.

Actividad C.   La historia de Ángel
Paso 1

As you know, Raquel has learned that Rosario has died. Her investigation must continue, however, and Arturo is willing to share information with her. The following events all form part of Ángel's story as told by Arturo, but . . . in what order did they occur? Put them in order, from 1 to 7. *Note*: All of the verbs are in the past tense.

a. _____ Martín murió de un ataque cardíaco.

b. _____ Ángel dejó los estudios y se dedicó a pintar.

c. _____ Ángel discutió (*fought*) con su padrastro.

d. _____ Martín, Rosario y el joven Arturo fueron a Buenos Aires para visitar a Ángel.

e. _____ Martín y Rosario supieron (*found out*) algo que no le gustó a Martín.

f. _____ Ángel se embarcó como marinero.

g. _____ Ángel se fue a la capital para estudiar ciencias económicas.

 ### Paso 2
Now listen to Arturo's version of the story and check your answers.

VOCABULARIO DEL TEMA

Los números de 100 a 1000

100 cien, ciento	400 cuatrocientos	700 setecientos	1.000 mil
200 doscientos	500 quinientos	800 ochocientos	
300 trescientos	600 seiscientos	900 novecientos	

- **Cien** is used in counting. To express the numbers 101 to 199, **ciento** is used: **ciento uno**, **ciento dos**, **ciento setenta y nueve**, and so on.
- **Cien** also precedes a noun: **cien iglesias**. When the numbers 200 through 900 precede a noun, they must agree in gender: **doscientas casas**, **trescientas calles**. **Mil** precedes a noun, with no change: **mil años**.
- These numbers are also used to express the year.

  799   setecientos noventa y nueve
  1997   mil novecientos noventa y siete

ROSARIO DEL VALLE DE IGLESIAS 1970 – 1987

 ### Actividad A.   ¿Hay una habitación disponible?
Listen as the hotel clerk tries to find out whether there is a room or suite available for Raquel today. Indicate the numbers you hear him say.

114   214   314   414   514   614   714   814   914

Actividad B. **Continúa la secuencia**

You will hear three numbers in each group. Write down the numbers you hear in numerals, in the order you hear them.

> MODELO: (*you hear*) —cien, doscientos, trescientos
> (*you write*)   100, 200, 300

1. _____   3. _____   5. _____
2. _____   4. _____   6. _____

Actividad C. **Hablando de la ropa**

Here is the laundry list for men's clothing from the Hotel Príncipe de Vergara. Listen as the speaker on the tape names an article of clothing, then tell how much it costs—in **pesetas**—to have the item washed or cleaned. Remember to make numbers agree with the feminine noun **pesetas** when necessary.

ROPA DE CABALLERO	
Camisa	450
Camisetas	250
Pijama	600
Pantalón	500
Chaqueta	900
Traje completo	1500
Pantalón corto	400

> MODELO: (*you hear*) —camisa
> (*you say*)   —cuatrocientas cincuenta pesetas

1. ...   2.   ...   3.   ...   4.   ...   5.   ...   6.   ...

Actividad D. **¿En qué año?**

Complete each of the following sentences with a year. Then compare your answers with those of your classmates. How many answers are the same? Who has different answers?

1. Yo nací (*was born*) en _____.
2. Creo que el profesor / la profesora nació (*was born*) en _____.
3. El año más importante en la historia de los Estados Unidos es _____.
4. El año más importante en la historia del mundo (*world*) es _____.
5. El año más desastroso (*disastrous*) en la historia del mundo es _____.
6. El año de mi graduación de la universidad es _____.

Nota cultural   The *vos* forms

In some countries, particularly in Argentina, Uruguay, and most of Central America, the pronoun **vos** is used instead of **tú**. Most verb forms used with **vos** are the same as the **tú** verb forms. However, in the present tense the endings **-ás**, **-és**, and **-ís** are generally used: **trabajás**, **comés**, **vivís**. Stem vowels do not change: **podés**, **querés**, **dormís**.

> Y vos, ¿qué **querés** hacer esta tarde?
> ¿**Vivís** en México?

Just as you heard **vosotros** forms in Spain, when Spaniards addressed each other, you will hear **vos** forms in the video episodes that take place in Argentina and whenever Argentine characters are talking. The **vos** forms will not, however, be practiced in the Textbook or Workbook/Study Guide.

4

UN POCO DE GRAMÁTICA

The Workbook/Study Guide contains more detailed explanation and practice of this grammar point.

Note: You may want to introduce the complete paradigms for regular *-ar*, *-er*, and *-ir* verbs in the preterite, even though the lesson focuses on third-person singular forms.

Optional: Practice recognition of third-person singular preterite forms by reading the following *Cierto/Falso* statements about *Destinos*. You may wish to use these as (part of) a (pop) quiz. 1. *Raquel habló con Ángel Castillo.* (F) 2. *Raquel conoció a un gaucho que se llama Cirilo.* (C) 3. *Raquel visitó la tumba de Rosario en el cementerio.* (C) 4. *El padre de Arturo se murió de un ataque cardíaco.* (C) 5. *Arturo abandonó sus estudios y se dedicó a pintar.* (F)

Using Verbs to Talk About the Past

Since the beginning of the *Destinos* series, you have been hearing verb forms that described things that happened in the past. In Spanish, as in English, there are a number of past-tense forms. In this section you will start to use forms of one of the Spanish past tenses, the preterite.

Most third-person singular preterite-tense Spanish verbs end in **-ó** (**-ar** verbs) or **-ió** (**-er** and **-ir** verbs). Note the verbs in this brief description.

> Rosario **vivió** en la estancia Santa Susana unos diez años. Luego se **mudó** a Buenos Aires.

-Ar and **-er** stem-changing verbs do not show the stem change in the preterite.

> Arturo **perdió** contacto con su hermano Ángel.

You will learn more about these verb forms in the Workbook/Study Guide. You will learn about the past-tense forms of **-ir** stem-changing verbs in a later lesson.

Act., *Paso 2,* **Variation:** Have students prepare *Cierto/Falso* statements rather than open-ended questions. It is probably easier for them to create statements such as *Raquel conoció a Ángel Castillo* rather than questions such as *¿A quién conoció Raquel?*

Actividad. La investigación sigue
Paso 1
Use the following verbs to tell what happened to Raquel or what she did in **Episodio 12**. Can you use them all? Write your sentences on a separate sheet of paper.

viajó	buscó
llegó	encontró
contó	volvió
habló	conoció*

Act., Note: Remind students of the proper placement of prepositions and the personal *a* in question formation: *¿Con quién... ? ¿A quién... ? ¿Adónde... ?*, etc.

Paso 2
Now, working with a partner, take turns asking and answering questions about the events in **Episodio 12**. Use your notes from **Paso 1**. You may also want to review interrogative words from **Lección 8**.

---

* Remember that **conocer** means both *to know (someone)* and *to meet (someone for the first time)*. What do you think is the more typical meaning of **conocer** in the preterite?

LECTURA CULTURAL

Lectura cultural, **Suggestion:** Assign as homework. Remind students that they should not expect to understand every word of the reading, but rather to get the main ideas.

La Pampa y los gauchos

Lectura cultural, Preguntas: Ask the following questions. 1. *¿Cuál es la capital de la Argentina?* (*Buenos Aires*) 2. *¿Cómo se llama la región que se asocia con los gauchos?* (*La Pampa*) 3. *¿Cómo se llaman las haciendas de la Argentina?* (*estancias*) 4. *¿Cierto o falso?* Los gauchos son famosos por su poesía. (F) 5. *¿Cierto o falso?* Los gauchos forman una parte importante del folklore de la Argentina. (C).

Before you read this **Lectura cultural**, refresh your memory about modern Argentina by listening to what the narrator told you about Argentina and Buenos Aires at the beginning of this video episode. As you listen, keep in mind the view of Buenos Aires that Raquel and Arturo enjoyed from the top of a tall building at the end of the episode.

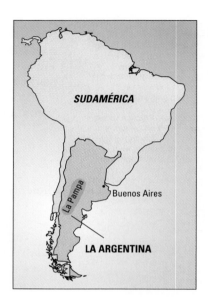

Buenos Aires es una ciudad grande y cosmopolita. Tiene bulevares elegantes y edificios y monumentos hermosos.[1] Es la capital de la República Argentina y es también un puerto,[2] el puerto más grande de la Argentina. Algunas personas la llaman el París de Sudamérica. Sin embargo, las personas que llegan a la Argentina por primera vez quieren ver gauchos.

La verdad es que los gauchos dejaron de existir[3] hace muchos años.[4] Hoy día, los gauchos forman parte de la herencia folklórica argentina. Para ver a un gaucho, es necesario visitar una estancia modelo como en la que trabaja Cirilo. Allí se puede admirar la habilidad del gaucho con el lazo y su caballo.[5] También es posible ver sus juegos[6] típicos, como «el pato», el polo de los gauchos. Además hay canciones[7] y comida típicas de la vida gauchesca.

Los gauchos eran los héroes de La Pampa, y La Pampa es la región más importante de la Argentina. Tiene una posición central en el país y es también una región especialmente adecuada para el ganado.[8] La unidad básica de la agricultura y de la ganadería[9] en La Pampa es la estancia. Las estancias son grandes haciendas, con viviendas,[10] almacenes[11] y enormes extensiones de terreno dedicado a la agricultura y a los pastos.[12]

Los amplios horizontes de La Pampa son la patria de un personaje ya mítico: el gaucho. Los gauchos eran jinetes[13] que cuidaban[14] el ganado. Vivían como nómadas, lejos de la civilización. Su vida era muy difícil y solitaria. Con frecuencia escapaban de un pasado no precisamente bueno.

La figura de los gauchos sigue viva[15] en la literatura y en el *folklore* de la Argentina y el Uruguay. Aquí hay unos datos sobre «Martín Fierro», el poema nacional de la Argentina. Su héroe es un gaucho.
Autor: José Hernández

[1]*beautiful* [2]*port* [3]*dejaron... disappeared* [4]*hace... many years ago* [5]*horse* [6]*games* [7]*songs* [8]*cattle* [9]*cattle raising* [10]*casas* [11]*storehouses* [12]*los... grazing* [13]*horsemen* [14]*cared for* [15]*alive*

Obras: el poema «Martín Fierro» (1872), compuesto de 2000 versos; la segunda parte
del poema, «La vuelta[16] de Martín Fierro» (1879)
Tema: la lucha[17] del héroe por la libertad contra adversidades, injusticias y prejuicios

[16]*return*   [17]*fight*

Actividad. El gaucho y su *folklore*

Does the story of the Argentine gaucho remind you of a folk hero from this
country? What are your country's equivalents for the following aspects of the
gaucho and his history?

1.   La Pampa   2.   la estancia   3.   el gaucho   4.   «el pato»

6

INTERCAMBIO

In this activity, you will talk about Raquel's and your instructor's past
activities.

Paso 1

What do you think your instructor and Raquel (or another *Destinos* character)
have both done in the past? What have they done differently? Write six statements in which you talk about their past activities. Note: You are not ex-
pected to know about Raquel's or your instructor's pasts; your statements
only need to be plausible.

> MODELO: Raquel estudió en la Universidad de California, Los Ángeles.
> Pero mi profesor(a) estudió en la Universidad de Wisconsin.

Paso 2

In groups of three, share your statements. Of all the statements, select eight
that you like the most.

Paso 3

Each group should read its statements out loud. Your instructor will respond
accordingly. Who seems to know more about your instructor? Is everyone
in agreement about the plausibility of statements about Raquel?

VOCABULARIO

Los verbos

ayudar	to help
contestar	to answer
mudarse	to move (*from one residence or city to another*)

Las personas

el medio hermano	half-brother
el padrastro	stepfather

Los adjetivos

desconocido/a	unknown

Las cosas

la puerta	door

Los lugares

la estancia	ranch
la habitación	room

Los conceptos

la revelación	revelation, unveiling

Los números: cien, doscientos, trescientos, cuatrocientos, quinientos, seiscientos, setecientos, ochocientos, novecientos, mil

LECCIÓN 13

LA BÚSQUEDA*

*The Search

OBJETIVOS

The materials in **Lección 13** of the Textbook and the Workbook/Study Guide will help you better understand the video episode and take you beyond it, giving you additional information about places and characters in the series. The Textbook will also help you to develop skill in using the Spanish language. In this lesson you will learn

- the Spanish words for seafoods and for some other food items
- ways to talk about what you did in the past

You will also learn about the regions of Argentina.

Be sure to work through all parts of the lesson. When you see a head-phones symbol in the margin, listen to the CD for **Lección 13**. Answers or hints for many activities are given in Appendix 1. Be sure to check your answers for each activity before going on to the next one.

The interactive CD-ROM to accompany *Destinos* contains additional practice with the video storyline and will help you improve your skills in Spanish.

BEFORE VIEWING . . .

1

PREPARACIÓN

 ## Actividad A.

Listen to the review of **Episodio 12** that you will hear at the beginning of this video episode. Then, based on the review and on what you remember, indicate whether the following events took place (**Sí**) or not (**No**) in the previous episode.

Sí No 1. No hay habitación para Raquel en el hotel de Buenos Aires.

Sí No 2. En la estancia, un joven le dice a Raquel que Rosario murió hace años (*years ago*).

Sí No 3. Un gaucho le dice que Rosario se mudó a la capital.

Sí No 4. Con el chofer, Raquel busca un número en la calle Gorostiaga.

Sí No 5. En una casa, Raquel conoce a un amigo de Rosario.

Sí No 6. Arturo le da a Raquel la nueva dirección de Rosario y de su hermano Ángel.

Actividad B.

As you prepare to watch this video episode, think about its title, **La búsqueda**. What does the title suggest to you? What does a search for a person entail? Indicate the most logical completion for the following sentences.

1. Mientras (*While*) buscan a Ángel, Raquel y Arturo
   a. _____ hablan con muchas personas.
   b. _____ hablan con pocas personas.

2. Raquel y Arturo comienzan la búsqueda
   a. _____ en la estación central de policía de Buenos Aires.
   b. _____ en el lugar donde Arturo vio a su hermano por última (*last*) vez.

3. Las personas que van a saber algo de Ángel, probablemente, son
   a. _____ los dependientes (*clerks*) y dueños de negocios (*shop owners*).
   b. _____ los viejos marineros.

Actividad C.

In this video episode, Raquel and Arturo will meet a man who is suspicious of strangers.

Paso 1

Listen to the conversation on the CD, trying to get the gist of it. Then read the following version of it to see whether you missed anything.

SEÑOR: Yo soy José, sí, señor.

ARTURO: Disculpe la molestia. Mario nos dijo que tal vez Ud. puede conocer a Ángel Castillo, mi hermano.

SEÑOR: ¿Ángel Castillo?

ARTURO: Sí, es mi hermano. Perdimos contacto hace muchos años. Tenía amigos acá. Pintaba. Le gustaban los barcos.[1]

SEÑOR: Lo siento. No lo conozco. ¿Ya hablaron con Héctor?

ARTURO: No. ¿Quién es?

SEÑOR: Sí. Tienen que hablar con Héctor. Él ha vivido siempre en este barrio. Conoce a todo el mundo.[2] Seguro que conoció a su hermano.

RAQUEL: ¿Y dónde podemos encontrar a Héctor?

[1]Le... *He liked boats.*   [2]todo... *everybody*

Now, indicate which of the following sentences is an accurate summary of the conversation you just heard.

Act. C, Answers: *Paso 1:* b; *Paso 3:* c

a. _____ José cree que Héctor es el hermano de Arturo.

b. _____ José no conoce a Ángel pero sí sabe el nombre de una persona que posiblemente lo conoció.

Paso 2

Now listen to the conversation again.

Paso 3

José is suspicious. For this reason, it is likely that he does not trust strangers. What do you think will happen after Raquel asks her question?

a. _____ José les da la dirección de Héctor en seguida.

b. _____ José piensa un momento y luego les da la dirección de Héctor.

c. _____ José les dice que él va a buscar a Héctor.

d. _____ José no quiere darles más información.

 . . . AFTER VIEWING

2

¿TIENES BUENA MEMORIA?

Act. A, Suggestion: Give students the opportunity to read items aloud as you go through the exercise.

Actividad A.   ¿Quiénes son? ¿Y qué hicieron?
Paso 1

As you probably predicted, Arturo and Raquel talk to a number of people in the course of their search for Ángel. Based on what you have seen in this video episode, who is the one person most likely to lead them eventually to Ángel?

a. _____ José, el marinero
b. _____ la dependienta de la tienda de comestibles (*grocery store*)
c. _____ Mario, el dueño de la tienda de antigüedades (*antiques*)
d. _____ el vendedor (*salesman*) de pescado
e. _____ Héctor, otro marinero
f. _____ doña Flora, la esposa de José
g. _____ Arturo

Paso 2

Now indicate which of the people in **Paso 1** made the following contributions to the search for Ángel.

1. _____ Mencionó a la señora del negocio de al lado (*next door*). ¿Por qué? Ella conoce a todo el mundo.
2. _____ Pensó en José. Llevó a Raquel y Arturo a la casa donde vive con su esposa.
3. _____ Encontró una foto de Ángel a los veinte años.
4. _____ Atendió a una clienta. Luego miró la foto varias veces pero no reconoció a Ángel.
5. _____ Mencionó dos lugares donde podían encontrar a José, en el bar o en el barco.
6. _____ Buscó a Héctor y sabe dónde va a estar mañana por la noche.

Paso 3

Select the statement that best describes what the next step in the search for Ángel will be.

a. _____ Héctor va a ir a la casa de Arturo.
b. _____ Arturo y Raquel van a buscar a Héctor en una fiesta.
c. _____ José va a hablar con Héctor para ver si conoce a Ángel.

Actividad B. ¡Un desafío!

If you were able to answer most of the items in **Actividad A**, you "caught" enough to watch the next episode. But were you also able to take note of some of the details, such as the names of places and of some foods? Your ability to hear and remember details of this kind will increase as you work through the *Destinos* materials. Work with a classmate to choose the best answer to complete each of the following statements.

1. Raquel y Arturo comenzaron la búsqueda en el barrio de
   a. _____ la Boca.   c. _____ Riachuelo.
   b. _____ Recoleta.

2. La última vez que Arturo vio a su hermano Ángel fue en la calle
   a. _____ Rivadavia.   c. _____ Caminito.
   b. _____ 9 de Julio.

3. Arturo y Raquel almuerzan en un restaurante que se llama
   a. _____ la Boca.   c. _____ la Vaca.
   b. _____ la Barca.

4. José les informó a Raquel y Arturo que mañana por la noche hay una fiesta en un bar-restaurante que se llama
    a. _____ Piccolo Navio.   c. _____ Puerto Escondido.
    b. _____ la Barca.

5. Arturo invitó a Raquel a comer (*eat*) en su casa. Va a preparar
    a. _____ pescado.   c. _____ pasta.
    b. _____ unas brochetas.

Nota cultural, Emphasis: Mention the influence of Europe on Argentine culture and the number of European immigrants there, which would explain Arturo's French pronunciation of *brochette*. Remind students that different varieties of Spanish are neither superior nor inferior to one another. They are simply different.

Nota cultural   ¿Cómo se dice...?

As you have already learned, the names for some foods are different in different parts of the Spanish-speaking world. Listen again as Arturo and Raquel discuss what Arturo is going to prepare for dinner.

Did you notice that, as they discuss the main course, Arturo and Raquel use slightly different words to describe it? Arturo uses a more French pronunciation, **unas brochettes**, while Raquel uses the term more frequently used in most of the Spanish-speaking world, **las brochetas**. Neither term is more "correct" than the other; they are merely different. You will find out what **brochetas** are in the next video episode.

You should also note that neither Arturo nor Raquel is confused or upset by the difference in terminology. Spanish is an international language, and there are differences in pronunciation, in vocabulary, and in usage throughout the Spanish-speaking world. These differences do not generally make communication difficult.

VOCABULARIO DEL TEMA

Many of the vocabulary sections in the video episodes from Argentina present food-related vocabulary. By the end of the Argentina episodes, you should be able to express which foods you like and dislike. If the words you need are not given, look them up in a dictionary or ask your instructor and make them part of your personal vocabulary. Don't try to learn all of the food vocabulary presented in the Textbook. Focus on those items you need to express your preferences and on those necessary for describing the story.

In the following list (and in those in subsequent Argentina episodes), the words on the left are from the video episode. Those in the right-hand column are additional vocabulary items for each category that you may want to learn.

Los mariscos

los calamares	squid	**el cangrejo**	crab
el langostino	prawn	**la langosta**	lobster
el mejillón	mussel	**la ostra**	oyster

El pescado

el lenguado	sole	**el atún**	tuna
el salmón	salmon	**la merluza**	hake

Otros comestibles

el aceite	oil
el arroz	rice
la ensalada	salad
la manteca (*Arg.*)	butter
la mantequilla	butter
el pan	bread

Remember that food vocabulary varies a good deal in the Spanish-speaking world. You may want to note these variations.

- **Mantequilla** generally means *butter*. For many Spanish speakers, **manteca** means *fat* or *lard*.
- Two frequently used words for *shrimp* are **la gamba** (in Spain) and **el camarón** (in Mexico and parts of Latin America).

Actividad A.   Los mariscos, el pescado y otros comestibles

Listen as the speaker on the CD talks about some of her food preferences. She will use the phrases **me gusta…** and **me gustan…** and the verb **prefiero…**. Write the number of the sentence next to the correct drawing.

Actividad B.   ¿Cuánto cuesta?
Paso 1

Listen as the grocery clerk from **Episodio 13** tallies the prices of a number of items her customer has bought. As you listen, write down the price of each item. *Note*: The monetary unit of Argentina is **el austral** (from the adjective **austral**, which means *southern*).

El arroz, son _____¹ australes; este pan, son _____² aus-

trales; este otro pan, _____³ australes, y este aceite,

_____⁴ australes. Total: _____⁵ australes.

Paso 2

Now state the prices yourself, item by item. You will hear the correct answer on the CD.

Actividad C.   Gustos y preferencias

Working with a partner, indicate your likes and dislikes. After stating your own preferences, use the phrase **¿Y tú?** to solicit similar information from your partner.

me gusta + *singular noun*	me gusta(n) mucho…
me gustan + *plural noun*	no me gusta(n) nada…

MODELO: Entre _____ y _____, yo prefiero… ¿Y tú?

The Workbook/Study Guide contains more detailed explanation and practice of this grammar point.

4

UN POCO DE GRAMÁTICA

More About Using Verbs to Talk About the Past

In **Lección 12** you learned to express what other people did in the past by adding **-ó/-ió** or **-aron/-ieron** to the stems of most verbs. To talk about your own actions in the past, add **-é** to the stems of most **-ar** verbs and **-í** to the stems of most **-er** and **-ir** verbs.

RAQUEL: Arturo volvió a su casa y yo **regresé** al hotel. **Llamé** a México y **hablé** con Pedro.
ARTURO: La última vez que **vi** a mi hermano fue aquí.

Remember that stem-changing verbs ending in **-ar** and **-er** do not have a stem change in the preterite. Note also that the first-person form of **ver** (**vi**) does not carry an accent mark.

Actividad.   ¿Quién fue?

Here are some statements a person might make about events that happened yesterday. Indicate who might have said each statement, a student, a professor, or a secretary. ¡OJO! Some statements may have more than one answer.

a. una estudiante   b. un profesor   c. un secretario

1. Me desperté a las seis de la mañana.
2. Fui a la biblioteca.

Act., Variation: Have a relay race using first-person forms in the preterite. Divide the class in half. You give the infinitive and subject pronoun and one student from each team writes the first-person preterite form of the verb. For instance, you say *hablar, yo,* and one student from each team quickly writes *hablé* on the board. The first one to write the correct form wins a point for the team.

3. Trabajé ocho horas.
4. Llegué a la universidad a la una de la tarde.
5. Conocí a la nueva profesora de francés.
6. Acepté una invitación para almorzar con una compañera de clase.
7. Almorcé en el parque debajo de (*underneath*) un árbol (*tree*).

5

 # LECTURA CULTURAL

Lectura cultural, **Suggestion:** Have students look at maps and text together in class before assigning listening activity as homework. It is helpful to have a large map of Argentina in front of the room or on an overhead.

 ## La Argentina, país de contrastes

At the beginning of **Episodio 13** you saw a brief introduction to Argentina and to its incredible geographical variety. Listen to the introduction again. Try to remember the images you saw in the video episode and locate the places named on these maps.*

Now listen to a series of statements about Argentina. Are they **Cierto (C)** or **Falso (F)**? You will hear the answers on the CD.

1. C F 2. C F 3. C F
4. C F 5. C F

¿Cómo es la Argentina? Para contestar, muchos pensamos en los gauchos… en el tango… en Juan Perón y Evita (¿te acuerdas de la obra musical que se montó[1] en Inglaterra y los Estados Unidos?)… en el fútbol[2]… Pero sobre todo pensamos en La Pampa. Es verdad que La Pampa ocupa la cuarta parte del territorio argentino y que da a la Argentina sus dos grandes riquezas:[3] la carne[4] y los cereales.

Pero la Argentina es mucho más que una inmensa llanura. Es también

- la selva[5] del norte, en la frontera con el Brasil
- las plantaciones de té de Misiones
- las viñas[6] de Mendoza (¡los vinos de la Argentina son fabulosos!)

[1]se… *was produced* [2]¡OJO! *soccer* (*football* = el fútbol americano) [3]*riches* [4]*meat* [5]*jungla* [6]*vineyards*

Las cataratas del Iguazú

Lectura cultural, **Preguntas:** 1. *¿Qué imágenes estereotipadas tenemos cuando pensamos en la Argentina?* (see first 2 sentences) 2. *¿Qué otras cosas también tiene este país de las que no hablamos normalmente?* (see list) *¿Dónde están las famosas estaciones de esquí?* (en Bariloche) 3. *¿De dónde son los vinos fabulosos de la Argentina?* (de Mendoza) 4. *¿Cómo se llama la gruta en donde un pueblo cubrió las paredes con huellas de mano?* (la Cueva de las Manos)

* As you look at the names on the maps and listen to the description of Argentina, note that the definite article is used with the names of some countries and not others: **la Argentina, el Brasil, el Uruguay, el Paraguay**; but: **Chile, Bolivia, Colombia** . . . . This isn't observed by all Spanish speakers.

- la impresionante cordillera de los Andes, con el Aconcagua, la cumbre[7] más alta de América, con sus 6.959 metros
- las famosas estaciones de esquí, como Bariloche
- los glaciares y grandes lagos —entre ellos, el lago Argentino— de la Patagonia, donde termina el continente americano.

La Argentina es también una nación marítima por excelencia. Tiene 4.500 kilómetros de costa con su riqueza marina. ¿Sabías,[8] por ejemplo, que la península de Valdés es el único asiento continental[9] de elefantes marinos del mundo? Y, por supuesto,[10] está también la Tierra del Fuego, separada del continente por el estrecho de Magallanes. Su capital, Ushuaia, es la ciudad más austral del mundo.

Todo esto ilustra el gran contraste que hay de una región a otra. ¿Cómo es posible que haya tanta variedad de climas y diversidad de paisajes[11]? Recuerda que la Argentina se extiende desde el Trópico de Capricornio hasta el Polo Sur. Aquí hay unas vistas más.

En las llanuras tropicales del noreste, entre la Argentina, el Brasil y el Paraguay, están las cataratas del Iguazú: unas 275 cascadas en medio de una vegetación exótica. Aunque la mayoría de los saltos[12] están en el lado argentino, las mejores vistas[13] se ven desde el Brasil: «Argentina pone el espectáculo[14] y Brasil cobra la entrada[15]», dicen allí.

Los pueblos[16] que habitaron en lo que hoy es la Argentina, no llegaron a desarrollar[17] civilizaciones como la inca, maya o azteca. Sin embargo, crearon[18] culturas muy interesantes con bellas manifestaciones artísticas. Una de las expresiones artísticas más interesantes y antiguas está situada en la provincia de Santa Cruz en la Patagonia. Hace unos diez mil años, un pueblo de esta región cubrió de huellas de mano las paredes de una gruta.[19] Hoy se llama la Cueva de las Manos.

La Cueva de las Manos

La cordillera de los Andes

[7]*peak*   [8]*Did you know*   [9]*asiento… continental shelf*   [10]*por… of course*   [11]*landscapes*   [12]*falls*   [13]*views*   [14]*pone… puts on the show*   [15]*price of admission*   [16]*peoples*   [17]*no… didn't develop*   [18]*they created*   [19]*cubrió… covered the walls of a cave with handprints*

Actividad.   La Argentina y los Estados Unidos

Do the following aspects of Argentine geography remind you of places in the United States? Are there American equivalents for some of them?

1. La Pampa
2. las viñas de Mendoza
3. los Andes
4. Bariloche
5. el Aconcagua
6. la península de Valdés
7. Ushuaia (¿Cuál es la ciudad más norteña de los Estados Unidos?)
8. las cataratas del Iguazú

6

INTERCAMBIO

In this activity, you will talk about things you might have done in the past.

Paso 1
Describe four activities from the following list that you have (supposedly) done in the past. You may add information to the phrase and expand on the idea if you like. Make sure at least one of the activities is *not* true. Embellish where you can!

MODELO: TÚ: Una vez comí ostras crudas (*raw*). ¡Qué deliciosas!

1. preparar langosta
2. pescar (*to fish*) salmón
3. conocer a una persona famosa
4. escribir un poema de amor (*love*)
5. recibir un poema de amor
6. llegar tarde a un examen
7. mentir (*to lie*) a un professor/una profesora
8. ¿ ?

Paso 2
Make your statements to the class. Can they tell which statements are true and which ones are not?

VOCABULARIO

Los verbos

almorzar (ue)	to have lunch
comenzar (ie)	to begin
comer	to eat
preferir (ie)	to prefer
reconocer (reconozco)*	to recognize

Las personas

el/la dependiente/a	clerk
el marinero	sailor
todo el mundo	everybody

Los lugares

el barco	boat
el negocio	business; shop
la tienda	store

Los conceptos

la búsqueda	search
la (primera/última) vez	(first/last) time

Los mariscos (Seafood)

los calamares	squid
el cangrejo	crab
la langosta	lobster
el langostino	prawn
el mejillón	mussel
la ostra	oyster

El pescado (Fish)

el atún	tuna
el lenguado	sole
la merluza	hake
el salmón	salmon

---

* Note that the first-person singular form of **reconocer** reflects the irregularity of **conocer** (**conozco**), from which it is derived.

Otros comestibles (Other Foods)

el aceite	oil
el arroz	rice
la ensalada	salad
la manteca (*Arg.*)	butter
la mantequilla	butter
el pan	bread

Las palabras adicionales

me gusta(n) (mucho)...	I like . . . (a lot)
no me gusta(n) (nada)...	I don't like . . . (at all)
en seguida	immediately
hace... (años, horas...)	. . . (years, hours . . .) ago
luego	then, next; later

EN EL EXTRANJERO*

*Abroad

OBJETIVOS

The materials in **Lección 14** of the Textbook and the Workbook/Study Guide will help you better understand the video episode and take you beyond it, giving you additional information about places and characters in the series. The Textbook will also help you to develop skill in using the Spanish language. In this lesson you will learn

- the Spanish words for some types of meat and for some other food items used to prepare **brochetas**
- some ways to talk about things you did with others in the past

You will also learn about the national hero of Argentina.

Be sure to work through all parts of the lesson. When you see a headphones symbol in the margin, listen to the CD for **Lección 14**. Answers or hints for many activities are given in Appendix 1. Be sure to check your answers for each activity before going on to the next one.

The interactive CD-ROM to accompany *Destinos* contains additional practice with the video storyline and will help you improve your skills in Spanish.

BEFORE VIEWING . . .

Preliminary: See Faculty Guide for additional information and activities for this lesson.
• **Variation:** For activities marked with the headphones icon, you may wish to read from the Audioscript instead of playing the CD.
• **Suggestion:** Make sure students are familiar with the activities before you read from the Audioscript or play the CD.

1

PREPARACIÓN

Suggestions:
• Before watching the video, go over the vocabulary list at the end of the chapter and have students pronounce the words after you.
• Assign *Preparación* activities as homework and then go over them quickly in class before viewing the video.

Act. A, Suggestion: You may want to have students do this activity in pairs.

Act. A, Answers: 1. c 2. b 3. c 4. a

Actividad A.

In the last video episode of *Destinos* Raquel and Arturo started their search for Ángel. What do you remember about the search? Complete the following statements.

1. Entre las cosas de su madre, Arturo encontró
   a. _____ una carta.
   b. _____ una pintura.
   c. _____ una foto... de Ángel.

2. En el barrio de la Boca, Raquel y Arturo hablaron con
   a. _____ pocas personas.
   b. _____ varias personas.
   c. _____ muchas personas.

3. Por fin encontraron a un marinero que
   a. _____ reconoció a Ángel.
   b. _____ tenía la dirección de Ángel.
   c. _____ les dio el nombre de otro marinero.

4. Arturo invitó a Raquel a
   a. _____ cenar en su casa.
   b. _____ ir al teatro.
   c. _____ ir a un parque.

 ## Actividad B.

Act. B, Variation: Have students role-play the dialogue between teacher and student, between one half of the class and the other, and in pairs.

In this video episode Raquel and Arturo will meet and talk with Héctor. Listen to part of their conversation on the CD, trying to get the gist of it. Then read it to see whether you missed anything. Afterwards, listen to the conversation again.

RAQUEL: ¿Se quedó[1] a vivir en el extranjero?

HÉCTOR: Sí. No recuerdo bien qué país era... ¿saben? Creo que era Puerto Rico, pero no estoy seguro. Era un país en el Caribe... no sé si Puerto Rico, pero estoy seguro que era en el Caribe... Sí, posiblemente Puerto Rico.

RAQUEL: ¿Y la carta?

HÉCTOR: ¡Claro! ¡La carta! La tengo que buscar.

ARTURO: Es muy importante para mí.

HÉCTOR: Sí, comprendo. Mire, Ud. sabe dónde encontrarme. Necesito un par de días para buscar la carta.

ARTURO: Bueno, se lo agradezco muchísimo.[2]

HÉCTOR: No hay de qué. Ángel era mi amigo.

[1]*Se... He stayed*   [2]*se... I'm very grateful. (I thank you very much for it.)*

Para pensar...*

¿Qué importancia puede tener el Caribe en esta historia? ¿Qué no recuerda muy bien Héctor? ¿Y por qué está interesada Raquel en una carta que tiene Héctor?

 . . . AFTER VIEWING

2

¿TIENES BUENA MEMORIA?

 Actividad A.   ¿Cuánto recuerdas?
Listen to part of Raquel's story review once again if you think you need to, then answer the following questions about **Episodio 14**.

Paso 1
All of the following events happened in **Episodio 14**, but . . . in what order did they occur? Put them in order, from 1 to 6. The understood subject of most of the sentences is **Arturo y Raquel**.

a. _____ Fueron al Piccolo Navio.
b. _____ Tomaron café y miraron unas fotos.
c. _____ Se sentaron a cenar en el jardín.
d. _____ Comieron brochetas y hablaron.
e. _____ Raquel llamó a su madre por teléfono.
f. _____ Conocieron a Héctor y hablaron con él.

Paso 2
Raquel found out some things about Arturo in this video episode. What were they? Indicate whether the statements are **Cierto (C)** or **Falso (F)**.

C   F   1. Arturo vive solo (*alone*).
C   F   2. Se casó una vez pero está divorciado.

C   F   3. Su esposa volvió a su país natal, el Perú.
C   F   4. Su profesión no es muy importante para él.

Actividad B.   El amigo de Ángel
So far, Héctor has been able to provide a little bit of information, and perhaps he might be of even more help later on. What do you remember about Héctor and the information he has given Arturo and Raquel? ¡OJO! More than one answer may be possible in some cases.

---

* **Para pensar**... means *Something to think about* . . . . This repeating feature will suggest things for you to think about as you work with the video, Textbook, or Workbook/Study Guide.

1. Héctor se acuerda muy bien de Ángel porque Ángel
   a. _____ lo ayudó cuando era niño.   c. _____ era su amigo.
   b. _____ vivió en el barrio.

2. También dice Héctor que recibió una carta de Ángel
   a. _____ hace dos días.   c. _____ hace muchos años.
   b. _____ hace unas semanas.

3. Héctor cree que Ángel
   a. _____ se casó muy joven.   c. _____ se fue a vivir en el
   b. _____ se preocupaba mucho por   extranjero, en Puerto
        su padre, don Fernando.   Rico.

Nota cultural Los brindis

As Arturo and Raquel have a glass of wine before dinner, they exchange a toast used throughout the Spanish-speaking world, with minor variations. You may have heard the toast on other
occasions, and you can probably guess its general meaning.

¡Salud, dinero y amor! Y tiempo para disfrutarlos.*

A shorter toast is simply **Salud**, the equivalent of *To your health*. It is considered polite to
use it even prior to drinking water, as in **Episodio 12** when Arturo brought up glasses of water for them both on the rooftop and began to tell Raquel about his city.

3

VOCABULARIO DEL TEMA

La carne

la carne de cerdo	pork	**el bistec**	steak	
la carne de vaca	beef	**el cordero**	lamb	
el chorizo	sausage	**la chuleta**	chop	
el jamón	ham	**de cerdo**	pork chop	
la panceta	bacon	**de cordero**	lamb chop	
el pollo	chicken	**la hamburguesa**	hamburger	
los riñones	kidney	**el pavo**	turkey	
el tocino	bacon	**la ternera**	veal	

---

* A frequent variation is: **Y tiempo para gozarlos**.

Otros comestibles

la cebolla	onion
el pimiento (morrón)	(red) pepper
el queso	cheese
el tomate	tomato
el vino	wine
el vino blanco	white wine
el vino tinto	red wine

Note some variations frequently used in other parts of the Spanish-speaking world.

la carne de vaca = la carne de res (*Mex.*)
el chorizo = la salchicha (*Lat. Am.*)
el pavo = el guajolote (*Mex.*)

Escalopines de Ternera con Setas a la Pimienta verde.- 1.800
Estofado de Rabo de Toro a la "Real Maestranza".- 1.600
Entrecot de Buey a la Bordalesa.- 1.800
Solomillo de Ternera al Estragón.- 1.950
Magre de Pato al Vino de Oporto.- 1.900
Salteado de Ternera a la Sevillana.- 1.600
Pollo con Champiñones al Ajillo.- 1.300

Actividad A. La carne y otros comestibles

Listen as the speaker on the CD talks about some of his food preferences. He will use the phrases **me gusta...** and **me gustan...** as well as the verb **prefiero...** . Write the number of the sentence next to the appropriate drawing.

Act. A, Answers: 1. beef, steak 2. hamburger, ham, cheese 3. bacon 4. turkey, chicken 5. kidney, pork

Act. A, Optional: Have students work with a partner to create sentences that describe what the speaker likes. They should use *le gusta …*, *le gustan …*, and *prefiere.*

Actividad B. Las brochetas y otros comestibles

Listen as Arturo and Raquel talk about how **brochetas** are prepared, as well as some other dishes. Try to provide the missing words without looking back at the list of foods.

Act. B, Answers: 1. *riñones (riñoncitos)* 2. *vaca* 3. *chorizos* 4. *panceta* 5. *tocino* 6. *pimiento* 7. *tomate* 8. *cebolla* 9. *jamones* 10. *pollo*

ARTURO: Preparo las brochettes con _____,¹ carne de

_____,² carne de cerdo, _____³ y panceta.

RAQUEL: ¿_____?[4] ¿Qué es eso?

ARTURO: Creo que Uds. le llaman «_____».[5]

RAQUEL: Ah, sí.

ARTURO: Y también… _____[6] morrón, _____,[7]

_____[8] y ciruela, para darle el toque artístico y agridulce.

RAQUEL: En España probé unos _____[9] deliciosos.

ARTURO: Sí, los jamones españoles tienen gran fama.

RAQUEL: La carne argentina también tiene gran fama, sobre todo la carne de vaca.

ARTURO: Si te gusta el _____,[10] tengo una receta fabulosa: pollo a la inglesa. Se prepara* con limón y mayonesa.

Actividad C. Las comidas (*meals*) especiales
Paso 1

Indicate which meats and other foods are most commonly served on the following special occasions.

Act. C, Follow-up: For homework, have students create a menu of foods they would like to prepare for a special guest.

1. Cuando hay una gran cena para celebrar algo especial, las comidas que

   preferimos en mi familia son _____ o _____.

2. Para celebrar el cuatro de julio, tradicionalmente se prepara una barbacoa

   (*barbeque*) de _____ o _____. Yo prefiero…

3. Para celebrar el Día de Dar Gracias en los Estados Unidos, se prepara(n)

   _____. La(s) comida(s) en esta cena que (no) me gusta(n)

   es/son…

Paso 2

Select an item from **Paso 1** and interview three classmates to see if their responses are similar. How do your tastes compare with those of your classmates?

Actividad D. Mis preferencias

Present to the class the following:

Act. D, Note: Mention other categories of food so that non-meat eaters can participate.

a. la carne que más me gusta (*I like the best*)
b. la carne que menos me gusta (*I like the least*)
c. una carne que como, pero con poca frecuencia

Your classmates will respond to you by agreeing (**Sí, me gusta[n] también/mucho**) or disagreeing (**No me gusta[n] para nada**). How similar or different is everybody regarding their preferences?

---

*Note the use of **se** before the verb in this sentence. **Preparo** expresses *I prepare*; **se prepara** in this context means *it is prepared*. You will hear and see the word **se** used frequently in this way throughout *Destinos*.

4 UN POCO DE GRAMÁTICA

The Workbook/Study Guide contains more detailed explanation and practice of this grammar point.

Suggestion: Write infinitives of several verbs across the top of the board and have students go up and conjugate the verbs in the preterite.

Extension: Mention time expressions that accompany the preterite (such as *ayer, anoche, hace _____, la semana pasada,* etc.) in order to provide examples of context for distinguishing when the *nosotros* form of *-ar* verbs is in the present tense or in the preterite.

More About Using Verbs to Talk About the Past

To talk about what you did in the past with others, add **-amos** to **-ar** verbs and **-imos** to **-er** and **-ir** verbs.

RAQUEL: Anoche **encontramos** a Héctor en el Piccolo Navio. Cuando lo **vimos**, se levantó para bailar. Por fin **hablamos** un poco con él. **Caminamos** con él hasta su casa. Nos **despedimos** de él y luego **volvimos** a la casa de Arturo.

RAQUEL: *Last night we found Héctor at the Piccolo Navio. When we saw him, he got up to dance. Finally we talked with him a bit. We walked to his house with him. We said good-bye to him and then we returned to Arturo's house.*

Did you notice that the present and preterite **nosotros** forms of most **-ar** verbs are identical, and that the same is true of most **-ir** verbs? Context will help you determine which tense is being used.

Actividad. Todos lo hicimos

Using **todos**, **casi** (*almost*) **todos**, or **sólo algunos** (*only a few*), make statements about what you and your classmates did last week. Is each statement you make correct? Your classmates will verify whether you are correct.

Todos / Casi todos / Sólo algunos

1. comimos pizza
2. salimos a bailar
3. hablamos con los padres por teléfono
4. vimos una película en el cine
5. trabajamos como voluntarios en algo
6. tomamos mucho café
7. fuimos a una fiesta
8. bebimos cerveza

5 LECTURA CULTURAL

José de San Martín, héroe nacional de la Argentina

Before reading the following passage about José de San Martín and his role in Latin American history, review what you know about him by listening again to information from the video episode. Pay particular attention to the names of the countries.

El general José de San Martín fue uno de los líderes militares de la independencia de América. Fue el héroe de la independencia de la Argentina, Chile y el Perú.

San Martín nació[1] el 25 de febrero de 1778 en Yapeyú, un pueblo[2] de las antiguas misiones jesuitas. (Hoy está en la provincia argentina de Corrientes.) En 1786 viajó con sus padres a España. En Madrid estudió en un colegio para futuros militares. A los doce años entró como cadete en un regimiento del ejército[3] español. Más tarde luchó[4] en la guerra de independencia española contra Napoleón.

A pesar de[5] su educación española, San Martín no se consideró nunca español, sino[6] americano.* Regresó a la Argentina en 1812, muy animado por el espíritu de la guerra de la independencia de los Estados Unidos y de la Revolución francesa. Muy pronto se puso al mando[7] de los movimientos independentistas de Sudamérica. La independencia de la Argentina se proclamó en 1816. Pero aún quedaban[8] muchas colonias en el continente.

En el norte, actuó Simón Bolívar, el Libertador de Venezuela, Colombia y Ecuador. Desde el sur, el general San Martín dirigió[9] personalmente la lucha por la independencia. Su talento militar era excepcional. En 1817 salió de la Argentina y cruzó los Andes con un ejército de 5.200 hombres. En 1818 se declaró la independencia de Chile.

En 1820 San Martín organizó la expedición del Perú. Avanzó desde el sur y conquistó Lima en 1821. Bolívar avanzó desde el norte. Por fin se consiguió la independencia del Perú en 1824.

Después de una larga carrera militar, San Martín decidió volver a Europa. Se instaló[10] en Francia, donde murió en 1850.

[1]*was born* [2]*village* [3]*army* [4]*he fought* [5]*A... In spite of* [6]*but rather* [7]*se... he took command* [8]*aún... there were still* [9]*directed* [10]*Se... He settled* [11]*You will be*

El general José de San Martín siguió toda su vida esta máxima: «Serás[11] lo que debes ser, y si no, no serás nada.»

Actividad.   **Sudamérica y este país**

Da el nombre de

1. dos libertadores de Sudamérica.
2. el héroe de la independencia de la Argentina.
3. un héroe de la independencia de este país.
4. un héroe argentino que fue militar.
5. un héroe de este país de la época moderna que fue militar.

---

* Note the use of the word **americano** in this context. It does not mean American in the sense of *from the United States of America*, but rather American in the sense of *from the Americas, North and South America.*

6

INTERCAMBIO

Paso 1

Fill in the following calendar with today's day in the right-hand column and then the previous four days. For example, if today is Wednesday, you write **miércoles** in the right-hand column, **martes** in the column immediately left, **lunes** in the next, and so on. Then, list any and all meats you have eaten for the meals indicated for today and the last four days. (Note: if you are a vegetarian, write **ninguna carne** in the blanks.)

					hoy:
desayuno					
almuerzo					
cena					

Paso 2

Now, ask questions in Spanish to find five classmates who ate what you ate prior to today. Jot down their names and the meat they ate in the chart from **Paso 1**. Be sure to have the information regarding day and meal!

> MODELO: ¿Comiste jamón esta semana (la semana pasada)? ¿En qué día? ¿Para qué comida del día? Gracias.

Intercambio, Paso 3., **Suggestion:** Gather the statements and randomly select a few. Read one out loud and then ask the person whose name is mentioned if he/she knows who wrote the statement. The object is to see if they paid attention and can remember or guess well to whom they supplied that information.

Paso 3

Write out four statements about what you and the classmates you interviewed ate. Turn the statements in to your instructor.

> MODELO: Roberto y yo comimos jamón. Pero yo lo comí el martes para el desayuno y Roberto lo comió el lunes para el almuerzo.

VOCABULARIO

Los verbos

llevarse (bien/mal) to get along (well/badly)
pasar to pass, spend (*time*); to happen
preparar to prepare

Las carnes (Meats)

el bistec steak
la carne de cerdo pork
la carne de vaca beef
el chorizo sausage

la chuleta chop
   de cerdo pork chop
   de cordero lamb chop
el cordero lamb
la hamburguesa hamburger
el jamón ham
la panceta bacon
el pavo turkey
el pollo chicken
los riñones kidneys
la ternera veal
el tocino bacon

Otros comestibles

la cebolla	onion
el pimiento (morrón)	(red) pepper
el queso	cheese
el tomate	tomato
el vino (blanco, tinto)	(white, red) wine

Los adjetivos

divorciado/a	divorced
juntos/as	together
solo/a	alone

Las palabras adicionales

en el extranjero   abroad

Palabras del texto

para pensar...   something to think about

Culpable*

*Guilty

Objetivos

The materials in **Lección 15** of the Textbook and the Workbook/Study Guide will help you better understand the video episode and take you beyond it, giving you additional information about places and characters in the series. The Textbook will also help you to develop skill in using the Spanish language. In this lesson you will learn

- how to express the names of many kinds of fruit in Spanish
- how to form additional preterite-tense verb forms

You will also learn about Buenos Aires and about one of Argentina's most important industries.

Be sure to work through all parts of the lesson. When you see a headphones symbol in the margin, listen to the CD for **Lección 15**. Answers or hints for many activities are given in Appendix 1. Be sure to check your answers for each activity before going on to the next one.

The interactive CD-ROM to accompany *Destinos* contains additional practice with the video storyline and will help you improve your skills in Spanish.

BEFORE VIEWING . . .

Preliminary: See Faculty Guide for additional information and activities for this lesson.
• **Variation:** For activities marked with the headphones icon, you may wish to read from the Audioscript instead of playing the CD.
• **Suggestion:** Make sure students are familiar with the activities before you read from the Audioscript or play the CD.

1

Preparación

Suggestions:
• Before watching the video, go over the vocabulary list at the end of the chapter and have students pronounce the words after you.
• Assign *Preparación* activities as homework and then go over them quickly in class before viewing the video.

Act. A, Answers: 1. b
2. b 3. a 4. c 5. b 6. b

Actividad A.

In the last video episode of *Destinos* Raquel and Arturo were finally able to make some progress in their search for Ángel. How much do you remember about **Episodio 14**? Complete the following statements.

1. En casa de Arturo, Raquel pasó una noche muy
   a. _____ aburrida (*boring*).   c. _____ triste (*sad*).
   b. _____ agradable.

2. Al día siguiente, en la cantina Piccolo Navio, Raquel y Arturo conocieron a este hombre. Se llama
   a. _____ José.   c. _____ Ángel.
   b. _____ Héctor.

3. Este hombre era (*was*) amigo de Ángel. Les dice a Raquel y Arturo que Ángel se fue a vivir a un país
   a. _____ del Caribe.   c. _____ de África.
   b. _____ de Europa.

4. El hombre tiene algo que da la dirección de Ángel. Es
   a. _____ un telegrama.   c. _____ una carta.
   b. _____ un libro.

5. Para buscarla, necesita
   a. _____ unos minutos.   c. _____ una semana.
   b. _____ un par de días.

6. Al final de su conversación, este hombre le da algo a Arturo como recuerdo (*memento*) de su hermano Ángel. Es
   a. _____ una foto.   c. _____ un poema.
   b. _____ un cuadro.

***Para pensar,* Suggestion:** Ask class in general these questions. Ask for a show of hands of those who believe there is a mutual attraction. This may stimulate a good bit of discussion. Do not reveal any new information, but allow the story to unfold naturally.

Para pensar...

¿Crees que hay una atracción mutua entre Raquel y Arturo? ¿Siente ella algo por él? Y él, ¿qué piensa de esta abogada norteamericana?

Actividad B.

In this video episode Arturo will express his concerns about Ángel's fate.

 ### Paso 1

Listen to part of a conversation between Arturo and Raquel without looking ahead in this activity. Then answer the question. You should listen to this section of the CD only once.

Which of the following statements best describes Arturo's mood in this conversation?

Act. B, Answers: *Paso 1:* b *Paso 2:* 1. c 2. *dime* = tell me 3. a

a. _____ Arturo está contento.

b. _____ Arturo está preocupado.

c. _____ Arturo está aburrido.

 Paso 2

Now listen to the conversation again. A written version of it is provided to help you understand it. Then answer the questions. This time you may listen to the CD as many times as you need to.*

RAQUEL: ¿En qué piensas?

ARTURO: En Ángel. ¿Qué quería de la vida? ¿Qué buscaba?

RAQUEL: ¿Te sientes bien? ¿Qué te pasa?

ARTURO: No te preocupes. No es nada.

RAQUEL: Ya verás. Pronto podrás hablar con tu hermano... Arturo, dime por favor qué es lo que te pasa.

ARTURO: Me tenés que perdonar, Raquel. Es que...

RAQUEL: ¿Sí...?

ARTURO: Tengo un mal presentimiento... ¿Qué pasa si Ángel...?

1. You should be able to understand the meaning of **¿Te sientes bien?** But what about **¿Qué te pasa?** What does Raquel want to know?
   a. _____ Where are you going?
   b. _____ What are you thinking about?
   c. _____ What's the matter?

2. The verb form **dime** is a command. Knowing that **me** means *me* or *to me* in English, what do you think Raquel is saying when she uses this verb form? (*Hint:* **Di** does not look very much like the infinitive from which it derives. Let the context in which **dime** is used be your guide.)

3. According to the context and to Arturo's mood, what do you think the word **presentimiento** means?
   a. _____ premonition
   b. _____ thought
   c. _____ headache

Para pensar, **Suggestion:** Ask class in general these questions. Accept any answers the students may have. The questions are designed to get students thinking but it is not necessary to answer them completely at this point. However, you may want to have them try to explain why they have a particular opinion.

Para pensar...

¿Qué presentimiento tiene Arturo? ¿Qué quiere decir él cuando le dice a Raquel «¿Qué pasa si Ángel...?» ¿A qué o a quién se refiere el título de este episodio?

---

*Some of the verb forms used in this conversation between Raquel and Arturo are probably unfamiliar to you. However, you should be able to follow the conversation by focusing on the verb stems and making logical guesses about whether the action described by the verb is in the present, past, or future.

. . . AFTER VIEWING

2

¿TIENES BUENA MEMORIA?

Actividad A.   ¿A quién se refiere?
Identify the character described in each sentence.

a.   Ángel Castillo   c.   Raquel Rodríguez
b.   Arturo Iglesias   d.   Héctor Condotti

1.   _____ Después de hablar con Héctor, está muy pensativo.
2.   _____ Va a buscar la carta que Ángel le escribió hace muchos años.
3.   _____ Probablemente tiene que hacer un viaje al Caribe.
4.   _____ Tiene vergüenza (*is embarrassed*) en el parque y no quiere andar en mateo (*ride in the carriage*).
5.   _____ Se fue a vivir al Caribe. Ahora tendrá* unos 52 años.
6.   _____ Se siente culpable porque nunca buscó a su hermano.

Actividad B.   ¿Qué pasó?
The following paragraphs are a summary of what Raquel and Arturo did in **Episodio 15**. Complete the paragraph with phrases from the following list.

tuvieron (*they had*) un *picnic*	no le interesó mucho
fue a la Cuadra	recibió un regalo (*present*)
compró una bolsa de cuero	de Arturo
decidieron ir a un parque	
llamó a Arturo	
encontró la carta	
no le gustó mucho	

Raquel visitó varias tiendas con Arturo y _____.[1] Más tarde, _____,[2] un centro comercial. Allí compró una blusa y unos pantalones. Luego regresó a su hotel. Mientras tanto,[a] Héctor _____[3] para decirle que _____.[4] Pero no puede ver a Arturo y Raquel hasta mañana. Esto _____[5] a Raquel. Empieza a ponerse[b] un poco impaciente y quiere terminar pronto la investigación.

[a]Mientras... *Meanwhile*   [b]*become*

---

* Remember that the phrase **tener... años** means *to be . . . years old* and that **tendrá** is a future form of **tener**. In this context it means *he is probably . . . .*

Para pasar el resto del día, Raquel y Arturo _____,[6] aunque[c] la idea _____[7] a Arturo. Pero lo pasaron muy bien.[d] Anduvieron[e] en bote y en mateo y también _____[8] con la comida que Arturo llevaba[f] en la canasta.[g] Por la noche, Raquel _____,[9] una linda chaqueta* de cuero. Parece que sí hay una atracción entre Arturo y Raquel, ¿no?

[c]*although*   [d]*lo… they had a good time*   [e]*They rode*   [f]*was carrying*   [g]*basket*

Now listen to the summary on the CD and check your answers.

Actividad C.   ¡Un desafío!

In this challenging game, one person tells something that happened in **Episodio 15**. The next person adds to the previous statement with connecting phrases such as **sí, pero antes…** , **sí, y después…** , **sí, y también…** , and tells about something else that happened. As the story goes on, it becomes difficult to think of additional details, so try not to be the last speaker!

Nota cultural   Tiendas y parques

In this video episode Raquel and Arturo visit a number of well-known places in Buenos Aires. It is obvious from the video episode that Buenos Aires is a cosmopolitan city on a par with Paris, Madrid, New York, and other major cities and capitals. In addition to its wide boulevards and many public buildings, Buenos Aires is also home to

- **La calle Florida**, an elegant pedestrian mall with expensive shops, designer boutiques, and restaurants that serve many ethnic foods as well as the varieties of **parrillada** (*grilling*) for which Argentina is famous. Additional shopping options in Buenos Aires include **centros comerciales**, that is, shopping centers like **la Cuadra** (which have begun to spring up in all major cities in the Spanish-speaking world), and smaller, less expensive **boutiques**, found in many neighborhoods.
- **El Rosedal**, the large park and recreational area in the center of Buenos Aires. It is similar to Central Park in New York, **el Parque Chapultepec** in Mexico City, and **el Retiro** in Madrid. All these parks are particularly crowded on the weekends. They are sites for family gatherings and picnics, and where young people can meet in groups or where couples can stroll. Why do you think Arturo was so reluctant to go there?

---

* In Argentina, a short jacket of the type Arturo buys for Raquel is called **una campera**. In Mexico, it's **una chamarra**.

3

VOCABULARIO DEL TEMA

Suggestions:
• Practice pronunciation with choral and individual repetition.
• Bring in photos, drawings, or plastic fruit to introduce the vocabulary. As you present each fruit, ask ¿*Les gustan las/los… ? A mí (no) me gustan/me encantan.*

Las frutas

la banana	banana	**la cereza**	cherry
el durazno	peach	**la ciruela**	plum
la frutilla (*Arg.*)	strawberry	**la fresa**	strawberry
la manzana	apple	**el limón**	lemon
el melón	melon	**el melocotón**	peach
la naranja	orange	**la pera**	pear
la uva	grape	**la piña**	pineapple
		el plátano	banana
		la sandía	watermelon
		la toronja	grapefruit

The names for fruits and vegetables are the most variable among all vocabulary groups in the Spanish-speaking world. Some specifically Argentine variations are noted in the preceding list. Additional words used in Argentina include **el pomelo** (= **la toronja**) and **el ananás** (= **la piña**).

Act. A, Answers: *la manzana, la naranja, la banana, el melón*

Actividad A. **El espectáculo de Jaime Bolas**

Listen again to Jaime's patter during his juggling act and indicate the fruits he mentions.

Actividad B. **En la canasta de Arturo**

Act. B, Answers: 1. *frutas* 2. *uvas, un melón, bananas, naranjas, manzanas* 3. *duraznos, frutillas (fresas)* 4. *pan, queso y vino*

As you know, Arturo goes shopping for a picnic lunch. Listen again to the conversation he has with the fruit-store clerk. Then complete the following summary with as much information as you can remember.

Para el *picnic*, Arturo sorprendió a Raquel con una variedad de

_____.[1] Él recordó lo que dijo Raquel[a] en la calle Florida: «Ahora

tengo ganas de[b] comer una ensalada de fruta.»

Arturo fue al Paseo Natural y compró _____.[2] El dependiente

también le ofreció _____,[3] pero no los compró. También compró

_____,[4] pero en otra tienda.

[a]lo… *what Raquel said*   [b]tengo… *I feel like*

Lección 15 Culpable

Actividad C.   ¿Qué te gusta?

Act. C, Suggestion: Have students find out and react to their partners, likes and dislikes as well as expressing their own. Tell them to use *¿Y tú?* to elicit their partner's statements. Also, rather than having them go through the entire list and becoming bored, set a time limit of 3–4 minutes.

With a partner, share what kinds of things you like and what you don't like. Use the items below along with the new vocabulary you have learned.

> MODELO: Me gusta mucho el chicle (*gum*) con sabor (*flavor*) a sandía.
> (No me gusta el chicle con sabor a limón.)

1. el chicle
2. el yogur
3. los refrescos (*soft drinks*)
    (¡OJO! me gustan)
4. el helado (*ice cream*)
5. los dulces (*candy*) (¡OJO!)
6. el licor

• Poll students to find out who likes/dislikes what foods. Compare student preferences. For example: *A Roberto y a Julia les gusta el helado de chocolate. Pero a Diana y a Pablo les gusta el helado de vainilla. A todos les gustan las bananas pero a sólo dos personas les gustan las toronjas.*

4

UN POCO DE GRAMÁTICA

The Workbook/Study Guide contains more detailed explanation and practice of this grammar point.

Note: You may wish to review the paradigms for regular *-ar, -er,* and *-ir* verbs in the preterite and/or introduce the complete paradigms for the irregular verbs presented in this lesson.

More About Using Verbs to Talk About the Past

Traer, decir, estar, tener, and **andar** belong to a group of Spanish verbs whose preterite forms are irregular. Here are some examples with first-person forms. Raquel is the speaker in each example.

No **traje** mucha ropa en este viaje. Por eso **tuve** que ir de compras varias veces.

I didn't bring a lot of clothes on this trip. That's why I had to go shopping several times.

Le **dije** a mi madre que conocí a un hombre muy simpático en Buenos Aires.

I told my mother that I met a very nice man in Buenos Aires.

Estuve en Buenos Aires sólo unos días. Entre otras cosas, **tuve** un *picnic* con Arturo en el Rosedal y **anduve** en mateo.

I was in Buenos Aires only a few days. Among other things, I had a picnic with Arturo in Rosedal and I rode in a carriage.

Did you notice the patterns of irregularity here?

• **Traer** and **decir** have a **j** in the stem of their preterite forms, while **estar, tener,** and **andar** have **uv** in the stem.

• All of these first-person forms, whether from **-ar, -er,** or **-ir** infinitives, end in *un*accented **e**.

See what other features you can spot in these irregular forms from the following activity, in which more than **yo** forms will appear. You will learn more about irregular preterite forms in the Workbook/Study Guide.

Act., Follow-up: Review answers by asking the class in general. Ask for a show of hands if statements are true for students.

Actividad.   ¿Qué pasó?

Select the verb that best completes each sentence. Then indicate whether the sentence is **Cierto (C)** or **Falso (F)** based on what you did recently.

C F 1. El domingo por la tarde (tuve/anduve/traje) por el parque.
C F 2. La semana pasada (tuve/dije/estuve) una fiesta en mi casa.
C F 3. Un día no (dije/anduve/traje) mi libro a la clase de español.

C F 4. Ayer le (traje/dije/estuve) «Buenos días» al profesor / a la profesora
        de español.
C F 5. La semana pasada (estuve/traje/tuve) en la biblioteca varias veces.
C F 6. El sábado (dije/estuve/tuve) un *picnic*.
C F 7. (Tuve/Dije/Anduve) en bicicleta por el parque.
C F 8. (Tuve/Estuve/Dije) un examen esta semana.

5

LECTURA CULTURAL

Lectura cultural, **Suggestion:** Assign as homework and then go over in class. Remind students that they should not expect to understand every word of the reading, but rather to get the main ideas.

Lectura cultural, **Note:** This is a good opportunity to review the ideas from the brainstorming session on Argentina (p. 115). Were students' ideas accurate? What would they change now after having seen a good bit of Buenos Aires and some other aspects of Argentina?

Buenos Aires, una ciudad europea en el Nuevo Mundo

At the end of **Episodio 12**, from the rooftop of a tall building Arturo pointed out some landmarks to Raquel. Listen again to his words, then complete the statement that follows.

La palabra *porteños* probablemente se refiere a

a. _____ personas que beben mucho vino.   b. _____ personas que viven en un puerto.

If you guessed *b*, you were correct. The word **porteños** is the name for people who live in the port city of Buenos Aires. Before reading the following passage about Buenos Aires, try to remember what you thought Buenos Aires would be like before you saw anything about the city in **Episodio 12**. Did you think Buenos Aires would be a modern or a colonial city? Would it be densely or sparsely populated? What would be the ethnic background of most of its inhabitants? You will find the answers to these questions in the reading passage.

«**B**uenos Aires… antes[1] morir que olvidarte»

Así dijo el famoso cantante[2] del tango Carlos Gardel, hablando[3] de su ciudad. Sin embargo,[4] cuando llegan a Buenos Aires, muchos visitantes se sienten un poco decepcionados. La ciudad es impresionante, pero no es exótica. No hay viejos monumentos históricos. No predomina el estilo colonial español. Y los habitantes de la ciudad podrían[5] ser de cualquier[6] nacionalidad. Uno tiene la impresión de estar en París, Londres, Milán o Madrid… en cualquier ciudad menos la capital de la Argentina, casi en el fin del mundo.

Dos factores importantes diferencian la Argentina de los demás países de la América Latina: su geografía y las características culturales de sus habitantes.

● Geográficamente la Argentina está aislada del resto de Hispanoamérica por los Andes al oeste y por el Brasil y la selva del Amazonas al norte. Por esta razón,

[1]*rather* [2]*singer* [3]*talking* [4]*Sin… Nevertheless* [5]*could* [6]*any*

la Argentina siempre miró más hacia[7] Europa que hacia sus vecinos. Y en Europa se sintió más cerca de Francia o de Inglaterra que de España.

- Además, la gran mayoría de los habitantes de la Argentina son descendientes de europeos. Desde mediados[8] del siglo XIX la Argentina recibió un gran número de emigrantes. Muchos de ellos eran europeos del área mediterránea, italianos y españoles, seguidos[9] a gran distancia por polacos, rusos, alemanes y gente de los países vecinos. Toda esta herencia étnica se refleja en la capital. Se puede decir que el porteño es «un italiano que habla español con acento napolitano y que se considera inglés o francés».

Esta gran capital es una metrópoli de unos trece millones de habitantes, más del 30 por ciento del total de la población del país. Es uno de los centros financieros y comerciales más importantes del continente.

Una plaza en el barrio de La Boca.

Pero al mismo tiempo[10] el nivel cultural y artístico que se respira en Buenos Aires es de excelente calidad. La ciudad tiene numerosos museos, galerías de arte, bibliotecas públicas, salas de cine y de teatro... Muy pocos teatros tienen el atractivo del Teatro Colón. En efecto, se dice que un artista no triunfa verdaderamente en Latinoamérica hasta que no triunfa en el Colón de Buenos Aires.

Lectura cultural, Optional: Rather than asking students follow-up questions, have them prepare several questions from the reading as homework. Then, have them ask their questions to the class or collect, edit, and use them as a culture quiz.

Hay que pasar unos días en Buenos Aires para tomarle el pulso a la ciudad. Andar por sus calles, hablar con su gente.[11] Siempre hay algo a la vuelta de la esquina[12] que llama la atención. La calle Rivadavia, que dicen que llega hasta la Patagonia (¿Es la más larga del mundo? ¿Y el Wilshire Boulevard?)... El obelisco blanco como el de Washington o la réplica del famoso Big Ben, regalo de Inglaterra... El barrio de San Telmo, donde viven muchos artistas y escritores, un barrio lleno de librerías, tiendas de antigüedades y artesanos[13]... La Boca, cuyas[14] casas color pastel y restaurantes populares recuerdan el sur de Italia... En el centro, la animación de las calles peatonales[15] y las avenidas con sus *boutiques.*

Es con razón que los porteños, como Arturo Iglesias, se sienten muy orgullosos[16] de su ciudad.

[7]*toward*   [8]*the middle*   [9]*followed*   [10]*al... at the same time*   [11]*people*   [12]a... *just around the corner*   [13]*craftspeople*   [14]*whose*   [15]calles... *pedestrian streets*   [16]*proud*

6

INTERCAMBIO

Paso 1
Imagine that you are going on a picnic and you are bringing fruit. List four fruits that you would pack to share in the picnic.

Paso 2
Now walk about the classroom and talk to your classmates to find out what they brought to the picnic.

> MODELO: Yo traje manzanas, un melón, uvas y bananas. ¿Qué trajiste tú?

Paso 3
Report back to the class who brought the same fruits as you.

> MODELO: Mark y yo tenemos el mismo gusto. Los dos trajimos las mismas frutas: manzanas, melón, uvas y bananas.

VOCABULARIO

Los verbos

andar	to walk

Las frutas (Fruits)

la banana	banana
la cereza	cherry
la ciruela	plum
el durazno	peach
la fresa	strawberry
la frutilla (*Arg.*)	strawberry
el limón	lemon
la manzana	apple
el melocotón	peach
el melón	melon
la naranja	orange
la pera	pear
la piña	pineapple
el plátano	banana
la sandía	watermelon
la toronja	grapefruit
la uva	grape

Los adjetivos

aburrido/a	bored; boring*
culpable	guilty
divertido/a	fun

La ropa

la bolsa	purse, handbag

Los otros sustantivos

la canasta	basket
el recuerdo	memento
el regalo	present

Los conceptos

el presentimiento	premonition
la sorpresa	surprise

Las palabras adicionales

andar en mateo	to take a carriage ride
ir de compras	to go shopping
tener... años*	to be . . . years old
tener vergüenza*	to be embarrassed, ashamed

---

* Use **aburrido** with **estar** to express *bored* and with **ser** to express *boring*.
** Note in each of these expressions that the Spanish verb **tener** (*to have*) is used to express English *to be*. **Jaime tiene diez años** literally means *Jaime has ten years*, i.e., *Jaime is ten years old*. You will learn more about expressions of this kind in **Lección 21** of the Workbook/Study Guide.

LECCIÓN 16

CARAS*

*Faces

OBJETIVOS

The materials in **Lección 16** of the Textbook and the Workbook/Study Guide will help you better understand the video episode and take you beyond it, giving you additional information about places and characters in the series. The Textbook will also help you to develop skill in using the Spanish language. In this lesson, you will learn

- how to express the names of many kinds of vegetables in Spanish
- how to form additional preterite-tense verb forms

You will also learn about other cities in Argentina.

Be sure to work through all parts of the lesson. When you see a headphones symbol in the margin, listen to the CD for **Lección 16**. Answers or hints for many activities are given in Appendix 1. Be sure to check your answers for each activity before going on to the next one.

The interactive CD-ROM to accompany *Destinos* contains additional practice with the video storyline and will help you improve your skills in Spanish.

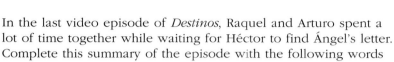

BEFORE VIEWING . . .

Preliminary: See Faculty Guide for additional information and activities for this lesson.
- **Variation:** For activities marked with the headphones icon, you may wish to read from the Audioscript instead of playing the CD.
- **Suggestion:** Make sure students are familiar with the activities before you read from the Audioscript or play the CD.

1

Preparación

Suggestions:
- Before watching the video, go over the vocabulary list at the end of the chapter and have students pronounce the words after you.
- Assign *Preparación* activities as homework and then go over them quickly in class before viewing the video.

Actividad A.
Paso 1

In the last video episode of *Destinos*, Raquel and Arturo spent a lot of time together while waiting for Héctor to find Ángel's letter. Complete this summary of the episode with the following words and phrases.

la atracción mutua   ya murió
un mal presentimiento   calmar
está pensativo   noticias de Héctor
pasan mucho tiempo juntos

Act. A, Answers: 1. *está pensativo* 2. *un mal presentimiento* 3. *ya murió* 4. *calmar* 5. *la atracción mutua* 6. *pasan mucho tiempo juntos* 7. *noticias de Héctor*

Al principio del episodio previo, Raquel nota que Arturo

_____.[1] Cuando ella le pregunta qué le pasa, Arturo le dice que

tiene _____.[2]

    —Arturo —dice Raquel— dime cuál es el mal presentimiento que tienes.

    —Es que —contesta Arturo— algo me dice que Ángel _____.[3]

    Raquel trata de[a] _____[4] a Arturo. Y cuando están por salir[b]

para el hotel, se dan cuenta de[c] _____[5] que sienten. Se besan[d] y

luego Arturo lleva a Raquel al hotel.

    Al día siguiente los dos _____.[6] Van de compras en la calle

Florida y más tarde van al parque Rosedal. Lo pasan muy bien. Ahora, en

este episodio, esperan tener _____[7]

[a]trata... *tries to*   [b]están... *they are ready to leave*   [c]se... *they become aware of*   [d]Se... *They kiss*

Paso 2
Now listen to the CD and check your answers.

Para pensar...

Ahora Raquel y Arturo están conscientes de su atracción mutua. ¿Crees que esta atracción va a convertirse en una relación seria?

    Parece que Raquel tendrá que (*will have to*) hacer un viaje al Caribe para seguir con la búsqueda de Ángel. ¿Qué va a hacer Arturo?

Act. B, Suggestion: You may want to have students do this activity in pairs, role-playing *Paso 2* and discussing their answers.

Act. B, Answers: Paso 1: 1. *pronto* 2. *muy serios* **Paso 2:** 1. b 2. b 3. b

Actividad B.

In this video episode Arturo will make an important decision.

Paso 1

Listen to part of a conversation between Arturo and Raquel without looking ahead in this activity. Then complete the statements according to what you understood. You should listen to this section of the CD only once.

1. Raquel sale para Puerto Rico... pronto / en unos días.
2. Los dos están... muy serios / muy alegres (*happy*)... durante esta conversación.

Paso 2

Now listen to the conversation again. Read the following portion of it before listening. Then answer the questions. This time you may listen to the CD as many times as you need to.

ARTURO: ¿Sabés? Ángel es el único pariente que tengo. ¿Ya decidiste cuándo te vas a ir?

RAQUEL: Debería tomar el primer vuelo... don Fernando está muy mal. Y no puedo tardarme mucho.

ARTURO: Hace unos pocos días que te conozco... y parece como si hiciera muchos años.

RAQUEL: Yo siento lo mismo.

ARTURO: Te voy a extrañar.

RAQUEL: Yo también a ti.

1. Arturo says, "Ángel es el único pariente que tengo." What do you think the word **pariente** means, according to the context?
   a. _____ friend
   b. _____ relative
   c. _____ enemy

2. Arturo says, "Hace unos pocos días que te conozco... y parece como si hiciera muchos años." What do you think he means?
   a. _____ I have known you for a few days, and I need more time to get acquainted.
   b. _____ I have known you for a few days, and it's as if I had known you for a long time.

3. A key word in this dialogue is the verb **extrañar**. Think about the context. Raquel has to travel to Puerto Rico to continue her search for Ángel. Given the mutual attraction that the two feel, when Arturo says to Raquel "Te voy a extrañar," and she responds "Yo también a ti," what do you think they are saying to each other?
   a. _____ I'm going to forget you.
   b. _____ I'm going to miss you.
   c. _____ I'm going to follow you.

. . . AFTER VIEWING

2

¿TIENES BUENA MEMORIA?

Actividad A. ¿Quién lo dijo?
Identify the character who makes the following statements in **Episodio 16**.

a. Raquel Rodríguez   c. Héctor Condotti
b. Arturo Iglesias   d. el ama de casa (*housekeeper*)

1. _____ «Salgo mal en las fotos y la cámara lo sabe.»
2. _____ «Mira. Me gusta mucho esta foto. ¿La has visto? El fotógrafo debe ser muy imaginativo.»
3. _____ «Disculpe, doctor, lo llaman por teléfono. Un Sr. Héctor…»
4. _____ «Señorita, ¿está bien el señor?»
5. _____ «Otra vez… este presentimiento… algo me dice que Ángel ya murió.»
6. _____ «Yo también tengo una sorpresa para ti… Pero me tienes que dar unos minutos para prepararla.»

Actividad B. ¿Qué pasó?
All of the following events happened in **Episodio 16**, but in what order did they occur? Put them in order, from 1 to 8.

a. _____ Héctor le da a Arturo la carta de Ángel.
b. _____ Raquel va al mercado para comprar legumbres y verduras.
c. _____ Arturo trata de tomar una foto con una cámara automática.
d. _____ Arturo lee la carta que Ángel le escribió a Héctor hace muchos años.
e. _____ Raquel encuentra una foto de una cara hecha de (*made of*) legumbres y verduras.
f. _____ Arturo le dice a Raquel que piensa viajar a Puerto Rico.
g. _____ Raquel le muestra (*shows*) dos caras de legumbres y verduras a Arturo.
h. _____ Arturo y Raquel van al puerto para buscar a Héctor.

Para pensar…

Arturo le dice a Raquel: «Tal vez (*Maybe*) yo podría ir a Puerto Rico y los dos continuar la búsqueda de Ángel.» ¿Por qué de repente (*suddenly*) quiere ir a Puerto Rico Arturo? ¿a causa de Ángel? ¿o a causa de Raquel?

Actividad C. ¿Quién soy?
Imagine that you are one of the characters from **Episodio 16**. Invent a line or two of dialogue your character (and only your character) might say or think. Be creative! Repeat your line(s) to a partner and have him or her guess who you are. Then switch roles and guess the character your partner is playing.

MODELOS: ¡Me gusta mucho esta señorita! (Arturo)

No sé quién es esta señorita que visita al doctor Iglesias. (el ama de casa)

VOCABULARIO DEL TEMA

Las legumbres y las verduras

la aceituna	olive	**el apio**	celery
la cebolla	onion	**los guisantes**	peas
los chícharos (*Mex.*)	peas	**la calabaza**	squash
el chile	chili pepper	**el champiñón**	mushroom
los ejotes (*Mex.*)	string beans	**los frijoles**	beans
la lechuga	lettuce	**las judías verdes**	string beans
la papa (*Lat. Am.*)	potato	**el maíz**	corn
el tomate	tomato		
la zanahoria	carrot		

Cognados: el brécol/el brocolí, la coliflor, las espinacas, la patata (*Spain*)

Remember that the names for fruits and vegetables are the most variable among all vocabulary groups in the Spanish-speaking world. Some specifically Mexican and Latin American variations are noted in the preceding lists.

Suggestions:
- Show pictures of the foods while going over the vocabulary.
- Bring examples of plastic foods to class to create your own Farmer's Market. Have students shop for different produce.

Follow-up: Have students cut food pictures out of magazines and label them.

Act A, Answers: Students should have marked the onions, peas, string beans, lettuce, tomatoes, carrots, potatoes, chile peppers, and olives.

Actividad A. **En el mercado**

Listen again to Raquel's shopping list and note the items she mentions.

___ ___ ___ ___ ___ ___

_____ _____ _____ _____ _____ _____ _____

Actividad B. Una cara hecha de legumbres y verduras
Paso 1

Listen again as Raquel shows Arturo the photograph she has found in one of his books and indicate the drawings of the vegetables you hear.

1. _____ _____

2. _____ _____

3. _____ _____

4. _____ _____

5. _____ _____

6. _____ _____

7. _____ _____

8. _____ _____

RAQUEL: Mira cómo ha usado las verduras. Ésta aquí es una hoja de

_____.[1] Y éste es un _____.[2]

ARTURO: ¿Un _____[2]? No puede ser.

RAQUEL: Sí, sí. Y éstas aquí son _____.[3] Éstas son

_____ .[4]

ARTURO: ¿_____[4]?

RAQUEL: Sí, _____ .[4] ¡No te hagas el tonto! Y éstos son

_____.[5]

ARTURO: ¿_____[5]?

RAQUEL: Sí, _____.[5] En México y en California los llamamos

_____.[5]

ARTURO: Aquí les decimos arvejas.

RAQUEL: Ésta es una _____[6] Y éstos son _____[7]

ARTURO: Y éstos son _____ .[8]

RAQUEL: ¿Cómo _____[8]?

ARTURO: Sí, pero Uds. les llaman chiles, ¿no?

RAQUEL: Sí.

Act. B, Answers: *Paso 1:* 1. *lechuga* 2. *tomate* 3. *cebollas* 4. *aceitunas* 5. *chícharos* 6. *zanahoria* 7. *ejotes* 8. *ajíes Paso 2: en la Argentina: arvejas; en México: chiles*

Act. B, Emphasis: This is a good moment to point out the diversity of the Spanish language and its speakers by showing how widely the names of food items vary from country to country.

Paso 2

Now fill in the following chart with some additional vocabulary variations you heard in the dialogue.

en la Argentina: _____   ____ajíes____

en México: ____chícharos____   _____

Act. C, Follow-up: To review food vocabulary, as well as *gustar,* prepare a *Firma aquí* activity with questions such as the following. *¿A ti te gusta(n) la ensalada / las papas / el pollo / … ?* Have students circulate in class asking and answering the questions and gathering the signatures of classmates who respond with *Sí.* Then have them report their findings to the class, using the model *A _____ le gusta la cebolla.*

Actividad C.   ¿Qué te gusta comer?

Indicate which vegetables and greens (and other things) you like to eat or combine with the following food items.

Palabras útiles: cocido/a (*cooked*), crudo/a (*raw*), frito/a (*fried*), al horno (*baked*), la mayonesa, la mostaza (*mustard*), la salsa (*dressing*), la salsa de tomate (*ketchup*), el puré de (papas, zanahorias…), la sopa de (legumbres, frijoles…)

1.   Las legumbres que como con más frecuencia son _____.

2.   En cuanto a (*As for*) legumbres, ¡no me gusta(n) nada _____!

3.   Con el pollo, me gusta comer _____. Prefiero el pollo

_____.

4.   A una hamburguesa siempre le pongo _____. También me

gusta comer _____ con una hamburguesa.

5.   A un sándwich de jamón le pongo _____.

6.   Mi sándwich favorito tiene _____.

7.   Una ensalada mixta (*tossed*) contiene _____. Se toma con

_____.

8.   Mi ensalada favorita contiene _____.

4

UN POCO DE GRAMÁTICA

The Workbook/Study Guide contains more detailed explanation and practice of this grammar point.

Suggestion. Have students write out full preterite conjugations for these verbs as homework after going over them. **Emphasis:** These verbs take on special meanings in the preterite. For example, *supe* means *to begin to know,* that is, *to discover* or *to find out.*

Optional: Write infinitives of several verbs across the top of the board and have students go up and conjugate the verbs in the preterite. **Variation:** Have a contest using irregular preterite forms. Divide the class in half. You give the infinitive and a subject pronoun and one student from each team writes the appropriate form of the verb. For instance, you say *querer, yo* or *poner, ella* and one student from each team quickly writes *quise* or *puso* on the board. The first one to write the correct form wins a point for the team.

More About Using Verbs to Talk About the Past

You already encountered some verbs with irregular preterite forms. Other verbs with irregular preterite forms include **querer**, **hacer**, **venir**, **poner**, **poder**, and **saber**. They use the same endings as the irregular verbs you learned in **Lección 15**. These examples are from Arturo's point of view.

Cuando Raquel **vino** a mi casa, **quise** tomar una foto de nosotros dos pero **no** lo **hice** bien.

When Raquel came to my house, I tried to take a photo of us two but I didn't do it well.

Raquel **puso** las verduras de forma que imitaban nuestras dos caras. ¡No lo **pude** creer!

Raquel arranged (placed) the vegetables so that they looked like our faces. I couldn't believe it!

¡Por fin **supimos** algo de Ángel!

We finally learned something about Ángel!

Can you identify the vowel common to the preterite stems of **querer**, **hacer**, and **venir**? And the vowel common to the preterite stems of **poner**, **saber**, and **poder**? You may also have noticed the slightly different meaning of some of these verbs in the preterite. You will learn more about these verbs in the Workbook/Study Guide.

Actividad.   La semana pasada
Paso 1

Make statements about yourself based on each of the following items. All your statements should refer to something that took place last week.

1. algo que hiciste
2. algo que supiste
3. algo que no pudiste hacer
4. algo que pusiste en tu mochila/bolsa
5. algo que no quisiste hacer

Paso 2

Now share your information with a partner, who will also share his or hers with you. Don't forget to jot down your partner's answers.

Paso 3

Report your partner's activities to the class. How many people in the class share the same experiences?

5

LECTURA CULTURAL

Otras ciudades argentinas

You have already learned a good deal about Buenos Aires, the political and economic capital of Argentina. In this video episode you learned a little bit about some other Argentine cities. Refresh your memory by listening to an excerpt from **Episodio 16** as you look at this map. Focus on the important characteristics of each city. Complete these sentences.

1. Buenos Aires es importante porque es
    a. _____ una ciudad histórica.   b. _____ un puerto.
2. Córdoba es
    a. _____ una ciudad histórica.   b. _____ un puerto importante.
3. La ciudad de Mendoza es
    a. _____ un centro industrial.   b. _____ un centro agrícola.
4. Tucumán y Rosario son
    a. _____ ciudades importantes al norte de Buenos Aires.
    b. _____ ríos que están en la parte central del país.

En qué ciudad vives? ¿Crees que esa ciudad es típica de las ciudades norteamericanas? Es probable que no. Los Estados Unidos y el Canadá son países muy grandes, con una variedad impresionante de paisajes,[1] centros industriales y costumbres[2] regionales. Además, muchas regiones tienen sus propios antecedentes[3] históricos: en el este y el sureste, la época colonial, la guerra de la independencia y la guerra civil; en Texas, la herencia mexicana, la República, la guerra con México; en California, también la herencia mexicana, la época de la búsqueda del oro[4]… Y así sucesivamente en muchos estados, provincias y regiones. Por eso no se puede decir que haya una ciudad ni una región típicas.

Lo mismo pasa en la Argentina, también un país muy grande con una gran variedad geográfica y demográfica. Ya sabes mucho de estos aspectos de la República Argentina y especialmente de Buenos Aires. Ahora vas a conocer otras ciudades argentinas. ¿Cuál te gustaría visitar?

- Córdoba y Rosario son las ciudades argentinas más importantes después de Buenos Aires. Córdoba cuenta con más de un millón de habitantes. Está situada en el centro del país. Fundada[5] en 1573, es una ciudad muy bella[6] con una rica herencia colonial. Su universidad, que se fundó en 1612, es la más antigua del país. En la actualidad, Córdoba es un centro industrial y comercial muy importante.

Viñas (*Vineyards*) cerca de Mendoza

[1]*landscapes*   [2]*customs*   [3]*beginnings, background*   [4]*gold*   [5]*Founded*   [6]bonita

Lectura cultural, Preguntas: 1. ¿Cuáles son las similaridades entre este país y la Argentina? (*Los dos tienen una gran variedad geográfica y demográfica.*) 2. ¿Cómo se llaman las ciudades argentinas más importantes después de Buenos Aires? (*Córdoba y Rosario*) 3. ¿Cuántas personas viven en Córdoba? (*un millón*) 4. ¿Dónde está situada? (*en el centro del país*) 5. ¿Qué tipo de ciudad es? (*industrial y comercial*) 6. ¿Qué tiene Rosario como ejemplos de su modernidad? (*edificios altos, bellas plazas y hermosos parques*) 7. ¿Cuándo fue fundada la ciudad de Mendoza? (*en 1561*) 8. ¿Por qué es famosa? (*por sus buenos vinos y su buena mesa*) 9. ¿En qué lugar celebran el Año Nuevo muchos argentinos? (*en las playas de Mar del Plata*) ¿En qué estación? (*en verano*)

- La ciudad de
Rosario está
situada a ori-
llas[7] del río
Paraná. Su
puerto tiene
mucha activi-
dad. Es tam-
bién un cen-
tro industrial
muy impor-
tante. Rosa-
rio es una
ciudad mo-
derna con
muchos edi-
ficios altos,
bellas pla-
zas y hermosos parques.

Una de las playas en mar del Plata

- Al oeste de la Argentina, al pie[8] de la cordillera de los Andes, se encuentra la ciudad de Mendoza. Fue fundada en 1561 y durante un tiempo estuvo bajo la jurisdicción de Chile. Es famosa por su buena mesa[9] y sus buenos vinos. Hay muy pocos monumentos antiguos en Mendoza, porque casi toda la ciudad fue destruida[10] el siglo pasado por un terrible terremoto.[11] Es un centro agrícola importante, especialmente por el cultivo de la uva.

- Mar del Plata, en la costa atlántica, es uno de los puertos más importantes del país, y el primero entre los puertos de pesca.[12] El mar, los deportes[13] náuticos, las discotecas, los mariscos y su casino atraen cada año a millones de turistas. En verano (¡OJO! los meses de diciembre, enero y febrero en el hemisferio sur), sus playas están totalmente llenas de gente. Muchos argentinos celebran el Año Nuevo en las playas de Mar del Plata.

[7]*a... on the banks* [8]*foot* [9]*food, cooking* [10]*destroyed* [11]*earthquake* [12]*fishing* [13]*sports*

Actividad. Ciudades argentinas y norteamericanas

Give one Argentine and one city from this country that correspond to the following descriptions.

1. el centro político del país
2. un centro económico del país
3. un puerto muy importante del país
4. una ciudad histórica
5. un centro de producción del vino
6. una ciudad industrial
7. un puerto de pesca
8. una ciudad con muchas playas bonitas
9. una ciudad destruida por un terremoto
10. una ciudad con una universidad muy antigua

INTERCAMBIO

Paso 1

Imagine that someone is cooking a stew with vegetables from the following list. When that person isn't looking, you remove the vegetable you like least and add more of the vegetable you like the most. Write out what you did.

tomate	ejotes/judías verdes	apio	guisantes
cebolla	papas	champiñones	maíz

MODELO: Al estofado le quité el apio y le puse más papas.

Paso 2

Your instructor will collect the statements and read half of them out loud. Based on what you know about your classmates, can you guess who did what? What do you think Raquel did to the stew?

VOCABULARIO

Los verbos

extrañar	to miss, long for
mostrar (**ue**)	to show
tratar de (+ *inf.*)	to try to (*do something*)

Las legumbres y las verduras
(Vegetables and Greens)

la aceituna	olive
el apio	celery
el brécol/brocolí	broccoli
la calabaza	squash
el champiñón	mushroom
los chícharos (*Mex.*)	peas
el chile	chile pepper
la coliflor	cauliflower
los ejotes (*Mex.*)	string beans
las espinacas	spinach
los frijoles	beans
los guisantes	peas
las judías verdes	string beans
la lechuga	lettuce
el maíz	corn
la papa (*Lat. Am.*)	potato
la patata (*Spain*)	potato
la zanahoria	carrot

Repaso: **la cebolla, el tomate**

Los lugares

el puerto	port

Las cosas

la foto*	photo

Otros sustantivos

la cara	face

Los adjetivos

pensativo/a	thoughtful, pensive

Las palabras adicionales

tal vez	perhaps

---

* Even though it ends in **-o,** the noun **foto** is feminine because it is derived from **la fotografía.**

LECCIÓN 17

INOLVIDABLE*

*Unforgettable

OBJETIVOS

The materials in **Lección 17** of the Textbook and the Workbook/Study Guide will help you better understand the video episode and take you beyond it, giving you additional information about places and characters in the series. The Textbook will also help you to develop skill in using the Spanish language. In this lesson, you will learn

- how to talk about written communication of all kinds
- more about how to talk about the past

You will also learn about the cultural and political history of Argentina.

Be sure to work through all parts of the lesson. When you see a head-phones symbol in the margin, listen to the CD for **Lección 17**. Answers or hints for many activities are given in Appendix 1. Be sure to check your answers for each activity before going on to the next one.

The interactive CD-ROM to accompany *Destinos* contains additional practice with the video storyline and will help you improve your skills in Spanish.

Preliminary: See Faculty Guide for additional information and activities for this lesson.
• **Variation:** For activities marked with the headphones icon, you may wish to read from the Audioscript instead of playing the CD.
• **Suggestion:** Make sure students are familiar with the activities before you read from the Audioscript or play the CD.

BEFORE VIEWING . . .

1

PREPARACIÓN

Suggestions:
• Before watching the video, go over the vocabulary list at the end of the chapter and have students pronounce the words after you.
• Assign *Preparación* activities as homework and then go over them quickly in class before viewing the video.

Actividad A.

What happened in the last video episode of *Destinos*? Indicate whether the following brief narratives contain information that is **Cierto** (**C**) or **Falso** (**F**). Can you correct the false information?

Act. A, Answers: 1. C 2. F 3. F 4. C (See Appendix 1 for expanded answers.)

C   F   1. Raquel y Arturo lo pasaron muy bien cuando Arturo trató de sacar una foto de los dos y tuvo problemas con la cámara.

C   F   2. Héctor llamó a Arturo por teléfono. Quería (*He wanted to*) pasar por (*by*) su casa para darle la carta de Ángel.

C   F   3. Cuando leyó la carta de Ángel, Arturo supo que Ángel decidió quedarse (*to stay*) en Puerto Rico. Pensaba (*He intended*) volver a la Argentina para sus vacaciones.

C   F   4. Raquel y Arturo sienten una atracción mutua. Les gusta mucho estar juntos.

Para pensar, **Suggestion:** Ask class in general these questions. Ask for a show of hands of those who believe that Arturo will go to Puerto Rico and whether this is a good idea or not. Do not reveal any new information, but allow the story to unfold naturally.

Para pensar...

Arturo dice que quiere ir a Puerto Rico con Raquel. ¿Crees que realmente va a poder acompañarla en su viaje? ¿Crees que esto es una buena idea? ¿No está pasando todo muy rápido?

Actividad B.

In this video episode Arturo and Raquel will each make a "wish upon a star," **una estrella**. In this activity you will first hear their wishes individually, then have the chance to listen to the complete conversation.

Paso 1

Pedir un deseo means *to ask for a wish*. Based on everything you know about Raquel and her personality, what do you think she will wish for?

Act. B, Answers: *Paso 1:* a; *Paso 2:* c; *Paso 4:* 1. *poder* 2. *estar* 3. *poder* 4. *ser*

a. _____ Pide a las estrellas que pueda encontrar a Ángel en Puerto Rico.

b. _____ Pide a las estrellas que Arturo pueda acompañarla a Puerto Rico.

Now listen to what Raquel actually says. Were you right?

Paso 2

Based on what you know about Arturo and on your observation of his behavior, what do you think he will wish for? Listen as he makes his wish.

Based on what you have heard Arturo say, which of the following do you think is the most appropriate title for this garden scene?

a. _____ La luna (*moon*)   c. _____ Declaración de amor
b. _____ El jardín por la noche

Paso 3
Now listen to the scene in its entirety.

Paso 4
Some of the verb forms used in this conversation between Raquel and Arturo are probably unfamiliar to you. You should be able to follow the conversation, however, by focusing on the verb stems. Can you give the infinitive for the following verb forms?

1. podamos   2. esté   3. pueda   4. sea

Para pensar...

¿Qué van a hacer Arturo y Raquel después de esta conversación? ¿darse la mano (*shake hands*)? ¿abrazarse? ¿besarse (*kiss*)?

  . . . AFTER VIEWING

2

¿TIENES BUENA MEMORIA?

Actividad A.   ¿Quién lo dijo?
Paso 1
Arturo and Raquel talk about a lot of things in this video episode. Indicate which of the two, Arturo (**A**) or Raquel (**R**), made each of the following statements.

A R 1. «Yo también les pido lo mismo. Que podamos encontrar a mi hermano y que él pueda conocer a su padre, don Fernando.»

A R 2. «Por favor, déjame terminar. Lo que quiero decir es que… no es fácil decir estas cosas. Todo ha sido tan… tan rápido… Necesito tiempo para pensar.»

A R 3. «Sabés, los argentinos somos más que la carne y el tango.»

A R 4. «Cuando volvamos con Ángel de Puerto Rico, los tres podremos venir a ver un espectáculo.»

A R 5. «¿Es posible que vuelvas entonces?»

Paso 2
Now indicate which of the preceding phrases expresses Raquel's answer to Arturo's declaration of his feelings. Is it an acceptance, a rejection, or something in between?

Actividad B.
Paso 1

Act. B, Suggestion: Give students about 5 minutes to complete the activity individually or in pairs and then compare answers as a whole class. Tell students to read through the entire passage before filling in any blanks in order to get the overall gist of the narrative.

In the last several video episodes you have learned information about Arturo and his half-brother Ángel. In this episode you learned more about Raquel. Listen again to Raquel's answers to Arturo's dinner table questions, then complete this summary with these words and phrases.

se fue a vivir	mucha gente interesante
en México	un estudiante joven
por un año entero	pasó los veranos
norteamericana	en la Universidad de California
don Pedro, hermano	Los Ángeles
de don Fernando	muy aburrida
muy contenta	

Act. B, Answers:
1. *norteamericana* 2. *pasó los veranos* 3. *por un año entero* 4. *en la Universidad de California* 5. *un estudiante joven* 6. *se fue a vivir* 7. *Los Ángeles* 8. *muy contenta* 9. *mucha gente interesante*

Raquel nació[a] en Los Ángeles, pero se siente tanto[b] mexicana como

_____.[1] Ella siempre _____[2] en México con la familia

mexicana de sus padres. Una vez fue a México _____.[3] Le gustó

mucho esa experiencia.

  Raquel estudió _____.[4] Allí conoció a _____,[5] quien

llegó a ser su novio.[c] Después de graduarse, él _____[6] a Nueva

York y ella se quedó en _____.[7] Ahora ella está _____[8]

con su trabajo, porque viaja mucho y conoce a _____.[9]

[a]*was born* [b]*as much* [c]*llegó... became her boyfriend*

Act. C, Suggestion: Give students about 5 minutes to complete the activity individually or in pairs and then have them present their statements to the class. Interesting regional differences may arise among students. Explain

Paso 2

Act. C, Note: If you have international students in your class, encourage them to make the statements for their home culture. If they mention aspects of their culture that are unknown to the class, ask them to describe these aspects.

Now listen to the correct answers on the CD.

Actividad C. «¡Somos más que la carne y el tango!»

Do you have a "national conscience"? That is, do you think that most people in this country feel the same way about many aspects of their culture?

  For each item on Argentine culture below, make a statement indicating what you believe to be a corresponding aspect of your culture. Follow the model and present your statements to the class. How many of your classmates say the same thing? Do you think you and your classmates have a "national conscience"?

that this highlights the difference between a country like Argentina, where much of the "high" culture (art, theater, film, architecture, etc.) is concentrated in one city, Buenos Aires, and the United States, where Washington, D.C. is the capital, but not necessarily the major center of culture. Important: allow free expression and try not to impose what you may feel are the "correct" answers.

  MODELO: _____ es para nosotros lo que el tango es para la
      gente (*people*) de Argentina.

1. el tango
2. el Teatro Colón
3. Jorge Luis Borges
4. Domingo Faustino Sarmiento
5. la carne

Nota cultural, Follow-up: For homework, send students to the library to research one of the Hispanic Nobel Prize winners mentioned. Have them find out what they earned the prize for and write a few sentences in Spanish about it. They can present their findings to the class or turn them in for a grade or extra credit.

Nota cultural Premios Nobel

Varios argentinos han ganado (*have won*) un premio Nobel. ¿Reconoces el nombre de alguno de ellos?

Carlos Saavedra Lamas, premio Nobel de la Paz en 1936; Bernardo Houssay, premio Nobel de Medicina en 1947; Luis Federico Lenoir, premio Nobel de Química en 1970; Adolfo Pérez Esquivel, premio Nobel de la Paz en 1980; César Milstein, premio Nobel de Medicina en 1984

¿Y el prestigioso premio Nobel de Literatura? No lo ha ganado todavía ningún argentino, aunque se sugirió con frecuencia el nombre de Jorge Luis Borges. Éstos son los escritores de lengua española que hasta la fecha (*until now*) han ganado este premio. ¿Los reconoces?

César Milstein, ganador del premio Nobel de Medicina

José Echegaray en 1904 (España); Jacinto Benavente en 1922 (España); Gabriela Mistral en 1945 (Chile); Juan Ramón Jiménez en 1956 (España); Miguel Ángel Asturias en 1967 (Guatemala); Pablo Neruda en 1971 (Chile); Vicente Aleixandre en 1977 (España); Gabriel García Márquez en 1982 (Colombia); Camilo José Cela en 1989 (España); Octavio Paz en 1990 (México)

3

VOCABULARIO DEL TEMA

Suggestion: Practice pronunciation with choral and individual repetition.

El arte de escribir

el artículo	article
la comedia	play; comedy
el cuento	short story
el ensayo	essay
la novela	novel
la obra	work
la poesía	poetry
el poema	poem

LOS CINCO LIBROS MAS LEIDOS

FICCION	NO FICCION
1° "Noticias de la tarde" Arthur Hailey - Emecé - ₳72.000	**1°** "Las trampas de la fe" Octavio Paz - FCE - ₳96.000
2° "La inmortalidad" Milan Kundera - Tusquets - ₳96.000	**2°** "Los intelectuales" Paul Johnson - Vergara - ₳82.700
3° "El huevo de Fabergé" Robert Upton - Sudamericana - ₳57.850	**3°** "Historia de la vida privada" Duby/Ariés - Taurus - ₳158.000
4° "La ciudad de la alegría" Dominique Lapierre - Planeta - ₳87.200	**4°** "Más grandes que el amor" Dominique Lapierre - Planeta - ₳89.000
5° "Fénix Rojo" Larry Bond - Emecé - ₳88.000	**5°** "Soy Roca" Félix Luna - Sudamericana - ₳98.000

Las personas

el autor/la autora	author	**el/la novelista**	novelist
el escritor/la escritora	writer	**el/la periodista**	journalist

Suggestion: Bring in an example of each type of literary work, preferably one in Spanish and one in English, and introduce the vocabulary by briefly showing and describing the work. Say: *Ésta es una novela. El autor/La autora es/fue _____. Ésta es otra novela, pero en español. El escritor/ La escritora es/fue _____. ¿A Uds. les gustan las novelas? ¿Quién es su autor(a) favorito/a? ¿Cuál es su novela favorita?* Introduce the other types of works in a similar fashion, mentioning type of work, types of writers, and the various means of communication.

Los medios de comunicación

la computadora (*Lat. Am.*)	computer	**el periódico**	newspaper
la máquina de escribir	typewriter	**la revista**	magazine
el ordenador (*Spain*)	computer		

Actividad A. ¿Quién era Borges?

The speaker on the CD will tell you more about Jorge Luis Borges, the great Argentine writer. Write the number of each sentence next to the appropriate drawing.

Act. A, Follow-up: Have students listen to the CD again and write down the sentences they hear. Then, taking turns with a partner, they read them aloud in random order so that their partner can match the sentences with the drawings.

Act. A, Answers: a. 5 b. 3 c. 1 d. 4 e. 2 f. 6

a. _____

b. _____

c. _____

d. _____

e. _____

f. _____

Actividad B. Más sobre Borges

Paso 1

Refresh your memory about Borges by listening again to what you learned about him in **Episodio 17**.

Paso 2

Now complete the following description of Borges based on what you just heard and on the information you learned about him in **Actividad A**. You will also need to make some logical guesses.

Borges comenzó su carrera como _____.[1] Trabajó para la

_____[2] *Nosotros* y también para el _____[3] *La Prensa*.

Más tarde fue director de la Biblioteca Nacional y profesor de inglés en la

Universidad de Buenos Aires.

Act. B, Paso 2, Answers:
1. *periodista* 2. *revista*
3. *periódico* 4. *ensayos*
5. *cuentos* 6. *cuentos*
7. *escritor (autor)* 8. *realidad*

Borges escribió poesías, pero sus obras más famosas son sus

_____⁴ y sus _____.⁵ En 1957 recibió un premio nacional por su libro *El Aleph*, una colección de _____.⁶

Este argentino fue un _____⁷ muy original. Sus temas favoritos eran la _____⁸ y la fantasía. También estaba obsesionado por el tema del tiempo, un tiempo circular en que todo se repite.

Act. C, Follow-up: Working in pairs and using any 4 items from the activity, students interview their partners to find out their preferences. They then tabulate the results and should be prepared to present to the class a brief comparison between themselves and their partner. Remind students that they will have to change the verb forms to the third-person singular to talk about their classmate.

Act. C, Optional: Have the whole class use the items from the activity to ask questions of the instructor. Then have each student write a brief comparison/contrast paragraph.

Actividad C.　**Me gusta...**

Indicate the things you like to read (**leer**) and write. Scan the list of **Palabras útiles** before you begin.

Palabras útiles: la novela (de amor, de aventuras, de ciencia-ficción, de horror, histórica, policíaca), el trabajo para las clases, escribir a mano (*by hand*)

1.　Me gusta leer _____ (tipo de libros).

2.　Me gustan en particular las obras de _____ (escritor). El/La _____ (obra) de él/ella que más me gusta es _____.

3.　En cuanto a (*As for*) periódicos y revistas, leo _____. Mi revista favorita es _____. El periódico que prefiero es _____.

4.　Escribo _____. Me gustaría escribir _____.

5.　Para mis clases, tengo que escribir _____.

6.　Cuando escribo trabajos para mis clases, prefiero usar / siempre _____.

4

UN POCO DE GRAMÁTICA

The Workbook/Study Guide contains more detailed explanation and practice of this grammar point.

Note: You may wish to review the verb paradigms for regular *-ar, -er,* and *-ir* verbs in the preterite and/or introduce the complete paradigms of the irregular verbs presented in this lesson.

More About Using Verbs to Talk About the Past

The preterite forms of **-ir** stem-changing verbs have a stem change in the third-person singular and plural. As you read the following examples, note that the **-e** of the stem changes to **-i** and the **-o** to **-u**.

Raquel y Arturo **prefirieron** cenar en casa. Arturo le **pidió** a Raquel que le contara algo de su pasado. **¿Murió** Ángel Castillo en Puerto Rico? Arturo tiene un mal presentimiento…	*Raquel and Arturo preferred to have dinner at home. Arturo asked Raquel to tell him a bit about her past. Did Ángel die in Puerto Rico? Arturo has a bad premonition . . .*

You will learn more about using these verbs in the Workbook/Study Guide.

Act., Suggestion: Assign *Paso 1* as homework the day before and then complete *Paso 2* in class.

Act., Follow-up: If students say *No, no tienes razón,* have them correct the statement with true information.

Actividad.   ¿Qué hicieron?

Paso 1

Use the following verbs to make statements about what some of your classmates did and how they felt recently. Write your statements on a sheet of paper.

MODELO: Mary Ann durmió doce horas el sábado.

1. (no) durmió
2. (no) siguió
3. (no) pidió
4. (no) se sintió
5. (no) prefirió
6. (no) se despidió de

Paso 2

Now read your sentences aloud to the class. Were you right about your classmates? The people spoken of should verify whether you are correct (**Sí, tienes razón.**) or not (**No, no tienes razón.**).

Lectura cultural, Suggestion: Assign as homework and go over in class. Remind students that they should not expect to understand every word of the reading, but rather to get the main ideas.

5

LECTURA CULTURAL

Las madres de la Plaza de Mayo

In **Episodio 17** you learned about part of Argentina's history. Listen again as the narrator tells you about one of the results of that era. Then read the following narration to find out more details.

Desgraciadamente la violencia se conoce en todas partes del mundo. Los derechos[1] humanos son violados durante guerras civiles, guerras de independencia y revoluciones, bajo[2] dictaduras y otros regímenes represivos o simplemente cuando hay enfrentamientos[3] entre grupos étnicos o entre grupos con ideas diferentes sobre cualquier tema.

La Argentina vivió en los años 70 uno de los períodos más tristes de su historia. Gobernaba[4] entonces la viuda[5] del general Perón, María Estela, su segunda esposa.

[1]*rights*   [2]*under*   [3]confrontaciones   [4]*Was in power*   [5]*widow*

La situación política y social del país se iba deteriorando.[6] Finalmente en 1976 un golpe militar[7] terminó con el gobierno de María Estela de Perón.

Como sucede en numerosos regímenes autoritarios, la Argentina sufrió muchos abusos durante los años de esta dictadura militar. El más grave,[8] sin duda, fue la «desaparición»[9] de miles de personas sospechadas de actividades en contra del gobierno. Se les llama[10] «desaparecidos» porque no fueron arrestados ni tampoco hubo ninguna orden judicial[11] contra ellos. Simplemente desaparecieron. No se comunicaba oficialmente su paradero[12] ni tampoco se sabía si estaban vivos o muertos. Aunque la dictadura terminó hace muchos años, la gran mayoría de los «desaparecidos» siguen sin aparecer. Es como si, *oficialmente*, nunca hubieran existido.[13]

El Movimiento de las Madres de la Plaza de Mayo empezó para protestar en contra de esas desapariciones. Todos los jueves del año y en silencio, un grupo de madres y personas solidarias[14] marchan frente a la Casa Rosada.[15] Llevan las fotos de sus desaparecidos.

Para muchas personas, esta actitud ya no tiene sentido.[16] El régimen político ha cambiado[17] y piensan que el país debe aceptar la tragedia y olvidar el pasado. Pero, para las madres, «no hay olvido ni perdón». Además de las madres, muchos argentinos también denunciaron la violación de los derechos humanos. Ése es el caso de Adolfo Pérez de Esquivel, que en 1980 recibió el premio Nobel de la Paz. En esta fecha todavía gobernaba en la Argentina la dictadura militar.

Dice Arturo: «Es un episodio horrible en nuestra historia. Y no debemos olvidarnos de que estas cosas ocurren.» ¿Qué crees tú?

[6]se... *was deteriorating*   [7]golpe... *coup d'état, military takeover*   [8]El... *The most serious (abuse)*   [9]*disappearance*   [10]Se... *They are called*   [11]ni... *nor was there any legal procedure*   [12]*whereabouts*   [13]Es... *It's as if they had never existed.*   [14]*sympathetic (to the cause)*   [15]la... *the "Pink House," the Argentine equivalent of the White House*   [16]ya... *no longer makes any sense*   [17]ha... *has changed*

6

INTERCAMBIO

Paso 1

This is a game to see which group can recall the most information in a short amount of time. Break up into groups of four and elect a secretary who will write down your ideas. You have ten minutes to jot down things that you remember have happened in **Episodios** 12 to 17. Your instructor will mark time.

Intercambio, Paso 2,
Suggestion: Keep a tally
of the following without
telling the class: 1. *lugares*
donde Raquel y Arturo
fueron juntos; 2. *comidas*
que comieron Raquel y
Arturo. You may invent or replace with others. Afterwards, announce to the class the categories
and which group remembered the most. Can anyone add more items to the categories?

Paso 2

Each group presents its ideas to the class. Your instructor will keep tally.
There is a surprise at the end.

VOCABULARIO

Los verbos

besar	to kiss
leer	to read
quedarse	to stay, remain

El arte de escribir (The Art of Writing)

el artículo	article
la comedia	play; comedy
el cuento	short story
el ensayo	essay
la novela	novel
la obra	work
el poema	poem
la poesía	poetry

Las personas

el autor/la autora	author
el escritor/la escritora	writer
el/la novelista	novelist
el/la periodista	journalist

Los medios de comunicación (Means of Communication)

la computadora (*Lat. Am.*)	computer
la máquina de escribir	typewriter
el ordenador (*Spain*)	computer
el periódico	newspaper
la revista	magazine

Más personas

| la gente* | people |

Los adjetivos

| inolvidable | unforgettable |

Los conceptos

| el amor | love |
| el trabajo | work, job; paper, assignment (*for a class*) |

---

* Note that, even though its English equivalent is plural, this Spanish word is singular and takes a
singular verb form: **La gente cree...**

LECCIÓN 18

ESTIMADA SRA. SUÁREZ*

*Dear Mrs. Suárez

OBJETIVOS

Part of this video episode is a review. Be sure to work through all parts of the lesson. When you see a headphones symbol in the margin, listen to the CD for **Lección 18**. Answers or hints for many activities are given in Appendix 1. Be sure to check your answers for each activity before going on to the next one.

The interactive CD-ROM to accompany *Destinos* contains additional practice with the video storyline and will help you improve your skills in Spanish.

BEFORE VIEWING . . .

Preliminary: See Faculty Guide for additional information and activities for this lesson.
Variation: For activities marked with the headphones icon, you may wish to read from the Audioscript instead of playing the CD.
Suggestion: Make sure students are familiar with the activities before you read from the Audioscript or play the CD.

1

PREPARACIÓN

Suggestions:
• Before watching the video, go over the vocabulary list at the end of the chapter and have students pronounce the words after you.
• Assign *Preparación* activities as homework and then go over them quickly in class before viewing the video.

Act. A, Suggestion: You may want to have students do this activity in pairs.

Actividad A.

Indicate whether the following events took place (**Sí, ocurrió**) or not (**No, no ocurrió**) in the previous video episode of *Destinos*.

¿Qué pasó en el episodio previo?

Sí	No	1.	Raquel y Arturo bailaron.
Sí	No	2.	Arturo le hizo a Raquel una declaración de amor.
Sí	No	3.	Decidieron salir a cenar.
Sí	No	4.	Raquel le dijo a Arturo que él era muy importante para ella.
Sí	No	5.	Arturo habló más de su ex esposa.
Sí	No	6.	Raquel le dijo a Arturo que lo amaba (*loved*).

Act. A, Answers: 1. *Sí* 2. *Sí* 3. *No* 4. *Sí* 5. *No* 6. *No* 7. *Sí* 8. *No* 9. *Sí* 10. *No* (See Appendix 1 for expanded answers.)

Al día siguiente, ¿qué hicieron Raquel y Arturo durante el día?

Sí	No	7.	Visitaron la casa de Jorge Luis Borges.
Sí	No	8.	Fueron a la ópera.
Sí	No	9.	Fueron a un parque.
Sí	No	10.	Comieron en un restaurante elegante.

Actividad B.
Paso 1

Look at the title of this lesson and at the photograph with which it begins. What do you think Raquel will do in this video episode?

a. _____ Llama por teléfono a la Sra. Suárez.
b. _____ Le escribe una carta a la Sra. Suárez.
c. _____ Le manda un telegrama a la Sra. Suárez.

Paso 2

If you selected *b* in **Paso 1**, you were correct. What might Raquel tell Sra. Suárez in her letter? Indicate all items that you think may be correct.

Act. B, Answers: *Paso 2:* a, b, c, e, g, h

a. _____ las tristes noticias de Rosario
b. _____ de cómo pudo por fin encontrar a un hijo de Rosario
c. _____ de su relación con Arturo
d. _____ más noticias de don Fernando
e. _____ unos detalles de la búsqueda de Ángel en Buenos Aires
f. _____ la dirección de Ángel en Puerto Rico
g. _____ de sus compras en Buenos Aires
h. _____ de lo que (*what*) comió

. . . AFTER VIEWING

2

¿TIENES BUENA MEMORIA?

Actividad A. **Raquel se va**

The following sentences describe what took place during Raquel's last hours in Argentina, but the words are out of order. Read all of the words in each group, then put them in the correct order to form complete sentences.

Act. A, Answers: 1. *Arturo llevó a Raquel al aeropuerto.* 2. *Los dos se despidieron en la entrada.* 3. *Se besaron con ternura.* 4. *La despedida fue triste.* 5. *Raquel tuvo que esperar un poco.* 6. *Le escribió una carta a la Sra. Suárez.*

1. llevó / Raquel / a / aeropuerto / Arturo / al
2. se / los dos / entrada / en / despidieron / la
3. con / besaron / se / ternura (*tenderness*)
4. despedida / fue / triste / la
5. un / tuvo / poco / Raquel / esperar / que
6. carta / le / a / Sra. Suárez / escribió / una / la

Actividad B. **¡Un desafío!**

With a partner, take turns asking and answering the following questions about events that took place in **Episodio 18.**

Act. B, Answers: 1. *Sí. Le dio un regalo (una pulsera de oro [gold bracelet]).* 2. *No. Le dijo «hasta pronto».* 3. *En un par de días.* 4. *Piensa en el deseo que les pidió a las estrellas: que la familia pueda reunirse definitivamente.*

1. ¿Le dio Arturo algo a Raquel en el aeropuerto? ¿Qué?
2. ¿Le dijo Arturo adiós a Raquel? ¿Qué le dijo Raquel a Arturo?
3. ¿Cuándo piensa Arturo reunirse con Raquel en Puerto Rico?
4. ¿En qué piensa Raquel al despegar el avión (*while the plane is taking off*)?

3

REPASO DE LOS EPISODIOS 12–17

Actividad A. **La búsqueda de Raquel**

The following summary of the first part of Raquel's search in Buenos Aires is adapted from her letter to Sra. Suárez. Complete it with phrases from the following list. ¡OJO! Not all of the phrases will be used.

se mudó a Puerto Rico
murió hace algunos años
era el hijo de Rosario y don
    Fernando
no me sirvió para nada
había muerto (*had died*)

perdió contacto con su hermano
se fue de la casa
se quedó en casa
me sirvió bastante (*a lot*)
ya no vivía allí

Estimada Sra. Suárez:

Ojalá que[a] cuando reciba esta carta se encuentre bien de salud.[b] Mi viaje a Buenos Aires ha resultado fructífero[c] gracias a su bondad en ayudarme, pues la dirección de la estancia _____.[1] Sin embargo,[d] me da mucha pena[e] tener que decirle que su buena amiga Rosario _____.[2]

En la estancia averigüé[f] que la familia Iglesias _____.[3] Un hombre me dio la dirección del hijo de Rosario. Fui a buscarlo, creyendo[g] que _____.[4] Imagínese Ud. la sorpresa que tuve al encontrarme con otro hijo de Rosario.

Fue durante esa conversación que el hijo, Arturo Iglesias que así se llama, me contó que Rosario _____.[5] En el cementerio conseguí pruebas[h] de la muerte de Rosario y allí Arturo me contó que Ángel Castillo _____[6] por una pelea[i] que tuvo con su padrastro. A causa de ese doloroso episodio, Arturo _____.[7] Al día siguiente, comenzamos juntos la búsqueda del paradero[j] de Ángel.

[a]Ojalá... *I hope that* [b]se... *you are well* [c]ha... *has had good results* [d]Sin... *Nevertheless* [e]me... *I'm very sorry* [f]*I found out* [g]*believing* [h]*proof* [i]*fight* [j]*whereabouts*

Actividad B. ¿Cierto o falso?

With a partner, take turns making up statements about events that took place in **Episodios 12–17**. Use the cues given below. ¡OJO! You should make up several false statements in your account of the events from the previous episodes. Your partner must guess which ones are true (**Cierto**) and which are false (**Falso**).

Personas	Acciones
Raquel	conocieron a un amigo de Ángel
Arturo	le escribió una carta a la Sra. Suárez
Héctor	hizo preparativos para salir de Buenos Aires
Cirilo	llamó a Arturo para decirle que había encontrado (*he had found*) la carta
	preguntaron por Ángel por todo el barrio de La Boca
	le dijo que Rosario murió
	conoció al hermano de Ángel
	les dijo que fue amigo de Ángel

Actividad C. Las actividades de Raquel
Paso 1

As you know, Raquel's visit to Buenos Aires involved more than just the search for Ángel. Here are the last paragraphs of Raquel's letter to Sra. Suárez, but some of the information has been changed. Read through the letter and indicate the incorrect information.

Tendría que decirle que mi estancia en Buenos Aires no ha sido nada más que[1] trabajo. En primer lugar, he tenido la oportunidad de conocer un poco el país. Pude hacer unas compras, pues como Ud. sabrá[2] en la Argentina hay muchos artículos de oro muy bonitos. Y, claro, también comí y comí y comí y comí... pero no me gustó.

Si me permite la confianza, quisiera decirle que no seguí sus consejos. El hermano de Arturo, Ángel, se ha hecho buen amigo mío.[3] Para decir la verdad, siento un amor muy especial por él. Resulta que Arturo me va a visitar en San Juan en un mes. Así concluye mi estancia en Buenos Aires.

Siento mucho la pelea que Ud. tuvo con su buena amiga tanto por Ud. como por[4] don Fernando. Ojalá[5] mi viaje a Puerto Rico tenga los resultados deseados, que encuentre a Rosario Castillo y que por fin se reúna con su madre.

Reciban Ud. y su familia un saludo cordial de
Raquel Rodríguez

[1]*nada... solamente*   [2]*Ud... you probably know*   [3]*se... has become a good friend of mine*
[4]*tanto... as much for your sake as for*   [5]*I hope*

Paso 2
Now check your answers by listening to the CD.

4

PARA ESCRIBIR

In this activity you will write a short narrative in which you describe Raquel and Arturo's relationship to someone who has not seen the video episodes. You want to tell the reader as much as you can about them and about what happened to them in Buenos Aires, include some interesting information, and make some suggestions about what you think will happen to them in future episodes. Your narrative should be no fewer than 200 and no more than 300 words long.

Go to the Workbook/Study Guide to begin this writing activity.

VOCABULARIO

Los verbos

reunirse (con)   to be reunited (with), get back together (with)

Los adjetivos

estimado/a   dear (*often used in letters*)
triste   sad

Las palabras adicionales

sin embargo   nevertheless

Un viaje a Puerto Rico

El Morro, San Juan

LECCIÓN 19

POR FIN...*

Preliminary: Recommend that students who have not used *Destinos* before watch Review Episodes 6, 11, and 18 to help them prepare for the second quarter of the course. Also, Spanish and English summaries of all previous episodes are printed in the Faculty Guide. You may wish to make these summaries available to students new to *Destinos*.
Suggestion: Have students look at the photo, describe what they see, and talk about what they think might happen. Ask questions about the photo to prompt student discussion.

*Finally . . .

OBJETIVOS

The materials in **Lección 19** of the Textbook and the Workbook/Study Guide will help you better understand the video episode and take you beyond it, giving you additional information about places and characters in the series. The Textbook will also help you to develop skill in using the Spanish language. In this lesson, you will learn

- to understand directions in Spanish
- to talk about the past in another way

You will also learn about the city of San Juan, Puerto Rico.

Be sure to work through all parts of the lesson. When you see a headphones symbol in the margin, listen to the CD for **Lección 19**. Answers or hints for many activities are given in Appendix 1. Be sure to check your answers for each activity before going on to the next one.

The interactive CD-ROM to accompany *Destinos* contains additional practice with the video storyline and will help you improve your skills in Spanish.

182

BEFORE VIEWING . . .

Preliminary: See Faculty Guide for additional information and activities for this lesson.
• **Variation:** For activities marked with the headphones icon, you may wish to read from the Audioscript instead of playing the CD.
• **Suggestion:** Make sure students are familiar with the activities before you read from the Audioscript or play the CD.

1

Preparación

Suggestions:
• Before watching the video, go over the vocabulary list at the end of the chapter and have students pronounce the words after you.
• Assign *Preparación* activities as homework and then go over them quickly in class before viewing the video.

Actividad A.

Here are some photographs of scenes from **Episodio 19** of *Destinos*. What do they suggest to you?

1. Esta mujer es la vecina (*neighbor*) de Ángel Castillo. ¿Qué le está preguntando* Raquel? ¿Qué información le está dando a Raquel?

2. Raquel se encuentra en el Viejo Cementerio de San Juan. ¿Por qué está allí? ¿Qué o a quién anda buscando?

2.

3. La mujer que está con Raquel se llama Ángela Castillo Soto. ¿Quién es? ¿Será (*Could she be*) pariente (*relative*) de Ángel Castillo?

Act. A, Point out: As a prediction exercise, this has no (in)correct responses. (See Appendix 1 for answers.)

Actividad B.

In this video episode Raquel has a conversation with the woman in the first photograph in **Actividad A**.

3.

Paso 1

In the conversation the woman will say the following: "Los dos están enterrados en el antiguo cementerio de San Juan." Read the line over a few times, so that you recognize it when you hear it.

Paso 2

Now listen to the dialogue on the CD. You should be able to obtain a lot of information from it.

Paso 3

Now answer the following questions about the dialogue you just heard.

1. **Enterrados** means *buried*. Now that you know that, what two people do you think the woman is talking about? *Hint*: What two people would be of interest to Raquel at this moment?

2. The neighbor also says: "Nunca se repuso de la muerte de su esposa." The verb form **se repuso** comes from the infinitive **reponerse**, meaning

Preparación, Optional: Brainstorm as a whole class or in small groups what students already know about Puerto Rico and what they think it is like. List the ideas on the board and have students copy them. As the unit in Puerto Rico unfolds over the next several episodes, have students refer to this list to see whether or not their ideas were accurate. Which ideas would they change? What did they see or hear that made them change their minds?

Act. B, Paso 3, Answers: 1. *Habla de Ángel Castillo y su esposa.* 2. *Describe a un hombre, a Ángel.*

---

* As you can probably guess, the verb form **preguntando** is derived from **preguntar**. You have been seeing forms ending in **-ndo** since the beginning of the *Destinos* series. The **-ndo** form corresponds to English *-ing*: **preguntando** = *asking*. This form is used with forms of **estar** to express an action that is happening right now. You will learn more about these forms in upcoming lessons of *Destinos*.

to get over or recover from (an illness). Who is the woman describing in this sentence, a man or a woman? Do you think she is talking about Ángel or about someone who knew him well?

 . . . AFTER VIEWING

Act. A, Answers: 1. *vecina* 2. *murió hace poco* 3. *escritora* 4. *hija* 5. *unos parientes* 6. *tiene un hermano*
Act. B, Suggestion: Give students about 5 minutes to complete the activity individually or in pairs and then compare answers as a whole class.

2 ¿TIENES BUENA MEMORIA?

Actividad A. Nuevos personajes

1.

4.

Act. A, Suggestion: Give students about 3 minutes to complete the activity individually or in pairs and then compare answers as a whole class.

Act. B, Answers: *Paso 1:* 1. *mudarse* 2. *debe ser muy triste para Ángela* 3. *llamar a sus tíos* 4. *visitar un lugar de interés histórico* 5. *mostrarle otros lugares interesantes* 6. *regresan al apartamento* 7. *está en Nueva York*

Act. B, Follow-up: Students create a brief paragraph, similar to those in the activity, that contains at least 2 blanks. They then give their paragraphs to a partner, who tries to fill in the blanks.

In this video episode of *Destinos* you have met some new characters. How much do you remember about them? Complete the following statements about the people shown in the photographs.

1. Esta señora es la... esposa / vecina / viuda... de Ángel Castillo.
2. La señora le dice a Raquel que Ángel... se mudó a otro país / volvió a España / murió hace poco.
3. Le dice también que la esposa de Ángel era... anciana / escritora / maestra de primaria.
4. Raquel descubre que esta señorita es la... hija / novia / viuda... de Ángel.
5. Ángela llama a... unos parientes / unos amigos / sus hermanos... para que vengan (*they come over*) a conocer a Raquel.
6. Hay otra sorpresa para Raquel al final del episodio. Ángela le dice que... ya sabe de don Fernando / tiene un hermano / ya conoce a Arturo.

Actividad B. La primera tarde en San Juan
Paso 1

Raquel's investigation gets off to a quick start in Puerto Rico. She finds a member of Ángel's family quickly, and it appears that she will soon meet more family members. Complete this summary of part of her afternoon with Ángela with the following phrases. ¡OJO! Not all of the phrases will be used.

encontrar una foto de su padre	está en Nueva York
tomar una foto	van al cementerio
llamar a sus tíos	hablan más
mudarse	debe ser muy triste para Ángela
visitar un lugar de interés histórico	regresan al apartamento
mostrarle otros lugares interesantes	va a México

En el apartamento, Ángela le dice a Raquel que piensa _____.[1]
«No quiero vivir sola en este apartamento», dice. Raquel queda sorprendida, porque el apartamento es muy bonito. Pero también comprende que el recuerdo de sus padres _____.[2]

Nota cultural, Suggestion: Give students about a minute to read. You may wish to discuss the idea of *inmediatez* with students, comparing different regions of the U.S. and their reputations for (un)friendliness. Discuss the perceptions students have of Spanish-speaking countries and their (un)friendliness and any experiences they may have had. One common stereotype is that the people of southern Spain are more open and friendly than those in the north, much like the U.S. stereotype.

Ángela trata de _____,³ pero no tiene suerte.ª Mientras sigue intentando,ᵇ Raquel sale a _____,⁴ la Casa Blanca. Luego Ángela se reúne con ella para visitar los jardines de la Casa Blanca y para _____.⁵ Van al Parque de las Palomas y a la Capilla de Cristo y finalmente _____.⁶

Allí es donde Raquel descubre que Ángela tiene novio. Pero no lo va a conocer pronto porque _____.⁷ Raquel también ve la foto de un joven atractivo. ¡Otro hijo de Ángel!

ª*any luck* ᵇ*sigue… she keeps on trying*

Paso 2
Now check your answers by listening to the CD.

Nota cultural La inmediatez puertorriqueña

You may have noticed that Raquel and Ángela have already developed a warm, comfortable relationship. This is partly because they are both women, not so far apart in age, and partly because Raquel has given Ángela some startling but potentially exciting news about her family.

There is another factor at work as well. Most visitors to the island of Puerto Rico comment on how friendly and open the people are and how quickly comfortable relationships are established. One phrase that describes this phenomenon is **la inmediatez de la gente**, related to the adjective **inmediato** (*immediate*).

Raquel responds warmly to this characteristic of the islanders. But even here, as in other parts of the Spanish-speaking world that Raquel has visited previously, another person—Ángela—initiates the use of **tú** with her.

3

VOCABULARIO DEL TEMA
Suggestion: Practice pronunciation with choral and individual repetition.

Las instrucciones

el bloque (*P.R.*)	city block	**la esquina**	corner	**doblar**	to turn
la bocacalle	intersection	**la ruta**	route, way	a la derecha	to the right
la calle	street			a la izquierda	to the left
la cuadra	city block	**bajar**	to go down	**seguir (i, i)**	to go straight
las escaleras	steps	**cruzar**	to cross	derecho	
				virar (*P.R.*)	to turn

baje...	go down . . .	**hacia**	toward
camine...	walk . . .	**hasta**	until
doble...	turn . . .	**por**	through;
siga...	continue . . . ,		along
	follow . . .		
tome...	take . . .		
vire...	turn . . .		

As with the names for fruits and vegetables, the words used for giving directions and naming parts of a city vary from area to area.

- Whereas in Puerto Rico you would walk **dos bloques**, in Spain you would walk **dos manzanas**, and in Mexico, **dos cuadras**.
- In Puerto Rico you can **virar a la izquierda**. In most other areas of the Spanish-speaking world, you would **doblar (a la izquierda)**. **Doblar** is also used in Puerto Rico.
- In Spain you would **seguir recto**, but in most of the western hemisphere you would **seguir derecho**.

For now, concentrate on learning the vocabulary listed here for giving directions. Note the verb forms **baje...**, **camine...**, and so on. They are command forms, used to give people directions. You will learn more about giving directions in the second half of *Destinos*. In this lesson you will practice recognizing the meaning of commands when you see and hear them.

Actividad A. Las instrucciones del taxista

As happens frequently in urban life, a road is closed off—**bloqueado**—due to construction work, and Raquel must reach Ángel's house on foot. Listen as the cab driver tells her how to get there and indicate in the following dialogue the words you hear.

EL TAXISTA: Mire. ¿Ve la _____[1]?

RAQUEL: Sí.

EL TAXISTA: Tome a la _____.[2]

RAQUEL: A la _____.[2]

EL TAXISTA: En el próximo bloque, vire a la _____.[3]

RAQUEL: A la _____.[3]

EL TAXISTA: Camine _____[4] hasta que encuentre unas escaleras a la _____.[5]

RAQUEL: A la _____.[5]

EL TAXISTA: Baje las escaleras y cuando encuentre le calle Sol... ¿cuál es el número que busca?

RAQUEL: El cuatro de la calle Sol.

EL TAXISTA: Entonces, creo que está a mano[a] _____.[6] Cuando encuentre la calle Sol, si se pierde, pregunte. Todo el mundo conoce esa calle.

[a]*a... on the . . . side*

Actividad B. **Otra ruta**
Paso 1

Listen as Ángel's neighbor gives Raquel directions to the cemetery. As you listen, fill in the missing words.

LA VECINA: Los dos están enterrados en el antiguo cementerio de San Juan.

RAQUEL: ¿El cementerio?

LA VECINA: Sí.

RAQUEL: ¿Podría decirme cómo llegar allí?

LA VECINA: Por supuesto. _____[1] por esta calle. Entonces _____[2] a la izquierda. Luego va a encontrar una _____[3] y vire a la _____[4] y allí está el Morro. Al lado está el cementerio.

RAQUEL: _____[5] por esta calle. Luego a la _____[6] encuentro una bocacalle. _____[7] a la derecha. Allí está el Morro y al lado el cementerio.

Paso 2

Now that you have all of the words to the dialogue, do you understand the directions? Select the right visual representation for each part of the directions.

1. _____ por esta calle.   a.   b.   c.

2. Entonces _____ a la izquierda.   a.   b.   c.

3. Luego va a encontrar una _____...   a.   b.   c.

4. ...y vire a la _____ y allí está el Morro.   a.   b.   c.

Actividad C. **¿Cómo se llega allí?**
Paso 1

Listen as your instructor gives you directions to get from your university campus to somewhere in your city. Can you tell where you are?

Paso 2

Now work with a partner to create directions to get from a given point on your campus to a familiar off-campus site. The two of you will give the directions to another pair of students, who will try to figure out the destination.

4

UN POCO DE GRAMÁTICA

The Workbook/Study Guide contains more detailed explanation and practice of this grammar point.

Note: You may wish to introduce the complete verb paradigm for the imperfect.

Describing What Was Happening While . . .

To describe an action that was taking place while something else was going on in the past, add **-aba** to the stem of all **-ar** verbs and **-ía** to the stem of almost all **-er** and **-ir** verbs.

Mientras **vivía** en San Juan,   *Ángel painted a lot while*
Ángel **pintaba** mucho.   *he was living in San Juan.*

Third-person plural forms have their characteristic final **-n**.

Mientras Ángel y su esposa   *While Ángel and his wife*
vivían en el Viejo San   *were living in Old San*
Juan, no **sabían** que don   *Juan, they didn't know that*
Fernando **guardaba** un   *don Fernando was keeping*
secreto.   *a secret.*

The past tense that you are learning to use is called the imperfect. Unlike the preterite, the imperfect signals that an action or event was in progress at a given point in the past. You will learn more about the forms and uses of the imperfect in the Workbook/Study Guide.

Act., Suggestion: Give students about a minute to read through and choose their answers. Then, have a student give his/her answer and ask the class if they agree or disagree.

Act., Optional: Prepare a *Firma aquí* activity with questions such as the following. 1. *¿Cenabas a las seis de la tarde ayer?* 2. *¿Dormías a las doce anoche?* 3. *¿Estudiabas el español a las ocho esta mañana?* 4. *¿Mirabas la televisión a las ocho anoche?* 5. *¿Charlabas con amigos a las diez de la noche el viernes?* Have students circulate in class asking and answering the questions and gathering the signatures of classmates who respond with *Sí.* Then have them report their findings to the class, using the model _____ *cenaba a las seis ayer.*

Actividad.   ¿Qué pasaba mientras... ?

Are you a good observer? Indicate what was going on when Spanish class was officially supposed to begin (at the assigned hour). Share your answers with the class.

Cuando era(n) la(s)... ,

1. el profesor
    a. hablaba con un(a) estudiante.
    b. escribía algo en la pizarra (*chalkboard*).
    c. leía algo.
    d. hacía otra cosa.

2. la persona a mi derecha/izquierda
    a. estudiaba la lección.
    b. hablaba con otro/a estudiante.
    c. dormía.
    d. hacía otra cosa.

5

LECTURA CULTURAL

San Juan, Puerto Rico

In **Episodio 19** you learned a little bit about the island of Puerto Rico as well as the city of San Juan. Listen again to the narrator's description as you look at this map. Then read the following narration to find out more about this capital city.

Los puertorriqueños quieren a la Isla donde viven. Es más que patriotismo. Se puede hablar de un verdadero amor al país y a sus lugares. Este amor se expresa en la forma de hablar de muchos puertorriqueños: «mi Isla», «mi Puerto Rico», «mi Viejo San Juan». De hecho[1] a esta última expresión se debe el título de una canción[2] famosa.

Muchas personas conocen San Juan como un centro turístico por excelencia. Pero pocas saben que es también una de las ciudades más antiguas[3] de América. Fue fundada en 1512 por Ponce de León, el explorador que buscaba en la Florida la fuente de la juventud.[4] Ponce de León fue también el primer gobernador español de la Isla. Así que[5] San Juan es a la vez una ciudad moderna y una ciudad histórica.

La ciudad histórica

Ya anduviste con Raquel por las calles de adoquines azulados[6] que caracterizan el Viejo San Juan. El barrio tiene muchos atractivos: restaurantes, bares, galerías de arte, museos, monumentos históricos… Lo que más llama la atención es el estilo colonial del barrio; es decir, el estilo que caracterizaba la arquitectura de la Isla cuando Puerto Rico era todavía una colonia española.

Gran parte de la historia del barrio tiene que ver[7] con la presencia española en la Isla.

La Catedral del Viejo San Juan

- Uno de los edificios históricos más importantes es la Casa Blanca. La arquitectura de esta casa es típica de la época colonial. Fue construida para Ponce de León, quien nunca vivió en ella.
- La Catedral de San Juan es uno de los pocos ejemplos de arquitectura europea medieval en América. Es un edificio crema y blanco, simple pero imponente. Allí fue ordenado el primer obispo[8] de la Iglesia Católica en el Nuevo Mundo.

Cerca de este barrio colonial están dos viejas fortificaciones: San Cristóbal y San Felipe del Morro (llamado el Morro). Estas fortalezas protegían a la ciudad contra los ataques de los enemigos del Imperio español.

[1]De… *In fact*   [2]*song*   [3]viejas   [4]fuente… *Fountain of Youth*   [5]Así… *So*   [6]adoquines… *bluish cobblestones*   [7]tiene… *has to do*   [8]*bishop*

La ciudad moderna

San Juan es una ciudad capital moderna. Tiene edificios altos (sobre todo en el distrito financiero), hoteles ultramodernos de gran lujo,[9] restaurantes internacionales, galerías de arte y exclusivas *boutiques* de moda. Sus residentes se quejan del[10] tráfico. ¡Y no hay que olvidar sus estupendas playas[11]!

Por eso San Juan es un lugar ideal para las vacaciones o para ir de compras. Pero San Juan es mucho más. Es también un centro cultural.

La Universidad de Puerto Rico en Río Piedras

- ¿Eres aficionado[12] a la música clásica? Todos los años se celebra en San Juan el internacionalmente famoso Festival de Música Casals. Fue fundado en 1973 por el violoncelista español Pablo Casals y su esposa Marta Istomín (ex directora del John F. Kennedy Center for the Performing Arts).
- Para los amantes[13] de la naturaleza y la historia, San Juan tiene un parque central muy atractivo, un museo arqueológico y un jardín botánico con más de 200 especies de plantas tropicales y subtropicales.
- Si quieres estudiar, en la ciudad vecina de Río Piedras se encuentra la Universidad de Puerto Rico, con 25.000 estudiantes. Allí han enseñado[14] muchos escritores famosos del mundo de habla española.

Si visitas San Juan, debes ir a la playa, eso sí. Pero... ¡no te debes perder las otras facetas de esta capital caribeña!

[9]*luxury*   [10]*se... complain about the*   [11]*beaches*   [12]*fan*   [13]*lovers*   [14]*han... have taught*

Lectura cultural, Preguntas: 1. ¿Quién fundó la ciudad de San Juan? (Ponce de León) 2. ¿En qué año fue fundada? (en 1512) 3. ¿Cómo se llama el estilo de arquitectura que caracteriza el Viejo San Juan? (colonial) 4. ¿Cuáles son los tres aspectos de cultura mencionados en la sección sobre la ciudad moderna? (la musica clásica, los parques y museos, la Universidad de Puerto Rico)

Actividad. San Juan y otras ciudades

What does San Juan have in common with other large cities? Answer based on your own experience and on the reading passage.

Piensa en

1. la población.
2. las partes de la ciudad.
3. los aspectos culturales.
4. los elementos modernos e históricos.

6

INTERCAMBIO

Paso 1

Work with a partner to prepare a list in Spanish of important events from *Destinos*. For example, **Raquel viajó a Sevilla, Arturo y Raquel empezaron la búsqueda de Ángel en la Boca.** Your list should contain at least ten items and should not be limited to any one episode or country.

Paso 2

Now pass your list to the group to your right. You will receive a list from the group to your left. Read the list you receive and try to add to the event. For example, **Raquel viajó a Sevilla pero la Sra. Suárez no vivía allí.** Return the list to the students who wrote it.

Paso 3
Take turns with other pairs of students to read some sentences to the class. After everyone has a turn, the class should decide on the ten most important events. When you have done this, you will have created a mini-synopsis of *Destinos.*

VOCABULARIO

Los verbos

bajar	to go down
cruzar	to cross
doblar	to turn
virar (*P.R.*)	to turn
baje...	go down . . .
camine...	walk . . .
doble...	turn . . .
siga...	continue . . ., follow . . .
tome...	take . . .
vire...	turn . . .

Repaso: **seguir (i, i)**

En la ciudad

el bloque (*P.R.*)	city block
la bocacalle	intersection
la cuadra	city block
las escaleras	steps
la esquina	corner
la ruta	route, way

Repaso: **la calle**

Las personas

el/la pariente	relative, family member
el/la vecino/a	neighbor

Los lugares

el apartamento	apartment
la isla	island

Las preposiciones

hacia	toward
por	through; along

Repaso: **hasta**

Las palabras adicionales

a la derecha	to the right
a la izquierda	to the left
derecho	straight
mientras	while

20

RELACIONES ESTRECHAS*

Suggestion: Have students look at the photo, describe what they see, and talk about what they think might happen. Ask questions about the photo to prompt student discussion.

*A Close Relationship

OBJETIVOS

The materials in **Lección 20** of the Textbook and the Workbook/Study Guide will help you better understand the video episode and take you beyond it, giving you additional information about places and characters in the series. The Textbook will also help you to develop skill in using the Spanish language. In this lesson, you will learn

- more vocabulary for talking about family members
- more ways to use the imperfect to talk about the past

You will also learn about the history of Puerto Rico.

Be sure to work through all parts of the lesson. When you see a headphones symbol in the margin, listen to the CD for **Lección 20**. Answers or hints for many activities are given in Appendix 1. Be sure to check your answers for each activity before going on to the next one.

The interactive CD-ROM to accompany *Destinos* contains additional practice with the video storyline and will help you improve your skills in Spanish.

BEFORE VIEWING . . .

Preliminary: See Faculty Guide for additional information and activities for this lesson.
- **Variation:** For activities marked with the headphones icon, you may wish to read from the Audioscript instead of playing the CD.
- **Suggestion:** Make sure students are familiar with the activities before you read from the Audioscript or play the CD.

1

PREPARACIÓN

Suggestions:
- Before watching the video, go over the vocabulary list at the end of the chapter and have students pronounce the words after you.
- Assign *Preparación* activities as homework and then go over them quickly in class before viewing the video.

Actividad A.
Paso 1

Refresh your memory about the events of the previous video episode by listening to the narrator's summary of it, which you will hear again when you watch **Episodio 20**.

Paso 2

Now complete the following statements about the previous video episode based on what you have just heard and on what you remember.

Act. A, Answers: *Paso 2:*
1. *Una vecina* 2. *la hija*
3. *estaba sorprendida*
4. *a los tíos* 5. *tenía un hermano también*

1. La hija de Ángel / Una vecina / Una amiga… le dio a Raquel la triste noticia de la muerte de Ángel y de su esposa.
2. Ángela es… la hija / la esposa / la sobrina (*niece*)… de Ángel.
3. Cuando Raquel le dijo a Ángela que tenía un abuelo en México, Ángela… estaba furiosa / estaba sorprendida (*surprised*) / no lo creía.
4. Al final del episodio, Ángela y Raquel esperaban… a los tíos / a los hermanos / al novio… de Ángela.
5. Mientras esperaban, Ángela le dijo a Raquel que… tenía un hermano también / no quería ir a México con ella / vendía su apartamento.

Act. B, Suggestion: You may want to have students do this activity in pairs, role-playing the dialogue.

Para pensar…

¿Cómo va a reaccionar la familia de Ángela cuando todos sepan las noticias? ¿Van a creer la historia? ¿Va a poder Ángela ir a México con Raquel?

Actividad B.
Paso 1

In this video episode you will meet one of Ángela's aunts, **la tía Olga**. Ángela calls her **la gruñona de la familia** (*the family grouch*). Listen to a conversation from **Episodio 20** between Raquel, Olga, and Ángela. You may follow along in the written text if you like.

RAQUEL: …y como don Fernando está gravemente enfermo en el hospital, es importante que Ángela vaya a México pronto.

OLGA: Creo que eso va a ser imposible.

ÁNGELA: ¿Por qué?

OLGA: Ángela, no conocemos a esa gente. Puede ser peligroso.

ÁNGELA: Titi Olga, por favor…

Paso 2

Now answer the following question.

Olga dice que un viaje a México «puede ser peligroso». ¿Qué significa **peligroso**?

Act. B, *Paso 2*, Answer: a

a. _____ dangerous   b. _____ exciting   c. _____ inconvenient

---

Para pensar...

¿Crees que la reacción de la tía Olga es razonable? Escucha con atención (*carefully*) las preguntas que Olga le hace a Raquel en este episodio. Nota también la reacción de Ángela a las preguntas de Olga. ¿Crees que su reacción es razonable?

Actividad C.
Paso 1

In this video episode you will hear Ángela read from a storybook that her father wrote for her when she was a child. Listen to the beginning of the story, following along in your textbook as needed. You should also look carefully at this illustration from the storybook.

El coquí y la princesa

A nuestra hija Ángela, nuestra princesa...

Érase una vez un coquí. Le gustaba pintar. Su padre y su madre querían mandarlo a la escuela. Pero el pequeño coquí no quería estudiar. Sólo quería pintar.

Paso 2

Act. C, *Paso 2*, Answers:
1. a 2. b 3. c

1. Según (*According to*) el dibujo ¿qué es un coquí?
    a. _____ un animal anfibio pequeño y verde
    b. _____ un animal grande y feroz
    c. _____ un animal grande pero dócil

2. El coquí representa a una persona de esta historia. ¿A quién representa? ¡OJO! ¿A quién le pasó lo mismo (*the same thing*)?
    a. _____ a Arturo   b. _____ a Ángel   c. _____ a don Fernando

3. ¿Qué significan las primeras palabras de la historia, «Érase una vez... »?
    a. _____ It was a cold and rainy   b. _____ Call me . . .
         night . . .   c. _____ Once upon a time . . .

. . . AFTER VIEWING

2

¿TIENES BUENA MEMORIA?

Act. A, Answers: 1. b 2. c
3. b 4. a 5. d 6. g 7. a 8. b
9. f 10. e 11. c

Actividad A. ¿Quiénes son?

Complete the following activity about some of the characters you met in this video episode.

1. Esta señora es
    a. _____ la tía de Raquel.
    b. _____ la abuela de Ángela.
    c. _____ la prima (*cousin*) de Ángel.

2. Se llama
    a. _____ María Luisa de Castillo.
    b. _____ Isabel Santana de Trujillo.
    c. _____ Carmen Contreras de Soto.

3. Vive en
    a. _____ San Juan, Puerto Rico.
    b. _____ San Germán, Puerto Rico.
    c. _____ Nueva York.

4. Ángela la llama porque
    a. _____ quiere su permiso para ir a México.
    b. _____ quiere pedirle dinero para viajar con Raquel.
    c. _____ Raquel quiere conocerla.

Now match Ángela's relatives with their names.

5. _____ la abuela de Ángela
6. _____ el tío Carlos
7. _____ el tío Jaime
8. _____ la tía Olga

9. _____ la tía Carmen
10. _____ la madre de Ángela
11. _____ Ángel Castillo, a los 50 años

a.   b.   c.   d.   e.   f.   g.

Nota cultural, **Suggestion:** Have students give examples of terms of endearment used for their own family members. Determine the Spanish equivalents for these terms as a whole-class activity.

Nota cultural, **Optional:** Mention the widespread use of nicknames in Hispanic countries and give examples, e.g., *Alberto → Beto,*

196   Ciento noventa y seis   *Lección 20 Relaciones estrechas*

Francisco → Pancho, Ignacio/a → Nacho/a, Guadalupe → Lupe, etc. Have students give examples of nicknames used for their own family members. Determine the Spanish equivalents, if any, as a whole-class activity.

Nota cultural   Las familias hispanas

Ángela is a young professional who lives alone and who is, for all intents and purposes, in charge of her own life. Yet a major topic of the family conference that takes place in her apartment concerns whether or not she should go to Mexico with Raquel to meet her paternal grandfather and to find out more about this "new" branch of the family. As you have learned, Ángela and Raquel will have to travel to San Germán to discuss the topic with Ángela's maternal grandmother.

It is very difficult to generalize about family customs in any culture. Depending on your particular situation, you may find the family unity shown in this video episode to be "normal" or "strange." It is fair to suggest, however, that Hispanic families are thought to be more close-knit than the average non-Hispanic U.S. family. Hispanic young people often live at home longer than their typical non-Hispanic U.S. counterparts, and the family is more often regarded as an important source of emotional support. You can read more about Ángela's family situation in the **Más allá del episodio** section of this lesson in the Workbook.

In Hispanic families, just as in families throughout the world, the use of terms of endearment to refer to family members is common. Ángela calls her Aunt Olga **titi** instead of **tía**. The use of the endings **-ito** or **-ita**, as appropriate, is also quite common: **abuelito**, **hermanita**, etc.

Actividad B. Yerno y suegra (*Son-in-law and mother-in-law*)

Ángel era el yerno de doña Carmen. ¿Cuánto recuerdas acerca de sus relaciones?

1.   Según Ángela, los dos
     a. _____ tenían unas relaciones muy estrechas.
     b. _____ no se llevaban bien.
     c. _____ se toleraban el uno al otro.

2.   Según el episodio, doña Carmen
     a. _____ no guarda nada de Ángel.
     b. _____ tiene algo que pertenecía (*belonged*) a Ángel.
     c. _____ realmente no quería mucho a su yerno.

Act. B, Suggestion: You may want to have students do this activity in pairs or small groups.

Act. B, Answers: 1. a 2. b

Actividad C. Llamadas de larga distancia
Paso 1

Work with a partner to describe the long-distance phone calls made in this episode. First, fill in the blanks.

1.   _____ llamó a _____ en México, pero no pudo hablar con él/ella.

2.   _____ llamó a _____ en San Germán y pudo hablar con él/ella.

3.   _____ llamó a _____ en México y pudo hablar con él/ella.

Act. C, Answers: *Paso 1:*
1. Ángela, Roberto, él
2. Ángela, su abuela, ella
3. Raquel, Pedro, él *Paso 2:* don Fernando

Act. C, Optional: Have each set of partners act out their version of call 2 or call 3 for the entire class.

Now you and your partner should act out a paraphrased version of the calls in items 2 and 3.

Paso 2

¡Un desafío! ¿Qué otra persona supo algo muy importante por una llamada telefónica?

Para pensar...

¿Quién llamaba a la habitación de Raquel al final del Episodio 20? ¿Era una llamada de México... con malas noticias?

3

VOCABULARIO DEL TEMA

Los parientes

You already know the following names for family members. Be sure that you recognize the meaning of these words.

el abuelo, la abuela   **el hijo, la hija**
el esposo, la esposa   **el padre, la madre**
el hermano, la hermana   **el tío, la tía**

Here are the names for other members of the family.

los nietos	grandchildren	**los suegros**	in-laws
el nieto,	grandson,	**el suegro,**	father-in-law,
la nieta	granddaughter	**la suegra**	mother-in-law
los primos	cousins	**el yerno**	son-in-law
el primo, la prima	male/female cousin	**la nuera**	daughter-in-law
los sobrinos	nieces and nephews	**el cuñado**	brother-in-law
el sobrino, la sobrina	nephew, niece	**la cuñada**	sister-in-law

el padrastro, la madrastra	stepfather, stepmother
el hijastro, la hijastra	stepson, stepdaughter
el hermanastro, la hermanastra	stepbrother, stepsister
el medio hermano, la media hermana	half brother, half sister

Note that the masculine plural form (**los nietos, los primos**...) of the names for family members is used to refer to everyone in that category, both male and female. The most frequently used plural terms are indicated in the list of additional family members.

If you can't find in the above list the name for a family member that you need in order to describe your own family, look it up in a dictionary or ask your instructor.

Actividad A. **Los parientes**

Listen to the definitions provided by the speaker on the CD. Can you provide the Spanish word that represents the relationship described? In each case the speaker describes how someone is related to him/herself.

1. a. _____ los sobrinos   b. _____ los nietos
2. a. _____ los sobrinos   b. _____ los primos
3. a. _____ los sobrinos   b. _____ los primos
4. a. _____ los cuñados   b. _____ los suegros
5. a. _____ los cuñados   b. _____ los yernos
6. a. _____ el hijastro   b. _____ el hermanastro

Actividad B. **La familia de Ángela**
Paso 1

As you listen to Ángela describe her family, complete her family tree. Fill each box with the appropriate name and indicate family relationships using connecting lines. Some hints are given for you.

doña Carmen   (Q.E.P.D.)

Ángel (Q.E.P.D.)   María Luisa (Q.E.P.D.)

Ángela   Roberto

Act. B, *Paso 2*, Answers:
1. *cinco* 2. *dos, dos*
3. *Tres* 4. *cinco* 5. *un, tres*
6. *Ángel, la suegra, suegro*

Act. B, Follow-up: Use students' family trees for a pair review the following day. You might have on an overhead questions such as *¿Cuántos tíos tienes? ¿Cómo se llama(n)? ¿Dónde vive(n)? ¿Tiene(n) hijos? ¿Cuántos años tienen tus primos?*, etc.

Paso 2

Now complete the following sentences based on the family tree you have just completed.

1. Doña Carmen y su esposo tuvieron _____ hijos.

2. María Luisa tenía _____ hermanos y _____ hermanas.

3. _____ personas serían (*would be*) sobrinas de María Luisa si ella estuviera viva (*were alive*).

4. Doña Carmen tiene _____ nietos en total.

5. Ángela tiene _____ hermano y _____ primas.

6. _____ era el yerno de doña Carmen. Doña Carmen era

    _____ de Ángel. El _____ de Ángel ya murió.

Actividad C. Más parentescos (*relationships*)

Complete the sentences with the appropriate words for the family relationships described.

1. ¿Qué parentesco tienen Ángela y Roberto con Arturo? Son sus

    _____.

2. ¿Qué parentesco tienen Mercedes, Ramón, Carlos y Juan con Ángela y

    Roberto? Ellos son los _____ de Ángela y Roberto.

3. ¿Qué parentesco hay entre Ángela y Maricarmen, la hija de Ramón y

    Consuelo? Ángela es la _____ de Maricarmen.

4. ¿Qué parentesco tiene Ángel con los hijos de don Fernando? Ellos son

    sus _____.

Actividad D. Mis parientes

For each of the following family members, indicate whether or not you have one, how many there are, and what their names are. Can you also indicate where they live and how old they are?

MODELOS: No tengo (primas, suegra…).

Tengo un/una/varios/varias _____. Se llama(n)

_____ y vive(n) en _____. Mi

_____ tiene _____ años.

1. primo/a   2. suegro/a   3. abuelo/a   4. sobrino/a
5. cuñado/a   6. hermanastro/a   7. padrastro/madrastra

4

UN POCO DE GRAMÁTICA

The Workbook/Study Guide contains more detailed explanation and practice of this grammar point.

Suggestion: Provide students with cards, each of which has a verb form written in the imperfect. Or, write in the infinitive with a subject pronoun and have students write the correct form in the imperfect. Then have students, working in pairs, groups, or teams, mime their verbs. Other students guess the verb in the imperfect.

More About Using the Imperfect

In **Lección 19** you learned to talk about what someone else *was doing* by adding **-aba(n)** or **-ía(n)** to the stems of most verbs. To talk about yourself, use the singular form of the same endings.

RAQUEL: Mientras yo **tomaba** una foto,   *While I was taking a photo,*
         Ángela Castillo llegó.   *Ángela Castillo arrived.*

> Mientras yo **visitaba** la Casa Blanca, Ángela trató de hablar con sus tíos.
>
> *While I was visiting the White House, Ángela tried to speak with her aunts and uncles.*

Did you notice that the imperfect was used along with the preterite in the preceding sentences? You will learn more about the forms of the imperfect and about its uses in the Workbook/Study Guide.

Actividad. ¡Firma aquí, por favor!

Paso 1

On a sheet of paper write down what you were doing yesterday at these times.

MODELO: 3:00 P.M. → A las tres de la tarde, estudiaba en la biblioteca.

1. 8:00 A.M.   2. 12:30 P.M.   3. 3:00 P.M.   4. 6:00 P.M.   5. 11:30 P.M.

Lectura cultural, **Suggestion:** It is helpful to have a large map of Puerto Rico in front of the room or on an overhead.

Lectura cultural, **Answers:** 1. P 2. P 3. I 4. I 5. P 6. I 7. I (See Appendix 1 for expanded answers.)

Paso 2

Using the verb form **hacías**, try to find people in the class who were doing the same thing as you at the same time. Ask each person who answers the same as you to sign his or her name (**¡Firma aquí, por favor!**) next to your sentence. The first person to collect five names wins!

MODELO: TÚ: ¿Qué hacías a las ocho de la mañana ayer?
COMPAÑERO/A: Dormía.
TÚ: ¡Yo también! ¡Firma aquí, por favor!

5

LECTURA CULTURAL

Puerto Rico, la «Isla del Encanto»

Before reading the following passage about the past and present of Puerto Rico, think about what you have seen in the video episodes and about what you already know about the island. Then indicate whether the following are **Probable (P)** or **Improbable (I)**.

P I 1. La población de la Isla es muy densa.
P I 2. La Isla tiene ríos y desiertos.
P I 3. El primer español que llegó a la Isla fue Ponce de León.
P I 4. Cuando llegaron los españoles, no había pueblos indígenas en la Isla.
P I 5. El oro (*gold*) fue muy importante en la historia de Puerto Rico.
P I 6. El inglés no es lengua oficial de la Isla.
P I 7. Puerto Rico está asociado con España políticamente.

After reading, check your answers. Are there any that you need to change?

Puerto Rico... la «Isla del Encanto»,[1] como la llaman los puertorriqueños y los que llegan a conocerla.[2] Es la más pequeña del archipiélago[3] que se llama las Antillas Mayores. A continuación[4] se presentan unos detalles acerca del presente y el pasado de esta isla tropical que tiene una relación especial con los Estados Unidos.

Datos importantes

Población: muy densa, cuatro millones de habitantes, en 9.000 kilómetros cuadrados[5]

Emigración: a Nueva York y otras ciudades del continente

Clima: cálido y soleado[6] casi todo el año

Geografía: playas, bosques,[7] colinas,[8] montañas, ríos abundantes, cascadas, áreas áridas,...

Historia

Cristóbal Colón llegó a la isla de Puerto Rico en 1493, en su segundo viaje a América. Le dio a la isla el nombre de San Juan. En aquel entonces[9] la isla estaba habitada por los indios taínos. La tribu era un pueblo pacífico y sedentario. Vivían de la pesca[10] y la agricultura. Se cree que llamaban a la isla Boriquén. (De allí[11] viene el nombre del himno nacional de Puerto Rico, «La Boriqueña».)

El explorador español Juan Ponce de León exploró la isla en 1508. Fundó la capital ese mismo año y la llamó Puerto Rico. (Más tarde se cambiaron[12] los nombres de la isla y de la capital.) Ponce de León fue nombrado gobernador de la isla al año siguiente.

Había poco oro en la Isla, pero el mito de su existencia atrajo[13] a muchos españoles. Obligaron a los taínos a buscar el oro. Entre el trabajo duro[14] de la búsqueda del metal precioso y las enfermedades[15] que contrajeron de los españoles, murió la mayoría de los indios en el siglo XVI.

Dentro de poco se extinguió el mito dorado,[16] y el cultivo del jengibre,[17] del azúcar[18] y del tabaco lo sustituyó. Para trabajar en los campos, los españoles trajeron a la isla a esclavos africanos. Y para defender los cultivos de los ataques de los piratas, construyeron fortificaciones como El Morro. La isla ganó así fama como una de las rutas comerciales más importantes del Imperio español.

Puerto Rico fue posesión española hasta finales del siglo XIX. Como resultado de la Guerra Hispanoamericana de 1898, la isla fue cedida a los Estados Unidos. Sus habitantes obtuvieron la ciudadanía[19] norteamericana en 1917. Años más tarde, los habitantes de la isla ganaron el derecho[20] a elegir a su propio gobernador.

Lectura cultural, Preguntas: 1. ¿Cómo se llama la gente de Puerto Rico? (*los puertorriqueños*) 2. ¿Cuál es el nombre que ellos le dan a Puerto Rico? (*la Isla del Encanto*) 3. ¿Qué tipo de geografía tiene Puerto Rico? (*playas, bosques, colinas, montañas, ríos, cascadas, áreas áridas*) 4. ¿Cuándo llegó Colón a la isla y qué nombre le dio? (*1493, San Juan*) 5. ¿Quién exploró la isla en 1508? (*Juan Ponce de León*) 6. ¿En qué siglo murió la mayoría de los indios? (*en el siglo XVI*) 7. ¿En qué guerra fue cedida Puerto Rico a los EEUU? (*en la Guerra Hispanoamericana de 1898*)

[1]*Enchantment* [2]*llegan... get to know her* [3]*grupo de islas* [4]*A... Here are* [5]*square* [6]*cálido... warm and sunny* [7]*forests* [8]*hills* [9]*En... At that time* [10]*fishing* [11]*De... From there* [12]*se... were transposed* [13]*attracted* [14]*hard* [15]*illnesses* [16]*el... the myth of the existence of gold* [17]*ginger* [18]*sugar* [19]*citizenship* [20]*ganaron... won the right* [21]*dry*

A partir de 1952, Puerto Rico es un Estado Libre Asociado de la comunidad estadounidense. Durante muchos años el idioma oficial de la Isla era el español, pero en 1993 el gobernador de Puerto Rico proclamó al inglés como segundo idioma oficial.

El Yunque es un bosque tropical en territorio estadounidense.

Act., Suggestion: You may want to have students work in pairs for this activity.

Actividad. **Puerto Rico y los Estados Unidos**

These areas of the world share a common history to some extent, starting with the arrival of explorers centuries ago. How many parallels can you find between the history of Puerto Rico and that of the United States? Think about these topics.

1. la geografía
2. la llegada de los españoles
3. la población indígena
4. la agricultura (y uno de los efectos importantes que tuvo en la historia)
5. el oro
6. la importancia de una guerra
7. los idiomas que se hablan

6

INTERCAMBIO

Paso 1
Select one of don Fernando's relatives from this lesson. Without saying who it is, describe the person in Spanish so your classmates might guess the character. They should respond by saying the name and the relationship to don Fernando.

Paso 2
Now imagine you are the person you described in **Paso 1**. Make up a series of four statements to talk about what you were doing when something else happened during one of the episodes of *Destinos*. Read your statements to the class and have the class decide whether what you say **Es posible** or **No es posible**.

VOCABULARIO

Los parientes

el cuñado/la cuñada	brother-in-law, sister-in-law
el hermanastro/ la hermanastra	stepbrother, stepsister
el hijastro/la hijastra	stepson, stepdaughter
la madrastra	stepmother
la media hermana	half sister
los nietos	grandchildren
el nieto/la nieta	grandson, granddaughter
los primos	cousins
el primo/la prima	male/female cousin
los sobrinos	nieces and nephews
el sobrino/ la sobrina	nephew, niece
los suegros	in-laws
el suegro/ la suegra	father-in-law, mother-in-law
el yerno, la nuera	son-in-law, daughter-in-law

Repaso: **el medio hermano, el padrastro**

Los adjetivos

estrecho/a	close-knit
sorprendido/a	surprised

Las palabras adicionales

según	according to

21

EL PEAJE*

Suggestion: Have students look at the photo, describe what they see, and talk about what they think might happen. Ask questions about the photo to prompt student discussion.

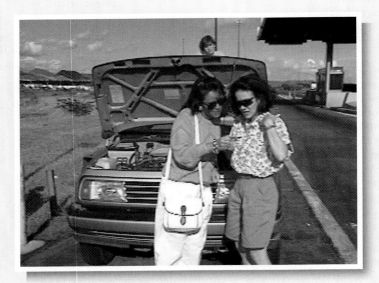

*The Tollbooth

OBJETIVOS

The materials in **Lección 21** of the Textbook and the Workbook/Study Guide will help you better understand the video episode and take you beyond it, giving you additional information about places and characters in the series. The Textbook will also help you to develop skill in using the Spanish language. In this lesson, you will learn

- how to talk about the weather and climates in Spanish
- more about how to use the imperfect to talk about the past

You will also learn about Puerto Rican cities other than San Juan and about the money used in Puerto Rico.

Be sure to work through all parts of the lesson. When you see a headphones symbol in the margin, listen to the CD for **Lección 21**. Answers or hints for many activities are given in Appendix 1. Be sure to check your answers for each activity before going on to the next one.

The interactive CD-ROM to accompany *Destinos* contains additional practice with the video storyline and will help you improve your skills in Spanish.

BEFORE VIEWING . . .

Preliminary: See Faculty Guide for additional information and activities for this lesson.
- **Variation:** For activities marked with the headphones icon, you may wish to read from the Audioscript instead of playing the CD.
- **Suggestion:** Make sure students are familiar with the activities before you read from the Audioscript or play the CD.

1

PREPARACIÓN

 Actividad A.
Paso 1

Suggestions:
- Before watching the video, go over the vocabulary list at the end of the chapter and have students pronounce the words after you.
- Assign *Preparación* activities as homework and then go over them quickly in class before viewing the video.

Refresh your memory about the events of the previous video episode by listening to the narrator's summary of it, which you will hear again when you watch **Episodio 21**.

Paso 2

Now answer the following questions about the previous video episode based on what you have just heard and on what you remember.

Act. A, Paso 2, Answers:
1. b 2. b 3. a 4. c 5. b 6. b

1. ¿Cuál era la actitud de los tíos de Ángela mientras escuchaban la historia de la investigación de Raquel?
   a. _____ Escuchaban sin gran interés.
   b. _____ Escuchaban con mucha atención.

2. ¿Cuál de los tíos tenía mucho que decir acerca de la historia de Raquel?
   a. _____ el tío Carlos
   b. _____ la tía Olga

3. En general, ¿cómo reaccionaban los tíos de Ángela ante las noticias?
   a. _____ Estaban preocupados.
   b. _____ Reaccionaban con indiferencia.

4. De los parientes de Ángela, ¿quién parecía ser el centro de la familia?
   a. _____ la tía Olga b. _____ el tío Jaime c. _____ la abuela

5. ¿Cómo eran las relaciones entre doña Carmen, la abuela y su yerno Ángel?
   a. _____ Eran problemáticas.
   b. _____ Eran muy estrechas.

6. ¿Con quién tiene que hablar ahora Raquel?
   a. _____ con la tía Olga
   b. _____ con doña Carmen

 Actividad B.

In this video episode Raquel has the following conversation with an employee at a tollbooth on the highway. Listen, and follow along in the text if you like. As you listen, keep in mind that the word **taller** means *repair shop*.

> RAQUEL: Perdone. Algo le pasó al carro. ¿Nos podría ayudar?
> EMPLEADA: Me gustaría mucho, señorita, pero no puedo. ¿Por qué no llaman a un taller en Ponce?

Now answer the following questions.

Act. B, Answers: 1. a
2. a

1. ¿Qué problema tienen Raquel y Ángela en el camino a San Germán?
   a. _____ No funciona el carro.
   b. _____ Paran (*They stop*) porque necesitan gasolina.

2. ¿Hay talleres en la autopista (*highway*)?
   a. _____ No, pero los hay en una ciudad que está cerca.
   b. _____ Sí, junto al peaje.

 . . . AFTER VIEWING

2

¿TIENES BUENA MEMORIA?

Act. A, Suggestion: Give students about 5 minutes to complete the activity individually or in pairs and then compare answers as a whole class.

Act. A, Optional: Students work in pairs. One student closes his/her book while the other reads the list of possible answers. The student with the closed book tries to choose the right answer.

Act. A, Answers: 1. b 2. c 3. b 4. c 5. c 6. b 7. b

Actividad A. La historia sigue

These statements are taken from Raquel's summary at the end of **Episodio 21**. Indicate the phrase that completes the statement or answers the question.

1. Esta mañana Ángela, su prima Laura y yo salimos de San Juan para ir a
   a. _____ Ponce.   b. _____ San Germán.   c. _____ Caguas.

2. En ruta a San Germán aprendí muchas cosas interesantes. Por ejemplo, ¿es una peseta puertorriqueña igual a una peseta española?
   a. _____ No. Vale un dólar. Es una moneda (*coin*) norteamericana.
   b. _____ Sí. Son iguales. Una peseta puertorriqueña y una peseta española valen lo mismo.
   c. _____ No. Vale veinticinco centavos. Es una moneda norteamericana.

3. En Puerto Rico una banana es **un guineo**. En España se dice **plátano**. Otra fruta con un nombre diferente es
   a. _____ la manzana.   b. _____ la naranja.   c. _____ la pera.

4. En camino a San Germán, cerca del peaje, tuvimos problemas con
   a. _____ la comida.   b. _____ mi sombrero.   c. _____ el carro.

5. La mujer del peaje me dio un número de un taller para llamar. ¿En dónde estaba el taller?
   a. _____ En San Juan.   b. _____ En Caguas.   c. _____ En Ponce.

6. Luego vino el señor del taller y remolcó (*towed*) el carro a Ponce. En el taller, supimos que el carro
   a. _____ simplemente no tenía   c. _____ era imposible de
       gasolina.   reparar.
   b. _____ estaba en muy malas
       condiciones.

7. Y aquí estamos, cansadas y listas para dormir. Ahora tendré que (*I'll have to*) esperar hasta mañana para conocer
   a. _____ al hermano de Ángela.   c. _____ al dueño (*owner*) del taller.
   b. _____ a Carmen Contreras.

 Now check your answers by listening to the CD.

Actividad B. **Un poco de historia. ¡Un desafío!**
Paso 1

In this and in previous video episodes of *Destinos,* as well as in the lessons of the Textbook and Workbook/Study Guide, you have learned a great deal about Puerto Rico. Can you supply the missing information in the following paragraphs?

> **Lugares:** La Habana, Ponce, San Juan, Cuba, Puerto Rico
> **Fechas:** 1859, 1898, 1911
> **Otras palabras:** español, inglés, la batalla, la guerra

Act. B, Suggestion: Give students about 4 minutes to complete the activity individually or in pairs and then compare answers as a whole class.

Act. B, Answers: 1. *español* 2. *San Juan* 3. *1898* 4. *guerra* 5. *Cuba* 6. *Puerto Rico*

Por más de 400 años, Puerto Rico formó parte del vasto Imperio _____.[1] Para el Imperio, _____[2] era uno de los puertos más importantes de todas las Américas.

En _____[3] estalló[a] la guerra entre los Estados Unidos y España. Al perder la _____,[4] España tuvo que concederle el resto de su imperio a los Estados Unidos. Las Filipinas, _____[5] y Puerto Rico pasaron a manos[b] norteamericanas.

En 1902 Cuba consiguió su independencia de los Estados Unidos. Las Islas Filipinas se independizaron en 1946, pero _____[6] siguió siendo[c] territorio norteamericano.

[a]empezó   [b]*hands*   [c]siguió... *continued to be*

Paso 2
Now check your answers by listening to the CD.

Nota cultural Los puertorriqueños, ciudadanos (*citizens*) de los Estados Unidos

When Raquel asks Ángela whether her passport is up to date, she has forgotten something of which many people are not aware: Puerto Ricans are U.S. citizens. They can travel back and forth freely from **la Isla** to the mainland, and, as U.S. citizens, they can go anywhere that other U.S. citizens are permitted to go without a passport, such as to Mexico.

Another result of Puerto Rico's relationship to the United States is the use of U.S. currency . . . some with Spanish names! Can you remember the value in cents (**centavos**) of the following coins?

una peseta   un vellón de 10   un vellón de 5   un chavo (un chavito)

3

VOCABULARIO DEL TEMA

¿Qué tiempo hace?

Hace (muy) buen tiempo.	The weather's (very) good.
Hace (muy) mal tiempo.	The weather's (very) bad.
Hace (mucho) frío.	It's (very) cold.
Hace (mucho) fresco.	It's (very) cool.
Hace (mucho) calor.	It's (very) hot.
Hace (mucho) sol.	It's (very) sunny.
Hace (mucho) viento.	It's (very) windy.
Está (muy) nublado.	It's (very) cloudy.
Está despejado.	It's clear (cloudless).

llover (ue):   to rain: **nevar (ie):**   to snow:
   Llueve. / **Está lloviendo.**   It's raining.   **Nieva.** / **Está nevando.**   It's snowing.

La temperatura está a ___ grados.   The temperature is ___ degrees.

Note the following about describing the weather in Spanish.

- **Hacer** (*to do* or *to make*) is used to describe many weather conditions. The adverb **muy** modifies the adjectives **buen** and **mal** + **tiempo**. The adjective **mucho** is followed by nouns (**frío, fresco**...) in a number of other expressions.
- The imperfect is generally used to talk about weather in the past: **Hacía mucho calor la semana pasada. La temperatura estaba a 38 grados.**

Actividad A. **En Ponce hace calor**

Listen again as the narrator uses a number of terms to describe weather conditions. Complete the statements with the terms you hear.

Actividad B. En el mes de diciembre

In **Episodio 9** you learned that the seasons are reversed in the southern hemisphere. That is, when it is winter in Spain, it is summer in Argentina, and vice versa. In the Caribbean, the weather conditions are fairly constant.

Working with a partner and using the cues below, make generalized statements about the weather in the cities indicated in column A. ¡OJO! Some of your statements should be true and some should be false. Can your partner detect the false ones?

> MODELO: TÚ: En Miami hace sol en abril.
>   COMPAÑERO/A: Sí, es cierto.
>   TÚ: En Búfalo hace calor en enero.
>   COMPAÑERO/A: No, no es cierto. Hace mucho frío.

A	B	C
1. Madrid	hace frío	enero
2. Chicago	hace fresco	abril
3. Ponce	hace calor	agosto
4. Buenos Aires	hace sol	octubre
5. San Diego		

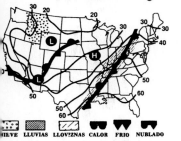

el 30 de marzo

Actividad C. ¿Qué tiempo hacía?

You will hear a series of questions about weather conditions in different parts of the United States. Indicate what the weather was like in those places last March 30, based on the following map. If no particular weather condition is depicted, answer by saying **Hacía buen tiempo.** Take a few seconds to scan the map and its legend. You will hear the legend on the CD. What known words can you associate with the unfamiliar words?

> MODELO: (*you hear*) —¿Qué tiempo hacía en la Florida? ¿Llovía?
>   (*you say*) —No, no llovía. Hacía buen tiempo.

1. …   2. …   3. …   4. …   5. …   6. …

Actividad D. ¿Qué tiempo hace?

Select one pair of cities below and compare and contrast the usual weather patterns in each for different times of the year.

> MODELO: Austin / Sacramento → En Austin, hace mucho calor en el verano. También hace mucho calor en Sacramento en el verano. En la primavera, hace…

1. Los Ángeles / Nueva York
2. Seattle / Palm Springs
3. Honolulu / Boston
4. ¿ ? / ¿ ?

Nota cultural Hablando de la temperatura

In most Spanish-speaking countries, temperature is measured by *Celsius* degrees, rather than by *Fahrenheit*. The following chart gives approximate correspondences between the two scales.

Celsius	100°	37°	30°	20°	10°	0°
Fahrenheit	212°	98.6°	86°	68°	50°	32°

4

UN POCO DE GRAMÁTICA

The Workbook/Study Guide contains more detailed explanation and practice of this grammar point.

Note: You may wish to review the verb paradigm for the imperfect.

More About the Imperfect

To describe what you and others *were doing,* add **-ábamos** or **-íamos** to the stems of regular verbs.

RAQUEL: Hacía mucho calor cuando **viajábamos** por las montañas. **Queríamos** llegar a San Germán esa noche, pero el carro no funcionaba bien.

Act., Follow-up: Have students number the items from 1 (most probable) to 10 (least probable) for themselves and their friends rather than for a "typical" student. Then, have them try to find classmates with similar habits by going around the classroom and comparing lists.

Actividad. ¿Qué hacíamos?

Imagine that you overhear two "typical" students from your campus talking about where they were and what they were doing last Friday afternoon at 5:00. Number the items from 1 (most probable) to 10 (least probable), depending on what you consider to be a "typical" student at your school.

a. _____ «Estábamos en la biblioteca. Estudiábamos.»
b. _____ «Practicábamos un deporte con unos amigos.»
c. _____ «Veíamos algo en la tele.»
d. _____ «Trabajábamos.»
e. _____ «Preparábamos la cena.»
f. _____ «Bebíamos cerveza en nuestro apartamento.»
g. _____ «Dormíamos la siesta.»
h. _____ «Manejábamos (*We were driving*) el coche para ir a un concierto.»
i. _____ «Hacíamos ejercicio.»
j. _____ «Salíamos para visitar a nuestros padres.»

5

LECTURA CULTURAL

Otras ciudades puertorriqueñas

In this video episode, due to Raquel, Ángela, and Laura's unscheduled stop in Ponce, you learned a bit about that city. **Ponceños** (people who live in Ponce) and other Puerto Ricans are fond of saying that **Ponce es Ponce**, which probably implies that people do things their own way in this relatively small, attractive city. Listen again to what the narrator told you about Ponce and try to recall the images in the video episode. Then read this passage about Ponce and other cities on **la Isla** and indicate them on the map.

En la Isla, las poblaciones típicas y los vestigios coloniales alternan con edificios modernos y complejos de hoteles y casinos. Esta gran variedad de ambientes[1] atrae el turismo de todas partes del mundo. Aquí hay algunos lugares que visitar. ¿Cuál te interesa más? ¿Puedes encontrarlos todos en el mapa, según la lectura? ¿Y puedes identificar la siguiente foto?

Lectura cultural, **Suggestion:** Assign as homework and go over answers quickly in class. Remind students that they should not expect to understand every word of the reading, but rather to get the main ideas.

- Una de las ciudades más importantes de Puerto Rico es Ponce, que está en la costa del Caribe. Es un antiguo centro agrícola, donde se cultiva la caña de azúcar[2] y el café. Ponce conserva su encanto provinciano. En el Parque Central está la Catedral de Guadalupe y el pintoresco[3] Parque de Bombas,[4] pintado de rojo y negro. Su museo de arte está entre los mejores del Caribe.

Mayagüez, Puerto Rico

- Al oeste de la Isla se encuentra Mayagüez, ciudad que fundaron los españoles en un lugar ya habitado por los indios taínos. Además de ser una ciudad histórica, tiene modernas fábricas[5] y hoteles. Su zoológico es fascinante, sobre todo para los niños.

- Cerca de Mayagüez, en el suroeste, está La Parguera, una pintoresca aldea[6] de pescadores.[7] Uno de sus atractivos es la llamada «bahía fosforescente»: de noche, cuando la luna se oculta,[8] y se agita el agua, brilla[9] con la luz de unos pequeños organismos marítimos unicelulares que viven en las aguas de la bahía. La Parguera tiene el mayor laboratorio marino de todo el Caribe.

[1]*environments* [2]*caña... sugar cane* [3]*picturesque* [4]Parque... *Fire Station* [5]*factories* [6]*village* [7]*fishermen* [8]la... *the moon is hidden* [9]*it glows*

• En la costa del norte, cerca de San Juan, está Arecibo. Se conoce por los carnavales, el ron y las piñas. Es también el centro de la industria farmacéutica. Y es famosa porque allí hay un observatorio con un enorme telescopio.

Actividad. La Isla del Encanto

Based on what you have just read, where would you most likely find the following people, animals, and events?

1. un estudiante de astronomía
2. una hacienda
3. viajes turísticos de noche, en bote
4. un biólogo marino
5. un estudiante de arte
6. un tigre
7. muchas personas que llevan máscaras y se divierten

6

INTERCAMBIO

Paso 1

Create four statements about what you were doing and/or where you were at 8:00 A.M., 12:00 noon, 3:00 P.M., and 7:00 P.M. yesterday.

Paso 2

Find people in the class who were doing the same thing as you. Your goal is to find at least two other people who were doing the same thing as you for any activity.

MODELO: ¿Qué hacías ayer a las 3:00 de la tarde?

Paso 3

Report to the class what you and the other students from **Paso 2** were doing at a particular time.

MODELO: Ayer a las 3:00 Sheryl, Tom y yo estudiábamos en la biblioteca.

Paso 4

As a class, what do you think Raquel was doing yesterday at the times mentioned in **Paso 1**?

VOCABULARIO

Los verbos

funcionar	to work, function (*machines*)
manejar	to drive
parar	to stop

En el camino

la autopista	highway; toll road
el carro	car
el peaje	tollbooth
el taller	repair shop (*automobiles*)

Los adjetivos

preocupado/a	worried

¿Qué tiempo hace? (What's the Weather Like?)

Hace (muy) buen tiempo.   The weather's (very) good.

Hace (mucho) calor.	It's (very) hot.
Hace (mucho) fresco.	It's (very) cool.
Hace (mucho) frío.	It's (very) cold.
Hace (muy) mal tiempo.	The weather's (very) bad.
Hace (mucho) sol.	It's (very) sunny.
Hace (mucho) viento.	It's (very) windy.
Está despejado.	It's clear (cloudless).
Está (muy) nublado.	It's (very) cloudy.
llover (ue)	to rain
Llueve./Está lloviendo.	It's raining.
nevar (ie)	to snow
Nieva./Está nevando.	It's snowing.
La temperatura está a ____ grados.	The temperature is ____ degrees.

LECCIÓN 22

Suggestion: Have students look at the photo, describe what they see, and talk about what they think might happen. Ask questions about the photo to prompt student discussion.

RECUERDOS*

Estos son
mis amigos del puerto...
los primeros en decirme que me dedicara a la pintura.

*Memories

OBJETIVOS

The materials in **Lección 22** of the Textbook and the Workbook/Study Guide will help you better understand the video episode and take you beyond it, giving you additional information about places and characters in the series. The Textbook will also help you to develop skill in using the Spanish language. In this lesson, you will learn

- how to describe changes in people's mood, condition, or state of being
- how to use the imperfect to talk about things you always used to do

You will also learn about the economy of Puerto Rico.

Be sure to work through all parts of the lesson. When you see a head-phones symbol in the margin, listen to the CD for **Lección 22**. Answers or hints for many activities are given in Appendix 1. Be sure to check your answers for each activity before going on to the next one.

The interactive CD-ROM to accompany *Destinos* contains additional practice with the video storyline and will help you improve your skills in Spanish.

BEFORE VIEWING . . .

Preliminary: See Faculty Guide for additional information and
activities for this lesson.
• **Variation:** For activities marked with the headphones icon, you
  may wish to read from the Audioscript instead of playing
  the CD.
• **Suggestion:** Make sure students are familiar with the activities
  before you read from the Audioscript or play the CD.

1

PREPARACIÓN

Suggestions:

Actividad.
Paso 1

• Before watching the video, go over the vocabulary list at the end of the chapter and
  have students pronounce the words after you.
• Assign *Preparación* activities as homework and then go over them quickly in class
  before viewing the video.

In the previous video episode, Raquel and her traveling companions set off
for San Germán, where Ángela's grandmother lives. Their trip was not un-
eventful, however. Complete the following summary of the previous episode.
No words are given from which to choose, but you should be able to complete the paragraph easily. Read it through at least once before you fill in the
blanks.

Act., *Paso 1,* **Answers:**
1. *prima* 2. *carro* 3. *taller*
4. *día siguiente (próximo
día)* 5. *Ponce*

En camino a San Germán, Raquel, Ángela y Laura, la _____¹ de

Ángela, tuvieron dificultades con el _____.² Llamaron a un

_____³ de reparaciones.ᵃ Vino un hombre y remolcó el carro a

Ponce. El mecánico les dijo que el carro no iba a estar listoᵇ hasta el

_____.⁴ Raquel y sus dos compañeras tuvieron que pasar la noche

en _____.⁵

ᵃ*repairs* ᵇ*ready*

 Paso 2

Now check your answers by listening to the CD.

Para pensar, **Suggestion:** You may want
to have students do this activity in pairs.

Para pensar...

Esto es un baúl. Contiene artículos personales
de alguien. ¿De quién?

¿Qué hay en la caja que le está dando doña Carmen
a Ángela? ¿Será (*Could it be*) algo relacionado
con la historia de Ángel?

... AFTER VIEWING

2

¿TIENES BUENA MEMORIA?

Actividad A. Las preguntas de Raquel
Paso 1

Listen again as Raquel asks questions at the end of the video episode while she is waiting for the family to say good-bye. Select the correct answer from the choices provided. Raquel will give the correct answer on the CD.

Act. A, *Paso 1,* Answers:
1. a 2. b 3. a *Paso 2:* 1. F
2. C 3. C 4. F *Paso 3:* 1. b
2. a (See Appendix 1 for
expanded answers.)

1. a. _____ Sí.   b. _____ No.
2. a. _____ Muy contenta. b. _____ Furiosa.
3. a. _____ En la iglesia. b. _____ En el mercado. c. _____ En el patio.

Paso 2

Now read the following statements and indicate whether they are **Cierto** (**C**) or **Falso** (**F**). Think about both what you have seen and heard in the video episode and what you know about the characters from other sources.

C F 1. Ángela estudió en la Universidad de Puerto Rico, en San Juan.
C F 2. Cuando la mamá de Ángela se enfermó, Ángela se quedó a vivir con la abuela.
C F 3. El padre de Ángela venía todos los fines de semana a San Germán.
C F 4. Pero en San Germán, Ángel no tenía interés en pintar.

Paso 3

Now listen again as Raquel gives the answers to the previous items. Then continue to answer her questions.

Act. B, Suggestion: You
may want to have students
do this activity in pairs.
Act. B, Answers: 1. *materna* 2. *una finca* 3. *ya
murió* 4. *sirvienta* 5. *yerno*
6. *muy estrechas* 7. *su
padre* 8. *una copa*

1. a. Poesías.   b. Recuerdos.   c. Fotografías.
2. a. Sí.   b. No.

Actividad B. Doña Carmen, suegra de Ángel

You have seen doña Carmen in a previous video episode of *Destinos.* How much do you remember about her from before and from this episode? Complete the following statements about her.

1. Doña Carmen es la abuela... paterna / materna... de Ángela.
2. Doña Carmen y su esposo eran dueños (*owners*) de... una finca / una farmacia.
3. El esposo de doña Carmen... ya murió / está ahora en otra ciudad.
4. Doña Carmen vive ahora en San Germán con una... nieta / sirvienta.
5. Ángel era el... hijastro / yerno... de doña Carmen.
6. Los dos tenían relaciones... poco estrechas / muy estrechas.
7. Doña Carmen sugiere que Ángela examine las cosas de... su padre / su hermano.
8. Doña Carmen le tiene una sorpresa a Ángela: un libro / una copa... de su abuela Rosario.

Nota cultural   La comida de Puerto Rico

Laura, Ángela's cousin, is still a growing girl who eats a lot. As her grandmother says, **¡Siempre tiene hambre esta chica!**

In this video episode, you saw the dessert course of a pleasant meal served in doña Carmen's house: **pasta de guayaba** (*guava paste*), which is served with cheese (**queso**). **La guayaba** is a tropical fruit from the West Indies, used in making preserves, jellies, and pastries of many kinds. Other fruits typical of Puerto Rican cuisine include **las piñas**, **los cocos**, **los mangos**, **los plátanos**, **la parcha** (*passion fruit*), and so on.

Bananas in particular appear in a number of dishes, including **el mofongo**, a type of fritter made with fried and baked bananas and served with a variety of sauces (shrimp or chicken, for example).

Actividad C.   ¿Qué pasó?

Paso 1

By now, you should be able to create simple sentences to talk about what happened in an episode of *Destinos*. Using the phrases below as a guide and taking turns with a classmate, talk about what happened in **Episodio 22** from beginning to end. Help each other to form the sentences when necessary. ¡OJO! The phrases are not in chronological order.

Personas: doña Carmen, Ángela, Raquel, Laura

1. darle una caja (que contiene algo especial)
2. revisar las cosas personales de Ángel
3. llegar a San Germán
4. pasar la noche en Ponce
5. hablar de las relaciones entre ella y su yerno
6. rezar (*to pray*) en la iglesia
7. ir al taller para recoger (*pick up*) el coche
8. leer *Recuerdos*, el libro de Ángel

Paso 2

Now, with your partner, take turns reading your sentences aloud to the class. Did everyone come up with more or less the same sentences in the same order?

3

VOCABULARIO DEL TEMA

Cambios de estado

Many Spanish verbs can be used with reflexive pronouns to express a change of state or condition. For example, the verb **casarse** expresses a change from single to marital status. Here are some additional verbs that express changes.

acostumbrarse	to become accustomed	**enfermarse**	to get sick
adaptarse	to adapt	**enojarse (con)**	to become angry (with)
alegrarse (de)	to become happy (about)	**molestarse**	to get irritated
cansarse (de)	to get tired (of)	**quedarse** + *adj.*	to become + *adj.*
divorciarse (de)	to get divorced (from)	**reponerse**	to get better; to get over (*an illness*)
enfadarse (con)	to become angry (with)		

Two other verbs that you already know are often used with adjectives to express similar changes: **ponerse**, **volverse**.

Don Fernando **se** va a **poner** muy contento.
A veces la gente **se vuelve** loca por las grandes tragedias.

- **Ponerse** means *to become*, *to get*, but in a physical or emotional sense: to become sick, sad, red (in the face), and so on.
- **Volverse** expresses *to become*, *to get* when the change is drastic and possibly permanent. It is frequently combined with the adjective **loco** (*crazy*).

Actividad A.   Ángela y Raquel
Paso 1
You now know even more about Ángela Castillo, and you have seen Ángela and Raquel interact over a number of video episodes. What have you observed about them? Start by indicating which of the following statements describe Ángela.

Act. A, *Paso 1*, Answers: 1, 5

1. _____ Se molesta fácilmente... y con frecuencia.
2. _____ No es muy enérgica y se cansa rápidamente.
3. _____ Quiere casarse y tener una familia grande.
4. _____ No se acostumbra fácilmente a vivir en ciertas situaciones o lugares nuevos.
5. _____ A veces se pone muy pensativa.

Act. A, *Paso 1*, Answer: 5

Paso 2
Now indicate which of the same statements you think apply to Raquel.

1. _____   2. _____   3. _____   4. _____   5. _____

Paso 3
Would you say that Raquel and Ángela are similar or very different? Listen to a brief description of them on the CD and see whether your observations were accurate.

Actividad B.   Adivinanzas (*Guesses*)
Most of the characters you have met or heard about so far in *Destinos* have undergone changes of one kind or another. Using the phrases below, create a statement about a character and present it to the rest of the class. Can your classmates guess or determine whom you are talking about? ¡OJO! Some statements may apply to more than one character.

Act. B, Variation: You make statements and students guess whom you are talking about. Use the *yo* form in your statements, as if you were the person, so that students are reminded of the contrast between first- and third-person forms in the preterite.

MODELO: se casó → Esta persona se casó dos veces. ¿Quién es?

1. se casó
2. se divorció
3. se enfermó
4. se enfadó
5. se molestó

6. se alegró
7. se puso muy triste
8. se acostumbró a
9. (no) se repuso

Act. C, Suggestion: You may want to have students work in pairs, sharing this personal information.

Actividad C.   ¿Y tú?

Which of the following statements are true for you? Change the statements that do not describe you to make them true for you.

1. _____ Me molesto por cualquier (*any*) cosa.
2. _____ Cuando me enfado con alguien, no digo nada. Me quedo callado/a (*silent*).
3. _____ Me enfermo fácilmente y con frecuencia de gripe (*flu*), de resfriados (*colds*), …
4. _____ No me adapto fácilmente a nuevas situaciones o lugares.
5. _____ Cuando me enfermo, me repongo rápidamente.
6. _____ Me vuelvo loco/a cuando los otros no hacen lo que (*what*) deben hacer.
7. _____ No pienso casarme.
8. _____ Me canso fácilmente. No tengo la energía de Ángela y Raquel.

Act. D, Suggestion: Assign as a mini-composition for homework. Have students share the information about themselves in pairs the following day.

Actividad D.   La última vez...

Describe the last time you became very angry, very sad, or very happy.

MODELO: La última vez que me enojé fue porque/cuando…
La última vez que me puse triste, estaba en…
La última vez que me alegré mucho fue porque/cuando…
La última vez que me molesté, estaba en…

4

UN POCO DE GRAMÁTICA

The Workbook/Study Guide contains more detailed explanation and practice of this grammar point.

Suggestions:
• After reviewing the imperfect, give out as homework a worksheet that requires students to review the present and the preterite [so that they won't forget previous forms when learning a new form]. You can have a list of infinitives, a list of subject pronouns, and an indication of the tense(s) in which you would like each verb to be conjugated.
• Review "used to" with the imperfect by getting students to be nostalgic about previous decades: *En los años 70, escuchábamos* _____, *bailábamos* _____, *usábamos las palabras* _____. *En los años 80, íbamos a* _____, *llevábamos* _____, etc.

More About Using the Imperfect

The imperfect tense is also used to talk about habitual or repeated events in the past. How often the event or action occurred is not expressed.

DOÑA CARMEN:

Éramos dueños de una gran finca de caña. A veces **empleábamos** más de doscientos hombres para los trabajos.

We were the owners of a large sugarcane plantation. At times we used to employ more than two hundred men to get the work done.

> El padre de Ángela **venía** todos los fines de semana.
>
> *Ángela's father would come every weekend.*
>
> You will learn more about using the imperfect in this way in the Workbook/Study Guide.

Actividad. **Hablando del pasado**

Using the cues provided, tell the class about something you *used to do* or something that *used to happen to you* often. Be sure to include a general time frame for your sentences **(cuando era niño/a, en la escuela primaria/secundaria, cuando tenía seis años…)**.

1. dormía
2. miraba/veía
3. (no) comía
4. me acostaba
5. estudiaba
6. (no) me gustaba
7. iba mucho a
8. leía
9. ¿ ?

ᵃ*flower pots*

5

LECTURA CULTURAL

La economía de Puerto Rico

Before reading the following selection about the economy of modern-day Puerto Rico, consider what you have already learned about the island. For what reason would many people from other countries come to visit it? If you thought of the tourist industry, you were correct. It is one of the mainstays of the present-day Puerto Rican economy. Now listen again as the narrator tells you about the history of San Germán. His description includes information about another important aspect of the economy of the Island.

Cuando ya había desaparecido[1] el mito del oro de América, los españoles empezaron la obra de sacarle a[2] su vasto territorio otro tipo de riqueza. Así es que, casi desde el principio, Puerto Rico fue un país agrícola. En la actualidad,[3] la agricultura sigue siendo importante para la economía puertorriqueña, junto con el desarrollo[4] in-

[1]había… *had disappeared*   [2]sacarle… *extracting from*   [3]En… *Currently*   [4]*development*

dustrial que ha traído[5] el siglo XX. Y, por fin, existe el turismo, una de las industrias más importantes del Puerto Rico moderno. Veamos estos tres aspectos de la economía puertorriqueña.

La agricultura

Por muchos años, el azúcar fue el producto más importante de Puerto Rico. Existían grandes fincas de caña, como la de doña Carmen y su esposo, y Puerto Rico era un gran exportador de azúcar. En la década de los años 40, el gobierno trató de diversificar la economía de Puerto Rico, para que la Isla no dependiera tanto de un solo producto. Pero muchos todavía siguen con el cultivo de la caña.

Plantación de bananas en Puerto Rico

El café también figura en la economía de la Isla desde muy temprano. En 1738 se empezó a cultivar en Puerto Rico un café aromático, de un suave sabor.[6] Este café era muy apreciado en las cortes reales de España y de otros países europeos. Actualmente las exportaciones anuales de café superan[7] los 70 millones de dólares.

¿Y otros productos? Hay plantaciones de arroz, de frutas tropicales —sobre todo de bananas— y algo de ganadería.[8]

La industria

Para la economía de la Isla, la industria moderna es lo que era la agricultura en siglos pasados. Hay más de dos mil fábricas[9] en la Isla, y Puerto Rico es hoy un gran productor de farmacéuticos, petroquímicas y productos metalúrgicos. Es necesario mencionar también la industria relacionada con la agricultura: ingenios[10] de azúcar, manufactura del tabaco y de textiles.

Y, por fin, sería imposible hablar de la industria puertorriqueña sin mencionar uno de sus productos más famosos: el ron. Famoso por su calidad, el ron puertorriqueño se produce cerca de San Juan. ¿No has visto[11] algunos anuncios[12] de la campaña publicitaria que se hacía al ron puertorriqueño, con personajes famosos?

La industria por excelencia

En las últimas décadas, Puerto Rico se ha convertido en[13] uno de los lugares más visitados del Caribe. La Isla ofrece al turista complejos hoteleros, casinos, restaurantes, y también campos de golf y facilidades para practicar todos los deportes acuáticos como el buceo[14] y el *surf*. Estos complejos modernos se encuentran sobre todo en San Juan —en las famosas playas de Isla Verde y Condado—, pero hay también hoteles y paradores[15] modestos en la capital y por todas partes de la Isla.

Nota al pie[16]

Con este retrato optimista de la economía de la Isla, no se quiere dar a entender[17] que Puerto Rico no tenga problemas económicos. De hecho, la tasa de desempleo[18] es alta, y muchos puertorriqueños emigran a las grandes ciudades industriales del este de los Estados Unidos —en Nueva York, Nueva Jersey y Pensilvania— en busca de trabajo.

[5]ha... *has brought*   [6]suave... *smooth flavor*   [7]*exceed*   [8]*cattle raising*   [9]*factories*   [10]*mills*   [11]¿No... *Haven't you seen*   [12]*ads*   [13]se... *has become*   [14]*snorkeling*   [15]*inns*   [16]Nota... *Footnote*   [17]no... *one does not imply*   [18]tasa... *unemployment rate*

Lectura cultural, Preguntas: 1. ¿*Desde el principio, qué tipo de país fue Puerto Rico?* (*un país agrícola*) 2. ¿*Cuáles son los tres contribuidores más importantes a la economía de Puerto Rico?* (*la agricultura, la industria, el turismo*) 3. *Identifiquen cuatro productos muy importantes de Puerto Rico.* (*el azúcar, el café, el arroz, las frutas tropicales*) 4. ¿*Cuántas fábricas hay en la Isla?* (*más de 2.000*) 5. ¿*Qué producen?* (*farmacéuticos, petroquímicas, productos metalúrgicos*) 6. ¿*Cuál es el producto más famoso?* (*el ron*) 7. ¿*Cuáles son algunas atracciones turísticas?* (*complejos hoteleros, casinos, restaurantes, el golf, deportes acuáticos como el buceo y el surf*) 8. ¿*Adónde emigran muchos puertorriqueños?* (*a Nueva York, a Nueva Jersey, a Pensilvania*) 9. ¿*Por qué quitan su país?* (*por la tasa de desempleo muy alta, para buscar trabajo*)

Actividad. Opiniones

The following questions ask for your opinions or ideas about Puerto Rico. Answer as best you can, making inferences when necessary.

1. En la actualidad, ¿se puede decir que la economía de Puerto Rico es más diversa que antes?
2. ¿En qué sentido se puede decir que Puerto Rico depende de ingresos (*income*) externos?
3. Si Puerto Rico depende del turismo, ¿qué cosas pueden tener un efecto negativo en esa industria?

6

INTERCAMBIO

Paso 1
Using the phrases below, create statements about what your instructor used to do.

1. Cuando era un/a niño/a de 5 años…
2. Durante su adoloscencia…
3. El semestre pasado…

Paso 2
Share your statements with two other classmates. Among the three of you, select the three statements most likely to be true.

Paso 3
Each group should read its statements out loud. Your instructor will say whether or not they are true. Which group was correct on all three?

VOCABULARIO

Los verbos

acostumbrarse	to become accustomed
adaptarse	to adapt
alegrarse (de)	to become happy (about)
cansarse (de)	to get tired (of)
divorciarse (de)	to get divorced (from)
enfadarse (con)	to become angry (with)
enfermarse	to get sick
enojarse (con)	to become angry (with)
molestarse	to get irritated
reponerse	to get better; to get over (*an illness*)

Los lugares

la finca	farm; ranch; hacienda
el mar	sea

Las personas

el/la dueño/a	owner

Las cosas

la caña de azúcar	sugar cane
la hoja	leaf; sheet

Los conceptos

el recuerdo	memory
quedarse + *adj.*	to become + *adj.*
volverse (ue) loco/a	to go crazy

Repaso: **ponerse** + *adj.*

LECCIÓN 23

VISTA AL MAR*

Suggestion: Have students look at the photo, describe what they see, and talk about what they think might happen. Ask questions about the photo to prompt student discussion.

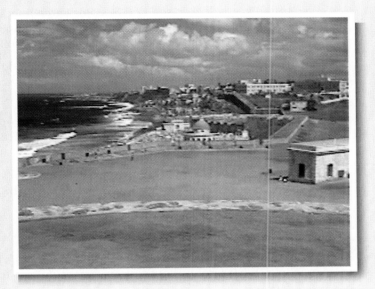

A View of the Sea

OBJETIVOS

The materials in **Lección 23** of the Textbook and the Workbook/Study Guide will help you better understand the video episode and take you beyond it, giving you additional information about places and characters in the series. The Textbook will also help you to develop skill in using the Spanish language. In this lesson, you will learn

*   ways to express in Spanish the parts of a house and some appliances
*   another way to describe what someone is doing right now

You will also learn about Puerto Ricans who live and work in the continental United States.

Be sure to work through all parts of the lesson. When you see a headphones symbol in the margin, listen to the CD for **Lección 23**. Answers or hints for many activities are given in Appendix 1. Be sure to check your answers for each activity before going on to the next one.

The interactive CD-ROM to accompany *Destinos* contains additional practice with the video storyline and will help you improve your skills in Spanish.

BEFORE VIEWING . . .

Preliminary: See Faculty Guide for additional information and activities for this lesson.
• **Variation:** For activities marked with the headphones icon, you may wish to read from the Audioscript instead of playing the CD.
• **Suggestion:** Make sure students are familiar with the activities before you read from the Audioscript or play the CD.

1

PREPARACIÓN

Suggestions:
• Before watching the video, go over the vocabulary list at the end of the chapter and have students pronounce the words after you.
• Assign *Preparación* activities as homework and then go over them quickly in class before viewing the video.

Act. A, Answers: 1. a
2. c 3. b

Actividad A.

In the last video episode of *Destinos* Raquel and Ángela spent time with doña Carmen, Ángela's grandmother. Do you remember the most important things that happened? Select the best answer for the following questions.

1. ¿Cómo reaccionó la abuela cuando Ángela le dijo que quería ir a México a conocer a don Fernando?
   Estaba _____. a. a favor b. en contra c. indiferente

2. ¿Qué encontró Ángela entre las cosas de su padre?
   Encontró _____. a. un álbum de fotografías b. un libro de poesías
   c. unas hojas con sus recuerdos

3. ¿Qué le dio la abuela a Ángela?
   Le dio _____. a. un retrato de Rosario b. la copa de bodas de Rosario c. una carta de Rosario

Act. B, Point Out: As a prediction activity, this has no (in)correct answers.

Actividad B.

As you know, Ángela wants to sell her parents' apartment in el Viejo San Juan. What kind of house or apartment do you think she will want to move into?

Ángela va a querer

a. _____ una casa antigua, en el Viejo San Juan, similar a la casa de sus padres.

b. _____ un apartamento en un edificio (*building*) muy moderno con una vista panorámica al mar.

c. _____ un apartamento pequeño pero cómodo, cerca de la universidad (donde trabaja su novio).

Para pensar...

¿Ha hablado (*Has . . . spoken*) Ángela con su hermano Roberto sobre la venta de la casa de sus padres? ¿Debe vender la casa sin consultar con él?

Actividad C.

Raquel will meet this person during this video episode. Look at the photograph carefully and consider the setting, then answer the following question.

Act. C, Answer: a   ¿Quién es esta persona? ¿Por qué aparece en este episodio?

a. _____ Ángela necesita pedirle permiso a su jefa (*boss*) para ausentarse de su trabajo. Quiere ir a México con Raquel por una o dos semanas.

b. _____ Además de ser su jefa, también es una buena amiga de Ángela y por eso quiere consultar con ella lo que (*what*) debe hacer en este caso.

c. _____ Ángela quiere renunciar (*quit*) a su trabajo en el banco. Raquel la acompaña para darle apoyo (*support*).

Para pensar, **Suggestion:** Ask students to describe Ángela's boyfriend in as much detail as possible, using what they know about Ángela to form a mental image. Encourage them to use their imaginations and take the description as far as they can.

Para pensar...

Además de su jefa, hay otra persona importante en la vida de Ángela que vas a conocer en este episodio: su novio. ¿Qué tipo de persona será (*will he probably be*)? ¿Será alto? ¿rubio? ¿extrovertido? ¿tímido? ¿Qué imagen tienes de él en este momento?

 . . . AFTER VIEWING

2

¿TIENES BUENA MEMORIA?

Act. A, Suggestion: Give students about 3 minutes to complete the activity individually or in pairs and then compare answers as a whole class.

Actividad A.   ¿Relaciones serias?
Paso 1

Part of the video episode you have just seen focused on Raquel's activities. Can you complete this summary of the episode without consulting the choices that follow?

Esta tarde Raquel está en la facultad[a] de la Universidad de Puerto Rico. Está esperando a Ángela, y ella _____[1] su novio Jorge.

Ángela y Raquel regresaron de San Germán _____.[2] Tan pronto como[b] Raquel llegó a su habitación, hizo una llamada de larga distancia _____.[3] Afortunadamente Arturo estaba en casa y los dos pudieron hablar un rato. Arturo le sorprendió a Raquel cuando le dijo que _____.[4]

Ahora Raquel está un poco perpleja. Arturo le gusta mucho, eso sí. Pero Raquel _____[5] quiere tener relaciones serias en estos momentos.

[a]*campus*   [b]Tan... *As soon as*

Act. A, Answers: 1. *está hablando afuera con* 2. *ayer por la noche* 3. *a Buenos Aires para hablar con Arturo* 4. *la quería mucho* 5. *no sabe si*

1. está hablando afuera (*outside*) con / está tratando de llamar a
2. ayer por la mañana / ayer por la noche
3. a Buenos Aires para hablar con Arturo / a México para hablar con Pedro
4. la quería mucho / ya no la quería como antes
5. no sabe si / está segura que

Paso 2

Now listen to part of Raquel's story review again and check your answers. Raquel's words are not identical to the written summary, but they are close enough to allow you to follow along with ease.

Actividad B. Ángela

By now, you should have a fairly good idea of who Ángela is as a person, where she works, who the important people in her life are, and so on. In groups of three, create a brief biography of Ángela. Then present it to the class. See if your group can think of at least one thing that the other groups might not say. Each group's biography should include at least five facts or observations about Ángela.

Act. B, Suggestion: Give students 5–10 minutes to write their biographies of Ángela.

Act. B, Follow-up: Keep track of the various facts and observations by listing each group's sentences on the board, perhaps with a student volunteer writing. Use the information for a brief true/false quiz or include it on a chapter quiz.

Act. B, Variation: Rather than writing facts or observations about Ángela, have students make up 5 true/false statements about her. Have each group present its statements to the class, who must identify them as true or false and correct the false statements. Or, collect the statements, edit them, and use them for a quiz.

3

VOCABULARIO DEL TEMA

Las partes de una casa

el baño	bathroom	**el balcón**	balcony	**la escalera**	stairway
la cocina	kitchen	**el jardín**	garden	**el piso**	floor
el comedor	dining room	**el patio**	patio	**la planta baja***	ground floor
el cuarto	bedroom	**la terraza**	terrace	**la puerta**	door
la sala	living room			**la ventana**	window
		el estacionamiento	parking		
		la vista (a)	view (of)		

---

* See the **Nota cultural** for an explanation of how floors of a building are named in Spanish.

Suggestions: • Practice pronunciation with choral and individual repetition. • Bring magazine pictures of the interiors of houses to introduce and practice the vocabulary. As you introduce each item, ask students *¿Tienen _____ en su casa?* or *¿Cuántos/as _____ hay en su casa?* Be sure to clarify whether they are talking about their parents' house or their own. Ask *¿Qué cosas hay en la casa de sus padres que no tienen Uds. aquí en la universidad?* Be prepared to supply additional vocabulary for rooms, household appliances, and related items.

Algunos aparatos domésticos

la estufa   stove
el horno (de microondas)
  (microwave) oven
la lavadora   clothes washer   **el estéreo**   stereo
el lavaplatos dishwasher   **el radio**   radio
la nevera   refrigerator   **el televisor**   television set
la secadora   clothes dryer   **la videocasetera**   VCR

Note the following information about the use of these terms in Spanish.

- The names of most rooms of a house are the same throughout the majority of the Spanish-speaking world. The word for *bedroom* does vary widely, however. The following terms may be used: **la alcoba** (Spain), **el cuarto** (used in Puerto Rico and in several other countries), **el dormitorio** (very widely used), **la recámara** (Mexico). **La habitación** is also used to mean *bedroom*, but for many native speakers of Spanish this term means only a hotel room.

- The feminine terms **la radio** and **la televisión** refer to the media. Thus one can say: **Me gusta mirar la tele(visión) y me gusta escuchar la radio**. The masculine nouns **el radio** and **el televisor** refer to the actual radio or TV set. Not all speakers of Spanish use these terms consistently, however.

Act. A, Answer: b

Apartamento Moderno
****
Sala/Comedor Aparte
Patio
Amplia cocina completa
Dos cuartos
Baño

a.

Se Alquila Apartamento
─────────────
2° Piso
Sala Grande, Comedor
Balcón/Terraza con vista al mar
Cocina completa
Dos cuartos
Tres baños

b.

Actividad A.   ¿Qué decide Ángela?

Listen again as Ángela, Raquel, and Blanca, the realtor, discuss the features of one of the apartments that Ángela is considering. Then indicate which of these two advertisements corresponds to the apartment. Take a few seconds now to scan both of them. As you listen to the conversation, you may want to check off features in the advertisements as you hear them, noting the number of each and any other factors.

Actividad B.   ¿Qué tiene el *Town House*?
Paso 1

Listen to the same three characters as they walk through the town house. Use the advertisement you didn't select in **Actividad A** to keep track of the features.

Paso 2

Now compare the features of the apartment (**Actividad A**) and the town house (this activity) by indicating whether the following statements are true (**Cierto**), false (**Falso**), or unable to be determined (**No se sabe**).

C   F   NSS   1. El apartamento tiene una vista hermosa al mar, el *town house* no.
C   F   NSS   2. Los dos tienen tres baños.
C   F   NSS   3. Los dos tienen estacionamiento.

Act. B, *Paso 2*, Variation: Have students work in pairs. One partner looks at the 2 advertisements on p. 227 while the other reads the true/false/don't know statements on p. 228. The person reading the statements marks the answers of the first person. You may want to go over the answers as a whole class or have student pairs look them up in the back of the book.

Act. B, *Paso 2*, Answers:
1. C 2. F 3. C 4. NSS 5. F
6. C 7. F 8. NSS (See
Appendix 1 for expanded
answers.)

C   F   NSS   4. Los dos tienen lavaplatos.

C   F   NSS   5. Los dos son de dos pisos.

C   F   NSS   6. La cocina del *town house* es más grande.

C   F   NSS   7. La sala y el comedor están juntos en el *town house*.

C   F   NSS   8. La estufa y la nevera son nuevas en los dos.

Act. C, Follow-up: Students ask each other questions about where things are located in their own residences. If students live in a residence hall, it is likely that they have only one room with no kitchen. If that is the case, tell them to base their responses on the place they consider their permanent home.

Actividad C.   ¿Dónde se encuentran?

With a partner, take turns asking about where certain appliances are usually found in a house. Use the replies (**respuestas**) to help create your answers.

MODELO: TÚ: ¿Se encuentra un estéreo en el garaje?

COMPAÑERO/A: Casi nunca se encuentra un estéreo en el garaje.

Aparatos	**Lugares**	**Respuestas**
un estéreo	el balcón	nunca
una estufa	el baño	casi nunca
una lavadora	la cocina	frecuentemente
una nevera	el cuarto	casi siempre
un teléfono	el garaje	siempre
un televisor	la sala	

Act. D, Suggestion: Assign as homework and have students compare their descriptions in the next class. Or, collect the descriptions for a grade.

Actividad D.   ¿Dónde vives? ¿Dónde te gustaría vivir?

Describe where you live now and what you would like a future dwelling to contain. Follow these models.

MODELOS: Vivo ahora en un(a) _____. Tiene _____,

_____, ... Los _____ (no) son grandes.

También tiene _____. No tiene _____.

El/La _____ (no) es moderno/a.

Me gustaría vivir en un(a) _____ con

_____...

Nota cultural, **Suggestion:** Assign as homework. If you have lived in a Spanish-speaking country, you may wish to describe your housing there and compare it with your present living quarters.

Nota cultural   Vivo en el segundo piso

Just as in this country, a wide range of types of housing is available in the Spanish-speaking world. In large cities the most common type of housing is an apartment or condominium, often in a high-rise building. An option available depending on the country is a separate house (generally called **una casa** but also called **un chalet** in Spain). Of the dwellings you have seen so far, Teresa Suárez's apartment best typifies middle-class housing. Héctor's apartment (seen only from the outside) is typical of people of more modest means.

The apartments Ángela looks at in this video episode, while luxurious by some standards, are relatively typical of modern apartments in most parts of the world. Note that Ángela and the agent use the term *town house*; in other parts of the Spanish-speaking world **el condominio** or **la casa adosada** would probably be used.

Something that is quite different about Hispanic buildings is the way the floors are numbered. The ground floor is generally **la planta baja**. The next floor up (the second floor in this country) is **el primer piso**; the next floor (the third floor in this country) is **el segundo piso**; and so on. (This usage does not occur in Puerto Rico.)

Look at this floor plan. Is it for the first floor (**la planta baja**) or the second floor (**el primer piso**)? How do you know?

4

UN POCO DE GRAMÁTICA

The Workbook/Study Guide contains more detailed explanation and practice of this grammar point.

Note: You may wish to review the verb paradigm for *estar* in the imperfect and/or the progressive.

Point out: Remind students that the progressive forms are used much less frequently in Spanish than in English, because the Spanish simple present and imperfect are often used where English would use present progressive and past progressive, respectively.

Describing What Someone Was Doing

To describe what someone was doing at a given moment, you can use the imperfect of **estar** + the **-ndo** form of the verb.

Arturo **estaba hablando** con Raquel por teléfono.
Arturo was talking on the phone with Raquel.

Ángela, Raquel y la agente **estaban mirando** un apartamento.
Ángela, Raquel, and the agent were looking at an apartment.

This construction is called the past progressive. Like the present progressive, it places special emphasis on the ongoing nature of the action. You will learn more about these forms in the Workbook/Study Guide.

Act., Suggestion: Assign as homework and have students present their sentences to the class the following day.

Act., Follow-up: Have students use the listed activities as points of departure for creating sentences about themselves that may be either true or false. Working in pairs, or as a whole class, students take turns reading their sentences aloud for others to guess whether they are true or false.

Actividad. **En ese momento...**
Paso 1

Decide who in the class was doing the following activities last night at the times indicated.

MODELO: Anoche a las diez, Susie estaba viendo la tele.

1. estaba viendo la tele / 10:00
2. estaba trabajando / 9:00
3. estaba estudiando en casa / 11:30
4. estaba leyendo una novela / 8:00
5. estaba comiendo algo / 6:00
6. estaba bebiendo algo / 9:30
7. estaba bailando / 12:30
8. estaba besando a su novio/a (esposo/a) / 8:30
9. estaba escuchando música / 11:00
10. estaba ¿ ? / 7:30

Paso 2
Were you right? Read your sentences aloud to the class. The people you talk about should tell you if you were right (**Sí, tienes razón**) or not (**No, no tienes razón**).

5

LECTURA CULTURAL

Los puertorriqueños en los Estados Unidos

In **Episodio 23** you learned about Puerto Ricans who live in the continental United States. Before you read this passage, refresh your memory about them by listening again to the narrator.

Lectura cultural, **Suggestion:** Assign as homework and go over answers quickly in class. Remind students that they should not expect to understand every word of the reading, but rather to get the main ideas.

Lectura cultural, **Preguntas:** 1. ¿Dónde vive la mayoría de los puertorriqueños en los EEUU? (en la costa este) 2. ¿Desde cuándo son los puertorriqueños ciudadanos de los EEUU? (desde 1917) 3. ¿Todos los puertorriqueños tienen derecho al voto en las elecciones presidenciales? (no, sólo los que residen en los EEUU).

Los puertorriqueños forman uno de los grandes grupos de hispanos que viven en los Estados Unidos continentales. Son más de dos millones. Viven sobre todo en la costa este, principalmente en las zonas metropolitanas de Nueva York, Connecticut, Nueva Jersey y Pensilvania.

Nueva York

Personas y personajes

Después de la Segunda Guerra mundial y junto con[1] la expansión económica de los Estados Unidos en esa época, los puertorriqueños llegaron al continente en gran número en busca de trabajo y de oportunidades para una vida mejor. En los últimos años, muchos de ellos han decidido[2] volver a la Isla, por varias razones. Pero hay también muchos que se quedan a vivir en el continente, y ellos, junto con la segunda y la tercera generaciones, forman parte integral de la economía y cultura de muchos estados. Muchos son bilingües y biculturales.

Muchos puertorriqueños hasta han encontrado[3] la fama en los Estados Unidos. ¿Puedes identificar a los siguientes puertorriqueños del pasado y del presente?

Marta Istomín	cantante[4]
José Ferrer y Jennifer López	jugador de béisbol que murió
Piri Thomas	trágicamente en un accidente de
Rita Moreno	aviación
Roberto Clemente	solista de la Ópera Metropolitana
Ricky Martin	de Nueva York
Justino Díaz	actores
	ex directora del John F. Kennedy
	Center for the Performing Arts
	escritor

[1]junto... *together with*   [2]han... *have decided*   [3]han... *have found*   [4]singer

La situación política

Puerto Rico es un Estado Libre Asociado de los Estados Unidos, y los puertorrique-ños son ciudadanos[5] estadounidenses desde 1917. Como tal[6] pueden ir y venir sin res-tricciones. Pero si viven en la Isla, no tienen derecho al voto en las elecciones presi-denciales. (En cambio, sí pueden votar si residen en el continente.) Puerto Rico tiene representantes en el Congreso estadounidense—se les llama *resident commissioners*—pero con poder[7] limitado ya que tienen voz pero no tienen voto.

En la actualidad, muchos puertorriqueños quieren que Puerto Rico se incorpore a los Estados Unidos como el estado número cincuenta y uno. Algunos prefieren que se independice. Otros desean que se mantenga el *status quo*.

[5]*citizens* [6]*Como... As such (As citizens)* [7]*power*

Actividad.   Opiniones
Answer the following questions about the Puerto Rican experience to the best of your knowledge.

1. Los puertorriqueños son ciudadanos de los Estados Unidos, pero se puede decir que su ciudadanía es «limitada». ¿En qué sentido es «limitada»?
2. Como sabes, muchos puertorriqueños llegan a los Estados Unidos conti-nentales para vivir. Según lo que sabes de sus motivos, ¿con qué otros grupos los asocias? Explica tus respuestas.
    a.   con los peregrinos (*pilgrims*)
    b.   con los irlandeses del siglo XIX y del comienzo del siglo XX
    c.   con los vietnameses de los años ochenta
    d.   ¿ ?

6

Intercambio

Paso 1
The class should divide itself into four groups and complete the tasks below.

> **Group 1:** Select six of the places in/around a house that appear on page 229 and number them 1–6.
> **Group 2:** Select six characters from the Puerto Rico episodes and number them 1–6.
> **Group 3:** Select six activities (e.g., **tomar un cerveza**) and number them 1–6.
> **Group 4:** Sit quietly and read something from your book.

Paso 2
Group 4 will now ask a series of questions. A member from each group must answer the question adhering to the numerical order in which the group se-lected places, characters, or activities. You may come up with some zany scenarios!

> MODELO:
>
>> GROUP 4: ¿Qué lugar tienen para el número 1?
>> GROUP 1: la terraza
>> GROUP 4: ¿Quién estaba en la terraza anoche?

GROUP 2: (*referring to item 1 on their list*) Olga estaba en la terraza.

GROUP 4: ¿Qué estaba haciendo Olga en la terraza?

GROUP 3: (*referring to item 1 on their list*) Estaba mirando la televisión.

Paso 3
Without looking at your notes or lists, which group can remember all six scenarios?

VOCABULARIO

Las partes de una casa
(Parts of a House)

el balcón	balcony
el baño	bathroom
la cocina	kitchen
el comedor	dining room
el cuarto	bedroom
el estacionamiento	parking
el jardín	garden
el patio	patio
el piso	floor
la planta baja	ground floor
la sala	living room
la terraza	terrace
la ventana	window
la vista (a)	view (of)

Repaso: **las escaleras, la habitación, la puerta**

Algunos aparatos domésticos
(Some Domestic Appliances)

el estéreo	stereo
la estufa	stove
el horno (de microondas)	(microwave) oven
la lavadora	clothes washer
el lavaplatos	dishwasher
la nevera	refrigerator
el radio	radio
la secadora	clothes dryer
el televisor	television set
la videocasetera	VCR

Las personas

el/la jefe/a	boss

24

EL DON JUAN*

*The Don Juan

OBJETIVOS

The materials in **Lección 24** of the Textbook and the Workbook/Study Guide will help you better understand the video episode and take you beyond it, giving you additional information about places and characters in the series. The Textbook will also help you to develop skill in using the Spanish language. In this lesson, you will learn

- vocabulary for talking about people's personality traits, both positive and negative
- more ways to use the preterite

You will also learn about a number of Puerto Rican musicians, artists, and literary figures.

Be sure to work through all parts of the lesson. When you see a headphones symbol in the margin, listen to the CD for **Lección 24**. Answers or hints for many activities are given in Appendix 1. Be sure to check your answers for each activity before going on to the next one.

The interactive CD-ROM to accompany *Destinos* contains additional practice with the video storyline and will help you improve your skills in Spanish.

BEFORE VIEWING . . .

Preliminary: See Faculty Guide for additional information and activities for this lesson.

● **Variation:** For activities marked with the headphones icon, you may wish to read from the Audioscript instead of playing the CD.

● **Suggestion:** Make sure students are familiar with the activities before you read from the Audioscript or play the CD.

1

PREPARACIÓN

Suggestions:
● Before watching the video, go over the vocabulary list at the end of the chapter and have students pronounce the words after you.
● Assign *Preparación* activities as homework and then go over them quickly in class before viewing the video.

Act. A, Suggestion: You may want to have students do this activity in pairs.

Act. A, Answers: Paragraph 1: *madre → padre; manda un telegrama → hace una llamada; hijos → hijas.* Paragraph 2: *de la tienda → del banco; meses → semanas; don Fernando va a enfadarse → es urgente.* Paragraph 3: *Los Ángeles → México; hermano → novio; del viaje → de la copa*

Actividad A.
Paso 1

Here is the text of the summary of **Episodio 23** that you will hear at the beginning of this video episode. But some of the details have been changed. Read through the text and correct as many details as you can. *Hint:* There are three incorrect details in each paragraph.

Al final de su estancia en San Germán, la abuela doña Carmen le da a Ángela un objeto muy especial… un regalo de su madre. Desde el hotel, Raquel manda un telegrama a Buenos Aires. Le cuenta a Arturo que Ángel ya murió… y que Ángel tenía dos hijos.

Ángela y Raquel hablan con la supervisora de la tienda donde Ángela trabaja. Le pide dos meses libres para ir a México a visitar a su abuelo don Fernando. Don Fernando está muy enfermo y Ángela le explica a la supervisora que don Fernando va a enfadarse.

Raquel y Ángela hacen los preparativos para salir mañana para Los Ángeles. Luego van a la universidad para ver a Jorge, el hermano de Ángela. En un patio de la universidad, Ángela y Jorge hablan del viaje.

 ### Paso 2
Now listen to the narration on the CD to discover whether you found all of the incorrect information.

Para pensar, Optional: You might refer students to the movie *Don Juan de Marco,* currently available on video.

Para pensar...

Piensa en el título de este episodio. ¿Qué es un «don Juan»? ¿A quién se podría referir este nombre en este episodio?

Una palabra importante que vas a oír en este episodio es **mujeriego** (*womanizer*). ¿Hay un hombre mujeriego en este episodio?

 ## Actividad B.

Listen to the following conversation between Ángela, Raquel, and Jorge on the CD. Then answer the question about it. A written version of the conversation is provided to help you understand it.

Act. B, Suggestion: You may want to have students do this activity in pairs, role-playing the dialogue.

> JORGE: ¿Por qué no nos vamos a vivir a Nueva York?
> ÁNGELA: No, gracias. Me gusta visitar esa ciudad, pero ¿vivir? No. Además, ¿no vas a formar una compañía de teatro acá en San Juan?
> JORGE: Hay en San Juan un cine[1] que puede funcionar como teatro.

[1]*movie theater*

Act. B, Answer: c

RAQUEL: Tiene que ser caro.[2]
JORGE: Sí, lo es. Pero es el mejor sitio. Perdónenme. Voy a cambiarme.

[2]*expensive*

Piensa bien en lo que (*what*) Jorge quiere hacer, porque esto va a provocar un conflicto. ¿Cuál podría (*could*) ser el conflicto?

a. _____ Ángela se opone a (*is opposed to*) la idea de Jorge. Por eso pelean (*they quarrel*).

b. _____ Jorge le pide consejos sobre asuntos legales a Raquel, pero ella se niega a (*refuses to*) dárselos.

c. _____ Ángela quiere ayudarle a Jorge, pero Raquel cree que no es una buena idea.

 . . . AFTER VIEWING

2

¿TIENES BUENA MEMORIA?

Actividad. Las preguntas de Raquel
Paso 1

As usual, Raquel recapped the most important moments of the video episode in her review at the end of the show. Here is a series of statements based on her review. Can you complete them with a few essential details? Your answers need not be long or involved.

Act. B, Answers *Possible answers:* 1. b 2. g 3. e 4. c 5. h, i 6. f, j 7. d, a (See Appendix 1 for more extended answers)

a. viajar a México en unos días
b. tutearla
c. Jorge las esperaba
d. estaba muy contento
e. lo esperaba un estudiante

f. el novio de Ángela
g. un don Juan
h. nadaban
i. hacía llamadas
j. se enojó con Raquel

1. Raquel fue con Ángela a la universidad para conocer a Jorge, el novio de Ángela. Para Raquel, fue una sorpresa cuando Jorge empezó a _____.

2. Por sus acciones, Raquel creía que Jorge era _____.

3. Cuando Ángela quería llevar a Raquel al museo de Oller, Jorge no quería acompañarlas porque _____.

4. Las dos mujeres vieron la colección de obras de Oller. _____ cuando salieron del museo. Todos fueron a unas tiendas cerca de la universidad, donde Raquel compró unos cassettes.

5. En el hotel, Jorge y Ángela _____ mientras Raquel _____. Habló con su madre y con Arturo.

Act., Follow-up: Have students work with a partner to create 2 more items similar to those in the activity. They should leave at least 2 blanks in each item and present their sentences to another pair of students to be completed.

6. Con su madre, Raquel habló sobre _____. Según su madre, Raquel no debe meterse (*get involved*) en la vida personal de otras personas. Efectivamente, cuando Raquel trató de hablar con Ángela, ésta (*the latter*) _____.

7. Con Arturo Raquel tuvo una conversación agradable porque Arturo _____. Raquel también se alegra, porque Arturo va a _____.

Paso 2
Now listen to Raquel's review and compare your answers with what she says.

Nota cultural   Más sobre la comida

In **Episodio 21**, on the road to San Germán, Ángela stopped the car to buy snacks at a small roadside store. Laura wanted **un pilón** (also calle d **un pirulí**), a fruit-based lollipop with seeds. Another popular Puerto Rican snack purchased by the characters in this video episode is **una piragua** (called a Sno Cone in parts of the United States), a small cone filled with chipped ice which is then flavored with a fruit syrup. Raquel and Ángela preferred **una piragua de frambuesa** (*raspberry*), while Jorge asked for **una piragua de tamarindo,** a tropical fruit popular in the Caribbean. Although Sno Cones are machine-made in the continental United States, in Puerto Rico **piragüeros** make them by hand and sell them from carts on the street.

Snack foods and treats are consumed all over the Spanish-speaking world and some places are famous for a particular food. Influenced by Italian culture, **heladerías** (*ice cream shops*) can be found on any street in Argentina, especially in Buenos Aires. In Spain **helados** of many kinds are also quite popular as a snack food, as are **patatas fritas** (*potato chips*). In Mexico street vendors routinely sell **chicle** (*chewing gum*) and **dulces** (*candy*) as well as **tacos**.

3 V**OCABULARIO DEL TEMA**

Emphasis: Remind students that, in Spanish, adjectives agree in number and gender with the nouns they modify and that they often answer the question *¿Cómo es?*

Para describir la personalidad

agresivo/a	aggressive	**desagradable**	disagreeable
alegre	happy	**desconfiado/a**	suspicious
cariñoso/a	affectionate	**egoísta**	selfish, egotistical
chistoso/a	funny	**encantador(a)**	charming
confiado/a	confident		

Suggestion: To review adjectives, prepare a *Firma aquí* activity with questions using the adjectives on the list: *¿Eres una persona agresiva/alegre/cariñosa/chistosa…?* Have students circulate in class asking and answering the questions and gathering the signatures of classmates who respond with *Sí*. Then have them report their findings to the class, using the model _____ *es una persona agresiva*. Point out that adjectives will be feminine, in agreement with *persona*, even when they refer to a male.

femenino/a	feminine	**optimista**	optimistic
grosero/a	crude, brutish	**pesimista**	pessimistic
gruñón/	grouchy, irritable	**sabio/a**	wise
gruñona		**simpático/a**	nice
ingenuo/a	naïve, ingenuous	**terco/a**	stubborn
inocente	innocent	**trabajador(a)**	hard-working
macho	manly, macho	**triste**	sad
mujeriego	womanizer,		
	a "don Juan" type		

You already know some of the preceding adjectives that describe people, and others are easy-to-learn cognates. Is an adjective that you often use to describe people missing from the list? Ask your instructor how to say it in Spanish or look it up in a dictionary. Think in particular about words that you need to describe family and friends.

   If you are describing someone's personality, use **ser** with these adjectives: **Arturo es encantador**. You can also say the following: **Esta persona es encantadora. Arturo es una persona encantadora.***

Actividad A.   ¿A quién se describe? (Parte 1)

Listen as the speaker on the CD describes one quality of each of the following characters from *Destinos*. Identify the person referred to, following the model. You will hear a possible answer on the CD. ¡OJO! More than one person may be correct for some items.

Act. A, Answers:
1. *Arturo es trabajador.*
2. *Jorge es muy macho.*
3. *Tía Olga es gruñona.*
4. *Ángela es ingenua.*
5. *Doña Carmen es sabia.*
6. *Jorge es agresivo.*
7. *Arturo es encantador.*
8. *Doña Carmen es cariñosa.* 9. *Laura es chistosa.* 10. *Raquel es simpática.*

> MODELO: (*you hear*) —Esta persona es trabajadora.
>   (*you say*) —Es Raquel.
>   (*you hear*) —Raquel es trabajadora.

Raquel Rodríguez   Jorge Alonso
Ángela Castillo   Arturo Iglesias
la tía Olga   Laura, la prima de Ángela
doña Carmen

1. …   2. …   3. …   4. …   5. …   6. …   7. …
8. …   9. …   10. …

Actividad B.   ¿A quién se describe? (Parte 2)

Now create your own descriptions of the same or other characters. With a partner, take turns presenting each description and identifying the person to whom it refers.

Act. B, Variation: Have student pairs describe themselves to each other.

Act. B, Follow-up: For homework, have students write a mini-composition describing a classmate.

---

* In these sentences the adjective is feminine because it agrees with the noun **persona**, even though Arturo is the person described.

Actividad C. ¿Cómo son?
What can you say about the following movie, TV, literary, and political personalities? Describe each of them as fully as you can. Then choose at least two well-known personalities and describe them.

> MODELO: Lucy → Lucy es una persona muy inocente y alegre. Su esposo Desi es un poco macho a veces. Sus aventuras con Ethel son siempre chistosas.

Act. C, Extension: You may want to pass out additional names of celebrities or pictures from magazines to enhance this activity.

1. Madonna
2. Kelsey Grammer («Frasier»)
3. Romeo y Julieta
4. Miss Piggy y Kermit la Rana
5. Scarlett O'Hara y Rhett Butler
6. el presidente (el vicepresidente) de los Estados Unidos
7. Cleopatra
8. Cristóbal Colón
9. ¿ ?

Actividad D. Mi pariente/amigo
Select at least one family member and a good friend, and describe them. Try to describe them as much as you can in general terms as well as give interesting details about their personality.

> MODELO: Mi _____ es _____, _____ y
> _____. Tiene _____ años y vive en/con
> _____. Le gusta(n) _____, pero no le
> gusta(n) nada _____.

4

UN POCO DE GRAMÁTICA

The Workbook/Study Guide contains more detailed explanation and practice of this grammar point.

Additional Uses of Some Preterite Forms

Use the preterite forms of **saber** (**supe, supiste...**) to describe the moment when someone learned or found out something.

Al final de este episodio, Ángela **supo** que hubo un accidente en la excavación.	*At the end of this episode Ángela found out that there was an accident at the excavation site.*

Use the preterite forms of **conocer** (**conocí, conociste...**) to indicate that someone met someone else for the first time.

En San Juan Raquel **conoció** a Ángela Castillo.	*Raquel met Ángela Castillo in San Juan.*

You will learn more about these uses of the preterite in the Workbook/Study Guide.

Suggestion: Remind students of the difference in the nature of the action of these verbs in the preterite vs. that in the imperfect. In the preterite, these verbs often point to the beginning of the action. For example, in the case of *saber,* to begin to know (a fact) = *to learn, to find out, to discover (a fact).* In the case of *conocer,* to begin to know (someone) = *to meet (someone).*

Actividad. **Personas y cosas importantes en la vida**
Paso 1

Make statements based on the following items. Use **conocí** or **supe** in each of your statements. Add details if you wish.

> MODELO: una persona importante que conociste en tu adolescencia →
> Conocí a mi mejor amiga en mi adolescencia. Teníamos doce años.

1. una persona importante que conociste en tu adolescencia
2. una persona importante en tu vida que conociste en la universidad
3. algo que supiste de adolescente que antes no sabías
4. algo que supiste de adulto que antes no sabías

Paso 2

Working with a partner, ask each other the questions from **Paso 1**. Write down your partner's answers and report them to the class.

5

LECTURA CULTURAL

El arte y la música en Puerto Rico

Lectura cultural, Preguntas: 1. *¿Cómo se llama el pintor más famoso de Puerto Rico?* (Francisco Oller) 2. *¿En qué año nació y cuándo murió?* (1833–1917). 3. *¿Dónde estudió?* (en Madrid y París) 4. *¿A quiénes conoció en Europa?* (Conoció a Cézanne y Pissarro) 5. *¿De regreso a Puerto Rico, qué estableció?* (la Academia Libre de Dibujo) 6. *Cuando abandonó la técnica impresionista, ¿a qué se dedicó?* (a un arte de Puerto Rico para los puertorriqueños) 7. *¿Cuáles son los elementos que crean una gran variedad de estilos populares en la música de Puerto Rico?* (los elementos africanos, los hispánicos y los autóctonos) 8. *¿Cómo se llama el ritmo más representativo de Puerto Rico?* (la salsa) 9. *¿De dónde es la madre de Pablo Casals?* (de Puerto Rico) 10. *¿Quiénes son dos escritores muy importantes de Puerto Rico?* (Julia de Burgos y René Marqués)

Throughout the Puerto Rican video episodes of *Destinos* you have caught glimpses of various aspects of the island's culture: popular and serious music, Jorge's interest in the theater, and works by a famous painter. The following reading will tell you more about music and the arts in Puerto Rico. Before you begin reading, listen again to Ángela's description of **El velorio** (*The Wake*) by Francisco Oller, as you look at this reproduction of it.

El mundo del arte

En Puerto Rico, Ángel Castillo encontró su verdadera inspiración como pintor. Lo inspiraba el colorido de la Isla, sus paisajes,[1] su gente... y sobre todo el mar. Pero eso pasó en la telenovela. En la realidad, el pintor puertorriqueño más famoso de todos es Oller.

Francisco Oller (1833–1917) fue uno de los primeros pintores americanos que se inspiró en el impresionismo francés. Estudió

El velorio de Francisco Oller

varios años en Madrid y París. Allí tuvo la oportunidad de conocer a pintores como

[1] *landscapes*

Cézanne y Pissarro, quienes ejercieron gran influencia en su pintura. De regreso a Puerto Rico, Oller estableció la Academia Libre de Dibujo[2] y Pintura en 1868. Su obra incluye retratos, paisajes y naturalezas muertas.[3] A partir de 1884 abandonó la técnica impresionista y se dedicó a la creación de un arte de Puerto Rico para los puertorriqueños. Se inspiró mucho en escenas de la cultura popular, como se ve en *El velorio*.

El mundo musical

Así como otras artes, la música ha sido[4] siempre muy importante en la vida de los puertorriqueños. Los elementos africanos se mezclaron[5] con los hispánicos y los autóctonos[6] para crear una gran variedad de estilos populares. En los últimos años, «la salsa», derivada de la vieja rumba, se ha convertido en el ritmo más representativo de Puerto Rico y del Caribe en general. El cantante de salsa va acompañado por un coro, piano, bajo[7] y varios instrumentos de percusión. La salsa ha contagiado a medio mundo[8] con su cálido[9] ritmo.

Al mismo tiempo, la música clásica tiene mucha importancia en la Isla, especialmente debido a la figura de Pablo Casals. Considerado uno de los mejores violoncelistas del mundo, Casals nació en Cataluña en 1876. Organizó un Festival de música en Francia, país en donde se exilió después de la Guerra Civil española. En 1957 trasladó[10] la celebración del Festival, y su residencia, a la tierra natal de su madre, Puerto Rico. En la Isla, desarrolló[11] una gran actividad musical. Murió en Río Piedras en 1973, a los noventa y siete años.

Todos los años, durante el mes de junio, el Festival Casals de Puerto Rico ofrece las interpretaciones musicales de los mejores virtuosos. Este Festival es, sin duda, uno de los acontecimientos[12] más importantes del mundo para los amantes de la música clásica.

El mundo literario

En cuanto a la literatura, un tema que les ha interesado a varios escritores es el de la identidad puertorriqueña. Entre los escritores puertorriqueños que escriben o escribieron en la Isla y en el continente, se destacan[13] especialmente dos.

- Julia de Burgos (1914–1953), poeta que escribió obras sobre su identidad como mujer y la identidad de Puerto Rico como país.
- René Marqués (1911–1979), autor de teatro contemporáneo que se preocupó por la identidad puertorriqueña en relación con los Estados Unidos.

[2]*Drawing* [3]naturalezas… *still lifes* [4]ha… *has been* [5]se… *mixed* [6]los… *native ones* [7]*bass*
[8]medio… *half the world* [9]*hot* [10]*he moved* [11]*he developed* [12]*events* [13]se… *stand out*

Actividad. ¿Probable o improbable?

Indica la oración que consideras más probable.

1. _____ Las obras de Oller son realistas.
   _____ Las obras de Oller son cubistas, como las de Picasso.
2. _____ La música de la salsa es buena para bailar.
   _____ La música de la salsa es buena para escuchar solamente.
3. _____ Julia de Burgos era una mujer muy tradicional.
   _____ Julia de Burgos tenía ideas feministas.

6

INTERCAMBIO

Paso 1
Prepare four to five statements about yourself. The statements should describe activities you have done or liked to do that reveal something about your personality. For example, saying that you once parachuted out of an airplane might suggest that you are daring and adventurous. The statements should address the following:

- at least three things you've done in the past that reflect something about you
- something that you used to do that you no longer do

Paso 2
In groups of four, take turns reading your statements. After hearing the statements, the others should discuss what personality traits the statements reveal.

VOCABULARIO

Los verbos

comunicarse (con)	to get in touch, contact (with)
meterse (en)	to get involved (with, in)
nadar	to swim
oponerse (a)*	to oppose

Para describir la personalidad
(To Describe Personality)

agresivo/a	aggressive
chistoso/a	funny
confiado/a	confident
desagradable	disagreeable
desconfiado/a	suspicious
egoísta	selfish, egotistical
encantador(a)	charming
femenino/a	feminine
grosero/a	crude, brutish
gruñón/ gruñona	grouchy, irritable
ingenuo/a	naïve, ingenuous
inocente	innocent
macho	manly, macho
mujeriego	womanizer, a "don Juan" type
optimista	optmistic
pesimista	pessimistic

sabio/a	wise
terco/a	stubborn
trabajador(a)	hard-working

Repaso: **alegre**, **cariñoso/a**, **simpático/a**, **triste**

---

* **Oponerse** is conjugated like **poner: me opongo, te opones...; me opuse, te opusiste...**

LECCIÓN 25

REFLEXIONES I*

*Reflections I

OBJETIVOS

This video episode is a review. Be sure to work through all parts of the lesson. When you see a headphones symbol in the margin, listen to the CD for **Lección 25**. Answers or hints for many activities are given in Appendix 1. Be sure to check your answers for each activity before going on to the next one.

The interactive CD-ROM to accompany *Destinos* contains additional practice with the video storyline and will help you improve your skills in Spanish.

BEFORE VIEWING . . .

Preliminary: See Faculty Guide for additional information and activities for this lesson.
•**Variation:** For activities marked with the headphones icon, you may wish to read from the Audioscript instead of playing the CD.
•**Suggestion:** Make sure students are familiar with the activities before you read from the Audioscript or play the CD.

1

PREPARACIÓN

Suggestions:
•Before watching the video, go over the vocabulary list at the end of the chapter and have students pronounce the words after you.
•Assign *Preparación* activities as homework and then go over them quickly in class before viewing the video.

Actividad.

Paso 1

All of the following events happened in **Episodio 24**, but in a different order. Read through all of the statements, then put them in order from 1 to 5.

Act., *Paso 1*, Answers:
a. 2 b. 3 c. 5 d. 1 e. 4

Act., Follow-up: After listening to the review, have students add as many events as they can to the original 5.

a. _____ Raquel, Ángela y Jorge hicieron unas compras en Río Piedras.

b. _____ Jorge y Ángela nadaban mientras Raquel hablaba por teléfono.

c. _____ Ángela y Raquel recibieron malas noticias.

d. _____ Raquel habló con Jorge, pero él no le cayó bien (*she didn't like him*).

e. _____ Raquel tenía una discusión muy fuerte (*nasty*) con Ángela.

Paso 2

Now listen to the review of **Episodio 24** that you will hear at the beginning of this video episode and check your answers. You will hear more information in the review than is given in the statements, so you will need to listen carefully.

***Para pensar*, Suggestion:** Have individual students prepare a list of the 5 most important events in the investigation so far, in their opinion. Then have them work in pairs or small groups to compare their lists and try to arrive at a consensus. Finally, compare lists as a whole class.

Para pensar...

Las noticias sobre Roberto dejan a Raquel en *shock*. En ese trance (*condition*), comienza a recordar y reflexionar sobre su difícil investigación. ¿Qué acontecimientos (*events*) de su investigación recuerda? ¿Cuáles son los acontecimientos más importantes desde su salida de México hasta su llegada a Puerto Rico?

. . . AFTER VIEWING

2

¿Tienes buena memoria?

Act., *Paso 1*, Suggestion: Give students about 3 minutes to complete the activity individually or in pairs and then compare answers as whole class.

Act., Answwers: *Paso 1:* 1. *No* 2. *No* 3. *Sí* 4. *Sí* 5. *Sí* 6. *Sí*

Act., *Paso 2*, Suggestion: Give students about 5 minutes to write their sentences. Circulate in the classroom, providing help where needed.

Actividad.   ¿Lo recuerda o no?

Paso 1

All of the following events have happened so far during Raquel's investigation, but did Raquel remember them as she thought back over the last few weeks? Indicate whether the following events were part of the review in **Episodio 25 (Sí)** or not **(No)**.

Sí   No   1. Raquel conoció a la familia de la persona que le escribió la carta a don Fernando.

Sí   No   2. Raquel viajó a Madrid en tren.

Sí   No   3. Conoció a Teresa Suárez y habló con ella sobre Rosario.

Sí   No   4. Supo que Rosario ya murió pero conoció a otro hijo de ella.

Sí   No   5. Raquel y Arturo se besaron por primera vez.

Sí   No   6. Héctor les dijo que Ángel se fue a vivir a Puerto Rico.

Paso 2

Create three more items that Raquel did not include but *could have* included in her review. Exchange lists with a partner and answer **Sí** or **No** for each new item.

Act., *Paso 2*, Point out: All of the items in *Paso 1* are in the preterite because they are events completed in the past. Items that students create for *Paso 2* should follow the same pattern.

3

Repaso de los Episodios 1–18

Actividad A.   Raquel habla con Teresa Suárez

You have now seen and heard several times the important conversation that takes place between Raquel and Teresa Suárez. It should be easier for you to understand most of it now. Here is part of the conversation, with all but the first of Teresa Suárez's lines missing. Complete the conversation with the appropriate lines from the following list of possibilities.

RAQUEL: En su carta Ud. le dice que Rosario no murió en la guerra.

TERESA: Es verdad. Rosario no murió. _____.[1]

RAQUEL: Ay...

TERESA: _____.[2]

RAQUEL: También en su carta Ud. le dice que Rosario tuvo un hijo.

TERESA: _____.[3]

RAQUEL: ¿Y qué nombre le puso?

TERESA: _____.[4]

RAQUEL: ¿Y dónde nació Ángel?

TERESA: _____.⁵

RAQUEL: ¿Y dónde vive Rosario ahora?

TERESA: _____.⁶

RAQUEL: ¿A la Argentina?

TERESA: _____.⁷

RAQUEL: ¿Y sabe dónde se estableció Rosario?

TERESA: _____.⁸

RAQUEL: ¿Se casó de nuevo?

TERESA: _____.⁹

RAQUEL: Sí, sí. Lo comprendo. ¿Y con quién se casó?

TERESA: _____.¹⁰

a.   Después de la guerra se fue a vivir a la Argentina.
b.   Sí. Todo este asunto es muy triste.
c.   Ángel… Ángel Castillo.
d.   Sí, sí. Como Ud. sabe, muchos españoles salieron del país después de la guerra.
e.   Pues sí. Rosario era muy atractiva… muy simpática. Y como ella creía que Fernando había muerto…
f.   Gracias a Dios, escapó de esa tragedia… pero ella creía que Fernando había muerto.
g.   Muy cerca de Buenos Aires. La última carta que recibí de ella fue cuando se casó de nuevo.
h.   Con un hacendado… un argentino llamado Martín Iglesias.
i.   Sí.
j.   En Sevilla, claro. Es allí donde conocí a Rosario.

Act. A, Answers:
1. f 2. b 3. i 4. c 5. j 6. a 7. d 8. g 9. e 10. h

Act. A, Follow-up: After students check their answers, have them act out the dialogue in pairs. Encourage them to be dramatic, like the actors in the original scene. You may want to replay the scene from the video to refresh students' memories.

Act. B, Answers: *Paragraph 1: un cuadro → una foto; artista → hombre Paragraph 2: él los invitó a entrar → los tres se quedaron fuera para hablar Paragraph 3: una foto → un cuadro; España → Puerto Rico Paragraph 4: tarjeta postal → carta*

Actividad B.   **La búsqueda en la Argentina**
Paso 1

In Argentina Raquel meets Arturo and the two search for Ángel, Arturo's half brother and the son of Rosario and don Fernando. Together they find Héctor Condotti, who once knew Ángel and who has some important information about him. The following narration about their meeting with Héctor contains some false information. Indicate the information you think is incorrect. *Hint:* There are one or two incorrect details in each paragraph.

Después de conocer a Héctor en el Piccolo Navio, Raquel y Arturo lo acompañaron a su casa. En la calle le mostraron a Héctor un cuadro de Ángel y le preguntaron si conocía al artista. «Ángel», respondió Héctor. «Claro que lo recuerdo bien. Era mi amigo.»

En el camino, empezaron a hablar de Ángel. Cuando llegaron a la casa de Héctor, él los invitó a entrar. Héctor les dijo que creía que Ángel consiguió trabajo en un barco. En ese momento, su esposa lo llamó y Héctor subió a su apartamento.

Act. B, Follow-up: Have students create a brief paragraph similar to those in the activity with information that followed the events described there. Have them include a few incorrect details. Then tell them to exchange paragraphs with a partner and try to find and correct the errors. Make sure students focus on errors of content, not on grammatical errors or mistakes in language.

Arturo y Raquel ya se iban, pero Héctor volvió con una foto de Ángel que le dio a Arturo. Muy conmovido,[1] Arturo le dio las gracias. Héctor también les dijo que creía que Ángel se quedó a vivir en el extranjero. No estaba seguro, pero creía que era en España.

Luego recordó una tarjeta postal que había recibido[2] de Ángel. Ésta debería[3] indicar la dirección de Ángel. Entonces Raquel y Arturo se fueron. Esa noche, los dos estaban muy pensativos, especialmente Arturo.

[1]*emotionally moved*   [2]había... *he had received*   [3]*would surely*

Paso 2
Now listen to the corrected narration on the CD and see whether you found all of the incorrect information.

Actividad C.   «Hay que dedicarle tiempo al corazón.»
During Raquel's stay in Argentina, she and Arturo begin to feel a strong attraction for each other. But Raquel must leave Buenos Aires to continue the search for Ángel. They begin to say their good-byes on a pier, after receiving Ángel's letter from Héctor. Complete their conversation with items from the lists.

Verbos: decir, dejar, estar, extrañar, me gustaría, recordar, te gustaría
Sustantivos: la búsqueda, el extranjero, el tiempo, trabajo, el primer vuelo
Adjetivos: muy bien, muy mal, regular
El tiempo: muchos años, unas semanas, unos pocos días

Act. C, Answers: 1. *el primer vuelo* 2. *muy mal* 3. *unos pocos días* 4. *muchos años* 5. *extrañar* 6. *la búsqueda* 7. *Te gustaría* 8. *trabajo* 9. *dejar*

ARTURO: ¿Ya decidiste cuándo te vas a ir?

RAQUEL: Debería tomar _____.[1] Don Fernando está

_____.[2] Y no puedo tardarme mucho.

ARTURO: Hace _____[3] que te conozco... y parece como si hiciera[a]

_____.[4]

RAQUEL: Yo siento lo mismo.

ARTURO: Te voy a _____.[5]

RAQUEL: Yo también a ti.

ARTURO: Aunque... tal vez...

RAQUEL: ¿Tal vez?

ARTURO: Tal vez... yo podría ir a Puerto Rico, y los dos continuar

_____[6] de Ángel.

RAQUEL: ¿Quieres decir que irías[b] a Puerto Rico?

ARTURO: ¿ _____[7]?

RAQUEL: ¡Claro que sí! Mucho. Pero, ¿tú puedes?

[a]como... *as if it had been*   [b]*you would go*

ARTURO: Creo que sí.

RAQUEL: ¿Y tu _____[8]? ¿tus pacientes?

ARTURO: Bueno, no sería fácil _____[9] todo. Pero... yo quiero ir.

Actividad D.   **Entrevista**

Imagine that you are conducting Raquel's investigation and a classmate is a reporter in Puerto Rico. The reporter has found out about your adventure and wants to know more. (You, unlike Raquel, have no problem divulging the secrets of your ongoing search!) Tell him or her about the story, supplying details for the parts of the series that you like the most. The reporter should ask interesting questions that will guide the lawyer's discussion of the events that took place.

Act. D, Suggestion: Brainstorm with the entire class before beginning the activity to generate a list of possible questions and answers. Students may use the list items as models and/or points of departure for their interviews.

Act. D, Emphasis: As this is a spontaneous oral activity, students should focus on communicating in Spanish, using whatever techniques and strategies they have at their disposal. Encourage them to act as if they did not understand English.

4

PARA ESCRIBIR

In this activity you will write a short letter that Raquel might send to a friend named Susan Winters, who lives in Los Angeles. Susan is a colleague at Raquel's law firm, and she is also interested in learning Spanish. Susan is currently taking a second-year Spanish course at a local college. Raquel will write to her in Spanish.

This is the first letter that Raquel has sent to Susan since leaving the United States, and, although Raquel and Susan are good friends as well as colleagues, she was not able to talk to Susan before she left. So Susan knows nothing about the case nor about Raquel's trip so far, and she has never traveled either to Spain or Argentina.

As you write from Raquel's point of view, tell Susan as much as you can about the important events that have happened, and include interesting information whenever you can. Your letter should be no fewer than 200 and no more than 300 words long.

Go to the Workbook/Study Guide to begin this writing activity.

26

REFLEXIONES II*

*Reflections II

OBJETIVOS

This video episode is a review. Be sure to work through all parts of the lesson. When you see a headphones symbol in the margin, listen to the CD for **Lección 26**. Answers or hints for many activities are given in Appendix 1. Be sure to check your answers for each activity before going on to the next one.

The interactive CD-ROM to accompany *Destinos* contains additional practice with the video storyline and will help you improve your skills in Spanish.

Preliminary: See Faculty Guide for additional information and activities for this lesson.
• **Variation:** For activities marked with the headphones icon, you may wish to read from the Audioscript instead of playing the CD.
• **Suggestion:** Make sure students are familiar with the activities before you read from the Audioscript or play the CD.

BEFORE VIEWING . . .

1

PREPARACIÓN

Suggestions:
• Before watching the video, go over the vocabulary list at the end of the chapter and have students pronounce the words after you.
• Assign *Preparación* activities as homework and then go over them quickly in class before viewing the video.

Act., Suggestion: You may want to have students do this activity in pairs or in small groups.

Act., Answers: 1. e, b 2. c, a 3. d, b 4. b, a 5. f, b 6. a, b

Actividad.

Look at the following photographs of people Raquel met or heard about in Puerto Rico and match the photos with the names given. Then read the statements that accompany them and indicate which is correct. Then add one true statement of your own about the character. Your statement can be factual or it can be your own opinion about the character.

1.

Act., Answers: 1. *Ángela Castillo*, b 2. *doña Carmen* a. 3. *Ángel, con su esposa y suegra*, b 4. *los tíos de Ángela y Roberto*, a 5. *Roberto Castillo*, b 6. *Jorge Alonso*, b.

3.

Jorge Alonso
los tíos de Ángela y Roberto
doña Carmen

Ángel, con su esposa y suegra
Ángela Castillo
Roberto Castillo

1. Es _____.
   a. Es una joven tranquila que sigue siempre lo que le dice la razón (*reason*).
   b. Es una joven impaciente e ingenua… y muy enamorada.
   c. ¿ ?

2. Es _____.
   a. Su opinión es muy importante para Ángela… y para los otros parientes también.
   b. Nadie en la familia le hace mucho caso (*pays much attention to her*).
   c. ¿ ?

2.

3. Es _____.
   a. Como en el estereotipo, este yerno no se llevó muy bien con su suegra.
   b. Este yerno era el hijo favorito de su suegra.
   c. ¿ ?

4. Son _____.
   a. Están ayudando a Ángela en esta época importante y difícil de su vida.
   b. No les importa la vida de Ángela en este momento.
   c. ¿ ?

4.

5. Es _____.
   a. Estudia comercio y trabaja en un banco en México.
   b. Estudia arqueología y trabaja en una excavación en México.
   c. ¿ ?

5.

6. Es _____.

   a. Este hombre le gusta mucho a Raquel… tanto que casi no piensa más en Arturo.

   b. Raquel le gusta mucho a él, pero él no le cae muy bien a ella (*she doesn't like him very much*).

   c. ¿?

6.

 . . . AFTER VIEWING

2

¿TIENES BUENA MEMORIA?

Actividad.   ¿A quiénes conoció Raquel?
Paso 1

Complete the following paragraphs with the names of people Raquel met or heard about while in Puerto Rico.

Act., Answers: 1. *Ángela* 2. *Olga* 3. *Laura* 4. *Carmen* 5. *Jorge* 6. *Jaime* 7. *Roberto*

Raquel conoció a _____[1] en el cementerio donde estaban enterrados Ángel y su esposa. Más tarde conoció a los cuñados de Ángel, incluyendo a la tía _____.[2] Ésta[a] no reaccionó bien al oír que su sobrina tenía otro abuelo en México.

   Raquel fue con Ángela y su prima _____[3] a San Germán a ver a su abuela, doña _____.[4] Al volver a San Juan, Ángela le presentó a Raquel a su novio _____,[5] quien acababa de regresar de Nueva York.

   Cuando estaban por salir para el aeropuerto Ángela y Raquel, el tío _____[6] vino a darle a su sobrina unas malas noticias. Su hermano _____[7] había tenido[b] un accidente en México.

[a]*The latter* [b]había… *had had*

 Paso 2

Now listen to the paragraphs on the CD and check your answers.

3

REPASO DE LOS EPISODIOS 19–24

Actividad A.   ¿En qué orden?

All of the following events took place in **Episodios 19–24**, but in what order did they occur? Put them in order, from 1 to 13.

Act. A, Suggestion: You may want to have students do this activity in pairs.

a. _____ En San Germán, doña Carmen le dio a Ángela una idea.

b. _____ Una vecina le dijo a Raquel: «Ángel Castillo murió hace poco.»

c. _____ Raquel y Ángela tenían que ir a San Germán.

d. _____ Doña Carmen también le dio a Ángela algo muy especial.

e. _____ Raquel conoció a los tíos de Ángela.

f. _____ Allí Ángela encontró unas hojas de su padre.

g. _____ Raquel trató de aconsejar a Ángela sobre sus relaciones con Jorge.

h. _____ Raquel tomaba una foto de la tumba de Ángel cuando Ángela apareció.

i. _____ Llegó el tío Jaime con unas malas noticias.

j. _____ Los tíos no sabían si Ángela debía hacer el viaje a México.

k. _____ ¿Por qué no revisaba (*look through*) lo que había entre las cosas de su padre?

l. _____ De regreso en San Juan, Raquel conoció al novio de Ángela.

m. _____ En San Juan, Raquel buscó una casa en la calle del Sol.

Be sure to check your answers in the Appendix, because the answers for this activity serve as the basis for the next one.

Actividad B.   ¿Y qué más?

The following sentences expand on the information given in the statements in **Actividad A**. Can you match these continuations with those statements? The first item is done for you.

1. _____ Era la copa de bodas de su abuela Rosario.

2. _____ Hubo un accidente en la excavación donde trabajaba Roberto.

3. _____ Pero Ángela se enfadó.

4. _____ También dijo que estaba enterrado en el cementerio del Viejo San Juan.

5. _____ Las hojas tenían sus recuerdos de la Argentina y de su vida en Puerto Rico.

6. __**m**__ Creía que Ángel Castillo vivía allí.

7. _____ Salieron en el carro de Ángela, con Laura, su prima.

8. _____ Fue al cuarto con Raquel y las dos encontraron un baúl.

9. _____ Raquel le contó la historia de su abuelo.

10. _____ No le gustó mucho.

11. _____ Debía ir al cuarto de su padre.

12. _____ Les contó la historia de Ángel Castillo.

13. _____ Creían que Ángela debía consultar con la abuela.

DESTINOS

Episodes 27–52

The story continues in a small town in the central meseta of Mexico, in Mexico City, and in the historic hacienda of La Gavia . . .

Un viaje a México:
El pueblo, la capital

EL OCÉANO ATLÁNTICO

la Ciudad
de México

San Juan

PUERTO
RICO

EL MAR CARIBE

Entremeses 2

Act. A, Suggestion: You may want to have students do this activity in pairs.

Act. A, Extension: You may want to list interrogative words on the board or on an overhead to help students get started: *¿cómo?, ¿de dónde?, ¿cuál?, ¿qué?*, etc.

Act. A, Follow-up: To help students get acquainted, prepare a *Firma aquí* activity with questions such as *¿Estudias francés / arte / biología / ...? ¿Vives en* (names of student residences)? *¿Te gusta el esquí acuático / nórdico / la natación / la pesca / ...? ¿Juegas al tenis / béisbol / fútbol (americano) / ...?* Have students circulate in class asking and answering the questions and gathering the signatures of classmates who respond with *Sí.* Then have them report their findings to the class, using the model _____ *juega al fútbol.*

Act. A, Optional: Have students bring in family group pictures and work in pairs to describe their families. For homework, have them write a brief composition describing the family picture and ask them to attach the photo to the paragraph.

Act. B, Suggestion: Before having students talk about their families, present your own (real or imaginary) family tree to the class, attaching pictures to the board. Ask the following types of question: *¿Quién es el padre de mi padre? ¿Cómo se llama la hermana de mi madre? ¿Cuál es la relación entre nosotras? ¿Cuántos tíos tengo? ¿Tengo hijos? ¿Quién es el esposo de mi hermana?* Using some famous people injects an element of humor into the activity.

Act. B, Extension: Have students create their own family trees as a homework assignment. They can draw family members or use photos.

Act. B, Follow-up:
• Use students' family trees to review vocabulary in pairs the following day. You may want to have questions such as *¿Cuántos tíos tienes? ¿Cómo se llama(n)? ¿Tienen hijos? ¿Cuántos años tienen tus primos?* on an overhead.
• To review family vocabulary, prepare a *Firma aquí* activity with questions such as *¿Tienes dos abuelas / un hijo / una cuñada / ... ?* Have students circulate in class asking and answering the questions and gathering the signatures of classmates who respond with *Sí.* Then have them report their findings to the class, using the model _____ *tiene tres hijas.*

Actividad A. ¡A conocernos!

Paso 1

¿Qué preguntas le harías (*would you ask*) a un compañero / una compañera para obtener la siguiente información?

1. nombre y apellido
2. origen
3. número de teléfono
4. especialización
5. cursos que tiene este semestre/trimestre
6. total de créditos/horas que tiene este semestre/trimestre
7. si estudió español con *Destinos* el semestre/trimestre pasado
8. si le gusta el español o no

Paso 2

Ahora entrevista a un compañero / una compañera que no conozcas (*you don't know*). Usa los siete temas del **Paso 1** como base de tu entrevista. Apunta (*Jot down*) la información en una hoja de papel aparte.

Paso 3

Escribe la información que obtuviste en el **Paso 2** y haz una copia para tu profesor(a). Ahora conoces a alguien que podrás (*you will be able to*) llamar si necesitas algo relacionado con la clase.

Actividad B. La familia

Paso 1

Piensa en los miembros de tu familia. En una hoja de papel aparte, escribe la siguiente información.

1. el nombre de tus padres y su edad
2. cuántos hermanos y hermanas tienes
3. la edad de tus abuelos (si es que todavía están vivos)
4. el nombre de la(s) mascota(s) (si es que la[s] hay)

Paso 2

Trata de encontrar a un compañero / una compañera de clase que tenga (*has*) en su familia algo similar a lo que se menciona en el **Paso 1.** (No tiene que ser la misma persona la que lo tiene todo.)

Paso 3

Presenta a la clase la información que obtuviste.

> MODELO: Tomás y yo tenemos algo parecido (*similar*) en cuanto a las mascotas. Yo tengo un perro y él también. El mío (*Mine*) se llama Jupiter y el de Tomás se llama Saturno.

Actividad C.   Repaso de los Episodios 1–26
Paso 1
Con toda la clase, identifiquen a las personas que *no* estudiaron español con *Destinos* el semestre/trimestre pasado. Luego, pasen al **Paso 2**. Si todos en la clase estudiaron con *Destinos*, sigan al **Paso 3**.

Paso 2
Los que estudiaron con *Destinos* deben dar descripciones de los siguientes personajes y del papel de cada uno en el programa. A continuacíon hay algunas preguntas que los pueden ayudar. Los que no estudiaron con *Destinos* deben escuchar y tomar apuntes. Después del **Paso 2**, pasen al **Paso 4**.

Preguntas
1.   ¿Cómo es este personaje? ¿viejo? ¿joven? ¿De qué color tiene el pelo? ¿los ojos?
2.   ¿Qué profesión u oficio tiene?
3.   ¿Qué papel tiene este personaje en la historia?

Personajes
don Fernando	Ramón	Arturo
Rosario	Carlos	Ángela
Raquel	Mercedes	Roberto
Pedro	Juan	Teresa Suárez

Act. C, *Paso 4*, **Suggestion:** If there are students in the class who have not previously used *Destinos*, have them try to identify people in the photos based on information they obtained in *Paso 2*. Those who are familiar with *Destinos* respond to their answers with *sí* or *no*.

Paso 3
Si todos estudiaron con *Destinos*, deben indicar cuáles son los cuatro o cinco acontecimientos más importantes de los **Episodios 1–26**. ¿Están todos de acuerdo?

Paso 4
Ahora, todos deben identificar a cada personaje en las siguientes fotos.

a.

b.

c.

d.

e.

f.

g.

h.

i.

EL RESCATE*

Suggestion: Have students look at the photo, describe what they see, and talk about what they think might happen. For example: *¿Qué es este lugar?* (*una excavación*); *¿Qué pasó allí?* (*un accidente*); *¿Quién trabaja en la excavación?* (*Roberto Castillo, el hermano de Ángela*).

*The Rescue

OBJETIVOS

The materials in **Lección 27** of the Textbook and the Workbook/Study Guide will help you better understand the video episode and take you beyond it, giving you additional information about places and characters in the series. The Textbook will also help you to develop skill in using the Spanish language. In this lesson, you will learn

• another way to talk about the future in Spanish

You will also learn information that will help you understand the background of Raquel's investigation and prepare you for future video episodes.

Be sure to work through all parts of the lesson. When you see a headphones symbol in the margin, listen to the CD for **Lección 27**. Answers or hints for many activities are given in Appendix 1. Be sure to check your answers for each activity before going on to the next one.

The interactive CD-ROM to accompany *Destinos* contains additional practice with the video storyline and will help you improve your skills in Spanish.

Suggestions:
• Before watching the video, go over the vocabulary list at the end of the chapter and have students pronounce the words after you.

BEFORE VIEWING . . .

Preliminary: See Faculty Guide for additional information and activities for this lesson.
• **Variation:** For activities marked with the headphones icon, you may wish to read from the Audioscript instead of playing the CD.
• **Suggestion:** Make sure students are familiar with the activities before you read from the Audioscript or play the CD.

1

• For the first episode of the new semester, you may wish to do the *Preparación* section in class, walking students through the activities, emphasizing that this section is designed to get them thinking about what they have already seen, as well as what they will see and hear in the upcoming episode. Some *Preparación* activities are prediction exercises that have no (in)correct answers, although the photos and previous events should help students make logical choices. Make sure that students read the entire introduction to the section before beginning the activities.

Optional: Brainstorm as a whole class or in small groups what students already know about Mexico and what they think it is like. How will it be similar to Spain, Argentina, and Puerto Rico? How will it be different? List the ideas on the board and have students copy them. As the unit in Mexico unfolds over the remainder of the series, have students refer to this list to see whether or not their ideas were accurate. Which ideas would they change? What did they see or hear that made them change their minds?

Act. A, Answers: 1. *La Gavia, don Fernando Castillo Saavedra, el hermano, Raquel Rodríguez* 2. *Teresa Suárez, la primera esposa* 3. *la Argentina, Madrid, San Juan* 4. *el cementerio* 5. *México, una excavación* 6. *el medio hermano, Rosario*

PREPARACIÓN

In this video episode you will watch a condensed version of Raquel's search for the truth about don Fernando's past. You will see highlights of the main events of **Episodios 1–26,** following Raquel's travels from Mexico to Spain, then on to Argentina, Puerto Rico, and back to Mexico (although not just yet to her exact point of departure!).

You may be surprised to realize how much more you can now understand from previous video episodes. What was challenging when you were watching **Episodio 5,** for example, may seem easier to you now. That is a measure of how much you have accomplished as you watched the first twenty-six video episodes and worked with the Textbook and Workbook/Study Guide.

Actividad A.

Antes de mirar el **Episodio 27,** trata de recordar algo de lo que (*what*) pasó en los episodios previos. ¿Puedes completar las respuestas a las siguientes preguntas?

Nombres: don Fernando Castillo Saavedra, Mercedes Castillo, Raquel Rodríguez, Rosario, Elena Ruiz, Teresa Suárez
Lugares: la Argentina, Córdoba, Costa Rica, Madrid, México, San Juan; el cementerio, la excavación, La Gavia, el puerto
Parientes: el hermano, el medio hermano, el hijo, la primera esposa

1. ¿Dónde comenzó esta historia? ¿Con qué comenzó? ¿Y con quiénes?

   La historia comenzó en una hacienda, _____, en México. Comenzó con una carta escrita por una mujer en España a _____, el dueño de la hacienda. Don Pedro Castillo, _____ de don Fernando, contrató a una abogada norteamericana, _____, para hacer la investigación.

2. ¿A quién buscaba Raquel? ¿Por qué?

   Al principio Raquel buscaba a la persona que escribió la carta, _____. La buscaba porque en la carta indicaba que sabía algo de Rosario, _____ de don Fernando.

3. ¿A qué países viajó? ¿Qué ciudades visitó?

   Raquel viajó a España, _____ y Puerto Rico. Visitó a Sevilla, _____, Buenos Aires, _____, Ponce y San Germán.

4. ¿Dónde conoció a Ángela Castillo?

   Raquel conoció a Ángela Castillo en ———————— del Viejo San Juan, en Puerto Rico.

5. ¿Adónde viajaron Ángela y Raquel? ¿Dónde está ahora el hermano de Ángela? ¿Qué le pasó?

   Viajaron a ————————. Roberto, el hermano de Ángela, está en ————————, donde hubo un accidente.

6. ¿Quién es Arturo Iglesias? ¿Sabe algo de lo que le pasó al hermano de Ángela?

   Arturo es ———————— de Ángel Castillo, el hijo de don Fernando y ————————. No sabe nada de lo que le pasó a Roberto.

Para pensar...

1. ¿Qué crees que va a pasar con Roberto, el hermano de Ángela? ¿Lo van a sacar de la excavación vivo o muerto?
2. Al final del **Episodio 26**, Raquel quería llamar a Arturo para decirle lo que pasaba con Roberto. ¿Crees que Raquel pudo comunicarse con Arturo? ¿Cómo va a reaccionar Arturo a las noticias de Roberto?

Actividad B.
Paso 1

Vas a escuchar una conversación entre Raquel y Ángela mientras manejan un carro alquilado (*rented*) hacia el sitio de la excavación. Puedes leer el diálogo al mismo tiempo que lo escuchas, si quieres. Después de escuchar, contesta la pregunta.

ÁNGELA: Roberto siempre quiso venir a México. Se pasaba los días y las noches estudiando las civilizaciones prehispánicas.

RAQUEL: Roberto y tú son muy unidos, ¿verdad? En Puerto Rico me decías siempre que tu hermano era un encanto.

ÁNGELA: La verdad es que... pues, desde que se vino para México, nos hemos alejado un poco.

RAQUEL: Comprendo... con la distancia.

ÁNGELA: No, no es por eso. Es que... Bueno, yo nunca le he dicho esto a nadie, Raquel. Pues, la verdad es que siempre le he tenido un poco de envidia a Roberto.

¿De quién habla Ángela en esta conversación?

a. ———— de su novio Jorge   c. ———— de su padre Ángel

b. ———— de su hermano Roberto

Act. B, *Paso 2*, Suggestion: Have students read through the questions and answers before replaying the CD.

Paso 2

Ahora escucha la conversación otra vez. Al escuchar, piensa en el verbo **alejarse**. **Nos hemos alejado** significa *we've grown apart*. Después de escuchar la conversación otra vez, contesta las siguientes preguntas.

1. ¿Qué materia siempre le gustó a Roberto?
   a. _____ las civilizaciones prehispánicas   c. _____ la geografía
   b. _____ la historia de México   mexicana

2. ¿Cómo son las relaciones entre Ángela y Roberto desde que él se va a vivir a México?
   a. _____ Se sienten más unidos.   c. _____ Nada cambió entre ellos.
   b. _____ Están un poco alejados.

3. ¿Qué secreto le revela Ángela a Raquel?
   a. _____ Le dice que no quiere a Roberto.
   b. _____ Le dice que Roberto no es realmente su hermano.
   c. _____ Le dice que siempre le ha tenido envidia (*she has always envied*) a Roberto.

***Para pensar*, Follow-up:** Personalize the questions by asking *¿Cuántos tienen hermanos? ¿Y cómo es la relación? ¿Son unidos o alejados? ¿Les tienen Uds. envidia a sus hermanos? ¿Y ellos a Uds.? ¿Es normal la relación entre Ángela y Roberto?*

Para pensar...

1. ¿Conoces a hermanos como Ángela y Roberto? ¿Son unidos o un poco alejados? ¿Tiene uno envidia al otro?
2. Imagina la conversación que va a tener Ángela con su hermano cuando lo vea. ¿Qué le va a decir?

 . . . AFTER VIEWING

2

¿TIENES BUENA MEMORIA?

Act., Suggestion: Give students about 10 minutes to complete the activity individually or in pairs and then compare answers as a whole class.

Actividad. El repaso de Raquel
Paso 1

Los siguientes párrafos son del repaso que hace Raquel al final del **Episodio 27**, pero faltan unas palabras. ¿Puedes completar el repaso?

buscar a Roberto
empezó a mirar la lista de nombres
era más inteligente y responsable que ella
está desesperada
estaba bloqueado y no podíamos pasar
le tenía un poco de envidia
no sabe nada del accidente
que era un error
se llevaban muy bien
un poco culpable

¡Qué día tuvimos hoy! Primero Ángela y yo llegamos a la Ciudad de México. Estábamos cansadas. Pero también estábamos muy preocupadas. Aunque estábamos cansadas, teníamos que venir a este pueblo. Teníamos que

_____,[1] el hermano de Ángela.

Mientras manejábamos, hablamos de Roberto. Ángela me decía que ella y su hermano _____.[2] Pero también me confesó que _____[3] a Roberto. Ángela le tenía envidia a Roberto porque sentía que él _____.[4] Pobre Ángela. Ahora se siente _____.[5]

Bueno, por fin llegamos al sitio de la excavación. ¿Y qué pasó? El camino _____.[6] Entonces, vinimos aquí, al hospital.

Le preguntamos a la recepcionista si estaba Roberto Castillo, y ella nos dijo que no. Entonces Ángela _____[7] y ¿qué encontró? Encontró el nombre R. Castilla. Por un momento tuvimos esperanzas.[a] Pensamos _____,[8] que debía ser R. Castilla. Pronto supimos que no. R. Castilla era Rodrigo Castilla.

¡Qué lástima! La pobre Ángela _____.[9] Y ahora estamos aquí. Quiero hablar con Arturo porque estará[b] esperándonos en el hotel y _____.[10] Pero no he podido[c] comunicarme con él.

[a]*hope*   [b]*he is probably*   [c]*no… I haven't been able*

 Paso 2
Ahora escucha el CD para verificar tus respuestas.

3

UN POCO DE GRAMÁTICA

The grammar previewed in most **Un poco de gramática** sections is used in the sentences that appear on-screen during Raquel's story review. This **Un poco de gramática** section is an exception. However, the form described here has been used many times in previous video episodes of *Destinos*.

Note: You may wish to introduce the complete verb paradigm for the future tense.

Another Way to Talk About the Future

To describe what another person will be doing in the future, add **-á** to most infinitives.

En unos días Raquel **estará** en la Ciudad de México.

In a few days Raquel will be in Mexico City.

To describe what more than one person will be doing, add **-án** to most infinitives.

Raquel y Ángela **llamarán** a los tíos en Puerto Rico.

Raquel and Ángela will call the aunts and uncles in Puerto Rico.

One useful verb that uses an irregular stem with these endings is **hacer.**

¿Qué **hará** Arturo si no puede comunicarse con nadie?

What will Arturo do if he can't get in touch with anyone?

You will learn more about these verb forms in the Workbook/Study Guide.

Act., *Paso 1*, **Suggestion:** Assign as homework and have students present their sentences to the class the following day. Tell them that more than one response is possible for each item.

Actividad. ¿Qué pasará?
Paso 1

Indica lo que crees que pasará en la clase este semestre/trimestre.

1. El profesor / La profesora…
    - _____ estará ausente (*absent*) varias veces.
    - _____ será más exigente (*demanding*) que el profesor / la profesora del semestre/trimestre pasado.
    - _____ no dará un examen final.
    - _____ se irá de (*will leave*) la universidad al terminar el semestre/trimestre.
    - _____ ¿ ?

2. Alguien en la clase…
    - _____ se enfermará y tendrá que dejar la clase.
    - _____ llegará tarde con mucha frecuencia.
    - _____ visitará México este año.
    - _____ se graduará al final del semestre/trimestre.
    - _____ ¿ ?

Act., *Paso 2*, **Suggestion:** Have individual students read items from each part of *Paso 1*. Ask the class in general to raise their hands if they agree; tally results on the board.

Paso 2

Ahora todos deben compartir sus ideas con la clase. ¿En qué están Uds. de acuerdo?

VOCABULARIO

Los adjetivos

unido/a   united, close

Los verbos

alejarse (**de**)   to draw away, grow apart (from)

Los conceptos

el rescate   rescue

Las palabras adicionales

lo que   what, that which
tenerle envidia (**a alguien**)   to envy (someone)

Entremeses 3

Act. A, *Paso 1*, Suggestion: Play *Veinte preguntas* (Twenty Questions). Assume the identity of at least one currently famous person, then of a deceased one, such as Oprah, a well-known current politician, Tom Cruise, Thomas Edison, *Isabel la Católica*, Jacqueline Kennedy Onassis.

Act. A, *Paso 2*, Suggestion: If students can't think of anyone to impersonate, whisper a name in their ear, such as *Pedro* (*el hermano de don Fernando*), *Roberto* (*el hermano de Ángela*), *Rosario*, Elizabeth Taylor, Robin Williams.

Act. A, Extension: You may prefer to save time by providing students with pictures of famous people or cards with names of famous people written on them, from which to choose the person whose identity they will assume.

Act. A, Variation: Tape or clip the name or a picture of a famous person to a student's back. The person with the name or picture on his/her back must ask questions such as *¿Estoy vivo/a / muerto/a?* to find out who he or she is supposed to be. The student's partner looks at the person's name so that he or she can answer the questions.

Act. B, *Paso 1*, Suggestion: Remind students to use *tú* forms of verbs when asking a question. You may wish to have them do the first 2 items aloud as models.

Act. B, *Paso 2*, Suggestion: If time permits, have 1 or 2 students share their paragraphs with the entire class.

Act. B, *Paso 2*, Extension: Have students write a composition in which they compare themselves with the 2 people they have interviewed.

Act. B, Follow-up: To help students get acquainted, prepare a *Firma aquí* activity with questions such as *¿Piensas tener hijos / graduarte este año / trabajar durante el semestre / … ?* Have students circulate in class asking and answering the questions and gathering the signatures of classmates who respond with *Sí*. Then have them report their findings to the class, using the model _____ *piensa tener dos hijos.*

Actividad A. ¿Quién es?

Paso 1

Tu profesor(a) asumirá la identidad de una persona famosa. La clase entera tiene que hacerle preguntas para saber quién es. ¡OJO! Solamente se puede hacer preguntas para responder con respuestas de **sí** o **no**.*

Preguntas útiles: ¿Estás vivo? / ¿Ya moriste?

¿Eres alguien importante en el mundo de la política / el cine / la música?

¿Eres hombre? / ¿Eres mujer?

Paso 2

Ahora te toca a ti. Mientras tú asumes la identidad de una persona famosa, tus compañeros de clase te harán preguntas para saber quién eres. (Si quieres, ¡puedes asumir la identidad de un personaje de *Destinos*!)

Actividad B. A conocernos un poco más

Ya sabes algo de tus compañeros por las actividades previas. Ahora los vas a conocer un poco más.

Paso 1

Entrevista a dos personas en la clase para obtener la siguiente información. Apunta (*Jot down*) lo que te dicen.

1. nombre y edad
2. cuándo se graduará
3. si piensa tener (más) hijos en el futuro
4. los planes que tiene para el final del semestre/trimestre
5. lo que piensa de *Destinos*

Paso 2

Escribe un breve ensayo de dos párrafos, haciendo una comparación de las dos personas. Puedes seguir el modelo si quieres.

MODELO: Párrafo 1: La primera persona que entrevisté se llama _____.

Tiene _____ años y se graduará en _____. En el futuro…

Párrafo 2: También entrevisté a _____. Tiene _____ años y/pero…

Palabras útiles: a diferencia de, igual que, pero, sin embargo, también, y

---

* Si tratas a tu profesor(a) de **Ud.**, debes cambiar las preguntas (¿Está vivo? / ¿Ya murió? ¿Cuándo murió?…).

265

Act. C, *Paso 1*, Suggestion: Go over name by name and have students brainstorm each character's description and important aspects of his/her life.

Act. C, *Paso 1*, Variation: Write the names of the characters listed in *Paso 1* on the board and have students brainstorm what they look like and what happened to each, or, have individual students come to the board and write each person's description and what happened to him/her under the names. Go over these with the entire class.

Act. C, *Paso 3*, Follow-up: After groups are finished, call upon one member from each group to comment upon what someone in that group said. Follow up with questions directed to the person whose ideas were talked about.

Act. D, Suggestion: Allow 6 or 7 minutes for the activity. Then call on one student to present item 1. Ask for a show of hands to see how many agreed and how many disagreed. Then repeat the process with the other items.

Actividad C.   ¿Te gustaría ser... ?

Paso 1

A continuación hay una lista de algunos personajes de *Destinos*. ¿Los conoces a todos?

Raquel
Arturo
don Fernando
Pedro

Ramón
Carlos
Mercedes
Juan

Teresa Suárez
Ángela

Paso 2

Ahora contesta las siguientes preguntas: De los personajes de *Destinos*, ¿quién te gustaría ser? ¿Quién *no* te gustaría ser? Da por lo menos una razón que explique tu respuesta.

Paso 3

En grupos de cuatro, presenten sus ideas del **Paso 2** a sus compañeros. Todos deben escuchar atentamente y apuntar lo que dicen los otros grupos.

Actividad D.   ¿Probable o no?

Indica cuáles de los siguientes acontecimientos son probables (**P**) y cuáles son improbables (**I**). Explica tu respuesta en cada caso.

MODELO: Roberto se morirá en la excavación. → Roberto no se morirá en la excavación. Va a ser rescatado.

1. _____ Raquel se casará con Arturo.
2. _____ Don Fernando se morirá antes de conocer a sus nietos.
3. _____ Juan y Pati se divorciarán.
4. _____ Mercedes tendrá una aventura romántica con un hombre.
5. _____ Ángela llegará a ser menos egoísta.

Actividad E.   ¿Quiénes son?

¿Quiénes son las personas de las siguientes fotos? ¿Qué sabes de su vida? ¿Te gustaría ser una de estas personas? ¿Por qué sí o por qué no?

1.

2.

3.

LECCIÓN 28

Suggestion: Have students look at the photo, describe what they see, and talk about what they think might happen. Ask questions about the photo to prompt student discussion: *¿Quiénes son estas personas? ¿Dónde están? ¿Qué papel tienen en la historia? ¿Son parientes? ¿amigos?*

ATRAPADOS*

Trapped

OBJETIVOS

The materials in **Lección 28** of the Textbook and the Workbook/Study Guide will help you better understand the video episode and take you beyond it, giving you additional information about places and characters in the series. The Textbook will also help you to develop skill in using the Spanish language. In this lesson, you will learn

- vocabulary for talking about parts of the body
- more ways to talk about the future

You will also learn about the geography and history of Mexico.

Be sure to work through all parts of the lesson. When you see a headphones symbol in the margin, listen to the CD for **Lección 28**. Answers or hints for many activities are given in Appendix 1. Be sure to check your answers for each activity before going on to the next one.

The interactive CD-ROM to accompany *Destinos* contains additional practice with the video storyline and will help you improve your skills in Spanish.

267

BEFORE VIEWING . . .

1

Preparación

 Actividad A.

Antes de mirar el **Episodio 28**, trata de recordar lo que pasó en los episodios previos y escucha el resumen del narrador al principio del episodio. Luego indica si los siguientes acontecimientos *(events)* ocurrieron (**Sí**) o no (**No**).

Sí No 1. Raquel y Ángela llegaron al área de la excavación donde trabajaba Roberto.

Sí No 2. Pudieron pasar en seguida al sitio del accidente.

Sí No 3. Llevaron a Roberto de urgencia al hospital.

Sí No 4. Arturo llegó a la casa de Pedro Castillo.

Sí No 5. Raquel no lo estaba esperando.

Sí No 6. Raquel quiso hablar con Arturo pero no pudo.

Actividad B.

En el **Episodio 28**, Raquel y Ángela pueden llegar a la excavación donde están atrapadas algunas personas. ¿Qué crees que pasará?

1. Roberto
   a. _____ morirá.
   b. _____ estará atrapado, vivo, en la excavación.

2. Arturo
   a. _____ seguirá sin saber lo que está pasando en la excavación.
   b. _____ se enterará *(will find out)* del accidente por la televisión y saldrá en seguida para el pueblo.

 Actividad C.
Paso 1

En este episodio y a lo largo del resto de la serie, vas a ver con frecuencia a los miembros de la familia Castillo Saavedra. Los conociste a todos en los primeros episodios, pero ¿recuerdas ahora quiénes son? Escucha las siguientes descripciones de algunos de ellos e identifícalos.

a. Mercedes   d. Carlos   g. Carmen
b. Ramón   e. Maricarmen   h. Juan
c. Pedro   f. Pati   i. Consuelo

1. …   2. …   3. …   4. …   5. …

Paso 2

Ahora completa el siguiente árbol de la familia, usando nombres de la lista y del CD del **Paso 1**.

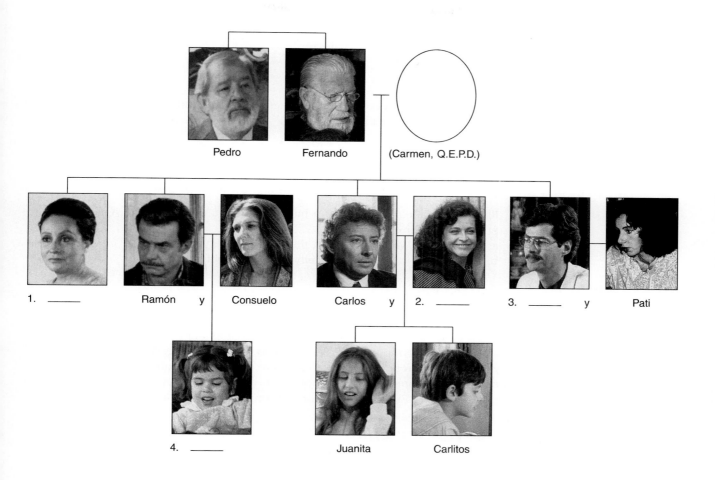

Pedro   Fernando   (Carmen, Q.E.P.D.)

1. _____   Ramón   y   Consuelo   Carlos   y   2. _____   3. _____   y   Pati

4. _____   Juanita   Carlitos

Actividad D.
Paso 1

Vas a escuchar una conversación entre el médico de don Fernando y sus hijos. Puedes leer el diálogo al mismo tiempo que lo escuchas, si quieres. Después de escuchar, contesta las preguntas del **Paso 2**.

DOCTOR: Su estado es muy delicado. Es necesario consultar a un especialista.

RAMÓN: ¿Y Ud. recomienda a alguien en particular?

DOCTOR: Conozco al mejor especialista en México, pero está de viaje. Está dando una serie de conferencias en Europa. No regresa hasta el fin del mes.

MERCEDES: ¿Y podemos esperar hasta entonces?

DOCTOR: No. Recomiendo que lo examine un especialista lo antes posible.

RAMÓN: ¿Y no hay otro, doctor? ¿Uno que sea de confianza?

DOCTOR: También conozco a otro muy bueno que radica[a] en la ciudad de Guadalajara. Tiene una clínica muy bien equipada en la Universidad de Guadalajara.

MERCEDES: ¿En Guadalajara? ¿Y aceptará venir a México?

DOCTOR: Eso no lo sé.

[a]vive, está situado

Paso 2

1. Según lo que dice el médico, ¿cómo está don Fernando?
   a. _____ mucho mejor   c. _____ igual que antes
   b. _____ muy mal

2. El médico recomienda a dos especialistas. ¿Es posible consultar al primero en este momento?
   _____ Sí.   _____ No.

3. Ramón quiere el nombre de un médico «que sea de confianza». ¿Qué puede significar esta frase?
   a. _____ one who can respect the confidentiality of the case
   b. _____ one in whom the family can have confidence

Actividad E.

En este episodio Carlos va a jugar (*play*) con sus hijos y su sobrina Maricarmen un juego muy divertido. Se llama «Simón dice» y, como seguramente lo sabes, en él se nombran muy rápidamente las partes del cuerpo. Lee las partes del cuerpo en la sección **Vocabulario del tema** en esta lección. Esto te ayudará a comprender más palabras, pero no necesitas saber los nombres del cuerpo para apreciar el juego porque lo más importante del juego es la frase «Simón dice». Escucha lo que dice tu profesor(a) para jugar.

 . . . AFTER VIEWING

2   ¿TIENES BUENA MEMORIA?

Actividad A.   En la excavación

Identifica al personaje a quien se refiere.

a. Raquel Rodríguez   d. Roberto Castillo
b. Ángela Castillo   e. el padre Rodrigo
c. Arturo Iglesias

1. _____ Le dio a Ángela noticias sobre su hermano.
2. _____ Se durmió sin ver las noticias de la televisión.
3. _____ Trató de llamar a Arturo, pero no pudo comunicarse con él.
4. _____ Todavía estaba vivo, aunque estaba atrapado en la excavación.
5. _____ Estaba angustiada, pero no podía hacer nada.
6. _____ Les recordó a todos que había que tener fe.
7. _____ Trató de apoyar (*support*) a su amiga tanto como pudo.

Actividad B. **En la capital**

Al mismo tiempo que Ángela y Raquel siguen con angustia los acontecimientos de la excavación, los miembros de la familia Castillo tienen sus propios problemas. Completa las siguientes oraciones sobre lo que pasa en la capital.

1. El médico les dice a los miembros de la familia que hay que consultar a un especialista... en dos o tres semanas. / en seguida.
2. El especialista está en... la capital. / Guadalajara.
3. Pedro y Mercedes están muy preocupados… por don Fernando. / por don Fernando y por otros asuntos familiares.

Para pensar, **Suggestion:** You may want to have students do this activity with you asking the questions and them answering, in pairs alternating questions and answers, or in small groups allowing for some discussion.

Para pensar...

En este episodio, Pedro y Mercedes hablan brevemente de tres asuntos que les preocupan en este momento. ¿Cuál crees que va a ser el resultado de cada uno de ellos?

1. ¿Qué le va a pasar a don Fernando? ¿Va a morir pronto? ¿sin conocer a sus nietos?
2. ¿Qué va a pasar entre Juan y Pati? ¿Cuáles son las dificultades que experimentan en esta época? ¿Las van a poder superar *(get through)*?
3. Y lo de la oficina en Miami, ¿en qué consiste? ¿Por qué no les ha dicho nada Carlos a sus hermanos y a su tío? ¿Es sólo porque don Fernando está enfermo?

3

VOCABULARIO DEL TEMA

Algunas partes del cuerpo

la boca	mouth	**el pecho**	chest	**el pie**	foot
el brazo	arm	**el pelo**	hair	**la pierna**	leg
la cabeza	head				
el corazón	heart				
la espalda	back				
el estómago	stomach				
la mano	hand				
la nariz	nose				
los ojos	eyes				
la oreja	ear				

Actividad A. Con el médico

Escucha otra vez mientras el médico del pueblo examina en la clínica,
cerca de la excavación, a un niño. Indica en el dibujo las partes del cuerpo
que examina.

Actividad B. Jugando con el Sr. Papa
Paso 1

Escucha otra vez mientras Pati y Maricarmen hablan del juguete que su prima
le ha dado (*given*). Completa las oraciones con las partes del cuerpo
apropiadas.

PATI:	¿Qué tienes allí, Maricarmen?
MARICARMEN:	Es un juguete que Juanita me trajo de los Estados Unidos. Se llama Sr. Papa.
PATI:	Ah, sí.
MARICARMEN:	Sí. Aquí está todo lo que necesitas, Pati. Dos (orejas/ojos),[1] una nariz, (una boca/un corazón),[2] dos orejas, (un brazo/una boca)[3] con una mano, otro brazo con otra (nariz/mano)[4] y los pies.
PATI:	Oye, Maricarmen, ¿y dónde están las piernas?
MARICARMEN:	Pati, el Sr. Papa no necesita (pies/piernas),[5] sólo (piernas/pies).[6]
PATI:	¿Y el resto del (corazón/cuerpo)[7]? ¿No tiene espalda ni (pecho/pie)[8]?
MARICARMEN:	No, Pati.
PATI:	Y ¿por qué se llama el Sr. Papa?
MARICARMEN:	Porque su (corazón/cabeza)[9] es una papa.
PATI:	¿No tiene (pelo/pierna)[10]?
MARICARMEN:	No, Pati. Las papas no tienen pelo.

Paso 2
Ahora indica lo que significan las palabras que indicaste.

Actividad C. Asociaciones

El Sr. Papa es un juguete norteamericano. ¿Con qué parte del cuerpo asocias
los siguientes productos norteamericanos?

1. Desenex
2. Slim-Fast
3. Tylenol
4. Vicks VapoRub
5. Visine
6. Listerine
7. Q-Tips
8. Lady Clairol
9. Vaseline Intensive Care
10. Kleenex
11. Ben-Gay

Nota cultural   Hablando de la familia Castillo

You initially met the members of the Castillo family at La Gavia, the rural estate owned by don Fernando. In this video episode you have seen them in the urban environment of Mexico City. The following aspects of their life and lifestyle are worthy of note.

- Although Ramón and his family live at La Gavia, they also have a home in Mexico City. It is not uncommon for well-to-do Hispanic families—Mexicans, in this case—to have several residences. In Mexico wealthy people often have two residences in the same city. One is viewed as the primary residence; the other may be used for entertaining or as a place for out-of-town guests to stay (rather than in a hotel).

- Carlos's children have been exposed to a number of elements of U.S. culture, such as **Simón dice** and **el Sr. Papa**, because they have been growing up in Miami. Because they also spend as much time as is practical in Mexico, they are also quite comfortable in that country. At this stage of their lives, it is fair to describe them as bicultural, participating in the language, culture, and cultural values of both the English-speaking and the Hispanic worlds.

4

UN POCO DE GRAMÁTICA

The Workbook/Study Guide contains more detailed explanation and practice of this grammar point.

Suggestions:
- Review the future tense of regular verbs before presenting irregular forms.
- Practice the irregular-stem futures and *habrá* in brief conversational exchanges. *¿Qué harás después de la clase? ¿Con quién saldrás esta noche?*, etc.
- **¡OJO!:** Mention the importance of stressing the accented syllables of the verbs to distinguish them from imperfect subjunctive forms, e.g., *hablará* vs. *hablara*.

More About Talking About the Future

The verbs **poder** and **tener** form the future with the irregular stems **podr-** and **tendr-**, respectively.

RAQUEL: **¿Podré** hablar con Arturo pronto? Si no, **tendré** que ponerme en contacto con él tan pronto como lleguemos a la capital.

RAQUEL: *Will I be able to speak with Arturo soon? If not, I'll have to get in touch with him as soon as we get to the capital.*

You will learn more about these and other verbs that use an irregular stem in the future in the Workbook/Study Guide.

Act., *Paso 1*, **Optional:** After students complete *Paso 1*, have them call out responses as you tally each item on the board. Is there a recognizable pattern of responses? Do many students rate the same items in the same way?

Act., Follow-up: For homework, have students write a mini-composition on what they learned about one classmate's opinions regarding the future.

Actividad.   Más sobre el futuro
Paso 1

Follow-up: To review future-tense forms, prepare a *Firma aquí* activity with questions such as *¿Estudiarás mucho esta noche? ¿Tendrás un hijo algún día?* Have students circulate in class asking and answering the questions and gathering the signatures of classmates who respond with *Sí.* Then have them report their findings to the class, using the model _____ *estudiará mucho esta noche.*

Indica con números tu opinión sobre las siguientes oraciones. Usa la siguiente escala.

     5 = sí   3 = tal vez   1 = no

1. En el futuro
   a. _____ podré ser buen esposo / buena esposa.
   b. _____ podré ser buen padre / buena madre.
   c. _____ podré contribuir con algo para mejorar la sociedad.
   d. _____ podré ganar lo suficiente para vivir bien.
   e. _____ podré hablar español como hablante (*speaker*) nativo.

2. En el futuro
   a. _____ tendré éxito en mi profesión.
   b. _____ tendré una casa grande y un auto de último modelo.
   c. _____ tendré mucho prestigio.
   d. _____ tendré muchas oportunidades para viajar al extranjero.
   e. _____ tendré que trabajar hasta los 65 años.

3. En el futuro
   a. _____ nosotros los seres humanos podremos comunicarnos con seres extraterrestres.
   b. _____ tendremos menos oxígeno para respirar bien.
   c. _____ no podremos salir al aire libre sin ponernos sombrero, gafas de sol (*sunglasses*) y loción protectora para el sol.
   d. _____ tendremos menos libertades políticas y personales.
   e. _____ podremos vivir en armonía y paz con todas las culturas del mundo.

Paso 2

Compara tus respuestas con las de un compañero / una compañera. Hablen de lo que sus respuestas indican sobre sus preocupaciones, valores y/o personalidad.

5

LECTURA CULTURAL

Lectura cultural, **Suggestion:** It is helpful to have a large map of Mexico in front of the room or on an overhead.

México, a vista de pájaro*

Throughout the first half of the Textbook a brief exercise before each extensive **Lectura cultural** helped you review what you already knew about the topic—generally information from the video episode—before beginning the reading. Keep that strategy in mind as you work with the readings in the second half of the text. The first few **Lecturas culturales** will have a brief reminder.

Antes de leer, escucha una vez más lo que dice el narrador sobre México y trata de completar este mapa. En la lectura, hay más detalles para que lo completes.

Para mucha gente de los Estados Unidos, México es un país al sur, grande y tal vez desconocido... excepto por la música de

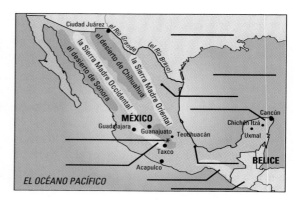

* a... *a bird's-eye view*

Lectura cultural, Preguntas: *1. ¿De qué mezcla cultural es México? (de lo autóctono con lo español y otros elementos internacionales, de lo antiguo y lo moderno) 2. ¿Cuántas personas viven en Mexico? (100 millones) 3. ¿Cómo se llama la capital? (la Ciudad de México, el Distrito Federal, [el D.F.]) 4. ¿En qué continente está situado México? (en el continente de la América del Norte) 5. ¿Cuáles son las características geográficas y culturales de México? (see list in text)*

sus mariachis y por sus hermosas[1] playas como las de Acapulco, Cancún y otras. Los que[2] se interesan por conocer a fondo[3] México se encuentran con una civilización compleja. México es ante todo una mezcla de lo autóctono[4] con lo español y otros elementos internacionales… de lo antiguo y lo moderno al mismo tiempo. A continuación se ofrece una fotografía de México a vista de pájaro.

México en cifras

Población:	100 millones de habitantes
Área:	761.605 millas cuadradas
Capital:	México = Ciudad de México, el Distrito Federal (el D.F.), a 7.575 pies de altura, en la meseta central con 21 millones de habitantes, la metrópoli más grande del mundo

México: una gran diversidad geográfica y cultural, pasado y presente

México es el único país de Latinoamérica situado en el continente de la América del Norte. Al norte, limita con[5] los Estados Unidos. El Río Grande (los mexicanos lo llaman el Río Bravo) sirve de límite natural desde Ciudad Juárez hasta el Golfo de México. Al sureste, México limita con Guatemala y Belice, en Centro América.

La diversidad geográfica y cultural de México es impresionante. De las siguientes características, ¿cuántas reconoces?

- un extenso litoral,[6] con hermosas playas como las de Acapulco y Cancún
- desiertos y regiones semiáridas, como el desierto de Sonora
- zonas de densa vegetación, como en Yucatán
- sierras altas
- la meseta central, el Altiplano Mexicano, donde está situada la capital
- ruinas precolombinas de las civilizaciones azteca y maya, en sitios como Uxmal y Chichén Itzá en Yucatán y Teotihuacán, cerca de la capital
- ciudades coloniales como Taxco o Guanajuato

En el D.F., hermosos edificios coloniales conviven[7] con edificios modernos, tiendas, teatros, cines y más. El mismo día se pueden visitar la Catedral Metropolitana de México, la más antigua de la América Latina, y la modernísima ciudad universitaria, la UNAM (Universidad Nacional Autónoma de México).

México… un país con un rico pasado y abierto al futuro, un país que busca mantener sus tradiciones y al mismo tiempo superar[8] los problemas del presente. En las siguientes lecciones de *Destinos*, llegarás a conocer este país más a fondo.

Arte mosaico en la UNAM

[1]*beautiful* [2]Los… Las personas que [3]*a… in depth* [4]lo… *indigenous elements* [5]limita… *borders on, has borders with* [6]*coastline* [7]*coexist* [8]*to overcome*

INTERCAMBIO

Paso 1

¿Has pensado alguna vez en la evolución y cómo serán los seres humanos dentro de un millón de años? Utilizando el modelo como guía, escribe cinco oraciones sobre lo que crees que serán los rasgos físicos de los seres humanos.

MODELO: No tendremos pelo en los brazos.

Paso 2

Comparte tus ideas con otras dos personas. Luego, deben escoger las cinco mejores ideas y presentarlas a la clase. ¿Hay ideas comunes en la clase?

VOCABULARIO

Los verbos

enterarse (de)	to find out (about)
jugar (ue) (al)	to play (*a game*)
rescatar	to rescue

Las personas

el padre	priest, father

Algunas partes del cuerpo
(Some Parts of the Body)

la boca	mouth
el brazo	arm
la cabeza	head
el corazón	heart
la espalda	back
la mano	hand
la nariz	nose
los ojos	eyes
la oreja	ear
el pecho	chest
el pelo	hair
el pie	foot
la pierna	leg

Los conceptos

el acontecimiento	happening, event
el asunto	matter, affair, business
la esperanza	hope

Los adjetivos

atrapado/a	trapped

LECCIÓN 29

¡SE DERRUMBÓ!*

It Collapsed!

OBJETIVOS

The materials in **Lección 29** of the Textbook and the Workbook/Study Guide will help you better understand the video episode and take you beyond it, giving you additional information about places and characters in the series. The Textbook will also help you to develop skill in using the Spanish language. In this lesson, you will learn

- more vocabulary for talking about parts of the body, as well as vocabulary and expressions related to medical examinations and conditions
- ways to talk about what people want others to do

You will also learn about several Mexican traditions.

Be sure to work through all parts of the lesson. When you see a headphones symbol in the margin, listen to the CD for **Lección 29**. Answers or hints for many activities are given in Appendix 1. Be sure to check your answers for each activity before going on to the next one.

The interactive CD-ROM to accompany *Destinos* contains additional practice with the video storyline and will help you improve your skills in Spanish.

BEFORE VIEWING . . .

Preliminary: See Faculty Guide for additional information and activities for this lesson.
• **Variation:** For activities marked with the headphones icon, you may wish to read from the Audioscript instead of playing the CD.
• **Suggestion:** Make sure students are familiar with the activities before you read from the Audioscript or play the CD.

1

PREPARACIÓN

Suggestions:
• Before watching the video, go over the vocabulary list at the end of the chapter and have students pronounce the words after you.
• Assign *Preparación* activities as homework and then go over them quickly in class before viewing the video.

Act. Answers: 1. c 2. a 3. c 4. c

Act., Follow-up: Have students create one true/false statement for Raquel and one for Ángela based on the events of the previous episode. Students read their statements to a partner or to the whole class who must determine whether they are true or false.

Actividad.

En el último episodio de *Destinos*, viste lo que pasó en la excavación y también conociste de nuevo a varios miembros de la familia Castillo. Completa las siguientes oraciones según lo que ocurrió en el episodio.

1. Después de completar el examen de don Fernando, el doctor que lo atendía le dijo a la familia que don Fernando
   a. _____ podía volver a La Gavia.
   b. _____ tenía que quedarse en la clínica una semana más.
   c. _____ necesitaba ver a un especialista.

2. En la familia Castillo
   a. _____ nadie sabía del accidente que ocurrió en la excavación donde trabajaba Roberto.
   b. _____ todos sabían lo del accidente en la excavación.
   c. _____ sólo Pedro sabía lo del accidente.

3. Roberto
   a. _____ logró (*was able*) escapar del derrumbe.
   b. _____ murió en el derrumbe.
   c. _____ es una de las personas atrapadas en el derrumbe.

4. Arturo
   a. _____ leyó la noticia del derrumbe en un periódico.
   b. _____ vio la noticia del derrumbe en la televisión.
   c. _____ se quedó dormido frente al televisor y no vio la noticia del derrumbe.

 . . . AFTER VIEWING

2

¿TIENES BUENA MEMORIA?

Act. A., Suggestion: Give students about 5 minutes to complete the activity individually or in pairs and then compare answers as a whole class.

Actividad A. En la excavación
Paso 1

Después de tomar un calmante, Ángela por fin se pudo dormir y Raquel también se durmió. Al despertarse, Raquel resume los acontecimientos más importantes que ocurrieron en la excavación. ¿Puedes completar el resumen?

1. teníamos pocas esperanzas
   teníamos muchas esperanzas
2. a un hombre y a una mujer
   a un profesor de Roberto
3. pero no fueron muchos los
   daños (*damage*)
   y se derrumbó todo otra vez
4. comenzó a salir
   comenzó a llorar (*cry*)
5. acostumbrarme al tiempo
   que hace aquí en la
   meseta
   comunicarme con la familia
   de don Fernando
6. Arturo
   Roberto

Pues, el calmante ha hecho[a] su efecto. Ángela está dormida. Pobre. Debe estar cansadísima… y con mucha razón. Han pasado[b] tantas cosas. Cuando volvimos al sitio de la excavación, _____.[1] Creíamos que sacaban a Roberto del túnel. ¿Y qué pasó? ¿Sacaron a Roberto? No sacaron a Roberto. Sacaron _____.[2]

Poco después, ocurrió algo inesperado. Ninguno de nosotros pensamos que esto ocurriría.[c] ¿Recuerdan qué pasó? Bueno, hubo un segundo derrumbe _____.[3]

Pues, esto fue demasiado para Ángela y _____.[4] Y tuvimos que traerla aquí. El doctor le dio un calmante. Poco después, entró el Padre Rodrigo con noticias.

Y aquí estamos. Ángela está dormida. Yo también tengo ganas de dormir, pero estoy muy preocupada. No he podido[d] _____.[5] ¿Sabrán ellos que estamos aquí? ¿Y cómo estará don Fernando?

Hmmm. Bueno, ya no puedo hacer nada más que esperar. Estoy muy cansada. ¡Ay! ¡Me olvidé de _____![6] Debe estar preocupadísimo.

[a]ha… *has had*   [b]Han… *Have happened*   [c]*would happen*   [d]No… *I haven't been able*

Paso 2
Ahora escucha el CD para verificar tus respuestas.

Actividad B. **En la capital**
Mientras Ángela y Raquel esperan noticias de Roberto, en casa de Pedro la vida sigue igual, con unos pequeños problemas.

Paso 1
Usando las siguientes indicaciones u otras, si quieres, describe algunas de las cosas que pasan esa noche y al día siguiente. Debes inventar diez oraciones originales. ¡OJO! Haz algunas oraciones falsas, con una o dos palabras o nombres incorrectos.

Personas: Carlitos, Juanita, Carlos, Gloria, Consuelo, Maricarmen, Mercedes, Arturo, Pedro, Raquel, don Fernando

Frases: decirle (algo a alguien), estar enfermo/a, llamar, ponerle una inyección, reunirse para cenar, sentirse bien/mal, tomarle la temperatura

Paso 2

Ahora, presenta tus oraciones a tu compañero/a. Túrnense para corregir las oraciones según lo que se dice en el **Episodio 29**.

MODELO: TÚ: Juanita no se siente bien.
                  COMPAÑERO/A: No es cierto. Carlitos no se siente bien.

¡Un desafío! Durante el desayuno, se menciona que una persona llegó tarde a casa anoche. ¿Recuerdas quién era?

Para pensar...

1. ¿Crees que Ángela es una persona fuerte? En tu opinión, ¿quién es mas fuerte, Ángela o Raquel?
2. ¿Crees que es bueno ocultarle (*to hide*) a don Fernando lo del accidente de Roberto? ¿O deben decirle los hijos lo que está pasando?

Nota cultural   Dos tradiciones mexicanas

In this video episode you learned some information about two very important Mexican traditions, one secular and the other religious.

- Not only does Arturo miss news of the excavation on TV, but he also misses an advertisement for the **Ballet Folclórico de México**. The spectacular performances of this dance troupe reflect the music and traditions of native Mexican peoples: the Mayans, the Aztecs, and many other civilizations that constitute the country's rich indigenous heritage, of which all Mexicans are aware and proud. You will learn more about **el Ballet Folclórico** in **Lección 39**.

- In Mexico, a European heritage exists alongside the indigenous culture. Father Rodrigo promises Ángela that "**la Virgen cuidará a tu hermano.**" The Virgin to whom he is referring is the Catholic **Virgen de Guadalupe,*** whose veneration started soon after the arrival in Mexico of the first Spanish priests and religious brothers. Today **la Virgen** is the patron saint not only of Mexico but also of all of Latin America. She is venerated as well by many Hispanic Catholics living in the United States. It is not a good idea to assume that all Hispanics are Catholic, however. In Mexico, for example, there are many Mexican Protestants and Jews, as well as members of other religious traditions.

---

* You will learn more about **la Virgen de Guadalupe** in the **Lectura cultural** of this lesson.

3

VOCABULARIO DEL TEMA

Los exámenes médicos

Las enfermedades

la fiebre	fever
la fractura	fracture
el resfriado	cold

Los tratamientos

la aspirina	aspirin
la medicina	medicine
la pastilla	pill
la receta	prescription
el termómetro	thermometer

Las personas

el doctor/la doctora, el/la médico	doctor
el enfermero/la enfermera	nurse
el/la paciente	patient

Verbos y expresiones útiles

bajar	to bring down (*a fever*)
curar	to heal, cure
examinar	to examine
guardar cama	to stay in bed
ponerle (a alguien) una inyección	to give (someone) a shot
respirar	to breathe
sacar la lengua	to stick out one's tongue
sacar rayos X (*equis*)	to take X-rays
sentirse (ie, i) bien/mal	to feel well/bad
tomarle (a alguien) la temperatura	to take (someone's) temperature
doler (ue)	to hurt, be painful
Me duele (la garganta).	*My (throat) hurts.*
Le duelen (los pies).	*His (feet) hurt.*
tener (*irreg.*)	to have
Tienes (una fiebre alta).	*You have (a high fever).*
Tienes (la lengua blanca).	*Your (tongue) is (white).*
Tienes (el brazo) hinchado.	*Your (arm) is swollen.*

R.F.C. MAAR 560224   CED. PROF. 162805
Dr. Alejandro Marroz R.
Médico Pediatra   Hospital Infantil
532-21-11
tels— 516-50-43
Rx.

¿PROBLEMAS DE SINUSITIS?
¿DOLOR DE CABEZA?
¿FIEBRE?
¿OBSTRUCCION NASAL?

TODOS ESTOS SINTOMAS PUEDEN ESTAR RELACIONADOS A UNA ALERGIA Y / O PROBLEMAS DE SINUSITIS

ALLERGY/SINUS CENTER
OFFERING COMPLETE DIAGNOSTIC SERVICES, including
• ALLERGY SKIN TESTING
• RAST ALLERGY BLOOD TESTING
• FIBEROPTIC EXAMINATION OF NOSE & SINUS
ALSO COMPLETE ALLERGY/SINUS TREATMENT
• FUNCTIONAL ENDOSCOPIC SINUS SURGERY (OUTPATIENT)
• ALLERGY DESENSITIZATION
BOARD CERTIFIED OTORHINOLARYNGOLOGIST AND HEAD & NECK SURGEON

LLAMENOS HOY
275-5550
GARY G. WIESMAN, M.D.,F.A.C.S.

1431 N. WESTERN AVE. SUITE 207 CHICAGO, IL 60622

1945 W. WILSON AVE. 3RD FLOOR CHICAGO, IL 60640

Note the following about the preceding health-related vocabulary.

- The terms **médico/doctor(a)** are not completely interchangeable. Both are used to speak about a doctor: **El médico/doctor vino a casa anoche**. But only **el doctor (la doctora)** can be used with the doctor's specific name: **Mi médico es la doctora Sánchez**.
- The verb **doler** is like **gustar**: the part of the body that hurts determines whether a singular verb form (**duele, dolía, dolió...**) or a plural one (**duelen, dolían, dolieron...**) is used.

Actividad A. **Carlitos tiene un resfriado**

Escucha las oraciones del CD. ¿A qué foto o dibujo se refiere cada oración?

a. _____ b. _____ c. _____ d. _____ e. _____ f. _____

Actividad B.

En el CD, escucha otra vez el examen que les hace el médico a las dos personas rescatadas de la excavación donde está atrapado Roberto. Luego indica la información correcta para cada paciente.

Primer paciente: El hombre

1. Se siente... bien/mal.
2. Le duele... la garganta/la espalda.
3. Tiene/No tiene... fiebre.
4. El doctor... le da una aspirina/le pone una inyección.

Segundo paciente: La mujer

5. Tiene hinchado... el brazo/el pie.
6. También le duele... la cabeza/la pierna.
7. Según el médico, necesita... un termómetro/rayos X.
8. Tiene/No tiene... fiebre.

Actividad C.   Cuando me enfermo...

¿Cuáles de las siguientes oraciones describen tu propia experiencia? Indícalas.

1. _____ Cuando me duele la cabeza, no tomo aspirinas. Simplemente espero... y siempre se me pasa.
2. _____ Cuando algo me duele, tomo alguna medicina en seguida. ¡No aguanto (*I can't stand*) el dolor!
3. _____ Tengo por lo menos un resfriado cada año.
4. _____ Nunca me resfrío (*catch a cold*).
5. _____ Nunca he tenido (*I've never had*) una fiebre muy alta.
6. _____ Tomo varias medicinas todos los días.
7. _____ Trago (*I swallow*) las pastillas fácilmente.
8. _____ Creo que es peligroso que a uno le tomen muchos rayos X en un año.
9. _____ Ningún tratamiento médico me molesta para nada.
10. _____ Tengo miedo de las inyecciones.

UN POCO DE GRAMÁTICA

The Workbook/Study Guide contains more detailed explanation and practice of this grammar point.

Talking About What People Want Others to Do

The following type of sentence is used to describe what someone wants another person to do.

Carlos **quiere que** Carlitos **se tome** la medicina. También **quiere que guarde** cama.

Carlos wants Carlitos to take his medicine. He also wants him to stay in bed.

The second half of each of these sentences contains an **-ar** verb, but with an **-e** ending. This is one form of a different verb system called the present subjunctive. It is formed by using the present-tense **yo** stem: **tom-** → **tome**.

To use an **-er** or **-ir** verb in this type of sentence, add an **-a** ending.

Carlitos no quiere que **venga** el médico.

Did you notice how the irregularity of the **yo** stem is reflected in this form? **Vengo** → **venga**, **pongo** → **ponga**, and so on. To form the third-person plural of the present subjunctive, add the characteristic **-n** ending to the **-a** or **-e**. You will learn more about these forms in the Workbook/Study Guide.

Actividad. ¿Qué quieren que hagas?
Paso 1

Indica lo que las siguientes personas e instituciones quieren —¡o no quieren!— que hagas. ¡OJO! También debes inventar algunas oraciones falsas.

> MODELOS: Mi profesora de español quiere que participe más en clase.
> Mi perro quiere que le dé más dinero.

Palabra útil: los impuestos (*taxes*)

Mis padres		trabaje _____
Mis profesores		lo(s) ayude (con) _____
Mis amigos		le(s) dé _____
Mis hermanos		sea _____
Mis parientes	(no) quiere(n) que	lo(s) llame _____
La universidad		lo(s) visite _____
La sociedad		pague _____
Mi país		¿ ?
Mi perro/gato		
¿ ?		

Paso 2

Ahora túrnate con tu compañero/a para leer algunas de las oraciones que inventaron en el **Paso 1**. Deben leer algunas de las oraciones falsas. ¿Puede adivinar (*guess*) tu compañero/a cuáles son las falsas?

> MODELO: TÚ: Mis padres no quieren que trabaje este semestre.
> COMPAÑERO/A: ¡Eso es falso!
>   TÚ: Sí, tienes razón.

5

LECTURA CULTURAL

La Virgen de Guadalupe

Remember that, throughout the first half of the Textbook, a brief exercise before each extensive **Lectura cultural** reading helped you review what you already knew about the topic (usually information from the video episode) before beginning the reading. Keep that strategy in mind as you work with the readings in the second half of the text. The first few **Lecturas culturales** will have a brief reminder.

Antes de leer, escucha una vez más lo que el narrador dice sobre la Virgen de Guadalupe. Hay más información sobre la Virgen en la lectura.

Lectura cultural, **Preguntas:** 1. *¿Cómo se llamaba el joven indio a quien apareció la Virgen María?* (Juan Diego) 2. *¿Qué le pidió la Virgen?* (que se construyera un templo) 3. *¿A quién contó su experiencia Juan Diego?* (al obispo) 4. *¿Qué planta apareció en el sitio de la aparición?* (un rosal) 5. *¿Cómo le convenció Juan Diego al obispo?* (con la imagen de la Virgen en la manta) 6. *¿Qué edificio está en el lugar sagrado hoy?* (la Basílica de Guadalupe).

Era el año 1531, pocos años después de la llegada de los primeros españoles a América. Un joven indio caminaba tranquilamente por el campo,[1] en lo que es hoy la capital de México. De repente, oyó una voz femenina que le decía: «Juan Diego, Juan Diego».

Era la Virgen María, quien es la madre de Jesucristo en la tradición[2] cristiana. La Virgen habló con Juan Diego. Le pidió que se construyera[3] un templo en su honor, en el mismo cerro[4] de Tepeyac. Juan Diego fue a ver al obispo de su pueblo, para contarle la increíble historia. Como era de esperar,[5] el obispo no le creyó. La madre de Dios no se le iba a aparecer a un pobre indio.

La Virgen persistió en su deseo de tener un templo en ese lugar. Hizo crecer un rosal[6] en el cerro, una región donde los rosales no crecían. Y se le apareció al joven otra vez. Le pidió al muchacho que le llevara al obispo unas rosas del rosal. Juan Diego las puso en una manta.[7] Al abrirla delante del obispo, apareció dibujada en la manta, junto a las rosas, la imagen de la Virgen.

Poco tiempo después se construyó en el sitio del milagro[8] una capilla. En el altar se colocó[9] la imagen de la Virgen indígena, Nuestra Señora de Guadalupe; también la llaman la Virgen Morena. Hoy día hay una catedral en este lugar, la Basílica de Guadalupe. Es un lugar sagrado[10] para todos los mexicanos católicos. Los pobres y los enfermos vienen a esta catedral a pedirle a la Virgen milagros.

En México y en las comunidades mexicoamericanas en los Estados Unidos, la imagen de la Virgen de Guada-

La Basílica de Guadalupe

lupe está en todas partes: en calendarios, en pinturas, en casas privadas y sitios públicos... no sólo en las iglesias y las catedrales. Ricos y pobres la veneran.

Es fácil de explicar esta devoción del pueblo mexicano por la Virgen de Guadalupe. Para muchos mexicanos, la Virgen tiene un valor simbólico porque representa la raza indígena y demuestra el valor que la cultura indígena tiene ante los ojos de Dios. Pero no sólo los mexicanos y sus descendientes participan del culto a la Virgen. Desde 1910 la Virgen es también la santa patrona de toda Hispanoamérica.

[1]*countryside* [2]*belief* [3]se... *he built* [4]en... *on that very hill* [5]era... *was predictable* [6]*rosebush*
[7]*cloak* [8]*miracle* [9]se... *was placed* [10]*sacred, holy*

Actividad.   **La historia de la Virgen de Guadalupe**

Los ocho dibujos a continuación narran la historia de la Virgen, pero un dibujo no pertenece a la narración que acabas de leer. ¿Puedes identificarlo?

1.   2.   3.   4.

5.   6.   7.   8.

6

INTERCAMBIO

Paso 1

Piensa en tres enfermedades o condiciones físicas y las recomendaciones de un médico.

> MODELO: una fiebre: «Quiero que tomes dos aspirinas cada cuatro horas.»

Paso 2

Ahora presenta sólo las recomendaciones del médico. No menciones la enfermedad. ¿Pueden adivinar tus compañeros cuál es la enfermedad?

Paso 3

Después de escuchar todas las recomendaciones, como clase decidan qué enfermedad es la más frecuente. ¿Cuál es la recomendación más común? ¿Es lo que Uds. hacen normalmente?

VOCABULARIO

Los verbos

derrumbarse	to collapse, cave in
llorar	to cry
lograr	to manage to, be able
sacar	to take out, get out

Las enfermedades (Illnesses)

la fiebre	fever
la fractura	fracture
el resfriado	cold

Los verbos relacionados con la salud
(Health-Related Verbs)

bajar	to bring down (*a fever*)
curar	to heal, cure
doler (ue)	to hurt, be painful
examinar	to examine
guardar cama	to stay in bed
ponerle (a alguien) una inyección	to give (someone) a shot
respirar	to breathe
sacar la lengua	to stick out one's tongue
sacar rayos X	to take X-rays
tomarle (a alguien) la temperatura	to take (someone's) temperature

Repaso: **sentirse (ie, i) bien/mal**

Los tratamientos (Treatments)

la aspirina	aspirin
el calmante	sedative
el examen	examination
la medicina	medicine
la pastilla	pill
la receta	prescription
el termómetro	thermometer

Otras partes del cuerpo

la garganta	throat
la lengua	tongue

Los adjetivos

hinchado/a	swollen
médico/a	medical

Las personas

el enfermero/la enfermera	nurse
el/la médico	doctor

Repaso: **el doctor/la doctora, el/la paciente**

LECCIÓN 30

PREOCUPACIONES*

*Worries

OBJETIVOS

The materials in **Lección 30** of the Textbook and the Workbook/Study Guide will help you better understand the video episode and take you beyond it, giving you additional information about places and characters in the series. The Textbook will also help you to develop skill in using the Spanish language. In this lesson, you will learn

- the names for many places in a city
- ways to use the subjunctive to discuss things about which you feel emotionally involved

You will also learn about the Cuban-American community.

Be sure to work through all parts of the lesson. When you see a headphones symbol in the margin, listen to the CD for **Lección 30**. Answers or hints for many activities are given in Appendix 1. Be sure to check your answers for each activity before going on to the next one.

The interactive CD-ROM to accompany *Destinos* contains additional practice with the video storyline and will help you improve your skills in Spanish.

BEFORE VIEWING . . .

Preliminary: See Faculty Guide for additional information and activities for this lesson.
• **Variation:** For activities marked with the headphones icon, you may wish to read from the Audioscript instead of playing the CD.
• **Suggestion:** Make sure students are familiar with the activities before you read from the Audioscript or play the CD.

1

PREPARACIÓN

Suggestions:
• Before watching the video, go over the vocabulary list at the end of the chapter and have students pronounce the words after you.
• Assign *Preparación* activities as homework and then go over them quickly in class before viewing the video.

Act. A, *Paso 1*, Suggestion: You may want to have students do this activity in pairs, then go over answers with whole class.

Actividad A.
Paso 1

A continuación tienes el texto del resumen del narrador que, como siempre, vas a escuchar al principio de este episodio, pero hay algunos detalles incorrectos. Indica la información equivocada. (Hay uno o dos detalles incorrectos en cada párrafo.)

Act. A, *Paso 1*, Answers: *Primer párrafo: murió → no se sabía nada de él. Segundo párrafo: hablaba del derrumbe en la excavación → hablaba de varios asuntos; Gloria → Carlos. Tercer párrafo: Muy contento porque ya sabía algo de Raquel → Muy preocupado porque no tenía noticias de Raquel*

En el episodio previo, cuando Raquel y Ángela llegaron al sitio de la excavación, ya sacaban a dos personas. Pero ninguna de las dos era el hermano de Ángela. Justo en ese momento, hubo otro derrumbe en la excavación. Roberto Castillo quedó atrapado de nuevo y murió. Ángela estaba desesperada.

Al día siguiente, en la Ciudad de México, la familia Castillo desayunaba y hablaba del derrumbe en la excavación. Mientras la familia desayunaba, Gloria hablaba con su hijo, quien estaba enfermo la noche anterior.

Muy contento porque ya sabía algo de Raquel, Arturo bajó a la recepción del hotel y preguntó por ella. Solo y sin amigos en esta ciudad grande, Arturo salió a la calle.

 ### Paso 2
Ahora escucha la narración en el CD para ver si encontraste todos los errores.

***Para pensar*, Suggestion:** Pose the same question to several students to elicit a variety of opinions.

> ### Para pensar...
>
> Imagina que eres Arturo y que te encuentras en la situación que se describe al final del episodio previo. ¿En qué estás pensando? ¿Cuáles son tus preocupaciones? ¿Qué necesitas? ¿Qué vas a hacer para tratar de resolver algunas de tus preocupaciones?

 ## Actividad B.
Paso 1

Act. B, ¡OJO!: Point out that, in many Caribbean dialects, certain final consonants are not pronounced (*más*) and intervocalic consonants sometimes disappear, particularly in past participles (*nađa, enojađa*).

En este episodio, vas a ver otra vez a un personaje que apareció mucho antes, en uno de los primeros episodios de *Destinos*. Es Ofelia, la secretaria de Carlos en Miami.

Como muchas personas que viven en la Florida, Ofelia es cubana. Su dialecto del español y acento son diferentes de los de los otros personajes de la serie. Escucha parte de una conversación telefónica entre Carlos y Ofelia para familiarizarte con el acento de ella. Puedes escuchar la conversación varias veces, si quieres. Luego contesta la pregunta.

¿De qué le habla Ofelia a Carlos?

a. _____ De su familia.

b. _____ De un nuevo restaurante.

c. _____ De un nuevo cliente.

¿Notas la diferencia en su acento? ¿Cómo es diferente, por ejemplo, del acento de Carlos? ¿de Raquel?

Paso 2

En este episodio, el Padre Rodrigo sigue muy preocupado por el bienestar (*well-being*) de Ángela y Raquel. Les hace una sugerencia sobre algo que cree que ellas deben hacer. Escucha su conversación con ellas. Luego completa la oración.

El Padre Rodrigo les

a. _____ recomienda a las dos mujeres que vayan a un hotel en el pueblo.

b. _____ recomienda que se queden con una persona religiosa.

Como en inglés, la palabra **hermana** se refiere no solamente a un miembro de la familia sino también a las mujeres que dedican su vida al servicio de Dios en una comunidad religiosa.

 . . . AFTER VIEWING

2 ¿TIENES BUENA MEMORIA?

Actividad A.   ¿Quiénes son?

Contesta las siguientes preguntas sobre dos mujeres que aparecen en este episodio. Una está relacionada con los asuntos de la capital; la otra, con los asuntos que ocurren en la excavación.

1. Esta mujer se llama
   a. _____ Pati.   c. _____ Ofelia.
   b. _____ Gloria.

2. Vive en… donde trabaja en la Compañía Industrias Castillo Saavedra, como secretaria de Carlos
   a. _____ Los Ángeles   c. _____ Nueva York
   b. _____ Miami

3. Después de hablar con ella, Carlos
   a. _____ está preocupado.   c. _____ empieza a llorar.
   b. _____ está muy contento.

Para pensar...

Sí, Carlos está muy preocupado después de hablar con Ofelia. ¿Crees que eran buenas o malas las noticias que Ofelia le dio?

4. La hermana María Teresa vive en el pueblo y trabaja
   a. _____ en la excavación.
   b. _____ en una escuela, con los niños del pueblo.
   c. _____ en un hotel para turistas.

5. La hermana les ofrece a Raquel y a Ángela
   a. _____ un lugar donde descansar y refrescarse.
   b. _____ algo de comer.
   c. _____ un teléfono que funciona.

Nota cultural, **Suggestion:** You may want to go over this note and have students compare the role of religion in Hispanic cultures with its role in this country.

Nota cultural Aspectos de la vida religiosa

As you have seen in previous video episodes and continued to observe in this one, various aspects of religion and religious life play an important role in Hispanic countries, especially in rural areas. People who belong to religious orders—priests, nuns (sisters), monks (brothers)—are integral parts of the communities in which they live and work.

Here at the excavation site, for example, **el Padre Rodrigo** is a source of comfort to all who are involved with the accident, whether they are Catholic or not. And **la hermana María Teresa** unquestioningly offers support to Ángela and Raquel, opening the facilities of the church to them.

An important service offered by members of religious orders in some countries is education. In rural areas many schools are run by the Catholic Church. Do you remember that Jaime and Miguel Ruiz attended a religious school in Sevilla? Religion was one of the subjects that they both studied.

Actividad B. En la excavación y en la capital
Paso 1

Los siguientes párrafos son un resumen de lo que pasó en este episodio. Complétalos con la forma correcta de las palabras y frases de las siguientes listas.

Lugares: la capital, la escuela del pueblo, el hotel, la iglesia del pueblo, Nueva York, Puerto Rico, el sitio de la excavación, la tienda del pueblo

Frases: le dejó un mensaje/una carta, descansar y almorzar, descansar y bañarse, durmió muy bien/muy mal, estaba ocupada la línea, no consiguió línea, hablando con alguien en la capital/Nueva York, llamar, tener noticias de Roberto/Arturo, tenía suficiente aire/comida

Act. B, Answers: *Paso 1:*
1. *durmió muy bien*
2. *tener noticias de Roberto* 3. *tenía suficiente aire* 4. *tienda del pueblo* 5. *estaba ocupada la línea* 6. *hablando con alguien en Nueva York* 7. *el hotel* 8. *le dejó un mensaje* 9. *Puerto Rico* 10. *la iglesia del pueblo* 11. *descansar y bañarse*

Ángela y Raquel pasaron la noche en la excavación. Ángela _____[1] porque el doctor le dio un calmante. Tan pronto como se despertó, Ángela quería _____.[2] Desgraciadamente, no había noticias. Ángela seguía muy preocupada, sobre todo porque pensaba que tal vez Roberto no _____.[3]

En una pequeña _____,[4] Raquel seguía tratando de comunicarse por teléfono con varias personas en la capital. No pudo hablar con Pedro, porque _____.[5] (Raquel no lo sabía, pero en esa ocasión Pati estaba _____.[6]) Pero Raquel sí pudo hablar con _____[7] en México. Arturo no estaba en su habitación, pero Raquel _____.[8] (Cuando leyó el mensaje, Arturo estaba muy preocupado.) Por su parte, Ángela pudo hablar con sus tíos en _____.[9]

Después de hacer estas llamadas telefónicas, Raquel y Ángela fueron a _____,[10] donde las esperaba la hermana María Teresa. Allí, pudieron _____.[11]

Paso 2
Escucha el CD para verificar tus respuestas.

3

VOCABULARIO DEL TEMA

Suggestion: As you go over vocabulary, ask questions related to your local urban area: *¿Cómo se llaman las afueras de _____? ¿En qué zona/barrio vives? ¿Cuáles son las tiendas más populares en el centro? ¿Hay (muchos) rascascielos en _____? ¿Dónde compras tu(s) ropa/comestibles/verduras?*

As in some previous lessons, the words on this page are from the video episode. Those on the next page are additional vocabulary items for each category that you may want to learn.

En una ciudad

las afueras	suburb; outskirts	**el hotel**	hotel
el barrio, la zona	neighborhood	**el mercado**	market
el centro	downtown	**el negocio**	business
la colonia (*Mex.*)	neighborhood	**la oficina**	office
		el supermercado	supermarket
el ayuntamiento	city hall	**la tienda**	store
el cine	movie theater	**la tienda de ropa para hombres**	men's clothing store
el edificio	building		
la iglesia	church	**la tienda de ropa para mujeres**	women's clothing store
la plaza	plaza, square		
el almacén	department store		
la farmacia	drugstore, pharmacy		

la escuela	school	el banco	bank
el jardín (botánico)	(botanical) garden	el centro comercial	shopping center
el (jardín) zoológico	zoo	el restaurante	restaurant
el parque	park		
el rascacielos	skyscraper		
el teatro	theater		

Actividad A. El Distrito Federal
Paso 1
Escucha otra vez la descripción de la Ciudad de México. Mientras escuchas, indica en este dibujo con la letra **C** (**ciudad**) los diferentes lugares de la ciudad mencionados por el narrador.

Act. A, *Paso 1,* Answers: Students should have written C on: the center of town, the suburbs, the outskirts, the group of tall buildings, the office building, the hotel, the market, the supermarket, the pharmacy, the small shop, the large department store. *Paso 2:* Students should have written P on: the center, the plaza, the city hall, the church, the pharmacy, the shop, the market. They should have written N on: the group of tall buildings, the supermarket, the department store. *¡Un desafío!:* Arturo mencionó una farmacia, una tienda para hombres, un almacén, un mercado, un supermercado.

Paso 2
Ahora escucha otra vez la descripción de un pueblo típico. Mientras escuchas, indica en el mismo dibujo con la letra **P** (**pueblo**) los lugares de la capital que también se encuentran en los pueblos o que solamente se encuentran en ellos. Con la letra **N** (**no**) indica los lugares que no se encuentran en los pueblos.

¡Un desafío! ¿Recuerdas los sitios que Arturo quería encontrar en la capital? Le mencionó cinco lugares al agente de turismo.

Actividad B. Lugares muy conocidos

Vas a escuchar una descripción breve de una serie de lugares. Pon el número del lugar junto al nombre apropiado de la siguiente lista.

MODELO: (*oyes*) Número uno: Un parque es un sitio donde hay mucho espacio, muchos árboles, muchas flores…

(*escribes*) __1__ el Rosedal

(*dices*) El Rosedal es un parque.

(*oyes*) El Rosedal es un parque.

a. _____ *the San Diego Zoo, the Bronx Zoo*

b. _____ la Torre Trump

c. _____ *Greenwich Village*

d. _____ *Macy's*

e. _____ La Barca

f. _____ La Cuadra

g. _____ *Radio City Music Hall*

h. _____ *A&P, Safeway, Lucky's…*

i. _____ el Rosedal

Actividad C. En mi ciudad...

Túrnate con un compañero / una compañera para escoger algunos de los lugares de la siguiente lista. Pregúntale a tu compañero/a si hay uno de esos lugares en la ciudad donde se crió (*was raised*). Si hay alguno, debe dar el nombre del lugar. Si no hay, debe decir «No hay».

MODELO: un parque grande →

TÚ: ¿Hay un parque grande en tu ciudad?

COMPAÑERO/A: Sí. Se llama el Parque Roosevelt. (No, no hay.)

un restaurante muy elegante

un rascacielos

un supermercado económico

un cine popular entre los estudiantes

un almacén no muy caro

un centro comercial nuevo

4

UN POCO DE GRAMÁTICA

The Workbook/Study Guide contains more detailed explanation and practice of this grammar point.

Expressing Your Feelings About Something

It is possible to express feelings or emotion about an event without using the subjunctive. But it is also common to use the subjunctive as the second verb in a sentence that starts out with an expression of emotion, feelings, or an attitude toward something.

Es lástima que Roberto todavía **esté** atrapado en el túnel.

It's a shame that Roberto is still trapped in the tunnel.

Carlitos **tiene miedo de que** el doctor le **ponga** una inyección.

Carlitos is afraid that the doctor will give him a shot.

• Review subjunctive in noun clauses with verbs of wishing before presenting subjunctive in noun clauses with verbs of emotion. Have students use the subjunctive triggers to give each other orders. Make expressions such as the following visible on an overhead: *Quiero que tú... , Es necesario que tú... , Deseo que tú... .* Pass out cards with infinitives on them for students to use in the subjunctive: *(cantar)* → *Quiero que tú cantes una canción de Bruce Springsteen.* The other student must act out the order.

Variation: Have students use the *Ud.* forms to give you orders that you must act out.

As you do the following activity, notice other expressions of emotion used at the beginning of the sentence that "trigger" the subjunctive. And be on the lookout for the subjunctive forms of some irregular verbs. You will learn more about these aspects of the subjunctive in the Workbook/Study Guide.

Actividad.   ¿Cuáles son tus sentimientos?

¿Cómo te sientes en distintas ocasiones? Expresa tus sentimientos utilizando los elementos a continuación.

MODELO: ¡Me alegro que el Sr. Smith sea nuestro profesor!

1. Siento (*I regret*) que…
2. Es una lástima que…
3. ¡Qué pena (*shame*) que…
4. (No) Me gusta que…

5. ¡Qué bueno que…
6. Tengo miedo de que…
7. Es extraño (*strange*) que…

Act. Follow-up: Have students create sentences that express wishing to follow up their original sentences. Model: *Es una lástima que mis padres sean malos cocineros. Quiero que aprendan a cocinar.*

a.   (no) haya _____.

b.   los estudiantes tengamos que _____.

c.   mi amigo/a _____ sea _____.

d.   mis padres sean _____.

e.   mi perro/gato esté _____.

f.   los profesores tengan _____.

g.   ¿ ?

5

LECTURA CULTURAL

Lectura cultural, **Suggestion:** It is helpful to have a large map of Cuba in front of the room or on an overhead.

Los cubanos en los Estados Unidos

Los cubanos que viven en los Estados Unidos son en su mayoría[1] inmigrantes.* Viven dispersos por varias partes del país. El lugar donde hay una mayor concentración de ellos es en el sur de la Florida, sobre todo en Miami. En esa ciudad, especialmente en el barrio que se llama La Pequeña Habana, es marcada la presencia de la exuberante cultura cubana. Se nota en todo: en el fuerte café cubano; en los juegos de dominó de los ancianos; en los ritmos caribeños que se escuchan en la televisión y en la radio; en los nombres de las calles y de las tiendas, y en las personas.

[1]en… *for the most part*

---

* Como inmigrantes, los cubanoamericanos son diferentes a los mexicoamericanos y a los puertorriqueños. Como ya lo sabes, los puertorriqueños son ciudadanos de los Estados Unidos. Los antepasados de algunos mexicoamericanos fueron los dueños de territorios en Texas, California, Arizona, Nuevo México… Otros mexicoamericanos están en este país porque quieren vivir aquí. No vinieron como refugiados políticos como muchos cubanos.

Lectura cultural, Preguntas: 1. *¿En qué parte de los EEUU hay una concentración de cubanos? (en Miami, Florida)* 2. *¿Cómo se llama el barrio cubano de Miami? (La Pequeña Habana)* 3. *¿Cuáles son los elementos cubanos de la cultura en este barrio? (el fuerte café, los juegos de dominó de los ancianos, los ritmos caribeños, los nombres de las calles y las tiendas, y las personas)* 4. *¿Quién fue el dictador antes de Fidel Castro? (Fulgencio Batista)* 5. *¿En qué año ocurrió la invasión de la Bahía de Cochinos? (en 1961)* 6. *¿Qué profesiones tienen Xavier Suárez y Gustavo Medina? (abogado, alcalde de Miami en 1985; escritor y guionista)*

Personas y personajes

Los cubanos comenzaron a llegar a los Estados Unidos en gran número hacia 1960. Fidel Castro ya había ganado[2] la revolución, y perseguía a las personas que tenían una buena posición económica y social bajo la dictadura de Fulgencio Batista.

Por eso, los cubanos que inmigraron en aquel entonces[3] eran en su mayoría profesionales de las clases media y alta: abogados, médicos, ingenieros,[4] hombres de negocio.* Como refugiados políticos, llegaron con poco más que su cultura y educación. En algunos casos sus títulos universitarios no eran válidos en los Estados Unidos, y tuvieron que volver a la universidad a estudiar.

Veamos algo de la historia de dos cubanoamericanos, uno ya famoso y el otro… todavía no.

- Xavier Suárez: elegido alcalde[5] de la ciudad de Miami en 1985

Xavier Suárez y su familia

Suárez nació en Cuba, el noveno[6] de catorce hijos. Llegó a los Estados Unidos a los once años, después de la invasión de la Bahía de Cochinos,[7] y pronto aprendió inglés. Como para muchos cubanoamericanos, la educación era muy importante para él. Por eso sacó un B.S. en ingeniería, un M.A. en administración pública y, por fin, el título de abogado en Harvard.

Aquí Suárez habla de una de sus primeras memorias en los Estados Unidos: «Yo fui a una iglesia el domingo y … no entendía nada de lo que decía el sacerdote[8] en el sermón. Nada. Nada. Y eso que estudié inglés como buen estudiante. ¡Vaya! Pensé que sabría[9] algo de lo que estaba diciendo. Nada. Nada. Nada. Dije 'Dios mío, ¿cómo yo voy a entender el idioma de este país?'»

- Gustavo Medina: escritor, guionista[10]

Medina también nació en Cuba. Tenía nueve años cuando salió de Cuba con su familia en 1959, el mismo año en que cayó[11] el gobierno de Batista. Ya en los Estados Unidos, sacó un M.S. en psicología y luego trabajó de corrector de libros y de programas para computadoras. Después de alcanzar[12] éxito en este campo, decidió sacar un título en cinematografía. Ahora aspira a hacer televisión.

Aquí Medina habla de un tema que le interesa mucho: «… es el tema de ser un exiliado en un país extranjero… [Uno] no pertenece[13] a una cultura ni pertenece a otra, pero tiene que acomodarse[14] y es muy difícil a veces…. Para mí un tema importante en mi vida es cómo resolver ese aislamiento[15] que yo siento, en esta cultura y en otras culturas hispánicas. Por ejemplo, yo voy a la Argentina, voy a México, voy a Colombia, voy a Puerto Rico, y la gente me dice, «Ah, tú eres cubano». Sí, claro, pero no lo soy… Cuando estoy en Europa y la gente me oye hablar inglés, me dice, *«Oh, you are American.»* Entonces yo digo, *«No, not really. I'm from Cuba, but I'm not really anymore.»*

[2]había… *bad won*   [3]en… *at that time*   [4]*engineers*   [5]*mayor*   [6]*ninth*   [7]Bahía… *Bay of Pigs*
[8]*priest*   [9]*would know*   [10]*script writer*   [11]*fell*   [12]*achieving*   [13]*belong*   [14]*adjust*   [15]*isolation*

---

* Ha habido otras olas de inmigración también: una, después de la invasión de la Bahía de Cochinos en 1961; otra, la llegada de los llamados «marielitos» en 1980.

La situación política actual

Se habla mucho de los aspectos positivos de la presencia de los cubanos en la Florida, sobre todo en Miami. Pero hay que reconocer al mismo tiempo que presenta problemas. Algunos anglosajones guardan resentimiento hacia lo que ellos ven como la «dominación» latina de la ciudad. Para otros, sobre todo para los que no hablan español, el vivir constantemente en contacto con este idioma representa una molestia. La otra cara de la moneda[16] es la actitud de los cubanos a quienes no les gusta —o que no saben— hablar inglés.

También hay controversias entre la misma comunidad cubanoamericana. Algunos, sobre todo los más ancianos, se consideran todavía cubanos y les gustaría volver a vivir en Cuba. Para ellos, es antipatriótico renunciar a esa esperanza. Pero los jóvenes son cubano*americanos,* sobre todo los que nacieron aquí. Es cierto que les interesa Cuba y todo lo hispánico, pero se van forjando[17] sus vidas en este país. Para ellos, Cuba es algo que vive en el recuerdo de sus padres o abuelos; no es parte de su realidad. Otros, como Suárez y Medina, comparten ambas experiencias.

[16]La… *The other side of the coin*   [17]*creating*

Actividad.   La experiencia de un inmigrante

En tu opinión, ¿cuáles son las ventajas (*advantages*) y las desventajas de ser un inmigrante en otro país? Piensa no sólo en lo que acabas de leer sino también en lo que sabes de Ángel Castillo, quien siendo español, fue después argentino y luego emigró a Puerto Rico.

6

INTERCAMBIO

Paso 1

Utilizando los modelos a continuación, inventa tres oraciones para expresar lo que es importante para ti y lo que no es importante. Cuando puedas, utiliza el nuevo vocabulario de las páginas 292–293 como **cine, teatro, supermercado,** etcétera.

1. Es importante que haya _____ cerca de mi casa porque…

2. Es poco importante que haya _____ cerca de mi casa porque…

Paso 2

Comparte tus ideas con la clase. ¿Qué ideas tienen en común? ¿Qué tendencias hay?

Paso 3

Según los resultados del **Paso 2**, ¿cuál de las siguientes ideas representa mejor lo que tienen en común?

_____ Tenemos más o menos las mismas necesidades. Nos importan las mismas cosas.

_____ No tenemos las mismas necesidades. Nos importan diferentes cosas.

VOCABULARIO

Los verbos

descansar	to rest
sentir (**ie**, **i**)	to regret

En una ciudad

las afueras	suburbs, outskirts
el almacén	department store
el ayuntamiento	city hall
el banco	bank
el centro	downtown
el cine	movie theater
la colonia (*Mex.*)	neighborhood
el edificio	building
la farmacia	pharmacy
el hotel	hotel
el jardín (**botánico**)	(botanical) garden
el (**jardín**) zoológico	zoo
el parque	park

el rascacielos	skyscraper
el restaurante	restaurant
el supermercado	supermarket
el teatro	theater
la tienda de ropa para hombres/mujeres	men's/women's clothing store
la zona	neighborhood

Repaso: **el barrio, la escuela, la iglesia, el mercado, el negocio, la oficina, la tienda**

Otros lugares

el pueblo	town

Las palabras adicionales

es extraño	it's strange
es (**una**) lástima	it's a shame

MEDIDAS DRÁSTICAS*

*Drastic Measures

OBJETIVOS

The materials in **Lección 31** of the Textbook and the Workbook/Study Guide will help you better understand the video episode and take you beyond it, giving you additional information about places and characters in the series. The Textbook will also help you to develop skill in using the Spanish language. In this lesson, you will learn

- the names for various businesses and types of shops in Spanish
- the use of the subjunctive to talk about things that have not happened yet

You will also learn about the Mexican-American community.

Be sure to work through all parts of the lesson. When you see a headphones symbol in the margin, listen to the CD for **Lección 31**. Answers or hints for many activities are given in Appendix 1. Be sure to check your answers for each activity before going on to the next one.

The interactive CD-ROM to accompany *Destinos* contains additional practice with the video storyline and will help you improve your skills in Spanish.

BEFORE VIEWING . . .

Preliminary: See Faculty Guide for additional information and activities for this lesson.
• **Variation:** For activities marked with the headphones icon, you may wish to read from the Audioscript instead of playing the CD.
• **Suggestion:** Make sure students are familiar with the activities before you read from the Audioscript or play the CD.

1

PREPARACIÓN

Suggestions:
• Before watching the video, go over the vocabulary list at the end of the chapter and have students pronounce the words after you.
• Assign *Preparación* activities as homework and then go over them quickly in class before viewing the video.

Act. A, *Paso 1*, Variation: Have students work in pairs. One student covers the second column, leaving only the characters' names visible. The partner then reads the statements from the second column and the first student tries to match the names with the actions.

Actividad A.
Paso 1

¿Recuerdas lo que hicieron estas personas en el **Episodio 30**? Haz oraciones completas tomando una frase de cada columna.

1. _____ Raquel
2. _____ Raquel y Ángela
3. _____ la hermana María Teresa
4. _____ Pati
5. _____ Carlos

a. se enteró de que había problemas en el teatro en Nueva York.
b. les dio a Ángela y Raquel dónde descansar y bañarse.
c. le dejó un mensaje a Arturo.
d. supo lo que pasa en la oficina en Miami.
e. fueron a una iglesia.
f. trató de comunicarse con Pedro y Arturo.

Act. A, Answers: *Paso 1:*
1. c, f 2. e 3. b 4. a 5. d

 ### Paso 2
Ahora escucha el CD para verificar tus respuestas.

***Para pensar*, Optional:** Have students prepare brief answers to the questions as homework or in class. Then have them compare answers in pairs or small groups. They must try to justify their ideas if they differ from the answers of others.

Para pensar...

1. ¿Qué hará Pati ahora que sabe que hay problemas con la producción de la obra? ¿Se quedará con la familia o volverá a Nueva York?
2. En los episodios previos, se ha sugerido que la familia Castillo tiene problemas. En tu opinión, ¿cuáles son esos problemas?
3. ¿Por qué se puso preocupado Carlos cuando habló con Ofelia, su secretaria?

 ## Actividad B.
Paso 1
Escucha parte de una conversación entre Juan y Pati. Es una discusión (*argument*) sobre algo. Después de escuchar, contesta la pregunta.

¿Cuál es el tema de la discusión entre Juan y Pati?

a. _____ el estado grave de la salud de don Fernando
b. _____ los problemas que tiene Pati en el teatro
c. _____ el hecho de que (*the fact that*) Pati cree que Juan no comprende su situación como mujer profesional

Si indicaste la letra *c*, tuviste razón.

Act. B, Answers: *Paso 1: c Paso 3: 1. b 2. b*

Paso 2

Lee las últimas líneas de la conversación que acabas de escuchar.

JUAN: ¿Pero por qué tienes que ir a Nueva York? ¿No lo puedes hacer desde aquí, por teléfono?

PATI: ¡Juan! ¡Estamos hablando de una obra de teatro! Lo que tú dices es como… como… pedirle a un doctor que cure a un enfermo por teléfono.

Paso 3

Ahora escucha toda la conversación de nuevo. Puedes leer las últimas líneas al mismo tiempo, si quieres. Luego contesta las preguntas.

1. ¿Qué quiere Juan que haga Pati?
   a. _____ Que vaya a Nueva York.   b. _____ Que se quede con él.

2. ¿Qué parece que va a hacer Pati?
   a. _____ Se va a quedar con Juan.   b. _____ Va a regresar a Nueva York.

. . . AFTER VIEWING

2

¿TIENES BUENA MEMORIA?

Actividad A.   En la excavación

Paso 1

¿Son ciertas (**C**) o falsas (**F**) las siguientes declaraciones sobre lo que pasó en la excavación en este episodio?

C F 1. Raquel y Ángela no saben nada de Roberto todavía.

C F 2. Ángela no se siente mejor después de descansar en la iglesia.

C F 3. La actitud de Ángela es pesimista en cuanto al rescate de Roberto.

Paso 2

Ahora escucha el repaso de Raquel para verificar tus respuestas.

> ### Para pensar…
>
> Al final del episodio algo tuvo lugar (*took place*) en los Estados Unidos. ¿Recuerdas lo que pasó? Una persona llamó a los padres de Raquel. ¿Recuerdas quién era esa persona? La madre de Raquel dijo que era «el novio de mi hija».
>
> 1. ¿Ha hablado (*Has spoken*) Raquel alguna vez de un novio, del pasado o del presente?
> 2. ¿Qué efecto es posible que esta persona tenga en las relaciones que están formando entre Raquel y Arturo?

Act. B, Suggestion: Give students about 2 minutes to complete the activity individually or in pairs and then compare answers as a whole class.

Act. B, Answers: *Paso 1:*
1. *Sí* 2. *Juan y Pati* 3. *Ramón y Pedro* 4. *Eran drásticas. ¡Un desafío!* 1. *Que cierren la oficina en Miami.* 2. *Que concentren en la producción de algo.* 3. *Que vendan la Gavia.* (See Appendix 1 for expanded answers.)

Actividad B. En la capital
Paso 1

Contesta las siguientes preguntas sobre lo que está pasando en la familia Castillo en la Ciudad de México.

1. ¿Sabe Pedro lo del accidente?
2. ¿Quiénes se pelearon (*had a fight*)?
3. ¿Quiénes hablaron con unos auditores?
4. ¿Eran mínimas o drásticas las recomendaciones de los auditores?

Paso 2

Ahora escucha el repaso del narrador para verificar tus respuestas.

¡Un desafío! ¿Recuerdas las tres recomendaciones de los auditores?

Act. B, Follow-up: Have students create one additional question similar to those in the activity, then exchange papers with a partner and answer each other's question.

3

VOCABULARIO DEL TEMA

Suggestions:
• Practice pronunciation with choral and individual repetition.
• Bring in pictures from magazines of products such as medicine, fish, shoes, etc. As you show them one by one to the class, ask ¿*Qué es esto?* (students respond with product name) ¿*Dónde se compra* _____? ¿*En la* _____ *o en la* _____?

Las tiendas y los comercios

la carnicería	butcher shop	**la barbería**	barber shop	**la papelería**	stationery store
la confitería	confectionery	**la droguería**	drugstore		
la farmacia	pharmacy	**la ferretería**	hardware store	**la peluquería**	beauty shop, hairdresser's
la panadería	bakery	**la frutería**	fruit store		
la pastelería	pastry shop	**la joyería**	jewelry store	**la pollería**	poultry shop
la pescadería	fish market	**la lavandería**	laundry	**la taquería**	taco stand
la zapatería	shoe store	**la librería**	bookstore	**la tortillería**	tortilla shop

Note the following about these store names.

- The names of many kinds of stores end in **-ería** in Spanish. Note that **la farmacia** is an exception.
- Many store names are derived from the names of the principal products sold in them or the service they perform. What product is sold in **una carnicería**? in **una librería**? Where would **dulces** or **confites** (*candies*) be sold? Where would you have clothing washed (**lavar**)? What other store-product relationships can you find, based on words you know?

Point out: In most Spanish-speaking countries, it is still more common to shop in small, specialized shops and markets than in large discount or department stores. Supermarkets are, however, becoming more and more common, especially in large cities. Most of the stores listed here are found in all Spanish-speaking countries. However, *taquerías* and *tortillerías* are found primarily in Mexico and in Mexican-American neighborhoods in the U.S.

- Just as store names and products are related, so are the names for people who work there. In what store do these people work? **un carnicero**, **una peluquera**, **un panadero**, **una zapatera**.

Actividad A. De compras con Lupe
Paso 1

Escucha otra vez mientras el narrador describe un día de compras con Lupe. Escribe los nombres de las tiendas que visita con los dibujos apropiados.

Act. A, Answers: Paso 1: 1. la pescadería 2. la carnicería 3. la zapatería 4. la confitería 5. la tortillería 6. la panadería 7. (la) pastelería 8. (la) farmacia

1. _____   2. _____   3. _____

4. _____   5. _____   6. _____

Nota cultural, **Suggestion:** This may be a good opportunity to note that mistakes are a natural part of language learning and that students should not feel overly discouraged by their mistakes. It may also be worthwhile to discuss opinions about bilingual education briefly.

Paso 2

Ahora escucha otra vez la lección de ortografía (*spelling*) que Carlos le da a Juanita y trata de corregir lo que tú escribiste. Carlos y Juanita van a hablar de dos tiendas cuyos (*whose*) nombres no escribiste en la primera parte de esta actividad. Escribe esos nombres cuando los oigas.

7. _____   8. _____

Nota cultural   La educación bilingüe

The spelling errors made by Juanita are natural for her age and are also typical of anyone—native or nonnative—who is learning how to write in Spanish. Compared with English, the number of sound or written symbol pairs that cause learners difficulty in Spanish is quite minimal. Spanish-speaking children, like speakers of English, also pass through periods in which they have difficulty using irregular forms consistently, if at all, and it is not unusual to hear Hispanic children say **yo sabo** instead of **yo sé**. Children, like older learners, soon learn the correct forms.

In Miami, Juanita attends a bilingual school in which she receives instruction in both English and Spanish. The concept of bilingual education is currently being debated in the United States. It may be years before the debate is resolved, if ever.

Act. B, Answers: 1. *pescadería* 2. *farmacia/droguería* 3. *carnicería* 4. *librería* 5. *zapatería* 6. *taquería* 7. *panadería* 8. *pollería* 9. *pastelería* 10. *frutería* 11. *confitería* 12. *tortillería*

Actividad B. ¿Adónde irás? (*Where will you go?*)

En el CD vas a oír los nombres de una serie de productos. Indica a qué tienda irás para comprarlas.

MODELO: (*oyes*) —las bananas
  (*dices*) —Iré a una frutería.
  (*oyes*) —Debes ir a una frutería.

1. ... 2. ... 3. ... 4. ... 5. ... 6. ...
7. ... 8. ... 9. ... 10. ... 11. ... 12. ...

Act. B., Variation: Play *Piccionario*. Prepare slips of paper, each of which has the name of a store on it. Divide the class into 2 teams. One member from the first team goes to the board. He or she has 30 seconds to draw things that the team identifies with the store named on his/her slip, while the team guesses what store the drawing represents. Give 5 points for a correct guess within 30 seconds but deduct one point for any incorrect guess to discourage random guessing. The second team then has a turn. A different team member should go to the board for each new round.

Actividad C. ¿Y tú?

Describe los comercios que hay en el lugar donde tú vives y también tus propias costumbres en cuanto a las compras. Completa solamente las oraciones que se relacionen con tus experiencias personales.

1. Por aquí (*Around here*) hay muchos/as _____, _____

   y _____.

2. No hay suficientes _____.

3. Casi nunca compro algo en un(a) _____.

4. Cuando necesito _____, siempre voy al/a la _____,

   que está en _____.

5. Casi siempre compro la comida en _____.

6. De joven, trabajaba en _____.

7. Hay un(a) _____ donde todos los estudiantes de la escuela

   superior se reúnen después de las clases.

8. Las tiendas están abiertas hasta las _____. Los supermercados

   como _____ están abiertos toda la noche.

Act. C, Suggestion: Assign as homework and then have students take turns presenting their statements to a partner.

Act. C, Follow-up: Have students work in pairs to invent a business or product and to come up with a slogan (*el lema*) for it. Model: *Pollería Quí Quí:* «*Más fresco, no hay*».

4

UN POCO DE GRAMÁTICA

The Workbook/Study Guide contains more detailed explanation and practice of this grammar point.

Note: You may wish to review the verb paradigms for the subjunctive.

Point Out: ¡OJO!: The subjunctive is used after *cuando* only when it refers to a future event or situation.

Another Way to Talk About the Future

As you know, it is possible to talk about future events by using the future forms, or forms of **ir** + **a** + an infinitive. But it is also common to use the subjunctive form of the verb when a sentence expresses future intent.

Ángela va a estar muy contenta **cuando rescaten** a Roberto.

Ángela is going to be very happy when they rescue Roberto.

> **Cuando hable** otra vez con Raquel, Arturo le quiere decir muchas cosas.
>
> *The next time he speaks with Raquel, Arturo wants to tell her lots of things.*

Did you notice that the subjunctive is used to express only the future event that directly follows **cuando**? You will learn more about this use of the subjunctive, as well as its use with other words such as **cuando**, in the Workbook/Study Guide.

Actividad.   ¿Qué pasará cuando... ?

Junta una frase del primer grupo con una del segundo para formar oraciones lógicas sobre lo que tú crees que va a pasar en el futuro. En el segundo grupo, puedes inventar tus propias frases, si quieres.

1. Cuando me gradúe en la universidad...
2. Cuando encuentren una cura para el cáncer...
3. Cuando viajemos al espacio...
4. Cuando yo esté casado/a...
5. Cuando una mujer suba a la posición de presidenta de los Estados Unidos...
6. Cuando mis hijos se casen...
7. Cuando yo gane la lotería...
8. Cuando mi familia y yo hagamos un viaje el próximo año...

a. ya será el siglo XXII.
b. daré un poco de dinero a todos mis parientes.
c. vamos a conocer a seres extraterrestres.
d. seré muy feliz.
e. tendré _____ años.
f. iremos a lugares exóticos.
g. estaré muy viejo/a.
h. voy a dar una gran fiesta.
i. ¿ ?

5

LECTURA CULTURAL

Los mexicoamericanos

La mayoría de los mexicoamericanos viven a lo largo de la frontera entre los Estados Unidos y México, de Texas a California. También hay una comunidad mexicana grande en Chicago. Pero la influencia mexicoamericana se nota por todas partes en este país. Son muy pocas las ciudades estadounidenses en donde no hay un restaurante mexicano. Y en todas las tiendas y mercados se venden productos típicamente mexicanos.

La influencia mexicana en muchos estados de los Estados Unidos es muy antigua. Hay que recordar que Texas fue territorio mexicano hasta 1836. Los actuales estados de Nuevo México, Arizona, Utah, Nevada, California, una parte de Colorado y de Wyoming fueron territorio mexicano hasta 1848. En aquella época, muchos mexicanos —y, con ellos, muchos descendientes de españoles que también vivían en ese territorio— prefirieron quedarse. Se hicieron ciudadanos americanos. En algunos casos sus descendientes todavía mantienen lazos muy estrechos[1] con la familia en México. Por otra parte mucha gente que hoy se considera mexicoamericana tiene raíces[2] familiares en España.

Edward James Olmos

Personas y personajes

Los mexicoamericanos sobresalen[3] en una gran variedad de carreras y campos. ¿Puedes identificar a los siguientes mexicoamericanos del pasado?

Lee Treviño	actor de televisión y cine
Linda Ronstadt	fundador de la UFWA (United Farm Workers Association)
César Chávez	jugador de golf que ha ganado en muchas competiciones
Luis Valdez	política californiana, la primera hispana que fue
Gloria Molina	elegida a la Cámara de Diputados[4] del estado de California
Edward James Olmos	director de teatro y cine (*Zoot Suit* es una de sus
Richard «Cheech» Marin	películas)
	cómico popular, cuya pareja[5] fue Chong
	cantante popular que canta las canciones de sus antepasados mexicanos

Mitos y verdades de la comunidad mexicoamericana

Como en el caso de todo grupo «minoritario» en los Estados Unidos, hay ciertos estereotipos que se aplican a los mexicoamericanos que la mayoría acepta como verdades. ¿Cuánto sabes tú de este grupo? En tu opinión, ¿son ciertas o falsas las siguientes declaraciones?

1. La gran mayoría de los mexicoamericanos son bilingües. El español es su primer idioma.
2. Mexicanos... mexicoamericanos... no hay gran diferencia entre ellos.

La oración número uno es falsa. Todo depende de la generación y de la crianza[6] de la persona. Muchos mexicoamericanos mayores sí son bilingües y para ellos el español es su primer idioma. Pero hay muchos, sobre todo entre los muy jóvenes, que hablan español muy poco o no lo hablan en absoluto.[7]

Estos jóvenes, de apellido y tipo hispánico, ni son bilingües ni son, en muchos casos, biculturales, al punto que estudian español en la escuela como lengua extranjera. ¿Te acuerdas de Ritchie Valens, el cantante que hizo famosa la canción «La Bamba»? Su hermano nació en los Estados Unidos, como él, y hablaba español, pero Ritchie no lo hablaba para nada.

[1]lazos... *very close ties*   [2]*roots*   [3]*excel*   [4]Cámara... *State Assembly*   [5]cuya... *whose partner*   [6]*upbringing*   [7]en... *at all*

La segunda oración es también falsa. Aunque el típico mexicoamericano —si es que tal persona existe— comparte muchas costumbres con el mexicano típico, también hay muchas diferencias entre ellos. En cuanto a semejanzas, hay que citar la unidad familiar, característica primordial[8] de las dos culturas.* Además hay la religión católica y el culto a la Virgen de Guadalupe que, para los dos grupos, son muy importantes.

Por otro lado, la comida que se conoce en este país con el nombre de «mexicana» no siempre tiene mucho que ver con la verdadera comida mexicana de México. Aun cuando a algunos platos se les da el mismo nombre en los dos países, los ingredientes que llevan y el sabor[9] que tienen son distintos. Y hay algunos platos «mexicanos» que son realmente de origen estadounidense, como los burritos y las sopaipillas.[10] Muchos estadounidenses se sorprenden cuando llegan a conocer la gran variedad de la comida mexicana propia de México. ¡Es mucho más que tacos y enchiladas!

[8]*very important*   [9]*flavor*   [10]*dessert of New Mexican origin, similar to a cream puff but made with honey*

Lectura cultural, **Preguntas:** 1. *¿En qué región de los EEUU vive la mayoría de los mexicoamericanos? (en el suroeste)* 2. *¿Qué estados o partes de estados formaban parte de México en el siglo XIX? (Texas, Nuevo México, Arizona, Utah, Nevada, California, Colorado y Wyoming)* 3. *¿Cuáles son algunos estereotipos de los mexicoamericanos? (que todos son bilingües y que son iguales a los mexicanos)* 4. *¿Cierto o falso? La comida mexicana en los EEUU es igual a la comida mexicana en México. (falso)* 5. *El burrito es una invención estadounidense. (cierto).*

Actividad.   Hablando de los mexicoamericanos

Contesta las siguientes preguntas sobre los mexicoamericanos.

1. ¿Qué imagen tenías de los mexicoamericanos antes de leer esta **Lectura cultural**? Y ahora, ¿qué piensas de ellos? ¿Tienes ahora diferentes opiniones de las que tenías?
2. ¿Puedes agregar (*add*) a la lista de mexicoamericanos famosos algunos otros nombres? Explica también por qué son famosos.

6

INTERCAMBIO

Paso 1

Muchos negocios pequeños o familiares están desapareciendo o son difíciles de encontrar. Mirando la lista de lugares en la página 302, completa las siguientes oraciones.

1. Muchos comercios pequeños desaparecerán en el futuro. Uno que seguramente no existirá por muchos años más es _____.
2. También _____.
3. En cambio, nunca desaparecerá(n) _____.

Paso 2

Comparte tus ideas con otras tres personas. ¿Han pensado en las mismas ideas?

---

* Se debe notar que la famosa unidad de la familia hispánica, tanto en las comunidades hispánicas de los Estados Unidos como en México y en otros países del mundo hispánico, viene debilitándose (*weakening*) un poco con las costumbres y presiones del mundo moderno.

Paso 3

Presenta tus ideas a la clase. ¿Hay tendencias? ¿Qué tipos de negocios desaparecerán primero? ¿Adónde vamos (o iremos) para obtener los servicios de ese negocio?

MODELO: Cuando ya no existan más _____, iremos a _____.

Vocabulario

Los verbos

pelearse   to fight

Las tiendas y los comercios

(Stores and Businesses)

la barbería	barber shop
la carnicería	butcher shop
la confitería	confectionery
la droguería	drugstore
la farmacia	pharmacy
la ferretería	hardware store
la frutería	fruit store
la joyería	jewelry store
la lavandería	laundry
la librería	bookstore
la panadería	bakery
la papelería	stationery store
la pastelería	pastry shop
la peluquería	beauty shop, hairdresser's
la pescadería	fish market
la pollería	poultry shop
la taquería	taco stand
la tortillería	tortilla shop
la zapatería	shoe store

Los conceptos

la discusión	argument, (verbal) fight
la medida	measure, step

Los adjetivos

drástico/a   drastic

LECCIÓN 32

HA HABIDO UN ACCIDENTE*

*There Has Been an Accident

OBJETIVOS

The materials in **Lección 32** of the Textbook and the Workbook/Study Guide will help you better understand the video episode and take you beyond it, giving you additional information about places and characters in the series. The Textbook will also help you to develop skill in using the Spanish language. In this lesson, you will learn

- vocabulary for talking about the natural world
- ways to give commands directly to someone whom you do not know well

You will also learn about the civilization of the Aztecs.

Be sure to work through all parts of the lesson. When you see a headphones symbol in the margin, listen to the CD for **Lección 32**. Answers or hints for many activities are given in Appendix 1. Be sure to check your answers for each activity before going on to the next one.

The interactive CD-ROM to accompany *Destinos* contains additional practice with the video storyline and will help you improve your skills in Spanish.

309

Preliminary: See Faculty Guide for additional information and activities for this lesson.
● **Variation:** For activities marked with the headphones icon, you may wish to read from the Audioscript instead of playing the CD.
● **Suggestion:** Make sure students are familiar with the activities before you read from the Audioscript or play the CD.

 BEFORE VIEWING . . .

1

PREPARACIÓN

Suggestions:
● Before watching the video, go over the vocabulary list at the end of the chapter and have students pronounce the words after you.
● Assign *Preparación* activities as homework and then go over them quickly in class before viewing the video.

Act. A, Suggestion: You may want to have students do this activity in pairs and go over answers with the entire class.

Act. A, Answers: 1. a 2. a 3. b

Act. B, Answers: 1. *Se llama Luis.* 2. *Vive ahora en Los Ángeles. (Acaba de mudarse para allí.)* 3. *Eran novios. (La madre de Raquel lo llama «el novio de mi hija».)*

Actividad A.

Contesta las siguientes preguntas sobre lo que pasó en el episodio previo.

1. ¿Por qué se pelearon Pati y Juan?
   a. _____ Porque ella tiene que volver a Nueva York por su trabajo.
   b. _____ Porque él quiere regresar a Nueva York con ella.

2. ¿Qué descubrieron Pedro y Ramón?
   a. _____ Que la familia tiene graves problemas económicos.
   b. _____ Que el gobierno mexicano investiga las finanzas de la familia.

3. ¿Se enteraron de algo Ángela y Raquel?
   a. _____ Sí. Encontraron a Roberto, muerto.
   b. _____ No. En la excavación no hubo noticias.

Actividad B.

En el episodio previo apareció un nuevo personaje. ¿Recuerdas algo de él? Contesta estas preguntas.

1. ¿Cómo se llama este señor?
2. ¿Dónde vive ahora?
3. ¿Qué clase de relaciones había entre él y Raquel?

Para pensar, ¡OJO!: Mention that *antiguo* means *former* when it precedes the noun and *old* when it follows the noun.

Para pensar...

Ya sabes que Luis es el antiguo (*former*) novio de Raquel. También sabes que ha vuelto (*he has returned*) a Los Ángeles. ¿Crees que todavía siente algo por Raquel? Y Raquel, ¿siente ella algo por él?

 . . . AFTER VIEWING

2

¿TIENES BUENA MEMORIA?

Act. A, Suggestion: You may want to have students do this activity in pairs or small groups.

Actividad A. ¿Qué pasó?
Paso 1

Indica si las oraciones describen o no lo que pasó en cada sitio. ¿Puedes hacer un comentario sobre cada oración incorrecta?

En el sitio de la excavación…

Sí No   1. Ángela y Raquel seguían esperando.
Sí No   2. No hubo mucha actividad.
Sí No   3. Por fin pudieron rescatar a Roberto.
Sí No   4. Hubo otro derrumbe.
Sí No   5. Roberto murió en el derrumbe.

En la capital…

Sí No   6. Por fin los hermanos supieron lo del accidente.
Sí No   7. Don Fernando se enteró del accidente también.
Sí No   8. Ramón y Consuelo también tienen problemas.
Sí No   9. Arturo le contó a Pedro todo lo que sabía.

En Los Ángeles…

Sí No   10. Luis visitó a los padres de Raquel.
Sí No   11. Luis les dijo que ellos debían ir a ver a Raquel a México.
Sí No   12. El padre de Raquel no estaba muy convencido en cuanto al viaje.

Paso 2
Ahora, escucha otra vez el repaso que hacen Raquel y el narrador del fin de este episodio y corrige tus repuestas.

Para pensar…

María, la madre de Raquel, le ha sugerido a Luis que vaya a México. Así podrá ver a Raquel otra vez. ¿Crees que es buena idea que Luis vaya a México? ¿Qué revelan las acciones de María acerca de su personalidad?

Nota cultural   El español en los episodios en México

On network TV in the United States, one does not hear a strong regional accent, by and large, unless it is required by the role an actor is playing. Otherwise, the English spoken on prime time is a standard Midwestern form of English that most people who wish to work in the industry learn to speak, regardless of their city—or accent—of origin.

In the same way, the Spanish of many of the major Mexican characters in *Destinos* is not totally characteristic of Mexican Spanish. Most Mexican actors who work in movies, the theater, and in television are trained to speak a relatively accent-free variety of Spanish. In real life, the Spanish spoken in Mexico, like the English of the United States, has many varieties, according to the geographical area, ethnic background, and social class of the speaker.

Of the major Mexican characters, Lupe and Carlos in particular have pronounced accents, along with a number of actors who have small roles or make one-time appearances.

Something that is characteristic of Mexican and Mexican-American Spanish is the more frequent use of **Ud.** forms between adults (as compared to the more generalized use of **tú** found in some other countries). In this video episode, Luis addresses Raquel's mother as **Ud.** (even though he used to be her daughter's boyfriend!).

Actividad B. ¿Quién sabe qué?

¿Tienes una idea muy clara de lo que sabe la mayoría de los personajes?
Indica el verbo correcto para cada frase. ¡OJO! Hay información de algunos
episodios previos.

1. Raquel… sabe/no sabe
    a. que Arturo llegó a México.
    b. nada sobre el estado de don Fernando.
    c. que sus padres hablaron con su antiguo novio.

2. Arturo… sabe/no sabe
    a. lo del accidente en la excavación.
    b. nada de Raquel.
    c. que Raquel tuvo un novio en otra época.

3. Don Fernando… sabe/no sabe
    a. que tiene dos nietos puertorriqueños.
    b. lo del accidente en la excavación.
    c. que hay problemas financieros en la Compañía Industrias Castillo
        Saavedra.

4. La madre de Raquel… sabe/no sabe
    a. lo del accidente en la excavación.
    b. mucho de las relaciones entre Arturo y Raquel.
    c. la historia de los nietos puertorriqueños de don Fernando.

Actividad C. Una civilización indígena

Completa los siguientes párrafos sobre la civilización de esta tribu indígena
de México.

En el centro de México había varias culturas indígenas. La más conocida era
la (azteca/maya).[1] Pero los aztecas no eran originarios del centro de México.
Eran del (este/norte),[2] de un lugar mítico llamado Aztlán.

En un (lago/río)[3] en el centro de la meseta, los aztecas fundaron la ciudad de Tenochtitlán. Eran una tribu fundamentalmente (pacífica/guerrera[a]).[4]
Por eso, lograron (colonizar/conquistar)[5] todo el centro de México.

[a]*warlike*

3

VOCABULARIO DEL TEMA

El mundo y su forma

el continente	continent	**el árbol**	tree	**el campo**	countryside
el mundo	world	**el arbusto**	shrub	**el cañón**	canyon
la tierra	earth	**el bosque**	forest	**el cerro**	hill
		la flor	flower	**la cordillera**	mountain
		la hierba (yerba)	grass		range
				la costa	coast
Los puntos cardinales: el norte, el sur, el este, el oeste				**el desierto**	desert

la pampa	pampa, grassland
la península	peninsula
la piedra	stone
la roca	rock
la selva	jungle
el valle	valley
el arroyo	stream
el golfo	gulf
el lago	lake
el mar	sea
el océano	ocean
el río	river

la isla	island	la montaña	mountain
la llanura	plain	el paisaje	countryside landscape
la meseta	plain, plateau		

Actividad A. La geografía de algunos países hispánicos

En el CD vas a escuchar la descripción de cuatro países hispánicos, pero no se da su nombre. ¿Puedes identificar el país que se describe?

1. …   2. …   3. …   4. …

Act. A, Answers: 1. *la Argentina* 2. *Puerto Rico* 3. *España* 4. *México*

Act. B, Suggestion: It is helpful to have a map of the world in front of the room or on an overhead.

Actividad B. Hablando del paisaje

Vas a escuchar uno de los sustantivos de la primera columna. Di un nombre de la segunda columna que lo ejemplifica.

MODELO: (*oyes*) una cordillera
(*dices*) los Andes
(*oyes*) Los Andes son una cordillera.

una cordillera, una montaña	el Titicaca
un golfo, un mar, un océano	Inglaterra (*England*)
un continente	el Atlántico
un desierto	Pike's Peak
una pampa	el Sahara
un cañón, un valle	los Andes
un lago, un río	el Nilo
una isla, una península	el Pérsico
	Sudamérica
	el Mediterráneo
	Napa
	Yucatán

Act. B, Answers: *¡Un desafío!* (See Appendix 1 for answers.)

1. …   2. …   3. …   4. …   5. …   6. …   7. …
8. …   9. …   10. …   11. …   12. …

¡Un desafío! ¿Puedes decir dónde quedan los lugares que acabas de identificar? Es decir, ¿en qué país o estado, cerca de qué lugar, en qué hemisferio? etcétera. Da todos los detalles que puedas.

Act. C, Note: Students may not know how to say many geographic place names in Spanish. Allow them to name the places in English.

Act. C, Suggestion: Have volunteers read some of their geographic points of interest aloud for the whole class to name the location.

Act. D, Optional: Have students present their information to the rest of the class.

Act. D, Follow-up: For homework, have students write a mini-composition about the geography of the area where one of their classmates lives.

Actividad C. La geografía de los Estados Unidos

Haz una lista de diez puntos geográficos de los Estados Unidos. Pregúntale a un compañero / una compañera en qué estado o región del país se encuentran. Identifica igualmente los puntos presentados por tu compañero/a. Si es posible, di los nombres en español.

MODELO: TÚ: ¿Dónde se encuentra el Gran Cañón del río Colorado?

COMPAÑERO/A: Se encuentra en Arizona.

Actividad D. Donde yo vivo...

Ahora describe el terreno y el paisaje en el lugar donde tú vives.

MODELO: Cerca de donde yo vivo, hay _____, _____

y _____. Me gusta(n) mucho _____ porque

allí _____. Es una lástima que no haya

_____.

En cuanto a las plantas, hay (mucho/a/os/as)

_____ y _____. No hay _____.

4

UN POCO DE GRAMÁTICA

The Workbook/Study Guide contains more detailed explanation and practice of this grammar point.

Emphasis: Review present subjunctive forms and emphasize that *Ud.* and *Uds.* command forms are identical to the third-person subjunctive forms.

Suggestions:
• Practice *Uds.* commands using Total Physical Response (TPR), telling students what to do and having them follow your commands: *¡Levántense! ¡Siéntense! ¡Vengan a la pizarra! ¡Escriban su nombre!,* etc.
• Pass out cards with infinitives on them for students to use in the imperative. Have students give each other orders using *Ud(s).* commands: (*cantar*→ *Cante una canción de los Beatles.*) The other student(s) must act out the order.

Variation: Have students give you orders that you must act out.

Telling Someone to Do Something

In Spanish, as you know, you must decide whether to address someone as **tú** or **Ud.** When you want to give a person a direct command (order), the same choice must be made.

Ud. (and **Uds.**) commands are identical to the third-person subjunctive forms you have already learned. Here are some **Uds.** commands from previous video episodes.

HOMBRE DEL PUEBLO: **¡Vengan, vengan!** Están a punto de rescatar a los hombres atrapados.

PADRE RODRIGO: **Esperen** aquí. **No se muevan.** Voy a ver qué pasa.

To form **Ud.** and **Uds.** commands, add to the **yo** stem of the present indicative the "opposite" vowel (**-e** for **-ar** verbs, **-a** for **-er/-ir** verbs). Add **-n** for **Uds.** commands. You will learn more in **Lección 32** of the Workbook/Study Guide. You will learn about **tú** commands in a later lesson.

Actividad. **Situaciones**

A continuación hay una serie de situaciones o circunstancias que ocurren todos los días. ¿Puedes encontrar un mandato apropiado de la siguiente lista
para cada caso?

1. _____ Un hombre se da con (*bumps into*) una mujer en el supermercado.
2. _____ Una abuela les habla a sus nietos por teléfono. Ella vive en la
Florida y sus nietos viven en California.
3. _____ Un señor enfermo está en un hospital. Intenta levantarse para buscar a su esposa. Le habla una enfermera.
4. _____ Unos niños miran atentamente la filmación de una película de
Hollywood. Les habla el asistente de la directora.
5. _____ Un médico llama por teléfono a un hombre en Chicago para decirle que su madre está enferma. No es nada grave, pero la persona de Chicago quiere estar cerca de ella.
6. _____ Una mujer corre por el aeropuerto. Acaban de anunciar su vuelo y
está todavía lejos de la puerta (*gate*). Un grupo de turistas está
directamente en su camino.
7. _____ Una pareja está en una agencia de viajes. Quieren hacer planes
para su luna de miel (*honeymoon*). Les habla el agente de viajes.
8. _____ Una profesora de historia les da instrucciones a sus estudiantes en
clase.

a. Por favor, déjenme pasar. ¡Voy a llegar tarde!
b. No, no. Quédese allí. Lo llamaré tan pronto como sepa algo.
c. Duérmase, por favor, señor. Ud. necesita descansar mucho.
d. Vengan a verme pronto. ¡Los echo de menos (*I miss you all*)!
e. Por favor, lean el segundo párrafo en la página 48.
f. Discúlpeme, señora. Lo hice sin querer (*I didn't mean to do it*).
g. Díganme, por favor, cuánto tiempo piensan quedarse en las islas.
h. Siéntense allí, para no estorbar (*to be in the way*), ¿eh?

5

LECTURA CULTURAL

La civilización de los aztecas

Entre todas las civilizaciones
indígenas de América, la azteca
era una de las más avanzadas.
La conquista sangrienta[1] de esta
civilización por los españoles,
encabezados por el conquistador Hernán Cortés, puso fin a

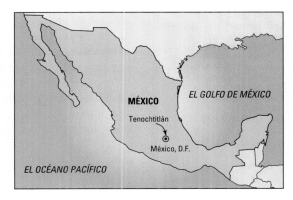

[1] *bloody*

uno de los imperios más grandes de América.

La sociedad azteca

La sociedad azteca estaba muy bien organizada, con un complejo sistema de jerarquías y clases sociales. A continuación se ofrecen unos detalles de las costumbres y creencias de esta gran civilización.

Hoy día en Teotihuacán se puede ver las ruinas de varios edificios ceremoniales. Los aztecas se apoderaron de (*took over*) la ciudad después de su abandono por los habitantes originales.

- Las jóvenes aztecas se casaban a los dieciséis años. Los chicos se casaban más tarde, como a los veinte. En teoría, los hombres podían tener más de una esposa, pero la mayoría tenía solamente una.
- El oficio de curandera[2] era importante en la cultura azteca. Según sus creencias, algunas enfermedades eran causadas por un enemigo o por los dioses, como castigo.[3] Una curandera tenía que saber usar artes mágicas para averiguar la verdad.
- Para curar las enfermedades, los aztecas usaban más de doscientas hierbas medicinales. Hoy día se ha comprobado[4] la eficacia de algunas de ellas. Sirven para bajar la fiebre y contener las hemorragias.
- Cuando los aztecas querían conquistar una ciudad, primero mandaban embajadores a ella. Les pedían tres cosas: hacer comercio con el imperio azteca, rendir culto[5] a los dioses aztecas y mandar regalos a Tenochtitlán todos los años. La ciudad tenía tres oportunidades para rendirse a estas demandas. Cada vez que una

Moctezuma era el emperador de los aztecas cuando llegaron los españoles. Según las cartas de Hernán Cortés, el emperador le dijo: «Por tanto vos sed cierto[11] que os obedeceremos y tendremos por señor... Y pues[12] estáis... en vuestra casa, holgad y descansad[13] del trabajo del camino y guerras que habéis tenido... »

Lectura cultural, Preguntas: 1. *¿Qué civilización indígena era muy avanzada?* (la azteca) 2. *¿Cómo se llama el conquistador español de este imperio?* (Hernán Cortés) 3. *¿Cuántos años tenían las jóvenes aztecas cuando se casaban?* (dieciséis) *¿los jóvenes aztecas?* (veinte) 4. *¿Para qué usaban las curanderas artes mágicas?* (para averiguar la verdad) 5. *¿Qué usaban para curar las enfermedades?* (más de doscientas hierbas medicinales) 6. *¿Cuándo se enojaban los dioses aztecas?* (cuando no se celebraban los sacrificios y fiestas tal como debían) 7. *¿A quién esperaban los aztecas cuando llegó Cortés?* (a un dios blanco y por eso no ofrecieron resistencia) 8. *¿Cómo se llamaba el emperador de los aztecas?* (Moctezuma) 9. *¿Qué año marcó el fin del imperio azteca?* (1521)

[2]*healer*   [3]*punishment*   [4]*se... has been shown, proven*   [5]*rendir... to pay homage*

ciudad se negaba[6] a aceptar esas condiciones, los aztecas le mandaban
un surtido de lanzas y escudos,[7] para que pudiera[8] defenderse en la batalla venidera.[9]

● Los dioses de los aztecas observaban constantemente a sus súbditos.[10]
Se enojaban si no se celebraban los sacrificios y fiestas tal como debían.

La conquista por los españoles: ¿Por qué fue posible?

Aquí hay una teoría que contesta esta pregunta. Los aztecas creyeron en la profecía
de la llegada de un dios blanco. Por eso cuando llegó Cortés en 1519 no ofrecieron
resistencia, creyendo que era el dios que esperaban. El mismo emperador Moctezuma se sometió a los españoles. En dos años, el gran imperio azteca se convirtió
en una colonia española. Moctezuma fue asesinado por algunos de sus hombres que
se oponían a la conquista española. La destrucción de la ciudad de Tenochtitlán por
los españoles en 1521 marcó el fin del imperio azteca.

---

[6]*se… refused*   [7]*un… a supply of lances and shields*   [8]*(the city) could*   [9]*upcoming*
[10]*subjects*   [11]*Por… For that reason, be certain*   [12]*since*   [13]*holgad… enjoy yourselves and rest*

Actividad.   Ahora, ¿cuánto sabes de los aztecas?

Según la **Lectura cultural**, ¿son ciertas o falsas las siguientes afirmaciones?

1. Tenía poca importancia para los aztecas el concepto de las clases
   sociales.
2. La religión tenía mucha importancia para ellos.
3. Eran muy astutos en cuanto a sus relaciones con otras tribus.
4. En la sociedad azteca, los hombres tenían más poder (*power*) que las
   mujeres.

6

INTERCAMBIO

Paso 1

En grupos de tres, escriban por lo menos tres oraciones que podrán utilizarse
en una campaña para atraer a turistas de habla española a los Estados Unidos.

> MODELO: ¡Vengan a visitar las montañas de Colorado! ¡Naden en las aguas
> del Golfo de México!

Paso 2

Cada grupo debe presentar sus ideas a la clase. Después, el grupo debe revisar sus ideas. ¿Hay otras en la clase que les han gustado?

Paso 3

Fuera de clase, cada grupo debe preparar un cartel (*poster*) turístico con fotos
de revistas y las oraciones que escribieron. Luego, todos deben exhibir sus
carteles en la clase.

Vocabulario

El mundo y su forma
(The World and Its Shape)

el árbol	tree
el arbusto	shrub
el arroyo	stream
el bosque	forest
el campo	countryside
el cañón	canyon
el cerro	hill
el continente	continent
la cordillera	mountain range
la costa	coast
el desierto	desert
la flor	flower
el golfo	gulf
la hierba (yerba)	grass
el lago	lake
la llanura	plain
la meseta	plateau
la montaña	mountain
el océano	ocean
el paisaje	countryside, landscape

la pampa	pampa, grassland
la península	peninsula
la piedra	stone
el río	river
la roca	rock
la selva	jungle
la tierra	earth
el valle	valley

Repaso: **la isla, el mar, el mundo**

Los puntos cardinales (Cardinal Directions)
el norte, el sur, el este, el oeste

Los adjetivos

antiguo/a	former*
guerrero/a	warlike

Los verbos

estorbar	to be in the way

---

* **Antiguo** has this meaning when it precedes a noun (**el antiguo novio**). It means *old* or *elderly* when it follows the noun (**una ciudad antigua**).

LECCIÓN 33

SI SUPIERAS...*

If You Only Knew . . .

OBJETIVOS

The materials in **Lección 33** of the Textbook and the Workbook/Study Guide will help you better understand the video episode and take you beyond it, giving you additional information about places and characters in the series. The Textbook will also help you to develop skill in using the Spanish language. In this lesson, you will learn

- the Spanish names for many careers and professions
- ways to give commands directly to someone whom you know well

You will also learn about the Mayan civilization.

Be sure to work through all parts of the lesson. When you see a headphones symbol in the margin, listen to the CD for **Lección 33**. Answers or hints for many activities are given in Appendix 1. Be sure to check your answers for each activity before going on to the next one.

The interactive CD-ROM to accompany *Destinos* contains additional practice with the video storyline and will help you improve your skills in Spanish.

319

BEFORE VIEWING . . .

Preliminary: See Faculty Guide for additional information and activities for this lesson.
• **Variation:** For activities marked with the headphones icon, you may wish to read from the Audioscript instead of playing the CD.
• **Suggestion:** Make sure students are familiar with the activities before you read from the Audioscript or play the CD.

1

PREPARACIÓN

Suggestions:
• Before watching the video, go over the vocabulary list at the end of the chapter and have students pronounce the words after you.
• **Assign** *Preparación* activities as homework and then go over them quickly in class before viewing the video.

Actividad A.
Paso 1

¿Recuerdas los acontecimientos más importantes del episodio previo? Completa las oraciones con la información correcta.

Act. A, Answers: *Paso 1:*
1. b 2. b 3. b 4. b 5. b

1. En el sitio de la excavación, Raquel y Ángela
   a. _____ decidieron regresar al pueblo.
   b. _____ seguían esperando el rescate de Roberto.

2. En la capital, Arturo por fin conoció a
   a. _____ Ramón.
   b. _____ Pedro.   c. _____ Carlos.

3. Arturo le contó algunos detalles de la búsqueda de
   a. _____ Roberto.
   b. _____ Ángel.   c. _____ Rosario.

4. En Los Ángeles, los padres de Raquel recibieron la visita de
   a. _____ un antiguo profesor de Raquel.
   b. _____ un antiguo novio de Raquel.
   c. _____ un colega de Raquel.

5. La madre de Raquel le sugirió a Luis, el antiguo novio de su hija, que sería (*it would be*) buena idea
   a. _____ esperar en Los Ángeles para ver a Raquel.
   b. _____ ir a México para verla.
   c. _____ volver a Nueva York sin verla.

 ### Paso 2
Ahora escucha el CD para verificar tus respuestas.

***Para pensar*, Optional:** Have students prepare brief answers to the questions as homework or in class. Then, have them compare answers in pairs or small groups. They must try to justify their ideas if they differ from answers of others.

Para pensar...

1. Como sabes, Raquel no sabe nada de lo que está pasando en Los Ángeles. ¿Crees que Luis irá a México para verla? ¿Qué pasará cuando Raquel lo vea después de tantos años? ¿Qué pasará si Luis y Arturo se conocen?
2. Al comienzo de este episodio, todavía no han rescatado a Roberto. En tu opinión, ¿en qué condiciones está él, después del segundo derrumbe?

Actividad B.
Paso 1

Escucha parte de una conversación entre Juan y Pati. Otra vez, discuten sobre algo. Debes leer la conversación al escuchar. Luego, contesta la pregunta.

JUAN: Pati, ya te lo dije. ¡No puedes irte justo ahora!

PATI: ¡No me grites así, Juan! Ya traté de explicarte los problemas de la producción en Nueva York. No entiendo por qué actúas como un niño mimado.

JUAN: ¿Cómo puedes hacerme esto?

PATI: ¿Ves? Todo te lo hacen a ti. Tus problemas son los más graves. A veces dudo que a ti te importen los demás.

JUAN: Me importa mi papá.

PATI: ¿Sí? Entonces, ¿por qué no estás más tiempo con él en el hospital? Te lo pasas aquí peleándote conmigo cuando él te necesita.

¿Cuál es el tema principal de la discusión entre Juan y Pati?

Act. B, Answers: *Paso 1:* b *Paso 2: 1.* C 2. F 3. C 4. c (See Appendix 1 for expanded answers.)

a. _____ el estado grave de la salud de don Fernando

b. _____ el hecho de que (*the fact that*) Pati cree que Juan es muy egoísta

c. _____ los problemas que tiene Pati en el teatro

Si indicaste la letra *b*, tuviste razón.

Paso 2

Ahora escucha toda la conversación de nuevo. Luego indica si las siguientes oraciones son ciertas (**C**) o falsas (**F**).

C F 1. Juan todavía no quiere que Pati se vaya a Nueva York.

C F 2. Pati se niega a explicarle a Juan los detalles de los problemas que tiene con la producción de la obra.

C F 3. Pati insinúa que Juan debe pasar más tiempo en el hospital con su padre.

En esta conversación, Pati acusa a Juan de ser un «niño mimado», porque sólo piensa en sí mismo.

4. ¿Qué significa **mimado**?

a. _____ memorable   b. _____ copy-cat   c. _____ spoiled

Para pensar, **Suggestion:** Ask the questions of the class in general. Ask for a show of hands to see how the class reacts. Students may have difficulty with the last question. Rephrase the question if necessary: *En esta situación, ¿la familia de Juan va a reaccionar a favor de Juan o de Pati?* Do not reveal any new information.

Para pensar...

Ya sabes que en este episodio Juan y Pati tendrán una gran discusión. ¿Cuál será el resultado de esa discusión? ¿Se irá Pati o se quedará? En tu opinión, ¿quién tiene razón, Juan o Pati? ¿A quién crees que va a apoyar la familia de Juan en esta discusión?

BEFORE VIEWING . . .

2

¿TIENES BUENA MEMORIA?

Actividad A.   En la excavación
Paso 1
Por fin hay buenas noticias en el sitio de la excavación. Completa las siguientes oraciones con la información correcta.

1. Al principio, Ángela y Raquel... podían ver lo que pasaba muy bien. / no sabían nada y tampoco podían ver bien lo que pasaba.
2. Mientras esperaban, las dos mujeres empezaron a hablar de... las profesiones. / la civilización maya.
3. Ángela dijo que pensaba que Roberto tenía una profesión... fascinante. / peligrosa (*dangerous*).
4. Raquel dijo que, de niña, pensaba en ser... abogada y médica. / veterinaria y profesora.
5. Ángela pensaba en ser... profesora y actriz. / abogada y dentista.

 ### Paso 2
Ahora escucha el CD para verificar tus respuestas.

 ## Actividad B.   ¿Y Roberto?
¿Qué le pasó a Roberto en este episodio? Inventa cinco oraciones ciertas o falsas sobre lo que le pasó. Puedes utilizar las palabras útiles a continuación, si quieres. Luego, intercambie (*exchange*) oraciones con un compañero / una compañera. Indica cuáles de sus oraciones son ciertas y cuáles son falsas.

Palabras útiles: consciente/inconsciente, lastimado (*injured*), llevar, rescatar, tratar

Actividad C.   En la capital
Paso 1
Completa el siguiente resumen de lo que pasaba en la Ciudad de México con los nombres de los personajes apropiados: Arturo, Pedro, Juan, Pati.

Mientras Raquel y Ángela esperaban en el sitio de la excavación,

_____¹ hablaba con Pedro sobre el accidente y otras preocupaciones. Al mismo tiempo, en la casa de Ramón, _____² y

_____³ seguían con su conflicto. _____⁴ quería regresar a Nueva York, pero para _____⁵ la familia es más importante que la profesión.

 ### Paso 2
Ahora escucha el CD para verificar tus respuestas.

3

Vocabulario del tema

Profesiones y oficios

el abogado/la abogada	lawyer	**el veterinario/**	veterinarian
el actor/la actriz	actor/actress	**la veterinaria**	
el ama* de casa	homemaker	**el arquitecto/la arquitecta**	architect
el/la dentista	dentist	**el/la artista**	artist
el enfermero/	nurse	**la azafata**	flight attendant
la enfermera			(female)
el hombre/la mujer	businessman/	**el camarero/la camarera**	waiter, waitress;
de negocios	woman		flight attendant
el ingeniero/	engineer	**el carpintero/la carpintera**	carpenter
la ingeniera		**el/la dependiente**	clerk
el maestro/la maestra	teacher	**el/la electricista**	electrician
el/la médico	doctor	**el escritor/la escritora**	writer
el/la periodista	journalist	**el hermano/la hermana**	brother/sister
el profesor/la profesora	teacher,		(*of a relig-*
	professor		*ious order*)
el/la programador(a)	computer	**el marinero/la marinera**	sailor
de computadoras	programmer	**el/la músico**	musician
		el piloto/la pilota	pilot
		el pintor/la pintora	painter
		el/la plomero	plumber
		el/la psiquiatra	psychiatrist
		el reportero/la reportera	reporter
		el sacerdote (padre)	priest (father)
		el secretario/la secretaria	secretary

Nota cultural   Los nombres de las profesiones

In the Spanish-speaking world there is some variation in the words that should be used to refer to women who hold certain professions.

The following patterns are generally followed:

• The masculine and feminine articles are used with nouns that end in **-ista**: **el dentista** → **la dentista**.

---

* **Ama** (**de casa**) is a feminine noun, but like **el agua**, it takes the masculine **el**. All feminine nouns that begin with stressed **a** or **ha** take the masculine article (**el**) in the singular and the feminine article (**las**) in the plural: **las amas de casa, las aguas**. If a feminine noun begins with an *unac-*cented **a** or **ha**, the feminine article (**la**) is used: **la abogada, la actriz, la artista, la hamaca**.

> - The feminine form of a noun is used:* **el pintor** → **la pintora**.
> - The masculine and feminine articles are used with the same noun: **el/la médico**.
> - The word **mujer** is used: **el hombre de negocios** → **la mujer de negocios**.
>
> Some forms, especially **la pilota** in the preceding list, are not accepted by all Spanish speakers. If you want to be sure to use the correct word to describe a person's profession, listen to the form he or she uses and follow that example.

Actividad A.   Hablando de carreras
Paso 1

Escucha otra vez mientras Raquel y Ángela hablan de las profesiones. Mientras escuchas, indica en la siguiente tabla las profesiones que las dos mencionan, en las categorías indicadas.

Act. A, Answers: *Paso 1: ÁNGELA pensaba en estudiar para profesora, actriz; se hizo programadora de computadoras. EL PADRE DE ÁNGELA quería que ella fuera abogada, mujer de negocios. RAQUEL pensaba en estudiar para profesora (de historia), veterinaria; se hizo abogada. LA MADRE DE RAQUEL quería que ella fuera abogada.*
Paso 2: 1. Ambas querían ser profesoras. 2. Raquel (Su madre quería que su hija fuera abogada.)

ÁNGELA pensaba en estudiar para...   _____   _____

se hizo...   _____

EL PADRE DE ÁNGELA quería que ella fuera (*wanted her to be*)...

_____   _____

RAQUEL pensaba en estudiar para...   _____   _____

se hizo...   _____

LA MADRE DE RAQUEL quería que ella fuera...   _____

Paso 2
Ahora contesta las siguientes preguntas sobre las profesiones y las dos mujeres.

1.   ¿Qué intereses compartían?
2.   ¿Cuál de ellas siguió el consejo de su padre o de su madre?

Actividad B.   Comentarios del narrador
Escucha otra vez mientras el narrador habla de las profesiones. Escribe el nombre de las profesiones que escuchas. Luego escribe el número de cuatro de las profesiones mencionadas con el dibujo apropiado.

Act. B, Answers: *1. abogada 2. programadora 3. médico 4. enfermera 5. ingeniero 6. profesora 7. hombre de negocios 8. profesores 9. ama de casa. Los dibujos: a. 3 b. 7 c. 1 d. 4*

Aquí, en la excavación, hay ejemplos de varias de las profesiones de que hablaban Raquel y Ángela. Claro, está presente una _____.[1] También hay una _____[2] de computadoras. Hay un _____,[3] una _____,[4] un _____[5] y una _____[6] de arqueología.

En la familia Castillo, hay ejemplos de un _____[7] de _____[8] y también de un _____.[9]

Act. C, Suggestion (p. 325): Have students take turns giving their partner a situation that requires a specific profession.

---

* The feminine form is usually avoided when it coincides with a word with the same form but a different meaning: **el músico** → **la músico** (not **la música** = *music*).

a. _____   b. _____   c. _____   d. _____

Act. C, Extension: 5. *Vas de viaje en un avión y necesitas algo.* 6. *Quieres dar una fiesta bailable para un amigo.* 7. *En el baño de tu apartamento, hay agua por todo el piso* (floor). 8. *Quieres comprar algo en una tienda.*
Act. C, Optional: Play *Veinte preguntas.* Have students form groups of 4. One student assumes the identity of a profession from the vocabulary list. Other students in group ask *Sí/No* questions until they discover the profession of the person.

Actividad C. Situaciones

En ciertas situaciones una persona necesita de un profesional en un campo específico. Preséntale a tu compañero/a una serie de situaciones de este tipo para que él/ella te diga qué profesional se necesita. Es posible necesitar más de un profesional en algunas situaciones.

> MODELO: (Tuviste un accidente de automóvil.) →
> TÚ: Tuve un accidente de automóvil.
> COMPAÑERO/A: Necesitas un médico (un enfermero, un abogado...).

Act. D, Suggestion: Read the following list of professions aloud. 1. *el escritor* 2. *la arquitecta* 3. *el periodista* 4. *la veterinaria* 5. *el dependiente* 6. *la mujer de negocios* 7. *el maestro.* Say each profession only once. Students immediately write an association. After you have said all seven, list the professions on the board and have students give their associations. Compare to see which ones produced common associations and which did not.

1. Tu perro está enfermo.
2. Te duele un diente (*tooth*).
3. Sientes mucho estrés y necesitas hablar con alguien.
4. Quieres construir una casa.

Actividad D. Asociaciones

El profesor / La profesora va a mencionar una profesión. En una hoja de papel aparte, escribe la primera palabra o idea relacionada con esa profesión que se te ocurra. ¿Hay ciertas profesiones que estimulan más asociaciones comunes que otras?

1. ...   2. ...   3. ...   4. ...   5. ...   6. ...   7. ...

Act. D, Optional: Play *¿Qué dicen?* In this game, slips of paper with the names of professions are randomly distributed in the class (or in groups). Each student with a slip of paper must say something that would be typical of that profession while the class (or group) guesses their profession. Model 1 or 2 professions for the class before beginning: *¿Quiere Ud. algo para tomar? ¿Un vino tinto? Muy bien. ¿Y para comer? Recomiendo el pescado hoy. Es muy fresco.* (*camarero/a*).

Actividad E. ¿Qué quieres hacer como profesión?
Paso 1

Completa las siguientes oraciones para nombrar las profesiones y oficios que tienen algo que ver con tus gustos.

1. De niño/a, pensaba en ser _____.

2. Ahora pienso hacerme _____.

3. No me interesa nada ser _____.

Act. E, Paso 1, Suggestion: Assign as homework. Complete *Paso 2* in class the following day.

Paso 2

Entrevista a un compañero / una compañera para saber su reacción a estas oraciones. Prepara un breve informe para la clase.

4

UN POCO DE GRAMÁTICA

The Workbook/Study Guide contains more detailed explanation and practice of this grammar point.

Note: You may wish to introduce the *tú* command forms for regular -*ar*, -*er*, and -*ir* verbs in paradigmatic form: *hablar → habla, no hables; comer → come, no comas; abrir → abre, no abras.*

Point out: When pronouns are attached to affirmative commands, a written mark is required to maintain the stress in its original position. Compare forms with and without attached pronouns and practice pronunciation with the class: *ayuda, ayúdame; explica, explícame,* etc.

Act., Suggestion: Have individual students read the commands aloud and the rest of the class respond with *niño, perro,* or *los dos.*

Act., Optional: Play *La verdad o las consecuencias* (Truth or Dare). Have each student prepare a personal question as well as a command for someone specific in the class (including you!). If the person receiving a question does not want to answer (*la verdad*), they must accept the dare (*las consecuencias*) in the form of a command. Give students a list of (safe) infinitives to help them write their commands: *correr, bailar, cantar, saltar, gritar,* etc.

Act., Optional: Provide students with paper, pens, crayons, etc. Tell them to make signs for their house or apartment to remind their roommates, spouses, friends, or themselves to do or not to do things. Brainstorm with students for a list of ideas and write them on the board: *Limpia tu cuarto; Lava los platos, No comas mi comida,* etc.

Telling Someone to Do Something

Tú commands are used to give a direct command to a person whom you address with **tú**. For most verbs the third-person singular *indicative* is the **tú** command. Pronouns are attached to the end of affirmative commands.

Espérame aquí.	*Wait for me here.*
Vuelve conmigo al pueblo.	*Go back to the town with me.*

Negative **tú** command forms are the same as the second-person singular subjunctive, but pronouns are placed in front of the verb.

No me esperes más.	*Don't wait for me anymore.*
No vuelvas a la excavación.	*Don't go back to the excavation.*

Some common irregular affirmative commands are **sal** (**no salgas**), **pon** (**no pongas**), **haz** (**no hagas**), and **di** (**no digas**).

You will learn more about **tú** commands as well as additional irregular forms in the Workbook/Study Guide.

Actividad. ¿A quién corresponde?

¿A quién se dan normalmente los siguientes mandatos, a un niño de cuatro años (**N**), a un perro (**P**) o a los dos (**D**)?

N   P   D   1. No subas al sofá.
N   P   D   2. No toques eso.
N   P   D   3. Habla.
N   P   D   4. No hagas tanto ruido.
N   P   D   5. ¡Mira por dónde vas!
N   P   D   6. ¡Sal de aquí!
N   P   D   7. Pórtate bien.
N   P   D   8. ¡Ven, ven aquí!
N   P   D   9. Dime la verdad.
N   P   D   10. Acuéstate ahora mismo.
N   P   D   11. No mires tanto la televisión.
N   P   D   12. ¡Cálmate, cálmate!
N   P   D   13. ¡Siéntate!
N   P   D   14. No hagas eso.
N   P   D   15. Límpiate las manos antes de comer.

5

LECTURA CULTURAL

La civilización de los mayas

Los mayas eran una familia de pueblos indios que habitaron durante unos 2.000 años la península de Yucatán y partes de Guatemala, Honduras y El Salvador. Su origen es muy incierto.

La sociedad maya

- Se cree que los mayas no vivían en sus ciudades. La gente llegaba a las ciudades sólo para las fiestas y los días de mercado. Luego todo quedaba desierto porque la gente vivía en el campo, donde practicaban la agricultura.

- Por mucho tiempo se creyó que los mayas, como otras tribus de la región, usaban un sistema de agricultura rudimentaria basado en las milpas.[1] Ahora se sabe que cultivaban la tierra con un complicado sistema de campos[2] elevados en forma de terrazas. Este sistema avanzado para practicar la agricultura sirvió de base para que la civilización maya llegara a su apogeo.

- Los mayas hicieron grandes avances en aritmética y astronomía. Mientras en el resto de México y Centroamérica se usaba un calendario de 260 días, los mayas tenían un calendario de 360 días. Su calendario empezaba en una fecha que corresponde al 13 de agosto de 3114 antes de Cristo[3] en el calendario gregoriano que usamos nosotros.

- En la cultura maya se empleaba un complejo sistema de escritura,[4] más avanzado que el de otros pueblos indígenas de la región. Los libros eran un elemento importante de su cultura y los escribientes[5] gozaban de una alta posición social. Desgraciadamente, al llegar los españoles a América, destruyeron[6] la gran mayoría de los libros y códices mayas.

- Por mucho tiempo no se pudo leer lo que quedaba de la escritura e inscripciones mayas. Se creía que los temas principales de estas obras eran la astronomía y la religión. Cuando por fin los arqueólogos pudieron desenredar[7] el misterio de ese sistema de escritura, descubrieron también una rica historia de dinastías: intrigas para heredar el trono, luchas entre herederos,[8] intentos de establecer la legitimidad de los reyes… historias muy parecidas a las que narró Shakespeare en algunas de sus obras.

- Una de las obras más importantes que dejaron los mayas se conserva hoy sólo en forma de una copia de una transcripción que se hizo de ella durante la época de los conquistadores españoles. Se llama el *Popol Vuh (Libro del Consejo)* y cuenta, entre otras cosas, la historia maya de la creación del mundo. Según el *Popol Vuh,* los dioses mayas tuvieron que hacer varios intentos antes de formar hombres que pudieran honrarlos tal como ellos querían. De uno de estos intentos fracasados nacieron los monos.[9]

Y dicen que la descendencia de aquéllos son los monos que existen ahora en los bosques; éstos son la muestra[10] de aquéllos, porque de palo[11] fue hecha su carne por el Creador y Formador.

Y por esta razón el mono se parece al hombre, es la muestra de una generación de hombres creados, de hombres formados que eran solamente muñecos[12] y hechos solamente de madera.[13]

---

[1]*fields cultivated with slash-and-burn agriculture* [2]*fields* [3]*antes…* B.C. [4]*writing* [5]*scribes* [6]*they destroyed* [7]*untangle*
[8]*heirs* [9]*monkeys* [10]*remains* [11]*sticks* [12]*dolls* [13]*wood*

Los mayas: ¿Por qué desaparecieron?

A partir del siglo X los mayas fueron desapareciendo de sus ciudades. Algunos creen que esto se debe a las constantes guerras e incursiones de los aztecas. Otros creen que las constantes guerras civiles y luchas dinásticas por fin debilitaron[14] la familia de pueblos mayas.

Realmente se ignora[15] el motivo por el cual una civilización tan avanzada desapareció sin causas aparentes. Sigue siendo hasta hoy un verdadero enigma. Sus grandes ciudades y templos quedaron ocultados por las selvas de Yucatán hasta que, a mediados del[16] siglo diecinueve, algunos arqueólogos descubrieron sus ruinas. Hay que imaginar su sorpresa al encontrar, bajo la densa vegetación tropical, toda una civilización «perdida».

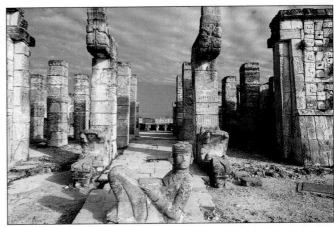

Chichén Itzá fue el mayor centro maya de Yucatán. En su apogeo, tenía explanadas, pirámides, terrazas y templos.

Lectura cultural, Preguntas: ¿Cierto o falso? 1. Los mayas vivían principalmente de la pesca. (F) 2. Los mayas sabían mucho de las ciencias, especialmente de las matemáticas y la astronomía. (C) 3. El calendario maya tenía 260 días. (F) 4. Los españoles enseñaron a escribir y leer a los mayas. (F) 5. Los libros mayas describen una larga historia de dinastías y reyes. (C) 6. El Popol Vuh es el equivalente maya de la Biblia. (C) 7. No se sabe exactamente por qué desaparecieron los mayas. (C)

[14]*weakened*   [15]*se... no se sabe*   [16]*a... in the middle of the*

Actividad.   Los mayas y los aztecas

Compara los siguientes aspectos de las civilizaciones maya y azteca.

Act., Suggestion: Have students prepare a 3 × 2 grid on a sheet of paper: 3 rows with *Dónde vivían; Organización social;* and *Razones por las que desaparecieron* and 2 columns headed with *Aztecas* and *Mayas*. Have them refer to Lesson 32 for information on the Aztecs. Fill in a large grid on the board or overhead with student responses.

1. donde vivían   2. razones de la caída de su imperio   3. organización social

6

INTERCAMBIO

Paso 1

La clase se va a dividir en seis grupos. A cada grupo se le va a asignar uno de los siguientes temas.

la personalidad	las destrezas y habilidades
la interacción con otras personas	los miedos
las cuestiones económicas	los intereses y pasatiempos

Paso 2

Cada grupo debe preparar por lo menos cinco preguntas que se podrían hacer a una persona. La idea es poder entender bien a la persona en cuanto a cada tema. Por ejemplo, **¿Cómo es su personalidad? ¿Qué adjetivos le describen? ¿Cómo se lleva con otras personas?** Las preguntas no deberían ser directas sino indirectas, por ejemplo, no se le debe preguntar **¿Eres paciente?** ni **¿Te irritas fácilmente?**, sino **¿Cuál de las siguientes situaciones te enfada más?**

Paso 3

Cuando terminen con las preguntas, deben compartirlas con la clase. Hagan revisiones según lo que dicen los compañeros.

Paso 4

Ahora, cada grupo debe hacerle las preguntas al profesor / a la profesora. Deben crear una descripción de su personalidad.

Paso 5

Luego, utilizando la información obtenida, miren la lista de profesiones y oficios en la página 323. ¿Qué profesiones serían apropiadas para su profesor(a)? ¿Cuáles no?

VOCABULARIO

Profesiones y oficios (Professions and Trades)

el actor/la actriz	actor/actress
el ama de casa	homemaker
el arquitecto/la arquitecta	architect
el/la artista	artist
la azafata	flight attendant (*f.*)
el camarero/la camarera	waiter/waitress; flight attendant
el carpintero/la carpintera	carpenter
el/la dentista	dentist
el/la electricista	electrician
el hermano/la hermana	brother/sister (*of a religious order*)
el hombre/la mujer de negocios	businessman/woman
el ingeniero/la ingeniera	engineer
el/la músico	musician
el piloto/la pilota	pilot
el/la plomero	plumber
el programador/la programadora de computadoras	computer programmer
el/la psiquiatra	psychiatrist
el sacerdote	priest
el secretario/la secretaria	secretary
el veterinario/la veterinaria	veterinarian

Los adjetivos

mimado/a	spoiled
peligroso/a	dangerous

Las palabras adicionales

sí mismo/a	oneself

Repaso: **el abogado/la abogada**; **el/la dependiente**; **el enfermero/la enfermera**; **el escritor/la escritora**; **el maestro/la maestra**; **el marinero/la marinera**; **el/la médico**; **el padre**; **el/la periodista**; **el pintor/la pintora**; **el profesor/la profesora**; **el reportero/la reportera**

ÉXITO*

*Success

OBJETIVOS

The materials in **Lección 34** of the Textbook and the Workbook/Study Guide will help you better understand the video episode and take you beyond it, giving you additional information about places and characters in the series. The Textbook will also help you to develop skill in using the Spanish language. In this lesson, you will learn

- vocabulary for talking about interpersonal relationships of many kinds
- ways to talk about what has happened

You will also learn about the social life typical of Hispanic young people.

Be sure to work through all parts of the lesson. When you see a headphones symbol in the margin, listen to the CD for **Lección 34**. Answers or hints for many activities are given in Appendix 1. Be sure to check your answers for each activity before going on to the next one.

The interactive CD-ROM to accompany *Destinos* contains additional practice with the video storyline and will help you improve your skills in Spanish.

BEFORE VIEWING . . .

Preliminary: See Faculty Guide for additional information and activities for this lesson.
• **Variation:** For activities marked with the headphones icon, you may wish to read from the Audioscript instead of playing the CD.
• **Suggestion:** Make sure students are familiar with the activities before you read from the Audioscript or play the CD.

1

PREPARACIÓN

Suggestions:
• Before watching the video, go over the vocabulary list at the end of the chapter and have students pronounce the words after you.
• Assign *Preparación* activities as homework and then go over them quickly in class before viewing the video.

Act. A, *Paso 1*, **Suggestion:** You may want to have students do this activity in pairs and then go over answers as whole class.

Act. A, Answers: *Paso 1:*
1. b 2. a 3. b 4. a

Actividad A.
Paso 1
Completa las siguientes oraciones con las frases apropiadas.

1. Después de mucho trabajo en el sitio de la excavación,
   a. ——— no pudieron rescatar a Roberto.
   b. ——— finalmente rescataron a Roberto.

2. En casa de Pedro, Juan y Pati
   a. ——— seguían discutiendo.   b. ——— se reconciliaron.

3. Juan quiere que Pati
   a. ——— regrese a Nueva York.   b. ——— se quede en México con él.

4. Pedro y Arturo decidieron tratar de averiguar (*find out*)
   a. ——— lo que pasó en el sitio de la excavación.
   b. ——— dónde estaban Raquel y Ángela.

 ### Paso 2
Ahora escucha el CD para verificar tus respuestas.

 ## Actividad B.
Paso 1
Escucha parte de una conversación entre Juan y Ramón. Después de escuchar, contesta la pregunta.

¿Cuál es el tema principal de la conversación entre Juan y Ramón?

Act. B, Suggestion: You may want to have students work in pairs, role-playing the dialogue.

Act. B, Answers: *Paso 2:*
1. F 2. C 3. F 4. C 5. C, c
(See Appendix 1 for expanded answers.)

a. ——— las relaciones que existen entre los hermanos Juan y Ramón, hijos de don Fernando
b. ——— las relaciones que hay entre Juan y Pati
c. ——— los problemas que tiene Pati en el teatro

Si indicaste la letra *b*, tuviste razón.

 ### Paso 2
Ahora escucha la conversación de nuevo. Puedes leer las últimas líneas al mismo tiempo, si quieres. Recuerda el significado de la palabra **éxito**, el título de este episodio, y ten en cuenta (*keep in mind*) que **celoso** significa *jealous*. Luego contesta las preguntas.

RAMÓN: Bueno, yo en tu lugar me sentiría celoso.
 JUAN: ¿Celoso? ¿De quién?
RAMÓN: No es de quién… sino de qué. Mejor debo decir tendría envidia.

JUAN: Yo sé que Pati es muy inteligente… que tiene mucho talento. Es escritora, productora y directora y también profesora de teatro. Ramón, ¿crees que tengo envidia del éxito de mi esposa?

Ahora indica si las siguientes oraciones son ciertas (**C**) o falsas (**F**), según la conversación.

C F 1. Ramón está de acuerdo con Juan.
C F 2. Ramón insinúa que Juan tiene envidia del éxito de Pati.
C F 3. Juan no lo quiere escuchar. Se niega a (*He refuses to*) pensar en lo que le dice Ramón.
C F 4. Juan se pone a pensar en lo que insinúa Ramón.
C F 5. Juan dice que su matrimonio es «un fracaso». ¿Qué significa «fracaso»?
      a. fricassee   b. fragile   c. failure

Para pensar, **Suggestion:** Pose the same questions to several different students to elicit a variety of opinions.

Para pensar…

Como sabes, la palabra **envidia** quiere decir *envy*. ¿Crees tú que Juan le tiene envidia a Pati? ¿Es egocéntrico Juan? ¿O es Pati la egocéntrica? ¿Son las relaciones entre Juan y Pati similares a las de alguna pareja que tú conoces?

 . . . AFTER VIEWING

2

¿TIENES BUENA MEMORIA?

Act. A, Suggestion: You may want to have students do this activity in pairs or small groups. **Act. A, Answers:** 1. *Sí* 2. *No* 3. *Sí* 4. *No* 5. *Sí* 6. *No* (See Appendix 1 for expanded answers.)

Actividad A. En la capital

Indica si los siguientes incidentes ocurrieron (**Sí**) o no (**No**) en el **Episodio 34**.

Sí No 1. Después de su pelea con Juan, Pati salió corriendo al jardín.
Sí No 2. El consejo de Mercedes es que Pati debe quedarse en México con Juan.
Sí No 3. Mercedes recordó con afecto el día de la boda (*wedding*) de Pati y Juan.
Sí No 4. Ramón le habló a Juan de una forma brutal sobre los problemas de su matrimonio.
Sí No 5. Ramón le dice a Juan que es posible que él, Juan, tenga envidia de Pati.
Sí No 6. Juan también le habló a Pedro, su tío, sobre los problemas que tiene en su matrimonio.

Actividad B.   **Camino al Distrito Federal**
Paso 1

Otra vez Raquel y Ángela se encontraron viajando juntas en un carro. Como ocurrió antes, pasaron el tiempo hablando de sus relaciones con varias personas. Indica todas las relaciones que mencionaron.

Act. B, Answers: *Paso 1: 2, 3, 5, 6 (¡OJO! Raquel habla de Jorge en su repaso, pero no lo mencionó cuando hablaba con Ángela en el carro.) Paso 3: (See Appendix 1 for possible answers.)*

Las relaciones entre...

1. —— Raquel y sus padres
2. —— Raquel y su antiguo novio
3. —— Raquel y Arturo
4. —— Raquel y Jorge (el novio de Ángela)

5. —— Ángela y Roberto
6. —— Ángela y Jorge
7. —— Ángela y sus tíos

Paso 2

Escucha el repaso de este episodio en el CD para verificar tus respuestas.

Paso 3

Ahora describe lo que recuerdas de estas relaciones, haciendo oraciones con una palabra o frase de cada columna. Añade todos los detalles que puedas.

Ángela	admira a	Arturo
Raquel	es amigo/a de	Roberto
Jorge	(no) es novio/a de	Jorge
Arturo	era novio/a de	Raquel
	quiere a	Ángela
	quiere casarse con	Luis
	recuerda a —— con cariño	
	se separó de	
	trató de ligar con (*pick up*)	

Para pensar...

Al final del episodio, un camión se acercaba rápidamente al coche que manejaba Raquel. ¿Qué crees que va a pasar? ¿Va a haber (*Is there going to be*) otro accidente, un choque?

Here are some notes of interest about some of the usages you have heard in this video episode.

- Did you notice the momentary difficulty that Arturo had in getting the desk clerk to pass him the newspaper? Arturo used the word **diario**, commonly used in Argentina to mean *newspaper*; the word **periódico** is more frequently used in other parts of the Spanish-speaking world. The two men do not focus at all on the brief misunderstanding; it is a normal incident in communication between speakers of a language that is used around the world.

• At the end of the flashback to Juan and Pati's wedding ceremony, the priest told the congregation: **Idos en paz**. (*Go in peace.*) The specific verb form used is a **vosotros** command (**ir** → **id**; **irse** → **idos**). As you know, **vosotros** forms are not generally used in Mexico. However, they survive in inscriptions on buildings, in documents that date back to the colonial era, and in religious services— like the wedding service—initiated in Mexico by the Spaniards. Even though the **vosotros** forms are not generally used in Mexico, their use in these situations does not cause any confusion.

3 VOCABULARIO DEL TEMA

Relaciones sociales

la amistad	friendship
el cariño, el afecto	affection
el amor (a primera vista)	love (at first sight)
la (primera) cita	(first) date
el noviazgo	engagement
la boda	wedding
el matrimonio	marriage
la luna de miel	honeymoon
el odio	hatred
el divorcio	divorce
el amigo/la amiga	friend
el compañero/la compañera	companion; "significant other"
el novio/la novia	boyfriend/girlriend; fiancé(e); groom/bride
la pareja	couple
el esposo/la esposa	husband/wife; spouse
el marido/la mujer	husband/wife
el matrimonio	married couple
llevarse bien/mal con	to get along well/badly with

tener envidia/celos (de)	to be envious/jealous (of)
tomarle cariño a alguien	to start to have affection for someone
enamorarse (de)	to fall in love (with)
estar enamorado/a (de)	to be in love (with)
casarse (con)	to get married (to)
odiar	to hate
divorciarse (de)	to divorce

Note the following about vocabulary used to describe marital relationships.

● Whereas the words **mujer** and **señora** can be used to mean *wife*, the words **hombre** and **señor** are never used to mean *husband*.

● The term **esposos** (in addition to meaning *husbands* or *husbands and wives*) can also mean *married couple*. **Maridos**, however, expresses only *husbands*.

Actividad A. Las relaciones: ¿Cómo se desarrollan?

Escucha mientras el narrador define por medio de una serie de características las siguientes relaciones. Indica la característica o características mencionadas que definen cada relación a continuación.

Act. A, Answers: 1. *el cariño* 2. *el cariño* 3. *el cariño, el amor* 4. *el amor, un período de tiempo* 5. *una ceremonia* 6. *un período de tiempo, el amor*

el cariño
el amor

1. la amistad
2. la familia
3. los novios

un período de tiempo
una ceremonia

4. el noviazgo
5. la boda
6. la luna de miel

Actividad B. Juan y Pati

Act. B, Suggestion: You may want to have students do this activity in pairs or small groups and go over their answers together.

Act. B, Answers: a. 7 b. 2 c. 3 d. 5 e. 1 f. 6 g. 8 h. 9 i. 4 j. 10

Pon en orden cronológico (del 1 a 10) los siguientes incidentes y acontecimientos tal como probablemente ocurrieron en las relaciones entre Juan y Pati.

a. _____ Los dos consiguieron puestos académicos al mismo tiempo, poco después de casarse.
b. _____ Tuvieron su primera cita al día siguiente.
c. _____ Se hicieron buenos amigos en seguida.
d. _____ Se casaron en La Gavia.
e. _____ Se conocieron en un teatro de Nueva York.
f. _____ Pasaron la luna de miel en Cancún.
g. _____ Pati empezó a tener mucho éxito en su carrera.
h. _____ Poco a poco Juan empezó a tenerle envidia a Pati.
i. _____ No se enamoraron hasta mucho más tarde.
j. _____ Empezaron a pelear por pequeñas cosas.

Actividad C.
Paso 1

¿Qué opinas de las relaciones entre Raquel y Arturo? Vas a escuchar las siguientes oraciones. Indica las oraciones que crees que mejor describen sus relaciones.

1. _____ Se han tomado mucho cariño.
2. _____ Ya son novios.
3. _____ Se enamoraron a primera vista.
4. _____ Realmente no han tenido (*they haven't had*) una «primera cita» todavía.
5. _____ Se van a casar algún día.
6. _____ Les gusta estar juntos.
7. _____ Se llevan muy, muy bien.
8. _____ Raquel tiene celos de la ex esposa de Arturo.

Paso 2

Ahora vas a escuchar estas oraciones. Indica solamente las oraciones que, para ti, describen las relaciones entre Raquel y Ángela.

1. _____ Raquel le tiene mucho cariño a Ángela.
2. _____ Le tiene un poco de envidia a Ángela porque ésta (*the latter*) tiene novio.
3. _____ Se llevan muy bien, aunque a veces se pelean.
4. _____ Les gusta estar juntas.
5. _____ Comparten confidencias, esperanzas, consejos…
6. _____ Ángela tiene celos de Raquel porque sabe que Jorge trató de ligar con ella.
7. _____ Sus relaciones van a durar mucho tiempo.
8. _____ Raquel cree que Ángela no debe casarse con Jorge.

Paso 3

Ahora haz diez oraciones que describan las relaciones entre Raquel y Arturo (**A**), entre Raquel y Ángela (**B**) o entre las dos parejas (**C**). Preséntaselas a tu compañero/a para que él/ella indique a cuál de las relaciones se refiere cada oración.

> MODELO: TÚ: Se tienen mucho cariño aunque se conocieron hace poco.
>
> COMPAÑERO/A: C

Actividad D. ¿Cómo deben ser las relaciones sociales?

Indica lo que piensas sobre cada tema a continuación. Luego, busca personas en la clase que tengan la misma opinión que tú.

1. El amor a primera vista: ¿existe o no?
2. ¿Es mejor tener uno o dos amigos íntimos o tener muchos amigos «superficiales»?
3. ¿Debe ser largo (seis meses o más) un noviazgo?
4. El matrimonio: ¿es esencial para la sociedad o no?
5. ¿Cuándo (¿A qué edad?) debe uno casarse?

Act. D, Suggestion: For the second part of the activity, have students prepare a *Firma aquí* activity with questions such as *¿Crees en el amor a primera vista? ¿Es bueno casarse a los veintiún años?* Have students circulate in class asking and answering the questions and gathering the signatures of classmates who respond with *Sí.* Then have them report their findings to the class, using the model _____ *cree en el amor a primera vista.*

4

UN POCO DE GRAMÁTICA

The Workbook/Study Guide contains more detailed explanation and practice of this grammar point.

Suggestions:
- Have students ask each other questions about what they have or have not done since arriving at the university. *¿Has bebido tequila? ¿Has visitado a tus padres? ¿Has recibido una mala nota? ¿Has ido al cine? ¿Has bailado?*, etc.
- Pass out pictures of famous people and have students create lists of events about the lives of these people, e.g., *Madonna: Ha tenido muchos novios. Ha ganado muchísimo dinero. Se ha casado,* etc.

Talking About What Someone Has Done

If you want to indicate that someone has done something, use the word **ha** with the past participle of another verb. The past participle of most verbs is formed by adding **-ado** to the stem of **-ar** verbs and **-ido** to the stems of **-er** and **-ir** verbs.

Pati **ha hablado** con Juan mil veces sobre este asunto.

Pati has talked with Juan about this matter a thousand times.

Ahora **ha perdido** la paciencia con él.

Now she has lost patience with him.

Some common irregular past participles are **dicho** (**decir**) and **hecho** (**hacer**). You will learn more about these verb forms in the Workbook/Study Guide.

Actividad.   ¿Qué ha hecho tu compañero/a?
Paso 1

Escoge a un compañero / una compañera de clase. ¿Crees que ha hecho cada acción a continuación? Indica lo que crees.

Mi compañero/a ———————————.

Sí   No   1. ha hecho un viaje a Europa
Sí   No   2. ha vivido en otro país
Sí   No   3. ha manejado un Porsche
Sí   No   4. se ha ofrecido como voluntario en la comunidad alguna vez
Sí   No   5. ya se ha graduado en otra especialización
Sí   No   6. ha estudiado español antes de tomar esta clase
Sí   No   7. ha hecho *autostop* (*hitchhiked*) alguna vez
Sí   No   8. no ha perdido (*missed*) ni una clase

Follow-up: For homework, have students write personal lists of events, using the present perfect. *He vivido en _____. He estudiado _____. He viajado en _____. Nunca he fumado un cigarrillo,* etc.

Act., Optional: Have students report their findings to the rest of the class.

Paso 2

Ahora lee tus respuestas a tu compañero/a. ¿Tenías razón?

Lectura cultural, Preguntas: 1. ¿Cuáles son algunas diversiones muy populares de los jóvenes hispánicos? (el cine, el baile, las fiestas, los deportes y hablar en las calles, los cafés, las reuniones y los clubes) 2. En general, ¿cómo es la vida nocturna en las grandes capitales del mundo hispánico? (muy activa) 3. ¿Cuándo comienza una noche de baile? (a las once o doce) 4. ¿Qué es una «Sin»? (una discoteca que no sirve bebidas alcohólicas) 5. ¿Cuál es una diferencia entre la cultura hispánica y la de los EEUU? (la distinción entre las relaciones amistosas y las amorosas) 6. El artículo dice que el típico joven hispano se interesa más por la cultura de otros países que el típico joven norteamericano y que también es más filosófico. ¿Estás de acuerdo?

5

LECTURA CULTURAL

La vida social de los jóvenes

Las diversiones de los jóvenes hispánicos son numerosas. Pueden variar según la clase social y el lugar, pero algunas gozan de[1] gran aceptación popular en todas partes: el cine, el baile, las fiestas, los deportes y hablar… en las calles, los cafés, en las reuniones y en los clubes.

Fiestas y bailes

Tal vez se puede decir que las diversiones más populares son las

Un café en Oaxaca, México

[1]gozan… *enjoy*

fiestas y los bailes. Es muy común reunirse con los amigos en la casa de alguien para hablar y bailar hasta muy tarde. Los jóvenes también van con frecuencia a los clubes nocturnos y a las discotecas. En las grandes capitales del mundo hispánico, la vida nocturna es muy activa. Ya que, según la costumbre, se cena relativamente tarde, es posible que una noche de baile con los amigos no empiece sino hasta las once o las doce.

Aun a los muy jóvenes, entre los quince y los dieciocho años, les gusta salir a bailar. Para ellos, en España se ha empezado a ver el fenómeno de las Discotecas «Sin», es decir en algunas discotecas una noche a la semana no se sirven bebidas alcohólicas. Los jóvenes vienen a estas discotecas solamente para escuchar música, bailar y conocer gente.

Amigos y novios

Como se ve, es muy frecuente entre los jóvenes hispánicos salir en grupos, con los «compas» (= los compañeros). Aun las parejas suelen salir con su grupo de amigos, tal vez despidiéndose más temprano para estar a solas.

Una diferencia interesante entre la cultura hispánica en general y la de los Estados Unidos se ve en la distinción que se hace entre las relaciones amistosas y las amorosas. Las palabras **amigo** y **novio** realmente no tienen un equivalente exacto en inglés. **Amigo/Amiga** sirven para definir las relaciones que en inglés se conocen por *friend* y *boy/girlfriend*. En cambio, los términos **novia/novio** solamente se aplican a los que tienen relaciones formales. También significan *fiancée/fiancé* y *bride/groom*.

La juventud: ¿Una cultura internacional?

¿Son realmente diferentes los jóvenes hispánicos y los de otras partes del mundo? Muchos creen que no. Actualmente[2] vivimos en una comunidad global. Las noticias, las ideas, las canciones, las modas[3]… todo se puede comunicar casi instantáneamente por medio de la televisión, la radio (sobre todo la música) y el cine. Los efectos de este fenómeno se notan —tal vez más que en otros grupos— en los jóvenes.

Si hace cuarenta años había gran diferencia entre, digamos, un joven español y un joven norteamericano de la misma edad, actualmente las diferencias no son tan marcadas. Están familiarizados con algunas de las mismas canciones y los mismos conjuntos[4] musicales, hablan de los mismos artistas de cine, quieren ver las mismas películas y se visten de una forma parecida —el estilo *punk* no es exclusivamente norteamericano.

Con todo, no se quiere decir que sean idénticos. Una de las grandes diferencias entre los jóvenes hispánicos y los norteamericanos es que el típico joven hispano, además de conocer su propia cultura, se interesa por la cultura estadounidense y de otros países; se informa de ellas por los medios de comunicación. El típico joven norteamericano, en cambio, sabe poco —y a veces también se interesa poco— por la cultura popular europea, mexicana o latinoamericana.

Mucha gente también cree que los jóvenes hispánicos son más filosóficos y más comprometidos[5] que los norteamericanos. Es decir, que se interesan más por las cuestiones éticas o políticas. Por eso los debates y las discusiones en los clubes y las cafeterías pueden durar hasta muy tarde… ¡y ser muy animados!

¿Qué opinas tú? Si tienes algunos amigos hispánicos, ¿qué opinan ellos?

[2]*Currently*   [3]*fashion*   [4]*(musical) groups*   [5]*involved, with strong ideas about issues*

Actividad. En tu ciudad

¿Adónde debe ir un joven hispánico en tu ciudad si quiere hacer lo siguiente?

1. ver una película reciente filmada en los Estados Unidos
2. ver una película hispánica o europea
3. bailar
4. hablar con unos amigos hasta muy tarde
5. hablar con otros jóvenes que se interesan en la política

6

INTERCAMBIO

Paso 1

Piensa en la relacion entre Raquel y Arturo. Utilizando vocabulario nuevo de esta lección, escribe por lo menos diez oraciones en las que describes cómo se ha desarrollado esa relación empezando con el primer momento en que se conocieron. Por ejemplo, ¿cuándo empezó Arturo a tenerle cariño a Raquel? ¿Crees que él se ha enamorado de ella? ¿Y Raquel?

Paso 2

En grupos de tres, compartan lo que han escrito para el **Paso 1**. Revisen sus oraciones y preparen una lista de diez oraciones para presentar a la clase.

Paso 3

Cada grupo debe presentar su lista de oraciones a la clase. Mientras tanto, el profesor / la profesora va a escribir las ideas en la pizarra.

Paso 4

Como clase, miren las ideas que aparecen en la pizarra. ¿Qué les parece lo que ha ocurrido hasta el momento? ¿Creen que es típico? ¿Están todos de acuerdo del estado actual de la relación entre Arturo y Raquel? ¿Cuál de las siguientes ideas expresa mejor lo que piensa Uds.?

a. Las relaciones entre Raquel y Arturo son típicas. No hay nada excepcional que ha pasado entre ellos.
b. Las relaciones entre Raquel y Arturo son más o menos típicas, pero hay ciertas cosas que no. Por ejemplo, …
c. Las relaciones entre Raquel y Arturo no son típicas porque…

VOCABULARIO

Los verbos

averiguar	to find out
ligar con	to "pick someone up"

Las relaciones sociales
(Social Relationships)

el afecto	affection
la amistad	friendship
el amor	love
(a primera vista)	(at first sight)
la boda	wedding
el cariño	affection
la (primera) cita	(first) date
el divorcio	divorce
la luna de miel	honeymoon
el noviazgo	engagement
el odio	hatred
enamorarse (de)	to fall in love (with)
estar enamorado/a (de)	to be in love (with)
odiar	to hate

tener celos (de)	to be jealous (of)
tomarle cariño a alguien	to start to have affection for someone

Repaso: **el amor, casarse (con), divorciarse (de), llevarse bien/mal con, el matrimonio** (*marriage*), **tener envidia**

Las personas

el compañero/ la compañera	companion; "significant other"
el marido/la mujer	husband/wife
el matrimonio	married couple
el novio/la novia	fiancé(e); groom/bride
la pareja	couple

Repaso: **el amigo/la amiga, el esposo/la esposa, el novio/la novia** (*boy/girlfriend*)

Los conceptos

el éxito	success
el fracaso	failure

Suggestion: Have students look at the photo, describe what they see, and talk about what they think might happen. Ask questions about the photo to prompt student discussion.

REUNIDOS*

*Reunited

OBJETIVOS

The materials in **Lección 35** of the Textbook and the Workbook/Study Guide will help you better understand the video episode and take you beyond it, giving you additional information about places and characters in the series. The Textbook will also help you to develop skill in using the Spanish language. In this lesson, you will learn

- additional vocabulary for making requests and recommendations
- ways to say that you hope something has happened

You will also learn about a popular Mexican drink, **tequila**.

Be sure to work through all parts of the lesson. When you see a headphones symbol in the margin, listen to the CD for **Lección 35**. Answers or hints for many activities are given in Appendix 1. Be sure to check your answers for each activity before going on to the next one.

The interactive CD-ROM to accompany *Destinos* contains additional practice with the video storyline and will help you improve your skills in Spanish.

BEFORE VIEWING . . .

1

Preparación

Actividad A.
Paso 1
Completa las siguientes oraciones con la información apropiada.

Act. A, *Paso 1,* Answers: 1. *a un hospital en la capital* 2. *en su propio carro* 3. *de sus novios* 4. *siguieron discutiendo sin resolver nada* 5. *el accidente*

1. Llevaron a Roberto... a un hospital en la capital. / a una clínica en los Estados Unidos.
2. Raquel y Ángela salieron... con Roberto. / en su propio carro.
3. Mientras manejaba Raquel, las dos mujeres hablaban... de sus novios. / de problemas familiares.
4. En la capital, Juan y Pati... pudieron resolver sus dificultades. / siguieron discutiendo sin resolver nada.
5. Arturo trataba de averiguar algo sobre... el paradero de Raquel. / el accidente.

 ### Paso 2
Ahora escucha el CD para verificar tus respuestas.

 ## Actividad B.
Paso 1
En este episodio, Carlos llama de nuevo a Miami. Al hablar con Ofelia, recibe noticias de cómo van las cosas en la oficina. Escucha la conversación entre Carlos y Ofelia y luego contesta la pregunta.

¿Cuál es el tema principal de la conversación entre Carlos y Ofelia?

a. _____ algunos problemas que hay con el personal de la oficina
b. _____ unos reportes que Carlos tiene que escribir
c. _____ los reportes de los auditores y sus recomendaciones

Si indicaste la letra *c,* tuviste razón.

 ### Paso 2
Ahora escucha la conversación de nuevo. Puedes leerla al mismo tiempo, si quieres. La palabra **gerente** es sinónimo de **jefe.** Trata de no fijarte en las palabras que no entiendes. Luego contesta las preguntas.

Act. B, *Paso 2,* Answers: 1. *Están en malas condiciones.* 2. b

CARLOS: ¿Ofelia? Habla Carlos. Mira, ¿no sabes algo más?
OFELIA: Sí, el gerente del banco que ha estado llamando muchas veces. Quiere hablar con Ud.
CARLOS: ¿No ha dicho para qué?
OFELIA: No, pero que quiere hablar con Ud. Yo le dije que andaba de viaje para México.
CARLOS: ¿Qué más?
OFELIA: Tengo una copia de los reportes de los auditores. No son muy buenos...

CARLOS: ¿Qué dicen?

OFELIA: Dicen que el balance general arroja fuertes pérdidas, que ponen en peligro las otras inversiones de la familia. Y pues… recomiendan cerrar la oficina.

1. Según los auditores, ¿están en buenas o malas condiciones las finanzas de la oficina de Miami?
2. La palabra **pérdidas** se relaciona con el verbo **perder**. ¿Qué significa?
   a. _____ profits   b. _____ losses

Para pensar…

Al saber las noticias que le da Ofelia, Carlos está muy agitado. ¿Por qué? ¿Qué secreto está ocultando? ¿Debe contárselo a la familia? Imagina que tú eres Carlos. ¿Qué vas a hacer?

 . . . AFTER VIEWING

2

¿TIENES BUENA MEMORIA?

Actividad A. En la capital
Paso 1

Ahora todos están por fin en la Ciudad de México. ¿Cuánto recuerdas de lo que pasó en el episodio? Contesta las siguientes preguntas. ¡OJO! A veces hay que elegir dos frases.

1. ¿Qué pasó mientras manejaba Raquel?
   a. _____ De repente apareció un perro en el camino…
   b. _____ De repente apareció un camión (*truck*) en el camino…
   c. _____ …y tuvieron un accidente.
   d. _____ …pero no tuvieron un accidente.

2. Cuando Ángela y Raquel llegaron al hospital, ¿quiénes estaban allí para ver a Roberto?
   a. _____ Pedro y Mercedes   c. _____ Arturo y Pedro
   b. _____ Ramón y Carlos

3. Ángela no los vio. Entró directamente al cuarto de Roberto. ¿Cómo estaba Roberto cuando entró?
   a. _____ Estaba dormido (*asleep*)…   c. _____ …y saludó con cariño.
   b. _____ Estaba despierto…   d. _____ …y no le habló.

4. ¿Qué hizo Arturo cuando vio a Raquel?
   a. _____ Gritó su nombre y le dio la mano.
   b. _____ Gritó su nombre y la besó.

5. ¿Cuál fue la reacción de Raquel?
    a. _____ Estaba un poco avergonzada (*embarrassed*)…
    b. _____ Estaba enojada con Arturo…
    c. _____ …y se peleó con él.
    d. _____ …pero no le dijo nada.

Paso 2
Ahora escucha el CD para verificar tus respuestas.

Actividad B.   Idas y venidas (*Comings and Goings*)
Paso 1
En el CD, escucha la segunda parte
del repaso de Raquel.

Paso 2
Ahora describe los incidentes más importantes que ocurren en este episodio, haciendo oraciones con una palabra o frase de cada columna. Añade
todos los detalles que puedas.

Pedro	se despidió de	Puerto Rico, Miami, Los
Raquel	saludó a	Ángeles, Nueva York
Arturo	conoció a	
Ángela	salió para	el hospital, el hotel,
Pati (no)	estaba (dormido/a) en	la casa de Pedro,
Ofelia	llamó a	la oficina
Carlos	fue a	
Roberto	le(s) contó algo a	Carlos, Carlos y Gloria,
	estaba preocupado/a por	toda la familia, Raquel,
	besó a	Pedro, Arturo, Juan,
		Ángela, Pati

Para pensar…

1. En la **Actividad B**, comentaste las actividades de casi todos los per-
    sonajes principales menos las de don Fernando. Parece que todos se
    han olvidado de él. ¿Cómo estará don Fernando? ¿En qué estará
    pensando? ¿Crees que sus nietos le van a causar una buena impre-
    sión?
2. ¿Crees que Arturo les ha causado una buena impresión a los miem-
    bros de la familia Castillo? ¿Por qué sí o por qué no? Piensa en sus
    interacciones con todos hasta ahora. Y la familia, ¿le ha causado una
    buena impresión a Arturo? ¿Está contento de conocer a su «nueva»
    familia?

3

VOCABULARIO DEL TEMA

Suggestion: Practice pronunciation with choral and individual repetition. Make sure that students understand the meaning of all of the words before continuing with the activities.

Consejos y sugerencias

el consejo	aconsejar	el requisito	requerir (ie)
	insistir (en)		rogar (ue)
el mandato	mandar	la sugerencia	sugerir (ie, i)
la recomendación	recomendar (ie)		

The preceding nouns and verbs express ways of influencing the behavior of others. You should be able to guess the meaning of almost all of them, except for **rogar** (*to beg*).

Actividad A. ¿Mandato o sugerencia?

Indica si lo que dice la persona es una recomendación, una sugerencia, un mandato o un requisito.

1. Arturo, hablando con Pedro: «¿Por qué no dejamos a Roberto, para que descanse?»
2. La doctora, hablando con Arturo: «Hay que dejarlo dormir y no despertarlo.»
3. La doctora, hablando con una enfermera: «Está muy agitado. Déle un calmante.»
4. Ofelia, hablando con Carlos: «Recomiendan cerrar la oficina.»
5. Arturo, hablando con Pedro: «Bueno, es mejor que salgamos, para no despertarlo.»
6. Arturo, hablando con Raquel y Ángela: «¿Por qué no vamos al hotel?»
7. Raquel, hablando con su madre: «Mamá, no comiences.»
8. Consuelo, hablando con los niños: «Ahora todos a la cama, sin chistar (*fussing*).»

Actividad B. En el episodio...
Paso 1

Completa las siguientes oraciones para describir los consejos y sugerencias del **Episodio 35**. ¡OJO! En algunos casos hay más de una respuesta.

1. ¿Qué sugiere Pedro en este episodio? Sugiere que
   a. _____ Carlos y Gloria le den las noticias sobre Roberto al resto de la familia.
   b. _____ Pati no se vaya a Nueva York.
   c. _____ Arturo despierte a Roberto.

2. ¿En qué insiste la madre de Raquel? Insiste en que
   a. _____ Luis vaya a México.
   b. _____ Raquel regrese a los Estados Unidos.
   c. _____ Raquel la presente a la familia Castillo.

3. ¿Qué recomiendan los auditores? (¿Tienes una memoria muy buena?)
   Recomiendan que
   a. _____ se cierre la oficina en Miami.
   b. _____ Ramón sea nombrado director de la compañía.
   c. _____ se venda La Gavia.

4. ¿Qué requiere la médico? Quiere que
   a. _____ le den un calmante a Roberto.
   b. _____ se saquen más rayos X.
   c. _____ dejen descansar a Roberto hasta mañana.

5. ¿Qué sugiere Arturo? Sugiere que
   a. _____ la familia prepare a don Fernando para conocer a sus nuevos
      parientes.
   b. _____ todos regresen al hotel.
   c. _____ Ángela no los acompañe a la casa de Pedro.

Paso 2
Ahora escucha el CD para verificar tus respuestas.

Act. C, *Paso 1*, Suggestions:
• Assign as homework and then complete *Paso 2* in class the following day.
• Have several students present their suggestions for both situations, then poll the class to see which one they think is the best.

Actividad C.   **Consejos**
Paso 1

Act. C, Follow-up: Have each student write a personal situation similar to those in the activity. It may be a true or an invented situation. Then have students circulate in class, recounting their situations in the first person and asking for recommendations. Sample: *Yo vi al novio de mi mejor amiga besando a otra mujer. ¿Qué debo hacer?* Write a model for responses on the board: *Recomiendo que tú* + subjunctive. Follow up by asking students *¿Cuál es tu situación? ¿Y qué recomendaciones te dieron? ¿Son buenas recomendaciones o no?*

¿Qué consejos o sugerencias darías (*would you make*) en estos casos? ¡OJO! No te olvides de usar el subjuntivo. Si no quieres ofrecer un consejo, di «No le aconsejo (sugiero...) nada porque _____.»

1. Un chico tiene problemas con sus padres. Se va de casa y no quiere volver. Tiene diecisiete años. ¿Qué recomendaciones le das a esta familia?

   Le aconsejo al chico que _____.

   Les recomiendo a sus padres que _____.

2. Una persona quiere dar una fiesta para todos sus amigos. Pero varios amigos suyos (*of his*) no se llevan bien. ¿Los invita a todos o no?

   Le sugiero que _____.

   Les recomiendo a sus amigos que _____.

Paso 2
Ahora presenta tus sugerencias a la clase. La clase debe decidir qué consejos son los mejores.

4

UN POCO DE GRAMÁTICA

The Workbook/Study Guide contains more detailed explanation and practice of this grammar point.

Note: You may wish to review the formation of past participles.

Expressing Hope

Use the phrase **ojalá (que)** to indicate what you hope will happen. You can also use this expression followed by **haya(n)** (the present subjunctive equivalent of **ha[n]**) plus the past participle to describe what you hope *has* happened.

Ojalá que Pati **haya llegado** a Nueva York sin problemas.	*It's to be hoped (I hope) that Pati has arrived in New York without any difficulty.*
Ojalá que don Fernando no se **haya enterado** del accidente.	*It's to be hoped (I hope) that don Fernando hasn't found out about the accident.*

You will learn more about using these forms in the Workbook/Study Guide.

Act., Optional: Read the following sentences and tell students *Éstos son pensamientos de los personajes de* Destinos. *¿Quién los pensaría?* 1. *Ojalá que Arturo les haya gustado a los miembros de la familia Castillo.* (Raquel) 2. *Ojalá que la familia Castillo me haya perdonado por no ir a su casa esta noche.* (Ángela) 3. *Ojalá que los auditores no hayan descubierto los problemas en la oficina de Miami.* (Carlos) 4. *Ojalá que Raquel no haya perdido interés por mí.* (Arturo)

Actividad. ¡Ojalá!
Paso 1

Indica si cada oración a continuación representa algo que esperas o no.

Cosas que posiblemente han pasado

Sí	No	1. Ojalá que mis padres me hayan mandado dinero esta semana.
Sí	No	2. Ojalá que yo haya salido bien en el último examen de _____.
Sí	No	3. Ojalá que haya apagado (*turned off*) la cafetera esta mañana.
Sí	No	4. Ojalá que hayan hecho una secuela (*sequel*) para *Destinos*.
Sí	No	5. Ojalá que las cuentas (*bills*) no hayan llegado hoy.

Act., Suggestion: Assign as homework and have students share their responses in class the following day.

Act., Follow-up: Have students create one item to add to each of the 2 sections. It may be something they would respond to affirmatively or negatively. Students exchange hopes/wishes with a partner and each decides whether the other would respond *Sí* or *No* to the sentence.

Cosas que posiblemente pasarán

Sí	No	6. Ojalá que no tengamos una prueba de sorpresa en esta clase mañana.
Sí	No	7. Ojalá que el verano llegue pronto.
Sí	No	8. Ojalá que yo pueda tomar otro curso de español el próximo semestre/trimestre.
Sí	No	9. Ojalá que mis padres no me llamen esta semana.
Sí	No	10. Ojalá que haga buen tiempo este fin de semana.

Paso 2

Ahora comparte (*share*) la información del **Paso 1** con otras personas en la clase. ¿Puedes explicar por qué esperas ciertas cosas?

LECTURA CULTURAL

El tequila

Al sentarse todos en la sala de la casa de Pedro, éste le pregunta a Arturo si ya ha probado el tequila. Esta bebida fuerte se asocia mundialmente con la cultura mexicana. Muchos creen que es la bebida favorita de las clases bajas. También se cree que se toma principalmente con el propósito de emborracharse.[1]

Sin embargo, para los mexicanos de las clases media y alta, como la familia Castillo, el tequila es una bebida fina. Se sirve solo, con sangrita[2] o con sal y limón como aperitivo o para celebrar las grandes ocasiones, como lo es la llegada de Arturo Iglesias a la casa de Pedro. El tequila que todos prueban en esta ocasión es añejo, es decir, es un tequila muy fino y muy viejo. Se aprecia[3] en la cultura mexicana como en otras culturas se aprecia un escocés[4] fino o el coñac.

La agave es una planta originaria de México.

La próxima vez que oigas hablar de las margaritas, piensa en los siguientes detalles de interés sobre esta bebida mexicana.

- El tequila se destila del jugo[5] del mezcal, un tipo de agave originario de México. Se cultiva sobre todo en el estado de Jalisco.
- El tequila se conocía ya en la época prehispánica. Fue inventado por la tribu de los tiquila. En esa cultura sólo lo bebían los sacerdotes[6] y los ancianos.
- En la época de la llegada de los españoles, los aztecas usaban el tequila para curar la rigidez de las articulaciones.[7] Se aplicaba frotándolo[8] en cuerpo. También se usaba en ceremonias religiosas.
- El primer tequila mexicano fue producido por la familia de José Antonio Cuervo en 1795. Hoy día el tequila es reconocido internacionalmente, como lo son otras bebidas alcohólicas como el coñac y el champaña.

[1]*to get drunk* [2]*spicy tomato-based drink* [3]*Se... It is held in high regard* [4]*Scotch* [5]*juice*
[6]*priests* [7]*rigidez... stiff joints* [8]*rubbing it*

Actividad.   Bebidas nacionales

¿Con qué país, estado o ciudad asocias las siguientes bebidas? Debes prepararte para explicar el por qué de la asociación.

1. el té
2. el jerez
3. el vino
4. el champaña
5. la Coca-Cola
6. el café
7. la cerveza (*beer*)
8. el vodka

6 INTERCAMBIO

Paso 1

En la lección anterior hicieron un análisis de las relaciones entre Raquel y Arturo. Ahora van a seguir comentando estas relaciones. Primero, como clase decidan en qué estado está la relación. ¿Se han enamorado? ¿Se han tomado mucho cariño solamente?

Paso 2

Ahora, las mujeres de la clase deben escribir tres consejos para Raquel en cuanto a sus relaciones con Arturo. Los hombres deben escribir tres consejos para Arturo. Pueden trabajar en grupos de tres o individualmente si prefieren.

MODELO: Sugiero/Sugerimos que Raquel...

Paso 3

Cada grupo o persona debe presentar sus consejos a la clase. En la pizarra, el profesor / la profesora escribirá en un lado los consejos para Raquel y en otro los consejos para Arturo.

Paso 4

Revisen los consejos. ¿Son similares para los dos personajes? ¿Piensan las mujeres y los hombres de la clase de la misma manera? ¿O dependen los consejos del sexo del personaje y la persona que da los consejos?

VOCABULARIO

Los verbos

aconsejar	to advise
insistir (en)	to insist (on)
mandar	to order
recomendar (ie)	to recommend
requerir (ie)	to require
rogar (ue)	to beg
sugerir (ie, i)	to suggest

Los conceptos

el mandato	order
la recomendación	recommendation
el requisito	requirement
la sugerencia	suggestion

Repaso: el consejo

En el camino

el camión (*Mex.*)	truck

Los adjetivos

avergonzado/a	embarrassed
dormido/a	asleep

Las palabras adicionales

ojalá (que)	it is to be hoped/I hope (that)

LECCIÓN 36

¿QUÉ ESTARÁN HACIENDO?*

*What Could They Be Doing?

OBJETIVOS

Most of this episode is a review. Be sure to work through all parts of the lesson. When you see a headphones symbol in the margin, listen to the CD for **Lección 36**. Answers or hints for many activities are given in Appendix 1. Be sure to check your answers for each activity before going on to the next one.

The interactive CD-ROM to accompany *Destinos* contains additional practice with the video storyline and will help you improve your skills in Spanish.

Preliminary: See Faculty Guide for additional information and activities for this lesson.
• **Variation:** For activities marked with the headphones icon, you may wish to read from the Audioscript instead of playing the CD.
• **Suggestion:** Make sure students are familiar with the activities before you read from the Audioscript or play the CD.

BEFORE VIEWING . . .

1 PREPARACIÓN

Suggestions: Assign *Preparación* activities as homework and then go over them quickly in class before viewing the video.

Actividad.

Los siguientes incidentes ocurrieron en el episodio previo. ¿Puedes dar el nombre del personaje o de los personajes apropiados que dijeron o hicieron estas cosas?

Act., Suggestion: You may want to have students do this activity in pairs or in small groups.

Act., Answers: 1. *Raquel y Ángela* 2. *Pati* 3. *Ofelia* 4. *Arturo* 5. *la médico* 6. *Arturo y Pedro* 7. *Roberto* 8. *Raquel y Arturo* 9. *Ángela* 10. *Raquel* 11. *Ángela* 12. *Raquel y Arturo* (See Appendix 1 for expanded answers.)

1. _____ por poco (*almost*) tuvieron un accidente en el camino.
2. _____ salió para Nueva York.
3. _____ le dio malas noticias a su jefe.
4. _____ llegó primero al hospital y vio a Roberto.
5. _____ dijo que Roberto no sufrió lesiones graves.
6. _____ conocieron a Ángela mientras estaban fuera del cuarto de Roberto.
7. _____ dormía durante todo el episodio.
8. _____ se besaron en el hospital (y también en el jardín en la casa de Pedro).
9. _____ llamó a Puerto Rico.
10. _____ habló con su madre.
11. _____ no quiso ir a la casa de Pedro.
12. _____ conoció a los miembros de la familia Castillo.

Para pensar, Suggestion: Write the names of the characters on the board and have students brainstorm what happened to each or come to the board and write what happened to each under the names.

Para pensar...

En este episodio alguien le va a contar a otra persona lo que le ha pasado recientemente. Otras personas van a pensar en lo que les ha pasado a ellos. Piensa tú un momento en los **Episodios 27–35**. ¿Qué les ha pasado a estas personas?

Raquel	Ramón	Juan
Arturo	Pedro	Roberto
Mercedes	Carlos	Ángela

. . . AFTER VIEWING

2

¿TIENES BUENA MEMORIA?

Actividad. ¿Qué pasó?

Contesta las siguientes preguntas sobre lo que pasó en este episodio.

1. Los miembros de la familia Castillo... se dan cuenta (*realize*) / no se dan cuenta... de la atracción entre Arturo y Raquel.
2. Raquel/Arturo... quería quedarse un poco más en el jardín antes de reunirse otra vez con los Castillo.
3. Arturo... sigue enamorado / ya no está enamorado... de Raquel.
4. En la sala... Consuelo/Gloria... habla sin parar mientras los demás piensan en sus propios problemas.

3

REPASO DE LOS EPISODIOS 27–35

Actividad A. Lo que le pasó a Raquel
Paso 1

Pon los siguientes incidentes en orden cronológico (del 1 a 7), según los contaba Raquel.

a. _____ Raquel y Ángela fueron manejando del pueblo a la capital.
b. _____ Al llegar al pueblo, no pudieron pasar al sitio de la excavación.
c. _____ Raquel y Ángela fueron manejando de la Ciudad de México a un pueblo.
d. _____ Por fin sacaron a Roberto y lo llevaron a la capital.
e. _____ Estaban a punto de rescatar a Roberto cuando hubo otro derrumbe.
f. _____ En un hospital conocieron a un cura que las ayudó mucho.
g. _____ Al regresar al sitio de la excavación, supieron que Roberto estaba vivo.

Paso 2
Ahora escucha el CD para verificar tus respuestas.

Actividad B. ¿Y la familia Castillo?
Varios miembros de la familia Castillo reflexionaron sobre problemas importantes mientras Gloria hablaba sin parar. ¿Te acuerdas de la información más importante?

Juan

¿Cuál es el motivo principal del conflicto entre él y Pati?

a. _____ A Pati no le gusta la familia de Juan.

b. _____ Juan quiere que Pati pase más tiempo con él y con su familia.

c. _____ Pati no sabe manejar sus proyectos profesionales y por eso no puede pasar tiempo suficiente con Juan.

Para pensar...

Ya sabes que Ramón le sugirió a Juan que tal vez él, Juan, le tenga envidia a Pati, su mujer. ¿Crees que Juan tomó en serio la sugerencia de Ramón? ¿Qué va a hacer Juan?

Mercedes
Paso 1

¿Cuál es el problema esencial de ella?

a. _____ Sufre por la enfermedad de su padre y porque sabe que hay otros problemas familiares también.

b. _____ Les tiene envidia a Consuelo y a Pati, porque éstas están casadas y ella no.

c. _____ Les tiene envidia a sus hermanos porque éstos tienen carreras y ella no.

Paso 2

Indica si las siguientes oraciones son ciertas (**C**) o falsas (**F**) con relación a Mercedes.

C F 1. Ha pasado la mayoría de su tiempo en el hospital.

C F 2. También habló con Juan sobre sus problemas matrimoniales.

C F 3. No sabe nada de lo que está pasando en la oficina en Miami. Pedro y Ramón no le han dicho nada del asunto.

Para pensar...

Algunas personas viven para sí mismas (*for themselves*). Otras viven para los demás. En tu opinión, ¿qué tipo de persona es Mercedes? ¿Por qué crees que es así? ¿Crees que es muy diferente de sus hermanos?

Pedro
Paso 1

¿De qué problema se entera él?

a. _____ Roberto y Ángela no son los verdaderos nietos de don Fernando.
b. _____ Don Fernando está arruinado económicamente por su enfermedad.
c. _____ Las finanzas de la compañía no están en buenas condiciones.

Paso 2

¿Qué recuerdas de la conversación que Pedro y Ramón tuvieron con los auditores? De las siguientes recomendaciones, ¿cuáles *no* fueron dadas por los auditores?

a. _____ vender La Gavia
b. _____ abrir otra oficina en la capital
c. _____ cerrar la oficina en Miami
d. _____ concentrarse en la producción de autos
e. _____ nombrar a Juan director de la compañía

Para pensar...

La situación económica de la compañía Castillo Saavedra realmente está grave. ¿Qué opinas tú? ¿Crees que Pedro y Ramón van a seguir las recomendaciones de los auditores? ¿Cuál es la causa de los problemas en la oficina de Miami? ¿Es culpa de Carlos? ¿O hay otra posibilidad?

4

PARA ESCRIBIR

In this activity, you will practice narrating events in the past, forming a cohesive account of what has happened in *Destinos* since Raquel and Ángela arrived in Mexico. You will be writing for a classmate who has missed some of the video episodes and needs to catch up on the plot before watching **Episodio 37.** Your composition should be no less than 300 words and no more than 500 words long.

Go to the Workbook/Study Guide to begin this writing activity.

UN VIAJE A MÉXICO:
LA CAPITAL

Un sector de la capital mexicana

Preliminary: Recommend that students who have not used *Destinos* before watch review Episodes 25, 26, and 36 to help prepare them for the third quarter of the course. Also, Spanish and English summaries of all previous episodes are printed in the Faculty Guide. You may wish to make these summaries available to students new to *Destinos*.

LLEVANDO CUENTAS*

Suggestion: Have students look at the photo, describe what they see, and talk about what they think might happen. Ask questions about the photo to prompt student discussion.

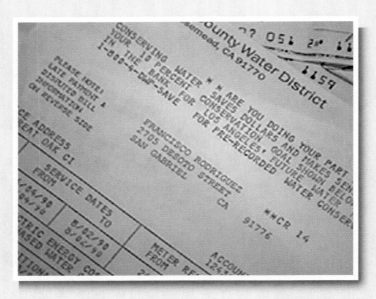

*Keeping the Books

OBJETIVOS

The materials in **Lección 37** of the Textbook and the Workbook/Study Guide will help you better understand the video episode and take you beyond it, giving you additional information about places and characters in the series. The Textbook will also help you to develop skill in using the Spanish language. In this lesson, you will learn

- vocabulary related to money and financial matters
- ways to use subjunctive forms to talk about the past

You will also learn about some important events in Mexican history.

Be sure to work through all parts of the lesson. When you see a headphones symbol in the margin, listen to the CD for **Lección 37**. Answers or hints for many activities are given in Appendix 1. Be sure to check your answers for each activity before going on to the next one.

The interactive CD-ROM to accompany *Destinos* contains additional practice with the video storyline and will help you improve your skills in Spanish.

Preliminary: See Faculty Guide for additional information and activities for this lesson.
• **Variation:** For activities marked with the headphones icon, you may wish to read from the Audioscript instead of playing the CD.
• **Suggestion:** Make sure students are familiar with the activities before you read from the Audioscript or play the CD.

📺 **BEFORE VIEWING . . .**

1

PREPARACIÓN

Suggestions:
• Before watching the video, go over the vocabulary list at the end of the chapter and have students pronounce the words after you.

• For the first episode of the new quarter, you may wish to do the *Preparación* section in class, walking students through the activities, emphasizing that this section is designed to get them thinking about what they have already seen, as well as what they will see and hear in the upcoming episode. Some *Preparación* activities are prediction exercises that have no (in)correct answers, although the photos and previous events should help students make logical choices.

Act. A, Answers: 1. *Arturo* 2. *Juan* 3. *Ramón, Pedro (tal vez Mercedes)* 4. *Pati* 5. *don Fernando* 6. *Carlos* 7. *Raquel* 8. *Mercedes* 9. *Raquel* 10. *Ángela*

Actividad A.

Al empezar esta serie de episodios de *Destinos,* varias situaciones están sin resolverse todavía. Otras están a punto de desarrollarse (*developing*). ¿Puedes dar el nombre de la persona que está enfrentando (*facing*) las siguientes situaciones? ¡OJO! Más de una persona está involucrada (*involved*) en algunas situaciones, y algunos personajes no tienen sólo un problema que resolver, sino (*but rather*) varios.

Personajes: Ángela, Arturo, Carlos, don Fernando, Gloria, Juan, Mercedes, Pati, Pedro, Ramón, Raquel, Roberto

Situaciones

1. Le ha declarado su amor a una persona, pero esa persona todavía no le ha dado una respuesta.
2. Esta persona está muy pensativa porque alguien le ha dicho que es egoísta.
3. Tiene que tomar decisiones relacionadas con los problemas financieros causados por un pariente.
4. Su trabajo es la causa de que se separa de una persona querida.
5. Todavía piensa en una persona de su pasado… y en unos parientes que no ha conocido todavía.
6. Hay serios problemas financieros en la oficina que esta persona dirige.
7. Un pariente se mete mucho en la vida de esta persona, lo cual (*which*) le molesta mucho.
8. Aunque el esposo de una pareja es miembro de su familia, esta persona apoya (*supports*) a la esposa.
9. Alguien le ha declarado su amor a esta persona, pero no sabe qué hacer. Por un lado, está el amor. Pero por otro, está la familia…
10. Esta persona tuvo una pelea con otra persona que ahora está inconsciente a causa de un accidente.

Act. B, Point out: Careful reading of Mercedes's explanations will prepare students for the spoken version from the video. Otherwise, they may have great difficulty in capturing this information directly from the video.

Actividad B.

En este episodio, Mercedes le va a explicar a Arturo el significado de algunas fiestas nacionales de México.

Paso 1

Primero, lee lo que Mercedes le va a decir sobre el 16 de septiembre.

MERCEDES: El 16 de septiembre se dio el grito de independencia. En ese día en el pueblo de Dolores, el padre Miguel Hidalgo supo que los españoles habían descubierto los planes de independencia del grupo de patriotas. El padre Miguel Hidalgo era uno de estos patriotas. Entonces, en la madrugada de ese día, el padre tocó las campanas de la iglesia, llamando a todos los habitantes del pueblo. Cuando llegaron, Hidalgo les habló otra vez de la igualdad entre los hombres. Les habló de cómo los indígenas, mestizos y criollos deberían tener los mismos derechos que los españoles que gobernaban las colonias. Dijo que era el momento de ser una nación independiente. Y así empezó la lucha por la independencia. Por ese motivo, cada 16 de septiembre hay grandes celebraciones en todo el país.

Paso 2
Ahora escucha el pasaje en el CD mientras lo lees otra vez al mismo tiempo.

Paso 3
Ahora escucha lo que Mercedes le dice a Arturo sobre el Cinco de Mayo. Luego contesta las preguntas.

Act. B, Answers: *Paso 3:*
1. b 2. a

1. En México, la celebración del Cinco de Mayo tiene que ver con (*has to do with*)…
   a. _____ una batalla contra tropas de los Estados Unidos.
   b. _____ una batalla contra tropas francesas.
   c. _____ una batalla contra tropas españolas.

2. El Cinco de Mayo conmemora…
   a. _____ la valentía de los mexicanos en esa batalla.
   b. _____ la independencia de México de España.
   c. _____ el comienzo de la primavera.

Paso 4
Ahora lee lo que Mercedes dice sobre el Cinco de Mayo. Luego escucha el pasaje otra vez, leyéndolo al mismo tiempo, si quieres. Vas a comprender más cada vez que lo repasas (*go over*).

MERCEDES: Como ya sabrás, Arturo, en 1861, los franceses invadieron México. Napoleón III siempre había soñado con poseer territorios en América. En esa época, Benito Juárez era presidente de México. Pero nuestro país estaba dividido. Había un gran conflicto entre los conservadores y los liberales. Llegaron las tropas francesas, y con la ayuda de los conservadores, Napoleón pudo instalar a Maximiliano de Austria como emperador de México. Pero el imperio de Maximiliano no duró mucho. Pues, las batallas con Juárez continuaban. En 1867, Maximiliano fue capturado y fusilado. Benito Juárez asumió su autoridad una vez más. Una de las batallas más importantes ocurrió el 5 de mayo de 1862 en la ciudad de Puebla. Allí, el general Zaragoza venció a las tropas francesas. Aunque la lucha contra los franceses duró varios años más, la batalla de Puebla representa el espíritu y la valentía con que los mexicanos luchaban. Cada año celebramos el Cinco de Mayo como un acontecimiento muy importante.

Para comprender, Suggestion: Ask whole class what these words probably mean. Encourage them to try to explain them using other Spanish words before resorting to an English translation. Make sure students understand the words before continuing with the video.

Para comprender un poco más

On occasion boxes such as this one will present vocabulary that may help you understand certain conversations more completely. Can you guess the meaning of the boldfaced vocabulary items from their brief context?

atrasado/a   El vuelo de Raquel está **atrasado**. Debe llegar a las siete y media, pero no va a llegar hasta las ocho.

darle de alta   Don Fernando desea regresar a La Gavia. ¿Cuándo **le** van a **dar de alta** sus médicos?

una pesadilla   Carlitos se despertó porque tuvo **una pesadilla** y ahora no quiere estar solo.

. . . AFTER VIEWING

2

¿TIENES BUENA MEMORIA?

Act. A, Suggestion: Give students about 3 minutes to complete the activity individually or in pairs and then compare answers as a whole class.

Act. A, Answers: 1. Mercedes 2. Ángela 3. La madre de Raquel 4. Pedro 5. Luis

Act. A, Optional: Have students make up 2 original descriptions like those in the activity. In pairs, students identify the people described.

Actividad A.   ¿Qué pasó?

¿Puedes identificar a los siguientes personajes?

1. Esta persona habló de las fiestas nacionales de México.
2. Esta persona revisó sus asuntos económicos y llegó a la conclusión de que maneja muy mal el dinero.
3. Esta persona también revisó sus asuntos económicos y encontró que tenía suficiente dinero para hacer un viaje.
4. Esta persona llamó al hotel y dejó un mensaje para Raquel.
5. Esta persona ha comprado su pasaje para ir a México.

Act. B, Answers: 1. Arturo a la familia Castillo. 2. Ángela a Roberto. 3. Carlitos a Arturo, Raquel y Carlos. 4. María Rodríguez a Luis. 5. Pedro a Raquel. (See Appendix 1 for expanded answers.)

Actividad B.   ¿Quién lo dijo?

Identifica al personaje que hizo cada una de las siguientes declaraciones. ¿Puedes identificar también al personaje con quien hablaba?

Raquel	Pedro	Luis
Ángela	Mercedes	Carlitos
Arturo	Ramón	María Rodríguez
Roberto	Juan	(la madre de Raquel)

MODELOS: _____ está conversando con _____.

_____ le(s) dijo esto a _____.

_____ está hablando por teléfono con

_____

Act. B, Suggestion: Give students about 3 minutes to complete the activity individually or in pairs and then compare answers as a whole class.

1. Bueno, mi madre era una mujer... llena de vida, afectuosa. A veces tenía momentos de tristeza y yo no entendía por qué...

Nota cultural, Optional: Introduce some common expressions from a variety of countries: ¡órale pues! (Mex.), ¡che! (Arg.), ¡jo! (Esp.), and explain their usage. (The first means ¡oiga!/¡venga!; the latter two are exclamations of surprise, annoyance, pleasure, etc.)

2. Ya verás las sorpresas que te esperan cuando despiertes, Roberto. Primero, conoceremos a nuestro abuelo, el padre de papá.
3. Tú eres el esposo de Raquel, ¿verdad?… Entonces, ¿son novios?… Porque sólo los novios o los esposos se besan en el jardín, ¿no es cierto?
4. Raquel se pondrá muy contenta de verte. … Será una completa sorpresa. … Yo creo que a ella también le gustará verte a ti.
5. Muy bien. Mañana le daré tus recibos (*receipts*) a mi secretaria y le diré que te haga un cheque.

Nota cultural   El español de María Rodríguez

The use of certain phrases by María, Raquel's mother, is in some ways typical of Mexican Americans and of Mexicans as well. Listen again as María works on the family's bills.

Did you note the following usages? Were you able to guess their meaning in context?

Anda, viejo.   **Anda** (also: **Ándale**, **Ándale pues**) is a common way to say *get going* or *get out of here* (in the literal and figurative sense). **Viejo** (also **vieja**) is an affectionate way to refer to one's spouse.

¡Híjole! ¡Caramba!   Frequently used interjections, roughly equivalent to English phrases such as *My God! Gosh!*

Para pensar…

Al final de este episodio, Raquel recibió un mensaje de Pedro. ¿Por qué quiere Pedro hablar con Raquel otra vez cuando acaba de verla en su casa? ¿Es posible que tenga que ver con don Fernando?

3
Suggestion: Practice pronunciation with choral and individual repetition.

VOCABULARIO DEL TEMA

El dinero

los ahorros	savings	**los gastos**	expenses
la cuenta	account; bill	**los ingresos**	income
la cuenta corriente	checking account		
la cuenta de ahorros	savings account	**ahorrar**	to save
		cargar	to charge (*on a credit card*)
el cheque	check	**ganar**	to earn
el efectivo	cash	**gastar**	to spend
el recibo	receipt	**manejar**	to manage
la tarjeta de crédito	credit card	**(bien/mal)**	(well/badly)
		pagar	to pay
		sacar	to take out, withdraw (*from an account*)

Note that English *to save* and *to spend* have specific Spanish equivalents when they refer to money.

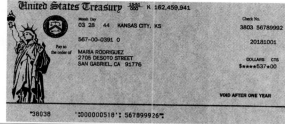

- **ahorrar** = to save (*money, time*)
  rescatar = to save, rescue
  (*a person or animal*)
  guardar = to save, keep (*things*)
- **gastar** = to spend (*money*)
  pasar = to spend (*time*)

Actividad A. **María lleva cuentas**

Escucha otra vez la descripción de la situación económica de los mayores. Indica con el número de la oración la foto o el dibujo a que corresponde cada oración.

Act. A, Answers: a. 7
b. 3, 4 c. 2, 5 d. 6 e. 1

a. _____

b. _____

c. _____

d. _____

e. _____

Actividad B. **Hablando de dinero**

Escucha otra vez mientras algunos personajes hablan de dinero. Luego indica si las oraciones son ciertas (**C**) o falsas (**F**) para los personajes. ¿Puedes corregir las oraciones falsas?

Primera conversación

Act. B, Answers: 1. F
2. C 3. F 4. F 5. C 6. F
7. F 8. F (See Appendix 1
for expanded answers.)

C F 1. Ángela tiene mucho dinero en su cuenta de ahorros.
C F 2. Sacó mucho dinero con su tarjeta de crédito.
C F 3. No tiene ninguna dificultad en pagar la cuenta.
C F 4. Maneja muy bien su dinero.

Segunda conversación

C F 5. Raquel tiene preparada para Pedro una lista de los gastos de su viaje.
C F 6. Usó poco su tarjeta de crédito en el viaje.
C F 7. No le van a pagar los gastos pronto.
C F 8. El jefe de Raquel se preocupa mucho por los gastos.

Actividad C. **El dinero y tú**
Paso 1

Act. C, *Paso 1*, Suggestion: Assign as homework and then complete *Paso 2* in class the following day.

Para ti, ¿son ciertas (**C**) o falsas (**F**) las siguientes oraciones?

C F 1. Tengo una cuenta de ahorros y una cuenta corriente.
C F 2. Casi todos los meses ahorro algún dinero.
C F 3. Escribo unos ocho cheques todos los meses.

C   F   4. Casi nunca uso las tarjetas de crédito. Lo pago todo en efectivo o con cheque.

C   F   5. Casi nunca gasto más de lo que gano.

C   F   6. Por lo general, si no tengo dinero en efectivo para pagar algo, no me lo compro.

C   F   7. Mis ingresos siempre alcanzan para pagar mis gastos.

Paso 2

Intercambia tus respuestas con un compañero / una compañera. Cada uno/a debe hacer una «evaluación» del otro / de la otra, contestando las siguientes preguntas.

1. ¿Cómo maneja tu compañero/a el dinero?
2. ¿Qué sugerencias tienes para él/ella?
3. ¿Cómo te comparas con él/ella?

4

UN POCO DE GRAMÁTICA

Talking About What You Wanted Someone to Do

You already know how to express your or someone else's wish that another person do something, using the present subjunctive.

Raquel **quiere que** Pedro le **pague** lo más pronto posible.	*Raquel wants Pedro to pay her as quickly as possible.*

To express the same thing in the past, you can use the past subjunctive. It is formed by adding -**a** to the third-person plural of the preterite minus -**on**: **trabajaron** → **trabajar-** → **trabajara**, **pidieron** → **pidier-** → **pidiera**.

María Rodríguez **quería que** Luis **viajara** a México.	*María Rodríguez wanted Luis to travel to Mexico.*
Carlos **quería que** su hijo **volviera** a la cama.	*Carlos wanted his son to go back to bed.*

You will learn more about the forms of the past subjunctive in the Workbook/Study Guide, and you will learn about its uses in this and subsequent lessons of the Textbook and Workbook/Study Guide.

Actividad.   Cuando era joven
Paso 1

Cuando eras joven, probablemente tenías que respetar algunas reglas y leyes en tu casa. ¿Cuáles eran? ¿Qué tenías que hacer? ¿Qué *no* debieras hacer? (*What weren't you supposed to do?*) Indica las frases que mejor describan cómo era tu vida de joven.

Act., *Paso 1*, Suggestion:
Assign as homework and
complete *Paso 2* in class
the following day. Have
students create at least
one original sentence for
each section.

Act., *Paso 2*, Follow-up:
Have students create in-
tentionally false sentences
similar to those in the activity and present them to
the class. Their class-
mates must correct them.
See who can make up the
most outrageous sen-
tences. Model one or two
before beginning: *Cuando
yo era niño, mis padres
querían que yo tomara
muchas drogas ilegales.*

*(No, tus padres querían
que tomaras mucha
leche.)*

1. Mis padres querían que yo
   a. —— leyera libros cada día.
   b. —— limpiara mi cuarto cada mañana.
   c. —— cuidara a mi perro/gato/¿ ?
   d. —— ayudara a preparar la cena.
   e. —— regresara pronto a casa después de la escuela.
   f. —— ¿ ?

2. Mis padres no querían que
   a. —— mirara la televisión.
   b. —— jugara en la calle.
   c. —— me acostara demasiado temprano.
   d. —— dejara mi bicicleta afuera.
   e. —— hablara con personas desconocidas.
   f. —— ¿ ?

Paso 2
Con un compañero / una compañera, lean en voz alta (*aloud*) sus oraciones.
Apunte las oraciones de tu compañero/a. ¿Son similares o distintas las ora-
ciones de Uds.?

5

LECTURA CULTURAL

***Lectura cultural*, Suggestion:** Assign as home-
work and go over answers quickly in class. Remind
students that they should not expect to understand
every word of the reading, but rather to get the
main ideas.

Episodios en la historia de México

En este episodio, los miembros de la familia Castillo le explicaron a Arturo algunos episodios muy importantes de la historia de México. ¿Te acuerdas de las
tres historias?

Lee los tres breves resúmenes que se dan a continuación y el siguiente bosquejo[1] de la historia de México. Luego trata de colocar las historias en su sitio
en el bosquejo. Para terminar, hay una nota sobre la celebración de uno de estos episodios en los Estados Unidos. ¿Sabes cuál es?

1. Época de la Revolución mexicana, iniciada por Francisco I. Madero. Lucharon[2]
   en la Revolución Pancho Villa y Emiliano Zapata.
2. El padre Miguel Hidalgo dio el grito[3] que inició la lucha para independizarse. Según
   el Padre Hidalgo, indígenas, mestizos[4] y criollos[5] debían tener los mismos derechos
   que los españoles que gobernaban las colonias.
3. En la ciudad de Puebla el cinco de mayo las fuerzas mexicanas ganaron una
   batalla importante contra los invasores franceses.

Bosquejo esencial de la historia de México

–1521	*Época precolombina*: civilizaciones azteca, maya, olmeca, tolteca
1521–1821	*Época colonial*

***Lectura cultural*, Answers:**
1810: 2 1862: 3 1910–1920: 1

---

[1]*outline* [2]*They fought* [3]*shout, cry* [4]*persons of Indian and Spanish extraction* [5]*persons born in
Mexico but of Spanish heritage*

1519	Llegada de Hernán Cortés.
1521	Destrucción de Tenochtitlán por Cortés y fundación de la Ciudad de México sobre sus ruinas. Se le dio al país el nombre de Nueva España.
1810	¿ ?
1810–1821	Guerras por la independencia.
1821	México se convierte en un país independiente.
1821–1910	*Época de consolidación del estado*
1836	El estado de Texas se separó de México tras una guerra de varios meses.
1846–1848	Guerra con los Estados Unidos en la que México perdió la mitad de su territorio: Nuevo México, alta California, Nevada, Utah, Arizona y partes de Colorado y Wyoming
1857	Benito Juárez llegó a ser el primer presidente mexicano de origen indígena
1861	La invasión de los franceses
1862	¿ ?
1867	Se reestableció la república.
1876–1910	Dictadura de Porfirio Díaz. Gobernó favoreciendo las clases elevadas de la sociedad.
1910–	*Época moderna*
1910–1920	¿ ?
1917	Promulgación de una constitución que sirve de base a la reconstrucción del país.
1938	Nacionalización de las compañías petrolíferas.[6]
1964	Reforma agraria que introduce la modernización de la explotación del campo.
1973	Descubrimiento de nuevas reservas de petróleo que dan un gran impulso a la economía del país.

Emiliano Zapata

Benito Juárez

El Cinco de Mayo

La fiesta del Cinco de Mayo conmemora la batalla que dio la victoria a los mexicanos contra los franceses en Puebla, durante la época del imperio francés en México. Curiosamente, esta fiesta mexicana realmente se celebra en los Estados Unidos de una manera muy diferente de la forma en que se celebra en México.

[6]*oil, petroleum*

Lectura cultural, Preguntas: 1. *¿Cuáles son las cuatro épocas principales de la historia de México?* (la precolombina, la colonial, la de la consolidación del estado, la moderna) 2. *¿Cómo se llamaba la ciudad indígena que ocupaba el sitio de la actual Ciudad de México?* (Tenochtitlán) 3. *¿Qué significado tiene el año 1821?* (año de la independencia) 4. *¿En qué año terminó la guerra de la Revolución?* (en 1920) 5. *¿Qué día feriado en los EEUU es el más parecido (semejante/similar) al Cinco de Mayo?* (el Día de los Veteranos).

En los Estados Unidos, muchos creen que el Cinco de Mayo es el Día de la Independencia de México, algo así como[7] el cuatro de julio. Pero el verdadero Día de la Independencia de México es el 16 de septiembre. El Cinco de Mayo es para los mexicanos lo que el Día de los Veteranos es para los estadounidenses: un día para celebrar la gran valentía nacional, pero no el Día de la Independencia.

En México las fiestas del Cinco de Mayo son primariamente patrióticas y se celebran de varias maneras en diferentes regiones del país. En los Estados Unidos, sin embargo, el Cinco de Mayo ha venido a ser[8] algo así como la celebración del orgullo[9] que siente por su raza de la comunidad mexicana y mexicoamericana. En muchas ciudades hay dos o tres días de fiestas, con canciones, bailes, comida típica, mercados, desfiles[10] y otros tipos de celebraciones. ¿Se celebra el Cinco de Mayo en tu comunidad?

[7]algo… *something like* [8]ha… *has come to be* [9]*pride* [10]*parades*

6

INTERCAMBIO

Paso 1

Prepara preguntas para entrevistar a un compañero / una companera sobre el siguiente tema: Al comenzar a estudiar en la universidad, ¿qué querían, en qué insistían y/o qué (no) permitían sus padres? Inventa dos preguntas más para cada categoría a continuación.

El permiso

1. ¿Permitían que utilizara la tarjeta de crédito de ellos?
2. ¿ ?
3. ¿ ?

Los deseos

1. ¿Querían que pagaras tus propios gastos?
2. ¿ ?
3. ¿ ?

Las exigencias

1. ¿Insistían en que los visitaras/llamaras a menudo?
2. ¿ ?
3. ¿ ?

Paso 2

Usando las preguntas del **Paso 1**, entrevista a tu compañero/a y contesta las preguntas que te hace él/ella. Apunta la información de las entrevistas.

Paso 3

Ahora, utilizando la información del **Paso 2**, escribe un párrafo de entre 100 y 150 palabras en que comparas los deseos y exigencias de tus padres con los de tu compañero/a.

VOCABULARIO

Los verbos

desarrollar	to develop
enfrentarse (con)	to deal with, face (*a problem*)
resolver (ue)	to solve, resolve

El dinero

los ahorros	savings
el cheque	check
la cuenta	account; bill
la cuenta corriente	checking account
la cuenta de ahorros	savings account
el efectivo	cash
los gastos	expenses
los ingresos	income

el recibo	receipt
la tarjeta de crédito	credit card
ahorrar	to save
cargar	to charge (*on a credit card*)
ganar	to earn
gastar	to spend
llevar cuentas	to keep the books; to keep track of expenses
manejar (bien/mal)	to manage (well/badly)
pagar	to pay

Repaso: **sacar**

Las palabras adicionales

en cuanto a	as far as . . . is concerned

LECCIÓN 38

OCULTANDO LA VERDAD*

*Hiding the Truth

OBJETIVOS

The materials in **Lección 38** of the Textbook and the Workbook/Study Guide will help you better understand the video episode and take you beyond it, giving you additional information about places and characters in the series. The Textbook will also help you to develop skill in using the Spanish language. In this lesson you will learn

- more vocabulary related to financial matters and to business questions
- more ways to use the past subjunctive

You will also learn about the Mexican economy and the economy of Latin America in general.

Be sure to work through all parts of the lesson. When you see a headphones symbol in the margin, listen to the CD for **Lección 38**. Answers or hints for many activities are given in Appendix 1. Be sure to check your answers for each activity before going on to the next one.

The interactive CD-ROM to accompany *Destinos* contains additional practice with the video storyline and will help you improve your skills in Spanish.

BEFORE VIEWING . . .

1

PREPARACIÓN

Actividad A.
Paso 1

¿Qué pasó en el episodio previo? Indica si las siguientes afirmaciones son ciertas (**C**) o falsas (**F**).

C F 1. La familia Castillo le pidió a Arturo que hablara un poco de su madre.

C F 2. También le dijeron a Arturo que regresara a México para conocer al resto de la familia.

C F 3. Arturo y Raquel salieron a bailar después de hablar con la familia.

C F 4. En el hospital Ángela revisaba sus cuentas.

C F 5. Al regresar por fin al hotel, Arturo le dio a Raquel un regalo, una foto.

C F 6. Raquel recibió un telegrama urgente.

 ### Paso 2
Ahora escucha el CD para verificar tus respuestas.

 ## Actividad B.

Ya sabes que la familia Castillo tiene problemas económicos. En este episodio, Ramón y Pedro le van a hablar de esos problemas a Mercedes. Luego van a hablar de posibles soluciones. Escucha una parte de su conversación y contesta las preguntas. Al escuchar, recuerda que **engañar** significa *to deceive.*

1. Cuando hablan de soluciones, Ramón habla de cerrar «la sucursal». ¿Qué significa esa palabra?
   a. _____ un tipo de investigación
   b. _____ oficina de una compañía

2. Ramón también propone otra solución para los problemas financieros: «poner a otra persona a cargo». ¿Qué crees que significa esa frase?
   a. _____ darle la dirección (*management*) de la oficina a otra persona
   b. _____ cambiar el personal de la oficina, por ejemplo, la secretaria

Para pensar...

1. Según lo que sabes en este momento, ¿se te ocurre otra solución para los problemas financieros de la familia Castillo?
2. ¿Cuándo crees que los hermanos deben hablar con Carlos sobre estos asuntos? Antes de contestar, piensa en todas las preocupaciones que la familia tiene en este momento.

Para comprender, Suggestion: Have students give personal examples for these vocabulary items. Ask *¿Conoces a un cabezón o a una cabezona? ¿Qué hace? ¿Quién te cae bien? ¿Quién te cae mal?*

Para comprender un poco más

cabezón/cabezona	Juan es **cabezón**. A veces no escucha los consejos que le dan y sigue con lo suyo (*what he wants to do*).
caerle bien/mal a alguien	Arturo **les** quiere **caer bien** a los Castillo. Es decir, quiere causarles una buena impresión.

 . . . AFTER VIEWING

2

¿TIENES BUENA MEMORIA?

Actividad A. Lo que sabe Raquel
Paso 1

Esta noche, en el hotel, Raquel ha hablado con una serie de personas que le son importantes de una forma u otra. ¿Puedes completar el siguiente resumen de sus conversaciones?

Frases útiles

> hablar de sí mismo / de nosotros, pasarlo bien/mal con, quedarse en Los Ángeles, venir a México
>
> una carta para él, un mensaje para mí, una llamada telefónica con don Fernando, con Roberto, en mí, en mi familia
> si Ángela había regresado, si Roberto se había despertado

Act. A, *Paso 1*, Answers: 1. *lo paso bien con* 2. *un mensaje para mí* 3. *con don Fernando* 4. *hablar de nosotros* 5. *en mí* 6. *una llamada telefónica* 7. *venir a México* 8. *si Ángela había regresado*

Me gusta mucho la foto que Arturo me dio. Yo siempre

_____¹ Arturo. Es muy amable y me hace sentir muy bien.

Cuando Arturo y yo regresamos al hotel, había

_____.² Pedro quería que yo lo llamara a su casa. Otra vez olvidé la cartera. Ya que el mensaje era urgente, Arturo y yo pensamos que tenía que ver _____.³ ¡Qué susto!ª

Luego Arturo y yo fuimos a tomar algo. Al sentarnos, Arturo empezó a

_____.⁴ Yo le dije que había pensado en él, pero que *no* había pensado _____.⁵ Nuestra conversación fue interrumpida por _____.⁶ Era mi madre, quien me quería decir que ella y mi padre sí iban a

_____.⁷

ª¡Qué... *What a fright!*

Al subir a mi habitación, llamé a la recepción para saber

_____,[8] pero parece que no. Ojalá Roberto

esté bien.

Paso 2
Ahora escucha el CD para verificar tus respuestas.

Actividad B. **Lo que Raquel no sabe**
Paso 1

Act. B, *Paso 1*, **Answers:** *Sí, Roberto se despertó.*

Act. B, *Paso 2*, **Suggestion:** Provide students with an outline on the board to help them write their summary. *Bosquejo* (Outline): 1. *Explica brevemente la situación.* 2. *Describe las opiniones o reacciones de los personajes.* 3. *Describe tu opinión o reacción con respecto al mismo.*

Act. B, **Optional:** Have students present their summaries in groups of 4.

Para pensar, **Suggestion:** Pose the same questions to several students to elicit a variety of opinions.

Para pensar, **Variation:** You may want to have students do this activity in pairs.

Raquel no ha podido hablar con Ángela, así que no sabe nada sobre Roberto. ¿Te acuerdas de lo que pasó con Roberto en este episodio? ¿Se despertó o no?

Paso 2

Raquel tampoco sabe lo que está pasando con varios miembros de la familia Castillo. Elige uno de los temas a continuación y haz un breve resumen de él.

Temas

a. el conflicto entre Juan y Pati
b. la situación económica de la compañía
c. Carlos, Gloria y «la verdad»

Para pensar...

1. En este episodio, Carlos le dijo a Gloria que no podía seguir ocultándole la verdad a su familia. ¿Qué «verdad» está ocultando Carlos? ¿Por qué crees que Carlos se enfadó con Gloria? ¿Es posible que ella tenga algo que ver con el dinero que ha sacado Carlos?
2. Al final del episodio, Carlos se enfadó muchísimo porque no encontró a Gloria en la casa. ¿Adónde crees que se fue? ¿Por qué se fue?

Nota cultural, **Suggestion:** You might want to talk about stereotypes concerning sex roles of Hispanics, and the concept of *machismo*. Remind students that inequality of the sexes is not limited to Hispanic cultures. Ask your students ¿*Conoces a un hombre machista? ¿Cómo es? ¿Es hispánico o norteamericano? ¿En tu familia, cuáles son las responsabilidades de tus padres? ¿Quién trabaja? ¿Quién cuida a los niños? ¿Quién toma las decisiones importantes?*, etc.

Nota cultural   La estructura familiar

In the Spanish-speaking world, as in many other cultures, the roles of men and women, and husbands and wives, are in a state of flux. In the Castillo family there are examples of a number of different roles:

• Ramón and Consuelo are a traditional couple. It appears that Consuelo is the primary caretaker of the children, and that Ramón is more involved with business matters.
• Juan and Pati are young urban professionals who do not have children yet, nor are there (apparently) any plans to have them.

- Carlos and Gloria are also somewhat nontraditional. Even though Carlos is a business executive, he takes great pleasure in spending time with his children; in fact, he appears to be more involved with child rearing than his wife is.

In short: No one image of family structure is typical for all Hispanic cultures. How would you describe Mercedes in this context? Raquel? María and Pancho (Raquel's parents)?

3

VOCABULARIO DEL TEMA

Suggestion: As you go over vocabulary, ask questions related to personal examples: *¿Cuándo se necesita un auditor/una auditora? ¿Quién es el dueño de tu casa? ¿Eres empleado/a? ¿Tienes un jefe o una jefa? ¿Andan bien las cosas con él/ella? ¿Cómo se llama la compañía o la empresa donde trabajas? ¿Trabajas en una oficina? ¿Cómo es? ¿Dónde está?*, etc.

El dinero y los negocios

el auditor/la auditora	auditor	**dirigir (dirijo)**	to run (*a business*)
el dueño/la dueña	owner	**economizar**	to economize
el empleado/la empleada	employee	**poner (a alguien)**	to put (someone)
el jefe/la jefa	boss	**a cargo (de)**	in charge (of)
el presupuesto	budget		
la compañía	company		
la empresa	firm, company, business		
la oficina	office		
la sucursal	branch office		
S.A. (Sociedad Anónima)	Inc.		
andar bien/mal	to be going well/badly		
despedir (i, i)	to fire (*an employee*)		

Actividad A. Preocupaciones financieras

Escucha otra vez mientras Pedro, Ramón y Mercedes hablan de los problemas económicos de Castillo Saavedra, S.A. Luego indica si las siguientes oraciones son ciertas (**C**) o falsas (**F**).

C F 1. En la oficina de Miami, todo anda bien económicamente.
C F 2. Hay irregularidades en el presupuesto.
C F 3. Los ingresos son mayores que los gastos.
C F 4. Mercedes no entiende el problema; dice que todo anda bien económicamente en los Estados Unidos.
C F 5. En total Carlos ha sacado un millón de dólares.
C F 6. El problema se encontraba en los libros de Carlos.

Actividad B. «Voy a cambiar.»
Paso 1
¿Te acuerdas de lo que decía Ángela mientras reflexionaba sobre sus problemas económicos? Completa el siguiente párrafo con las palabras apropiadas.

Sustantivos: los gastos, los ingresos, el presupuesto
Verbos: economizar, ganar, manejar

Bueno. Cuando regresemos a Puerto Rico voy a hacer

_____.[1] No sé por qué manejo tan mal el dinero.

Pero voy a cambiar. Quizás[a] eso lo heredé de papá. Mamá decía que papá

tampoco sabía _____[2] el dinero. Me acuerdo que

una vez me dijo: «No sé lo que haría[b] tu padre sin mí. Sabe

_____[3] el dinero, pero no sabe manejarlo.» Mamá

sí tenía cabeza para el dinero. Ella sabía _____[4]

cuando _____[5] no alcanzaban[c] para cubrir

_____.[6]

[a]*Perhaps* [b]*would do* [c]*no... were not enough*

Paso 2
Ahora escucha el CD para verificar tus respuestas.

Actividad C. Hablando de negocios
¿Puedes dar el nombre de una compañía con una de las siguientes características?

1. El apellido del dueño de la compañía es el nombre de la compañía.
2. La compañía tiene sucursales en muchos países extranjeros.
3. La empresa tiene una jefa.
4. El director de la compañía es muy famoso.
5. Es una empresa extranjera que tiene muchas sucursales en los Estados Unidos.

Actividad D. El gran plan
Con un compañero / una compañera de clase, escojan una de las dos situaciones a continuación y hagan un plan de economización. Luego, los/las dos deben presentar su plan a la clase. El resto de la clase comentará las posibles consecuencias de su plan.

1. Uds. son estudiantes universitarios. Necesitan economizar porque es difícil trabajar (más) y seguir estudiando. ¿Cuáles son cuatro de las cosas más importantes que pueden hacer para economizar?
2. Están encargados (*in charge*) de revisar el presupuesto del departamento de español de su universidad para ver cómo pueden economizar en ese departamento. ¿Cuáles son las cosas que necesitan investigar?

4

UN POCO DE GRAMÁTICA

The Workbook/Study Guide contains more detailed explanation and practice of this grammar point.

Point out: For the past subjunctive to occur in noun clauses, 3 elements are necessary: 1) a subjunctive trigger in the past (usually imperfect or preterite); 2) the word *que*; 3) a change of subject between the first and the second clauses.
• Review present subjunctive in adjectival and adverbial clauses: *No hay nadie que sepa* (adjectival). *Ángela quiere llegar antes de que Roberto se despierte* (adverbial).
• Review past subjunctive forms in noun clauses with brief conversational exchanges: *¿Qué querían tus padres que estudiaras? ¿Qué deseabas que tu novio/a te diera? ¿De qué tenías miedo de que el doctor te pusiera?*, etc. Indicate the presence of the 3 essential elements: subjunctive trigger in past tense; *que*; change of subject between first and second clause.

Suggestions: Review present subjunctive in noun clauses, using verbs of wishing as subjunctive triggers. Have students give each other polite commands using Ud. verb forms and acting out the responses. Pass out cards with infinitives on them for students to use in their commands: *comer → Deseo que coma espagueti con los dedos.* Then, list each command situation on the board or overhead in past tense to review past subjunctive. *María quería que Dan comiera… . Era necesario que Lori hiciera la tarea. Ana deseaba que Gabe leyera… .*

More About Talking About the Past

The past subjunctive is used in most of the same contexts as the present subjunctive. The difference is that the time frame is the past.

Le **pidieron** a Arturo que les **hablara** de Rosario. — *They asked Arturo to talk to them about Rosario.*

Arturo **esperaba** que Raquel **pensara** mucho en él. — *Arturo was hoping that Raquel would think a lot about him.*

Ángela **quería** llegar al hospital antes de que Roberto **se despertara**. — *Ángela wanted to get to the hospital before Roberto woke up.*

No **había** nadie que **supiera** cuál era el problema de Gloria. — *No one knew what Gloria's problem was.*

You will learn more about the uses of the past subjunctive in the Workbook/Study Guide.

Act., Suggestion: You may want to have students do this activity in pairs and then share their answers with the rest of the class.

Act., Optional: Have students present their information to the rest of the class.

Actividad.   Al comenzar la clase de español

Piensa en tu primer día o primera semana de la clase de español. ¿Cuáles de las siguientes oraciones se te aplican? Explica por qué.

1. a. Quería que el ritmo de la clase fuera más lento (*slower*).
   b. Quería que el ritmo de la clase fuera más rápido.
2. a. Esperaba que no tuviera que hablar mucho en clase.
   b. Esperaba que el hablar (*speaking*) fuera algo muy importante en clase.
3. a. Tenía miedo de que los demás supieran más que yo.
   b. Tenía miedo de que yo supiera más que los otros.
4. a. Quería que todos trabajáramos mucho en grupos.
   b. Quería que trabajáramos solos, sin la interacción entre compañeros.
5. a. Esperaba que el profesor / la profesora nos diera más tarea.
   b. Esperaba que el profesor / la profesora no nos diera ninguna tarea.

Lectura cultural, **Preguntas:** 1. ¿Cuáles son los productos típicamente explotados del mundo hispanoamericano? (el café, el banano, el azúcar, el tabaco) 2. ¿Cuándo comenzó esta explotación? (en la época colonial cuando España explotaba el oro y la plata de sus colonias americanas)

5

LECTURA CULTURAL

3. ¿En qué insisten los hispanoamericanos ahora? (en su derecho a manejar su propio destino económico) 4. ¿Cuáles son los recursos naturales de Hispanoamérica que necesitará el mundo del futuro? (el petróleo, el cobre, la plata, el hierro, el plomo, el estaño, el tungsteno) 5. ¿Cuál es la verdadera riqueza de México? (la mineral).

La economía de Hispanoamérica

Tradicionalmente, el sistema económico de algunos países de Hispanoamérica se ha basado en un solo producto: el café, el banano, el azúcar, el tabaco… Esta situación es resultado de la explotación económica de los productos hispanoamericanos más valiosos[1] por los intereses internacionales.

Esta historia comenzó en la época colonial, cuando España explotaba el oro y la plata[2] de sus colonias americanas. Después de conseguir la independencia de España en el siglo XIX, las diez naciones hispanoamericanas —políticamente débiles— fueron lugares de fácil

El petróleo, el «oro negro» del lago Maracaibo, Venezuela

explotación económica para los países industrializados de Europa y para los Estados Unidos. El caso clásico es el banano centroamericano.

Actualmente los hispanoamericanos tienen una clara consciencia[3] de este pasado de explotación extranjera. Insisten cada vez más en su derecho[4] a manejar su propio destino económico. Por eso, cabe[5] hacer la siguiente pregunta: ¿Será algún día Hispanoamérica una de las regiones económicamente más importantes del mundo?

Cuando se considera la gran cantidad de recursos naturales que quedan aún por explotar, es muy fácil decir que sí. Un ejemplo de la riqueza natural que posee Hispanoamérica es el petróleo. Además, las tierras hispanoamericanas cuentan con grandes depósitos de cobre,[6] plata, hierro, plomo, estaño[7] y tungsteno. Todos éstos son productos que necesitará el mundo del futuro.

Será importante también el aprovechamiento[8] de la riqueza agrícola y pesquera.[9] Con sus vastos territorios cultivables y con la pesca —en especial a lo largo de la costa del Pacífico— las naciones hispanoamericanas, con un desarrollo apropiado, podrán producir suficiente comida para su propio consumo y también para la exportación.

Un vistazo a México

Tradicionalmente, México ha sido un país agrícola. Sus productos más importantes han sido el maíz, el café y el algodón.[10] Sin embargo, hoy en día la verdadera riqueza de México es la mineral. Es uno de los más importantes productores de plata del mundo. Además, desde 1973 México se ha convertido en un gran productor de petróleo. Sus principales depósitos se encuentran en la bahía de Campeche. La producción de gas natural es también considerable, y el comercio y la industria están en constante desarrollo.

EL GOLFO DE MÉXICO

MÉXICO

la bahía de Campeche

EL OCÉANO PACÍFICO

[1]*valuable*   [2]*oro… gold and silver*   [3]*awareness*   [4]*right*   [5]es apropiado   [6]*copper*   [7]hierro… *iron, lead, tin*   [8]*utilization*
[9]*fishing*   [10]*cotton*

6

INTERCAMBIO

Paso 1
Piensa en la última vez que tuviste que dirigir algo. Luego contesta las siguientes preguntas en una hoja de papel aparte.

¿Quién te puso a cargo? ¿Qué querían o esperaban que hicieras? ¿Tuviste que dirigir a otras personas? ¿manejar algo importante? ¿Cómo salió todo?

Paso 2
Ahora, busca a otra(s) persona(s) en la clase que tuvo/tuvieron que hacer lo mismo. Puedes utilizar la pregunta de modelo.

MODELO: ¿Alguna vez te pusieron a cargo de

_____ ?

Paso 3
Compara lo que te pasó con lo que pasó a otro(s) de la clase. Luego, debes presentar tus experiencias a la clase. Después de las presentaciones, todos deciden quién en la clase tuvo la experiencia más interesante o más rara.

VOCABULARIO

Los verbos

ocultar	to hide

El dinero y los negocios
(Money and Business)

la empresa	firm, company, business
el presupuesto	budget
la sucursal	branch office
S.A. (Sociedad Anónima)	Inc.
andar bien/mal	to be going well/badly
despedir (i, i)	to fire (*an employee*)
dirigir (dirijo)	to run (*a business*)
economizar	to economize
poner (a alguien) a cargo (de)	to put (someone) in charge (of)

Repaso: **la compañía, la oficina**

Las personas

el auditor/la auditora	auditor
el empleado/la empleada	employee

Repaso: **el dueño/la dueña, el jefe/la jefa**

Las palabras adicionales

caerle* bien/mal a alguien	to make a good/bad impression on someone

---

* Note the irregular first person of **caer**: **caigo**.

LA MISMA SONRISA*

*The Same Smile

OBJETIVOS

The materials in **Lección 39** of the Textbook and the Workbook/Study Guide will help you better understand the video episode and take you beyond it, giving you additional information about places and characters in the series. The Textbook will also help you to develop skill in using the Spanish language. In this lesson you will learn

- vocabulary related to real estate transactions
- more ways to use the past subjunctive

You will also learn about the **Ballet Folclórico de México** and about Mariachi music.

Be sure to work through all parts of the lesson. When you see a headphones symbol in the margin, listen to the CD for **Lección 39**. Answers or hints for many activities are given in Appendix 1. Be sure to check your answers for each activity before going on to the next one.

The interactive CD-ROM to accompany *Destinos* contains additional practice with the video storyline and will help you improve your skills in Spanish.

BEFORE VIEWING . . .

Preliminary: See Faculty Guide for additional information and activities for this lesson.
• **Variation:** For activities marked with the headphones icon, you may wish to read from the Audioscript instead of playing the CD.
• **Suggestion:** Make sure students are familiar with the activities before you read from the Audioscript or play the CD.

1

Preparación

Suggestions:
• Before watching the video, go over the vocabulary list at the end of the chapter and have students pronounce the words after you.
• Assign *Preparación* activities as homework and then go over them quickly in class before viewing the video.

Actividad.
Paso 1

Aquí está el resumen del narrador que vas a escuchar al principio de este episodio. ¿Puedes completar las oraciones?

En el episodio previo,

Act., *Paso 1,* **Answers:**
1. *una reunión en la casa de Pedro* 2. *Raquel* 3. *Pedro* 4. *Arturo; Raquel* 5. *los problemas económicos de la oficina en Miami* 6. *Carlos* 7. *seriamente* 8. *Gloria había desaparecido*

1. Raquel y Arturo regresaron al hotel después de… ver a don Fernando en el hospital. / una reunión en la casa de Pedro.
2. Había un mensaje para… Raquel./Arturo.
3. Ellos, alarmados, llamaron en seguida a… Puerto Rico./Pedro.

En el bar,

4. Arturo/Raquel… le preguntó a… Arturo/Raquel… si había pensado… en ellos… en su futuro.

Mientras tanto,

5. Pedro, Ramón y Mercedes hablaban de… los problemas que tienen Juan y Pati. / los problemas económicos de la oficina en Miami.
6. Pedro y los demás no sabían que… Juan/Carlos… los escuchaba.

En casa de Ramón,

7. Carlos habló… seriamente/alegremente… con Gloria.
8. Más tarde, Carlos descubrió que… los niños habían desaparecido. / Gloria había desaparecido.

Paso 2
Ahora escucha el CD para verificar tus respuestas.

Para pensar, **Suggestion:** If beginning a third quarter course, make sure students know who each person in the photos is before continuing with the video.

Para pensar…

Las siguientes fotos representan algunas de las escenas que vas a ver en este episodio. ¿Quiénes son los personajes que se ven? ¿Qué te sugiere cada foto?

Para comprender, **Suggestion:** Ask whole class what the word *boleto* probably means. Encourage them to try to explain in other Spanish words before resorting to an English translation. Make sure students understand the word before continuing with the video.

Para comprender un poco más

el boleto   Si quieres ver una película o una obra de teatro, tienes que comprar **el boleto** para poder entrar.

 . . . AFTER VIEWING

2

¿TIENES BUENA MEMORIA?

 Actividad A.   ¿Qué hicieron?

En la siguiente tabla se encuentran los nombres de los personajes principales de este episodio. Vas a escuchar una serie de oraciones. Escribe el número de cada oración junto a los nombres apropiados.

Act. A, Answers: *Raquel y Arturo:* 3, 5, 6, 8 *Carlos y Gloria:* 1 *Ángela y Roberto:* 2 *Juan, Ramón y Pedro:* 4, 7

Raquel y Arturo	Carlos y Gloria
Ángela y Roberto	Juan, Ramón y Pedro

Actividad B.   Encuentros

En este episodio, ¿recuerdas lo que decían Arturo y sus sobrinos puertorriqueños? Indica todos los temas de que hablaron en el episodio.

Act. B, Suggestion: Give students about 2 minutes to complete the activity individually or in pairs and then compare answers as whole class.

Act. B, Answers: 2, 3, 5, 6, 7

1. _____ El accidente en la excavación
2. _____ La condición de Roberto
3. _____ El parecido (*resemblance*) entre Roberto y su padre Ángel
4. _____ La esposa de Ángel
5. _____ Las cosas que trajo Arturo desde la Argentina
6. _____ La muerte del padre de Arturo
7. _____ El sentido de culpabilidad de Ángel
8. _____ El sentido de culpabilidad de Arturo

Act. C, Suggestion: Give students about 5 minutes to prepare their ideas or assign as homework and complete the activity in groups the following day.

Act. C, Point out: Students can use the following lead-ins to answer the questions.

Write on the board *Me interesa más... (la relación entre Arturo y Raquel)*. *No me interesa... (el conflicto entre Juan y Pati)*. *Espero que... (Arturo y Raquel se casen)*.

Actividad C.   Conflictos y situaciones

Piensa en todos los conflictos, las situaciones y posibles situaciones que confrontan a los personajes de *Destinos*. ¿Cuál te interesa más? ¿Cuál te interesa menos? ¿Qué resolución esperas que haya para la situación que más te interesa? Presenta tus ideas a tres compañeros. ¿Están de acuerdo con tus ideas? ¿Qué ideas tienen ellos?

Act. C, Follow-up: Students form small groups. Ask one group *¿Qué situaciones les interesan más? ¿Qué situaciones les interesan menos? ¿Qué resolución esperan?* Then ask the rest of the class *¿Están de acuerdo? ¿Por qué sí? ¿Por qué no?*

Para pensar...

En este episodio, Juan pensaba en hacer una llamada telefónica, pero no lo hizo. ¿A quién pensaba llamar? ¿Por qué? ¿Qué le quería decir?

Suggestions:
• Practice pronunciation with choral and individual repetition.
• Provide vocabulary for *to own* (*ser dueño/a*). As you introduce

3

VOCABULARIO DEL TEMA

vocabulary, ask *¿Alquilan un apartamento o son dueños de una casa? ¿Cómo encontraron su casa o apartamento? ¿Usaron un agente de bienes raíces? ¿Les gustaría comprar La Gavia? ¿Cuál sería una buena oferta?*

Los bienes raíces

el apartamento	apartment	**el precio**	price
la propiedad	property	**el préstamo**	loan
		la venta	sale
el alquiler	rent		
la oferta	offer	**el/la agente de**	real estate
		bienes raíces	agent
alquilar	to rent	**se alquila**	for rent
estar intersado/a en,	to be	**se vende,**	for sale
interesarse en	interested in	**en venta**	
hacer una oferta	to make an offer		
aceptar la oferta	to accept the offer		
rechazar la oferta	to reject the offer		

The word **apartamento** is understood throughout most of the Spanish-speaking world to mean *apartment*. Other frequently used words include **el departamento** (*Mexico and other Latin American countries*) and **el piso** (*Spain*). In other parts of the Spanish-speaking world, the word **piso** means *floor*.

Act. A, Answers: *Primera conversación: 1. C 2. F 3. F 4. C (See Appendix 1 for expanded answers.) Segunda conversación: la casa → el apartamento; comprarla → comprarlo; Es una mala oferta → Es una buena oferta; Ángela debe rechazarla → Ángela debe decidir; ...que lo hable con Arturo → ...que lo hable con Roberto*

Actividad A.   En venta

En este episodio, se habla de vender dos propiedades. Escucha las conversaciones otra vez y luego contesta las preguntas.

Act. A, Optional: Test students' knowledge of *Destinos* by asking ¿*A cuál de los personajes de Destinos se refieren estas oraciones?* 1. *Son dueños del apartamento de sus padres.* (*Ángela y Roberto*) 2. *Es el dueño de una hacienda histórica.* (*don Fernando*) 3. *Una agente de bienes raíces tiene un cliente interesado en comprar su propiedad.* (*la familia Castillo / don Fernando*) 4. *Hay una oferta para comprar su apartamento.* (*Ángela y Roberto*) 5. *Tiene una oficina en su casa.* (*Arturo*) 6. *Debe consultar con un pariente antes de aceptar una oferta.* (*Ángela*) 7. *Vio varios apartamentos con una agente de bienes raíces.* (*Ángela*).

Primera conversación

Indica si las siguientes oraciones son ciertas (**C**) o falsas (**F**).

C F 1. Una agente de bienes raíces llamó a la familia Castillo.

C F 2. El cliente que se interesa en comprar la propiedad es de la Argentina.

C F 3. Mercedes quiere aceptar la oferta inmediatamente.

C F 4. Pedro cree que es bueno saber cuál puede ser el precio.

Segunda conversación

Aquí está la conversación que acabas de escuchar. ¿Puedes encontrar la información equivocada?

TÍO JAIME: ¡Ah! Y hay algo muy importante. El hombre interesado en la casa ha hecho una oferta.

RAQUEL: ¿Para comprarla?

TÍO JAIME: Sí. Es una mala oferta. Ángela debe rechazarla. Pídale que se comunique conmigo.

RAQUEL: Por supuesto, yo se lo digo.

TÍO JAIME: Ah, y también hay que recordarle que lo hable con Arturo.

RAQUEL: Sí, por supuesto.

TÍO JAIME: Ángela, a veces, es un poco apresurada.

RAQUEL: Comprendo.

Act. B, Suggestion: Assign as homework and then go over answers quickly in class.

Act. B, Answers: a. 5 b. 8 c. 3 d. 1 e. 6 f. 9 g. 4 h. 10 i. 2 j. 7

Actividad B. Se compra

Imagina que vives en un apartamento y que quieres comprar una casa. ¿En qué orden vas a hacer las siguientes cosas?

a. _____ Hago una oferta, que es rechazada por los dueños.

b. _____ Firmo todos los documentos legales y, más importante, escribo el cheque más grande de mi vida.

c. _____ Miro varias casas, sin poder decidirme.

d. _____ Pienso en todas las cualidades que quiero que la casa tenga.

e. _____ Hago otra oferta ¡y la aceptan!

f. _____ El antiguo dueño se va por fin de la casa.

g. _____ Por fin encuentro la casa ideal para mí/mi familia.

h. _____ Yo me mudo / Mi familia y yo nos mudamos a la nueva casa.

i. _____ Me pongo en contacto con un agente de bienes raíces.

j. _____ Pido un préstamo en el banco.

Act. C, Suggestion: Assign as homework and then compare answers as whole class. Tell students to contact a real estate agent and a bank to research their answers if they do not already know.

Act. C, Extension: 4. ¿*Cuál es el precio medio en tu ciudad de una casa de tres dormitorios con dos baños?* 5. ¿*de un coche usado?*

Actividad C. ¿Cuánto sabes?

Di lo que sabes de cada tema o situación a continuación.

1. Si se vende una casa *sin* la ayuda de un agente de bienes raíces, ¿cuánto dinero se ahorra?

2. ¿Cuál es el porcentaje (*percentage*) del interés para un préstamo para (a) comprar un auto, (b) comprar una casa, (c) estudiar en la universidad?

3. ¿Cuál es el alquiler medio (*average*) en tu ciudad para un apartamento de dos cuartos?

4

UN POCO DE GRAMÁTICA

The Workbook/Study Guide contains more detailed explanation and practice of this grammar point.

Note: You may wish to review the verb paradigms for the past subjunctive and/or review compound sentences with adjectival and adverbial clauses.

More About Talking About the Past

Use the past subjunctive in adjectival and adverbial clauses with time conjunctions when the time frame of the conversation is in the past.

Ángela llegó al hospital antes de que Roberto **se despertara**.

Ángela arrived at the hospital before Roberto woke up.

La agente de bienes raíces buscaba a alguien que **quisiera** comprar La Gavia.

The real estate agent was looking for someone who wanted to buy La Gavia.

You will learn more about this usage in the Workbook/Study Guide.

Act., Suggestion: Assign as homework and have students present their sentences to the class or to a partner the following day.

Act., Follow-up: Have students create original completions for the 5 sentences. The completions may be true or false for them. Working with a partner, students take turns reading their original sentences and trying to guess which are true or false.

Actividad.   En el pasado

Indica cada frase que completa la oración correctamente según tu experiencia.

1. Cuando era niño/a, no había nadie en mi barrio que
    a. _____ hablara español.
    b. _____ tuviera una familia con más de tres hijos.
    c. _____ viviera sin auto.

2. De niño/a, no podíamos cenar en mi casa antes de que
    a. _____ volviera mi madre/padre del trabajo.
    b. _____ todos estuviéramos presentes.
    c. _____ nos laváramos las manos.

3. De adolescente, no me quería asociar con nadie que
    a. _____ no fuera de mi clase social.
    b. _____ tuviera mala reputación.
    c. _____ participara en el Club de _____.

4. De adolescente, pensaba que mi vida sería mejor sólo cuando
    a. _____ aprendiera a manejar un auto.
    b. _____ saliera para la universidad.
    c. _____ ganara mucho dinero.

5. Al comenzar este año escolar, sólo podía relajarme después de que
    a. _____ hubiera conseguido todas mis clases.
    b. _____ conociera a todos mis profesores.
    c. _____ comprara todos mis libros.

5

LECTURA CULTURAL

México, música y baile

Lectura cultural, **Suggestion:** Assign as homework and go over answers quickly in class. Remind students that they should not expect to understand every word of the reading, but rather to get the main ideas.

Lectura cultural, **Preguntas:** 1. ¿Cómo se llama el grupo de baile más famoso de México? (*el Ballet Folclórico*). 2. En México, ¿dónde se presenta esta obra? (*en el Palacio de Bellas Artes en la Ciudad de México*) 3. ¿Cómo se llama el baile probablemente más famoso del Ballet Folclórico? (*el jarabe tapatío*) 4. ¿Cómo se llaman los grupos de músicos que se encuentran en las calles? (*mariachis*) 5. ¿Cuáles son los temas típicos de las canciones de los mariachis? (*la vida diaria y el amor*).

Como muchos turistas que llegan a la capital, Raquel se interesa por ver el gran espectáculo del Ballet Folclórico. Esta obra, que se presenta en el elegante Palacio de Bellas Artes, es famosa en todo el mundo. Las funciones consisten en lujosas[1] imitaciones de fiestas típicas de diferentes regiones de México. También se presentan danzas de la tradición indígena, tal como se cree que se presentaban en la época precolombina.

El Palacio de Bellas Artes

El baile nacional de México

Entre todos los bailes que se presentan en el Ballet Folclórico, tal vez el más famoso sea el jarabe tapatío.[2] Es derivado de bailes españoles. Se conocía ya en México en el siglo XVIII y fue prohibido durante los últimos años del dominio español, por su extrema desenvoltura.[3] Por su antigüedad y por su popularidad, es considerado el baile nacional de México.

La música de los mariachis

Ay, ay, ay, ay.
Canta y no llores
porque cantando,
se alegran,
cielito lindo,[4]
los corazones.

El Ballet Folclórico de Guadalajara

Para muchos, la música que mejor ejemplifica a México es la de los mariachis. Estos músicos ambulantes se contratan para que den serenatas,[5] para que toquen en las fiestas o sencillamente para que les canten unas canciones a los clientes que están sentados en los cafés al aire libre. Cantan las canciones típicas del pueblo, con historias de la vida diaria y del amor.

---

[1]*lavish*   [2]*jarabe… Mexican Hat Dance (tapatío = from the state of Jalisco)*
[3]*liveliness, naturalness*   [4]*cielito… pretty little heaven (term of affection)*   [5]*serenades*

INTERCAMBIO

Paso 1

Toda la clase va a entrevistar al profesor / a la profesora sobre el primer apartamento o casa que tuvo después de salir de la casa de sus padres. La clase debe dividirse en cuatro grupos. A cada grupo se le asignará una de las siguientes categorías.

1. lo que quería
2. cómo lo encontró
3. cómo lo consiguió
4. cuándo se mudó después y bajo qué circunstancias

Paso 2

Los grupos deben formular por lo menos cinco preguntas sobre la categoría. La idea es sacar todos los detalles posibles haciendo sólo preguntas de tipo sí/no.

Paso 3

La clase debe hacerle las preguntas al profesor / a la profesora. Todos deben apuntar la información. ¡OJO! Su profesor(a) les va a dar respuestas falsas para una de las categorías.

Paso 4

En grupos, revisen la información. ¿Pueden identificar la información falsa?

VOCABULARIO

Los bienes raíces (Real Estate)

alquilar	to rent
estar interesado/a en, interesarse en	to be interested in
rechazar	to reject
se alquila	for rent
se vende, en venta	for sale
el/la agente de bienes raíces	real estate agent
el alquiler	rent
la oferta	offer
el precio	price

el préstamo	loan
la propiedad	property
la venta	sale

Repaso: **el apartamento**

Sustantivos

la sonrisa	smile

Los adjetivos

mismo/a	same

40

Suggestion: Have students look at the photo, describe what they see, and talk about what they think might happen. Ask questions about the photo to prompt student discussion.

ENTRE LA ESPADA Y LA PARED*

*Between a Rock and a Hard Place

OBJETIVOS

The materials in **Lección 40** of the Textbook and the Workbook/Study Guide will help you better understand the video episode and take you beyond it, giving you additional information about places and characters in the series. The Textbook will also help you to develop skill in using the Spanish language. In this lesson, you will learn

- vocabulary useful to tourists traveling abroad
- ways to talk about what would happen

You will also learn about Hispanic theater.

Be sure to work through all parts of the lesson. When you see a headphones symbol in the margin, listen to the CD for **Lección 40**. Answers or hints for many activities are given in Appendix 1. Be sure to check your answers for each activity before going on to the next one.

The interactive CD-ROM to accompany *Destinos* contains additional practice with the video storyline and will help you improve your skills in Spanish.

BEFORE VIEWING . . .

Preliminary: See Faculty Guide for additional information and activities for this lesson.
• **Variation:** For activities marked with the headphones icon, you may wish to read from the Audioscript instead of playing the CD.
• **Suggestion:** Make sure students are familiar with the activities before you read from the Audioscript or play the CD.

1

PREPARACIÓN

Suggestions:
• Before watching the video, go over the vocabulary list at the end of the chapter and have students pronounce the words after you.
• Assign *Preparación* activities as homework and then go over them quickly in class before viewing the video.

Act. A, Suggestion: You may want to have students do this activity in pairs and go over answers as whole class.

Act. A, Answers: 1. *desapareció* 2. *buscarla* 3. *se sentía muy bien, con mucha hambre* 4. *su tío* 5. *la posible venta de La Gavia* 6. *regresó al hospital para estar con su padre*

Actividad A.

¿Puedes completar el siguiente resumen de lo que pasó en el episodio previo?

1. se acostó / desapareció
2. buscarla / dar un paseo
3. se sentía muy bien, con mucha hambre / estaba muy cansado y sin apetito
4. su abuelo / su tío
5. la posible venta de La Gavia / la enfermedad de don Fernando
6. se quedó en casa / regresó al hospital para estar con su padre

En el episodio previo, Carlos le dijo a Ramón que Gloria

_____.¹ Después de pedirle el carro a Ramón,

Carlos salió a _____.²

   Mientras tanto, en el hospital, Roberto, ya despierto,

_____.³ Después de comerse dos desayunos,

Roberto conoció a _____.⁴

   En casa de Pedro, los hermanos también desayunaron y hablaron de

_____.⁵ Luego, Ramón, Pedro y Juan salieron para

la hacienda. Mercedes, como de costumbre,

_____.⁶

Act. B, Suggestion: You may want to have students work in pairs.

Act. B, Answers: *Paso 1:* b *Paso 2:* 1. a 2. c

Actividad B.

Ya sabes que Pati se ha ido a Nueva York para resolver los problemas que tiene con la producción de su obra. En este episodio, va a hablar de esos problemas con su productor.

Paso 1

Escucha una parte de su conversación y luego contesta la pregunta.

   De las siguientes oraciones, ¿cuál describe mejor la conversación entre Pati y el productor?

a. Es una conversación calmada. Pati y el productor se llevan bien y pueden resolver algunos asuntos.
b. Es una conversación animada. Es obvio que Pati y el productor tienen ideas diferentes sobre una serie de asuntos.

Paso 2

Escucha la conversación por lo menos una vez más y luego contesta las preguntas. Al escuchar, ten en cuenta que **patrocinadores** significa *sponsors* (*people who give money to fund productions*).

1. Según el productor, ¿qué cosa importante tiene que hacer Pati?
    a. _____ hacer unos cambios en la obra
    b. _____ pasar más tiempo hablando con los patrocinadores
    c. _____ darle una entrevista a un reportero del periódico de la universidad

2. Según el productor, ¿qué pasará si Pati no sigue sus consejos?
    a. _____ La obra no tendrá éxito.   c. _____ La obra se cancelará.
    b. _____ Él buscará a otro director.

Para pensar...

En tu opinión, ¿cuál va a ser la respuesta de Pati a las demandas del productor? ¿Hará ella los cambios? ¿Qué sabes de Pati que te ayudará a determinar lo que hará?

Para comprender un poco más

me/le cansa	Algunas personas siempre se quejan de las mismas cosas. Realmente **me cansa** estar con ellas.
mandón/mandona	La mamá de Raquel es una persona muy **mandona**. Siempre les dice a todos lo que deben hacer.
me importa un comino	¡**Me importa un comino** lo que puedan decir los demás! ¡No me importa para nada!

  . . . AFTER VIEWING

2

¿TIENES BUENA MEMORIA?

Actividad A. ¿A quién se refiere?

Indica al personaje descrito en cada oración.

a.	Raquel	d.	Carlos	g.	la agente de bienes raíces
b.	Arturo	e.	Mercedes	h.	Pati
c.	Roberto	f.	don Fernando	i.	el productor de Pati

1. _____ Le dan de alta (*They release him*) en el hospital.
2. _____ Lo tienen que llevar a otro hospital.
3. _____ No quiere hacer ningún cambio en un proyecto.
4. _____ Amenaza con cancelar un proyecto.
5. _____ Confiesa que su madre es un poco mandona a veces.
6. _____ Tiene un cliente que quiere comprar La Gavia.
7. _____ Tiene que ir de compras porque no tiene ropa.
8. _____ Va a ir con su padre a Guadalajara.
9. _____ Se sentó a hablar con su ayudante.
10. _____ No puede acompañar a su padre a Guadalajara.

Actividad B.   **Pati y su ayudante**

Como sabes, después de hablar con el productor, Pati también habló largamente con Guillermo, su ayudante en el teatro. ¿Cuánto recuerdas de su conversación?

1. ¿Quién inició la conversación, Pati o Guillermo?
2. ¿De qué hablaron, de la obra o de Juan?
3. ¿Cree Guillermo que era necesario que Pati regresara a Nueva York, por la obra?
4. ¿Qué idea le dio Guillermo a Pati, que Juan tiene miedo o envidia de ella?

Para pensar...

Piensa un momento en la conversación entre Pati y su ayudante. ¿Qué tipo de relaciones existe entre ellos? ¿Crees que hace mucho tiempo que se conocen?

Actividad C.   **Raquel y sus padres**

Usando las preguntas a continuación como base, describe brevemente las relaciones que tiene Raquel con sus padres.

1. ¿Cómo describe Raquel a su madre?
2. ¿Cómo describe Raquel a su padre?
3. ¿Se lleva mejor con uno que el otro?

Para pensar...

¿Qué opinas de las relaciones entre Raquel y su madre? ¿Son parecidas a las relaciones que tienes (o tenías) tú con tu propia madre? ¿con tu padre? ¿Es muy común entre padres e hijos el tipo de tensión que describe Raquel?

Suggestion: As you go over vocabulary, ask questions related to personal examples: *¿Cuándo se necesita cambiar dinero? ¿Adónde vas para enviar/mandar cosas? ¿Dónde dicen la palabra* timbre *en vez de* sello *o* estampilla? ¿Cómo se llama tu banco? ¿Sabes a cuánto está el peso mexicano ahora? ¿Cuánto cuesta mandar una tarjeta postal? ¿Dónde está el correo más cerca? ¿Qué cheques de viajero prefieres?, etc.*

3

VOCABULARIO DEL TEMA

Para los turistas

cambiar	to change (*money*)	**el sobre**	envelope
enviar	to send	**la tarjeta postal**	postcard
mandar	to send	**la estampilla**	stamp
		el sello	stamp
el banco	bank	**el timbre** (*Mex.*)	stamp
el cheque de viajero	traveler's check		
el correo	mail; post office		
el correo aéreo	air mail		
el giro	money order		
el paquete	package		
el recibo	receipt		

ESTAMPILLAS

Quisiera cambiar…	I would like to change . . .
¿A cuánto está (el dólar, el peso…)?	What's the exchange rate on (the dollar, peso . . .)?
Está a…	It's at (It's worth) . . .
¿Cuánto es/cuesta mandar… ?	How much is it / does it cost to send . . . ?

 Actividad A.   Con Ángela y Raquel

Vas a escuchar otra vez tres breves conversaciones del episodio. Pon el número de la conversación con la foto a la que corresponde.

Act. A, Answers: a. 3 b. 2 c. 1

a. _____   b. _____   c. _____

Act. B, Suggestion: You may want to have students do this activity in pairs or small groups, then check answers as whole class.

Actividad B.   Más necesidades turísticas
Paso 1
Aquí hay dos conversaciones que has escuchado en este episodio, pero hay que poner las oraciones en un orden lógico. ¿Puedes hacerlo?

Primera conversación

Habla primero Ángela.

DEPENDIENTE

a. _____ Cómo no. ¿Cuántos?
b. _____ Muy bien. Aquí tiene su recibo, señorita.
c. _____ A 2.900 pesos.

ÁNGELA

d. _____ Gracias.
e. _____ ¿A cuánto está el dólar?
f. _____ Quisiera cambiar unos dólares, por favor.
g. _____ Bueno. Quiero cambiar cien dólares entonces.

Segunda conversación

En esta conversación intervienen tres personas. Empieza a hablar primero Ángela.

ÁNGELA

a. _____ Gracias, Raquel. Pero yo tengo que mandar muchas postales a mi familia. ¿Venden sellos, ay, digo, timbres aquí?
b. _____ Necesito comprar sellos.
c. _____ ¿Y está muy lejos el correo?

DEPENDIENTE

d. _____ No, está aquí, cerquita. A la vuelta nada más.
e. _____ Normalmente, sí, señorita, pero ahora no tenemos. Tendrá que ir al correo.

RAQUEL

f. _____ Ángela, aquí no se dice sellos. Se dice timbres. Yo guardé unos de antes. Mira.

Paso 2
Ahora escucha el CD para verificar tus respuestas.

Actividad C. Cosas de los viajeros
Escoge una de los siguientes temas o situaciones y explícale a un compañero / una compañera cómo era, según tu experiencia.

1. el último paquete que enviaste (qué era, cuánto costó…)
2. la última tarjeta postal que recibiste (de quién era, de dónde, qué decía…)
3. la estampilla que más te ha gustado y por qué
4. si has utilizado cheques de viajero y para qué
5. la última vez que un recibo te era muy importante (para los impuestos [*taxes*], para devolver algo…)
6. la última vez que cambiaste dinero en un banco (dónde estabas, qué monedas recibiste, a cuánto estaba el dólar…)

Suggestion: Before introducing the conditional, review all the indicative and subjunctive verb forms that have been studied. Provide a handout with subject pronouns and infini-

4

UN POCO DE GRAMÁTICA

The Workbook/Study Guide contains more detailed explanation and practice of this grammar point.

tives (or pictures of actions) down the left-hand side of the page and either triggers and time expressions (*ojalá que, ayer, de niño, mañana, siempre,* etc.) or names of verb tenses and modes (*subjuntivo, pretérito, imperfecto, futuro, presente,* etc.) across the top of the page. Have students fill in the verb forms. They should be comfortable with those before moving on to the conditional.
Note: Remind students of the irregular-stem verbs for the future and the imperfect endings of -*er* and -*ir* verbs before teaching conditional forms.
Point out: Mention to students that the *would* used for English equivalents of the conditional differs from the *would* meaning *used to* in some imperfect equivalents.
Variation: Write names of famous people, animals, and objects on cards and distribute to students. Have individual students say what they would do if they were the person or thing named on the card. The rest of the class tries to guess who or what they are. This may be done in pairs, small groups, or the entire class. As they have not yet learned *si* clauses, they can replace *si* with *como.* For example, a student with a card reading *Bush* says *Sería presidente.* The class says *Como (George W.) Bush.* A student with a card reading *pájaro* says *Podría volar.* The class says *Como pájaro.*

Act., Follow-up: Survey the class to find out how each student answered each item. Tally the numbers on the board and compare what different students would and wouldn't do. Ask for volunteers to explain why they would or would not do the things mentioned.

Talking About What You Would Do

To describe what would happen or what someone would do, add endings with **-ía** to most infinitives.

Ángela dijo que **compraría** sellos y que les **mandaría** postales a sus familiares.

Ángela said that she would buy stamps and that she would send postcards to her relatives.

CLIENTE: Sí, **estaría** interesado en comprar La Gavia.

CLIENT: *Yes, I would be interested in buying La Gavia.*

MARÍA: Luis, ¿**podrías** ir a México con nosotros?

MARÍA: *Luis, would you be able to come to Mexico with us?*

RAMÓN: Claro, **hablaríamos** con don Fernando antes de vender la hacienda.

RAMÓN: *Of course, we would speak with don Fernando before selling the estate.*

You will learn more about composing and using these forms in the Workbook/Study Guide.

Act., Optional: To review conditional forms, prepare a *Firma aquí* activity with questions such as ¿*Irías a una película extranjera / una discoteca /… ?* ¿*Comerías el pescado crudo / tofu /… ?* Have students circulate in class asking and answering the questions and gathering the signatures of classmates who respond with *Sí.* Then have them report their findings to the class, using the model _____ *comería el pescado crudo.*

Actividad. ¿Qué harías?
Paso 1

Indica tus reacciones a las oraciones a continuación.

5 = Sí, lo haría.   3 = Bueno, probablemente lo haría.   1 = No, no lo haría nunca.

1. _____ Comería un plato de gusanos (*worms*) por $10.000.
2. _____ Pasaría la noche solo/a en una casa encantada (*haunted*).
3. _____ Viviría en un lugar donde no sabía hablar el idioma y donde no conocía a nadie.
4. _____ Acompañaría a mis amigos a una fiesta de piscina en donde llevar el traje de baño era optativo.
5. _____ Nadaría en una playa donde se había reportado la presencia de tiburones (*sharks*).

Paso 2

Suma (*Add*) los números y compara el total de tus respuestas con el de tus compañeros de clase. ¡Cuanto más alto el número, más arriesgado/a (*daring*) eres!

5

LECTURA CULTURAL

El teatro hispánico, una larga tradición

Como autora de su propia obra de teatro, Pati representa la continuación de una larga tradición literaria en el mundo hispánico. En esta tradición, hay de todo: teatro popular, para el público; teatro clásico (que sigue más o menos el estilo del teatro griego[1]); teatro experimental, de vanguardia; teatro de evasión, para las masas. A continuación[2] se encuentran tres ejemplos de esta tradición teatral.

Lope de Vega, español (1562–1635)

Lope fue el padre del teatro popular español. Contemporáneo de Shakespeare, fue el primero en romper[3] con la tradición del teatro clásico. Sus obras tenían como fin divertir y enseñar al público. Gracias a sus obras, el teatro se hizo popular en España. Su producción fue enorme: unas mil quinientas obras de teatro. Algunas de las mejores todavía se representan en todas partes del mundo.

Lope de Vega

    Una de sus obras más conocidas es *Fuenteovejuna*,[4] que se basa en un acontecimiento histórico. El protagonista principal es todo el pueblo de Fuenteovejuna, en Andalucía. El pueblo entero se levantó[5] contra la tiranía de su Comendador,[6] quien había cometido numerosos abusos, y le dio muerte. Poco después un representante del rey llegó al pueblo para investigar el caso. «¿Quién mató al Comendador?» preguntó. Todos contestaron al mismo tiempo: «¡Fuenteovejuna, señor!»

Emilio Carballido, mexicano (1925–)

Carballido es sin duda una de las figuras cumbre[7] del teatro contemporáneo mexicano y de toda Hispanoamérica. Ha sabido representar e interpretar la realidad contemporánea, así que sus obras les hablan a las masas. Al mismo tiempo, se ha aprovechado de la temática[8] de la tragedia clásica y la ha adaptado al mundo contemporáneo.

    En su pieza corta *El censo,* un empadronador[9] trata de recoger unos datos sobre un taller de costura[10] clandestino. Pero los empleados y Paco, el dueño, no se dejan contar fácilmente.

EL EMPADRONADOR: (*Desesperado.*) Es como… Mire, la Nación se pregunta: ¿Cuáles son mis riquezas? Y hace la cuenta.[11] Como usted, ¿no le importa saber cuánto dinero hay en su casa?

PACO: No.

---

[1]*Greek* [2]A… *Following* [3]*breaking* [4]*Sheep Well* [5]*se… rose up* [6]*Knight Commander* [7]más importantes [8]*characteristic themes or topics* [9]*census taker* [10]*taller… tailor shop* [11]*hace… it counts them*

EL EMPADRONADOR: Pero… tiene que contar cuánto gastan, cuánto ganarán…

PACO: Nunca.

EL EMPADRONADOR: ¡Pero cómo no! Bueno, ustedes no, pero un país debe saber… cuánta riqueza tiene, debe publicarlo…

PACO: ¿Para que cuando lo sepan los demás países le caigan encima?[12] ¡Yo no voy a ayudar a la ruina de mi Patria!

Luis Valdez

El Teatro Campesino

Este teatro popular nació dentro de la huelga[13] contra los viñadores[14] de California. Al principio era un teatro de improvisación: algunos campesinos[15] improvisaron escenas de la huelga para enseñar y para llevar la huelga a otros. Los problemas trágicos de los campesinos pobres se presentaban con humor y sátira, y se utilizaban en sus espectáculos elementos de la tradición mexicana, como calaveras y esqueletos.[16] Los actores del Teatro Campesino viajaron a todas partes de los Estados Unidos para transmitir su mensaje político al público.

Ahora el Teatro Campesino es una compañía de teatro, todavía localizada en California. En la compañía, jóvenes actores, escritores y directores pueden aprender y practicar su arte. Luis Valdez, el fundador y director artístico del Teatro, ha escrito obras de teatro y películas, como, por ejemplo, *Zoot Suit,* una obra controvertida que tuvo mucho éxito, especialmente en California, y *La Bamba,* la historia de Ritchie Valens.

[12]¿Para… *So that when other countries find out about it they will attack?* [13]*strike* [14]*grapegrowers* [15]*farm laborers* [16]calaveras… *skulls and skeletons*

Lectura cultural, Preguntas: 1. ¿Cuáles son cuatro tipos de teatro? (*el popular, el clásico, el experimental, el de evasión*) 2. ¿Cuándo vivió Lope de Vega? (*1562–1635*) 3. ¿De dónde fue? (*de España*) 4. ¿Cómo se llama una de sus obras más conocidas? (*Fuenteovejuna*) 5. ¿En qué año nació Emilio Carballido? (*en 1925*) 6. ¿Cuál es su nacionalidad? (*mexicana*) 7. ¿Cuál es el nombre de su pieza corta? (*El censo*) 8. ¿Dónde se encuentra el Teatro Campesino? (*en California*) 9. ¿Cómo se llama el fundador y director artístico del Teatro? (*Luis Valdez*) 10. ¿Qué obras famosas ha escrito? (*Zoot Suit y La Bamba*).

6

INTERCAMBIO

Paso 1

Imagínate que, entre las cosas de un pariente recién fallecido (*deceased*), encuentras unos sellos. Consultas con un experto y averiguas que valen un total de $50,000. ¿Venderías los sellos o te quedarías (*keep*) con ellos?

Paso 2

Con otras dos personas, discutan la situación y explica lo que harías. ¿Harían todos lo mismo? ¿Bajo qué circunstancias harías lo opuesto?

Paso 3

Un grupo debe presentar sus ideas a la clase. Los demás deben decir después si están de acuerdo o no. Como clase, discutan los factores que influyen en sus decisiones.

VOCABULARIO

Para los turistas (For Tourists)

cambiar	to change (*money*)
enviar	to send

el cheque de viajero	traveler's check
el correo	mail; post office
el correo aéreo	air mail
la estampilla	stamp
el giro	money order
el paquete	package
el sello	stamp
el sobre	envelope
el timbre (*Mex.*)	stamp

Quisiera cambiar...	I would like to change . . .
¿A cuánto está (el dólar, el peso...)?	What's the exchange rate on (the dollar, peso . . .)?
Está a...	It's at (It's worth) . . .

¿Cuánto es/cuesta mandar... ?	How much is it / does it cost to send . . . ?

Repaso: **el banco, mandar, el recibo, la tarjeta postal**

Los adjetivos

mandón, mandona	bossy

Las palabras adicionales

darlo/la de alta	to release someone (*from an institution*)
entre la espada y la pared	between a rock and a hard place

41

ALGO INESPERADO*

*Something Unexpected

OBJETIVOS

The materials in **Lección 41** of the Textbook and the Workbook/Study Guide will help you better understand the video episode and take you beyond it, giving you additional information about places and characters in the series. The Textbook will also help you to develop skill in using the Spanish language. In this lesson, you will learn

- more travel-related vocabulary
- more about using the conditional

You will also learn about the city of Guadalajara.

Be sure to work through all parts of the lesson. When you see a headphones symbol in the margin, listen to the CD for **Lección 41**. Answers or hints for many activities are given in Appendix 1. Be sure to check your answers for each activity before going on to the next one.

The interactive CD-ROM to accompany *Destinos* contains additional practice with the video storyline and will help you improve your skills in Spanish.

📺 BEFORE VIEWING . . .

1

PREPARACIÓN

Actividad A.
Paso 1

¿Te acuerdas de lo que pasó en el **Episodio 40**? Indica si las siguientes oraciones son ciertas (**C**) o falsas (**F**).

C F 1. A Roberto le dieron de alta en el hospital.
C F 2. Antes de ir a conocer a don Fernando, Roberto quería ir al hotel para cambiarse de ropa.
C F 3. En Nueva York Pati tenía problemas graves con el productor de su obra.
C F 4. El productor quería que Pati hiciera unos cambios en la obra.
C F 5. Más tarde Pati le contaba a su esposo los problemas que tenía en el teatro.
C F 6. En México, le informaron a la familia Castillo que el especialista vendría a la capital para examinar a don Fernando.

Paso 2
Ahora escucha el CD para verificar tus respuestas.

Actividad B.

En este episodio, Ángela y Roberto comienzan a hablar de la venta del apartamento en San Juan. Como sabes, el tío Jaime le dijo a Raquel por teléfono que había una oferta para comprarlo.

Paso 1
Escucha la conversación y trata de captar los puntos más importantes. Luego contesta las preguntas.

1. ¿Cuál es la reacción de Roberto?
   a. _____ Roberto está de acuerdo con la venta del apartamento.
   b. _____ Roberto se opone a la idea de venderlo.

2. ¿Cuál es el intento de Arturo?
   a. _____ Quiere calmar a sus sobrinos.
   b. _____ Trata de convencer a Ángela de su error.

Paso 2
Escucha la conversación otra vez y contesta las siguientes preguntas.

1. ¿Sabe Roberto por cierto que Ángela quiere darle dinero a Jorge, su novio?
2. ¿Qué les aconseja Arturo?
   a. _____ Que esperen, que dejen el asunto por el momento.
   b. _____ Que piensen bien lo que quieren hacer.
   c. _____ Que lo consulten con un abogado.

Para pensar...

1. ¿Has notado que Raquel no dijo nada durante la conversación? ¿Por qué crees que se queda callada (*silent*)?
2. ¿Qué opinas de la forma en que Arturo se comportaba (*behaved*) con sus sobrinos? Acaba de conocerlos. ¿Crees que es apropiado que les esté aconsejando de esta manera?

Para comprender un poco más

gruñón, gruñona   La tía Olga es la **gruñona** de la familia. Siempre se queja o encuentra defectos en todo.

rezongón, rezongona   No me gusta levantarme. Por eso por la mañana soy la persona más **rezongona** del mundo. Después de las diez, es otra cosa.

 . . . **AFTER VIEWING**

2

¿TIENES BUENA MEMORIA?

Actividad A. El repaso de Raquel

Al final de cada episodio de *Destinos,* has escuchado el repaso de Raquel. En esta actividad, vas a escuchar el repaso del **Episodio 41** otra vez, pero ¡ahora tú tienes que dar las respuestas!

Escucha las preguntas de Raquel con cuidado y contéstalas. Luego, como siempre, vas a oír la respuesta de ella. Tu respuesta no tiene que ser idéntica a la de Raquel, pero sí debe contener la misma información.

1. ...   2. ...   3. ...   4. ...

Actividad B. La familia Castillo

Como sabes, al principio de este episodio, don Fernando sale para Guadalajara, acompañado por Mercedes. Pero había otros acontecimientos importantes también. ¿Puedes completar las siguientes oraciones?

Verbos: jugar al *bridge,* jugar por dinero (*to gamble*), llamar a Pati, llevar a don Fernando a Guadalajara, salir para el aeropuerto, vender La Gavia
Sustantivos: una enfermedad física, un vicio
Lugares: Guadalajara, Nueva York
Personas: don Fernando, Gloria, Pati
Adjetivos: culpable, preocupado

1. Carlos le revela a su familia su secreto: Gloria tiene… . Tiene que… .
2. En este momento, Carlos se siente… . Cree que hablan de… por lo que él ha hecho con el dinero de la oficina en Miami.
3. Juan escucha parte de la confesión de Carlos, pero luego se levanta y… . Va a… para ver a… .

Para pensar…

Algunas personas fácilmente llegan a ser adictas al juego. ¿Conoces tú a alguien que tenga este problema? ¿Conoces a alguien que tenga otro tipo de adicción? Habla con algunos amigos para ver lo que piensan de la adicción de Gloria.

Actividad C. ¡Un desafío!

Hay varias acciones simultáneas en este episodio. ¿Cuántas recuerdas?

1. Tres personas o grupos de personas llegan en taxi o toman un taxi. ¿Quiénes son?

   _____ toma(n) un taxi para ir a _____.

   _____ llega(n) a _____ en taxi.

2. Dos personas toman el ascensor (*elevator*) del hotel al mismo tiempo. ¿Quiénes son?

Nota cultural   El regateo

Bargaining (**regatear**, **el regateo**) is a common custom in many Spanish-speaking countries, but only in certain locations: in markets, in some small shops and stalls, with street vendors who are selling objects (but not food). In other places—supermarkets, boutiques, department stores—prices are fixed (**los precios son fijos**) and one must pay the stated price. If objects in a store do not have a price written on a tag, it is possible that the seller will bargain. You can ask: **¿Son fijos los precios?** The worst that can happen is that the vendor will say yes.

In the video episode there is a brief example of the bargaining process. It can be as simple as giving a counter offer when a price is quoted. At times the seller will accept your offer. If not, he or she will make another offer, which you can accept, reject, or counter. If the price is not reduced to an acceptable level, you can walk away in the expectation that the seller might call after you to accept your last offer.

Bargaining can be fun, but you can also lose out on an item that you really want . . . unless you are prepared to take the seller's last offer!

3

VOCABULARIO DEL TEMA

You have seen and heard a good deal of travel-related vocabulary throughout the previous video episodes of *Destinos*. Here is a listing of useful words and phrases.

Hablando de los viajes

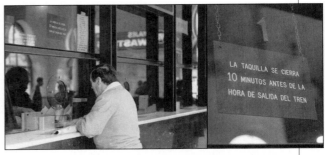

la aduana	customs office
la agencia de viajes	travel agency
el billete (*Spain*)	ticket
el boleto (*Span. Amer.*)	ticket
...de ida	. . . one-way
...de ida y vuelta	. . . round-trip
la (primera, segunda) clase	(first, second) class
la clase turística	tourist class
el equipaje	luggage
la gira	tour
la maleta	suitcase
el mapa	(*road, geographical*) map
el pasaje	passage, fare; ticket
el pasaporte	passport
el plano	map (*of a city*)
la reserva (*Spain*)	reservation
la reservación	reservation
la sección de (no) fumar	(non)smoking section
el vuelo	flight

el/la agente de viajes	travel agent
el/la guía	guide
hacer/cancelar una reservación	to make/cancel a reservation
hacer la maleta	to pack one's suitcase
hacer una gira	to take a tour
tomar un (autobús, avión, barco, taxi, tren)	to take a (bus, plane, boat, taxi, train)

 Actividad A.   Juan se va, Luis ha llegado...

En *Destinos,* los personajes viajan mucho. Vas a escuchar una serie de descripciones de varios aspectos de los viajes. Pon el número de la descripción con la foto o el dibujo apropiado.

a. _____   b. _____

la
Ciudad
de
México

MÉXICO

c. _____   d. _____   e. _____

Actividad B. Haciendo los arreglos

¿Cuánto sabes de arreglar un viaje? Completa los siguientes párrafos con las palabras apropiadas.

Para hacer un viaje en avión: Llamo a la (gira/agencia)[1] de viajes para (reservar/cancelar)[2] un (plano/billete)[3] de clase turística en un vuelo. Tomo (un barco/un taxi)[4] al aeropuerto, facturo[a] (el equipaje/el plano)[5] y espero en la sala, en la sección de no (pasar/fumar).[6]

Para ir de un país a otro: Al llegar a la frontera,[b] tengo que pasar por (la gira/la aduana).[7] Saco (el pasaporte/el plano)[8] y el agente de la aduana lo revisa. También tengo que abrir (el mapa/las maletas)[9] para que el inspector lo inspeccione todo.

Para ver las atracciones turísticas en una ciudad: Llamo a (la aduana/la agencia de viajes)[10] para reservar un plazo[c] en una (sección/gira).[11] (El barco/El autobús)[12] me recoge en el hotel y, con un grupo de viajeros, veo todo lo que hay que ver en la ciudad. No necesito comprar un (mapa/plano)[13] de la ciudad, porque nos dan uno en el autobús. Al fin de la gira, le doy una propina[d] al (agente/guía).[14]

Actividad C. Un viaje ideal
Paso 1

Imagina que tienes el dinero y el tiempo necesarios para hacer cualquier viaje. Contesta estas preguntas sobre tu viaje ideal.

1. ¿Adónde te gustaría ir más?   Me gustaría ir a _____.
2. ¿Cómo viajarías?   Iría en _____.
3. ¿Qué atracciones turísticas visitarías?   Visitaría _____.

Paso 2

Usando las mismas preguntas del **Paso 1**, entrevista a cinco compañeros de clase para saber cuáles son los viajes más populares entre ellos. Prepara un breve informe para la clase sobre cada punto. ¿Es el destino ideal el mismo para muchos?

[a]*I check*   [b]*border*   [c]*seat*   [d]*tip* (*monetary*)

Act. B, Answers:
1. *agencia* 2. *reservar* 3. *billete* 4. *un taxi* 5. *el equipaje* 6. *fumar* 7. *la aduana* 8. *el pasaporte* 9. *las maletas* 10. *la agencia de viajes* 11. *gira* 12. *El autobús* 13. *plano* 14. *guía*

Act. C, Paso 1, Suggestion: Assign as homework and then complete *Paso 2* in class the following day.

Act. C, Paso 2, Suggestion: Have students prepare a 3 × 5 grid on a sheet of paper: 3 rows with the 3 questions and 5 columns headed with the names of 5 classmates. As they interview their classmates, they simply fill in the grid. Make a model grid on the board as an example.

Act. C, Follow-up: Have students summarize their findings in a paragraph, comparing and contrasting the various trips that their classmates told them about. This may be prepared as homework and turned in for a grade.

4

UN POCO DE GRAMÁTICA

The Workbook/Study Guide contains more detailed explanation and practice of this grammar point.

Note: You may wish to review the verb paradigms for the conditional.

Reporting Events Projected in the Past

Use the conditional to quote indirectly what someone said in the past.
Note the verb forms used in this pair of sentences. The future is used to tell what *will* happen, the conditional to tell what *would* happen.

Mercedes le **dice** a don Fernando que **conocerá** a sus nietos pasado mañana.	*Mercedes tells don Fernando that he will meet his grandchildren the day after tomorrow.*
Mercedes le **dijo** a don Fernando que **conocería** a sus nietos en dos días.	*Mercedes told don Fernando that he would meet his grandchildren in two days.*

You will learn more about this use of the conditional in the Workbook/Study Guide.

Actividad. ¿Qué dijiste que harías?
Paso 1
Completa cada oración con algo apropiado según tu experiencia. ¡OJO!
Usarás una forma del condicional en cada oración.

Act., *Paso 1*, Suggestion: Assign as homework and have students present their sentences to the class the following day.

Act., *Paso 1*, Point out: The second part of each sentence is as important as the first to establish context and complete the sentences logically. Make sure students understand the complete context before filling in the blanks.

1. Una vez dije que algún día yo _____, pero todavía no lo he hecho.
2. Una vez dije que yo nunca _____, pero ahora pienso de una manera diferente.
3. De adolescente, mis padres creían que yo _____, pero realmente no es así.
4. De niño/a, yo sabía que, para la edad que tengo ahora, yo _____. ¡Y es toda la verdad!
5. Nunca pensaba que yo _____, pero así es.
6. Al entrar en la universidad, pensaba que yo _____, pero todavía no me es posible.
7. De adolescente, mis amigos pensaban que yo _____, pero no tenían razón.

Paso 2

Todos los estudiantes en la clase deben presentar sus oraciones mientras el
profesor / la profesora escribe sus ideas en la pizarra. ¿Tienen Uds. muchas
respuestas en común?

LECTURA CULTURAL

Toluca y Guadalajara

De su cuarto en el hospital de
la capital llevan a don Fernando…
no a Toluca, para después ir en
coche a La Gavia, sino a otro hospital, en la Universidad de
Guadalajara. ¿Cómo son estas
dos ciudades, de momento
tan importantes para el señor
Castillo?

Toluca

Esta ciudad es la capital de es-
tado más alta de México. Por su altitud, en un valle a los pies del volcán Xinantécatl
(= *Nevado*), su clima es seco y frío, con una temperatura promedia[1] anual de 12°C
(53°F). Según un viejo dicho,[2] en Toluca sólo hay dos estaciones al año: invierno y la
estación del tren.

A pesar de su clima áspero,[3] Toluca tiene sus encantos. Es un centro industrial y
comercial que ofrece a sus habitantes algunas de las ventajas de una metrópoli sin todas las desventajas. Su calendario de fiestas típicas es largo, y larga es también su
tradición culinaria. Hay otro dicho que llama a esta ciudad «Toluca, ciudad choricera[4]
y dulcera[5]». La industria cho-
ricera se remonta[6] a la época
de los españoles, como
también algunos de sus dulces típicos: yemitas,[7] mazapa-
nes,[8] frutas cristalizadas…

Pero don Fernando no ha
regresado a Toluca, para
luego seguir el camino bien
conocido a la hacienda. Lo
han llevado en avión a otra
ciudad señorial.

En una escalera del Palacio de Gobierno, José Clemente
Orozco pintó al Padre Hidalgo empuñando una tea.[9] Su
figura es a la vez inspirada y amenazante.

Guadalajara

Guadalajara es la segunda
ciudad de México y capital del estado de Jalisco. Situada a 580 kilómetros al noroeste
de la capital, cuenta con una población de unos tres millones y medio de habitantes.

[1]*average* [2]*saying* [3]*harsh* [4]*of the* chorizos (*sausages*) [5]*of sweets* (*candy*) [6]*dates back* [7]*candied egg yolks* [8]*marzipan* (*almond-based candy*) [9]empuñando… *brandishing a torch*

Guadalajara es una hermosa ciudad colonial que, a pesar de las construcciones modernas, ha sabido mantener una atmósfera muy agradable. Pasear por la ciudad es una delicia, pues entre otras cosas tiene un clima templado, muy excepcional, durante todo el año. La ciudad también recibe el nombre de «ciudad de las rosas» y está llena de flores, árboles y fuentes.

Además de ser un importante y moderno núcleo económico para el país, Guadalajara es un centro histórico y cultural.

En el centro histórico de Guadalajara, hay una hermosa catedral que fue construida durante los siglos XVI–XVIII. Está rodeada de cuatro plazas.

- La Universidad de Guadalajara se fundó en 1792.
- Fue uno de los principales núcleos independentistas. Allí el Padre Hidalgo proclamó la abolición de la esclavitud en 1810.
- Se considera cuna[10] de los mariachis (los famosos conjuntos musicales), del rodeo mexicano o «charreada»* y del jarabe tapatío.

[10] *birthplace* (*cradle*)

6

INTERCAMBIO

Paso 1

Completa cada oración con algo lógico. Las oraciones no se refieren a ningún episodio en particular así que no tienes que limitarte al episodio actual. Pero trata de apuntar también cuándo y dónde ocurrió cada situación.

1. Pedro le dijo a Raquel que ella tendría que

   _____ .

2. En un momento, Raquel pensó que sería necesario

   _____ .

3. Ángela decidió que tendría que

   _____ .

* The members of mariachi bands wear costumes typical of Mexican **charros**, skilled horsemen who perform in the rodeos.

4.   Arturo pensó que Raquel necesitaría

_____.

5.   Pati se dio cuenta de que tendría que

_____.

Paso 2

En grupos de tres, cada persona debe leer sus oraciones. ¿Pueden los otros dos dar la información de cuándo y dónde ocurrió cada situación? Después, escojan las tres situaciones más difíciles de deducir para luego presentárselas a la clase. ¿Pueden los demás decir cuándo y dónde habría pasado cada situación? En general, ¿cuánto recuerdan de los episodios previos?

VOCABULARIO

Hablando de los viajes

la aduana	customs office
la agencia de viajes	travel agency
el/la agente de viajes	travel agent
el billete (*Spain*)	ticket
el boleto (*Span. Amer.*)	ticket
...de ida	. . . one way
...de ida y vuelta	. . . round-trip
la (primera, segunda) clase	(first, second) class
la clase turística	tourist class
el equipaje	luggage
la gira	tour
el/la guía	guide
la maleta	suitcase
el mapa	(*road, geographical*) map
el pasaje	passage, fare; ticket
el pasaporte	passport
el plano	map (*of a city*)
la reserva (*Spain*)	reservation
la reservación	reservation
la sección de (no) fumar	(non)smoking section

hacer/cancelar una reservación	to make/cancel a reservation
hacer la maleta	to pack one's suitcase
hacer una gira	to take a tour
tomar un (autobús, avión, barco, taxi, tren)	to take a (bus, plane, boat, taxi, train)

Repaso: el vuelo

Los lugares

el ascensor	elevator

Las condiciones

el vicio	bad habit

Los adjetivos

inesperado/a	unexpected

Las palabras adicionales

jugar (ue) (a las cartas) por dinero	to gamble (at cards)

42

YO INVITO*

Suggestion: Have students look at the photo, describe what they see, and talk about what they think might happen. Ask questions about the photo to prompt student discussion.

*My Treat

OBJETIVOS

The materials in **Lección 42** of the Textbook and the Workbook/Study Guide will help you better understand the video episode and take you beyond it, giving you additional information about places and characters in the series. The Textbook will also help you to develop skill in using the Spanish language. In this lesson, you will learn

- how to order a meal in a restaurant
- how to express *What would happen if . . .* in Spanish

You will also learn about Mexican food.

Be sure to work through all parts of the lesson. When you see a headphones symbol in the margin, listen to the CD for **Lección 42**. Answers or hints for many activities are given in Appendix 1. Be sure to check your answers for each activity before going on to the next one.

The interactive CD-ROM to accompany *Destinos* contains additional practice with the video storyline and will help you improve your skills in Spanish.

Preliminary: See Faculty Guide for additional information and activities for this lesson.
• **Variation:** For activities marked with the headphones icon, you may wish to read from the Audioscript instead of playing the CD.
• **Suggestion:** Make sure students are familiar with the activities before you read from the Audioscript or play the CD.

BEFORE VIEWING . . .

1

PREPARACIÓN

Suggestions:
• Before watching the video, go over the vocabulary list at the end of the chapter and have students pronounce the words after you.
• Assign *Preparación* activities as homework and then go over them quickly in class before viewing the video.

Actividad A.
Paso 1

Escucha el repaso que va a presentar el narrador al principio del **Episodio 42**.

Paso 2

Ahora contesta las siguientes preguntas sobre el **Episodio 41**.

1. ¿Sí o no? ¿Han llegado Ángela y Roberto a un acuerdo sobre la venta del apartamento?
2. ¿Cierto o falso? Ángela y Roberto no pueden conocer a su abuelo todavía.
3. En casa de Pedro, Carlos
   a. _____ confesó que había sacado fondos de la oficina.
   b. _____ admitió que tenía problemas en manejar el dinero.

Act. A, Suggestion: You may want to have students do this activity in pairs and review answers as whole class.

Act. A, *Paso 2,* Answers: 1. *No* 2. *Cierto* 3. a

Para pensar...

Cuando Raquel baje para ir a cenar con Arturo, se va a encontrar con Luis y con Arturo. ¿Qué harías tú en esta situación? ¿Cómo le presentarías a Luis a Arturo? ¿Invitarías a Luis a cenar?

Actividad B.
Paso 1

Luis les va a hablar a Raquel y Arturo de su vida profesional. Escucha una parte de lo que les dice y luego contesta la pregunta.

Según lo que acabas de escuchar, Luis es una persona

a. vanidosa.　　b. discreta.　　c. sencilla (*simple*).

Act. B, Suggestion: You may want to have students work in pairs, roleplaying the dialogue.

Act. B, Answers:
Paso 1: a
Paso 2: 1. *mucho*
2. *impresionar*

Paso 2

Escucha la conversación una vez más. Puedes leerla al mismo tiempo, si quieres. Luego completa las oraciones.

RAQUEL: Y tú, Luis, ¿qué has hecho durante todos estos años? ¿Sigues trabajando en la misma compañía?

LUIS: No. Al poco tiempo de estar en Nueva York, encontré una mejor oferta de trabajo. Así que renuncié a mi antiguo puesto y me fui a esta nueva compañía. Me ha ido muy bien; no me puedo quejar. Soy ahora vicepresidente de la compañía.

1. En su vida profesional, Luis ha tenido... mucho/poco... éxito.
2. La intención de Luis al decir esto es irritar/impresionar... a Raquel.

. . . AFTER VIEWING

2

¿TIENES BUENA MEMORIA?

Actividad A. En este episodio

¿Te acuerdas de los acontecimientos más importantes de este episodio? Completa el siguiente resumen.

Personas: Arturo, Luis, Raquel
Verbos: esperaba a Pati, había salido a tomar algo, hablaba con Pati, hablando mucho, pagando la cuenta, salieron a cenar

Act. A, Answers: 1. *Luis* 2. *Raquel* 3. *salieron a cenar* 4. *pagando la cuenta* 5. *esperaba a Pati* 6. *había salido a tomar algo*

Cuando Raquel bajó en el ascensor para reunirse con Arturo, para su gran sorpresa _____¹ estaba allí también.

_____² invitó a Luis a acompañarlos, y los tres

_____³ Raquel terminó[a]

_____⁴ Más tarde, poco antes de acostarse Raquel, sonó[b] el teléfono. ¿Quién sería?[c]

En Nueva York, Juan _____⁵ en su apartamento, pero ella no regresó. Después de ensayar[d] con los actores, _____⁶ con su asistente.

[a]*ended up* [b]*rang* [c]¿Quién... *Who could it be?* [d]*rehearsing*

 ## Actividad B. Momentos importantes

¿Recuerdas estas escenas? Escúchalas en el CD y escribe la letra de la foto a que corresponde.

Act. B, Answers: 1. b 2. c 3. a 4. c 5. b

a.

b.

c.

1. _____
2. _____
3. _____
4. _____
5. _____

Act. C, Answers: 1. *Luis* 2. *Arturo* 3. *Arturo* 4. *Raquel* 5. *Raquel*

Act. C, Follow-up: Have students, working in small groups, brainstorm characteristics of Luis and Arturo and decide whom Raquel should be with, whom she shouldn't be with, and why.

Actividad C. ¿Qué recuerdas?

Con dos compañeros/as, hagan un resumen de lo que pasó durante la cena que tuvieron Raquel, Arturo y Luis. Las siguientes oraciones son sólo sugerencias de lo que pueden comentar.

1. Alguien habló de su trabajo y de su éxito.
2. Alguien tuvo que defenderse de una crítica de su profesión.
3. Alguien recordó una conversación previa.

4. Alguien insistió en pagar la cuenta.
5. Alguien jugaba con algo y dijo que era un regalo.

Para pensar...

1. Después de esta cena, ¿qué impresión tienes de Luis? ¿Cómo es su personalidad? ¿Crees que Raquel todavía siente algo por él? Y Arturo, ¿qué estará pensando esta noche?
2. Al final del episodio, el teléfono suena en la habitación de Raquel. ¿Quién será?

3 VOCABULARIO DEL TEMA

En un restaurante

el camarero/la camarera (el mesero/la mesera, el mozo/la moza)	waiter/waitress	
el/la cliente	customer, client	
la cuenta	bill, check	
la orden	order	**la taza** cup
la propina	tip	**el vaso** glass
el antojito (*Mex.*)	appetizer	**los cubiertos** silverware
el aperitivo	appetizer	**la cuchara** spoon
el plato principal	entrée	**el cuchillo** knife
el postre	dessert	**el tenedor** fork
la copa	wine goblet	**invitar** to invite (*with the intention of paying*)
el pimentero	pepper shaker/grinder	**ordenar** (*Mex.*), **pedir (i, i)** to order (*a meal*)
el plato	plate	**tomar** to have something to eat/drink
el salero	salt shaker	
la servilleta	napkin	

¿Me pasa el salero / el pimentero, por favor?   *Will you pass me the salt/pepper shaker, please?*

¿Me trae la cuenta / otra servilleta, por favor?   *Will you bring me the check / another napkin, please?*

Note the following about the preceding vocabulary and expressions.

- **Camarero** is the most widely accepted term for *waiter*. The term **mesero** is used primarily in Mexico.
- The term **ordenar** is widely used in Mexico. In other parts of the Spanish-speaking world, **pedir** is more common.
- To refer to hors d'oeuvres, use the terms **los antojitos** or **la botana** in Mexico, but **tapas** in Spain. You will hear other words in other parts of the Spanish-speaking world.

Actividad A.   ¿En qué consiste una cena?
Paso 1

Pon las siguientes oraciones en orden numérico (del 1 al 7), según ocurren cuando uno come fuera.

a. _____ Después de comer, el cliente pide la cuenta.

b. _____ Luego les pregunta si quieren pedir el plato principal.

c. _____ El camarero les pregunta a los clientes si quieren tomar algo.

d. _____ Para terminar, les sirve a los clientes el café y el postre, si es que ellos quieren.

e. _____ Luego les pregunta si quieren un plato para empezar.

f. _____ Después de servir la comida, un buen camarero quiere saber si todo está bien o si los clientes necesitan algo.

g. _____ Si la propina está incluida, el cliente deja una propina adicional cuando el servicio ha sido muy bueno.

Paso 2

Ahora escucha el CD para verificar tus respuestas. ¡OJO! Las oraciones que oirás no son idénticas a las del **Paso 1**.

Actividad B.   En un restaurante

Empareja las siguientes oraciones con el dibujo que sugieren.

1. Mesero, me trae otra copa de vino tinto, por favor.
2. Mozo, faltan dos cubiertos en esta mesa.
3. Me pasas el salero y el pimentero, por favor.
4. Ese camarero es muy bueno. Vamos a dejarle una buena propina. ¿Te parece?
5. Todo estaba excelente. ¿Nos trae la cuenta, por favor?
6. Este tenedor está sucio. ¿Me trae otro, por favor?
7. Necesito otra cuchara, por favor.
8. Dejé caer la servilleta. ¿Me trae otra, por favor?

a. _____   b. _____   c. _____   d. _____

e. _____   f. _____   g. _____   h. _____

Actividad C.   Los restaurantes y yo

Indica solamente las oraciones que te describen a ti.

1. Siempre dejo de propina la menor cantidad de dinero posible.
2. Si no me ha gustado el servicio, no dejo ninguna propina.
3. Siempre pongo la servilleta en mis rodillas (*knees*), no importa donde sea: un restaurante elegante, McDonald's…

4. Creo que la costumbre de incluir la propina en la cuenta es buena.
5. Cuando como pollo frito, uso tenedor y cuchillo.
6. Creo que no es bueno llevarse la comida a la boca con las manos.
7. Casi ninguno de mis amigos invita a nadie a comer. Cuando comemos juntos, compartimos la cuenta.
8. Si faltan cubiertos en la mesa, los «robo» de otra mesa.

Nota cultural, ¡OJO!: Differentiate between *to invite* in English and in Spanish. In English, the person doing the inviting has no obligation to pay for the person being invited. In Spanish, the person who does the inviting fully expects to and wants to pay for the person being invited. It is sometimes inappropriate and often futile to insist that the person who invited you allow you to pay for your share of the meal.

Nota cultural, Optional: Have students interview native speakers about tipping customs in the Spanish-speaking world and report their findings to the class. Have them ask what the standard tip is for taxi drivers, delivery people, bellhops, food servers, etc.

Nota cultural   En un restaurante hispánico

The customs related to eating out in the Hispanic world do not vary as greatly as the names for different food items. You may wish to note the following.

- In Spain and in other parts of the Spanish-speaking world, the term **servicio** (which often appears on a restaurant check) refers to the waiter. **El servicio está incluido** means that the tip has been included in the bill.
- When the tip is included, it is customary to leave the waiter any small change that is returned to the table (unless service has been really awful). Only if the service has been especially good or if the waiter has had to do something extraordinary does one add a substantial amount to the tip.
- Raquel orders a bottle of red wine with a direct command to the waiter: **Traiga una botella de vino tinto**. However, one should not limit oneself to direct commands only, because in many places this would seem abrupt or even impolite. Note the examples given in the **Vocabulario del tema** section: **¿Me trae (un tenedor), por favor?** A request can also be made with a direct statement: **Me trae (un tenedor), por favor**.
- When Hispanic friends go out, it is customary for one of them (the person who says **Yo invito**) to pay the check. When the check is shared, the occasion is referred to as going out **a la americana**.

UN POCO DE GRAMÁTICA

The Workbook/Study Guide contains more detailed explanation and practice of this grammar point.

Expressing What Would Happen If . . .

Here are two questions that Raquel asked herself during the story review.

RAQUEL: ¿Cómo **sería** mi vida **si**...   RAQUEL: *What would my life be like if . . .*

todavía **estuviera** con Luis?   *I were still with Luis?*
yo **viviera** en Nueva York?   *I lived in New York?*

Did you notice the verb forms used in each part of the sentences? The past subjunctive follows the word **si** (*if*) and the conditional is used in the other part of the sentence. You will learn more about sentences like these in the Workbook/Study Guide.

Suggestions: Before introducing the conditional with *si* clauses, review the conditional forms that have been studied. Have students form human sentences. Write out several conditional sentences on strips of paper and cut them in half, separating the *si* clauses from the main clauses. Distribute the *si* clauses to half the class, and the main clauses to the other half. Have students with the *si* clauses read their parts. Students with the appropriate main clause must read their parts in order to form a complete sentence. You may want to have students circulate to find their match. **Variation:** Write names of famous people, animals, and objects on cards and distribute to students. Have individual students say what they would do if they were the person or thing named on the card. The rest of the class tries to guess who or what they are. This may be done in pairs, small groups, or the entire class. For example, the student says *Podría volar.* The class says *Si fueras pájaro.*

Actividad.   ¿Qué pasaría si... ?
Paso 1

Pon números (del 1 al 4) en los espacios en blanco para indicar cuál es más importante (1) y cuál es menos importante (4) para ti en cada grupo de posibilidades.

1. Yo estaría muy contento/a si
   - _____ pudiera encontrar un nuevo trabajo.
   - _____ sacara una A en esta clase.
   - _____ tuviera un auto nuevo.
   - _____ viera a mi familia con más frecuencia.

2. Al graduarme de la universidad, aceptaría un trabajo sólo si
   - _____ estuviera cerca de mi familia.
   - _____ el sueldo fuera muy bueno.
   - _____ ofreciera muchos beneficios y un buen plan de jubilación (*retirement*).
   - _____ la compañia (el lugar, la escuela...) tuviera mucho prestigio.

3. Esta clase sería major si
   - _____ hubiera menos tarea fuera de clase.
   - _____ fuera más pequeña (es decir, si no hubiera tantas personas).
   - _____ el profesor / la profesora explicara más la gramática.
   - _____ *Destinos* tuviera menos episodios.

Paso 2

Ahora compara tus respuestas con las de dos o tres compañeros. ¿Qué revelan las respuestas sobre la vida de Uds.? ¿sobre su personalidad?

5 LECTURA CULTURAL

La comida mexicana... dentro y fuera de México

Hace mucho tiempo que[1] la comida mexicana es[2] muy popular en los Estados Unidos. En casi todas las ciudades hay restaurantes que la sirven. Una de las grandes cadenas[3] de «comida rápida» se especializa en lo que se conoce en este país como platos mexicanos, y en las cafeterías y restaurantes de todas partes se sirven nachos y tacos.

Pero ¡cuidado! Toda comida que se conoce por el nombre de «mexicana» no lo es necesariamente...

La comida mexicana en México

La cocina[4] mexicana es muy rica y variada. Su origen se remonta[5] a antes de la llegada de los españoles. Los indios ya cultivaban el maíz, que servía de base para la preparación de una gran variedad de platos.

[1]Hace... *For a long time* [2]*has been* [3]*chains* [4]*cuisine, cooking* [5]se... *dates back*

Lectura cultural, Preguntas: 1. *¿Cómo es la comida mexicana?* (*muy rica y variada*) 2. *¿Qué ingrediente sirve de base para muchos platos?* (*el maíz*) 3. *¿Qué influencias cambiaron la comida mexicana?* (*las frutas y los cereales de los españoles, las crepas de los franceses, la comida mexicoamericana como los burritos*) 4. *¿De qué es hecha una tortilla?* (*de maíz o de harina de trigo*) 5. *¿Cuáles son los ingredientes de mole poblano?* (*una salsa de chocolate y ajíes, se sirve con pollo o con guajolote*) 6. *¿Por qué no va a conocer un burrito o unas sopaipillas el mesero en un restaurante mexicano?* (*porque no es comida mexicana auténtica*) 7. *¿De dónde vienen los burritos y las fajitas?* (*del estado de Texas*).

Después de la llegada de los españoles, la cocina de México cambió, ya que se introdujeron nuevos productos como frutas y cereales. La fusión de las dos cocinas dio como resultado la mayoría de los platos que se comen hoy en día. En la época del emperador austríaco Maximiliano (1861–1867), la cocina local se vio influida otra vez, ahora por la cocina francesa. Esto explica en parte la frecuente presencia de las crepas en los menús mexicanos.

El mole poblano

La base de la comida mexicana es la tortilla. Es un tipo de pan que se hace por lo general de maíz o de harina de trigo.[6] Las tortillas no sólo se sirven como acompañantes de la comida principal, como el pan, sino que también se usan para hacer varios otros platos. Por ejemplo:

- la enchilada: carne picada[7] bien condimentada[8] y envuelta[9] en una tortilla enrollada;[10] se sirve con una salsa de ají[11] (enchiladas verdes)
- el taco: una tortilla rellena de carne picada, lechuga, tomate y queso blanco; se sirve a menudo con una salsa picante.[12]

Pero hay otros platos —menos conocidos en los Estados Unidos— que también son típicos de la cocina mexicana.

- el mole poblano: una salsa hecha, entre otras cosas, de chocolate y ajíes; se sirve a veces con pollo o guajolote[13]
- el filete de guachinango relleno de huitlacoche[14]

En total, la cocina mexicana ofrece una cantidad de platos apetitosos y llenos de color: antojitos, sopas, carnes y pescados que varían según las regiones. Pero si tú pides en un restaurante mexicano un burrito o, de postre, unas sopaipillas, el mesero probablemente no va a conocer esos platos. ¿Por qué? Porque no son comida mexicana auténtica.

La comida mexicana en los Estados Unidos

No es extraño que la comida mexicana haya influido mucho en la cocina del suroeste de los Estados Unidos. Esta región perteneció a México en una época, y con el cambio de gobierno no se cambiaron las costumbres de los habitantes.

Tampoco es de extrañar[15] que los habitantes de esta región —texanos, nuevomexicanos, etcétera— hayan hecho sus propios inventos muy a la mexicana. Un buen ejemplo son los burritos, un plato de origen texano. Hoy día los burritos (tortillas enrolladas y rellenas de frijoles, queso, pollo o carne) se encuentran hasta en la sección de comida congelada[16] de los supermercados en los Estados Unidos.

Otro plato de invención texana es la fajita: una tortilla de maíz rellena de carne en escabeche[17] preparada rápidamente en una parrilla. Al principio la palabra fajita se refería al tipo de carne que se usaba, el llamado *skirt steak*. Ahora, en los Estados Unidos, la palabra fajita ha venido a significar una manera de preparar algo; es decir, cortado en largas fajas.[18] Por eso se puede hablar de fajitas de pollo, de cerdo, de salmón…

Ahora las fajitas son populares en todas partes de los Estados Unidos… ¡y también en el norte de México! Así que representan una manera en que la cultura mexicoamericana ha influido en la cocina de México.

[6]harina… *wheat flour* [7]*chopped* [8]*seasoned* [9]*wrapped* [10]*rolled* [11]*chile* [12]*hot, spicy*
[13]*turkey* [14]el… *fillet of red snapper filled with, among other ingredients, a mushroom that grows on corn stalks* [15]Tampoco… *Nor is it strange* [16]*frozen* [17]*marinade* [18]*strips*

6 **INTERCAMBIO**

Paso 1
Contesta cada pregunta a continuación.

1. Si estuvieras en un restaurante y al camarero se le olvidó algo en la cuenta, ¿qué harías?
2. Si estuvieras con unos amigos en un restaurante y vieras que un cliente salió sin pagar la cuenta, ¿qué harías?
3. Si estuvieras de primera cita con alguien y esa persona ofreciera pagar la cuenta, ¿qué harías?
4. Si tú fueras Raquel en este momento sabiendo que Luis todavía te tenía un cariño especial, ¿qué harías?
5. Si tú fueras Pati (o Juan) con los mismos problemas matrimoniales, ¿qué harías?

Paso 2
Cada persona debe presentar sus respuestas a la clase mientras el profesor / la profesora anota la información en la pizarra y marca ideas repetidas.

Paso 3
Como clase, analicen la información en la pizarra. ¿Qué tendencias morales y éticas indican las respuestas de la clase a los números 1 a 3? ¿Qué indican las respuestas a 4 y 5 en cuanto a la manera en que resolverían estos tipos de conflictos personales?

VOCABULARIO

En un restaurante (In a Restaurant)

el/la cliente	customer, client
la cuenta	bill, check
el mesero/la mesera, el mozo/la moza	waiter/waitress
la orden	order
la propina	tip
el antojito (*Mex.*)	appetizer
el aperitivo	appetizer
el plato principal	entrée
el postre	dessert
los cubiertos	silverware
la cuchara	spoon
el cuchillo	knife
el tenedor	fork

la copa	wine goblet
el pimentero	pepper shaker/grinder
el plato	plate
el salero	salt shaker
la servilleta	napkin
la taza	cup
el vaso	glass
ordenar (*Mex.*), pedir (**i, i**)	to order (*a meal*)
¿Me pasa... , por favor?	Will you please pass me . . . ?
¿Me trae... , por favor?	Will you please bring me . . . ?
yo invito	(it's) my treat

Repaso: **el camarero/la camarera**

LECCIÓN 43

SEREMOS CUATRO*

*There Will Be Four of Us

OBJETIVOS

The materials in **Lección 43** of the Textbook and the Workbook/Study Guide will help you better understand the video episode and take you beyond it giving you additional information about places and characters in the series. The Textbook will also help you to develop skill in using the Spanish language. In this lesson, you will learn

- vocabulary related to staying in hotels
- ways to express what you had done

You will also learn about women in the Hispanic world.

Be sure to work through all parts of the lesson. When you see a headphones symbol in the margin, listen to the CD for **Lección 43**. Answers or hints for many activities are given in Appendix 1. Be sure to check your answers for each activity before going on to the next one.

The interactive CD-ROM to accompany *Destinos* contains additional practice with the video storyline and will help you improve your skills in Spanish.

413

Preliminary: See Faculty Guide for additional information and activities for this lesson.
● **Variation:** For activities marked with the headphones icon, you may wish to read from the Audioscript instead of playing the CD.
● **Suggestion:** Make sure students are familiar with the activities before you read from the Audioscript or play the CD.

 BEFORE VIEWING . . .

1

PREPARACIÓN

Suggestions:
● Before watching the video, go over the vocabulary list at the end of the chapter and have students pronounce the words after you.
● Assign *Preparación* activities as homework and then go over them quickly in class before viewing the video.

Act. A, *Paso 1,* **Answers:**
1. e 2. a 3. c or d 4. a 5. a
Paso 2: 1. Pati 2. Arturo y Luis 3. Luis o Arturo 4. Luis 5. *su madre, Luis*

Actividad A.
Paso 1
Identifica a las personas a quienes se refieren las siguientes oraciones. Primero, identifica el sujeto de la oración con la letra (a–e) correspondiente.

a. Raquel   c. Arturo   e. Juan
b. Pati   d. Luis

1. ____ Esperaba a *alguien* en un apartamento en los Estados Unidos.
2. ____ Durante una cena, se encontraba entre *dos personas que se observaban con atención.*
3. ____ Durante una cena, observaba a *un posible rival.*
4. ____ Le sorprendió la llegada de *una persona de su pasado.*
5. ____ Se enteró del papel (*role*) de *otra persona* en el viaje de *alguien* a México.

Paso 2
Ahora escucha el CD para verificar tus respuestas. ¿Puedes sustituir la información indicada con letras itálicas por el nombre de una persona o personas?

Act. A, *Paso 1,* **Follow-up:** Have students create an additional statement similar to those in the activity, then exchange papers with a partner and identify the person(s) referred to in each other's statements.

Para pensar, **Suggestion:** Ask questions of whole class. Accept any possibilities as there are no (in)correct responses.

> ### Para pensar...
>
> La madre de Raquel la ha puesto en una situación complicada... difícil. Si tú fueras Raquel, ¿qué harías?
>
> 1. ¿Llamarías a tu mamá para hablar con ella? ¿Qué le dirías?
> 2. ¿Hablarías con Arturo en seguida? ¿O esperarías que él no supiera quién era Luis?

Actividad B.
En este episodio varios personajes van a hablar con un agente de viajes en una agencia. Si quieres, lee brevemente el vocabulario relacionado con los hoteles en la sección **Vocabulario del tema** en esta lección. No tienes que aprender el vocabulario de memoria antes de ver el episodio.

> ### Para pensar...
>
> Al final del **Episodio 42**, alguien llamó a Raquel por teléfono. En tu opinión, ¿quién fue?

Para comprender, **Suggestion:** Ask whole class what the words probably mean. Encourage them to try to explain them using other Spanish words before resorting to an English translation. Make sure students understand the words before continuing with the video.

Para comprender un poco más

la censura   En algunos países los escritores no pueden decir siempre lo que piensan porque hay un sistema de **censura** oficial.

se hace tarde   En un momento Raquel ve que **se** le **hace tarde**. Se va en seguida para no llegar tarde.

 . . . AFTER VIEWING

2

¿TIENES BUENA MEMORIA?

Act. A, *Paso 1,* **Suggestion:** Give students about 2 minutes to complete *Paso 1* individually.

Actividad A.   ¿A quién se refiere?
Paso 1

Act. A, *Paso 1,* **Answers:** 1. *Arturo, Luis y Raquel* 2. *Luis, Ángela y Juan*

Identifica a los personajes que corresponden a las siguientes descripciones. Las descripciones se refieren a lo que pasó en el **Episodio 43**.

1. tres personajes que hicieron reservaciones
2. tres personajes que recibieron una sorpresa

Act. A, *Paso 2,* **Suggestion:** Give students about 4 minutes to complete *Paso 2.* You may wish to write a model sentence on the board: *Hizo reservaciones en un hotel de Zihuatanejo.* (*Luis*)

Paso 2
Ahora escoge uno de los grupos (1 ó 2). Tu compañero/a usará el otro. Identifica con una oración a cada personaje de tu grupo. (La oración debe relacionarse con el tema del episodio.) ¿Cuáles fueron las reservaciones que hicieron los unos y qué sorpresas recibieron los otros?

Act. A, *Paso 2,* **Point out:** Students do not use the names of characters in their sentences. Instead, the actions described must be specific enough to identify the person.

Paso 3
Presenta tus oraciones a tu compañero/a para que te dé el nombre del personaje descrito (*described*).

Act. A, *Paso 3,* **Suggestion:** Give pairs of students 2 minutes to present their sentences to each other and try to name the characters described.

Actividad B.   Detalles
Completa las oraciones con la información apropiada.

1. Juan le confiesa a Pati que no está muy contento con su carrera porque
   a. _____ quiere trabajar en el teatro y no ha tenido éxito.
   b. _____ no tiene una posición estable en la universidad.
   c. _____ los libros que ha escrito no le han producido suficiente dinero.

Act. B, Suggestion: Give students about 3 minutes to complete the activity individually or in pairs and then compare answers as whole class.

Para pensar, **Suggestion:** Put the questions to the whole class. Ask for a show of hands to see how the class reacts to each possibility. Do not reveal any new information.

Para pensar...

¿Qué va a pasar con Juan y Pati, ahora que Juan le ha confesado a ella lo que realmente le pasa? ¿Es posible que se separen por un tiempo? ¿que se divorcien? ¿O crees que ahora se podrán reconciliar?

2. Cuando piensa en Luis, Raquel recuerda el momento en que
    a. _____ se conocieron en una fiesta.
    b. _____ Luis le dijo que se iba a Nueva York.
    c. _____ se besaron por primera vez.

3. En la agencia de viajes, Arturo
    a. _____ sólo hizo las reservaciones; no compró los billetes.
    b. _____ lo arregló todo, sin haber hablado con Raquel.
    c. _____ llamó a Raquel al hotel para consultarla.

4. En la agencia de viajes, Luis
    a. _____ sólo hizo las reservaciones; no compró los billetes.
    b. _____ lo arregló todo, sin haber hablado con Raquel.
    c. _____ llamó a Raquel al hotel para consultarla.

Para pensar...

Arturo y Luis (y también Raquel) han ido a la misma agencia de viajes, pero no hicieron la misma cosa. ¿Qué diferencias de su personalidad revelan las acciones de Arturo y Luis en esta situación? ¿Cómo crees que Raquel va a reaccionar cuando sepa lo que los dos han hecho?

---

5. Hoy Ángela, Roberto y Arturo piensan
    a. _____ hacer una gira por México.
    b. _____ ir a Guadalajara a conocer a don Fernando.
    c. _____ hablar más del asunto del apartamento.

3

VOCABULARIO DEL TEMA

En un hotel

el baño privado (con ducha)	private bath (with shower)
la cabaña	bungalow; cabana
la habitación (individual/doble)	(single/double) room
el hotel de (cinco) estrellas	(five)-star hotel
el plan económico/ de lujo	economy/deluxe plan
la tarifa	rate, price
el buceo	snorkeling
la cancha de tenis	tennis court
la piscina	swimming pool
la playa (privada)	(private) beach

alojarse (en) to stay (at) (*accommodations*) **confirmar** to confirm	**hacer una reservación (para el próximo fin de semana)** to make a reserva- tion (for next weekend)

Actividad A. Los planes de Arturo y Luis

Vas a escuchar otra vez la conversación entre Arturo y el agente de viajes, luego la conversación entre Luis y el mismo agente.

Paso 1

Primero, lee las siguientes oraciones. En el **Paso 2**, vas a indicar a quién se refieren, a Luis (**L**) o a Arturo (**A**).

L A   1. Quiere información sobre un hotel con cabañas.
L A   2. Le interesa conocer una playa.
L A   3. Hace reservaciones, pero no las paga todavía.
L A   4. Lo arregla todo porque no piensa consultar con nadie.
L A   5. Hace reservaciones para dos personas.
L A   6. Hace reservaciones para cuatro personas.
L A   7. Pide tres habitaciones.
L A   8. Parece que quiere solamente una habitación.
L A   9. Quiere ir a Cozumel.
L A 10. Le interesa ir a Zihuatanejo.
L A 11. No le interesan los planes económicos.

Paso 2

Ahora escucha las conversaciones y completa el **Paso 1**.

Actividad B. Lo que planea Raquel

Escucha otra vez la conversación entre Raquel y el mismo agente de viajes. Luego contesta las preguntas.

1. ¿Adónde quería viajar Raquel, a Guadalajara o a Toluca?
2. ¿Cuántas personas van a viajar en total, dos, tres o cuatro? (¡OJO!)
3. ¿Cómo quería Raquel que viajaran, en avión o en tren?
4. ¿Quiere o no quiere que le recomienden un hotel?
5. ¿Compró Raquel los pasajes o solamente quería informarse?

Actividad C. En el hotel
Paso 1

Escribe definiciones de cinco palabras o frases del **Vocabulario del tema**.

MODELO: la piscina → Es un lugar donde se nada.

Paso 2

Presenta cada definición a tu compañero/a para que te dé la palabra o frase definida.

Actividad D.   Planeando un viaje

Imagina que vas a una agencia de viajes para planear un viaje. Decide adónde quieres ir. Luego completa las oraciones para indicar las preguntas que le harías al agente.

1. Quiero información sobre _____, por favor.

2. ¿Cuál es la manera más _____ de llegar a

    _____?

3. ¿Me puede informar sobre los horarios de

    _____?

4. Quiero alojarme en _____. ¿Qué posibilidades

    hay?

5. En _____, me interesa

    _____ (actividades). ¿Qué me puede decir

    de eso?

4

UN POCO DE GRAMÁTICA

The Workbook/Study Guide contains more detailed explanation and practice of this grammar point.

Talking About What Had Happened Before . . .

To describe what had already happened before another event took place, use the imperfect of **haber** (**había, habías**...) with the past participle (the form that ends in **-do**).

Raquel ya **había cenado** con Luis y Arturo cuando volvió a su habitación.	*Raquel had already eaten dinner with Luis and Arturo when she returned to her room.*

Remember that a few past participles are irregular: **hecho** (**hacer**), **dicho** (**decir**), and so on.

Actividad.   ¿Qué había pasado?
Paso 1

Indica cuáles de las siguientes oraciones describen tu propia experiencia. Rellena (*Fill in*) también los espacios en blanco con información verdadera para ti.

1. A los quince años, yo
    a. _____ ya había viajado en avión.
    b. _____ ya había visitado otro país.

    c. ____ ya había decidido a qué universidad quería ir.

    d. ____ nunca había vivido en un apartamento.

    e. ____ nunca había tenido novio/a.

    f. ____ ya había estudiado una lengua extranjera.

    g. ____ ya había aprendido a _____.

    h. ____ nunca había ido a _____.

Act., *Paso 2,* Point out: Questions in the *tú* form are created by simply changing *había* to *habías*.

2. Antes de tomar esta clase, yo

    a. ____ ya había estudiado español.

    b. ____ nunca había oído nada sobre *Destinos*.

    c. ____ ya había visitado un país de habla española.

    d. ____ no había tomado ninguna clase de lenguas extranjeras.

    e. ____ ya había visto algunos programas en español en la tele.

    f. ____ ya había aprendido algo sobre las culturas hispánicas.

    g. ____ ya había sabido _____.

    h. ____ nunca había sabido _____.

Paso 2

Ahora escoge por lo menos dos de tus respuestas del número 1 y dos del número 2 en el **Paso 1**. Luego, hazle preguntas a tu compañero/a para saber si dieron las mismas respuestsas.

    MODELO: TÚ: A los quince años, ¿tú ya habías viajado en avión?

                COMPAÑERO/A: No, pero sí había viajado en crucero (*cruise ship*).

Act., *Paso 2,* Variation: To practice the past perfect, play a *Firma aquí* activity. Have student choose 3 or 4 items from each section of *Paso 1* to use as questions, such as *A los quince años, ¿ya habías viajado en avión?* Have students circulate in class asking and answering the questions and gathering the signatures of classmates who respond with *Sí.* Then have them report their findings to the class, using the model *A los quince años, _____ había viajado a la Florida en avión.*

5

LECTURA CULTURAL

Lectura cultural, **Suggestion:** Assign as homework and go over quickly in class. Remind students that they should not expect to understand every word of the reading, but rather to get the main ideas.

La mujer en el mundo hispano

La situación de la mujer en la sociedad hispana, igual que la de la mujer en este país, ha cambiado mucho en este siglo. Hoy en día, la posibilidad de quedarse en casa y ocuparse de la familia todavía existe. Además, en los países menos desarrollados[1] económica y socialmente, hay mujeres que todavía trabajan en el campo (a veces, al lado de los hombres). Pero muchas mujeres ahora tienen a su disposición otras alternativas.

La voz[2] del presente

El cambio se ha notado mucho en los últimos treinta años, y ahora se puede hablar de varias generaciones de mujeres que han recibido un mejor trato en general y han tenido más oportunidades. Leamos lo que dijo una mujer peruana que ha tenido éxito en los Estados Unidos como directora de un instituto lingüístico.

[1]*developed*   [2]*voice*

[Mi padre] no quería que fuéramos al colegio. Porque él no tuvo buena educación. Mi madre… ella quería que estudiáramos, y realmente somos productos de mi madre porque ella tenía un carácter muy fuerte. No podíamos faltar[3] [a la escuela]. Teníamos que hacer tarea. Ella es la que nos ha empujado[4] a entrar a la universidad. Mi papá decía: «¿Para qué van a estudiar si realmente me van a ayudar en el campo?» Mi madre decía: «No, mis hijos tienen que hacer algo más.»

Cuando la estructura social y económica del país lo permite,* muchas mujeres han tenido éxito en el mundo profesional. Trabajan en grandes empresas y ocupan puestos que hace poco estaban reservados a los hombres. Hoy día es común ver a mujeres ejecutivas, abogadas, profesoras universitarias, periodistas, médicos o arquitectas. Al mismo tiempo, muchas se interesan o intervienen activamente en la vida económica y política de su comunidad.

El pasado en el presente

Al mismo tiempo, hay mucho por hacer todavía. Ya en el siglo XVII una monja[5] mexicana, Sor Juana Inés de la Cruz, escribió los siguientes versos:[6]

¿Cuáles crees que son los papeles[12] de esta pareja española? ¿Quién trabaja fuera de casa? ¿Quién cuida al niño? Hoy día es difícil contestar estas preguntas. Hace cincuenta años hubiera sido[13] más fácil.

> Hombres necios[7] que acusáis
> a la mujer sin razón,
> sin ver que sois la ocasión
> de lo mismo que culpáis[8]…

Lectura cultural, Preguntas: ¿Cierto o Falso? 1. El papel de la mujer en los países hispanos es siempre lo de ama de casa. (F) 2. En los países hispanos, es más difícil que las mujeres consigan un buen trabajo que los hombres. (C) 3. Como en este país, las mujeres en los países hispanos todavía no reciben un trato igual en el mundo profesional. (C)

Así denunció la actitud intransigente y represiva de los hombres de su época y del hombre en general. Otra poeta famosa, la argentina Alfonsina Storni (1892–1938), siguió esa temática con una voz más moderna:

> Hombre pequeñito, hombre pequeñito,
> Suelta[9] a tu canario que quiere volar…
> Yo soy el canario, hombre pequeñito,
> Déjame saltar.[10]

Para algunas mujeres hispanas de este década, el grito de estas dos autoras todavía conserva su vigencia.[11]

[3]*skip classes, not attend*   [4]*nos… pushed us*   [5]*nun, sister*   [6]*lines (of poetry)*   [7]*stupid*   [8]*la… the cause of what you criticize*   [9]*Set loose, Free*   [10]*fly away*   [11]*vigor*   [12]*roles*   [13]*hubiera… it would have been*

---

* En los países menos industrializados, la posición de la mujer media (*average*) no ha cambiado tan radicalmente como ha pasado en países como España, la Argentina y Chile.

***Intercambio*, Suggestion:** Prepare a table on the board to compare the kinds of hotels students have stayed in. Use categories to indicate the kind of hotel, the kind of room and room accommodations, the city or area, and the available activities. Have students make generalizations based on the information.

INTERCAMBIO

Paso 1

Si has quedado en un hotel durante las vacaciones, apunta información sobre el hotel (económico, de lujo, con baño privado, etcétera), el lugar (en la playa, en las montañas, cerca de un parque temático, etcétera) y las actividades disponibles en el hotel. Si no has quedado en un hotel nunca, inventa información sobre un hotel interesante. Prepara también preguntas sobre hoteles.

Paso 2

Entrevista a tu compañero/a sobre un hotel en el que se ha alojado. Contesta sus preguntas sobre tu experiencia. Comparen los hoteles que describen y presenten la información a la clase.

VOCABULARIO

En un hotel

el baño privado (con ducha)	private bath (with shower)
el buceo	snorkeling
la cabaña	cabin
la cancha de tenis	tennis court
la habitación (individual/doble)	(single/double) room
el hotel de (cinco) estrellas	(five)-star hotel
la piscina	pool
el plan económico/ de lujo	economy/deluxe plan

la playa (privada)	(private) beach
la tarifa	rate, price
alojarse (en)	to stay (at) (*accommodations*)
confirmar	to confirm
hacer una reservación (para el próximo fin de semana)	to make a reservation (for next weekend)

LECCIÓN 44

UNA PROMESA Y UNA SONRISA*

*A Promise and a Smile

OBJETIVOS

The materials in **Lección 44** of the Textbook and the Workbook/Study Guide will help you better understand the video episode and take you beyond it, giving you additional information about places and characters in the series. The Textbook will also help you to develop skill in using the Spanish language. In this lesson, you will learn

- vocabulary for talking about sports
- some additional ways to use the past perfect

You will also learn about the work of some extraordinary muralists.

Be sure to work through all parts of the lesson. When you see a headphones symbol in the margin, listen to the CD for **Lección 44**. Answers or hints for many activities are given in Appendix 1. Be sure to check your answers for each activity before going on to the next one.

The interactive CD-ROM to accompany *Destinos* contains additional practice with the video storyline and will help you improve your skills in Spanish.

BEFORE VIEWING . . .

1

PREPARACIÓN

Suggestions:
• Before watching the video, go over the vocabulary list at the end of the chapter and have students pronounce the words after you.
• Assign *Preparación* activities as homework and then go over them quickly in class before viewing the video.

Actividad.
Paso 1

¿Cuánto recuerdas de lo que pasó en el episodio previo? Contesta las preguntas.

1. ¿Quién llamó a Raquel por la noche después de cenar con Arturo y Luis?
2. ¿Qué quería esa persona? ¿Quería ver a Raquel o sólo quería hablar con ella por teléfono?
3. ¿Qué le prometió Raquel a esa persona?
    a. _____ reunirse con él en cinco minutos
    b. _____ verla* al día siguiente
4. ¿Quién fue a la agencia de viajes para pedir información, Arturo o Luis? ¿Y cuál de los dos compró pasajes para dos a un lugar romántico?
5. ¿Sabe Raquel algo de lo que pasó en la agencia de viajes?

Paso 2
Ahora escucha el CD para verificar tus respuestas.

Para pensar...

1. En el episodio previo, Raquel recordó una conversación que tuvo con Luis hace unos años. ¿Recuerdas de qué hablaron en esa conversación? ¿Qué noticias le dio Luis a Raquel en aquel entonces (*back then*)?
2. Si tú fueras Raquel, ¿le recordarías a Luis esa conversación en la presente situación? ¿Cómo influiría en ti esa conversación al pensar en él ahora? ¿al pensar en Arturo?

Para pensar...

Al final del episodio previo, Ángela llamó a Puerto Rico, al apartamento de Jorge, su novio. Para su gran sorpresa, una mujer contestó al teléfono. ¿Quién era esa mujer? ¿Crees que por fin Ángela va a comprender por qué a los demás (*other people*) no les gusta Jorge?

---

* **La** is used as the object pronoun because the grammatical referent is **persona**.

. . . AFTER VIEWING

2

¿TIENES BUENA MEMORIA?

Actividad.   ¿Qué pasó?

Paso 1

¿Qué pasó en el episodio? Indica si las oraciones son ciertas (**C**) o falsas (**F**). Corrige las que son falsas. Inventa otras oraciones (ciertas o falsas) para los espacios indicados.

Raquel y Luis

C   F   1. Luis sorprendió a Raquel con dos boletos para un viaje romántico a Zihuatanejo.
C   F   2. ¿ ?

Ángela, Roberto y Arturo

C   F   3. Ángela se enfadó con Jorge porque había una mujer en el apartamento de él.
C   F   4. Roberto llevó a su hermana y a su tío a ver un poco la Ciudad de México.
C   F   5. ¿ ?

La familia Castillo

C   F   6. Para el final del episodio, Gloria todavía no había regresado.
C   F   7. Los niños de Carlos no saben bien lo que pasa con su mamá. (¡OJO! Piensa también en los episodios previos.)
C   F   8. Cuando Juan se levantó, vio que Pati estaba por salir. Se abrazaron y después ella se fue a dar unas clases.
C   F   9. ¿ ?
C   F 10. ¿ ?

Paso 2

Presenta tus oraciones a tu compañero/a para que él/ella indique si son ciertas o falsas. También debe corregir las oraciones falsas.

Para pensar...

1. Como sabes, cuando Luis le dio a Raquel los pasajes para el viaje de vacaciones con él, ella se molestó. ¿Qué piensas de la reacción de ella? ¿Crees que tenía razón o que debería haber reaccionado de otra manera? ¿Cómo va a influir este incidente en lo que Raquel le va a decir a su mamá?

2. Ahora que has visto este episodio, ¿puedes explicar el significado del título, «Una promesa y una sonrisa»? ¿Significa lo que tú creías que significaba antes de ver el episodio?

3

VOCABULARIO DEL TEMA

Hablando de los deportes

el baloncesto/básquetbol	basketball
el béisbol	baseball
el buceo	snorkeling, scuba diving
el esquí (acuático/ alpino/nórdico)	(water/downhill/cross-country) skiing
el fútbol	soccer
el fútbol americano	football
el golf	golf
la natación	swimming
la navegación	sailing
la pesca	fishing
el tenis	tennis
el vólibol	volleyball
el/la atleta	athlete
el campeón/la campeona	champion
el entrenador/ la entrenadora	coach
el jugador/la jugadora	player
el barco	boat
la cancha	court
la caña de pescar	fishing pole
el equipo	team; equipment
el estadio	stadium

el gimnasio	gymnasium
la pelota	ball
la piscina	swimming pool
la pista	track
correr	to run
esquiar	to ski
hacer ejercicio (aeróbico)	to do (aerobic) exercise
jugar (ue) (a)	to play (*a game or sport*)
montar a caballo	to ride horseback
nadar	to swim
practicar un deporte	to play a sport

Note the use of **a** with **jugar** (**jugar al golf, al tenis…**). Not all Spanish speakers observe this usage.

Suggestion: As you go over vocabulary, ask questions related to personal examples. *¿Cuáles son tus deportes favoritos para practicar? ¿y para mirar? ¿Cómo se llaman los equipos del básquetbol / del fútbol americano / del béisbol en nuestro estado? ¿A quién (no) le gusta correr/esquiar/montar a caballo/nadar … ? ¿Qué tipo de esquí prefieres? ¿Cómo se llama tu jugador favorito de _____? ¿Dónde fueron los Juegos Olímpicos en el verano de 2000? ¿Dónde van a ser en el año 2004?*

Act. A, Suggestions: You may want to have students do this activity in pairs or small groups, then check answers as whole class.

Actividad A.   ¿Practicabas algún deporte?
Paso 1
Escucha otra vez la conversación entre Carlos y Juanita. Luego contesta las preguntas en el **Paso 2**.

Paso 2

1. ¿A qué jugaba Carlos de niño, al básquetbol o al fútbol?
2. Indica cuáles de los siguientes deportes o actividades son parte de la educación física que se da en la escuela de Juanita en Miami.

_____ el tenis   _____ nadar
_____ el béisbol   _____ el buceo
_____ el fútbol   _____ el esquí acuático
_____ el baloncesto
_____ correr

3. ¿Qué deporte quiere aprender Juanita? ¿el tenis, el esquí o el buceo? (¿También recuerdas por qué le interesa este deporte?)

Actividad B.   Cosas relacionadas con los deportes

Haz una lista de diez personas y/o cosas relacionadas con varios deportes. Preséntaselas a tu compañero/a para que él/ella nombre el deporte con que se relacionan.

MODELOS: TÚ: ¿Con qué deporte se relaciona Michael Jordan?
            COMPAÑERO/A: Él juega al baloncesto.
                    TÚ: ¿Con qué deporte se relaciona una piscina?
            COMPAÑERO/A: Con la natación.

Actividad C.   ¡Un desafío! La historia de los deportes

¿Cuántas de las siguientes preguntas puedes contestar?

1. Los Juegos Olímpicos modernos empezaron a celebrarse en el siglo XIX. ¿En qué país del mundo antiguo se habían celebrado antes?
   a. _____ Grecia   b. _____ Turquía   c. _____ Babilonia

2. Antes de 1968, año en que se celebraron los Juegos Olímpicos en la Ciudad de México, ¿habían tenido lugar (*taken place*) ya en otro país de habla española?
   Sí _____   No _____

3. El famoso actor Johnny Weismuller, quien hizo el papel (*role*) de Tarzán en muchas películas, había participado en los Juegos Olímpicos. ¿Cuál era su deporte?
   a. _____ el béisbol   b. _____ la natación   c. _____ la gimnasia

4. En 1984, la Unión Soviética se negó a (*refused to*) participar en los Juegos Olímpicos de Los Ángeles. ¿Qué nación había hecho lo mismo antes (en 1980), cuando los Juegos Olímpicos tuvieron lugar en Moscú?
   a. _____ España   b. _____ los Estados Unidos c. _____ el Canadá

5. ¿Qué deporte habían inventado los aztecas que después se desarrolló y se hizo popular en los Estados Unidos y otros países?
   a. _____ el golf   b. _____ el baloncesto   c. _____ correr

Act. D, Suggestion: You
may want to have students
do this activity in pairs.

***Nota cultural*, Point out:**
The term *football* is used
for the sport of soccer all
over the world. In the
United States, we use the
term *soccer* to distinguish
the game from American
football.

***Nota cultural*, Optional:**
You may want to have stu-
dents discuss or debate
the ethics of bullfighting. As an extension, solicit opinions about the use of animals for sport
and entertainment in this country, and elsewhere. Examples: rodeos, horse and dog races,
cock fights, dog fights, pigeon shoots, etc.

Actividad D. **Los deportes y yo**

Escoge uno de los temas a continuación. Contesta las preguntas del tema en
una hoja de papel aparte. Luego, presenta tus respuestas sobre el tema al
resto de la clase.

1. ¿Practicas algún deporte? ¿Cuál? ¿Dónde lo practicas? ¿Cuándo lo practicas?
   ¿Con quién? ¿Es necesario tener equipo especial para practicar este deporte?
2. ¿Qué deporte no te gusta para nada? Explica por qué no te gusta.
3. ¿Qué deporte no practicas pero te gusta verlo en la televisión o en el estadio? ¿Por qué te interesa este deporte? ¿Tienes un equipo favorito? ¿un
   jugador favorito / una jugadora favorita?

Nota cultural   Los deportes en el mundo hispánico

In addition to being a matter of individual taste, preferences in sports are also a matter of social class and location. Many families, like their counterparts in this country, like to go into the
countryside to have a picnic or a cookout and to play sports like soccer, volleyball, or badminton. In urban areas, jogging is becoming more common, as are the oriental martial arts such
as kung fu and tai chi.

   With regard to team sports, soccer is definitely one of the favorite sports in the Spanish-speaking
world. Games are not telecast as often as they are in this country, but **la Copa Mundial de fútbol** (the World Soccer Cup) is a major television event that few fans miss. In addition to international competition, many countries have leagues, and fans are fiercely loyal to their city's team.

   In the Caribbean, baseball is without question the leading sport, and
many Hispanic baseball players come to the United States to play in the
major and minor leagues.

   Finally, although not as popular as it once was, **la corrida de toros**
(*bullfighting*) is still the favorite sport of many people, especially in
Spain (where the bull is killed) and in Mexico (where it is not). The
question of whether bullfighting is a sport or an art is still debated by
some. Nevertheless, it seems fair to say that younger generations are
less taken with this sport than their parents and grandparents have been.

Representación de jugadores hispanos en las grandes ligas	
República Dominicana	33
Puerto Rico	21
Venezuela	13
Cuba	5
México	4
Panamá	3
Nicaragua	1
Honduras	1

4

U**N POCO DE GRAMÁTICA**

The Workbook/Study Guide contains more
detailed explanation and practice of this
grammar point.

Suggestion: For home-
work, have students write
a chronological list of 5 or
6 past events in their
lives. Then, in class, have
them work in pairs, using
past perfect verb forms,
cuando and *antes de* +
inf. to write sentences
about each other's lives.
Variation: On the board
or overhead, write a
chronological list of infinitives that represent events
in your past, e.g., *nacer,
vivir en Nueva York, viajar,
mudarme a Washington,
estudiar, enseñar,
casarme,* etc. Write a
model sentence about the order of events in your past, using past perfect and the time expressions *cuando* or
antes de + *inf.*: *Ya había viajado cuando me mudé al estado de Washington. Ya había estudiado antes de enseñar.* Have students complete your biography as an entire group.

More About Talking About What Had Happened

You have learned that the imperfect of **haber** + **-do** can be used to express past events.

Juanita ya **había aprendido**
a nadar cuando empezó el
primer año.

*Juanita had already learned
to swim when she started
first grade.*

De niño, Carlos **había jugado**
al fútbol en la escuela.

*As a child, Carlos had played
soccer in school.*

Variation: On the board or overhead, write a chronological list of infinitives that represent events in your past, e.g., *nacer, vivir en Nueva York, viajar, mudarme a Washington, estudiar, enseñar, casarme,* etc. Write a model sentence about the order of events in your past, using past perfect and the time expressions *cuando* or *antes de* + *inf.: Ya había viajado cuando me mudé al estado de Washington. Ya había estudiado antes de enseñar.* Have students complete your biography as an entire group.

You now have four verb forms that can be combined to describe the past or narrate in the past.

the preterite: Raquel **viajó** a España porque
the imperfect: don Fernando **quería** saber la verdad de su pasado.
the past perfect: **Había viajado** al extranjero antes, y ahora
the conditional: le **gustaría** viajar más, especialmente por Sudamérica.

In the Workbook/Study Guide you will review how these four verb forms function. For now, continue to use the imperfect of **haber** + **-do** to talk about an event in the past that had occurred prior to another event.

Actividad.   ¿Lo habías hecho antes?
Paso 1

Utilizando el modelo como guía y las indicaciones a continuación, inventa oraciones en que expresas lo que has hecho o no has hecho recientemente. Si contestas afirmativamente, también debes decir si lo habías hecho antes.

> MODELO: Recientemente he comido *sushi*. Nunca había comido algo similar antes.

1. algo que (no) has comido/bebido
2. algo que (no) has visto
3. algo que (no) has aprendido a hacer
4. alguna actividad que (no) has hecho
5. algún deporte que (no) has practicado
6. alguna noticia que has oído
7. ¿ ?

Act., Follow-Up: To review past perfect, prepare a *Firma aquí* activity with questions such as *Cuando cumpliste once años, ¿habías tenido un perro / un gato / un caballo / ... de mascota? Antes de llegar a la universidad, ¿habías ido a una película extranjera / un concierto de música clásica / un salón de billar / ...?*

Have students circulate in class asking and answering the questions and gathering the signatures of classmates who respond with *Sí.* Then have them report their findings to the class, using the model *Cuando ____ cumplió once años, había tenido un «hamster» de mascota.*

Paso 2

Ahora pregúntale a tu compañero/a cuáles son sus respuestas a las frases en el **Paso 1**. Él/Ella te va a preguntar lo mismo. ¿Son similares las respuestas de los/las dos? ¿Cómo difieren?

> MODELO: TÚ: ¿Qué has comido recientemente?
>   COMPAÑERO/A: He comido caracoles (*snails*).
>   TÚ: ¿Los habías comido antes?
>   COMPAÑERO/A: No, ¡y no pienso comerlos otra vez!

5

LECTURA CULTURAL

El arte mural y los muralistas

(Antes de leer esta sección, te conviene ver una vez más los murales que se encuentran en las **Lecciones 32** y **41** de este libro. También debes pensar en los cuadros de estas páginas.)

Por horribles que sean, las guerras tienen la capacidad de servir de inspiración a las mentes creadoras: novelistas, pintores, dramaturgos y, ahora en el siglo XXI, cineastas.[1] La Revolución mexicana no fue una excepción. La época de esta guerra civil, de 1910 a 1920, fue uno de los períodos más sangrientos[2] de toda la historia de México. Ha inspirado muchas novelas y películas famosas, pero sobre todo inspiró a tres pintores a utilizar y popularizar la pintura mural. Ellos convirtieron este arte en un gran instrumento social.

En *Hispano-América* Orozco pinta al campesino revolucionario con las fuerzas que lo oprimen:[9] los banqueros, los soldados… Es toda una alegoría.

¿Por qué la pintura mural?

En los países donde el índice de analfabetismo[3] es muy alto, el artista puede servir de maestro a su pueblo. Desde el principio, el arte muralista se destinó a las masas.

- Por una parte, los artistas querían compartir con el pueblo la historia de los grandes acontecimientos de la Revolución y sus héroes, así como[4] los ideales de la Revolución.
- Por otra parte se buscaba enseñarles a las grandes masas las maravillas de la historia de la raza indígena: la grandeza de las civilizaciones azteca, maya, tolteca…

El campesino que ignoraba la palabra escrita podía mirar los dibujos, interpretar las figuras y así aprender. ¿Quién no se inspira al ver al *Padre Hidalgo*, en el mural de Orozco, en Guadalajara? No queda duda[5] sobre la fuerza y verdad de su mensaje.

Las grandes figuras del arte mural mexicano

- **Diego Rivera (1886–1957)**

Para este artista, quien se declaraba comunista, la historia de México no es más que una lucha de clases sociales: por una parte, el campesino, el obrero, el indio y el soldado; por otra, los militares, el clero[6] y los capitalistas. Más que ningún otro pintor, fue capaz de poner en alto[7] la herencia indígena mexicana.*

- **José Clemente Orozco (1883–1949)**

Este muralista pensaba que los artistas no debían tener convicciones políticas. Sin embargo sus murales expresan la tristeza de la guerra y denuncian los errores del sistema capitalista y de los militares.

- **David Alfaro Siqueiros (1896–1974)**

Hay que participar en los murales y cuadros de Siqueiros. En ellos se destacan[8] con frecuencia los brazos y las manos, símbolos de la dignidad del hombre trabajador.

[1]*people who work in the movie industry* [2]*bloody* [3]*índice… level of illiteracy* [4]*así… as well as* [5]*No… There is no doubt* [6]*clergy* [7]*poner… putting on display* [8]*se… stand out* [9]*oppress*

* En los últimos años, la fama de Diego Rivera ha crecido en los Estados Unidos por otra razón: fue el esposo de la pintora mexicana Frida Kahlo.

En *Nuestra imagen actual,* de Siqueiros, una figura anónima suplica[13] la devolución[14] de una identidad humana.

El arte mural en los Estados Unidos

Estos grandes pintores no sólo crearon en México sus obras maestras. La obra de Orozco que se reproduce con esta **Lectura** se pintó, y se encuentra todavía, en Dartmouth College. Pero Rivera no tuvo tanta suerte. Un fresco que pintó para el Centro Rockefeller en 1932 provocó manifestaciones anticomunistas. Esta obra fue destruida, pero luego se recreó[10] en la Ciudad de México.

Hoy día todavía se puede afirmar que la tradición de la pintura mural sigue vigente[11] en los Estados Unidos. En los barrios mexicoamericanos de Los Ángeles, Chicago, San Diego, San Francisco y otras ciudades, se ven murales pintados por una nueva generación de muralistas. En ellos hay una temática basada en la experiencia de lo que es ser latino en los Estados Unidos.

Uno de los mayores proponentes del estilo mural es la profesora Judy Baca, de la Universidad de California en Irvine. Para ella, como para los maestros mexicanos de este arte, un mural es ante todo[12] comunicación, un lenguaje visual que puede unir a un pueblo. En su proyecto más famoso, *Great Wall of Los Angeles,* hay escenas de la historia de California.

[10]se… *it was recreated*   [11]*vital, alive*   [12]ante… *above all else*   [13]*begs for*   [14]*return*

6

INTERCAMBIO

Paso 1

Pensando en lo que sabes de los otros compañeros de clase, ¿a quién o quiénes podrían corresponder las siguientes oraciones? Apunta los nombres de los compañeros que, en tu opinión, habían hecho cada una de las siguientes cosas.

Antes de llegar a la universidad, alguien…

1. había hecho viaje en barco.
2. había roto (*broken*) una pierna esquiando.
3. había aprendido a jugar al golf o tenis muy joven.
4. no había jugado al fútbol nunca.
5. había sido atleta en la escuela secundaria.
6. había nadado en el Océano Pacífico.
7. había ¿ ?

Intercambio, Paso 2,
Suggestion: Create a
chart to tally guesses.
Write the numbers of the
items across the top row.
Write the names given un-
der the corresponding
numbers. For *Paso 3*, circle the correct guesses.

Paso 2

Túrnense para dar los nombres que apuntaron para cada número del **Paso 1**.
Deben seguir el orden para comparar sus ideas.

Paso 3

Ahora, túrnense para decir qué habían hecho del **Paso 1** y para qué sus
compañeros lo adivinaron.

VOCABULARIO

Hablando de los deportes

(Talking About Sports)

el baloncesto/básquetbol	basketball
el barco	boat
el béisbol	baseball
la caña de pescar	fishing pole
el equipo	team; equipment
el esquí (acuático/alpino/ nórdico)	(water/downhill/ cross-country) skiing
el estadio	stadium
el fútbol	soccer
el fútbol americano	football
el gimnasio	gymnasium
el golf	golf
la natación	swimming
la navegación	sailing
la pelota	ball
la pesca	fishing
la pista	track
el tenis	tennis
el vólibol	volleyball

el/la atleta	athlete
el campeón/la campeona	champion
el entrenador/la entrenadora	coach
el jugador/la jugadora	player
esquiar	to ski
hacer ejercicio (aeróbico)	to do (aerobic) exercise
montar a caballo	to ride horseback
practicar un deporte	to play a sport

Repaso: **el buceo, la cancha, correr, jugar (ue) (a), nadar, la piscina**

Las personas

los/las demás	others, other people

Los conceptos

la promesa	promise

¡ESTOY HARTA!*

*I'm Fed Up!

OBJETIVOS

The materials in **Lección 45** of the Textbook and the Workbook/Study Guide will help you better understand the video episode and take you beyond it, giving you additional information about places and characters in the series. The Textbook will also help you to develop skill in using the Spanish language. In this lesson you will learn

- vocabulary for talking about relationships with family and friends
- ways to use another perfect tense to talk about what someone should have done

You will also learn about Hispanic families.

Be sure to work through all parts of the lesson. When you see a headphones symbol in the margin, listen to the CD for **Lección 45**. Answers or hints for many activities are given in Appendix 1. Be sure to check your answers for each activity before going on to the next one.

The interactive CD-ROM to accompany *Destinos* contains additional practice with the video storyline and will help you improve your skills in Spanish.

BEFORE VIEWING . . .

Preliminary: See Faculty Guide for additional information and activities for this lesson.
• **Variation:** For activities marked with the headphones icon, you may wish to read from the Audioscript instead of playing the CD.
• **Suggestion:** Make sure students are familiar with the activities before you read from the Audioscript or play the CD.

1

Preparación

Suggestions:
• Before watching the video, go over the vocabulary list at the end of the chapter and have students pronounce the words after you.
• Assign *Preparación* activities as homework and then go over them quickly in class before viewing the video.

Actividad.
Paso 1

Act., *Paso 1*, Answers:
1. b 2. c 3. b 4. b

Act., Follow-up: Have students create an additional question and set of options similar to those in the activity, then exchange papers with a partner and answer each other's questions.

Contesta las siguientes preguntas según lo que recuerdas del episodio previo.

1. ¿Quiénes fueron a conocer la Ciudad de México?
   a. _____ Arturo, Raquel y Ángela   c. _____ Raquel, Luis y Arturo
   b. _____ Ángela, Arturo y Roberto

2. ¿Con qué sorprendió Luis a Raquel?
   a. _____ con su plan de mudarse a Los Ángeles
   b. _____ con su plan de casarse con ella lo antes posible
   c. _____ con su plan de pasar el fin de semana con ella en Zihuatanejo

3. ¿Qué pasó con don Fernando?
   a. _____ El especialista lo autorizó a volver a su casa.
   b. _____ El especialista quería hacerle otros exámenes.
   c. _____ Su condición mejoró muchísimo.

4. ¿Qué pasó con Gloria?
   a. _____ Regresó a casa por fin.
   b. _____ La seguían esperando todos.
   c. _____ Llamó para decir que regresaría pronto.

 Paso 2
Ahora escucha el CD para verificar algunas de tus respuestas.

Para pensar, **Suggestion:** Ask questions of whole class. Accept any possibilities as there are no (in)correct responses.

Para pensar...

1. En este episodio, Juan va al teatro donde Pati está ensayando (*rehearsing*) con los actores. ¿Qué le va a decir Juan a ella? ¿Crees que él ha llegado a una conclusión sobre lo que él debería hacer?

2. También en este episodio, los padres de Raquel llegan a México. ¿Cuál ha sido la actitud de María, la madre de Raquel, hacia Arturo hasta ahora? (Recuerda que Raquel le ha hablado por teléfono varias veces.) ¿Crees que su actitud será igual cuando María y Arturo se conozcan por fin? ¿Y qué le va a decir Raquel a su madre en cuanto al viaje de Luis a México?

. . . AFTER VIEWING

2 ¿TIENES BUENA MEMORIA?

Actividad A. ¿Que pasó?
Paso 1

Indica si las siguientes oraciones son ciertas (**C**) o falsas (**F**).

Raquel

C F   1. Raquel se enteró de que Luis es la causa de su situación difícil.

C F   2. Raquel y su madre se enojaron la una con la otra.

C F   3. Arturo habló con Raquel sobre un viaje a Cozumel, posiblemente con sus padres.

C F   4. De momento, Raquel piensa que Luis es más considerado que Arturo.

Ángela y Roberto

C F   5. No tenían ningún interés en las relaciones entre Arturo y Raquel.

C F   6. Bajaron para ir a cenar con los padres de Raquel y los demás.

La familia Castillo

C F   7. Las noticias sobre la salud de don Fernando eran buenas.

C F   8. Juan decidió regresar a México sin Pati.

C F   9. Gloria todavía no ha vuelto a casa.

C F   10. Don Fernando regresará a La Gavia mañana.

 Paso 2

Ahora escucha el CD para verificar algunas de tus respuestas.

Paso 3

Ahora lee el siguiente párrafo para verificar las otras respuestas.

Ángela y Roberto tenían muchas ganas de saber lo que Arturo pensaba hacer con respecto a sus sentimientos por Raquel. Pero cuando se lo preguntaron, Arturo les dijo que sus planes eran un secreto. Cuando Ángela y Roberto llegaron a la habitación de Raquel, conocieron a los padres de ella. También vieron la manera en que María se portó (*behaved*): muy fría con Arturo... y muy emotiva con Luis. Más tarde, decidieron no salir a cenar con el grupo. ¿Crees que fue porque, como dijeron, tenían muchas cosas de que hablar? ¿O fue por otra razón?

 ### Actividad B. Raquel y su mamá
Paso 1

Con un compañero / una compañera, revisen la conversación entre Raquel y su mamá. Utilicen las siguientes preguntas como base de su conversación.

Act. B, *Paso 1*, Suggestion: Replay the conversation between Raquel and her mother on the video if possible, or play the CD. Make sure students know what specific information to listen for before they review the conversation.

Act. B, *Paso 1*, Answers: See Appendix 1.

Act. B, *Paso 2*, Suggestion: Have students form groups of 4 or 5 and present their opinions to the others in the group, who agree or disagree. Encourage students to explain as best they can in Spanish why they agree or disagree.

1. ¿De qué acusa Raquel a su mamá?
2. ¿Qué actitud muestra su mamá al principio de la conversación? ¿y al final?
3. ¿Qué hace su papá durante esta discusión?

Paso 2

Indiquen si Uds. están de acuerdo o no con las siguientes ideas. Luego presenten sus reacciones a la clase.

1. Raquel tiene razón.
2. Raquel reacciona a las acciones de su mamá de una manera exagerada.
3. Su papá debería haber intervenido (*should have intervened*).
4. La mamá de Raquel debe buscarla y confiarle sus sentimientos.

Note: The two columns of words in the *Vocabulario* are not necessarily positive in the first column versus negative in the second column. They are merely set up as contrasting pairs.

3

VOCABULARIO DEL TEMA

Point out: Almost all of these verbs will have a person as their direct object, thus requiring use of the personal *a*.

Suggestion: Practice pronunciation with choral and individual repetition.

Las relaciones interpersonales

Por un lado...	*Por otro lado...*
aceptar	**perdonar**
acusar	**insultar**, **ofender**
alabar (to praise)	**odiar**
amar, querer (ie)	**desconfiar* (de)**
confiar* (en) (to trust)	**disculpar** (to excuse; to make excuses for)
culpar (to blame)	
decir la verdad	**engañar, mentir (ie, i)**
rechazar	
llevarse bien (con)	**llevarse mal (con), discutir** (to argue), **pelear(se) (con)**
prestar atención (a) (to pay attention [to])	**no hacer caso (de)**
respetar, estimar, venerar	**despreciar, desdeñar**
ser amigo íntimo/amiga íntima de	**ser distante de**
ser unido/a	**ser desunido/a**
tratar (to deal with, treat)	**no hacerle caso a alguien**

actuar†/portarse + *adverb* (to act + *adverb*)
    actuar†/portarse amigablemente/hostilmente

You already know the meaning of some of the preceding verbs and phrases. Others are easily recognizable cognates. Still others are "guessable" when seen in the context of the word(s) with which they are grouped. If you are unsure of the meaning of any of these verbs, check their meaning in the **Vocabulario** at the end of this lesson or in the Spanish-English dictionary at the back of the Textbook.

---

* Note the patterns of accentuation in these verbs: **confiar: confío, confías... confiamos...** ; **desconfiar: desconfío, desconfías... desconfiamos...**
† Note the pattern of accentuation in this verb: **actuar: actúo, actúas... actuamos...**

Actividad A. Opiniones

Escucha las siguientes descripciones o predicciones. Luego indica si estás de acuerdo (**Sí**) con ellas o no (**No**).

La familia Castillo Soto

Act. A, Point out: These statements are subject to interpretation. If students disagree on a given item, ask them to explain why.

Sí   No   1. Ángela y Roberto no son muy unidos.

Sí   No   2. Ángela no hace caso de las opiniones y consejos de los demás.

Sí   No   3. En la familia de Ángela y Roberto, todos veneran a la abuela y respetan sus opiniones.

La familia Rodríguez

Sí   No   4. Raquel y su madre se llevan bien en general.

Sí   No   5. Como ocurre entre todas las madres e hijas, a veces Raquel y su madre discuten porque son de distintas generaciones y tienen diferentes ideas sobre algunas cosas.

Sí   No   6. Al fin y al cabo (*In the end*), Raquel va a disculpar a su madre.

Sí   No   7. María (la madre de Raquel) no le hace mucho caso a su esposo.

Sí   No   8. María se portó hostilmente con Arturo porque no le caen muy bien los argentinos.

La familia Castillo Saavedra

Sí   No   9. Los miembros de la familia Castillo se mantienen distantes los unos de los otros.

Sí   No   10. Carlos trató de engañar a la familia por razones económicas.

Sí   No   11. Es obvio que Juan no quiere a Pati, pues le tiene envidia.

Sí   No   12. Gloria hace lo que hace porque los hermanos de Carlos no la aceptan.

Actividad B. Tú y los demás

Act. B, Follow-up: Have students change the statements into questions to ask a partner. Remind them to use *tú* forms in phrasing their questions.

Para cada una de las siguientes oraciones, da una respuesta: **siempre**, **muchas veces**, **a veces**, **muy poco**, **nunca**.

1. Me llevo muy bien con mi familia.
2. Le he mentido a una persona a quien quiero mucho.
3. Mis profesores me tratan amigablemente.
4. Actúo de una forma cortés y considerada con los otros.
5. Alabo a los demás por sus triunfos y éxitos.
6. Los demás me prestan atención cuando hablo u ofrezco una opinión.
7. Me peleo con un pariente.
8. Me han acusado de ser desleal.
9. Rechazo a los demás por sus opiniones políticas.
10. Me ha insultado un buen amigo/una buena amiga.

Actividad C. Tu vida

Act. C, Suggestion: Have students working in pairs take turns asking the questions.

De las siguientes preguntas, contesta las que tengan algo que ver con tu vida.

1. ¿Con quién(es) te llevas muy bien? ¿Por qué razón? ¿Qué han hecho Uds. juntos?
2. ¿Hay alguien con quien te lleves muy mal? ¿Puedes explicar por qué? ¿Qué ha pasado entre Uds.?

Act. C, Optional: Have individual students choose one group of questions and search for classmates who answered that group of questions. Have them compare answers to find out how similar or different they are.

3. ¿Quiénes son tus amigos íntimos? ¿Hace mucho que los/las conoces? ¿Dónde conociste a tu mejor amigo/a? ¿En qué circunstancias?

4. ¿Es tu familia muy unida? ¿Cuántas veces a la semana (al mes/al año) se ven? ¿Hay un pariente de quien *des*confías?

5. ¿Qué días acostumbras pasar con tu familia? ¿Qué hacen Uds. cuando se reúnen?

6. ¿En quién confías mucho? ¿A quién le confiesas tus secretos más íntimos?

4   UN POCO DE GRAMÁTICA

The Workbook/Study Guide contains more detailed explanation and practice of this grammar point.

> ### Talking About What Someone Should Have Done
>
> To express what someone should—or should *not*!—have done in the past, use the conditional of **deber** + the infinitive of **haber** + the **-do** form.
>
> Luis no **debería haber comprado** los pasajes sin consultar a Raquel primero.
>
> *Luis should not have bought the tickets without consulting with Raquel first.*
>
> Gloria no **debería haber estado** ausente tanto tiempo… y sin llamar.
>
> *Gloria should not have been away from home for so long . . . and without even calling.*
>
> You will learn more about using these forms in the Workbook/Study Guide.

Act., Suggestion: Assign as homework. In class the following day, have students working in pairs try to guess how their partner responded to the statements.

Act., Follow-up: Have students create a sentence following the pattern of those in the activity, but based on the life of a famous person or fictional character. Their partner must try to guess who the person is. Model: *Yo no debería haber ido a Dallas en 1963.* (*el presidente John F. Kennedy*)

Actividad.   Más opiniones

Indica si estás de acuerdo o no con cada oración a continuación. Usa la siguiente escala en tus respuestas.

5 = Estoy de acuerdo.   3 = En cierto sentido, estoy de acuerdo.   1 = No estoy de acuerdo.

a. _____ Yo debería haber estudiado francés en vez de español.

b. _____ Debería haber elegido otra universidad.

c. _____ Debería haber tomado más cursos este semestre/trimestre.

d. _____ Debería haber trabajado (más) el verano pasado para tener más dinero ahora.

e. _____ Debería haber leído más durante mi adolescencia.

f. _____ No debería haber salido con mis amigos anoche.

g. _____ Debería haber estudiado más para el último examen.

h. _____ No debería haber visto tanto la televisión la semana pasada.

i. _____ No debería haberle dicho tantas atrocidades a mi compañero/a de cuarto la última vez que me enfadé con él/ella.

5

LECTURA CULTURAL

Facetas de la familia hispana

La familia Castillo tiene una vida privilegiada en el sentido económico. Pero también goza de[1] otra circunstancia envidiable: la unidad de la familia. Los nietos tienen la oportunidad de pasar mucho tiempo con su abuelo. Dos hijos de don Fernando viven con él en la hacienda, por lo menos parte del tiempo. Parece que todos los hermanos se llevan bien y que se apoyan en todo. En realidad, de lo único que culpan a Carlos cuando se descubre lo de la oficina en Miami es de no haber confiado en la familia.

¿Telenovela o realidad?

Esta visión de la familia modelo muy bien puede servir de fondo[2] para una telenovela, como *Destinos*. Pero no representa necesariamente una realidad compartida por la mayoría de la gente de habla española. Entre los hispanos, como en toda cultura, hay familias unidas y desunidas, familias grandes y chicas, familias cariñosas y violentas. En algunas familias, muchos parientes viven en una misma vivienda[3] (la llamada «familia extendida»). Pero hay también familias nucleares (sólo padres e hijos) y también familias donde hay sólo uno de los padres.

Escuchemos lo que nos dice un niño chileno «moderno» de su familia. El chico tiene siete años.

> Los papás siempre llegan muy tarde. Solamente los fines de semana salimos. Casi siempre vamos a andar en bicicleta en las mañanas y a veces jugamos o vamos al estadio. Y cuando vamos donde mis abuelitos, hacemos lo que queremos. Si queremos un helado, el tata[4] va a comprarlo al tiro. Y siempre que vamos, nos tiene pasteles y cosas ricas. Pero ahora los veo menos, porque voy poco. Antes iba todos los viernes, y ahora me invitan y me invitan, y yo les digo «cuando pueda».

¿Te fijaste en las diferencias entre lo que dice este chico y la familia del estereotipo? (Piénsalo un poco antes de seguir leyendo.)

Aquí, los padres llegan tarde (¿trabajan los dos fuera de casa?) y realmente pasan con los niños solamente los fines de semana. Los abuelos no viven con los hijos. Y ya hay cierta distancia entre el niño y sus abuelos, pues ya, a los siete años, no tiene tiempo para ellos.

¿Lo pasado, pasado?[5]

No era antes así —ni en las culturas hispanas ni en este país. En todas partes del mundo moderno se ha notado en los últimos años una serie de cambios en la estructura de la familia y en la calidad de la vida familiar. ¿El ideal norteamericano del pasado? La familia de Ozzie y Harriet. ¿La realidad del presente? Piensa en los programas en la televisión esta semana.

El ideal de otras épocas de la familia hispana se parece en algunos detalles al ideal de la familia que se tenía en este país. Veamos esto en las palabras de una chilena de mediana edad.[6]

> La mamá de mi papá, mi abuela paterna, vivía con nosotros. La familia nuestra era los tres niños y los tres adultos. Es muy común que —sea un tío o los abuelos— vivan en el mismo lugar. Las familias son mucho más grandes en este sentido, más extendidas. La familia es un núcleo muy importante dentro de la sociedad, a todo nivel, en la clase más alta y en la clase más baja también. Y también los tíos que no son tíos, son amigos que también son muy próximos a la familia…

En los países menos industrializados, en donde se conservan las tradiciones, es posible que este tipo de familia todavía exista y hasta sea común. En las grandes ciudades, sin embargo, para bien o para mal,[7] entre la gente joven el patrón[8] se parece más al de los países industrializados. ¿Cómo será la familia dentro de veinticinco años? No se sabe, pero seguramente seguirá cambiando.

[1]goza… *they enjoy* [2]de… *as a background* [3]*dwelling* [4]*abuelo* [5]¿Lo… *Is the past gone forever?* [6]de… *middle-aged* [7]para… *for better or worse* [8]*pattern, model*

6 **I**NTERCAMBIO

Paso 1

Piensa en la discusión entre Raquel y su mamá María. Luego, escribe una respuesta breve a las siguientes preguntas. Trata de utilizar el vocabulario nuevo de esta lección si puedes.

1. ¿Debería haber hecho Raquel algo diferente?
2. ¿Debería haber reaccionado María tal como reaccionó?
3. ¿Qué debería haber hecho el papá de Raquel, Pancho?

Paso 2

En grupos de tres, compartan sus ideas. ¿Están de acuerdo? Luego, decidan qué respuestas quieren presentarle al resto de la clase. Sólo pueden presentar una respuesta para cada pregunta.

Paso 3

Cada grupo debe presentar sus ideas a la clase. ¿Hay ideas semejantes? ¿Qué piensan todos del papel de Pancho en la discusión?

VOCABULARIO

Las relaciones interpersonales
(Interpersonal Relationships)

acusar	to accuse
alabar	to praise
amar	to love
confiar (en)	to trust
culpar	to blame
desconfiar (de)	to distrust
desdeñar	to disdain, scorn
despreciar	to hold in low esteem
disculpar	to make excuses for
discutir	to argue
estimar	to hold in high esteem
insultar	to insult
mentir (ie, i)	to lie
no hacer caso (de)	to pay no attention (*to an issue*)
no hacerle caso a alguien	to ignore someone
ofender	to offend
perdonar	to pardon
prestar atención (a)	to pay attention (to)
respetar	to respect
tratar	to treat, deal with
venerar	to venerate

ser...	to be...
amigo íntimo/amiga íntima	a close friend
distante	distant
desunido/a	fragmented
actuar/portarse + *adverb*	to act + *adverb*
amigablemente/hostilmente	in a friendly/ hostile manner

Repaso: **aceptar, decir la verdad, engañar, llevarse bien/mal (con), odiar, pelear(se) (con), querer (ie), rechazar, unido/a**

Las palabras adicionales

estar harto/a (de/con)	to be fed up (with)

LECCIÓN 46

LAS EMPANADAS*

*The Turnovers (Pies)

OBJETIVOS

The materials in **Lección 46** of the Textbook and the Workbook/Study Guide will help you better understand the video episode and take you beyond it, giving you additional information about places and characters in the series. The Textbook will also help you to develop skill in using the Spanish language. In his lesson you will learn

- ways to talk about hobbies and pastimes
- ways to talk about what would happen if . . .

You will also learn about a popular park in Mexico City.

Be sure to work through all parts of the lesson. When you see a headphones symbol in the margin, listen to the CD for **Lección 46**. Answers or hints for many activities are given in Appendix 1. Be sure to check your answers for each activity before going on to the next one.

The interactive CD-ROM to accompany *Destinos* contains additional practice with the video storyline and will help you improve your skills in Spanish.

Preliminary: See Faculty Guide for additional information and activities for this lesson.
● **Variation:** For activities marked with the headphones icon, you may wish to read from the Audioscript instead of playing the CD.
● **Suggestion:** Make sure students are familiar with the activities before you read from the Audioscript or play the CD.

 BEFORE VIEWING . . .

1

PREPARACIÓN

Suggestions:
● Before watching the video, go over the vocabulary list at the end of the chapter and have students pronounce the words after you.
● Assign *Preparación* activities as homework and then go over them quickly in class before viewing the video.

Act. A, *Paso 1*, Suggestion: You may want to have students do this activity in pairs, then check answers as whole class.
Act. A, *Paso 1*, Answers: 1. b 2. a 3. a 4. c 5. b

Actividad A.
Paso 1
Completa las siguientes oraciones según lo que recuerdas del episodio previo.

1. En el episodio previo, Arturo le sugirió a Raquel que
   a. _____ fuera a Buenos Aires con él.
   b. _____ ellos fueran a Cozumel con sus padres.
   c. _____ invitaran a sus padres a cenar.

2. Raquel estaba muy impresionada por
   a. _____ el interés que Arturo mostraba en sus padres.
   b. _____ la fineza de Arturo al elegir un lugar tan bonito para su fin de semana.
   c. _____ el interés que Arturo tenía en ella.

3. En el hospital de Guadalajara, le dieron de alta a don Fernando,
   a. _____ pero su estado de salud no era bueno.
   b. _____ porque su estado de salud había mejorado mucho.
   c. _____ pero él no quería volver a La Gavia.

4. Juan le dijo a Pati que había decidido volver a México y que
   a. _____ ella tenía que volver con él.
   b. _____ ella tenía que elegir entre su carrera y su esposo.
   c. _____ entendía por fin por qué ella tuvo que volver a Nueva York.

5. Gloria volvió a casa de Ramón, y Carlos
   a. _____ se enojó mucho con ella.
   b. _____ le dijo que era hora de hablar seriamente.
   c. _____ le dijo que esta vez no pagaría sus deudas.

 ### Paso 2
Ahora escucha el CD para verificar tus respuestas.

Act. B, Answers: *Paso 1:* 1, 4, 5, 6 ***Paso 2:*** 2. *La madre de Raquel actuó muy fríamente con Arturo.* 3. *Cuando llegó Luis, la madre lo saludó con mucho cariño.*

Actividad B.
Paso 1
¿Cuánto recuerdas de la llegada de los padres de Raquel? Indica solamente las oraciones que la describan.

1. _____ Raquel y sus padres conversaban en la habitación de Raquel cuando llegaron Ángela, Roberto y Arturo.
2. _____ Arturo actuó muy fríamente con sus padres.
3. _____ Cuando llegó Luis, la madre de Raquel ni lo saludó.
4. _____ Raquel se enojó con su madre y fue a su habitación para hablarle de su conducta.
5. _____ Arturo se sentía apenado (*distressed*); no quería intervenir entre Raquel y sus padres.
6. _____ Luis sospecha que Raquel está enamorada de (*in love with*) Arturo.

Paso 2

¿Puedes modificar las oraciones que no indicaste para que sean verdaderas?

Para pensar...

¿Recuerdas cómo reaccionó Arturo ante la conducta de María Rodríguez? En su lugar, ¿cómo te sentirías tú? ¿Te sentirías como ella? ¿Qué harías tú si fueras Arturo? ¿Buscarías a los padres de Raquel para hablar con ellos? ¿Tratarías de hablar primero con Raquel?

Para comprender un poco más...

fastidiar   A veces los niños **fastidian** a sus padres, sobre todo cuando hacen muchas preguntas… sólo por preguntar.

  . . . AFTER VIEWING

2

¿TIENES BUENA MEMORIA?

Actividad A.   Raquel: Discusión, confesión
Paso 1

Hoy ha sido un día difícil e importante para Raquel. ¿Puedes completar el siguiente resumen de su repaso?

1. Le había hecho
   Le había comprado
2. disculparse con su hija
   empezar una conversación seria
3. cenar con ellos la otra noche
   venir a México
4. de las relaciones entre Raquel y Arturo
   del impacto que tuvo la investigación en la carrera de Raquel
5. Raquel se casara con Arturo
   Raquel se fuera a vivir a la Argentina
6. una llamada de Luis
   un mensaje de Luis
7. no lo quiere ver más en su vida
   sí está enamorada de Arturo

Esta mañana, la madre de Raquel vino a verla a su habitación.

_____[1] unas empanadas. Esto fue como una señal[a]

para Raquel porque su madre las usaba para

_____[2]

　Mientras comían las empanadas, María le explicó a Raquel por qué había

invitado a Luis a _____.[3] En realidad lo hizo

porque tenía miedo _____.[4] No quería que

_____.[5]

　María no debía de haberse preocupado.[b] Raquel no quiere irse a vivir a

la Argentina, pero todavía no ha hablado con Arturo de todo esto.

　Al bajar a la recepción con su madre, Raquel recibió

_____.[6] Él ha regresado a Los Ángeles. Para

Raquel, es mejor así porque ahora no le tiene que decir que

_____.[7]

[a]*sign, signal*　[b]*no… needn't have worried*

Paso 2
Ahora escucha el repaso de Raquel otra vez en el CD para verificar tus
respuestas.

Para pensar...

Raquel ha dicho algo muy importante al final de este episodio: «Estoy
enamorada de Arturo.» Ahora ella tiene que tomar una decisión, ¿no? O,
tal vez, varias decisiones. ¿Cuáles son las alternativas que tiene? ¿Qué harías
tú si fueras ella?

Actividad B.　Las otras actividades
Paso 1

Mientras Raquel iba resolviendo algunos de sus problemas, los asuntos de los
otros personajes también se iban resolviendo. Completa las siguientes oraciones con algo lógico.

1.　Ángela y Roberto decidieron que _____.

2.　El padre de Raquel le dijo a Arturo _____

3.　Mientras paseaba con su esposo y su hija, María

_____.

4. Por fin don Fernando _____.

5. Los otros miembros de la familia Castillo

    _____.

6. Al comentar con sus hermanos la posible venta de La Gavia, Mercedes

    les _____.

7. Raquel, Arturo y sus sobrinos _____.

Paso 2
Compara tus oraciones del **Paso 1** con las de un compañero / una compañera. ¿Están Uds. de acuerdo (más o menos) el uno con el otro?

Actividad C. **Dos conversaciones muy importantes**
Paso 1
En este episodio, el padre de Raquel le ofrece un consejo al amigo de su hija. Al mismo tiempo, la madre de Raquel está hablando con su hija. Escucha las dos conversaciones otra vez.

Paso 2
Ahora di si estás de acuerdo (**Sí**) o no (**No**) con las siguientes oraciones.

Sí No 1. A Pancho le gusta mucho Arturo.
Sí No 2. Parece que el padre de Raquel comprende bien a las personas.
Sí No 3. Es dudoso que Arturo se sintiera aliviado después de hablar con Pancho.
Sí No 4. Pancho quiere que Arturo y su esposa se lleven bien.
Sí No 5. Ésta es la primera vez que Raquel y su madre han tenido una conversación seria.
Sí No 6. Es probable que Raquel se mude a la Argentina.
Sí No 7. Raquel siente que Luis se haya ido.
Sí No 8. La madre de Raquel se va a portar mejor con Arturo en el futuro.

3

VOCABULARIO DEL TEMA

Diversiones y pasatiempos

al aire libre	outdoors
el tiempo libre/los ratos libres	free time
cocinar	to cook
coleccionar estampillas/monedas...	to collect stamps/coins . . .
coser	to sew
dar/hacer fiestas	to give/have parties
dar paseos, pasear	to take walks
hacer un *picnic*	to have a picnic
ir al cine/a una función de teatro	to go to the movies/to a show at the theater
ir a un parque/al campo	to go to a park/the country
jugar (ue) a las cartas/al ajedrez/ al póquer/juegos de salón	to play cards/chess/poker/parlor games
leer revistas/novelas...	to read magazines/novels . . .
mirar la televisión	to watch television
pasarlo bien con los amigos	to have a good time with friends
sacar fotos/vídeos	to take photos/videos
salir con los amigos	to go out with friends
salir de la ciudad	to get out of the city
trabajar en el jardín	to work in the garden
ver una película	to see a movie
visitar un museo/a los parientes	to visit a museum/relatives
disfrutar (de), gozar (de)	to enjoy
divertirse (ie, i)	to have a good time
entretenerse	to entertain oneself
llevar una vida activa	to have an active life
llevar una vida sedentaria	to have a sedentary life

You already know many of the preceding words and phrases, especially the verbs in the second section. If a hobby or pastime of yours is not given here, find out how to say it in Spanish by looking it up in a dictionary or asking your instructor. You should pay particular attention to the names of activities that are important to you and to your friends and family.

Actividad A. El pasatiempo apropiado

Junta el objeto o concepto de la primera columna con los pasatiempos de la segunda. ¡OJO! Algunos conceptos admiten más de una asociación.

1. _____ las flores y las plantas
2. _____ las reuniones familiares y toda ocasión importante
3. _____ un rey y una reina
4. _____ un parque, una calle residencial tranquila
5. _____ objetos raros o especiales por alguna razón
6. _____ recetas para cocinar platos mexicanos, italianos…
7. _____ la barbacoa, el badmintón, las hormigas (*ants*)
8. _____ los dibujos animados, sobre todo el sábado por la mañana
9. _____ hacer su propia ropa
10. _____ historias de amor

a. cocinar
b. dar una fiesta
c. sacar vídeos
d. mirar la televisión
e. trabajar en el jardín
f. jugar al ajedrez
g. coser
h. hacer un *picnic*
i. leer novelas
j. coleccionar
k. dar un paseo

Actividad B. Cómo nos divertimos
Paso 1

Entre todas las actividades, ¿cuáles te gustan más? Haz una lista de diez actividades (pueden ser del **Vocabulario del tema** o no) en orden de importancia para ti (10 = la más importante).

MODELOS: (10) Mi actividad favorita es hacer un *picnic* en el campo.
(9) También me gusta sacar vídeos.

Paso 2

Ahora entrevista a cinco compañeros/as para saber cuáles son las diez actividades favoritas de cada uno/a. ¿Les gustan las mismas actividades? Apunta la posición de cada actividad en la lista de los otros.

Paso 3

Con un compañero / una compañera, hagan una lista de las actividades más populares entre los compañeros a quienes Uds. entrevistaron. Asignen puntos para cada actividad según su posición en cada lista. ¿Cuál es la actividad favorita del grupo?

Actividad C. Cuando tengo tiempo libre…

Explica lo que te gusta hacer en tus ratos libres.

1. Cuando tengo tiempo libre, me gusta _____

   porque…

2. Pienso que es aburrido/divertido _____

   porque…

3. Cuando era niño/a, pasaba mucho tiempo en/con

   _____.

4. Una cosa que nunca he aprendido a hacer —¡y que me gustaría mucho aprender!— es _____.

5. Para mí, lo mejor de vivir en esta ciudad / en el campo es que uno puede _____.

6. Yo no estaría contento/a si no pudiera _____.

Nota cultural, **Suggestion:** Ask students whether there are any activities in this country that compare with *el paseo* and café-sitting in Spanish-speaking countries. If so, what are they, and if not, why might that be?

Nota cultural Las diversiones en el mundo hispánico

As with sports activities, preferences in hobbies and pastimes—alone, with friends, or with family—are highly individual and are also greatly affected by social class and location. It is fair to suggest, however, that activities such as going to the movies and watching television are universally popular in the Spanish-speaking world.

Many families, like their counterparts in this country, simply enjoy going out to the country to have a picnic or a cookout and to play sports such as soccer, volleyball, or badminton.

Two activities that are not widely practiced in this country but that are an intimate part of Hispanic cultures throughout the world include **el paseo** and café-sitting.

- Going out for a walk with the family is a common, regular pastime for Hispanics wherever and whenever the weather permits. Especially around the midday meal and in the late afternoon, before the evening meal, the streets of many Hispanic cities are filled with people out for a walk. Sometimes errands and tasks are completed during the walk. Hispanics who come to this country are often struck by the absence of people in the streets, especially at those times when Hispanic customs tell them that the streets should be bustling with people.
- Hispanics often combine the pleasant custom of café-sitting with the **paseo**. They have a cup of coffee (or tea, a beer, mineral water, **un jerez** …), chat with their companions, and watch people walk by. This is a relaxing way to run into friends and enjoy the sun on a warm day. Many individuals make it their habit to have an after-lunch cup of coffee or drink (**copa**) at a local café or bar.

4 UN POCO DE GRAMÁTICA

The Workbook/Study Guide contains more detailed explanation and practice of this grammar point.

Suggestion: Before introducing the conditional perfect, review all the indicative and subjunctive verb forms that have been studied. Provide a handout with subject pronouns and infinitives (or pictures of actions) down the left-hand side of the page and either triggers and time expressions (*ojalá que, ayer, de niño, mañana, siempre*) or names of verb tenses and modes (*subjuntivo, pretérito, imperfecto, futuro, presente*) across the top of the page. Have students fill in the verb forms. They should be comfortable with those before moving on to *si* + past perfect subjunctive + the conditional perfect to express contrary-to-fact situations.

Expressing *If . . . , then . . .*

Use **Si (no) hubiera** + **-do** to express *If . . . , then . . .* statements such as the following.

Si Raquel **no hubiera ido** a Buenos Aires, nunca **habría (hubiera) conocido** a Arturo.

If Raquel had not gone to Buenos Aires, she never would have met Arturo.

Variation: On the board or overhead, write a *si* clause in past perfect subjunctive, based on *Destinos: Si Raquel no hubiera ido a Buenos Aires...* . Use it to initiate a chain game. One student begins by completing the statement, using a verb in conditional perfect: *Si Raquel no hubiera ido a Buenos Aires, nunca habría conocido a Arturo.* The next student creates a *si* clause from the preceding main clause and adds a new conditional perfect: *Si no hubiera conocido a Arturo, habría salido con Luis.* Student 3: *Si hubiera salido con Luis, su madre habría estado muy contenta.* Make sure that students change the conditional perfect from the main clause to a past perfect subjunctive in the new *si* clause.

Si Carlos **hubiera hablado** con la familia, tal vez **no habría (hubiera) sido** necesario cerrar la oficina en Miami.

If Carlos had spoken with his family, perhaps it would not have been necessary to close the Miami office.

Note that either the **habría** or **hubiera** form can be used in the "then" part of the sentence. You will learn more about these usages in the Workbook/Study Guide.

Act., Answers: 1. *México* 2. *Fernando e Isabela* 3. *Kennedy* 4. *franceses* 5. *John Wilkes Booth*

Actividad. Un poco de historia

¿Cuánto sabes de historia? Complete cada oración con información verdadera. ¡Cuántas más completes, más historia sabes!

1. Si los Estados Unidos no hubiera tenido una guerra con _____, California no sería uno de los estados hoy día.
2. Si _____ no le hubiera(n) ayudado económicamente, Cristóbal Colón no habría llegado a este continente.
3. Si el presidente _____ no hubiera soñado con la exploración del espacio en 1961, no habríamos llegado a la luna en 1969.
4. Si los _____ no hubieran colonizado la región de Quebec, los ciudadanos de esa región hablarían sólo inglés.
5. Si _____ no hubiera asesinado al presidente Lincoln en 1865, Andrew Johnson no habría sido presidente de los Estados Unidos.

5

LECTURA CULTURAL

El Parque de Chapultepec... y algunas notas sobre la historia de Texas

En los pueblos del mundo hispánico, casi siempre hay una plaza central donde se reúne la gente para ver a sus amigos, hablar con ellos y pasear. En las grandes ciudades de todos los países hay muchas plazas, pero también suele haber[1] una zona verde que es un parque público, por ejemplo, el famoso Parque Central en Nueva York, el Parque del Retiro en Madrid, el Rosedal en Buenos Aires. En México, está el Parque de Chapultepec.

El Parque de Chapultepec es un inmenso bosque de cipreses, con colinas[2] y espacios abiertos donde se reúne la gente —familias con sus niños, novios, esposos jóvenes y viejos—, sobre todo los fines de semana. Los domingos por la tarde hay conciertos gratis al aire libre. Toda el área del parque es una importante zona ecológica. Hay zoológicos, lagos y otros lugares de distracción. Hay también varios museos. En el Museo de Arte Moderno hay obras de los grandes pintores mexicanos del siglo XX. Y el famoso Museo de Antropología está al lado del Parque.

[1]*suele... there usually is* [2]*hills*

Lectura cultural, **Preguntas:** 1. ¿Cómo se llaman cuatro parques famosos? (*el Parque Central en Nueva York, el Parque del Retiro en Madrid, el Rosedal en Buenos Aires, el Parque de Chapultepec en México*) 2. ¿Cuándo hay conciertos gratis en Chapultepec? (*los domingos*) 3. ¿Qué cosas hay en el parque? (*zoológicos, lagos, varios museos y un castillo de la época colonial*) 4. ¿En qué año ganó Texas su independencia de México? (*en 1836*) 5. ¿Por qué hay un monumento que se llama los Niños Héroes? (*para conmemorar a los jóvenes que se tiraron de una muralla, prefiriendo la muerte a ser capturados*).

Se cree que el área de Chapultepec es el lugar donde se estableció por primera vez el pueblo mexicano en el valle de México. Durante muchos años las fuentes termales[3] de la zona abastecieron[4] de agua a la ciudad. Hoy día la zona se encuentra en el centro de la Ciudad de México.

En el Parque, hay también un castillo que data de la época colonial. Es ahora un museo que, con la estatua de los Niños Héroes, nos recuerda un episodio triste en la historia de México. ¿Sabes lo que es? Para contestar esa pregunta, hay que saber un poco de la historia de... Texas.

La República de Texas y lo que causó

El actual estado de Texas, antes territorio mexicano, ganó su independencia de México, tras[5] varios meses de conflicto armado, en 1836. (La famosa derrota[6] de El Álamo fue un episodio de esa guerra.) Nueve años más tarde, en 1845, Texas quedó incorporado a los Estados Unidos. Esto desencadenó[7] una guerra entre los dos países. Cuando terminó la guerra, México se vio obligado a cederles a los Estados Unidos dos quintas partes de su territorio.

Los Niños Héroes

La campaña final de esta guerra tuvo lugar en lo que es hoy el Parque de Chapultepec. En la cima de la colina de Chapulín, había un antiguo castillo que era en esa época una academia militar. Las tropas norteamericanas lo atacaron y, después de tres días de lucha, lo capturaron. Los jóvenes cadetes que lo defendían no querían entregarles[8] a las tropas la bandera[9] mexicana. Por eso uno de esos jóvenes se envolvió[10] en la bandera y se tiró de una muralla[11] del castillo. Los demás jóvenes lo siguieron, prefiriendo la muerte a ser capturados. El monumento a los Niños Héroes conmemora su valentía.[12]

El monumento a los Niños Héroes

[3]fuentes... *hot springs*   [4]*supplied*   [5]*after*   [6]*defeat*   [7]*set off*   [8]*hand over*   [9]*flag*   [10]se... *wrapped himself*   [11]se... *threw himself off a wall*   [12]*bravery*

6

INTERCAMBIO

Paso 1

Escribe cuatro oraciones sobre Raquel, una para cada país que visitó, describiendo lo que le ha pasado allí.

> MODELO: Si Raquel no hubiera aceptado la investigación al principio, nunca habría conocido a Arturo en Buenos Aires.

Paso 2

Túrnense para presentar oraciones sobre los cuatro países: España, la Argentina, Puerto Rico y México. Un voluntario debe marcar en la pizarra si cada oración describe un aspecto de la vida profesional de Raquel, de sus relaciones con Arturo, de sus relaciones con sus padres o de sus intercambios con otros personajes.

Paso 3
Ahora indica en qué aspecto de la vida de Raquel la clase se ha fijado más. Traten de explicar por qué.

VOCABULARIO

Diversiones y pasatiempos (Diversions and Pastimes)

al aire libre	outdoors
el tiempo libre/los ratos libres	free time
cocinar	to cook
coleccionar estampillas/monedas...	to collect stamps/coins . . .
coser	to sew
dar/hacer fiestas	to give/have parties
dar paseos, pasear	to take walks
hacer un *picnic*	to have a picnic
ir al cine/a una función de teatro	to go to the movies/to a show at the theater
ir a un parque/al campo	to go to a park/the country
jugar (ue) a las cartas/al ajedrez/ al póquer/juegos de salón	to play cards/chess/poker/parlor games
mirar la televisión	to watch television
sacar fotos/vídeos	to take photos/videos
salir con los amigos	to go out with friends
salir de la ciudad	to get out of the city
trabajar en el jardín	to work in the garden
ver una película	to see a movie
entretenerse	to entertain oneself
gozar (de)	to enjoy
llevar una vida activa	to have an active life
llevar una vida sedentaria	to have a sedentary life

Repaso: **disfrutar de, divertirse (ie, i), leer revistas/novelas, pasarlo bien con los amigos, visitar un museo/a los parientes**

Los adjetivos
enamorado/a (de)   in love (with)

47

Suggestion: Have students look at the photo, describe what they see, and talk about what they think might happen. Ask questions about the photo to prompt student discussion.

TENGO DUDAS*

*I Have Doubts

OBJETIVOS

The materials in **Lección 47** of the Textbook and the Workbook/Study Guide will help you better understand the video episode and take you beyond it, giving you additional information about places and characters in the series. The Textbook will also help you to develop skill in using the Spanish language. In this lesson, you will learn

- One way to express relationships between events

Be sure to work through all parts of the lesson. When you see a headphones symbol in the margin, listen to the CD for **Lección 47**. Answers or hints for many activities are given in Appendix 1. Be sure to check your answers for each activity before going on to the next one.

The interactive CD-ROM to accompany *Destinos* contains additional practice with the video storyline and will help you improve your skills in Spanish.

BEFORE VIEWING . . .

Preliminary: See Faculty Guide for additional information and activities for this lesson.
• **Variation:** For activities marked with the headphones icon, you may wish to read from the Audioscript instead of playing the CD.
• **Suggestion:** Make sure students are familiar with the activities before you read from the Audioscript or play the CD.

1

Preparación

Suggestions:
• Before watching the video, go over the vocabulary list at the end of the chapter and have students pronounce the words after you.
• Assign *Preparación* activities as homework and then go over them quickly in class before viewing the video.

Actividad.
Paso 1

Completa el siguiente resumen del episodio previo con las palabras y frases apropiadas.

1. iban a poder curar a
   ya no había nada que hacer para
2. pasar sus últimos días con su familia
   pasarlo bien con sus nietos
3. Tampoco le caía muy bien a Pancho
   Le caía muy bien a Pancho
4. se fuera a vivir a la Argentina
   nunca más volviera a Los Ángeles
5. caerle bien a Arturo
   conocer a Arturo
6. venderlo al regresar a San Juan
   no venderlo por el momento
7. conocer a su abuelo paterno
   hablar de la venta de La Gavia

Act. *Paso 1*, Answers:
1. *ya no había nada que hacer para* 2. *pasar sus últimos días con su familia* 3. *Le caía muy bien a Pancho* 4. *se fuera a vivir a la Argentina* 5. *conocer a Arturo* 6. *no venderlo por el momento* 7. *conocer a su abuelo paterno*

Act., Follow-up: Have students create additional true/false sentences about the previous episode, using details not included in the activity, then exchange papers with a partner and respond to each other's sentences.

En Guadalajara, el médico le dijo a Mercedes que

_____ [1] don Fernando. Por eso le dieron de alta.

Don Fernando sabía que regresaba a La Gavia para

_____.[2]

Mientras tanto, Arturo pudo hablar con Pancho, el padre de Raquel.

_____,[3] quien le dio un consejo sobre María, la madre de Raquel. Al mismo tiempo que hablaban los dos hombres, Raquel y su madre también estaban conversando. María pudo confesarle a su hija que temía que _____ [4] Más tarde, todos dieron un paseo juntos y María empezó a _____.[5]

Cuando Ángela y Roberto hablaron del apartamento, decidieron

_____.[6] Por la tarde, fueron a La Gavia con Arturo y Raquel para _____.[7]

 Paso 2
Ahora escucha el CD para verificar tus respuestas.

Para pensar...

1. Al final del episodio previo, Ángela y Roberto entraron al cuarto de don Fernando. ¿Qué les va a decir su abuelo? Si tú fueras uno de sus nietos, ¿qué le querrías decir a don Fernando?
2. ¿Crees que los otros miembros de la familia tendrán dificultades en aceptar a Ángela y Roberto?

Para comprender un poco más

el orfanato Cuando los padres de un niño se mueren, éste generalmente va a vivir con otros parientes. Cuando eso no es posible, mandan al niño a **un orfanato**, donde vive con otros huérfanos como él.

 . . . AFTER VIEWING

2

¿TIENES BUENA MEMORIA?

Actividad A.　¿Qué pasó con Raquel?
Paso 1

¿Puedes poner en orden cronológico los siguientes acontecimientos en que Raquel participó en este episodio?

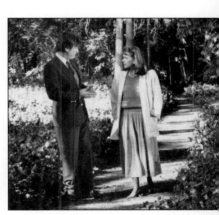

a. _____ Arturo le contestó que él se iría a vivir a Los Ángeles.

b. _____ Raquel le dijo a Arturo que no podía irse a vivir a la Argentina.

c. _____ Hubo un encuentro emocionante entre don Fernando, Ángela, Roberto y Arturo.

d. _____ Raquel les dejó un mensaje a sus padres para decirles que no regresaba al hotel esta noche.

e. _____ Durante el paseo, Arturo le quería hablar de algo importante.

f. _____ Les dijo que iba a quedarse en La Gavia para cenar con la familia.

g. _____ Arturo y Raquel salieron a dar un paseo.

 ### Paso 2
Ahora escucha el CD para verificar tus respuestas.

Para pensar…

Arturo le ha dicho a Raquel que está dispuesto a irse a vivir a Los Ángeles. Raquel le dice que debería pensarlo más, pero él no quiere. «Quiero actuar», le ha dicho a Raquel. ¿Crees que es una buena decisión? ¿Qué harías si tú fueras Raquel? ¿Y cómo van a reaccionar los padres de Raquel?

Actividad B.   ¿Y la familia Castillo?
Paso 1

Haz oraciones completas para describir lo que pasó con los miembros de la familia Castillo en este episodio.

1. Al llegar a La Gavia, don Fernando…
2. Los hermanos le dijeron a Carlos que…
3. Mercedes les propuso a todos que…
4. Carlos le confesó a Arturo…
5. Roberto y Ángela discutieron sobre…
6. Al final del episodio, don Fernando sorprendió a todos cuando les dijo que…

Paso 2

Ahora convierte las indicaciones del **Paso 1** en preguntas para hacerle a un compañero / una compañera. ¿Llegaron Uds. a las mismas conclusiones?

Para pensar…

¿Por qué tendrá don Fernando dudas? ¿Qué más podrán hacer Raquel y los demás para demostrarle que Ángela y Roberto son verdaderamente sus nietos?

3 UN POCO DE GRAMÁTICA

Expressing Relationships Between Events

The Spanish conjunction **para que**, meaning *in order that* (*for*), *so that*, expresses the relationship between the events in each part of a sentence. It is always followed by the subjunctive.

Para que don Fernando no **tenga** dudas, Raquel le va a decir cómo llegó a conocer a Ángela y Roberto.

So that don Fernando doesn't have any doubts, Raquel is going to tell him how she met Ángela and Roberto.

Raquel viajó a cuatro países y superó muchos obstáculos **para que** don Fernando **pudiera** conocer a sus nietos.	*Raquel traveled to four countries and overcame many obstacles so that don Fernando could meet his grandchildren.*

Note in the two examples that the present subjunctive is used in present-tense contexts and the past subjunctive in past-tense contexts. You will learn more about conjunctions such as **para que** in the Workbook/Study Guide.

Act., Suggestion: Assign as homework and have students present their sentences to the class the following day.

Act., Point out: Remind students that the expression *tendré que + infinitive = I will have to (do something).*

Act., Variation: Have students complete the sentences with true or false information, then take turns with a partner reading them and trying to determine which are true and which are false.

Actividad. ¿Qué necesita pasar?

Indica lo que necesita pasar para que cada situación se realice (*is accomplished*).

1. Para que me gradúe en la universidad, tendré que

    _____.

2. Para que yo pueda hablar español con facilidad, tendré que

    _____.

3. Para que mi vida sea completa, necesitaré

    _____.

4. Para que no exista la discriminación, todos deberíamos

    _____.

5. Para que yo pueda viajar por todo el mundo, tendré que

    _____.

6. Para que saque una buena nota en esta clase, tendré que

    _____.

7. Para que mis padres sean felices, tendré que

    _____.

8. Para que yo llegue a ser famoso/a, tendré que

    _____.

4

INTERCAMBIO

Paso 1

Como clase, piensen en las cosas que dos personas tienen que hacer para que sean felices como pareja. Un voluntario debe apuntar las ideas en la pizarra.

MODELO: Para que una pareja sea feliz, cada uno debe tener respeto para el otro.

Paso 2

En grupos de tres, revisen las ideas en la pizarra. ¿Cuántos pueden tener que ver con Raquel y Arturo? ¿Hay cosas particulares en cuanto a la relación entre ellos que no se reflejan en las ideas del **Paso 1**? Traten de decidir si Raquel y Artura serán felices.

Paso 3

Ahora, cada grupo debe presentar sus conclusiones del **Paso 2**. Al final, la clase debe decidir si Raquel y Arturo serán felices o no. ¿En qué se basan sus ideas?

VOCABULARIO

Los verbos

superar   to overcome, conquer

Los lugares

el orfanato   orphanage

Los conceptos

la duda   doubt

Las conjunciones

para que   in order that (for), so that

LECCIÓN **48**

Así fue* (i)

*That's How It Happened

Objetivos

All of this video episode is a review. Be sure to work through all parts of the lesson. Answers or hints for many activities are given in Appendix 1. Be sure to check your answers for each activity before going on to the next one.

 The interactive CD-ROM to accompany *Destinos* contains additional practice with the video storyline and will help you improve your skills in Spanish.

BEFORE VIEWING . . .

1

PREPARACIÓN

No es necesario hacer nada especial antes de ver el **Episodio 48**. Todo lo que ocurre lo has visto varias veces, pues son escenas de la investigación de Raquel en España. Raquel les va a contar a don Fernando y los demás lo que le pasó en esta parte de su viaje.

Antes de ver el episodio, piensa en todos los episodios que has visto y escuchado hasta ahora. ¿Te es más fácil ahora entender lo que dicen los personajes cuando hablan? ¿Captas más detalles ahora que antes? Es probable que entiendas mucho más ahora en comparación con lo que pudiste comprender cuando miraste los episodios por primera vez.

Para pensar...

En tu opinión, ¿quiénes son los personajes más importantes de la investigación de Raquel en España? Cuando piensas tú en el viaje de Raquel a España, ¿a quién(es) recuerdas inmediatamente? ¿Qué acontecimientos o información son de gran importancia para su investigación?

Algunos personajes de España

. . . AFTER VIEWING

2

REPASO DE LOS EPISODIOS 3–11

Act. A, Suggestion: You may want to have students do this activity in small groups.

Act. A, *Paso 1*, Answers: 2, 4, 5, 7, 8, 9, 10, 11, 12, 14, 15, 16

Actividad A.　Lo que pasó en España
Paso 1

De los siguientes acontecimientos, ¿cuáles son los que Raquel les menciona a los demás?

1. _____ su llegada al hotel en Sevilla
2. _____ cómo fue que no encontró a la Sra. Suárez en la calle Pureza
3. _____ su visita a una iglesia en el barrio de Triana
4. _____ cómo y dónde conoció a Elena Ramírez
5. _____ su conversación con Miguel Ruiz, hijo de Teresa Suárez
6. _____ el tiempo que pasó con la familia Ruiz y su aventura con Jaime y Osito, el nuevo perro del niño, cuando se perdieron en las calles del barrio de Santa Cruz
7. _____ cómo y dónde conoció a Alfredo Sánchez, el reportero
8. _____ el interés de Alfredo en el caso de don Fernando
9. _____ cómo perdió y luego recuperó su cartera
10. _____ la confusión de Alfredo sobre la maestra de Sevilla que había ganado un premio de la lotería
11. _____ cómo y dónde conoció a Federico Ruiz y luego a la Sra. Suárez
12. _____ la conversación que tuvo con Teresa Suárez
13. _____ la cena que tuvo con Federico y Teresa Suárez en su apartamento
14. _____ cómo y dónde se despidió de la Sra. Suárez
15. _____ su visita al Museo del Prado
16. _____ su llamada a Elena Ramírez para pedirle que le consiguiera el certificado de nacimiento de Ángel Castillo

Paso 2

¿Puedes explicar por qué Raquel omitió algunos acontecimientos? En tu opinión, ¿debería haberlos incluido en la narración que le hizo a don Fernando? ¿Por qué sí o por qué no?

Act. B, Suggestion: Assign as homework after watching the video. The following day, check answers in small groups, then as whole class.

Act. B, Answers: See Appendix 1.

Actividad B.　Reflexiones
Paso 1

¿Puedes contar lo que le pasó a Raquel en su viaje a España? Siguiendo este modelo, haz una breve narración. No están incluidos todos los detalles de la **Actividad A**.

Cuando Raquel llegó a Sevilla, no tardó en buscar a la Sra. Suárez. Fue a

_____, pero _____. Conoció a dos chicos en la calle. Ellos

_____. Luego llevaron a Raquel al mercado para _____.

Elena no sabía nada del caso, pero le sugirió a Raquel que sería buena

idea _____. Esa noche Raquel _____, pero Miguel tampoco sabía nada del caso. Sin embargo, le dijo a Raquel que había hablado con su madre, quien había dicho que _____.

A los dos días, Raquel salió para Madrid. En el tren, _____. El reportero _____. Como no tuvo éxito, se interesó en _____. Raquel, respetando la confidencialidad de su cliente, _____.

En su hotel en Madrid, Raquel bajaba de su habitación cuando _____. La invitó a su casa a cenar y por fin Raquel _____. Ésta le contó la triste historia de _____, quien al final de la Guerra Civil _____, pensando que don Fernando había muerto. La Sra. Suárez también le dio a Raquel _____. Ahora Raquel podía seguir con su investigación. Se preparó para otro viaje, esta vez a Buenos Aires.

Paso 2
Ahora compara tu narración con la del Apéndice 1. ¿Son muy similares?

Actividad C.   Juego de nombres
Trabajando en grupos de tres o cuatro personas, piensen en todos los personajes de los **Episodios 3–11**. Den el nombre de cada personaje y describan su apariencia física y su función en la historia completa. El profesor / La profesora va a decidir si la descripción es adecuada o no.

1. Cuando es su turno, cada grupo debe nombrar a un personaje y presentar la descripción de él/ella. Si la descripción es adecuada, el profesor / la profesora va a escribir el nombre en la pizarra. Si no es adecuada, el grupo pierde su turno.
2. Siguen los grupos uno por uno. Cuando un grupo ya no pueda nombrar a otro personaje distinto, se retira del juego y los otros siguen describiendo a los personajes. El grupo que nombra al último personaje gana el juego.

Act. C, Follow-up: Write the names of the characters on the board and have students brainstorm what they look like and what happened to each, or come to the board and write their descriptions and what happened to each under the characters' names. Go over as whole class.

3

PARA ESCRIBIR

Raquel did not tell don Fernando about Jaime's losing Osito, nor did she talk about the fact that she left her wallet in a taxi in Madrid. But it's a fact that people lose things all the time. Osito escaped, which is one way that things "get lost." In the taxi, however, Raquel just left her wallet behind.

What kinds of objects do people tend to lose or leave somewhere, forgetting about them? What items *don't* people tend to forget or lose? In this composition, you will answer these questions and also explain why you think people forget the things they do. You will be writing for a classmate who will be answering the same questions. If possible, you should compare your composition with what another person taking the course has written. Your composition should be no fewer than 300 and no more than 500 words long.

Go to the Workbook/Study Guide to begin this writing activity.

ASÍ FUE* (II)

*That's How It Happened

OBJETIVOS

All of this video episode is a review. Be sure to work through all parts of the lesson. Answers or hints for many activities are given in Appendix 1. Be sure to check your answers for each activity before going on to the next one.

The interactive CD-ROM to accompany *Destinos* contains additional practice with the video storyline and will help you improve your skills in Spanish.

BEFORE VIEWING . . .

1

PREPARACIÓN

En este episodio, Raquel sigue contándoles a don Fernando y los demás de su investigación. Ahora les va a decir lo que pasó cuando estaba en Buenos Aires, Argentina.

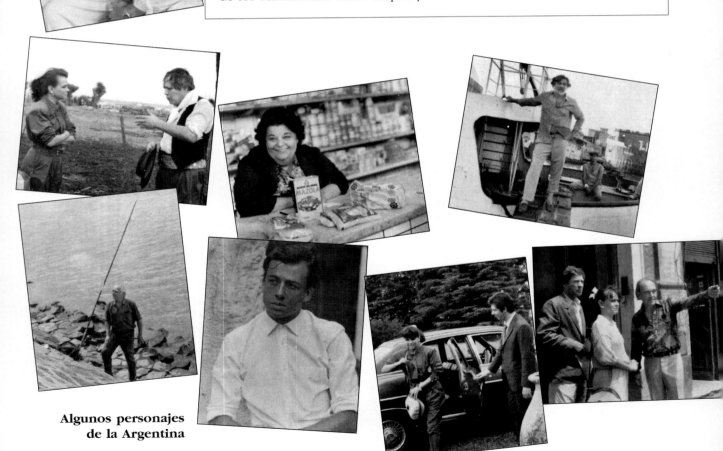

Para pensar...

Seguramente que Raquel les va a hablar de la muerte de Rosario y de cómo llegó a saber del paradero de Ángel. ¿Crees tú que también les va a hablar de sus relaciones con Arturo? Ya sabes que Ángela está al tanto de todo (*knows all about it*), pero ¿crees que los demás se han dado cuenta de los sentimientos entre Raquel y Arturo?

Algunos personajes de la Argentina

. . . AFTER VIEWING

2

Repaso de los Episodios 12–18

Act. A, Suggestion: Give students about 3 minutes to complete the activity individually or in pairs, then check answers as whole class.

Actividad A.   ¿Quién la ayudó?

En la Argentina, varios personajes hicieron algo para ayudar a Raquel en su investigación. ¿Puedes encontrar el nombre de la persona que la ayudó con lo siguiente?

a. José
b. Arturo
c. Héctor
d. Cirilo
e. Mario
f. doña Flora
g. el venddor de pescado

Act. A, Answers: 1. b 2. d 3. a 4. a 5. b 6. c 7. c 8. e

Act. A, Variation: Have students work in pairs. One student covers the sentences but not the names. The other student reads the sentences aloud and the first tries to match the description with one of the names.

1. _____ Le dijo a Raquel que Rosario ya había muerto.
2. _____ Le dio a Raquel información sobre dónde podía encontrar a Rosario y su hijo en Buenos Aires.
3. _____ Conocía a Héctor y les dijo a Raquel y Arturo que era posible que Héctor conociera a Ángel.
4. _____ Les dijo dónde podían encontrar a Héctor.
5. _____ Quiso ayudar a Raquel en su búsqueda.
6. _____ Reconoció al joven de la foto, Ángel a los veinte años.
7. _____ Tenía una carta con la dirección de Ángel en Puerto Rico.
8. _____ Pensó en José y habló con su esposa, doña Flora, para averiguar dónde podían encontrar a José esa tarde.

Actividad B.   Reflexiones
Paso 1

Act. B, Suggestion: Allow students about 15 minutes to complete the activity individually or in pairs, then have them compare their answers with those in Appendix 1. Circulate in the classroom offering clarifications and other help as needed, while students complete the narration.

Act. B, Point out: The narration is in past tense. Students should use past-tense verb forms, particularly preterite and imperfect, as well as attending to content.

Act. B, Answers: See Appendix 1.

¿Puedes tú contar lo que le pasó a Raquel en su viaje a la Argentina? Siguiendo este modelo, haz una breve narración. No están incluidos todos los detalles de la **Actividad A**.

Cuando Raquel llegó a Buenos Aires, alquiló un coche con un chofer para ir a la estancia Santa Susana, la dirección que Teresa Suárez _____. Tenía muchas esperanzas de encontrar a Rosario. Llamó a la puerta y _____. Éste no sabía nada de Rosario, pero le dijo a Raquel que _____. Cirilo sí _____ y _____. También se acordaba de _____.

Raquel regresó a Buenos Aires y buscó la dirección que Cirilo le había dado. Por fin, en una casa en la calle Gorostiaga, _____. Raquel quedó muy sorprendida al encontrar por fin a un miembro de la familia. Desgraciadamente, _____. Arturo también le contó a Raquel que no sabía nada de Ángel porque _____.

Los dos fueron al cementerio donde estaba enterrada Rosario. Allí _____. Más tarde Arturo le dijo _____. Con una foto de Ángel a los veinte años, los dos _____. Preguntaron en varias tiendas, pero

_____. Por fin, Mario, el dueño de una tienda de antigüedades, dijo que era posible que un tal José lo conociera. Encontraron a José en su barco. José _____. Más tarde les dijo dónde y cuándo podrían encontrar a Héctor.

En un bar llamado el Piccolo Navio, Raquel y Arturo encontraron a Héctor con sus amigos. Al acompañarlo a casa, le mostraron la foto de Ángel. Héctor _____. Pensaba que Ángel se había embarcado para _____. A los dos días Héctor le dio a Arturo una carta de Ángel que tenía en su casa. La carta _____. Era verdad: Ángel _____.

Ahora, para seguir su investigación, Raquel tenía que ir a Puerto Rico. Fue _____. Se despidió de Arturo en el aero-puerto. Mientras esperaba su vuelo, _____.

Paso 2
Ahora compara tu narración con la del Apéndice 1. ¿Son muy similares?

Actividad C.   ¿Cómo ocurrió?
Trabajando en grupos de tres o cuatro personas, representen las escenas más importantes de los **Episodios 12–18**. Claro, el diálogo no tiene que ser idéntico, pero debe contener lo esencial de la escena representada. Cada grupo debe informarle al profesor / a la profesora qué escena va a escoger para que no se repitan las escenas. Después de cada representación, los otros grupos tienen que identificar la escena y los personajes en ella.

3

PARA ESCRIBIR

Although Raquel told don Fernando many of the details of the search for Rosario and Ángel in Buenos Aires, she did not give him any information at all about her feelings for Arturo nor about any of the intimate things that happened between them. Some people would say that things moved too quickly between Arturo and Raquel, and, in fact, even Raquel has commented on this.

What do you think? Did their relationship progress too quickly? Or perhaps not quickly enough? In this composition, you will answer these questions and also express what you think about the way their relationship has developed thus far. You will be writing for a classmate who will be answering the same questions. If possible, you should compare your composition with what another person taking the course has written. Your composition should be no fewer than 300 and no more than 500 words long.

Go to the Workbook/Study Guide to begin this writing activity.

Así fue* (iii)

*That's How It Happened

Objetivos

All of this video episode is a review. Be sure to work through all parts of the lesson. Answers or hints for many activities are given in Appendix 1. Be sure to check your answers for each activity before going on to the next one.

The interactive CD-ROM to accompany *Destinos* contains additional practice with the video storyline and will help you improve your skills in Spanish.

BEFORE VIEWING . . .

Preliminary: See Faculty Guide for additional information and activities for this lesson.
• **Variation:** For activities marked with the headphones icon, you may wish to read from the Audioscript instead of playing the CD.
• **Suggestion:** Make sure students are familiar with the activities before you read from the Audioscript or play the CD.

1

Preparación

Suggestion: Before watching the video, have students look at the photos from the episodes in Puerto Rico. See if they can name or describe all of the individuals pictured.

En este episodio, Raquel sigue contándoles a don Fernando y los demás los incidentes de su investigación. Ahora les va a decir lo que pasó cuando fue a Puerto Rico.

> ### Para pensar...
>
> Ya tienes una idea, más o menos, del tipo de información que Raquel está incluyendo en su narración para la familia Castillo. Piensa en lo que sucedió en Puerto Rico. ¿Qué incidentes o detalles crees que Raquel incluirá y qué omitirá en la narración de este episodio? ¿Qué omitirías tú y qué incluirías?

Algunos personajes de Pueto Rico

. . . AFTER VIEWING

2

REPASO DE LOS EPISODIOS 19–26

Actividad A.   ¿Qué pasó en Puerto Rico?
Paso 1

Contesta las siguientes preguntas sobre los acontecimientos en Puerto Rico.

1. ¿Cómo se enteró Raquel de la muerte de Ángel? ¿Se lo dijo alguien o encontró la tumba por casualidad (*by chance*) mientras visitaba el cementerio?

2. ¿Cuándo supo Raquel que Ángela tenía un hermano? ¿cuando hablaban en el apartamento de Ángela, antes de la llegada de los tíos, o cuando los tíos hablaban con ella?

3. ¿Sabían los tíos algo del pasado de Ángel? ¿O fue la primera vez que oían los nombres de Rosario y don Fernando?

4. Los tíos pensaron que era importante que Ángela hablara con alguien. ¿Con quién? ¿Con la abuela de Ángela o con su hermano?

5. Camino a San Germán, Ángela, Raquel y Laura tuvieron problemas con el carro. ¿Pudieron llegar a San Germán esa noche o tuvieron que quedarse en Ponce?

6. En casa de la abuela, ésta le recordó a Ángela que había algo relacionado con su padre que Ángela no había hecho. ¿A qué se refería la abuela, a limpiar el cuarto de Ángel o a leer su testamento (*will*)?

7. ¿Qué encontraron Ángela y Raquel entre las cosas de Ángel, unas fotos de su familia en Buenos Aires o uno dibujos que él había hecho con recuerdos de su pasado?

8. ¿Qué pasó justo cuando Raquel y Ángela salían para el aeropuerto? ¿Se pelearon o recibieron noticias importantes?

Paso 2

¿Qué partes de lo que le pasó en Puerto Rico omitió Raquel en su narración? Haz una lista de los personajes y situaciones omitidos.

> ### Para pensar...
>
> ¿Notaste que Raquel no mencionó nada de Jorge, el novio de Ángela? ¿Por qué todavía no le ha dicho nada de lo que le pasó con Jorge en San Juan?

Actividad B.   **Reflexiones**
Paso 1
¿Puedes tú contar lo que le pasó a Raquel en su viaje a Puerto Rico? Siguiendo este modelo, haz una breve narración. No están incluidos todos los detalles de la **Actividad A**.

Cuando llegó a San Juan, Raquel fue directamente a la dirección que estaba en la carta de Héctor. Tocó a la puerta, pero _____. Desde su balcón, una vecina le dijo que _____. En el cementerio Raquel _____. Allí en el cementerio, Raquel se lo explicó todo.

Raquel y Ángela regresaron al apartamento donde vivía ella, que era el antiguo apartamento de sus padres. Desde allí Ángela _____ para que vinieran a conocer a Raquel. Mientras los esperaban, seguían hablando. Raquel supo que _____.

Cuando llegaron los tíos de Ángela, Raquel les contó la historia de don Fernando y les habló de su investigación. También les dijo que Ángela _____. La tía Olga, la gruñona de la familia, _____. Por eso Ángela llamó a _____ para pedirle consejo. Ésta quería que Ángela y Raquel fueran a verla a San Germán.

Al día siguiente Raquel y Ángela, acompañadas por Laura, la prima de Ángela, salieron para San Germán. En un peaje tuvieron _____. Se quedaron por la noche en Ponce y a la mañana siguiente _____.

En San Germán, almorzaron con la abuela y hablaron de Ángel y su esposa. La abuela le recordó a Ángela que _____. Allí, en un viejo baúl, Ángela _____. Eran _____. Al salir para San Juan, la abuela salió corriendo de la casa y _____.

De regreso en San Juan, Raquel y Ángela pasaron por el banco donde trabajaba Ángela para _____. También vieron unos apartamentos con una agente de bienes raíces, porque Ángela _____. Al día siguiente, cuando salían para el aeropuerto, llegó el tío Jaime con malas noticias: _____.

Paso 2
Ahora compara tu narración con la del Apéndice 1. ¿Son muy similares?

Actividad C. **Otra perspectiva**

Trabajando en grupos de tres o cuatro personas, escojan a un personaje de los **Episodios 19–26** y preparen una descripción de lo que pasó en esos episodios desde la perspectiva de ese personaje. Los miembros de los grupos deben consultarse para determinar cuál sería la perspectiva del personaje. ¡OJO! Recuerden que varios personajes no saben toda la historia y pueden tener perspectivas muy distintas de las de Raquel y de Ángela, por ejemplo. Cada grupo debe presentar su descripción a la clase.

3

PARA ESCRIBIR

Although Raquel told don Fernando many of the details of her visit to Puerto Rico, she did not give him any information at all about her dealings with Jorge nor about her fight with Ángela. In fact, Raquel didn't even tell Ángela about what happened with Jorge.

What do you think? Should Raquel say something to Ángela now? Or should she have said more earlier on? Why or why not? What might the implications be of telling her (or not telling her)? In this composition, you will answer these questions. You will be writing for a classmate who will be answering the same questions. If possible, you should compare your composition with what another person taking the course has written. Your composition should be no fewer than 300 and no more than 500 words long.

Go to the Workbook/Study Guide to begin this writing activity.

51

ASÍ FUE* (IV)

*That's How It Happened

OBJETIVOS

All of this video episode is a review. Be sure to work through all parts of the lesson. Answers or hints for many activities are given in Appendix 1. Be sure to check your answers for each activity before going on to the next one.

The interactive CD-ROM to accompany *Destinos* contains additional practice with the video storyline and will help you improve your skills in Spanish.

BEFORE VIEWING . . .

Preliminary: See Faculty Guide for additional information and activities for this lesson.
• **Variation:** For activities marked with the headphones icon, you may wish to read from the Audioscript instead of playing the CD.
• **Suggestion:** Make sure students are familiar with the activities before you read from the Audioscript or play the CD.

1

PREPARACIÓN

Suggestion: Before watching the video, have students look at the photos from the episodes in Mexico. See if they can name or describe all of the individuals pictured.

En este episodio Raquel concluye la narración de los incidentes de su investigación. Va a contarle a don Fernando lo que le ha pasado hasta ahora en México. ¿Hasta qué punto llega la narración de Raquel? ¿Cuáles son los acontecimientos más importantes para el caso?

Algunos personajes de México

. . . AFTER VIEWING

2

REPASO DE LOS EPISODIOS 27–36

Actividad A.   En el sitio de la excavación
Paso 1

Pon en orden cronológico (del 1 al 10) los siguientes sucesos.

a. _____ Se derrumbó todo otra vez.

b. _____ Por fin Raquel pudo dejarle un mensaje a Arturo en el hotel.

c. _____ Fueron al hospital para ver si Roberto era uno de los accidentados.

d. _____ Ángela se puso histérica y el médico le dio un calmante.

e. _____ Raquel y Ángela llegaron por primera vez al sitio de la excavación.

f. _____ Sacaron a varias personas de la excavación, pero ninguna era Roberto.

g. _____ Raquel y Ángela se fueron a la capital y en el camino por poco chocan con un camión blanco.

h. _____ Rescataron a Roberto y lo llevaron a México.

i. _____ Allí conocieron a un padre, quien les ayudó mucho durante su estancia en el pueblo.

j. _____ Conocieron a la hermana María Teresa, quien les dio donde descansar y refrescarse.

Paso 2

Imagina que eres don Fernando y que Raquel acaba de resumirte su investigación. ¿Estás satisfecho ahora con lo que ella ha dicho? ¿Todavía tienes dudas?

Actividad B.   Reflexiones
Paso 1

¿Puedes tú contar lo que le pasó a Raquel en el sitio de la excavación? Siguiendo este modelo, haz una breve narración. No están incluidos todos los detalles de la **Actividad A**.

Tan pronto como llegaron a México, Raquel y Ángela alquilaron un auto y salieron para un pueblo cerca de la excavación donde trabajaba Roberto. En el camino, Ángela le habló a Raquel de _____ y le confesó que _____.

Al llegar al sitio, no las dejaron pasar. Entonces _____. Allí les dieron la lista de los accidentados. Por un momento, _____.

En el hospital conocieron a un padre que las ayudó mucho a lo largo de su estancia en el pueblo. Por medio del padre, Ángela y Raquel pudieron

_____. Tenían muchas esperanzas de que rescataran a Roberto pronto. Por fin sacaron a dos personas, pero _____. Antes de que pudieran sacar a otras personas, _____. Ángela comenzó a llorar y le tuvieron que dar un calmante. Por fin se pudo dormir, y Raquel _____.

Por la mañana, mientras seguían esperando el rescate de Roberto, Raquel y Ángela hicieron varias llamadas. Raquel _____. Y Ángela _____. Después fueron a la iglesia del pueblo, donde _____.

Por fin encontraron a Roberto… ¡y _____! Antes de que pudieran rescatarlo, sin embargo, _____. Pero lo pudieron sacar de todas formas. Lo examinaron en seguida; por suerte _____. Sin embargo _____. Raquel y Ángela salieron para México en su auto, y en el camino _____. Al llegar al hospital, Ángela entró corriendo al cuarto de Roberto. Arturo, quien estaba allí con Pedro, vio a Raquel y _____.

Paso 2
Ahora compara tu narración con la del Apéndice 1. ¿Son muy similares?

Actividad C.   El diario secreto de Raquel
Paso 1
Como se sabe, Raquel ha escrito los acontecimientos de la historia en su diario. Trabajando en grupos de tres o cuatro personas, hagan una lista de temas que ella habrá tratado desde el principio de su investigación.

Paso 2
Los miembros de cada grupo deben ponerse de acuerdo respecto a un solo tema sobre el cual van a escribir. Consulten con el profesor / la profesora para que no se repitan los temas. ¡OJO! Recuerden que este tema forma una parte ocultada (*hidden*) del diario. Es decir, trata de algo que Uds. no vieron en los episodios.

Paso 3
Como grupo, escriban una página de las observaciones posibles (usando lo que saben de las actitudes y la personalidad de Raquel) sobre el tema escogido.

3

PARA ESCRIBIR

In a previous video episode Raquel asked herself: **¿Cómo sería mi vida si todavía estuviera con Luis?** Many people asked themselves "What would happen if . . . ?" or "What if I were . . . ?", especially when they are thinking about important moments or events in their lives.

In this composition, you will answer a "What if . . . ?" question.

¿Cómo sería el mundo si todos habláramos el mismo idioma?

You will be writing for a classmate who will be answering the same questions. If possible, you should compare your composition with what another person taking the course has written. Your composition should be no fewer than 300 and no more than 500 words long.

Go to the Workbook/Study Guide to begin this writing activity.

52

Suggestion: Have students look at the photo, describe what they see, and talk about what they think might happen. Ask questions about the photo to prompt student discussion.

SIEMPRE LO AMÓ*

*She Always Loved You

OBJETIVOS

The materials in **Lección 52** of the Textbook will help you better understand the video episode. There is no corresponding Workbook/Study Guide lesson for this episode.

Be sure to work through all parts of the lesson. When you see a head-phones symbol in the margin, listen to the CD for **Lección 52**. Answers or hints for many activities are given in Appendix 1. Be sure to check your answers for each activity before going on to the next one.

The interactive CD-ROM to accompany *Destinos* contains additional practice with the video storyline and will help you improve your skills in Spanish.

BEFORE VIEWING . . .

Preliminary: See Faculty Guide for additional information and activities for this lesson.
• **Variation:** For activities marked with the headphones icon, you may wish to read from the Audioscript instead of playing the CD.
• **Suggestion:** Make sure students are familiar with the activities before you read from the Audioscript or play the CD.

1

PREPARACIÓN

Note: There is no corresponding Workbook/Study Guide lesson for this episode.

Suggestion: Assign the *Preparación* activity as homework and then go over it quickly in class before viewing the video.

Act., Suggestion: You may want to have students do this activity in pairs.

Act., Paso 1, Answers:
1. b 2. a 3. a 4. a 5. b

Actividad.
Paso 1

En los **Episodios 48–51** de *Destinos,* has escuchado la narración de Raquel para don Fernando y no hubo información nueva. En este episodio la historia sigue. ¿Te acuerdas de lo que pasó en el **Episodio 47**? Completa las siguientes oraciones.

1. Ángela y Roberto por fin conocieron
   a. _____ al médico de don Fernando.
   b. _____ a don Fernando.

2. Raquel decidió quedarse en La Gavia esa noche porque
   a. _____ había una gran cena y todos querían que se quedara.
   b. _____ no quería ver a sus padres.

3. Mientras Arturo y Raquel daban un paseo en la hacienda, Arturo le pidió a Raquel que
   a. _____ se fuera a vivir a Buenos Aires con él.
   b. _____ hablara con la madre de ella sobre él.

4. Al oír la respuesta negativa de Raquel, Arturo le dijo que
   a. _____ él se iría a vivir a Los Ángeles.
   b. _____ entendía por qué ella no quería hablar con su madre.

5. Durante la cena, todos se sorprendieron cuando don Fernando se presentó y dijo que
   a. _____ tenía dudas sobre la identidad de Ángel y Arturo.
   b. _____ tenía dudas sobre la identidad de Ángela y Roberto.

 ### Paso 2
Ahora escucha el CD para verificar tus respuestas.

Para pensar, **Suggestion:** Pose the same questions to several students to elicit a variety of opinions.

Para pensar...

Don Fernando los sorprendió a todos cuando les dijo que tenía grandes dudas. ¿Qué otra(s) prueba(s) quiere? ¿Qué pueden hacer o decir Ángela y Roberto para que él esté seguro de su identidad?

. . . AFTER VIEWING

2

¿TIENES BUENA MEMORIA?

Actividad.   En el episodio final
Paso 1

¿Puedes tú contar lo que pasó en el episodio final? Siguiendo este modelo, haz una breve narración.

Don Fernando tenía dudas de la identidad de Ángela y Roberto, y quería estar seguro de que eran sus nietos. Raquel le recordó a Ángela lo de la copa de bodas de Rosario, que _____.

Al día siguiente, llegó la agente de bienes raíces. El deseo de su cliente de comprar La Gavia no fue realizado, porque _____. Entonces Mércedes reveló su plan para fundar un orfanato en la hacienda. Todos quedaron sorprendidos cuando don Fernando reveló que _____. Según don Fernando, Carlos y Mercedes _____. Juan debería regresar a Nueva York, porque _____.

Más tarde, en el cuarto de don Fernando, cuando todos estaban presentes, Ángela _____. Cuando don Fernando la abrió, se puso muy emocionado. Entonces le pidió a Mercedes que le diera a Ángela una caja que él tenía allí en su cuarto, en un armario. Cuando Ángela la abrió, _____. Así ya no había dudas: _____.

Raquel y Arturo se despidieron de don Fernando y estaban para salir. Pero el patriarca quería hablar con Raquel a solas. Le dijo que no se la había escapado cómo _____. Raquel le confesó que _____. Entonces don Fernando le dio unos consejos: o ella _____ o él _____, que no debían perder un amor verdadero. Se abrazaron una vez más.

Antes de salir, Raquel se volvió y le dijo a don Fernando que Rosario nunca dejó de pensar en él, que _____. Con las dos copas reunidas, don Fernando se quedó en su cuarto a solas, pensando en el día en que, hace años, en un país lejano, dos jóvenes españoles las habían usado para celebrar el día de su boda.

Paso 2
Ahora compara tu narración con la del Apéndice 1. ¿Son muy similares?

CINCO AÑOS DESPUÉS

Suggestion: You may want to have students discuss these questions in pairs or small groups before they write.

Imagina que han pasado cinco años desde ese día en que Raquel se despidió de don Fernando. ¿Qué ha pasado? ¿En qué situación o condición están los varios personajes? ¿Qué ha pasado entre Arturo y Raquel, Juan y Pati, Carlos y Gloria y los demás? ¿Qué le ha pasado a don Fernando? ¿Y La Gavia? ¿Todavía pertenece a la familia Castillo? ¿Quién(es) vive(n) allí ahora?

Escribe una breve composición (100–200 palabras) con este título: «*Destinos*: Cinco años después».

APPENDIX 1: ANSWER SECTION

In many of the **Preparación** sections, "prediction" activities encourage you to guess at the content of upcoming video episodes. The answers to these types of activities will be found not with the answers to other **Preparación** activities but at the end of the answers to the **¿Tienes buena memoria?** sections. This has been done to discourage you from checking your answers before you watch the video episode.

You should always go back and look at your answers to those activities *after* you have watched the video episode. If you are still unsure of an answer, that is the time to check it at the end of the **¿Tienes buena memoria?** section.

ENTREMESES

Actividad A. 1. c 2. a 3. b 4. b 5. a **Actividad B.** A. 3, 5, 1, 2, 4 B. 2, 5, 1, 4, 3

LECCIÓN 1

¿TIENES BUENA MEMORIA?

Actividad A. 1. c 2. b 3. a **Actividad B.** *Paso 1* 1. Julio 2. Juan 3. La Gavia 4. Raquel 5. Mercedes 6. Ramón 7. Carlos **Actividad C.** 1. b. El nombre completo de Raquel es Raquel Rodríguez. 2. b. Raquel es mexicoamericana. 3. a. Raquel vive en Los Ángeles.
Preparación. **Actividad A.** 3 **Actividad B.** 2 **Actividad C.** 1

VOCABULARIO DEL TEMA

Actividad. 1. b. Es un concepto. 2. d. Es una persona. 3. d. Es una persona. 4. d. Es una persona. 5. d. Es una persona. 6. c. Es una cosa. 7. b. Es un concepto.

LECCIÓN 2

PREPARACIÓN

Actividad A. 1. de España. 2. El secreto tiene que ver con la vida privada de don Fernando. **Actividad B.** Ramón va a llamar a otras personas de la familia.

¿TIENES BUENA MEMORIA?

Actividad A. *Paso 1* 1. e 2. f 3. g 4. a 5. c 6. d 7. b *Un desafío* 1. b 2. c 3. h 4. d 5. e 6. a 7. f 8. g
Actividad B. *Paso 1* 1. Pedro vive en la Ciudad de México. 2. Lupe vive en La Gavia. 3. Juan vive en Nueva York. 4. Julio vive en la Ciudad de México. 5. Raquel vive en Los Ángeles. 6. Pati vive en Nueva York. 7. Ramón vive en La Gavia. 8. Carlos vive en Miami. **Actividad C.** Don Fernando tiene otra esposa. Don Fernando tiene otro hijo. *Paso 2* 1. Pedro es abogado. 2. Lupe es cocinera en La Gavia. 3. Juan es profesor de literatura en la universidad. 4. Julio es el médico de la familia. 5. Raquel es abogada. 6. Pati es profesora de teatro en la universidad. 7. Ramón es administrador de la hacienda. 8. Carlos es director de la Compañía Castillo Saavedra, S.A.
Preparación. **Actividad C.** b. Ramón le dice a Carlos que hoy vino el médico para ver a don Fernando. b. Ramón desea que Carlos venga a la hacienda.

UN POCO DE GRAMÁTICA

Actividad. *Paso 1* *If you answered with the names only of the people described, that is fine. But you should read the full sentences anyway when you check your answers for this activity.* 1. Sus hijos fueron Jack (John F.) Kennedy y Bobby (Robert) Kennedy. 2. Su padre fue Pablo Picasso. 3. Su madre fue Eva (*Eve*) (y su padre fue Adán [*Adam*]). 4. Su esposa fue Eleanor Roosevelt. 5. Su hermana fue Gretel. 6. Su hermano es Michael Jackson. 7. Su hermano es Peter Fonda. Su padre fue Henry Fonda. 8. Su esposo fue Ulises (*Ulysses*). 9. Su hermano fue Remo (*Remus*). 10. Su hija fue la reina Isabel (*Elizabeth*). 11. Su quinto esposo fue Richard Burton. 12. Sus hijos son Emilio Estevez y Charlie Sheen.

LECCIÓN 3

PREPARACIÓN

Actividad A. 1. Falso. Raquel no es miembro de la familia Castillo. 2. Cierto. 3. Cierto. 4. Cierto. 5. Cierto. Es lógico, ya que (*since*) la carta es de España.

¿TIENES BUENA MEMORIA?

Actividad A. *Paso 1* 1. c 2. b 3. d ***Paso 2*** 1. e 2. d 3. d, e 4. d, e 5. a 6. c 7. b 8. e **Actividad C. *Paso 1*** 1. c 2. b 3. a 4. b
Preparación.* Actividad B.** 1. España. *This is the best answer based on what you know now. But don't rule out the possibility of other destinations in a series called* Destinos. 2. Rosario, la primera esposa de don Fernando; la persona que escribió la carta; otro hijo de don Fernando. *Three of the answers are possible. Raquel needs to find the letter writer in order to find out whether Rosario is alive and whether don Fernando has another child.* 3. el nombre de la persona que escribió la carta; el nombre de la calle donde la persona vive. *It is logical for Raquel to know this, because don Fernando has a letter from this person. The possible existence of a child is the mystery, thus no name is known.* **Actividad C. *Paso 1 b ***Paso 2*** a, c

LECTURA CULTURAL

Actividad. 1. Falso. España es un país de contrastes. 2. Cierto. 3. Falso. Otros idiomas que se hablan son el catalán, el gallego y el vascuence. 4. Cierto. 5. Falso. España es una monarquía constitucional.

LECCIÓN 4

PREPARACIÓN

Actividad A. 1. Sevilla 2. Teresa Suárez 3. Teresa Suárez 4. dos chicos 5. Madrid 6. Elena Ramírez 7. la madre 8. no tiene

¿TIENES BUENA MEMORIA?

Actividad A. *Por la noche:* a. 1 b. 3 c. 2 *Al día siguiente:* a. 3 b. 2 c. 4 d. 1 **Actividad B. *Paso 1*** 1. d 2. b 3. c 4. a ***Paso 2*** 1. Cierto. 2. Falso. Miguel no sabe nada. 3. Cierto. 4. Falso. Los chicos no toman un fino. 5. Cierto. Acepta la responsabilidad, pero... ¿realmente cumple con ella (*does he live up to it*)? 6. Cierto. 7. Cierto. 8. Cierto. Por eso (*That's why*) desea ponerle *Einstein* al perro. 9. Falso. Miguel es buen estudiante. ***Preparación.* Actividad B.** 1. b 2. a **Actividad C. *Paso 1*** a, c ***Paso 2*** c

VOCABULARIO DEL TEMA

Actividad A. 1. los dos 2. Jaime 3. los dos 4. Miguel 5. Jaime *Otras materias: business* = el comercio; *foreign languages* = las lenguas extranjeras; *accounting* = la contabilidad; *chemistry* = la química **Actividad B.** a. 3 b. 2 c. 4 d. 1 **Actividad G.** *Fish:* (peces) tropicales *Birds:* canarios, loros (*parrots*), patitos (*ducklings*)

LECTURA CULTURAL

1. Cierto. 2. Falso. En Sevilla, hay tradiciones judías, árabes y cristianas. 3. Cierto 4. Cierto 5. Falso. Hay barrios modernos, pero no son tan (*as*) interesantes como las otras partes de la ciudad, según (*according to*) algunas personas.

LECCIÓN 5

PREPARACIÓN

Actividad A. *Paso 3* 1. No saben nada 2. por teléfono 3. con otro hijo 4. compra un perro 5. se pierde en **Actividad C.** 1. c 2. b

¿TIENES BUENA MEMORIA?

Actividad A. 1. Jaime, Raquel 2. Jaime, Raquel 3. el ciego, Jaime 4. Raquel, Jaime 5. el ciego 6. Raquel 7. el ciego 8. Raquel 9. Jaime, Raquel. ¡OJO! *Neither one is actually "lost," but they are not with each other, and the rest of the family doesn't know where they are either!* 10. Raquel **Actividad C.** 1. d. A las once y media. Pero no todos llegan a las once y media. 2. c. A la una. Cierran (*They close*) el Alcázar a la una menos cuarto (12:45). 3. d. A las once y media. Llegan a la estación a las once y cinco.
***Preparación.* Actividad B.** 1. Jaime encuentra a su perro. 2. Jaime se pierde también en el Barrio de Santa Cruz. 3. Raquel decide quedarse en Sevilla otro día.

VOCABULARIO DEL TEMA

Actividad A. 1. el domingo 2. el viernes 3. el jueves 4. el sábado 5. el martes 6. el miércoles 7. el lunes **Actividad B.** el lunes: en casa de su abuela (visita a su abuela); el martes: en casa (estudia mucho) el miércoles: con su padre (trabaja, acompaña a su padre); el jueves: en el mercado (camina con su madre); el viernes: en casa de un amigo (cena); el sábado: en casa con su madre ayuda [*he helps out*]; el domingo: en la iglesia (con la familia) **Actividad D.** 1. las once y media 2. las ocho de la mañana, la una, las cuatro de la tarde, las ocho, las ocho y media de la tarde 3. las tres, las tres y cuarto, las cuatro, las cuatro y cuarto **Actividad F.** 1. d. a las doce. 2. f. a las siete y media 3. a. a las ocho y cinco 4. e. hasta las siete y veinte 5. b. a las nueve 6. g. a las ocho y veinte 7. c. a las once y cuarto 8. h. a las nueve y diez

LECTURA CULTURAL

1. Cierto. 2. Cierto. 3. Cierto. 4. Cierto. *Photos:* 2, 3, 1 **Actividad.** 1. los árabes 2. los judíos 3. los cristianos

LECCIÓN 6

PREPARACIÓN

Actividad A.   1. a   2. a   3. b

¿TIENES BUENA MEMORIA?

Actividad A.   1. Alfredo Sánchez   2. la ganadora de un premio, una maestra de primaria   3. no encuentra   4. rechaza
5. desea investigar más   **Actividad B.**   En el compartimiento de Raquel… a. 3 b. 2 c. 1 d. 4 Luego… a. 3 b. 4 c. 2 d. 1 En
la estación del tren… a. 3 b. 2 c. 1 d. 4
Actividad B.   1. Es un reportero.   2. Desea entrevistar a Raquel.   **Actividad C.**   *Paso 1*   1. b   2. b   3. a

REPASO DE LOS EPISODIOS 1–6

Actividad.   1. don Fernando   2. Rosario   3. hermano   4. España   5. Sevilla   6. Teresa Suárez   7. vive   8. esposo
9. hijo   10. saben   11. compra   12. Jaime   13. encuentra   14. vende   15. toma   16. nada

LECCIÓN 7

PREPARACIÓN

Actividad A.   *Paso 1*   1. b   2. a   *Paso 2*   1. Cierto.   2. Falso. Raquel le dice al reportero que investiga un caso para
un cliente mexicano.   3. Falso. El reportero se llama Alfredo Sánchez.   4. Falso. El reportero tiene mucho interés en el
caso.   **Actividad B.**   *Note: Now that you have seen the episode, you will know whether the events happened. For this reason,
answers are given here as* **Cierto** *(C) or* **Falso** *(F).*   1. F   2. C   3. F   4. F   **Actividad C.**   3

¿TIENES BUENA MEMORIA?

Actividad A.   *Paso 1*   1. b   2. a   3. d   *Paso 2*   1. d   2. b   3. a, b   4. a, e   5. c, d   6. d   **Actividad C.**   *Paso 2*
Hint: If you have trouble doing this activity, reread the **Nota cultural** in *Lección 5*. It will give you an overview of the
history of Spain. Then try to do the activity again, keeping in mind that the monarchs are listed *in chronological
order.*   1. b   2. c   3. d   4. b, c   5. a

VOCABULARIO DEL TEMA

Actividad A.   *You should have indicated the following items of clothing: 2 blouses, 2 sweaters, 1 skirt, 1 dress, 2 pairs of
shoes, a few pairs of stockings (number not specified), 1 pair of pants.* Raquel decide que *no tiene suficiente ropa.*   **Actividad B.**   *You should have indicated the following items of clothing: shirt, T-shirt, socks, tie, jacket, pants, scarf, sweater.* La
Sra. Suárez *no* está muy contenta con su hijo.   **Actividad C.**   Raquel lleva pantalones, una chaqueta, zapatos, medias…
Alfredo lleva pantalones, una chaqueta, una corbata, una camisa…   **Actividad E.**   1. 73 2. 81 3. 36 4. 45   **Actived F.**
1. 3-45-33-60   2. 5-99-24-68   3. 7-36-64-85   4. 3-75-53-91   5. 5-59-25-44   6. 7-15-49-42

LECTURA CULTURAL

Actividad.   1. d   2. b   3. e   4. c   5. g   6. a   7. f

LECCIÓN 8

PREPARACIÓN

Actividad A.   a. Raquel Rodríguez (con el recepcionista)   d. Alfredo Sánchez (con Raquel)   c. el recepcionista (con el Sr.
Díaz)   d. Alfredo Sánchez (con Raquel)   a. Raquel Rodríguez (con Alfredo)   f. Federico Ruiz (con Raquel)

¿TIENES BUENA MEMORIA?

Actividad A.   1. a   2. a, b   3. b   4. a   5. b. Teresa. Y ahora, Raquel tiene una carta para Rosario.   6. a, b, c   7. a
8. c   9. a   10. a   **Actividad B.**   1. Raquel   2. Raquel   3. Raquel   4. Raquel   5. el Sr. Díaz   6. Alfredo Sánchez   **Actividad C.**   *Paso 1*   1, 4, 6   *Paso 3*   1. no murió   2. un hijo   3. la Argentina   4. se casó
Preparación.   **Actividad B.**   1. Improbable. Raquel desea saber información acerca de Rosario, no acerca de la Sra. Suárez.   2. Probable.   3. Improbable. Raquel no sabe nada de su esposo.   4. Probable. Pero Raquel no hace esta pregunta.
5. Probable.   **Actividad C.**   *Paso 2*   c   *Paso 4*   b

LECTURA CULTURAL

Actividad.   1. Cataluña, el País Vasco   2. Castilla-León   3. Segovia (Castilla-León)   4. Extremadura   5. las islas Canarias,
Andalucía   6. Andalucía, Asturias   7. el País Vasco   8. Andalucía, Extremadura

LECCIÓN 9

PREPARACIÓN

Actividad A.   1. a. Cierto.   b. Falso. Rosario sí tuvo un hijo.   c. Cierto.   d. Falso. Sí se casó de nuevo, con un hacendado
argentino llamado Martín Iglesias.   e. No se sabe todavía.   2. a. Cierto.   b. Falso. Raquel ya sabe la dirección de Rosario.
c. Cierto.   d. Falso. Raquel no tiene la cartera todavía; el reportero tiene la cartera.   e. Falso. Raquel recibe un TELEX.

¿TIENES BUENA MEMORIA?

Actividad A.   1. b   2. e   3. b, d   4. b, e   5. c   6. b   7. b, e   8. b
Preparación.   **Actividad B.**   La respuesta correcta es 1.

VOCABULARIO DEL TEMA

Actividad B.   1. julio   2. octubre   3. noviembre   4. enero   5. junio   6. mayo   7. febrero   8. marzo   9. septiembre
10. diciembre   **Actividad D.**   *Possible answers.* 1. el blanco, el gris…   2. el amarillo, el azul…   3. el rosado, el rojo, el

verde… 4. el amarillo, el anaranjado, el rojo… 5. el anaranjado, el amarillo… 6. el negro 7. el blanco (el vestido de Rosario) 8. el negro 9. el rojo, el rosado 10. el verde

LECTURA CULTURAL

1. Falso. Hay música de todos tipos en España. 2. Falso. Al contrario, les gusta mucho la música importada. 3. Cierto. 4. Cierto. Es la zarzuela. 5. Falso. Es el *rock*.

LECCIÓN 10

PREPARACIÓN

Actividad A. 1. Cierto. 2. Falso. El reportero le da a Raquel la cartera perdida. 3. Falso. Necesita comprar ropa porque es primavera en la Argentina. 4. Falso. Pero ahora el reportero puede hablar con «la maestra», el Sr. Díaz, sobre el premio de la lotería. 5. Falso. Raquel no sabe nada de esto todavía.

¿TIENES BUENA MEMORIA?

Actividad B. 1. en taxi 2. a las cinco 3. Goya 4. a su mamá y papá
Preparación. **Actividad B.** 1. sí 2. sí 3. sí 4. un museo (Pero no puedes saber eso sólo por el título. Todos los lugares son posibles.) **Actividad C.** 1. su vida personal 2. su trabajo 3. un novio **Actividad D.** *You should have indicated the following words:* alto; delgado; con barba; del pelo corto, no largo; ojos expresivos

VOCABULARIO DEL TEMA

Actividad A. *Many answers are possible. Here is one answer for each item.* 1. San Francisco tiene barba. 2. La princesa tiene pelo rubio. 3. El pintor es delgado. 4. Las Meninas son bajas. 5. San Andrés es alto. 6. San Andrés tiene pelo blanco. 7. San Andrés es viejo. 8. San Francisco tiene ojos expresivos. 9. La princesa es bonita. 10. La enana (*dwarf*) tiene pelo largo. **Actividad B.** a. 4 b. 6 c. 5 d. 1 e. 8 f. 2 g. 3 h. 7

LECCIÓN 11

PREPARACIÓN

Actividad A. *Paso 1* 1. Cierto. 2. Falso. Raquel sí se despide de ellos. 3. Cierto. 4. Falso. Ve las obras de El Greco, Velázquez y Goya. 5. Cierto. 6. Cierto. 7. Falso. Llama, pero nadie contesta. 8. Cierto.

¿TIENES BUENA MEMORIA?

Actividad A. a. 4 b. 2 c. 1 d. 5 e. 6 f. 3 **Actividad B.** 1. Es el Hotel Príncipe de Vergara. 2. El número de su habitación es 631 (seiscientos treinta y uno; también, seis tres uno). 3. Raquel le da una foto de Jaime y Miguel con Osito. 4. La señora le da una carta para Rosario. 5. El vuelo sale a las nueve. 6. El número del vuelo es el 897 (ocho nueve siete).
Preparación. **Actividad B.** La agencia no puede confirmar su reservación. b. Raquel debe preguntarle al recepcionista…

REPASO DE LOS EPISODIOS 7–10

Actividad A. 1. empieza 2. conoce 3. reportero 4. busca 5. cree 6. dice 7. empieza 8. dice 9. cartera 10. salen (van) 11. encuentran 12. llegan (vuelven) 13. da 14. toman 15. puede 16. Pero 17. debe 18. cliente **Actividad B.** 1. b 2. b 3. a 4. a 5. a

LECCIÓN 12

PREPARACIÓN

Actividad A. 1. Falso. Raquel está en el avión cuando sale el vuelo. 2. Cierto. 3. Falso. Raquel no habla con él. No habla con nadie de México en el Episodio 11. 4. Cierto. 5. Cierto. ¿Recuerdas el consejo? 6. Cierto. ¿Recuerdas la dirección? 7. Es el consejo de la Sra. Suárez.

¿TIENES BUENA MEMORIA?

Actividad A. 1. a 2. c 3. c 4. a 5. c 6. b 7. a 8. b **Actividad B.** 1. Sí. 2. No. Raquel está exhausta cuando llega. No sale para la estancia hasta el día siguiente. 3. No. Un joven desconocido contesta la puerta. 4. Sí. 5. Sí. **Actividad C. *Paso 1*** a. 6 b. 2 c. 5 d. 3 e. 4 f. 7 g. 1
Preparación. **Actividad B.** 1. b 2. c 3. a 4. c

VOCABULARIO DEL TEMA

Actividad A. You should have indicated 314, 414, 514, 614, 714, and 814. **Actividad B.** 1. 200, 400, 600 2. 500, 600, 700 3. 100, 300, 500 4. 200, 220, 240 5. 150, 200, 250 6. 511, 512, 513

LECCIÓN 13

PREPARACIÓN

Actividad A. 1. Sí ocurrió. Pero el recepcionista le da a Raquel una suite. 2. No, no ocurrió. El joven no sabe nada de Rosario. 3. Sí ocurrió. 4. Sí ocurrió. 5. No, no ocurrió. Raquel conoce a un hijo de Rosario. 6. No, no ocurrió. Arturo le cuenta que Rosario ya murió y que perdió contacto con su hermano hace años.

¿TIENES BUENA MEMORIA?

Actividad A. *Paso 1* e ***Paso 2*** 1. d 2. c 3. g 4. b, d 5. f 6. a ***Paso 3*** b **Actividad B.** 1. a 2. c 3. b 4. a 5. b

Preparación. **Actividad B.** 1. a 2. b 3. b **Actividad C.** *Paso 1* b *Paso 3* c

VOCABULARIO DEL TEMA

Actividad A. 1. prawns, crab 2. squid, rice 3. salmon 4. tuna 5. salad, oil, bread 6. butter **Actividad B.** 1. 440 2. 220 3. 460 4. 1.050 5. 3.200 ¡OJO! What do you think of the shopkeeper's math?

LECCIÓN 14

PREPARACIÓN

Actividad A. 1. c 2. b 3. c 4. a

¿TIENES BUENA MEMORIA?

Actividad A. *Paso 1* a. 5 b. 3 c. 1 d. 2 e. 4 f. 6 *Paso 2* 1. Cierto. 2. Cierto. 3. Cierto. 4. Falso. Su profesión es muy importante para él (pero ya no es una obsesión). **Actividad B.** 1. b, c 2. c 3. c

VOCABULARIO DEL TEMA

Actividad A. 1. beef, steak 2. hamburger, ham, cheese 3. bacon 4. turkey, chicken 5. kidney, pork **Actividad B.** 1. riñones (riñoncitos) 2. vaca 3. chorizos 4. panceta 5. tocino 6. pimiento 7. tomate 8. cebolla 9. jamones 10. pollo

LECCIÓN 15

PREPARACIÓN

Actividad A. 1. b 2. b 3. a 4. c 5. b 6. b

¿TIENES BUENA MEMORIA?

Actividad A. 1. b 2. d 3. c 4. b 5. a 6. b **Actividad B.** 1. compró una bolsa de cuero 2. fue a la Cuadra 3. llamó a Arturo 4. encontró la carta 5. no le gustó mucho 6. decidieron ir a un parque 7. no le interesó mucho 8. tuvieron un *picnic* 9. recibió un regalo de Arturo

Preparación. **Actividad B.** *Paso 1* b *Paso 2* 1. c 2. dime = *tell me* 3. a

VOCABULARIO DEL TEMA

Actividad A. You should have checked the apple, the orange, the banana, and the melon. **Actividad B.** 1. frutas 2. uvas, un melón, bananas, naranjas, manzanas 3. duraznos, frutillas (fresas) 4. pan, queso y vino

LECCIÓN 16

PREPARACIÓN

Actividad A. 1. está pensativo 2. un mal presentimiento 3. ya murió 4. calmar 5. la atracción mutua 6. pasan mucho tiempo juntos 7. noticias de Héctor

¿TIENES BUENA MEMORIA?

Actividad A. 1. a 2. a 3. d 4. c 5. b 6. a **Actividad B.** a. 4 b. 7 c. 2 d. 5 e. 1 f. 6 g. 8 h. 3

Preparación. **Actividad B.** *Paso 1* 1. pronto 2. muy serios *Paso 2* 1. b 2. b 3. b

VOCABULARIO DEL TEMA

Actividad A. You should have marked the onions, peas, string beans, lettuce, tomatoes, carrots, potatoes, chile peppers, and olives. **Actividad B.** *Paso 1* 1. lechuga 2. tomate 3. cebollas 4. aceitunas 5. chícharos 6. zanahoria 7. ejotes 8. ajíes *Paso 2* en la Argentina: arvejas / en México: chiles

LECTURA CULTURAL

1. b 2. a 3. b 4. a

LECCIÓN 17

PREPARACIÓN

Actividad A. 1. Cierto. 2. Falso. Héctor sí llama a Arturo por teléfono, pero quiere hablar con ellos en el puerto de Buenos Aires. 3. Falso. Ángel sí decidió quedarse en Puerto Rico, pero no pensaba volver a la Argentina nunca más. 4. Cierto.

¿TIENES BUENA MEMORIA?

Actividad A. *Paso 1* 1. A 2. R 3. A 4. A 5. A *Paso 2* 2. Something in between. **Actividad B.** *Paso 1* 1. norteamericana 2. pasó los veranos 3. por un año entero 4. en la Universidad de California 5. un estudiante joven 6. se fue a vivir 7. Los Ángeles 8. muy contenta 9. mucha gente interesante

Preparación. **Actividad B.** *Paso 1* a. *Paso 2* c *Paso 4* 1. poder 2. estar 3. poder 4. ser

VOCABULARIO DEL TEMA

Actividad A. a. 5 b. 3 c. 1 d. 4 e. 2 f. 6 **Actividad B.** *Paso 2* 1. periodista 2. revista 3. periódico 4. ensayos 5. cuentos 6. cuentos 7. escritor (autor) 8. realidad

LECCIÓN 18
PREPARACIÓN
Actividad A.   1. Sí.   2. Sí.   3. No. Cenaron en casa de Arturo.   4. Sí.   5. No. Raquel habló de su ex novio.   6. No. Raquel le dijo que necesitaba (*she needed*) más tiempo.   7. Sí.   8. No. Pero sí fueron al Teatro Colón, donde presentan óperas.   9. Sí.   10. No. Por lo menos no se vio en el episodio. Sí comieron un helado en el parque.

¿TIENES BUENA MEMORIA?
Actividad A.   1. Arturo llevó a Raquel al aeropuerto.   2. Los dos se despidieron en la entrada.   3. Se besaron con ternura.   4. La despedida fue triste.   5. Raquel tuvo que esperar un poco.   6. Le escribió una carta a la Sra. Suárez.
Actividad B.   1. Sí. Le dio un regalo (una pulsera de oro [*gold bracelet*]).   2. No. Le dijo «hasta pronto». Raquel le dijo «adiós» primero.   3. En un par de días.   4. Piensa en el deseo que les pidió a las estrellas: que la familia pueda reunirse definitivamente.
Preparación.   **Actividad B.**   *Paso 2*   a, b, c, e, g, h
REPASO DE LOS EPISODIOS 12–17
Actividad A.   1. me sirvió bastante   2. murió hace algunos años   3. ya no vivía allí   4. era el hijo de Rosario y don Fernando   5. había muerto   6. se fue de la casa   7. perdió contacto con su hermano   **Actividad C.**   Correct wording: mi estancia en Buenos Aires ha sido más... , conocer un poco la ciudad, artículos de cuero... , y me gustó mucho, que seguí sus consejos... , El hermano de Ángel, Arturo... , siento un afecto... , en un par de días, Siento mucho la muerte de... , que encuentre a Ángel Castillo... , se reúna con su padre

LECCIÓN 19
PREPARACIÓN

¿TIENES BUENA MEMORIA?
Actividad A.   1. vecina   2. murió hace poco   3. escritora   4. hija   5. unos parientes   6. tiene un hermano   **Actividad B.**
Paso 1   1. mudarse   2. debe ser muy triste para Ángela   3. llamar a sus tíos   4. visitar un lugar de interés histórico   5. mostrarle otros lugares interesantes   6. regresan al apartamento   7. está en Nueva York
Preparación.   **Actividad A.**   1. Raquel le está preguntando dónde está Ángel Castillo. La vecina le está diciendo que Ángel ya murió.   2. Está allí porque busca la tumba de Ángel Castillo.   3. Es hija de Ángel Castillo.   **Actividad B.**
Paso 3   1. Habla de Ángel Castillo y su esposa.   2. Describe a un hombre, a Ángel.

VOCABULARIO DEL TEMA
Actividad A.   1. esquina   2. izquierda   3. derecha   4. derecho   5. izquierda   6. derecha   **Actividad B.**   *Paso 1*
1. Siga   2. vire   3. bocacalle   4. derecha   5. Sigo   6. izquierda   7. Allí   *Paso 2*   1. a   2. b   3. c   4. c

LECCIÓN 20
PREPARACIÓN
Actividad A.   *Paso 2*   1. Una vecina   2. la hija   3. estaba sorprendida   4. a los tíos   5. tenía un hermano también

¿TIENES BUENA MEMORIA?
Actividad A.   1. b   2. c   3. b   4. a   5. d   6. g   7. a   8. b   9. f   10. e   11. c   **Actividad B.**   1. a   2. b   **Actividad C.**
Paso 1   1. Ángela, Roberto   2. Ángela, su abuela, doña Carmen   3. Raquel, Pedro Castillo   *Paso 2* don Fernando
Preparación.   **Actividad B.**   *Paso 2*   1. a
Actividad C.   *Paso 2*   1. a   2. b   3. c

VOCABULARIO DEL TEMA
Actividad B.   *Paso 2*   1. cinco   2. dos, dos   3. Tres   4. cinco   5. un, tres   6. Ángel, la suegra, suegro   **Actividad C.**
1. sobrinos   2. tíos   3. prima   4. medio hermanos
LECTURA CULTURAL
Actividad.   1. Probable.   2. Probable.   3. Improbable. Fue Cristóbal Colón.   4. Improbable. Había tribus indígenas que se llamaban los taínos.   5. Probable.   6. Improbable. El español y el inglés son los idiomas oficiales.   7. Improbable. Puerto Rico es un Estado Libre Asociado a los Estados Unidos.

LECCIÓN 21
PREPARACIÓN
Actividad A.   *Paso 2*   1. b   2. b   3. a   4. c   5. b   6. b
¿TIENES BUENA MEMORIA?
Actividad A.   1. b   2. c   3. b   4. c   5. c   6. b   7. b   **Actividad B.**   1. español   2. San Juan   3. 1898   4. guerra   5. Cuba   6. Puerto Rico
Preparación.   **Actividad B.**   1. a   2. a
VOCABULARIO DEL TEMA
Actividad A.   1. calor, más, mucho   2. frío, más, mucho   3. fresco

LECCIÓN 22

PREPARACIÓN

Actividad.   *Paso 1*   1. prima   2. carro   3. taller   4. día siguiente (próximo día)   5. Ponce

¿TIENES BUENA MEMORIA?

Actividad A.   *Paso 1*   1. a   2. b   3. a   ***Paso 2***   1. Falso. Ángela estudió en la Universidad Interamericana, en San Germán.   2. Cierto.   3. Cierto.   4. Falso. En San Germán, Ángel pintaba constantemente.   ***Paso 3***   1. b   2. a
Actividad B.   1. materna   2. una finca   3. ya murió   4. sirvienta   5. yerno   6. muy estrechas   7. su padre   8. una copa
Actividad C.   *Possible answers:*   4. Ángela, Raquel y Laura pasaron la noche en Ponce.   7. Las tres fueron al taller para recoger el coche.   3. Por fin llegaron a San Germán.   6. Doña Carmen rezó en la iglesia.   5. Doña Carmen habló de las relaciones entre ella y su yerno.   2. Ángela y Raquel revisaron las cosas personales de Ángel.   8. Luego, Ángela leyó *Recuerdos*, el libro de Ángel.   1. Al final, doña Carmen le dio a Ángela una caja que contiene algo especial (la copa de bodas de Ángel y Rosario).

VOCABULARIO DEL TEMA

Actividad A.   *Paso 1*   1, 5   ***Paso 2***   5   **Actividad B.**   *Possible answers:*   1. Esta persona se casó dos veces. (don Fernando, Rosario)   2. Esta persona se divorció y ahora vive solo/a. (Arturo)   3. Esta persona se enfermó. (don Fernando)   4. Esta persona se enfadó con un pariente. (Martín Iglesias, Ángel, tía Olga, Ángela)   5. Esta persona se molestó por una cosa pequeña. (Ángela)   6. Esta persona se alegró al saber (*upon learning*) cierta noticia. (Raquel, Ángela)   7. Esta persona se puso muy triste al saber cierta noticia. (Arturo, don Fernando, Raquel)   8. Esta persona se acostumbró a vivir en otro país. (don Fernando, Rosario, Ángel)   9. Esta persona nunca se repuso de la muerte de su esposo/a. (Rosario, Ángel)

LECCIÓN 23

PREPARACIÓN

Actividad A.   1. a   2. c   3. b

¿TIENES BUENA MEMORIA?

Actividad A.   1. está hablando afuera con   2. ayer por la noche   3. a Buenos Aires para hablar con Arturo   4. la quería mucho   5. no sabe si
***Preparación.*   Actividad C.**   a

VOCABULARIO DEL TEMA

Actividad A.   You should have selected *b*.   **Actividad B.   *Paso 2***   1. Cierto.   2. Falso. El *town house* tiene solamente un baño.   3. Cierto.   4. No se sabe. Sólo sabes que el *town house no* tiene lavaplatos.   5. Falso. Sólo el *town house* es de dos pisos.   6. Cierto.   7. Falso. Están juntos en el apartamento.   8. No se sabe. Sólo sabes que las dos cocinas son modernas, pero no sabes si estos aparatos son nuevos.

LECCIÓN 24

PREPARACIÓN

Actividad A.   *Paragraph one:* madre → padre; manda un telegrama → hace una llamada; hijos → hijas   *Paragraph two:* de la tienda → del banco; meses → semanas; don Fernando va a enfadarse → es urgente   *Paragraph three:* Los Ángeles → México; hermano → novio; del viaje → de la copa

¿TIENES BUENA MEMORIA?

Actividad.   *Possible answers:*   1. b   2. g   3. e   4. c   5. h, i   6. f, j   7. d, a
***Preparación.*   Actividad B.**   c

VOCABULARIO DEL TEMA

Actividad A.   1. Arturo es trabajador.   2. Jorge es muy macho.   3. Tía Olga es gruñona.   4. Ángela es ingenua.   5. Doña Carmen es sabia.   6. Jorge es agresivo.   7. Arturo es encantador.   8. Doña Carmen es cariñosa.   9. Laura es chistosa.   10. Raquel es simpática.

LECCIÓN 25

PREPARACIÓN

Actividad.   a. 2   b. 3   c. 5   d. 1   e. 4

¿TIENES BUENA MEMORIA?

Actividad.   *Paso 1*   1. No.   2. No.   3. Sí.   4. Sí.   5. Sí.   6. Sí.

REPASO DE LOS EPISODIOS 1–18

Actividad A.   1. f   2. b   3. i   4. c   5. j   6. a   7. d   8. g   9. e   10. h   **Actividad B.**   *Paragraph one:* un cuadro → una foto; artista → hombre   *Paragraph two:* él los invitó a entrar → los tres se quedaron fuera para hablar   *Paragraph three:* una foto → un cuadro; España → Puerto Rico   *Paragraph four:* tarjeta postal → carta   **Actividad C.**   1. el primer vuelo   2. muy mal   3. unos pocos días   4. muchos años   5. extrañar   6. la búsqueda   7. Te gustaría   8. trabajo   9. dejar

LECCIÓN 26

PREPARACIÓN
Actividad. 1. Ángela Castillo, b 2. doña Carmen, a 3. Ángel, con su esposa y suegra, b 4. los tíos de Ángela y Roberto, a 5. Roberto Castillo, b 6. Jorge Alonso, b.

¿TIENES BUENA MEMORIA?
Actividad. 1. Ángela 2. Olga 3. Laura 4. Carmen 5. Jorge 6. Jaime 7. Roberto

REPASO DE LOS EPISODIOS 19–24
Actividad A. a. 7 b. 2 c. 6 d. 10 e. 4 f. 9 g. 12 h. 3 i. 13 j. 5 k. 8 l. 11 m. 1 **Actividad B.** 1. d 2. i 3. g 4. b 5. f 6. m 7. c 8. k 9. h 10. l 11. a 12. e 13. j

LECCIÓN 27

PREPARACIÓN
Actividad A. 1. La Gavia, don Fernando Castillo Saavedra, el hermano, Raquel Rodríguez 2. Teresa Suárez, la primera esposa 3. la Argentina, Madrid, San Juan 4. el cementerio 5. México, una excavación 6. el medio hermano, Rosario
Actividad B. *Paso 1* b *Paso 2* 1. a 2. b 3. c

¿TIENES BUENA MEMORIA?
Actividad. 1. buscar a Roberto 2. se llevaban muy bien 3. le tenía un poco de envidia 4. era más inteligente y responsable que ella 5. un poco culpable 6. estaba bloqueado y no podíamos pasar 7. empezó a mirar la lista de nombres 8. que era un error 9. está desesperada 10. no sabe nada del accidente

LECCIÓN 28

PREPARACIÓN
Actividad A. 1. Sí. 2. No. No pudieron pasar. Tuvieron que ir al hospital de un pueblo cercano. 3. No. Ni se sabe todavía si Roberto es uno de los hombres atrapados. 4. No. Arturo llegó a un hotel en la Ciudad de México. 5. Sí. 6. Sí.
Actividad C. *Paso 1* 1. d 2. b 3. a 4. f 5. c *Paso 2* 1. Mercedes 2. Gloria (esposa de Carlos) 3. Juan (esposo de Pati) 4. Maricarmen (hija de Ramón y Consuelo)

¿TIENES BUENA MEMORIA?
Actividad A. 1. e 2. c 3. a 4. d 5. b 6. e 7. a **Actividad B.** 1. en seguida 2. Guadalajara 3. por su padre y por otros asuntos familiares
Preparación. **Actividad B.** 1. b 2. a **Actividad D.** *Paso 2* 1. b 2. No. 3. b

VOCABULARIO DEL TEMA
Actividad A. You should have indicated these body parts: eyes, nose, ears, both hands, arms, legs, heart, chest, back.
Actividad B. *Paso 1* 1. ojos 2. una boca 3. un brazo 4. mano 5. piernas 6. pies 7. cuerpo 8. pecho 9. cabeza 10. pelo; *Paso 2* 1. eyes 2. mouth 3. arm 4. hand 5. legs 6. feet 7. body 8. chest 9. head 10. hair
Actividad C. 1. los pies 2. todo el cuerpo 3. la cabeza 4. el pecho 5. los ojos 6. la boca 7. las orejas 8. el pelo 9. las manos 10. la nariz 11. los brazos, las piernas, la espalda, etcétera

LECCIÓN 29

PREPARACIÓN
Actividad. 1. c 2. a 3. c 4. c

¿TIENES BUENA MEMORIA?
Actividad A. *Paso 1* 1. teníamos muchas esperanzas 2. a un hombre y a una mujer 3. y se derrumbó todo otra vez 4. comenzó a llorar 5. comunicarme con la familia de don Fernando 6. Arturo **Actividad B.** **¡Un desafío!** La persona que llegó tarde fue Gloria.

VOCABULARIO DEL TEMA
Actividad A. a. 1 b. 3 c. 2 d. 6 e. 4 f. 5 **Actividad B.** 1. mal 2. la espalda 3. Tiene 4. y le pone una inyección 5. el brazo 6. la pierna 7. rayos X 8. No tiene

LECTURA CULTURAL
Actividad. drawing 4

LECCIÓN 30

PREPARACIÓN
Actividad A. *Primer párrafo:* murió → no se sabía nada de él *Segundo párrafo:* hablaba del derrumbe en la excavación → hablaba de varios asuntos; Gloria → Carlos *Tercer párrafo:* Muy contento porque ya sabía algo de Raquel → Muy preocupado porque no tenía noticias de Raquel

¿Tienes buena memoria?

Actividad A. 1. c 2. b 3. a 4. b 5. a **Actividad B.** **Paso 1** 1. durmió muy bien 2. tener noticias de Roberto 3. tenía suficiente aire 4. tienda del pueblo 5. estaba ocupada la línea 6. hablando con alguien en Nueva York 7. el hotel 8. le dejó un mensaje 9. Puerto Rico 10. la iglesia del pueblo 11. descansar y bañarse
Preparación. **Actividad B.** **Paso 1** b **Paso 2** b

Vocabulario del tema

Actividad A. **Paso 1** *You should have written the letter C on these places: the center of the town, the suburbs, the outskirts, the group of tall buildings, the office building, the hotel, the market, the supermarket, the pharmacy, the small shop, the large department store.* **Paso 2** *You should have written P on the following parts of the drawing: the center, the plaza, the city hall, the church, the pharmacy, the shop, the market. You should have written N on the following parts of the drawing: the group of tall buildings, the supermarket, the department store.* **¡Un desafío!** Arturo mencionó los siguientes lugares: una farmacia, una tienda para hombres, un almacén, un mercado, un supermercado. **Actividad B.** a. 4 b. 1 c. 5 d. 3 e. 2 f. 8 g. 9 h. 6 i. 7

LECCIÓN 31

Preparación

Actividad A. **Paso 1** 1. c, f 2. e 3. b 4. a 5. d **Actividad B.** **Paso 1** c **Paso 3** 1. b 2. b

¿Tienes buena memoria?

Actividad A. **Paso 1** 1. Cierto. 2. Falso. Ángela se siente mucho mejor. 3. Falso. Ángela es optimista. Es Raquel quien es pesimista. **Actividad B.** **Paso 1** 1. Sí. Pedro lo sabe (porque Arturo se lo dijo por teléfono). 2. Juan y Pati se pelearon. 3. Ramón y Pedro hablaron con los auditores. 4. Eran drásticas. **¡Un desafío!** Que cierren la oficina en Miami. Que concentren en la producción de algo (el acero = *steel*). Que vendan La Gavia (porque hace falta capital).

Vocabulario del tema

Actividad A. **Paso 1** 1. la pescadería 2. la carnicería 3. la zapatería 4. la confitería 5. la tortillería 6. la panadería 7. (la) pastelería 8. (la) farmacia

LECCIÓN 32

Preparación

Actividad A. 1. a 2. a 3. b **Actividad B.** 1. Se llama Luis. 2. Vive ahora en Los Ángeles. (Acaba de mudarse para allí.) 3. Eran novios. (La madre de Raquel lo llama «el novio de mi hija».)

¿Tienes buena memoria?

Actividad A. **Paso 1** 1. Sí. 2. No. Hubo actividad. Llegaron más personas para ayudar con el rescate. 3. No. Pero casi han sacado (*they've gotten out*) a Roberto. 4. Sí. 5. No se sabe todavía. 6. Sí. 7. No. Mercedes no quería contarle lo que pasaba. 8. No. Están muy contentos en su matrimonio. 9. Sí. 10. Sí. 11. No. Al contrario, la madre de Raquel le dijo a Luis que debía ir a México a ver a Raquel. 12. No. No se sabe todavía la actitud del padre de Raquel. **Actividad B.** 1. a. sabe b. no sabe c. no sabe 2. a. sabe b. no sabe c. sabe (Raquel se lo dijo en la Argentina.) 3. a. sabe b. no sabe c. no sabe (Aunque hay que admitir que es posible que, siendo dueño de la compañía, sepa algo del asunto, inclusive algo que Pedro y Ramón no saben. Pero no se dice nada de esto en el episodio.) 4. a. no sabe b. no sabe (Raquel le dijo algo, pero no se lo contó todo.) c. sabe **Actividad C.** 1. azteca 2. norte 3. lago 4. guerrera 5. conquistar

Vocabulario del tema

Actividad B. **¡Un desafío!** El Titicaca está en Sudamérica, entre Bolivia y el Perú. Inglaterra está en el Océano Atlántico, al oeste de Europa. El Atlántico está entre América y Europa y África. Pike's Peak está en los Estados Unidos, en Colorado. El Sahara está en África, en el norte. Los Andes están en Sudamérica, en el oeste. El Nilo está en África, en Egipto. El Golfo Pérsico está entre Irán y Arabia. Sudamérica está en el hemisferio sur. El Mediterráneo está al sur de Europa y al norte de África. Napa está en el norte de California. Yucatán está en el sureste de México.

Un poco de gramática

Actividad. 1. f 2. d 3. c 4. h 5. b 6. a 7. g 8. e

LECCIÓN 33

Preparación

Actividad A. 1. b 2. b 3. b 4. b 5. b

¿Tienes buena memoria?

Actividad A. 1. no sabían nada y tampoco podían ver bien lo que pasaba 2. las profesiones 3. peligrosa 4. veterinaria y profesora 5. profesora y actriz **Actividad C.** 1. Arturo 2. Juan 3. Pati 4. Pati 5. Juan [Note that answers 2 and 3 may be transposed.]
Preparación. **Actividad B.** **Paso 2** 1. Cierto. 2. Falso. Ya trató de explicárselos. 3. Cierto. 4. c

Vocabulario del tema

Actividad A. **Paso 1** ÁNGELA pensaba en estudiar para profesora, actriz; se hizo programadora de computadoras. EL PADRE DE ÁNGELA quería que ella fuera abogada, mujer de negocios. RAQUEL pensaba en estudiar para profesora (de historia), veterinaria; se hizo abogada.   LA MADRE DE RAQUEL quería que ella fuera abogada.   *Paso 2*   1. Ambas querían ser profesoras.   2. Raquel (Su madre quería que su hija fuera abogada.)   **Actividad B.**   1. abogada   2. programadora   3. médico   4. enfermera   5. ingeniero   6. profesora   7. hombre de negocios   8. profesores   9. ama de casa   *Los dibujos:* a. 3   b. 7   c. 1   d. 4

Un poco de gramática

Actividad.   1. D   2. N   3. D   4. D   5. N   6. P   7. D   8. D   9. N   10. N   11. N   12. D   13. D   14. D   15. N

LECCIÓN 34

Preparación

Actividad A.   *Paso 1*   1. b   2. a   3. b   4. a

¿Tienes buena memoria?

Actividad A.   1. Sí.   2. No. Mercedes cree que Pati debe regresar a Nueva York.   3. Sí.   4. No. Ramón le habló con tacto, con cariño.   5. Sí.   6. No. Juan sólo habló con Ramón.   **Actividad B.**   *Paso 1*   2, 3, 5, 6 (¡OJO! Raquel habla de Jorge en su repaso, pero no lo mencionó cuando hablaba con Ángela en el carro.)   *Paso 3*   *Possible answers:* **Ángela** admira a Roberto. Es amiga de Raquel. Es novia de Jorge. Quiere a Jorge. Quiere casarse con Jorge. Recuerda a Roberto con cariño. Se separó de Roberto. **Raquel** admira a Arturo. Es amiga de Ángela. Era novia de Luis. ¿Quiere a Arturo? ¿Quiere casarse con Arturo? Recuerda a Arturo y a Luis con cariño. Se separó de Arturo. **Jorge** es novio de Ángela. ¿Quiere a Ángela? ¿Quiere casarse con Ángela? Trató de ligar con Raquel. **Arturo** admira a Raquel. Es amigo de Raquel. Quiere a Raquel. ¿Quiere casarse con Raquel? Recuerda a Raquel con cariño. Se separó de Raquel.
Preparación.   **Actividad B.**   *Paso 2*   1. Falso. Ramón cree que Juan está exagerando.   2. Cierto.   3. Falso. Juan considera lo que Ramón le ha dicho (*has told him*).   4. Cierto.   5. Cierto; c

Vocabulario del tema

Actividad A.   1. el cariño   2. el cariño   3. el cariño, el amor   4. el amor, un período de tiempo   5. una ceremonia   6. un período de tiempo, el amor   **Actividad B.**   a. 7   b. 2   c. 3   d. 5   e. 1   f. 6   g. 8   h. 9   i. 4   j. 10

LECCIÓN 35

Preparación

Actividad A.   *Paso 1*   1. a un hospital en la capital   2. en su propio carro   3. de sus novios   4. siguieron discutiendo sin resolver nada   5. el accidente

¿Tienes buena memoria?

Actividad A.   *Paso 1*   1. b, d   2. c   3. a, d   4. b   5. a, d   **Actividad B.**   *Paso 2*   *Possible answers:* **Pedro** se despidió de Pati. Les contó algo a Carlos y Gloria. Fue al hospital. Conoció a Ángela. **Raquel** saludó a Arturo y a Pedro. Besó a Arturo. Llamó a Los Ángeles. Fue a la casa de Pedro. Conoció a toda la familia. **Arturo** saludó a Raquel. Besó a Raquel. Conoció a Ángela en el hospital. Les contó algo a Raquel y Pedro. Fue a la casa de Pedro. Conoció a toda la familia. **Ángela** conoció a Arturo. Llamó a Puerto Rico. No fue a la casa de Pedro y no conoció a toda la familia. Fue al hospital. Estaba preocupada por Roberto. **Pati** se despidió de Pedro y Juan. Salió para Nueva York. **Ofelia** le contó algo a Carlos. **Carlos** llamó a Miami. Estaba preocupado por la oficina. Conoció a Arturo y a Raquel. **Roberto** estaba dormido en el hospital.
Preparación.   **Actividad B.**   *Paso 2*   1. Están en malas condiciones.   2. b

Vocabulario del tema

Actividad A.   1. una sugerencia   2. un requisito   3. un mandato   4. una recomendación   5. una recomendación   6. una sugerencia   7. un mandato   8. un mandato

LECCIÓN 36

Preparación

Actividad.   1. Raquel y Ángela   2. Pati   3. Ofelia (la secretaria de Carlos)   4. Arturo   5. la médico (También Arturo les dijo esto a Pedro, Raquel y Ángela. También Ángela se lo dijo a su tío Jaime.)   6. Arturo y Pedro   7. Roberto   8. Raquel y Arturo   9. Ángela   10. Raquel   11. Ángela   12. Raquel y Arturo

¿Tienes buena memoria?

Actividad.   1. se dan cuenta   2. Arturo   3. sigue enamorado   4. Gloria

Repaso de los episodios 27–35

Actividad A.   *Paso 1*   1. c   2. b   3. f   4. g   5. e   6. d   7. a   **Actividad B.**   **Juan.**   b. **Mercedes.**   *Paso 1*   a
Paso 2   1. Cierto.   2. Falso. Mercedes habló con Pati sobre sus problemas matrimoniales.   3. Cierto. **Pedro.**   *Paso 1*   c
Paso 2   c, d, e

LECCIÓN 37

Preparación

Actividad A.   1. Arturo   2. Juan   3. Ramón, Pedro (Tal vez Mercedes también. No sabes hasta qué punto ella se interesa en los asuntos financieros de Castillo Saavedra, S.A.)   4. Pati   5. don Fernando   6. Carlos   7. Raquel   8. Mercedes   9. Raquel   10. Ángela

¿TIENES BUENA MEMORIA?

Actividad A. 1. Mercedes 2. Ángela 3. La madre de Raquel 4. Pedro 5. Luis. **Actividad B.** 1. Arturo les dijo esto a los miembros de la familia Castillo. 2. Ángela le dijo esto a Roberto. 3. Carlitos les dijo esto a Raquel, Arturo y Carlos. 4. María Rodríguez está hablando por teléfono con Luis. 5. Pedro está conversando con Raquel. *Preparación.* **Actividad B.** *Paso 3* 1. b 2. a

VOCABULARIO DEL TEMA

Actividad A. a. 7 b. 3, 4 c. 2, 5 d. 6 e. 1 **Actividad B.** 1. Falso. No tiene casi nada en su cuenta de ahorros. 2. Cierto. 3. Falso. No sabe cómo va a pagar la cuenta. 4. Falso. Lo maneja muy mal. 5. Cierto. 6. Falso. La usó mucho. 7. Falso. La secretaria de Pedro le dará un cheque mañana. 8. Falso. Una secretaria en la oficina de Raquel se preocupa mucho por las gastos.

LECCIÓN 38
PREPARACIÓN

Actividad A. 1. Cierto. 2. Falso. Le dijeron que regresara para las fiestas nacionales. 3. Falso. Regresaron al hotel. 4. Cierto. 5. Cierto. 6. Falso. Raquel recibió un mensaje de Pedro.

¿TIENES BUENA MEMORIA?

Actividad A. *Paso 1* 1. lo paso bien con 2. un mensaje para mí 3. con don Fernando 4. hablar de nosotros 5. en mí 6. una llamada telefónica 7. venir a México 8. si Ángela había regresado **Actividad B.** *Paso 1* Sí, Roberto se despertó. *Preparación.* **Actividad B.** 1. b 2. a

VOCABULARIO DEL TEMA

Actividad A. 1. Falso. Hay irregularidades en esa oficina. 2. Cierto. 3. Falso. Los gastos son mayores que los ingresos. 4. Cierto. 5. Falso. Ha sacado cien mil dólares. 6. Falso. Los auditores hicieron sus propias cuentas. **Actividad B.** *Paso 1* 1. un presupuesto 2. manejar 3. ganar 4. economizar 5. los ingresos 6. los gastos

LECCIÓN 39
PREPARACIÓN

Actividad. *Paso 1* 1. una reunión en la casa de Pedro 2. Raquel 3. Pedro 4. Arturo; Raquel 5. los problemas económicos de la oficina en Miami 6. Carlos 7. seriamente 8. Gloria había desaparecido.

¿TIENES BUENA MEMORIA?

Actividad A. Raquel y Arturo: 3, 5, 6, 8 Carlos y Gloria: 1 Ángela y Roberto: 2 Juan, Ramón y Pedro: 4, 7 **Actividad B.** 2, 3, 5, 6, 7

VOCABULARIO DEL TEMA

Actividad A. *Primera conversación:* 1. Cierto. 2. Falso. Es de los Estados Unidos. 3. Falso. Quiere esperar para ver si su padre se mejora. 4. Cierto. *Segunda conversación:* la casa → el apartamento; comprarla → comprarlo; Es una mala oferta → Es una buena oferta; Ángela debe rechazarla → Ángela debe decidir; ...que lo hable con Arturo → ...que lo hable con Roberto. **Actividad B.** a. 5 b. 8 c. 3 d. 1 e. 6 f. 9 g. 4 h. 10 i. 2 j. 7

LECCIÓN 40
PREPARACIÓN

Actividad A. 1. desapareció 2. buscarla 3. se sentía muy bien, con mucha hambre 4. su tío 5. la posible venta de La Gavia 6. regresó al hospital para estar con su padre

¿TIENES BUENA MEMORIA?

Actividad A. 1. c 2. f 3. h 4. i 5. a 6. g 7. c 8. e 9. h 10. d **Actividad B.** 1. Guillermo inició la conversación. 2. Pati quería hablar de la obra, pero Guillermo insistió en que hablaran de la vida de ella, de sus relaciones con Juan. 3. Sí, cree que era necesario. 4. Que Juan tiene envidia de ella. **Actividad C.** 1. Según Raquel, su madre es un poco mandona. 2. Su padre es una persona muy tranquila. 3. Sí. Raquel se lleva mejor con su padre. *Preparación.* **Actividad B.** *Paso 1* b *Paso 2* 1. a 2. c

VOCABULARIO DEL TEMA

Actividad A. a. 3 b. 2 c. 1 **Actividad B.** *Paso 1* 1. f 2. a 3. e 4. c 5. g 6. b 7. d *Paso 2* 1. b 2. f 3. a 4. e 5. c 6. d

LECCIÓN 41
PREPARACIÓN

Actividad A. 1. Cierto. 2. Falso. Roberto no tenía ropa en el hotel porque la había dejado en la excavación. Quería ir de compras para comprar ropa. 3. Cierto. 4. Cierto. 5. Falso. Pati le hablaba a un amigo, su ayudante. 6. Falso. Le dijeron que don Fernando tendría que ir a Guadalajara.

¿Tienes buena memoria?
Actividad A. 1. Arturo creía que sería mejor si yo entrara primero. 2. Cuando entré, vi que don Fernando no estaba. Luego una enfermera nos dijo que lo habían llevado a Guadalajara. 3. Ángela tenía que llamar a su tío Jaime. 4. A Roberto no le gustó. **Actividad B.** 1. un vicio, jugar por dinero 2. culpable, vender La Gavia 3. sale para el aeropuerto, Nueva York, Pati **Actividad C.** 1. Raquel, Arturo, Ángela y Roberto toman un taxi para ir al hotel. Luis llega al mismo hotel en taxi. Juan toma un taxi para ir al aeropuerto. 2. Luis y Arturo toman el ascensor al mismo tiempo. *Preparación.* **Actividad B.** *Paso 1* 1. b 2. a *Paso 2* 1. Sí, lo sabe. 2. a y b (¡OJO! B es también correcto porque Arturo les dice que no se dejen tentar por la primera oferta.)

Vocabulario del tema
Actividad A. a. 3 b. 2 c. 1 d. 5 e. 4 **Actividad B.** 1. agencia 2. reservar 3. billete 4. un taxi 5. el equipaje 6. fumar 7. la aduana 8. el pasaporte 9. las maletas 10. la agencia de viajes 11. gira 12. El autobús 13. plano 14. guía

LECCIÓN 42
PREPARACIÓN
Actividad A. *Paso 2* 1. No. 2. Cierto. 3. a

¿Tienes buena memoria?
Actividad A. 1. Luis 2. Raquel 3. salieron a cenar 4. pagando la cuenta 5. esperaba a Pati 6. había salido a tomar algo **Actividad B.** 1. b 2. c 3. a 4. c 5. b **Actividad C.** 1. Luis 2. Arturo 3. Arturo 4. Raquel 5. Raquel *Preparación.* **Actividad B.** *Paso 1* a *Paso 2* 1. mucho 2. impresionar

Vocabulario del tema
Actividad A. *Paso 1* a. 6 b. 3 c. 1 d. 5 e. 2 f. 4 g. 7 **Actividad B.** a. 2 b. 6 c. 7 d. 8 e. 1 f. 5 g. 3 h. 4

LECCIÓN 43
PREPARACIÓN
Actividad A. *Paso 1* 1. e 2. a 3. c *or* d 4. a 5. a *Paso 2* 1. Pati 2. Arturo y Luis 3. Luis o Arturo 4. Luis 5. su madre, Luis

¿Tienes buena memoria?
Actividad A. *Paso 1* 1. Raquel, Arturo, Luis 2. Luis, Ángela, Juan **Actividad B.** 1. b 2. b 3. a 4. b 5. a

Vocabulario del tema
Actividad A. *Paso 1* 1. L 2. A 3. A 4. L 5. L 6. A 7. A 8. L 9. A 10. L 11. A **Actividad B.** 1. Quería viajar a Guadalajara. 2. Iban a viajar tres, posiblemente cuatro. 3. Quería que viajaran en avión. 4. Sí, quiere que le recomienden un hotel, aunque tiene parientes en Guadalajara. 5. Solamente quería informarse.

LECCIÓN 44
PREPARACIÓN
Actividad. *Paso 1* 1. La llamó Luis. 2. Quería ver a Raquel. 3. b 4. Los dos fueron a la agencia de viajes. Luis hizo esas reservaciones. 5. No, Raquel no sabe nada de lo que pasó.

¿Tienes buena memoria?
Actividad. 1. Cierto. 3. Falso. Ángela pareció aceptar la explicación que Jorge le ofreció. 4. Cierto. 6. Cierto. 7. Cierto. No saben los detalles, pero sospechan que hay algún problema. 8. Falso. Cuando Juan se levantó, Pati ya había salido.

Vocabulario del tema
Actividad A. *Paso 2* 1. al fútbol 2. el béisbol, el fútbol, el baloncesto, correr, nadar 3. el tenis (Quiere hacerse rica y famosa.) **Actividad C.** 1. a 2. No. 3. b 4. b 5. b

LECCIÓN 45
PREPARACIÓN
Actividad. 1. b 2. c 3. b 4. b

¿Tienes buena memoria?
Actividad A. *Paso 1* 1. Falso. Raquel se enteró del papel (*role*) de su madre en esta situación difícil. 2. Cierto. 3. Cierto. 4. Falso. Raquel piensa que Arturo es considerado y que Luis no lo es. 5. Falso. Se interesan mucho. Incluso se lo preguntaron a Arturo. 6. Falso. Dijeron que no querían salir a cenar. 7. Falso. Las noticias eran malas. 8. Cierto. 9. Falso. Gloria ya regresó. 10. Cierto. **Actividad B.** *Paso 1* *Possible answers:* 1. Raquel la acusa de haber actuado como si Arturo fuera un extraño. 2. Al principio, su mamá se defiende y muestra una actitud de superioridad. Al final, no cambia de idea y actúa igual. 3. Su padre no hace nada durante esta discusión.

LECCIÓN 46

PREPARACIÓN

Actividad A. *Paso 1* 1. b 2. a 3. a 4. c 5. b **Actividad B.** *Paso 1* 1, 4, 5, 6 *Paso 2* 2. La madre de Raquel actuó muy fríamente con Arturo. 3. Cuando llegó Luis, la madre de Raquel lo saludó con mucho cariño.

¿TIENES BUENA MEMORIA?

Actividad A. *Paso 1* 1. Le había comprado 2. empezar una conversación seria 3. venir a México 4. de las relaciones entre Raquel y Arturo 5. Raquel se fuera a vivir a la Argentina 6. un mensaje de Luis 7. sí está enamorada de Arturo **Actividad B.** *Paso 1* *Possible answers:* 1. no iban a vender el apartamento por el momento 2. que su esposa cambiaría... a su manera 3. caminaba y hablaba muy amigablemente con Arturo 4. pudo regresar a La Gavia 5. llegaron a la hacienda también 6. dijo quo tenía una idea 7. ...llegaron a La Gavia y conocieron a todos de la familia.

VOCABULARIO DEL TEMA

Actividad A. 1. e, k 2. b, c 3. f 4. k 5. j 6. a, h, j 7. h 8. d 9. g 10. d, i

UN POCO DE GRAMÁTICA

Actividad. 1. México 2. la reina Isabel, los Reyes Católicos (Fernando e Isabel) 3. Kennedy 4. franceses 5. John Wilkes Booth

LECCIÓN 47

PREPARACIÓN

Actividad. *Paso 1* 1. ya no había nada que hacer para 2. pasar sus últimos días con su familia 3. Le caía muy bien a Pancho 4. se fuera a vivir a la Argentina 5. conocer a Arturo 6. no venderlo por el momento 7. conocer a su abuelo paterno

¿TIENES BUENA MEMORIA?

Actividad A. *Paso 1* a. 5 b. 4 c. 1 d. 6 e. 3 f. 7 g. 2 **Actividad B.** *Paso 1* *Possible answers:* 1. podía pasar un poco de tiempo con Arturo y sus nietos. 2. no podían salvar la oficina en Miami. 3. convirtieran La Gavia en un orfanato. 4. lo del problema de Gloria. 5. Jorge y sus relaciones con Ángela. 6. tenía grandes dudas sobre la identidad de Ángela y Roberto.

LECCIÓN 48

REPASO DE LOS EPISODIOS 3–11

Actividad A. *Paso 1* 2, 4, 5, 7, 8, 9, 10, 11, 12, 14, 15, 16 **Actividad B.** *Possible answer:* Cuando Raquel llegó a Sevilla, no tardó en buscar a la Sra. Suárez. Fue a *la calle Pureza*, pero *no encontró a la señora*. Conoció a dos chicos en la calle. Ellos *le dijeron que Teresa Suárez era su abuela pero que ahora vivía en Madrid*. Luego llevaron a Raquel al mercado para *conocer a su madre, Elena Ramírez*.

Elena no sabía nada del caso, pero le sugirió a Raquel que sería buena idea *reunirse con su esposo por la noche para ver si él sabía algo*. Esa noche Raquel *conoció a Miguel Ruiz, hijo de Teresa Suárez*, pero Miguel tampoco sabía nada del caso. Sin embargo, le dijo a Raquel que había hablado con su madre, quien había dicho que *Raquel fuera a Madrid para que hablara con ella personalmente*.

A los dos días, Raquel salió para Madrid. En el tren, *conoció a un reportero*. El reportero *buscaba a una maestra (y creía que Raquel era esa persona)*. Como no tuvo éxito, se interesó en *el caso que Raquel investigaba*. Raquel, respetando la confidencialidad de su cliente, *no le dijo nada (¡aunque el reportero era muy persistente!)*.

En su hotel en Madrid, Raquel bajaba de su habitación cuando *encontró a otro hijo de Teresa Suárez, Federico Ruiz*. La invitó a su casa a cenar y por fin Raquel *conoció a Teresa Suárez*. Ésta le contó la triste historia de *Rosario*, quien al final de la Guerra Civil *se fue con su hijo Ángel a la Argentina*, pensando que don Fernando había muerto. La Sra. Suárez también le dio a Raquel *la dirección de Rosario en la Argentina*. Ahora Raquel podía seguir con su investigación. Se preparó para otro viaje, esta vez a Buenos Aires.

LECCIÓN 49

REPASO DE LOS EPISODIOS 12–18

Actividad A. *Paso 1* 1. b 2. d 3. a 4. a 5. b 6. c 7. c 8. e **Actividad B.** *Pasos 1 y 2* *Possible answer:* Cuando Raquel llegó a Buenos Aires, alquiló un coche con un chofer para ir a la estancia Santa Susana, la dirección que Teresa Suárez *le había dado*. Tenía muchas esperanzas de encontrar a Rosario. Llamó a la puerta y *un joven contestó*. Éste no sabía nada de Rosario, pero le dijo a Raquel que *hablara con Cirilo, un gaucho*. Cirilo sí *recordaba a Rosario y le dijo a Raquel que Rosario y su hijo se habían mudado a la capital*. También se acordaba *del nombre de la calle*.

Raquel regresó a Buenos Aires y buscó la dirección que Cirilo le había dado. Por fin, en una casa en la calle Gorostiaga, *conoció a Arturo Iglesias, psiquiatra que es hijo de Rosario y medio hermano de Ángel*. Raquel quedó muy sorprendida al encontrar por fin a un miembro de la familia. Desgraciadamente, *Arturo le contó que Rosario había muerto y que hacía mucho tiempo que él no sabía nada de Ángel*. Arturo también le contó a Raquel que no sabía nada de Ángel porque *perdió contacto con él hace mucho tiempo*.

Los dos fueron al cementerio donde estaba enterrada Rosario. Allí *Raquel sacó una foto de la tumba para don Fernando*. Más tarde Arturo le dijo *que la quería ayudar con la búsqueda de Ángel*. Con una foto de Ángel a los veinte años, los dos *empezaron la búsqueda en La Boca, un barrio de Buenos Aires donde Arturo creía que Ángel tenía amigos*. Preguntaron en varias tiendas, pero *nadie lo conocía*. Por fin, Mario, el dueño de una tienda de antigüedades, dijo que era posible que un tal José lo conociera. Encontraron a José en su barco. José *no reconocía a Ángel, pero pensaba que era posible que Héctor lo conociera.* Más tarde les dijo dónde y cuándo podrían encontrar a Héctor.

En un bar llamado el Piccolo Navio, Raquel y Arturo encontraron a Héctor con sus amigos. Al acompañarlo a casa, le mostraron la foto de Ángel. Héctor *sí lo recordó, porque era su amigo.* Pensaba que Ángel se había embarcado para *Puerto Rico, pero no estaba muy seguro.* A los dos días Héctor le dio a Arturo una carta de Ángel que tenía en su casa. La carta tenía la dirección de Ángel. Era verdad: Ángel *se había mudado a Puerto Rico.*

Ahora, para seguir su investigación, Raquel tenía que ir a Puerto Rico. Fue *de compras en Buenos Aires porque necesitaba ropa para su viaje al Caribe y, con Arturo, vio un poco de la ciudad.* Se despidió de Arturo en el aeropuerto. Mientras esperaba su vuelo, *le escribió una carta a la Sra. Suárez, dándole las malas noticias de la muerte de su amiga Rosario.*

LECCIÓN 50
REPASO DE LOS EPISODIOS 19–26

Actividad A. *Paso 1* 1. Se lo dijo alguien, una vecina de la familia. 2. Raquel supo que Ángela tenía un hermano cuando hablaba con ella antes de la llegada de los tíos. 3. Fue la primera vez que oían los nombres de Rosario y don Fernando. 4. Pensaron que era importante que hablara con su abuela. 5. Tuvieron que quedarse en Ponce. 6. Ángela no había limpiado el cuarto de Ángel. 7. Encontraron unos dibujos que él había hecho con recuerdos de su pasado. 8. Recibieron noticias importantes. Supieron del derrumbe en el sitio de la excavación. **Actividad B. *Pasos 1 y 2*** Cuando llegó a San Juan, Raquel fue directamente a la dirección que estaba en la carta de Héctor. Tocó a la puerta, pero *no contestó nadie.* Desde su balcón, una vecina le dijo que *Ángel había muerto y que estaba enterrado en el cementerio del Viejo San Juan.* En el cementerio Raquel *conoció a Ángela Castillo Soto... la hija de Ángel Castillo.* Allí en el cementerio Raquel se lo explicó todo.

Raquel y Ángela regresaron al apartamento donde vivía ella, que era el antiguo apartamento de sus padres. Desde allí Ángela *llamó a sus tíos* para que vinieran a conocer a Raquel. Mientras los esperaban, seguían hablando. Raquel supo que *Ángela tenía un hermano, Roberto Castillo, que era estudiante de arqueología y estaba trabajando en una excavación en México.*

Cuando llegaron los tíos de Ángela, Raquel les contó la historia de don Fernando y les habló de su investigación. También les dijo que Ángela *iba a ir a México con ella a conocer a su abuelo.* La tía Olga, la gruñona de la familia, *no reaccionó bien a las noticias de Raquel.* Por eso Ángela llamó a *su abuela* para pedirle consejo. Ésta quería que Ángela y Raquel fueran a verla a San Germán.

Al día siguiente Raquel y Ángela, acompañadas por Laura, la prima de Ángela, salieron para San Germán. En un peaje tuvieron *problemas con el carro y por eso no pudieron llegar a San Germán.* Se quedaron por la noche en Ponce y a la mañana siguiente *recogieron el carro y empezaron el viaje de nuevo.*

En San Germán, almorzaron con la abuela y hablaron de Ángel y su esposa. La abuela le recordó a Ángela que *no había limpiado el cuarto de su padre.* Allí, en un viejo baúl, Ángela *encontró unos dibujos que su padre había hecho.* Eran *recuerdos de su vida en Puerto Rico y también de su vida en España y la Argentina.* Al salir para San Juan, la abuela salió corriendo de la casa y *le dio a Ángela otro recuerdo de su padre: la copa de bodas de Rosario, madre de Ángel y primera esposa de don Fernando.*

De regreso en San Juan, Raquel y Ángela pasaron por el banco donde trabajaba Ángela para *pedirle a su jefa permiso de ausentarse unas semanas.* También vieron unos apartamentos con una agente de bienes raíces, porque Ángela *quería vender el apartamento de sus padres y mudarse a otro sitio.* Al día siguiente, cuando salían para el aeropuerto, llegó el tío Jaime con malas noticias: *había habido un derrumbe en la excavación donde trabajaba Roberto.*

LECCIÓN 51
REPASO DE LOS EPISODIOS 27–36

Actividad A. *Paso 1* a. 5 b. 7 c. 2 d. 6 e. 1 f. 4 g. 10 h. 9 i. 3 j. 8 **Actividad B. *Pasos 1 y 2*** *Possible answer:* Tan pronto como llegaron a México, Raquel y Ángela alquilaron un auto y salieron para un pueblo cerca de la excavación donde trabajaba Roberto. En el camino, Ángela le habló a Raquel de *sus relaciones con Roberto,* y le confesó que *le tenía un poco de envidia.*

Al llegar al sitio, no las dejaron pasar. Entonces *fueron al hospital del pueblo.* Allí les dieron la lista de los accidentados. Por un momento *pensaron que un tal R. Castilla era Roberto, pero no era así.*

En el hospital conocieron a un padre que las ayudó mucho a lo largo de su estancia en el pueblo. Por medio del padre, Ángela y Raquel pudieron *llegar al sitio de la excavación.* Tenían muchas esperanzas de que rescataran a Roberto pronto. Por fin sacaron a dos personas, pero *ninguno era el hermano de Ángela.* Antes de que pudieran sacar a otras personas, *hubo un derrumbe.* Ángela comenzó a llorar y le tuvieron que dar un calmante. Por fin se pudo dormir, y Raquel *pasó la noche a su lado.*

Por la mañana, mientras seguían esperando el rescate de Roberto, Raquel y Ángela hicieron varias llamadas. Raquel *no pudo ponerse en contacto con Arturo, pero sí le dejó un mensaje.* Y Ángela *pudo hablar con sus tíos en Puerto Rico.* Después fueron a la iglesia del pueblo, donde *una hermana muy amable les dio dónde descansar y refrescarse.*

Por fin encontraron a Roberto... ¡y *estaba vivo!* Antes de que pudieran rescatarlo, sin embargo, *hubo un segundo derrumbe.* Pero lo pudieron sacar de todas formas. Lo examinaron en seguida; por suerte *no tuvo lesiones graves.* Sin embargo *era necesario llevarlo a un hospital en la capital.* Raquel y Ángela salieron para México en su auto, y en el camino *casi chocaron con un camión.* Al llegar al hospital, Ángela entró corriendo al cuarto de Roberto. Arturo, quien estaba allí con Pedro, vio a Raquel y *gritó su nombre y la besó.*

LECCIÓN 52

PREPARACIÓN

Actividad.   1. b   2. a   3. a   4. a   5. b

¿TIENES BUENA MEMORIA?

Actividad. *Pasos 1 y 2*   Don Fernando tenía dudas de la identidad de Ángela y Roberto, y quería estar seguro de que eran sus nietos. Raquel le recordó a Ángela lo de la copa de bodas de Rosario, que *seguramente sería la prueba definitiva.*

Al día siguiente, llegó la agente de bienes raíces. El deseo de su cliente de comprar La Gavia no fue realizado, porque *don Fernando llegó y les dijo a todos que La Gavia no estaba en venta.* Entonces Mercedes reveló su plan para fundar un or-fanato en la hacienda. Todos quedaron sorprendidos cuando don Fernando reveló que, *hace años, había establecido una fundación para hacer precisamente eso.* Según don Fernando, Carlos y Mercedes *administrarían el orfanato.* Juan debería regresar a Nueva York porque *allí estaba su vida y allí tenía su carrera.*

Más tarde, en el cuarto de don Fernando, cuando todos estaban presentes, Ángela *le dio la caja al patriarca.* Cuando don Fernando la abrió, se puso muy emocionado. Entonces le pidió a Mercedes que le diera a Ángela una caja que él tenía allí en su cuarto, en un armario. Cuando Ángela la abrió, *encontró otra copa igual.* Así ya no había dudas: *Ángela y Roberto eran sus nietos.*

Raquel y Arturo se despidieron de don Fernando y estaban para salir. Pero el patriarca quería hablar con Raquel a solas. Le dijo que no se le había escapado cómo *Arturo y ella se miraban.* Raquel le confesó que *lo que sentía por Arturo era se-rio.* Entonces don Fernando le dio unos consejos: o ella *tenía que irse a Buenos Aires* o él *tenía que ir a Los Ángeles,* que no debían perder un amor verdadero. Se abrazaron una vez más.

Antes de salir, Raquel se volvió y le dijo a don Fernando que Rosario nunca dejó de pensar en él, que *siempre lo amó.* Con las dos copas reunidas, don Fernando se quedó en su cuarto a solas, pensando en el día en que, hace años, en un país lejano, dos jóvenes españoles las habían usado para celebrar el día de su boda.

APPENDIX 2: VERB CHARTS

A. Regular Verbs: Simple Tenses

INFINITIVE / PRESENT PARTICIPLE / PAST PARTICIPLE	INDICATIVE					SUBJUNCTIVE		IMPERATIVE
	PRESENT	IMPERFECT	PRETERITE	FUTURE	CONDITIONAL	PRESENT	IMPERFECT	
hablar	hablo	hablaba	hablé	hablaré	hablaría	hable	hablara	
hablando	hablas	hablabas	hablaste	hablarás	hablarías	hables	hablaras	habla tú,
hablado	habla	hablaba	habló	hablará	hablaría	hable	hablara	no hables
	hablamos	hablábamos	hablamos	hablaremos	hablaríamos	hablemos	habláramos	hable Ud.
	habláis	hablabais	hablasteis	hablaréis	hablaríais	habléis	hablarais	hablemos
	hablan	hablaban	hablaron	hablarán	hablarían	hablen	hablaran	hablen
comer	como	comía	comí	comeré	comería	coma	comiera	
comiendo	comes	comías	comiste	comerás	comerías	comas	comieras	come tú,
comido	come	comía	comió	comerá	comería	coma	comiera	no comas
	comemos	comíamos	comimos	comeremos	comeríamos	comamos	comiéramos	coma Ud.
	coméis	comíais	comisteis	comeréis	comeríais	comáis	comierais	comamos
	comen	comían	comieron	comerán	comerían	coman	comieran	coman
vivir	vivo	vivía	viví	viviré	viviría	viva	viviera	
viviendo	vives	vivías	viviste	vivirás	vivirías	vivas	vivieras	vive tú,
vivido	vive	vivía	vivió	vivirá	viviría	viva	viviera	no vivas
	vivimos	vivíamos	vivimos	viviremos	viviríamos	vivamos	viviéramos	viva Ud.
	vivís	vivíais	vivisteis	viviréis	viviríais	viváis	vivierais	vivamos
	viven	vivían	vivieron	vivirán	vivirían	vivan	vivieran	vivan

B. Regular Verbs: Perfect Tenses

INDICATIVE									
PRESENT PERFECT		PAST PERFECT		PRETERITE PERFECT		FUTURE PERFECT		CONDITIONAL PERFECT	
he		había		hube		habré		habría	
has	hablado	habías	hablado	hubiste	hablado	habrás	hablado	habrías	hablado
ha	comido	había	comido	hubo	comido	habrá	comido	habría	comido
hemos	vivido	habíamos	vivido	hubimos	vivido	habremos	vivido	habríamos	vivido
habéis		habíais		hubisteis		habréis		habríais	
han		habían		hubieron		habrán		habrían	

SUBJUNCTIVE			
PRESENT PERFECT		PAST PERFECT	
haya		hubiera	
hayas	hablado	hubieras	hablado
haya	comido	hubiera	comido
hayamos	vivido	hubiéramos	vivido
hayáis		hubierais	
hayan		hubieran	

C. Irregular Verbs

INFINITIVE PRESENT PARTICIPLE PAST PARTICIPLE	INDICATIVE					SUBJUNCTIVE		IMPERATIVE
	PRESENT	IMPERFECT	PRETERITE	FUTURE	CONDITIONAL	PRESENT	IMPERFECT	
andar andando andado	ando andas anda andamos andáis andan	andaba andabas andaba andábamos andabais andaban	anduve anduviste anduvo anduvimos anduvisteis anduvieron	andaré andarás andará andaremos andaréis andarán	andaría andarías andaría andaríamos andaríais andarían	ande andes ande andemos andéis anden	anduviera anduvieras anduviera anduviéramos anduvierais anduvieran	anda tú, no andes ande Ud. andemos anden
caer cayendo caído	caigo caes cae caemos caéis caen	caía caías caía caíamos caíais caían	caí caíste cayó caímos caísteis cayeron	caeré caerás caerá caeremos caeréis caerán	caería caerías caería caeríamos caeríais caerían	caiga caigas caiga caigamos caigáis caigan	cayera cayeras cayera cayéramos cayerais cayeran	cae tú, no caigas caiga Ud. caigamos caigan
dar dando dado	doy das da damos dais dan	daba dabas daba dábamos dabais daban	di diste dio dimos disteis dieron	daré darás dará daremos daréis darán	daría darías daría daríamos daríais darían	dé des dé demos deis den	diera dieras diera diéramos dierais dieran	da tú, no des dé Ud. demos den
decir diciendo dicho	digo dices dice decimos decís dicen	decía decías decía decíamos decíais decían	dije dijiste dijo dijimos dijisteis dijeron	diré dirás dirá diremos diréis dirán	diría dirías diría diríamos diríais dirían	diga digas diga digamos digáis digan	dijera dijeras dijera dijéramos dijerais dijeran	di tú, no digas diga Ud. digamos digan
estar estando estado	estoy estás está estamos estáis están	estaba estabas estaba estábamos estabais estaban	estuve estuviste estuvo estuvimos estuvisteis estuvieron	estaré estarás estará estaremos estaréis estarán	estaría estarías estaría estaríamos estaríais estarían	esté estés esté estemos estéis estén	estuviera estuvieras estuviera estuviéramos estuvierais estuvieran	está tú, no estés esté Ud. estemos estén
haber habiendo habido	he has ha hemos habéis han	había habías había habíamos habíais habían	hube hubiste hubo hubimos hubisteis hubieron	habré habrás habrá habremos habréis habrán	habría habrías habría habríamos habríais habrían	haya hayas haya hayamos hayáis hayan	hubiera hubieras hubiera hubiéramos hubierais hubieran	
hacer haciendo hecho	hago haces hace hacemos hacéis hacen	hacía hacías hacía hacíamos hacíais hacían	hice hiciste hizo hicimos hicisteis hicieron	haré harás hará haremos haréis harán	haría harías haría haríamos haríais harían	haga hagas haga hagamos hagáis hagan	hiciera hicieras hiciera hiciéramos hicierais hicieran	haz tú, no hagas haga Ud. hagamos hagan

C. Irregular Verbs (continued)

INFINITIVE / PRESENT PARTICIPLE / PAST PARTICIPLE	INDICATIVE					SUBJUNCTIVE		IMPERATIVE
	PRESENT	IMPERFECT	PRETERITE	FUTURE	CONDITIONAL	PRESENT	IMPERFECT	
ir / yendo / ido	voy	iba	fui	iré	iría	vaya	fuera	
	vas	ibas	fuiste	irás	irías	vayas	fueras	ve tú,
	va	iba	fue	irá	iría	vaya	fuera	no vayas
	vamos	íbamos	fuimos	iremos	iríamos	vayamos	fuéramos	vaya Ud.
	vais	ibais	fuisteis	iréis	iríais	vayáis	fuerais	vayamos
	van	iban	fueron	irán	irían	vayan	fueran	vayan
oír / oyendo / oído	oigo	oía	oí	oiré	oiría	oiga	oyera	
	oyes	oías	oíste	oirás	oirías	oigas	oyeras	oye tú,
	oye	oía	oyó	oirá	oiría	oiga	oyera	no oigas
	oímos	oíamos	oímos	oiremos	oiríamos	oigamos	oyéramos	oiga Ud.
	oís	oíais	oísteis	oiréis	oiríais	oigáis	oyerais	oigamos
	oyen	oían	oyeron	oirán	oirían	oigan	oyeran	oigan
poder / pudiendo / podido	puedo	podía	pude	podré	podría	pueda	pudiera	
	puedes	podías	pudiste	podrás	podrías	puedas	pudieras	
	puede	podía	pudo	podrá	podría	pueda	pudiera	
	podemos	podíamos	pudimos	podremos	podríamos	podamos	pudiéramos	
	podéis	podíais	pudisteis	podréis	podríais	podáis	pudierais	
	pueden	podían	pudieron	podrán	podrían	puedan	pudieran	
poner / poniendo / puesto	pongo	ponía	puse	pondré	pondría	ponga	pusiera	
	pones	ponías	pusiste	pondrás	pondrías	pongas	pusieras	pon tú,
	pone	ponía	puso	pondrá	pondría	ponga	pusiera	no pongas
	ponemos	poníamos	pusimos	pondremos	pondríamos	pongamos	pusiéramos	ponga Ud.
	ponéis	poníais	pusisteis	pondréis	pondríais	pongáis	pusierais	pongamos
	ponen	ponían	pusieron	pondrán	pondrían	pongan	pusieran	pongan
querer / queriendo / querido	quiero	quería	quise	querré	querría	quiera	quisiera	
	quieres	querías	quisiste	querrás	querrías	quieras	quisieras	quiere tú,
	quiere	quería	quiso	querrá	querría	quiera	quisiera	no quieras
	queremos	queríamos	quisimos	querremos	querríamos	queramos	quisiéramos	quiera Ud.
	queréis	queríais	quisisteis	querréis	querríais	queráis	quisierais	queramos
	quieren	querían	quisieron	querrán	querrían	quieran	quisieran	quieran
saber / sabiendo / sabido	sé	sabía	supe	sabré	sabría	sepa	supiera	
	sabes	sabías	supiste	sabrás	sabrías	sepas	supieras	sabe tú,
	sabe	sabía	supo	sabrá	sabría	sepa	supiera	no sepas
	sabemos	sabíamos	supimos	sabremos	sabríamos	sepamos	supiéramos	sepa Ud.
	sabéis	sabíais	supisteis	sabréis	sabríais	sepáis	supierais	sepamos
	saben	sabían	supieron	sabrán	sabrían	sepan	supieran	sepan
salir / saliendo / salido	salgo	salía	salí	saldré	saldría	salga	saliera	
	sales	salías	saliste	saldrás	saldrías	salgas	salieras	sal tú,
	sale	salía	salió	saldrá	saldría	salga	saliera	no salgas
	salimos	salíamos	salimos	saldremos	saldríamos	salgamos	saliéramos	salga Ud.
	salís	salíais	salisteis	saldréis	saldríais	salgáis	salierais	salgamos
	salen	salían	salieron	saldrán	saldrían	salgan	salieran	salgan

C. Irregular Verbs (continued)

Infinitive / Present Participle / Past Participle	Present	Imperfect	Preterite	Future	Conditional	Subjunctive Present	Subjunctive Imperfect	Imperative
ser siendo sido	soy eres es somos sois son	era eras era éramos erais eran	fui fuiste fue fuimos fuisteis fueron	seré serás será seremos seréis serán	sería serías sería seríamos seríais serían	sea seas sea seamos seáis sean	fuera fueras fuera fuéramos fuerais fueran	sé tú, 　no seas sea Ud. seamos sean
tener teniendo tenido	tengo tienes tiene tenemos tenéis tienen	tenía tenías tenía teníamos teníais tenían	tuve tuviste tuvo tuvimos tuvisteis tuvieron	tendré tendrás tendrá tendremos tendréis tendrán	tendría tendrías tendría tendríamos tendríais tendrían	tenga tengas tenga tengamos tengáis tengan	tuviera tuvieras tuviera tuviéramos tuvierais tuvieran	ten tú, 　no tengas tenga Ud. tengamos tengan
traer trayendo traído	traigo traes trae traemos traéis traen	traía traías traía traíamos traíais traían	traje trajiste trajo trajimos trajisteis trajeron	traeré traerás traerá traeremos traeréis traerán	traería traerías traería traeríamos traeríais traerían	traiga traigas traiga traigamos traigáis traigan	trajera trajeras trajera trajéramos trajerais trajeran	trae tú, 　no traigas traiga Ud. traigamos traigan
venir viniendo venido	vengo vienes viene venimos venís vienen	venía venías venía veníamos veníais venían	vine viniste vino vinimos vinisteis vinieron	vendré vendrás vendrá vendremos vendréis vendrán	vendría vendrías vendría vendríamos vendríais vendrían	venga vengas venga vengamos vengáis vengan	viniera vinieras viniera viniéramos vinierais vinieran	ven tú, 　no vengas venga Ud. vengamos vengan
ver viendo visto	veo ves ve vemos veis ven	veía veías veía veíamos veíais veían	vi viste vio vimos visteis vieron	veré verás verá veremos veréis verán	vería verías vería veríamos veríais verían	vea veas vea veamos veáis vean	viera vieras viera viéramos vierais vieran	ve tú, 　no veas vea Ud. veamos vean

D. Stem-changing and Spelling Change Verbs

INFINITIVE PRESENT PARTICIPLE PAST PARTICIPLE	INDICATIVE					SUBJUNCTIVE		IMPERATIVE
	PRESENT	IMPERFECT	PRETERITE	FUTURE	CONDITIONAL	PRESENT	IMPERFECT	
construir (y) construyendo construido	construyo construyes construye construimos construís construyen	construía construías construía construíamos construíais construían	construí construiste construyó construimos construisteis construyeron	construiré construirás construirá construiremos construiréis construirán	construiría construirías construiría construiríamos construiríais construirían	construya construyas construya construyamos construyáis construyan	construyera construyeras construyera construyéramos construyerais construyeran	construye tú, 　no construyas construya Ud. construyamos construyan
dormir (ue, u) durmiendo dormido	duermo duermes duerme dormimos dormís duermen	dormía dormías dormía dormíamos dormíais dormían	dormí dormiste durmió dormimos dormisteis durmieron	dormiré dormirás dormirá dormiremos dormiréis dormirán	dormiría dormirías dormiría dormiríamos dormiríais dormirían	duerma duermas duerma durmamos durmáis duerman	durmiera durmieras durmiera durmiéramos durmierais durmieran	duerme tú, 　no duermas duerma Ud. durmamos duerman

D. Stem-changing and Spelling Change Verbs (continued)

INFINITIVE / PRESENT PARTICIPLE / PAST PARTICIPLE	INDICATIVE					SUBJUNCTIVE		IMPERATIVE
	PRESENT	IMPERFECT	PRETERITE	FUTURE	CONDITIONAL	PRESENT	IMPERFECT	
pedir (i, i) / pidiendo / pedido	pido / pides / pide / pedimos / pedís / piden	pedía / pedías / pedía / pedíamos / pedíais / pedían	pedí / pediste / pidió / pedimos / pedisteis / pidieron	pediré / pedirás / pedirá / pediremos / pediréis / pedirán	pediría / pedirías / pediría / pediríamos / pediríais / pedirían	pida / pidas / pida / pidamos / pidáis / pidan	pidiera / pidieras / pidiera / pidiéramos / pidierais / pidieran	pide tú, no pidas / pida Ud. / pidamos / pidan
pensar (ie) / pensando / pensado	pienso / piensas / piensa / pensamos / pensáis / piensan	pensaba / pensabas / pensaba / pensábamos / pensabais / pensaban	pensé / pensaste / pensó / pensamos / pensasteis / pensaron	pensaré / pensarás / pensará / pensaremos / pensaréis / pensarán	pensaría / pensarías / pensaría / pensaríamos / pensaríais / pensarían	piense / pienses / piense / pensemos / penséis / piensen	pensara / pensaras / pensara / pensáramos / pensarais / pensaran	piensa tú, no pienses / piense Ud. / pensemos / piensen
producir (zc) / produciendo / producido	produzco / produces / produce / producimos / producís / producen	producía / producías / producía / producíamos / producíais / producían	produje / produjiste / produjo / produjimos / produjisteis / produjeron	produciré / producirás / producirá / produciremos / produciréis / producirán	produciría / producirías / produciría / produciríamos / produciríais / producirían	produzca / produzcas / produzca / produzcamos / produzcáis / produzcan	produjera / produjeras / produjera / produjéramos / produjerais / produjeran	produce tú, no produzcas / produzca Ud. / produzcamos / produzcan
reír (i, i) / riendo / reído	río / ríes / ríe / reímos / reís / ríen	reía / reías / reía / reíamos / reíais / reían	reí / reíste / rió / reímos / reísteis / rieron	reiré / reirás / reirá / reiremos / reiréis / reirán	reiría / reirías / reiría / reiríamos / reiríais / reirían	ría / rías / ría / riamos / riáis / rían	riera / rieras / riera / riéramos / rierais / rieran	ríe tú, no rías / ría Ud. / riamos / rían
seguir (i, i) (ga) / siguiendo / seguido	sigo / sigues / sigue / seguimos / seguís / siguen	seguía / seguías / seguía / seguíamos / seguíais / seguían	seguí / seguiste / siguió / seguimos / seguisteis / siguieron	seguiré / seguirás / seguirá / seguiremos / seguiréis / seguirán	seguiría / seguirías / seguiría / seguiríamos / seguiríais / seguirían	siga / sigas / siga / sigamos / sigáis / sigan	siguiera / siguieras / siguiera / siguiéramos / siguierais / siguieran	sigue tú, no sigas / siga Ud. / sigamos / sigan
sentir (ie, i) / sintiendo / sentido	siento / sientes / siente / sentimos / sentís / sienten	sentía / sentías / sentía / sentíamos / sentíais / sentían	sentí / sentiste / sintió / sentimos / sentisteis / sintieron	sentiré / sentirás / sentirá / sentiremos / sentiréis / sentirán	sentiría / sentirías / sentiría / sentiríamos / sentiríais / sentirían	sienta / sientas / sienta / sintamos / sintáis / sientan	sintiera / sintieras / sintiera / sintiéramos / sintierais / sintieran	siente tú, no sientas / sienta Ud. / sintamos / sientan
volver (ue) / volviendo / vuelto	vuelvo / vuelves / vuelve / volvemos / volvéis / vuelven	volvía / volvías / volvía / volvíamos / volvíais / volvían	volví / volviste / volvió / volvimos / volvisteis / volvieron	volveré / volverás / volverá / volveremos / volveréis / volverán	volvería / volverías / volvería / volveríamos / volveríais / volverían	vuelva / vuelvas / vuelva / volvamos / volváis / vuelvan	volviera / volvieras / volviera / volviéramos / volvierais / volvieran	vuelve tú, no vuelvas / vuelva Ud. / volvamos / vuelvan

SPANISH-ENGLISH VOCABULARY

The Spanish-English Vocabulary contains all the words that appear in the Textbook and Workbook/Study Guides I and II (and their corresponding audio program materials), with the following exceptions: (1) most close or identical cognates that do not appear in the chapter vocabulary lists; (2) most conjugated verb forms; (3) diminutives ending in **-ito/a**; (4) absolute superlatives ending in **ísimo/a**; (5) most adverbs ending in **-mente** (if the corresponding adjective is listed); and (6) most vocabulary that is glossed in the Text and Workbook/Study Guides. Only meanings that are used in the Textbook and Workbook/Study Guides are given.

The gender of nouns is indicated, except for masculine nouns ending in **-o** and feminine nouns ending in **-a**. Stem changes and spelling changes are indicated for verbs: **dormir (ue, u)**; **llegar (gu)**; **seguir (i, i) (g)**.

Words beginning with **ñ** are found under separate headings, following the letter **n**. Similarly, **ñ** within words follows **l, n**. For example, **añadir** follows **anuncio**.

The following abbreviations are used:

adj.	adjective		*m.*	masculine
adv.	adverb		*Mex.*	Mexico
approx.	approximately		*n.*	noun
Arg.	Argentina		*obj. (of prep.)*	object (of a preposition)
C. Am.	Central America		*pers.*	personal
conj.	conjunction		*pl.*	plural
def. art.	definite article		*poss.*	possessive
d.o.	direct object		*p.p.*	past participle
f.	feminine		*P.R.*	Puerto Rico
fam.	familiar		*prep.*	preposition
form.	formal		*pron.*	pronoun
gram.	grammatical term		*refl. pron.*	reflexive pronoun
inf.	infinitive		*s.*	singular
interj.	interjection		*Sp.*	Spain
inv.	invariable form		*sub. pron.*	subject pronoun
i.o.	indirect object		*U.S.*	United States
irreg.	irregular		*v.*	verb
L.A.	Latin America			

A

a to; at (*with time*); **a base de** on the basis of; **a bordo** aboard, on board; **a cargo (de)** in charge (of); **a causa de** because of, on account of; **a continuación** following, below, immediately after; **a dieta** on a diet; **a diferencia de** unlike; **a favor** in favor; **a fondo** completely, thoroughly; **a la vez** at the same time; **a la vuelta** around the corner; **a la(s) ...** at (*hour*); **a lo mejor** maybe; **a más tardar** at the latest; **a menos que** unless; **a menudo** often; **a nombre de** in the name of; **a orillas de** on the banks of; **a partir de** starting from; **a pesar de** in spite of; **a punto de** at the point of; about to; **¿a quién?** to whom? **a ratos** at times; **a sus órdenes** at your service; **a través de** through, across; **a veces** at times, sometimes; **a ver** let's see, let's have a look

abandonar to abandon
abanico fan
abastecer (zc) to supply, provide
abierto/a (*p.p. of* **abrir**) open(ed)
abogado/a lawyer
abolición *f.* abolition
abrazarse (c) to embrace
abrigador(a) heavy, warm (*of a coat*); sheltering
abril *m.* April
abrir (*p.p.* **abierto/a**) to open
absoluto/a absolute; **en absoluto** (not) at all
abuelo/a grandfather, grandmother, *pl.* grandparents
abundante abundant
abundar to abound, be plentiful
aburrido/a: ser (*irreg.*), **aburrido/a** to be boring; **estar** (*irreg.*) **aburrido/a** to be bored
aburrirse (de) to get bored (*with*)

abuso abuse
acá here
acabar to finish; **acabar de** + *inf.* to have just (*done something*)
academia academy
académico/a academic
acatarrarse to catch a cold
accidentado/a *person involved in an accident*
accidente *m.* accident
acción *f.* action
aceite *m.* oil
aceituna olive
acento accent
aceptación *f.* acceptance
aceptar to accept
acerca de *prep.* about, concerning
acercarse (qu) (a) to approach, draw near
acero steel
aclaración *f.* clarification

A21

acoger (j) to welcome, bring in, receive
acomodarse (a) to adapt oneself (to)
acompañar to accompany
aconsejable advisable
aconsejar to advise
acontecimiento event
acordarse (ue) (de) to remember
acostar (ue) to put to bed; **acostarse** to go to bed
acostumbrarse (a) to get accustomed to
actitud *f.* attitude
actividad *f.* activity
activo/a active
actor *m.* actor
actriz *f.* (*pl.* **actrices**) actress
actual current
actualidad present time; **en la actualidad** at this time, nowadays
actualmente currently
actuar to act, perform; **actuarse** to behave
acuático/a *adj.* aquatic, related to water; **esquí** (*m.*) **acuático** water skiing
acueducto aqueduct
acuerdo agreement; **de acuerdo** OK, I agree; **estar** (*irreg.*) **de acuerdo (con)** to agree, be in agreement (with)
acusación *f.* accusation
acusar to accuse
Adán Adam
adaptar(se) to adapt
adecuado/a adequate; suitable
adelantarse to get ahead
además (de) besides, in addition (to)
adicción *f.* addiction
adicional additional
adicto/a addict
adiós good-bye
adivinanza riddle, puzzle
adjetivo *n.* adjective; **adjetivos posesivos** (*gram.*) possessive adjectives; **adjetivos demostrativos** demonstrative adjectives
administración *f.* administration; **administración de empresas** business administration
administrador(a) administrator
admiración *f.* admiration
admirar to admire
admitir to admit
adolescente *m., f.* adolescent
adonde where
¿adónde? (to) where?
adoquín *m.* cobblestone
adorar to adore
aduana *s.* customs
adulto/a adult
adversario adversary
adversidad *f.* adversity
aéreo: (por) correo aéreo (by) airmail
aeróbico: ejercicio aeróbico aerobic exercise
aeropuerto airport
afectar to affect
afectivo/a emotional
afecto affection
afectuoso/a affectionate
aficionado/a fan, enthusiast
afirmación *f.* affirmation
afirmar to affirm
afirmativamente affirmatively

afortunadamente fortunately
africano/a *n., adj.* African
afuera *adv.* outside
afueras suburbs, outskirts
agave *f.* agave (*Mexican plant from which tequila is made*)
agencia agency; **agencia de viajes** travel agency
agente *m., f.* agent; **agente de bienes raíces** real estate agent; **agente de viajes** travel agent
agitado/a upset, worried; shaky; excited
agosto August
agradable agreeable, pleasant
agradar to be pleasing
agradecer (zc) to thank
agradecido/a grateful
agraria: reforma agraria agrarian reform
agravarse to worsen
agregar (gu) to add
agresivo/a aggressive
agrícola *m., f.* agricultural; **estudios agrícolas** agricultural studies
agricultura agriculture
agridulce bittersweet
agua *f.* (*but* **el agua**) water; **agua mineral** mineral water; **pasar por agua** to boil (*eggs*)
aguacate *m.* avocado
aguantar to put up with, endure, tolerate
águila *f.* (*but* **el águila**) eagle
ahí there
ahora now; **ahora mismo** right now; **justo ahora** right now, just now
ahorrar to save (*money, time*)
ahorros savings; **cuenta de ahorros** savings account
aire *m.* air; (**estar** [*irreg.*]) **al aire libre** (to be) outdoors
aislado/a isolated
aislamiento isolation
ajedrez *m.* chess; **jugar (ue) (gu) al ajedrez** to play chess
ajeno/a distant, detached
ají *m.* pepper, chili
al (*contraction of* **a** + **el**) to the; **al** + *inf.* upon, while, when + *verb form;* **al anochecer** at nightfall, dusk; **al borde de** on the edge of; **al comienzo** at the beginning; **al contrario** on the contrary; **al día siguiente** the next day; **al fin y al cabo** after all, when all is said and done; **al final** in the end; **al final de** at the end of; **al horno** baked; **al menos** at least; **al (mes, año, ...)** per (month, year, . . .); **al mismo tiempo** at the same time; **al parecer** apparently; **al pie de** at the bottom of; **al poco tiempo** shortly after; **al principio** at first, at the beginning; **al terminar ...** when . . . is/was over; **al tiro** immediately
alabar to praise
alargado/a elongated, lengthened
alarmado/a alarmed
alcalde *m.* mayor
alcanzar (c) to reach; to amount to
alcázar *m.* fortress; castle
alcoba bedroom
alcohólica: bebida alcohólica alcoholic beverage

aldea village
alegoría allegory
alegrarse (de) to be glad, be happy (about)
alegre happy
alegría happiness; happy nature
alejarse (de) to go far away (from); to separate (from); to draw away, grow apart (from)
alemán, alemana *n., adj.* German
Alemania Germany
alérgico/a allergic
aleta rudder
alfabeto alphabet
álgebra *f.* (*but* **el álgebra**) algebra
algo something, anything
algodón *m.* cotton
alguien someone; **caerle** (*irreg.*) **bien/mal a alguien** to like (not like), make a good/bad impression on someone; **darle** (*irreg.*) **de alta a alguien** to release someone (*from an institution*); **poner** (*irreg.*) **a alguien a cargo (de)** to put someone in charge (of)
algún, alguno/a some; any; **alguna vez** ever
aliado/a *n.* ally; *adj.* allied
alianza wedding ring
alicantino/a from Alicante (*region of Spain*)
aliviar to alleviate, relieve
allá there; **más allá de** *prep.* beyond
allí there
alma *f.* (*but* **el alma**) soul
almacén *m.* department store; storehouse
almorzar (ue) (c) to have lunch
almuerzo lunch
alojado/a *adj.* staying, lodged (*at a hotel*)
alojarse to stay, lodge
alpino: esquí (*m.*) **alpino** downhill skiing
alquilado/a rented
alquilar to rent
alquiler *m.* rent
alta: darle (*irreg.*) **de alta (a alguien)** to release (someone) (*from an institution*)
alternar to alternate
alternativa alternative
altiplano high plateau
altitud *f.* altitude
alto *n.* height; **de alto** in height
alto/a *adj.* tall; high; loud; **clase** (*f.*) **alta** upper class; **alta cocina** haute cuisine; **en voz alta** out loud
altura height
ama (*f.* [*but* **el ama**]) **de casa** homemaker; housekeeper
amabilidad *f.* kindness
amable nice, kind
amaestrar to train
amante *m., f.* lover
amar to love
amarillo/a yellow
ambición *f.* ambition
ambicionar to desire
ambicioso/a ambitious
ambiental environmental
ambiente *m.* atmosphere; **medio ambiente** environment

ambos/as both
ambulancia ambulance
ambulante: músicos ambulantes strolling musicians
amenaza threat
amenazante threatening
amenazar (c) to threaten
ameno/a pleasant, agreeable
América Latina Latin America
americano/a n. adj. American; **fútbol** (*m.*) **americano** football
amigablemente amicably, in a friendly way
amigo/a friend; **amigo/a íntimo/a** close friend; **mejor amigo/a** best friend; **salir** (*irreg.*) **con los amigos** to go out with friends
amistad *f.* friendship
amistoso/a friendly
amor *m.* love; **amor a primera vista** love at first sight
amoroso/a affectionate, loving; amorous
amplio/a ample
analfabetismo illiteracy
análisis *m.* analysis
analizarse (c) to analyze
ananás *m. s.* pineapple (*Arg.*)
anaranjado/a orange (*color*)
anciano/a elderly person
¡anda! *interj.* move it!; go on!
Andalucía Andalusia
andaluz, andaluza (*pl.* **andaluces**) Andalusian
andar (*irreg.*) to walk; to go; **andar bien/mal** to be going well/badly; **andar buscando** to be looking for; **andar en barco** to take a boat ride; **andar en bicicleta** to go for a bicycle ride; **andar en bote** to take a rowboat ride; **andar en mateo** to take a carriage ride
anfibio: animal (*m.*) **anfibio** amphibian
anglosajón, anglosajona *n., adj.* Anglo-Saxon
angustia anguish
angustiado/a anguished
animación *f.* animation, liveliness
animado/a lively, animated, spirited; **dibujos animados** cartoons
animal *m.* animal; **animal anfibio** amphibian; **animal doméstico** pet
animar to encourage
ánimo strength
aniversario anniversary
anoche last night
anochecer: al anochecer at nightfall, dusk
anónimo/a anonymous; **sociedad** (*f.*) **anónima** incorporated; stock company
ansiedad *f.* anxiety
ansioso/a anxious
Antártida Antarctica
ante before, in the presence of; with regard to; **ante todo** above all
antecedentes (*m.*) **históricos** *pl.* historical record; background
antemano: de antemano beforehand
antepasado ancestor
anterior previous, preceding
antes *adv.* before, formerly; **antes de** *prep.* before (*in time*); **antes (de)**

que *conj.* before; **antes de Cristo** B.C.; **lo antes posible** as soon as possible
anticipación: con anticipación in advance
anticipar to anticipate
anticomunista *m., f.* anticommunist
antigüedad *n. f.* antique; **tienda de antigüedades** antique store
antiguo/a former; old, ancient
antipatriótico/a unpatriotic
antojito appetizer (*Mex.*)
antropología anthropology
anual annual
anuncio announcement, advertisement
añadir to add
añejo/a old, aged
año year; **al año** per year; **hace muchos años** many years ago; **de primer año** *adj.* freshman; **tener** (*irreg.*) ... **años** to be ... years old; **una vez al año** once a year
añorar to long for
apacionado/a *n.* admirer
aparato apparatus, appliance; **aparato doméstico** household appliance
aparecer (zc) to appear
aparente apparent
apariencia appearance
apartamento apartment
apellido surname, last name
apenado/a grieved
apenas scarcely
apéndice *m.* appendix
aperitivo appetizer
apetito appetite
apetitoso/a: plato apetitoso appetizing dish
apio celery
aplicar (qu) to apply
apoderarse (de) to take possession (of)
apogeo height, summit
apoyar to support
apoyo support
apreciado/a esteemed
apreciar to appreciate, esteem
aprender to learn; **aprender a** + *inf.* to learn to (*do something*)
apresurado/a in a hurry
aprieto difficulty, fix
aprobar (ue) to approve, confirm
aprobarse (ue) to be approved
apropiado/a appropriate
aprovechamiento use; exploitation
aprovechar to take advantage of
aproximadamente approximately
aptitud *f.* aptitude
apuntar to note, write down
apuro difficulty, jam
aquel, aquella *adj.* that (*over there*); **aquél, aquélla** *pron.* that one (*over there*); **en aquel entonces** back then, at that time, in those days
aquello that, that thing, that fact
aquellos/as *adj.* those (*over there*); **aquéllos/as** *pron.* those (ones) (*over there*)
aquí here
árabe *n. m., f.* Arab; *adj.* Arabic
arador *m.* plowman
árbol *m.* tree

arbusto shrub
archipiélago archipelago
arcilla (bruta) (unworked) clay
área *f.* (*but* **el área**) area
arena: duna de arena sand dune
argentino/a Argentine
árido/a arid, dry; barren
aritmética arithmetic
armado: conflicto armado armed conflict
armario closet
aromático/a aromatic
arqueología archeology
arqueólogo/a archeologist
arquitecto/a architect
arquitectura architecture
arreglar to arrange; to fix
arreglo arrangement
arrestado/a arrested
arrestar to arrest
arriba upstairs
arrogante arrogant
arrojar to indicate, show
arrollada: tortilla arrollada rolled tortilla
arroyo stream
arroz *m.* rice
arruinado/a ruined
arte *m.* (*but* **las artes**) art; **artes** (*f.*) **liberales** liberal arts; **bellas artes** (*f.*) fine arts
artesano/a artisan, craftsperson
articulación *f.* joint
artículo article
artista *m., f.* artist
artístico/a artistic
arvejas peas
ascendencia descent
ascender (ie) to advance
ascenso promotion
ascensor *m.* elevator
asco: dar (*irreg.*) **asco a (alguien)** to disgust (someone)
asegurar to assure
asentir (ie, i) to assent, agree
asesinar to assassinate
asesinato assassination, murder
asesino/a assassin, murderer
así *adv.* so, thus; that way; therefore, consequently; **así que** *conj.* so, then
asiento seat; breeding ground; site; **asiento de atrás** back seat
asignatura (school) subject
asimilar to assimilate
asistente/a assistant
asistir (a) to attend
asociación *f.* association
asociar to associate
aspecto aspect
áspero/a harsh
aspiración *f.* aspiration
aspirar (a) to aspire (to)
aspirina aspirin
astronomía astronomy
astrónomo/a astronomer
Asturias *region of Spain*
asunto issue, matter
asustar to frighten
atacar (qu) to attack
ataque *m.* attack; **ataque cardíaco** heart attack
atención *f.* attention; **llamar la**

atención to attract attention; **prestar atención (a)** to pay attention (to)
atender (ie) to attend to, take care of
atentamente attentively
atlántico/a Atlantic; **Océano Atlántico** Atlantic Ocean
atleta *m., f.* athlete
atmósfera atmosphere
atracción *f.* attraction; **atracción turística** tourist attraction
atractivo *n.* attraction
atractivo/a *adj.* attractive
atraer (*like* **traer**) to attract
atrapado/a trapped
atrás behind; **asiento de atrás** back seat
atrasado/a *adj.* late, arriving late
atreverse (a) to dare (to)
atún *m.* tuna
auditor(a) auditor
aumentar to increase; **aumenta tu vocabulario** increase your vocabulary
aumento increase
aun *adv.* even
aún *adv.* still, yet
aunque although
ausencia absence
ausente absent
austral *n. former monetary unit of Argentina; adj.* southern
autobús *m.* bus
autóctono/a native
automático/a automatic
automóvil *m.* automobile, car
autonomía autonomy
autónomo/a autonomous
autopista highway; toll road
autor(a) author
autoritario/a authoritarian
autorizar (c) to authorize
avanzado/a advanced
avanzar (c) to advance, get ahead
avenida avenue
aventura adventure
avergonzado/a embarrassed
avería breakdown
averiguar (gü) to find out, ascertain
avión *m.* airplane
avisar to advise, notify; to warn
¡ay! *interj.* oh!
ayer yesterday
ayuda help, assistance
ayudante *m., f.* assistant
ayudar to help, assist
ayuntamiento city hall
azafata (female) flight attendant
azteca *n. m., f.; adj.* Aztec
Aztlán *legendary place of origin of the Aztecs*
azúcar *m.* sugar; **caña de azúcar** sugar cane; **ingenio de azúcar** sugar mill
azul blue
azulado/a bluish

B
bachillerato high school diploma
bahía bay; **Bahía de (los) Cochinos** Bay of Pigs
bailar to dance
baile *n. m.* dance; **baile de gala** formal dance

bajar to go down(stairs); to bring down (*a fever*); **bajar de peso** to lose weight
bajo *n.* bass; *prep.* under
bajo/a, *adj.* short (*in height*); low; **clase** (*f.*) **baja** lower class; **planta baja** ground floor, first floor
balcón *m.* balcony
ballet *m.* ballet
baloncesto basketball
balsa raft
banca banking
banco bank; bench
bandera flag
banquero/a banker
bañarse to bathe, take a bath
baño bath; bathroom, **baño privado (con ducha)** private bath, (with shower); **traje** (*m.*) **de baño** bathing suit
bar *m.* bar
barato/a inexpensive, cheap
barba beard
barbacoa barbecue
barbaridad: ¡qué barbaridad! *interj.* how awful!
barbería barber shop
barca boat, barge
barco boat; **andar** (*irreg.*) **en barco** to take a boat ride; **navegar (gu) en barco** to sail
barrera barrier
barril *m.* barrel
barrio district; neighborhood
basarse to be based; **basarse en** to base one's ideas or opinions on
base *f.* base; basis; **a base de** on the basis of
básico/a basic
básquetbol *m.* basketball
bastante enough; a great deal; rather, quite
bastar to be enough
batalla battle
baúl *m.* trunk
bebé *m.* baby
beber to drink
bebida *n.* drink, beverage; **bebida alcohólica** alcoholic beverage
béisbol *m.* baseball
belleza beauty
bello/a beautiful; **bellas artes** *f.* fine arts
besar to kiss
beso kiss
biblioteca library
bicicleta: andar (*irreg.*) **en bicicleta** to ride a bicycle
bien *adv.* well; **andar** (*irreg.*) **bien** to be going well; **caerle** (*irreg.*) **bien a (alguien)** to like, make a good impression on (someone); **llevarse bien (con)** to get along well (with); **manejar bien** to manage well; **muy bien** very well; **pasarlo bien** to have a good time; **por bien o por mal** for better or worse; **sentirse (i, i) bien** to feel well
bien *n., m.* good; *pl.* goods; **agente** (*m., f.*) **de bienes raíces** real estate agent; **bienes raíces** *pl.* real estate
bienestar *m.* well-being
bienvenido/a welcome

bilingüe bilingual; **educación** (*f.*) **bilingüe** bilingual education
bilingüismo bilingualism
billete *m.* ticket (*Sp.*); **billete de ida y vuelta** round-trip ticket
biología biology
biólogo/a biologist
bistec *m.* steak
blanco/a white
bloque *m.* city block (*P.R.*)
bloqueado/a blocked, closed off
blusa blouse
boca mouth
bocacalle *f.* intersection (*of a street*)
boda wedding
bohemio/a bohemian
boleto ticket (*L.A.*)
bolsa purse, handbag
bomba *traditional Puerto Rican dance*
bombardeo bombing
bondad *f.* goodness; kindness
bonito/a pretty, attractive
borde: al borde de on the edge of
bordo: a bordo aboard, on board
Borinquen *f. aboriginal and poetic name of Puerto Rico*
borinqueño/a *n. adj.* Puerto Rican
borrar to erase
bosque *m.* forest; **bosque tropical** tropical forest
bosquejo outline
botana appetizer (*Mex.*)
botánico/a botanical; **jardín** (*m.*) **botánico** botanical garden
bota boot
botar to throw away
bote *m.* rowboat; **andar** (*irreg.*) **en bote** to take a rowboat ride
botella bottle
botones *m. s.* bellhop
brazalete *m.* bracelet
brazo arm
brécol *m.* broccoli
breve brief
brevísimamente very briefly
brillante brilliant
brillar to shine
brindar to (drink a) toast
brindis *m. s.* toast
brocheta brochette, skewer
brocolí *m.* broccoli
broma joke; **en broma** as a joke, jokingly
brujo/a magician
bruta: arcilla bruta unworked clay
buceo snorkeling; scuba diving
buen, bueno/a *adj.* good; **buen día** good day (*greeting*) (*Arg.*); **buena suerte** good luck; **buenas noches** good evening/night; **buenas tardes** good afternoon; **buenos, buenas** good day, good afternoon/evening; **buenos días** good morning; **hace buen tiempo** it's good weather; **bueno** (*when answering the telephone*) hello (*Mex.*); **bueno** *adv.* all right
bufanda scarf
bufete *m.* lawyer's office
bulevar *m.* boulevard
burlarse (de) to ridicule, make fun (of)
busca search; **en busca de** in search of

buscar (qu) to look for, seek; **andar** (*irreg.*) **buscando** to be looking for; **en busca de** in search of
búsqueda search, quest

C
caballero gentleman
caballo horse; **montar a caballo** to ride horseback
cabaña cabin
caber (*irreg.*) to fit; to go; to be possible; **no cabe duda** there is no doubt
cabeza head; **dolor** (*m.*) **de cabeza** headache; **me/le duele la cabeza** I/he/she/you (*form.*) have/has a headache
cabezón, cabezona stubborn, hard-headed
cabezonería stubbornness
cabo end; **al fin y al cabo** after all, when all is said and done
cacahuete *m.* peanut
cada *inv.* each, every; **cada vez más** more and more
cadena chain
cadete *m.* cadet
caer (*irreg.*) to fall; **caerle bien/mal a (alguien)** to like (not like), make a good/bad impression on (someone)
café *m.* (cup of) coffee; **café,** coffee shop; **café con leche** *strong coffee served with warm or hot milk;* **café solo** black coffee
cafeína caffeine
cafetería cafeteria
calabaza squash
calamar *m.* squid; **calamares fritos** fried squid rings
calavera skull
calcetines *m. pl.* socks
calculador(a) calculating
calcular to calculate
cálculo calculus
calendario calendar; **calendario gregoriano** Gregorian calendar
calidad *f.* quality
cálido: clima (*m.*) **cálido** hot climate
caliente hot
califato *region governed by an Islamic leader*
callado/a silent, quiet
calle *f.* street; **calle peatonal** pedestrian mall
calmado/a quiet, calm
calmante *m.* sedative
calmar to calm
calor *n. m.* heat; **hace un calor de mil demonios** it's a hellishly hot day; **hace (mucho) calor** it's (very) hot; **tener** (*irreg.*) **(mucho) calor** to be (very) hot
cama bed; **cama matrimonial** double bed; **guardar cama** to stay in bed
cámara camera
camarero/a waiter, waitress
camarón *m.* shrimp (*Mex. and parts of L.A.*)
cambiar (de) to change; **cambiarse de ropa** to change one's clothes; **quisiera cambiar ...** I would like to change . . . (*money*)

cambio change; exchange; **en cambio** on the other hand
caminar to walk
camino street, road; way; **camino a** on the way to; **a lo largo del camino** along the way
camión *m.* truck; bus (*Mex.*)
camisa shirt; **camisa de noche** nightshirt
camiseta T-shirt
campana bell
campanada ringing of a bell
campaña campaign
campeche *m.* logwood
campeón, campeona champion
campera short jacket (*Arg.*)
campesino/a farm worker, peasant; **teatro campesino** farm worker's theater
campo field; countryside; **campo de golf** golf course
cana gray hair
canal *m.* canal
canario canary; **Islas Canarias** Canary Islands
canasta basket
cancelar to cancel
cáncer *m.* cancer
cancha court; playing field; **cancha de tenis** tennis court
canción *f.* song
cangrejo crab
canoso/a gray-haired; **pelo canoso** gray hair
cansado/a tired
cansar to tire; **cansarse** to get tired
Cantábrico: Mar (*m.*) **Cantábrico** Bay of Biscay
cantante *m., f.* singer
cantar to sing
cantidad *f.* quantity, amount
cantina bar
canto song
caña cane; **caña de azúcar** sugar cane; **caña de pescar** fishing pole
cañón *m.* canyon
caos *m. s.* chaos
capacidad *f.* capacity
capaz (*pl.* **capaces**) capable, able
capilla chapel
capital *f.* capital (city); *m.* capital (*money*)
capitalista *m., f.* capitalist
capítulo chapter
capricho whim; desire
Capricornio: Trópico de Capricornio Tropic of Capricorn
captar to grasp; to depict; to pick up (*sound*)
capturar to capture
cara face; side; **la otra cara de la moneda** the other side of the coin
carácter *m.* character
característico/a *adj.* characteristic
caracterizar (c) to characterize
¡caramba! *interj.* my God! gosh!
caramelo caramel; candy
¡caray! *interj.* damn!
cárcel *f.* prison
cardíaco/a *adj.* cardiac, heart; **ataque** (*m.*) **cardíaco** heart attack

cardinales: direcciones (*f.*) **cardinales** cardinal points
carga load
cargar (gu) to carry; to charge (*on a credit card*)
cargo position; **poner** (*irreg.*) **a alguien a cargo (de)** to put (someone) in charge (of)
Caribe *n. m.* Caribbean
caribeño/a *n., adj.* Caribbean
cariño affection; **tomarle cariño a (alguien)** to start to have affection for (someone)
cariñoso/a affectionate
carisma *m.* charisma
carnaval *m.* carnival
carne *f.* meat; **carne de cerdo** pork; **carne de res** beef (*Mex.*); **carne de vaca** beef; **carne picada** ground meat
carnicería butcher shop
carnicero butcher
caro/a expensive
carpintero/a carpenter
carrera career, profession; course of study
carretera highway
carro car
carta letter; **jugar (ue) (gu) a las cartas por dinero** to gamble on cards
cartel *m.* sign
cartera wallet
casa house; home; **ama** (*f.* [*but* **el ama**]) **de casa** homemaker; **en casa** at home
casado/a married; **recién casado/a** recently married, newly wed
casar(se) (con) to marry (someone); to get married (to)
cascada cascade
casero/a home, homemade
casi almost
casino casino
caso case; **en caso de que** in case; **en todo caso** in any case; **hacer** (*irreg.*) **caso a** to pay attention to; **no hacer caso (de)** to pay no attention (to an issue); **no hacerle caso (a alguien)** to ignore (someone)
castaño/a brown, brunet(te)
castigo punishment
Castilla Castile (*region of Spain*)
castillo castle
casualidad: dar (*irreg.*) **la casualidad** to just happen; **por casualidad** by chance
catalán *m.* Catalan (*language of Catalonia* [*region of Spain*])
catalán, catalana *n., adj.* Catalonian
Cataluña Catalonia (*region of Spain*)
catarata waterfall
catarro común common cold
catecismo catechism
catedral *f.* cathedral
categoría category
catolicismo Catholicism
católico/a *n., adj.* Catholic
catorce fourteen
causa cause; **a causa de** because of, on account of
causar to cause, be the cause of; **causar una buena impresión** to make a good impression

cautivar to captivate
cautivo *n.* captive
cebolla onion
ceder to give up, hand over
ceiba silk-cotton tree
celebración *f.* celebration
celebrar to celebrate
célebre *m.* celebrity
celos jealousy; **tener** (*irreg.*) **celos (de)** to be jealous (of)
celoso/a jealous; **estar** (*irreg.*) **celoso/a (de)** to be jealous (of)
cementerio cemetery
cena dinner, supper
cenar to have dinner
censo census
censura censorship
centavo cent
céntrico/a central
centro center; downtown; **centro comercial** shopping center
Centroamérica Central America
cerámica ceramic
cerca *adv.* near, nearby, close; **cerca de** *prep.* near (to); **de cerca** from a short distance
cercano/a *adj.* close
cerdo pig; **carne** (*f.*) **de cerdo** pork; **chuleta de cerdo** pork chop
cereal *m.* cereal; grain
ceremonia ceremony
cereza cherry
cero zero
cerrado/a closed
cerrar (ie) to close
cerro hill
certificado certificate; **certificado de nacimiento** birth certificate
cervecería beer tavern, pub
cerveza beer
champán *m.* champagne
champaña *m.* champagne
champiñón *m.* mushroom
Chanuka Chanukah, Hanukkah
chapulín *m.* grasshopper (*L.A.*)
chaqueta jacket
charlar to chat
charrada charro dance
chau ciao, 'bye, good-bye
chavo money, "dough" (*P.R.*)
cheque *m.* check; **cheque de viajero** traveler's check
chequear to check
chico/a *adj.* little, small; *n.* boy, girl; *pl.* boys, girls; children
chícharos peas (*Mex.*)
chile *m.* chili pepper
chileno/a *n., adj.* Chilean
chimpancé *m.* chimpanzee
chino/a *n., adj.* Chinese
chismear to gossip
chistar: sin chistar without saying a word
chistoso/a funny
chocar (qu) (con) to run into, collide (with)
chocolate *m.* (hot) chocolate
chófer *m.* chauffeur, driver
choque *m.* accident, collision
choricero/a sausage maker or seller
chorizo sausage

chuleta chop; **chuleta de cerdo** pork chop; **chuleta de cordero** lamb chop
ciclo cycle
ciego/a *n.* visually impaired person, blind person; *adj.* visually impaired, blind
cielo heaven; sky
cien, ciento (one) hundred
ciencia science; **ciencia-ficción** science fiction; **ciencias económicas** economics; **ciencias naturales** natural sciences; **ciencias sociales** social sciences
científico/a scientist
cierto/a true; certain; **es cierto** it's certain, true; **por cierto** by the way, certainly
cifra figure, number
cigarrillo cigarette
cima summit, top
cinco five
cincuenta fifty
cine *m.* cinema, movie theater; **ir** (*irreg.*) **al cine** to go to the movies; **sala de cine** theater
cinematografía cinematography, filmmaking
cinematógrafo filmmaker
cinta tape
ciprés *m.* cypress tree
círculo circle
circunstancia circumstance
ciruela plum
cita date; appointment; **primera cita** first date
ciudad *f.* city; **Ciudad de México** Mexico City
ciudadanía citizenship
ciudadano/a citizen
civil: guerra civil civil war
civilización *f.* civilization
clandestino/a secret, clandestine
clarín *m.* bugle
claro/a clear; light (*colors*); **claro** *interj.* of course; **claro que sí** of course; **ojos claros** light-colored eyes
clase *f.* class; kind; **clase alta** upper class; **clase baja** lower class; **clase elevada** upper class; **clase media** middle class; **clase obrera** working class; **clase social** social class; **clase trabajadora** working class; **clase turística** tourist class; **dar** (*irreg.*) **una clase** to teach a class; **primera clase** first class; **salón** (*m.*) **de clase** classroom
clásico *n.* classic
clásico/a *adj.* classic(al)
cláusula (*gram.*) clause
clero clergy
cliente/a client
clima *m.* climate; clime; **clima cálido** hot climate
climático/a climatic
clínica clinic
cobrar to cover; to charge; **cóbreme** charge me (for)
cobre *m.* copper
coche *m.* car
coche-comedor *m.* dining car (*on a train*)

cochinita pibil roast suckling pig
cochino: Bahía de (los) Cochinos Bay of Pigs
cocido/a cooked
cocina kitchen; cooking
cocinar to cook
cocinero/a *n.* cook, chef
coco coconut
cocotero coconut palm tree
códice *m.* body of laws; manuscript volume
cofradía *f.* brotherhood
cognado *n.* cognate
coincidencia coincidence
cola line (*of people*)
colaboración *f.* collaboration
colección *f.* collection
coleccionar to collect
colega *m., f.* colleague
colegio grade or high school
colgar (ue) (gu) to hang up
coliflor *f.* cauliflower
colina hill
colmo last straw
colocar (qu) to place
colombiano/a Colombian
Colón: Cristóbal Colón Christopher Columbus
colonia colony; neighborhood (*Mex.*)
colonial colonial
colonizar (c) to colonize
color *m.* color; **color claro** pastel colored; **de color salmón** salmon-colored
colorido *n.* coloring, color
columna column
combatir to fight
combinación *f.* combination
combinar to combine
comedia comedy; play
comedor *m.* dining room; **coche-comedor** (*m.*) dining car (*on a train*)
comendador *m.* commander
comentar to comment (on); to discuss
comentario comment; commentary
comenzar (ie) (c) to begin
comer to eat; **comerse** to eat up
comercial *adj.* commerical; **centro comercial** shopping center
comerciante *m., f.* merchant
comercio commerce, business
comestible *n. m.* food; *adj.* edible; **tienda de comestibles** food store
cometer to commit
cómico/a comical
comida food; meal; **comida congelada** frozen food; **comida rápida** fast food
comienzo *n.* beginning; **al comienzo** at the beginning
comino: me importa un comino I couldn't care less
como as (a); like; since; **como consecuencia** as a result; **como tal** as such; **tal como** just as, exactly the same as; **tan ... como** as ... as; **tan pronto como** as soon as; **tanto/a/os/as ... como** as much/many ... as
¿cómo? how?, how's that?, what?, I didn't catch that
comodidades *f.* comforts
cómodo/a comfortable

compañero/a companion; mate, "significant other"

compañía company (*business*)

comparación *f.* comparison

comparar to compare

compartimiento compartment

compartir to share

compas *m. pl. shortened form of* **compañeros**

compasión *f.* compassion

competición *f.* competition

complacer (zc) to please

complejo/a complex, complicated

completar to complete

completo/a complete, full; **por completo** completely

complicación *f.* complication

complicado/a complicated

componerse (*like* **poner**) **(de)** to be composed (of)

comportamiento behavior

comportarse to behave oneself

composición *f.* composition

compositor(a) composer

compra purchase; **hacer** (*irreg.*) **las compras** to shop; **ir** (*irreg.*) **de compras** to go shopping

comprar to buy

comprender to understand

comprensión *f.* comprehension, understanding

comprensivo/a understanding

comprobar (ue) to check

comprometido/a committed; involved

compromiso obligation, commitment

compuesto/a (*p. p. of* **componer**) composed

compulsivo/a compulsive

computación *f.* computer science

computadora computer (*L.A.*); **programación** (*f.*) **de computadoras** computer programming; **programador(a) de computadoras** computer programmer (*L.A.*)

común common; **catarro común** common cold; **en común** in common; **sentido común** common sense

comunicación *f.* communication; **medios de comunicación** means of communication, media

comunicarse (qu) (con) to communicate (with); to get in touch (with), contact

comunidad *f.* community

comunismo communism

comunista *n., m., f., adj.* communist

con with; **con anticipación** in advance; **con destino a** bound for; **con frecuencia** frequently; **con más frecuencia** most frequently, most often; **con permiso** may I pass by?; **¿con qué frecuencia?** how often?; **¿con quién?** with whom?; **con razón** understandably so; **con respecto a** with respect to; **con tal (de) que** so that

conceder to grant, concede

concentración *f.* concentration

concentrar(se) to concentrate

concepto concept

concesión *f.* granting, concession

conciencia moral conscience

concierto concert

conciliador(a) conciliatory

concluir (y) to conclude

conclusión *f.* conclusion

concreto/a concrete

concurso contest

condición *f.* condition; **buenas/malas condiciones** *pl.* good/bad shape, condition

condimentado/a: bien condimentado/a well-seasoned

conducta conduct

conductor(a) conductor

conferencia lecture

confesar (ie) to confess

confesión *f.* confession

confiado/a confident

confianza confidence; **de confianza** trustworthy, reliable

confiar (en) to trust (in); to confide (in)

confidencialidad *f.* confidentiality

confirmación *f.* confirmation

confirmar to confirm

confitería confectionery

conflicto conflict; **conflicto armado** armed conflict; **en conflicto** in conflict

confundir to confuse

confusión *f.* confusion

confuso/a confused

congelado/a frozen; **comida congelada** frozen food

congestión *f.* congestion

congresista *m., f.* congressperson, member of congress

congreso convention; congress

conjunción *f.* conjunction

conjunto ensemble, outfit: group, ensemble (*musical*)

conmemorar to commemorate

conmigo with me

conmovido/a moved (*emotionally*)

conocer (zc) to know, be acquainted with; to meet

conocido/a well-known

conocimiento(s) knowledge

conquista conquest

conquistador(a) conqueror

conquistar to conquer

consciencia awareness

consciente conscious

consecuencia consequence; **como consecuencia** as a result

conseguir (i, i) (g) to get, obtain, attain; to succeed in

consejero/a counselor

consejo(s) advice

conservar to conserve, save, preserve

considerar to consider

consigo with himself, with herself; with it; with them

consistir (en) to consist (of)

consolar (ue) to console

consolidación *f.* consolidation, strengthening

constante constant

constar (de) to consist, be composed (of)

constitución *f.* constitution

constitucional constitutional

construcción *f.* construction

constructor (a) builder, manufacturer

construir (y) to build

consulta *s.* consulting hours

consultar to consult

consumidor(a) consumer

consumir to consume, use

consumo consumption

contabiladad *f.* accounting

contacto contact

contagiar to infect

contar (ue) to tell (about); to count; **contar con** to have; to rely on; to have available

contemplar to contemplate; to look at, study

contemporáneo/a contemporary

contener (*like* **tener**) to contain

contenido *n. s.* contents

contentarse (con) to be content, satisfied (with)

contento/a happy, content

contestar to answer

contexto context

contigo with you (*fam.*)

continental continental; **desayuno continental** continental breakfast

continente *m.* continent

continuación *f.* continuation; **a continuación** below, immediately after, following

continuar to continue, go on; to follow

contra against; **en contra (de)** against

contradicción *f.* contradiction

contradictorio/a contradictory

contraer (*like* **traer**) to contract (*an illness*)

contrario: al contrario on the contrary

contraste *m.* contrast

contratar to hire

contrato contract

contribución *f.* contribution

contribuir (y) to contribute

controlar to control

controversia controversy; **de controversia** controversial

controvertido/a controversial

convencer (z) to convince

convencido/a convinced

conveniente convenient

convenir (*like* **venir**) to be suitable, convenient for; to be desirable; to be worth one's while

conversación *f.* conversation

conversar to converse

convertirse (ie, i) (en) to become; to change (into); to convert

convicción *f.* conviction

convivencia coexistence, living together

convivir to coexist, to live together

coñac *m.* cognac, brandy

cooperar to cooperate

copa goblet, wineglass; drink (*slang*)

copado/a taken, filled up

copia copy

coquetear to flirt

coquí *small tree frog indigenous to Puerto Rico that makes a characteristic musical sound*

coraje *m.* courage

Corán *m.* Koran

corazón *m.* heart

corbata necktie
cordero lamb; **chuleta de cordero** lamb chop
cordillera mountain range
coriza head cold
coro chorus
correcto/a correct, right
corredor *m.* corridor, hall
corregir (i, i) (j) to correct
correo mail; post office; **(por) correo aéreo** (by) airmail
correr to run; **correr riesgo** to run a risk
corresponder to correspond, match
correspondiente *adj.* corresponding
corriente common, ordinary; **cuenta corriente** checking account
corrupción *f.* corruption
cortado/a cut (up)
cortapisas *pl.* restrictions
corte *f.* court (*of law*)
cortés courteous, polite
cortesía courtesy
corto/a brief, short (*in length*); **pantalón** (*m.*) **corto, pantalones** (*m. pl.*) **cortos** shorts
cosa thing; **cualquier cosa** anything
coser to sew
cosmopolita *m., f.* cosmopolitan
costa coast
costar (ue) to cost; **costarle trabajo (a alguien)** to be hard, take a lot of effort (for someone)
costumbre *f.* custom, habit; **como de costumbre** as usual; **es costumbre** it is customary
costura *n.* sewing
creación *f.* creation
creador(a) creator
crear to create
creatividad *f.* creativity
crecer (zc) to grow
crédito: tarjeta de crédito credit card; **dar** (*irreg.*) **crédito** to believe
creencia belief
creer (y) (en) to think, believe (in); **creer que sí/no** to think (not think) so; **ya lo creo** I should say so
crema cream(-colored)
crepa crepe
criado/a servant
crianza upbringing
criar to raise; **criarse** to grow up
criollo/a creole
crisis *f.* crisis
crisol *m.* crucible; melting pot
cristalizadas: frutas cristalizadas candied (crystallized) fruit
cristiano/a *n., adj.* Christian
Cristo Christ; **antes de Cristo** B.C.
Cristóbal Colón Christopher Columbus
crítica criticism
criticar (qu) to criticize
crítico/a critical
cronológico: en orden cronológico in chronological order
crudo/a raw
crueldad *f.* cruelty
cruz *f.* (*pl.* **cruces**) cross
cruzar (c) to cross
cuaderno notebook

cuadra city block
cuadrado/a *adj.* square
cuadro painting; picture
cual *relative pron.* whom, which; **con el cual** with whom; **el motivo por el cual** the reason why; **lo cual** which; **para lo cual** for which; **la razón por la cual** the reason why
¿cuál? what?, which?; **¿cuál(es)?** which one(s)?
cualidad *f.* quality
cualquier(a) whatever, whichever; any; **cualquier cosa** anything
cuando when
¿cuándo? when?
cuanto: en cuanto as soon as; **en cuanto a ...** as for, as far as . . . is concerned
cuánto/a how much, how many **¿cuánto/a?** how much?; **¿cuántos/as?** how many?; **¿a cuánto está el dólar?** what is the exchange rate for the dollar?; **¿a cuánto estaba la temperatura?** how high was the temperature?; **¿cuánto tiempo hace que ... ?** how long has it been that . . . ?
cuarenta forty
cuartel *m.* barracks, quarters
cuarto *n.* fourth; quarter (*hour*); (bed)room
cuarto/a *adj.* fourth
cuatro four
cuatrocientos/as four hundred
cubano/a *n., adj.* Cuban
cubanoamericano/a *n. adj.* Cuban American
cubierto *n.* place setting; *pl.* silverware
cubierto/a (*p.p. of* **cubrir**) **(de)** covered (with)
cubismo cubism
cubrir (*p.p.* **cubierto/a**) to cover
cuchara spoon
cuchillo knife
cuenta account; bill, check; calculation; **cuenta corriente** checking account; **cuenta de ahorros** savings account; **darse** (*irreg.*) **cuenta (de)** to realize, become aware (of); **hacer** (*irreg.*) **cuentas** to do the accounts; **llevar (las) cuentas** to keep the books; **por su propia cuenta** on his/her/its/your (*form.*)/their own account; **revisar las cuentas,** to audit the accounts; **tener** (*irreg.*) **en cuenta** to keep in mind
cuentista *m., f.* storyteller
cuento short story
cuero leather
cuerpo body
cuestión *f.* question; problem; matter
cueva cave
cuidado care; **¡cuidado!** be careful; **con cuidado** carefully; **tener** (*irreg.*) **cuidado** to be careful
cuidar(se) to take care of (oneself)
culinario/a culinary
culpa fault; blame; **tener** (*irreg.*) **la culpa (de)** to be to blame for, to be guilty (of)
culpabilidad *f.* guilt; **sentido de**

culpabilidad sense of guilt or responsibility
culpable *n. m., f.* guilty person; responsible person; *adj.* guilty, responsible
culpar to blame
cultivar to cultivate
cultivo cultivation
culto worship, cult; **rendir (i, i) culto (a)** to worship
cultura culture
cumbre *n.f.* peak; *adj.* top
cumpleaños *m. s.* birthday
cumplir to perform; to keep (*a promise*); **cumplir años** to have a birthday; **cumplir con** to live up to; to meet, fulfill
cuna birthplace
cuñado/a brother/sister-in-law
cupón *m.* ticket
cura *m.* priest; *f.* cure
curación *f.* cure, recovery
curandero/a healer; witch doctor
curar to heal, cure
curiosidad *f.* curiosity
curioso/a curious
curso course, class
curvas: líneas curvas curved lines
cuyo/a whose

D

danza dance
daño: hacerle (*irreg.*) **daño (a alguien)** to hurt (someone)
dar (*irreg.*) to give; **darle asco (a alguien)** to disgust, to nauseate (someone); **dar una clase** to teach a class; **dar con** to meet up with; **dar crédito** to believe; **dar una fiesta** to give a party; **dar las gracias** to thank; **dar muerte a** to put to death; **dar un paseo** to take a walk; **darle de alta (a alguien)** to release (someone) (*from an institution*); **darse cuenta (de)** to realize, become aware (of); **darse la mano** to shake hands; **darse prisa** to hurry; **Día** (*m.*) **de Dar Gracias** Thanksgiving Day; **me da pena** I'm sorry
datar to date
dato fact
de *prep.* of; from; **de acuerdo** OK, I agree; **de alto** in height; **de antemano** beforehand; **de confianza** trustworthy, reliable; **de controversia** controversial; **de fondo** thoroughly; **de joven** as a youth; **de memoria** by heart; **de moda** fashionable; **de momento** for the moment; **de nacimiento** by birth; **de nada** you're welcome; **de niño/a** as a child; **de noche** at night, by night; **de la noche** in the evening, at night; **de nuevo** again; **de primer año** *adj.* freshman; **de prisa** quickly, in a hurry; **¿de quién?** whose?; **de regreso** *adj.* return (*flight*); **de regreso a** on returning to; **de repente** suddenly; **de (la) tarde** P.M., in the afternoon; **de todas formas** in any case; **de una vez** now, right away; **¿de verdad?**

really?; **de vez en cuando** sometimes; **estar** (*irreg.*) **de acuerdo (con)** to agree, be in agreement (with); **más allá de** *prep.* beyond; **más de** more than; **vivir de** to live off of, support oneself by

deber *v.* should, ought to; to owe; **deber + inf.** should, must, ought to (*do something*); **deberse a** to be due to

deber *n. m.* duty

debido/a proper; right

débil weak

debilidad *f.* weakness

debilitar to weaken, debilitate

década *f.* decade

decadencia decadence, decline

decente decent

decepcionado/a disappointed

decidir to decide; **decidirse** to make up one's mind

decir (*irreg.*) to say, tell; **decir la hora** to tell time; **decir la verdad** to tell the truth; **decir que sí/no** to say yes/no; **es decir** that is to say

decisión *f.* decision; **tomar decisiones** to make decisions

decisivo/a decisive

declamación *f.* declamation, speech

declaración *f.* declaration

declarar to declare; **declararse** to declare (one's) love

dedicar (qu) to dedicate; **dedicarse** to dedicate oneself

defender (ie) to defend; **defenderse** to defend oneself; to get along/by

defensa defense

definición *f.* definition

definido a definite

definir to define

definitivo/a final, definitive

dejar to leave (behind); to let, allow; to quit; **dejar de + inf.** to stop (*doing something*); **dejar de existir** to disappear

del (*contraction of* **de** + **el**) of the; from the

delante *adv.* ahead; **por delante** ahead (of one); **delante de** *prep.* in front of

deletrear to spell

deletreo *n.* spelling

delgado/a thin, slender

delicado/a delicate

delicia delight

delicioso/a delicious

demanda demand

demás: los/las demás the rest, the others, others, other people

demasiado *adv.* too, too much

democracia democracy

demócrata *n. m., f.* democrat

demográfico/a demographic

demonios: hace un calor de mil demonios it's a hellishly hot day

demora delay

demostrar (ue) to show, demonstrate

demostrativos: adjetivos demostrativos demonstrative adjectives

denominación *f.* denomination, name

densidad *f.* density

denso/a dense

dentista *m., f.* dentist

dentro de inside, within; **dentro de poco** very soon

denunciar to denounce; to expose

depender (de) to depend (on)

dependiente *adj.* dependent

dependiente/a *n.* clerk

deporte *m.* sport; **practicar (qu) un deporte** to play a sport

deportivo/a *adj.* sports

depósito deposit

depresión *f.* depression

deprimir to depress

derecha: a la derecha to the right; **a mano derecha** on the right(-hand) side

derecho *n.* law; right **derechos humanos** human rights; **derecho** *adv.* straight ahead; **seguir (i, i) (g) (todo) derecho** to continue straight (ahead)

derivado/a derived

derrota defeat

derrumbarse to collapse, cave in

derrumbe *m.* collapse; caving in

desafío challenge

desagradable disagreeable

desamparado/a abandoned

desaparecer (zc) to disappear

desaparecido/a *n.* person who has disappeared; *p.p.* disappeared

desaparición *f.* disappearance

desarrollar to develop

desarrollo development

desastre *m.* disaster

desayunar to have breakfast

desayuno breakfast; **desayuno continental** continental breakfast

descansar to rest; **que en paz descanse** may he/she rest in peace

descanso rest; relaxation

descendencia descent

descendiente *m., f.* descendant

descomponer (*like* **poner**) to break down

desconfiado/a suspicious

desconfiar (en) to distrust

desconocido/a unknown

describir (*p.p.* **descrito/a**) to describe

descripción *f.* description

descriptivo/a descriptive

descrito/a (*p.p. of* **describir**) described

descubierto/a (*p.p. of* **descubrir**) discovered

descubrimiento discovery

descubrir (*p.p.* **descubierto/a**) to discover

desde *prep.* from; **desde hace años** for a number of years; **desde luego** of course; **desde pequeño/a** since he/she was small; **desde que** *conj.* since

desdeñar to disdain, scorn

deseado/a desired

desear to want, wish; **desear (+ inf.)** to wish, want to (*do something*)

desechable disposable

desembarcarse (qu) to land; to disembark

desempeñar to play, fulfill (*a role*)

desempleo: tasa de desempleo unemployment rate

desencadenar to unchain; to let loose, free

desenredar to untangle, unravel

desenvoltura self-confidence, assurance; eloquence

deseo desire, wish

desesperado/a desperate

desfilar to file past; to parade

desfile *m.* parade

desgracia: por desgracia unfortunately

desgraciadamente unfortunately

desierto desert

desilusión *f.* disappointment

desilusionado/a disillusioned

desleal disloyal

desnudez *f.* nudity

desobediente disobedient

despedida *n.* farewell, leave-taking, good-bye; **regalo de despedida** going-away present

despedir (i, i) to fire (*an employee*); **despedirse (de)** to say good-bye (to), take leave (of)

despegarse (gu) to take off (*airplane*)

despejado clear (*weather*)

desperdiciado/a wasted

despertar (ie) (*p.p.* **despierto/a**) to wake (*someone up*); **despertarse** to awaken, wake up

despierto/a awake; alert

despreciar to hold in low esteem

después *adv.* later, afterwards; **después de** *prep.* after; **después de que** *conj.* after

destacarse (qu) to stand out

destilar to distill

destino destiny; destination; **con destino a** bound for

destrozar (c) to destroy

destrucción *f.* destruction

destruir (y) to destroy

desunido/a fragmented, disunited; separated

desventaja disadvantage

detalle *m.* detail; **con detalle** in detail

detective *m.* detective

detenidamente carefully

deteriorar to deteriorate

determinado/a specific

determinar to determine

detestar to detest

detrás de *prep.* behind

deuda debt

devoción *f.* devotion

devolución *f.* return

devolver (ue) to return (*things to a place or to someone*)

devorar to devour

devoto/a devout

día *m.* day; **al día siguiente** the next day; **buen día** good day (*greeting*) (*Arg.*); **buenos días** good morning; **Día de Dar Gracias** Thanksgiving Day; **Día de los Enamorados** Valentine's Day; **Día de la Independencia** Independence Day; **Día de la Madre** Mother's Day; **Día del Padre** Father's Day; **Día de los Reyes** Epiphany; **Día de San Patricio** St. Patrick's Day; **Día de San Valentín** Valentine's Day; **día de la semana** day of the week;

Día del Trabajo Labor Day; **hoy día** today, nowadays; **todos los días** every day; **un par de días** a few days
diablos: ¿qué diablos? what the devil?
diagnosis *f.* diagnosis
diagnóstico diagnosis
dialecto dialect
diálogo dialogue
diario/a daily; **vida diaria** *adj.* daily life; *n. m.* daily newspaper
dibujar to draw; **dibujarse** to take form
dibujo drawing; sketch; **dibujos animados** cartoons
diccionario dictionary
dicho *n.* saying
dicho/a (*p.p. of* **decir**) said
diciembre *m.* December
dictador *m.* dictator
dictadura dictatorship
diecinueve nineteen
dieciocho eighteen
dieciséis sixteen
diecisiete seventeen
diente *m.* tooth
dieta diet; **estar** (*irreg.*) **a dieta** to be on a diet
diez ten
diferencia difference; **a diferencia de** unlike
diferente different
difícil difficult, hard
dificultad *f.* difficulty
difunto/a defunct, dead
dignidad *f.* dignity
dilema *m.* dilemma
dinamismo dynamism
dinámico/a dynamic
dinastía dynasty
dinero money; **dinero en efectivo** cash
Dios *m. s.* God; **¡Dios mío!** *interj.* my God!; **gracias a Dios** *interj.* thank God; **por Dios** *interj.* for heaven's sake
diplomático/a *n.* diplomat
diputado/a representative; congressman, congresswoman
dirección *f.* address; direction; **direcciones cardinales** cardinal points
directamente directly
director(a) director; head, leader
dirigir (j) to direct, run
discar (qu) to dial
disciplina discipline
disciplinado/a disciplined
discoteca disco(theque)
discreto/a discreet
discriminación *f.* discrimination
discriminar to discriminate
disculpar to excuse, make excuses for; **disculparse** to apologize; **disculpe** pardon me, excuse me
disculpas: pedir (i, i) disculpas to apologize
discurso speech
discusión *f.* discussion; argument, (*verbal*) fight
discutir to discuss; to argue; to fight (*verbally*)
diseño design
disfrutar (de) to enjoy
disgustar to dislike; **disgustarse** to get annoyed

disgusto quarrel
disiparse to disappear
disperso/a dispersed, scattered
disponible available
disposición: a su disposición at their service, at their disposal
dispuesto/a (a) ready, willing (to)
disputa dispute
distancia distance; **llamada de larga distancia** long-distance call
distante distant
distinguir (g) to distinguish
distinto/a distinct, different
distracción *f.* recreation
distrito district; **distrito federal** federal district
diversidad *f.* diversity
diversificar (qu) to diversify
diversión *f.* pastime, recreation
diverso/a diverse
divertido/a amusing, fun
divertir (ie, i) to entertain; **divertirse** to have a good time
dividirse to be divided
divino/a divine
divorciarse (de) to divorce, get divorced (from)
divorcio divorce
doblar to turn
doble double; **habitación** (*f.*) **doble** double room
doce twelve
dócil docile
doctor(a) doctor
doctrina doctrine
documento document, paper
dogma *m.* dogma
dólar *m.* dollar; **¿a cuánto está el dólar?** what is the exchange rate for the dollar?
doler (ue) to hurt, be painful; to ache; **me/le duela la cabeza** I/he/she/you (*form.*) have/has a headache
dolor *m.* pain; **dolor de cabeza** headache
doloroso/a painful
doméstico/a domestic; **animal** (*m.*) **doméstico** pet; **aparato doméstico** household appliance
dominación *f.* domination, dominion; rule
dominante dominant
dominar to dominate; to master
domingo Sunday
dominio dominion, domain
dominó *s.* dominoes
don *title of respect used with a man's first name;* **don** *m.* gift; **don de gentes** charm
donde where
¿dónde? where?; **¿de dónde?** from where?
doña *title of respect used with a woman's first name*
dorado/a golden
dormido/a asleep
dormir (ue, u) to sleep; **dormir la siesta** to take a siesta, nap; **dormirse** to fall asleep
dormitorio bedroom
dos two

doscientos/as two hundred
dosis *f.* dose
drama *m.* drama, play
dramático/a dramatic
dramaturgo/a playwright
drástico/a drastic
droga drug
droguería drugstore
ducha shower; **baño privado con ducha** private bath with shower
ducharse to take a shower
duda doubt; **no cabe duda** there is no doubt; **sin duda** no doubt, without a doubt
dudar to doubt; to hesitate
dudoso: es dudoso que it's doubtful that
dueño/a owner; **dueño/a de negocios** shop owner
dulce *adj.* sweet
dulces *n. m. pl.* sweets, candy; **dulce de leche** spread made from sweetened condensed milk
dulzura sweetness
duna de arena sand dune
durante during; for (*period of time*)
durar to last
durazno peach (*Arg.*)
duro/a hard; harsh

E

e and (*used instead of* **y** *before words beginning with* **i** *or* **hi**)
echar to throw out; **echar de menos** to miss, long for
eclesiástico/a ecclesiastical
eclipse *m.* eclipse
ecológico/a ecological
economía economy
económico/a economic; economical; **ciencias económicas** economics
economista *m., f.* economist
economizar (c) to economize
edad *f.* age; **edad mediana** middle age
edificio building
editor(a) editor; publisher
educación *f.* education; **educación bilingüe** bilingual education; **educación física** physical education
educado/a educated
efectivamente actually, in fact
efectivo cash; **(dinero) en efectivo** cash
efecto effect
eficacia efficiency
Egipto Egypt
egocéntrico/a egocentric, self-centered
egoísmo selfishness, egoism
egoísta *m., f.* egotistical, selfish
¿eh? *tag phrase with approximate English equivalent of* **okay?**
ejecutivo/a executive
ejemplificar (qu) to exemplify
ejemplo example; **por ejemplo** for example
ejercer (z) to exert; to practice (*a profession*)
ejercicio exercise; **ejercicio aeróbico** aerobic exercise; **hacer** (*irreg.*) **ejercicio** to exercise, get exercise
ejército army

ejote *m.* string bean (*Mex.*)
el the (*m. def. art.*)
él *sub. pron.* he; *obj. of prep.* him
elección *f.* election
electricista *m., f.* electrician
elefante *m.* elephant; **elefante marino** elephant seal
elegancia elegance
elegante elegant
elegido/a elected
elegir (i, i) (j) to select, choose
elemento element
elevado/a raised; elevated; **clase** (*f.*) **elevada** upper class
ella *sub. pron.* she; *obj. of prep.* her
ello *pron. neut.* it
ellos/as *sub. pron.* they; *obj. of prep.* them
elogiar to praise
elogio praise
embajador *m.* ambassador
embarazada pregnant
embarcarse (qu) to embark, board ship
embargo: sin embargo nevertheless
emborracharse to get drunk
emigración *f.* emigration
emigrado/a emigrant
emigrante *m., f.* emigrant
emigrar to emigrate
emoción *f.* emotion
emocionado/a moved, emotional
emocionante exciting
emotivo/a emotional
empadronador *m.* census taker
empanada turnover, pie
emparejar to match
empeñar to pawn
empeño undertaking
emperador *m.* emperor
empezar (ie) (c) to begin; **empezar a** + *inf.* to begin to (*do something*)
empleado/a employee
emplear to employ
empresa firm, company, business; **administración** (*f.*) **de empresas** business administration
empresario/a employer, contractor
empujar to urge; to push
empuñar to seize, grasp
en in, on, at; **en la actualidad** at this time, nowadays; **en aquel entonces** back then, at that time, in those days; **en broma** as a joke, jokingly; **en busca de** in search of; **en cambio** on the other hand; **en casa** at home; **en común** in common; **en conflicto** in conflict; **en contra (de)** against; **en cuanto a …** as far as . . . is concerned; **en este momento, en estos momentos** right now, currently; **en fin** in short; after all; **en el fondo** deep down, at heart; **en forma** in good shape; **en general** generally, in general; **en ninguna parte** not anywhere, nowhere; **en punto** on the dot (*with time*); **en realidad** actually, really; **en seguida** right away, immediately; **¿en serio?** seriously?; **en teoría** in theory; **en venta** for sale; **en voz alta** out loud; **pensar (ie) en** to think about

enamorado/a *n.* sweetheart; **Día** (*m.*) **de los Enamorados** Valentine's Day; **estar** (*irreg.*) **enamorado/a (de)** to be in love (with)
enamorarse (de) to fall in love (with)
enano/a dwarf
encabezado/a (por) led (by)
encantado/a in seventh heaven
encantador(a) charming
encantar to enchant, charm; to love, like
encanto *n.* charm, enchantment; delight
encarcelado/a imprisoned
encima *adv.* above; over; overhead; moreover; **encima de** *prep.* on top of
encontrar (ue) to meet; to find; **encontrarse** to find (*oneself*); **encontrarse con** to meet with
encuentro meeting, encounter
encuesta poll, survey
enemigo/a enemy
energía energy
enérgico/a energetic
enero January
enfadado/a angry
enfadarse (con) to get angry (at, with)
enfermarse to get sick
enfermedad *f.* illness
enfermero/a nurse
enfermo/a *n.* sick person; *adj.* sick, ill
enfocar (qu) to focus
enfrentamiento confrontation
enfrentar to face, confront; **enfrentarse (con)** to deal with, face (*a problem*)
enfrente de *prep.* in front of
enfriarse to become cold
engañar to deceive
engaño deception
engordar to gain weight
enigma *m.* puzzle, mystery
enojado/a angry
enojarse (con) to get angry (at)
enorme enormous
enrollado/a rolled up
ensalada salad
ensayar to rehearse
ensayista *m., f.* essayist
ensayo *n.* essay; rehearsal
enseñar to teach; to show
entender (ie) to understand
enteramente entirely
enterarse (de) to find out (about)
entero/a entire, whole
enterrado/a buried, interred
entonces then, at that time; **en aquel entonces** at that time, back then, in those days
entrada entrance; price of admission
entrar (en/a) to enter, go (in)
entre between, among; **entre la espada y la pared** between a rock and a hard place
entregar (gu) to surrender; to hand over
entrenador(a) coach
entrenar to train
entretenerse (*like* **tener**) to amuse oneself
entrevista interview
entrevistar to interview
entrometerse to meddle
entrometido/a nosy

entusiasmar to cause enthusiasm
entusiasmo enthusiasm
enviar to send
envidia envy; **tenerle** (*irreg.*) **envidia (a alguien)** to envy (*someone*)
envidiable enviable
envidioso/a: estar (*irreg.*) **envidioso/a (de)** to be envious (of)
envolverse (ue) (*p.p.* **envuelto/a**) (**en**) to wrap oneself up (in)
envuelto/a (*p.p. of* **envolver**) wrapped
episodio episode
época epoch, period, era
equipado/a equipped
equipaje *m.* luggage
equipo team; equipment
equis: sacar (qu) rayos equis to take X rays
equivalente *m.* equivalent
equivocación *f.* mistake
equivocado/a mistaken
equivocarse (qu) to make a mistake
érase una vez once upon a time
error *m.* error
escabeche *m.* marinade
escala scale
escalera step, stair; stairway; ladder; *pl.* stairs, steps
escándalo scandal
escandaloso/a scandalous
escapada escapade
escapar(se) to escape
escaparate *m.* display window
escasez *f.* (*pl.* **escaseces**) lack, shortage
escena scene; stage
escenario scene
esclavitud *f.* slavery
esclavo/a slave
escocés *m.* Scotch (*whiskey*)
escoger (j) to choose
escondido/a hidden
escribir (*p.p.* **escrito/a**) to write; **escribir a mano** to write by hand; **máquina de escribir** typewriter
escrito/a (*p.p. of* **escribir**) written
escritor(a) writer
escritura *n.* writing
escrúpulo scruple
escuchar to listen (to)
escudo shield
escuela school; **escuela primaria** elementary school; **escuela secundaria** high school; **escuela superior** high school
escultor(a) sculptor
escultura sculpture
ese, esa *adj.* that; **ése, ésa** *pron.* that one
esencia essence
esencial essential
esforzarse (ue) (c) to strive, make an effort
esfuerzo effort
esmero great care
eso that, that thing, that fact; **por eso** for that reason, that's why
esos/as *adj.* those; **ésos/as** *pron.* those (ones)
espacial: transbordador (*m.*) **espacial** spaceship
espacio space

espada: entre la espada y la pared
between a rock and a hard place
espalda back
España Spain
español *m.* Spanish (*language*)
español(a) *n.* Spaniard; *adj.* Spanish;
mundo de habla española Spanish-
speaking world
especial special
especialidad *f.* specialty
especialista *m., f.* specialist
especialización *f.* specialization; major
especializarse (c) (en) to specialize
(in); to major (in)
especialmente especially
especie *f.* species; type
espectacular spectacular
espectáculo spectacle, show
espectador(a) spectator
especulación *f.* speculation
esperanza(s) hope
esperar to wait (for); to hope; to expect
espinaca(s) spinach
espíritu *m.* spirit; **espíritu de hierro**
iron will
esplendor *m.* splendor
espontaneidad *f.* spontaneity
espontáneo/a spontaneous
esposo/a husband/wife; spouse; *m. pl.*
husband and wife, spouses
esqueleto skeleton
esquí *m.* skiing; **esquí acuático** water
skiing; **esquí alpino** downhill skiing;
esquí nórdico cross-country skiing;
estación (*f.*) **de esquí** ski resort
esquiar to ski
esquina corner (*of a street*)
estable *adj.* stable
establecer (zc) to establish; **establecerse**
to establish oneself, get settled
establo *n.* stable
estación *f.* station; season; resort;
estación de esquí ski resort; **estación
de gasolina** gas station; **estación del
tren** train station
estacionamiento parking lot
estadio stadium
estado state
Estados Unidos *pl.* United States
estadounidense *of or from the United
States*
estallar to break out (*war*)
estampilla stamp
estancia ranch; stay, visit
estaño tin
estar (*irreg.*) to be; to be located; **¿a
cuánto está el dólar (el peso)?**
what's the exchange rate for the dollar
(the peso)?; **está a** it's at (it's worth);
está nublado it's cloudy, overcast;
estar a dieta to be on a diet; **estar a
punto de** to be about to; **estar al
aire libre** to be outdoors; **estar al
tanto** to be informed, up to date;
estar de acuerdo (con) to agree, be
in agreement (with); **estar de vuelta**
to be back; to have returned; **estar
enamorado/a de** to be in love with;
estar envidioso/a (celoso/a) (de) to
be envious (jealous) (of); **estar
harto/a (de/con)** to be fed up (with);

estar listo/a to be ready; **estar mal**
to be ill; **estar por** (+ *inf.*) to be
about to (*do something*); to be ready
to (*do something*); **(no) estar
seguro/a** (not) to be sure; **la
temperatura está a … grados** the
temperature is . . . degrees
estatua statue
estatura height; **de estatura mediana**
of average height
este *n. m.* east
este/a *adj.* this; **éste/a** *pron.* this one;
en este momento right now,
currently; **esta noche** tonight
estéreo stereo
estereotipo stereotype
estilizado/a stylized; slender
estilo style
estimado/a dear (*correspondence
salutation*)
estimar to hold in high esteem
estímulo stimulus
esto this, this thing, this matter
estorbar to hinder; to get in the way of
estos/as *adj.* these; **éstos/as** *pron.* these
(ones); **en estos momentos** right
now, currently
estrecho *n.* strait
estrecho/a *adj.* narrow; close-knit;
relación (*f.*) **estrecha(s)** close,
intimate relationship
estrella star
estrenar to debut, perform for the first
time
estricto/a strict
estructura structure
estudiante *m., f.* student
estudiar to study
estudio study; **estudios agrícolas**
agricultural studies
estudioso/a studious
estufa stove
estupendamente stupendously
estupendo/a wonderful, marvelous,
stupendous, great
estupidez (*pl.* **estupideces**) stupid
remark or action
etapa stage
ético/a ethical
etiqueta: de etiqueta formal (*dress*)
étnico/a ethnic
Europa Europe
europeo/a *n., adj.* European
evasión *f.* escape, evasion
evidente evident
evitar to avoid
evolucionar to evolve, change
exacto *adv.* exactly, that's exactly right
exacto/a *adj.* exact
exagerar to exaggerate
examen *m.* exam; examination
examinar to examine
excavación *f.* excavation
excavar to excavate
excelencia: por excelencia par
excellence
excelente excellent
excepción *f.* exception; **con excepción
de** with the exception of
excepcional exceptional
excepto except

exceso excess
exclamar to exclaim
excluido/a excluded
exclusivo/a exclusive
excursión *f.* excursion, trip
excusa excuse
excusarse to excuse oneself
ex esposo/a ex-husband/wife
exhausto/a exhausted
exhibir to exhibit
exiliado/a *n.* exile, exiled person
exiliarse to be exiled
exilio exile
existencia existence
existir to exist; **dejar de existir** to
disappear
éxito success; **tener** (*irreg.*) **éxito** to be
successful
exótico/a exotic
expansión *f.* expansion
expedición *f.* expedition
experiencia experience; experiment
experimentar to experience
experto/a expert
explanada esplanade
explicación *f.* explanation
explicar (qu) to explain
explorador(a) explorer
explorar to explore
explotación *f.* exploitation
explotar to exploit
exportación *f.* exportation, export
exportador(a) exporter
exportar to export
exposición *f.* exhibition, exposition;
show
expresar to express
expresión *f.* expression
expresionista *adj.* expressionist
expresivo/a expressive
expulsar to expel
exquisito/a exquisite
extenderse (ie) to extend
extendido/a extended; **familia
extendida** extended family
extensión *f.* extension, stretch, expanse
extenso/a extensive
exterior exterior, outer
externo/a external
extinguir (g) to die out
extranjero *n.* abroad; **en el extranjero**
abroad
extranjero/a *n.* foreigner; *adj.* foreign;
lengua extranjera foreign language
extrañar to miss, long for
extraño/a *n.* stranger; *adj.* strange; **es
extraño** it's strange; **¡qué extraño!**
how strange!
extraordinario/a extraordinary
extravagancia folly
extravío loss of one's way
extremo/a extreme
extrovertido/a extrovert
exuberante exuberant, abundant

F
fábrica factory
fabricar (qu) to manufacture, make
fabuloso/a fabulous
faceta facet
fácil easy

facilidad *f.* facility
fácilmente easily
factor *m.* factor
facturar to check (*luggage*)
facultad *f.* faculty, school
faja strip
fajita *tortilla filled with strips of marinated meat and condiments*
falda skirt
fallar to fail
fallecimiento death
falso/a *adj.* false
falta lack; **hacer** (*irreg.*) **falta** to be lacking, needed; **hacerle** (*irreg.*) **falta a alguien** to need (*something*)
faltar to be missing, lacking; to be absent
fama fame, reputation
familia family; **familia extendida** extended family; **familia nuclear** nuclear family
familiar *n. m.* relation, member of the family; *adj.* family, related to the family
familiarizarse (c) to familiarize oneself
famoso/a famous
fantasía fantasy
farmacéutico/a pharmaceutical
farmacia pharmacy, drugstore
fascinante fascinating
fascinar to fascinate
fascismo fascism
fastidiar to "drive up a wall"
fatal fatal; disastrous
fatiga fatigue
favor *m.* favor; **a favor** in favor; **por favor** please
favorecer (zc) to favor
favorito/a favorite
fe *f.* faith
febrero February
fecha date; **hasta la fecha** so far, to date, up until now
fechado/a dated
federal: distrito federal federal district
felicidad *f.* happiness
felicitaciones *f. pl.* congratulations
feliz (*pl.* **felices**) happy
femenino/a feminine
feminista *m., f.* feminist
fenomenal phenomenal
fenómeno phenomenon
feo/a ugly
feria fair
feroz (*pl.* **feroces**) ferocious
ferretería hardware store
ferrocarril *m.* railroad
ficción *f.* fiction; **ciencia-ficción** science fiction
fiebre *f.* fever; **bajar la fiebre** to bring down one's fever; **tienes una fiebre alta** you (*fam.*) have a high fever; **tener** (*irreg.*) **una fiebre** to have a fever
fiel loyal, faithful
fiesta party; holiday; festival; **dar** (*irreg.*) **una fiesta** to give a party
figura figure
figurar (en) to be important (in)
fijamente: mirar fijamente to stare
fijarse en to pay attention to, take notice of, concentrate on

fijo/a fixed
filete *m.* fillet
Filipinas: (Islas) Filipinas Philippine (Islands)
filmado/a filmed
filosofía philosophy; **filosofía y letras** liberal arts
filosófico/a philosophical
filósofo/a philosopher
fin *m.* end; **al fin y al cabo** after all, when all is said and done; **en fin** in short; after all; **fin de semana** weekend; **por fin** at last, finally; **tener** (*irreg.*) **como fin** to have as a goal
final *n. m.* end; *adj.* final; **al final** in the end; **al final de** at the end of; **hasta finales de** until the end of
financiero/a financial
finanzas finances
finca farm, ranch
fineza class, good taste
fino sherry
fino/a fine; dry (*liquor*)
firma signature
firmar to sign
física *n.* physics
físico/a *adj.* physical; **educación** (*f.*) **física** physical education
flan *m.* baked custard, flan
flirtear to flirt
flojo/a slack, sluggish
flor *f.* flower
florecer (zc) to flower; to prosper, flourish
folclórico/a *adj.* folk
folklore *m.* folklore
folklórico/a *adj.* folk
fondo background; *pl.* funds; **a fondo** completely, thoroughly; **de fondo** thoroughly; **en el fondo** deep down, at heart
forjar to forge, make
forma form; **de todas formas** in any case; **en forma** in good shape
formación *f.* (professional) training; education
formado/a (por) formed, made up (of)
formador *m.* maker, former
formar to form; to make; to shape; **formar parte de** to be or form a part of
fortaleza fortress
fortificación *f.* fortification, fort
fosforescente phosphorescent
foto(grafía) *f.* photo(graph); **tomar/sacar (qu) una foto** to take a picture, photograph
fotografiar to photograph
fotográfico/a photographic
fracasado/a unsuccessful
fracasar to fail
fracaso failure
fractura fracture
frágil fragile
frambuesa raspberry
francamente frankly
francés *n. m.* French (*language*)
francés, francesa *n.* Frenchman, Frenchwoman; *adj.* French
Francia France

frase *f.* phrase; sentence
frecuencia frequency; **con frecuencia** often; frequently **con más frecuencia** most frequently, most often; **¿con qué frecuencia?** how often?
frecuentar to frequent, go regularly to
frecuente frequent
frecuentemente frequently
frente a opposite, facing; **en frente** opposite
fresa strawberry
fresco/a fresh; **hace (mucho) fresco** it's (very) cool (*weather*)
fríamente coolly, coldly
frijol *m.* bean
frío *n.* cold; **hace (mucho) frío** it's (very) cold (*weather*)
frío/a *adj.* cold; **tener** (*irreg.*) **(mucho) frío** to be (very) cold
frito/a fried; **calamares fritos** fried squid rings, **papas fritas** French fries (*L.A.*); **patatas fritas** French fries (*Sp.*)
frívolo/a frivolous
frontera border
frotación *f.* rubbing
fructífero/a fruitful
frustrado/a frustrated
fruta fruit; **frutas cristalizadas** candied (crystallized) fruit
frutería fruit store
frutilla strawberry (*Arg.*)
fue: se fue he/she went away
fuego fire
fuente *f.* fountain; source; **fuente de la juventud** fountain of youth
fuera *adv.* out, outside; **fuera de** *prep.* out(side) of
fuerte strong; nasty; hard
fuerza strength; *pl.* strength; forces
fumar to smoke; **sección** (*f.*) **de (no) fumar** (non)smoking section
función *f.* performance, show, function
funcionar to function, work (*machines*)
fundación *f.* foundation
fundador(a) founder
fundamentalmente fundamentally
fundar to found
funerario/a *adj.* funeral
furioso/a furious
furtivo/a sneaky
fusión *f.* fusion; merging
fútbol *m.* soccer; **fútbol (norte)americano** football
futuro *n.* future
futuro/a *adj.* future

G

gabinete *m.* cabinet
gala: baile (*m.*) **de gala** formal dance
galería gallery
gallego Galician (*language of Galicia* [*region of Spain*])
gamba shrimp (*Sp.*)
gana: de buena gana willingly
ganadería cattle raising
ganado cattle; herd
ganador(a) winner
ganar to win; to earn; to gain
ganas: tener (*irreg.*) **ganas de** + *inf.* to feel like (*doing something*)
garaje *m.* garage

garganta throat
gas *m.* gas; heat
gasolina gasoline; **estación** (*f.*) **de gasolina** gas station
gastar to spend (*money*)
gastos expenses
gato/a cat
gauchesco/a *pertaining to gauchos*
gemelo/a twin
generación *f.* generation
general *n. m., adj.* general; **en general** generally, in general; **por lo general** generally, in general
generalización *f.* generalization
generoso/a generous
genial pleasant; congenial
gente *f. s.* people; **don** (*m.*) **de gentes** charm
geografía geography
geográfico/a geographic(al)
geométrico/a geometric
gerente *m., f.* manager
gigante giant, gigantic
gimnasia *s.* gymnastics
gimnasio gymnasium
gira tour
giro money order
gitano/a gypsy
globo globe
gobernador(a) governor
gobernar (ie) to govern, rule
gobierno government
golf: campo de golf golf course
golfo gulf
golpe *m.* blow (*injury*); **golpe militar** military coup
golpear to bang
gordito/a plump, fat
gordo/a fat
gorra cap
gótico/a Gothic
gozar (c) (de) to enjoy
grabado etching
gracias thank you; **dar** (*irreg.*) **las gracias** to thank; **Día** (*m.*) **de Dar Gracias** Thanksgiving Day; **gracias a Dios** *interj.* thank God; **muchas gracias** thank you very much
gracioso/a funny
grado grade; degree (*temperature*)
graduado/a *adj.* graduate
graduarse (en) to graduate (from)
gramática grammar
gran, grande large, big; great
grandeza greatness
granja farm
gratis *inv.* free (*of charge*)
grave grave, serious
Grecia Greece
grecorromano/a Greco-Roman
gregoriano: calendario gregoriano Gregorian calendar
griego/a *n., adj.* Greek
gripe *f.* influenza, flu
gris gray
gritar to shout
grito shout; cry
grosero/a crude, brutish
grotesco/a grotesque
grueso/a heavy (*clothing*)
gruñón, gruñona grouchy, irritable

grupo group
gruta grotto, cave
guachinango red snapper (*Mex.*)
guajolote *m.* turkey (*Mex.*)
guantes *m.* gloves
guapo/a handsome; pretty
guardar to save, keep (*things, a secret*); to have; **guardar cama** to stay in bed
guardia *m.* guard
guerra war; **guerra civil** civil war; **guerra mundial** world war
guerrero/a *adj.* warlike; *n.* warrior
guía *m., f.* guide; **guía turístico/a** tour guide
guineo banana (*P.R.*)
guionista *m., f.* scriptwriter
guisantes *m.* peas
guisar to cook
guitarra guitar
guitarrista *m., f.* guitarist
gurú *m.* guru
gustar to like; to be pleasing to; **me gustaría** + *inf.* I would really like to (*do something*); **(no) gustarle** + *inf.* to (dis)like to (*do something*); **no me gusta(n) nada ...** I don't like . . . at all
gusto pleasure; like, preference; taste; **mucho gusto** pleased to meet you

H

Habana: la Habana Havana
habanero/a from Havana
haber (*irreg.*) *inf. form of* **hay;** to have (*auxiliary*); to be; **va a haber** there's going to be
había there was, there were (*imperfect of* **hay**)
habilidad *f.* ability
habitación *f.* room; **habitación doble** double room; **habitación individual** single room
habitante *m., f.* inhabitant
habitar (en) to inhabit, live (in)
habla *f.* (*but* **el habla**) speech; language; **(mundo) de habla española** Spanish-speaking (world)
hablador(a) talkative
hablar to talk; to speak
hacendado/a wealthy rancher
hacer (*irreg.*) to do; to make; **¿cuánto tiempo hace que ... ?** how long has it been that . . . ?; **desde hace años** for a number of years; **hace un calor de mil demonios** it's a hellishly hot day; **hace (mucho) calor (fresco, frío, sol, viento)** it's (very) hot (cool, cold, sunny, windy) (*weather*); **hace muchos años** many years ago; **hacer buen/mal tiempo** it's good (bad) weather; **hacer caso a** to pay attention to; **hacer las compras** to shop; **hacer las cuentas** to do the accounts; **hacer ejercicio** to exercise, get exercise; **hacerle daño (a alguien)** to hurt (someone); **hacer falta** to be lacking, needed; **hacer la maleta** to pack one's suitcase; **hacer una oferta** to make an offer; **hacer el papel (de)** to play the role (of); **hacer un *picnic*** to have a picnic;

hacer planes to make plans; **hacer una reservación** to make a reservation; **hacer televisión** to work in television; **hacer un viaje** to take a trip; **hacerle preguntas (a alguien)** to ask (someone) questions; **hacerse** to become (*a member of a profession*); **hacerse tarde** to be getting late; **hacerse el tonto** to play dumb; **no hacer caso (de) ...** to pay no attention (*to an issue*); **no hacerle caso (a alguien)** to ignore (someone); **¿qué tiempo hace?** what's the weather like?; **se me hace tarde** it's getting late
hacia toward
hacienda estate, hacienda
hada *f.* (*but* **el hada**): **hada madrina** fairy godmother
hallazgo find; discovery
hamaca hammock
hambre *f.* (*but* **el hambre**) hunger; **tener** (*irreg.*) **hambre** to be hungry
hamburguesa hamburger
hámster *m.* hamster
harina flour
harto/a: estar (*irreg.*) **harto/a (de/con)** to be fed up (with)
hasta *prep.* until; **hasta la fecha** so far, to date; up until now; **hasta finales de** until the end of; **hasta luego** until later, see you later; **hasta mañana** until tomorrow, see you tomorrow; **hasta pronto** see you soon; **hasta** *conj.* even; **hasta que** *conj.* until; **¿hasta qué punto?** up to what point?
hay there is, there are; **no hay** there is not/are not; **no hay de qué** you're welcome (*form.*)
hecho fact; **de hecho** in fact
hecho/a (*p.p. of* **hacer**) made, done
helado ice cream
helicóptero helicopter
hemisferio hemisphere
hemorragia hemorrhage
heredar to inherit
heredero/a heir, heiress
herencia heritage; inheritance
herido/a wounded
hermanastro/a stepbrother, stepsister
hermano/a brother, sister (*family; religious vocation*); *m. pl.* brothers and sisters; **medio/a hermano/a** half brother, half sister
hermoso/a beautiful
héroe *m.* hero
hierba grass; herb
hierro iron; **espíritu** (*m.*) **de hierro** iron will
hijastro/a stepson, stepdaughter
hijo/a son, daughter; child; *m. pl.* children; **hijo/a único/a** only child
¡híjole! my God! gosh!
himno nacional national anthem
hinchado/a swollen
hipnotizar (c) to hypnotize
hipócrita *m., f.* hypocrite
hispánico/a *adj.* Hispanic
hispano/a *n., adj.* Hispanic
Hispanoamérica Spanish America

hispanoamericano/a Spanish American
histérico/a hysterical
historia history; story
histórico/a historic(al); **antecedentes** (*m.*) **históricos** *pl.* historical record, background
hoja leaf; sheet of paper
hojear to leaf through, glance through; to scan
hola hello, hi
holgar (ue) (gu) to rest, enjoy oneself
hombre *m.* man; **hombre de negocios** businessman; **tienda de ropa para hombres** men's clothing store
honestidad *f.* honesty
honesto/a honest
honrar to honor
hora hour; time; **¿a qué hora?** at what time?; **decir** (*irreg.*) **la hora** to tell time; **¿qué hora es?** what time is it?; **¿qué horas son?** (*Mex.*) what time is it?
horario schedule; timetable
horizonte *m.* horizon
hormiga ant
horno oven; **al horno** baked; **horno de microondas** microwave oven
horrorizar (c) to terrify; to horrify
horroroso/a horrible
hospital *m.* hospital; **hospital de urgencia** emergency hospital
hostilmente in a hostile manner
hotel *m.* hotel
hotelero/a *adj.* hotel
hoy today; **hoy día** nowadays
huelga *n.* strike (*labor*)
huella mark; print; trace; track; **huella de mano** handprint
huérfano/a *n., adj.* orphan
huésped(a) guest
huevo egg; **huevos pasados por agua** soft-boiled eggs; **huevos revueltos** scrambled eggs
humanidades *f.* liberal arts, humanities
humano/a human; **derechos humanos** human rights; **ser** (*m.*) **humano** human being
húmedo/a humid
humilde humble; relatively poor
humor *m.* mood; **de mal humor** in a bad mood

I

Ibérico/a: Península Ibérica Iberian Peninsula
ida *n.* departure; **billete** (*m.*) **de ida** one-way ticket; **pasaje** (*m.*) **de ida y vuelta** round-trip ticket (fare)
idealista *n. m., f.* idealist; *adj.* idealistic
idéntico/a identical
identidad *f.* identity
identificar (qu) to identify
idioma *m.* language
iglesia church
ignorar not to know; to be unaware of
igual equal; the same
igualmente likewise; so am I (*pleased to meet you*)
iluminar to illuminate

ilustrar to illustrate
imagen *f.* image
imaginación *f.* imagination
imaginar(se) to imagine
imaginativo/a imaginative
imitación *f.* imitation
imitar to imitate; to look like
impaciencia impatience
impaciente impatient
impacto impact
impedimento impediment, obstacle
impedir (i, i) to prevent
imperfecto (*gram.*) imperfect tense
imperio empire
impetuoso/a impetuous
implicar (qu) to mean
imponente *adj.* imposing
imponer (*like* **poner**) to impose
importación *f.* import
importado/a imported
importancia importance
importante important
importar to be important, matter; **me importa un comino** I couldn't care less
imposible impossible
impresión *f.* impression; **causar una buena impresión** to make a good impression
impresionado/a impressed; **quedar bien impresionado/a (con)** to have or be left with a good impression (by/with)
impresionante impressive
impresionar to impress, make an impression on
impresionismo Impressionism
impresionista *n. m., f., adj.* Impressionist
improbable improbable
impropio/a inappropriate
improvisación *f.* improvisation
improvisar to improvise
impuesto tax
impulsivo/a impulsive
impulso impulse; thrust
inapropiado/a inappropriate
inca *n. m.; adj. m., f.* Inca
incapaz (*pl.* **incapaces**) incapable
incidente *m.* incident
incierto/a uncertain
incitar to cause, motivate
inclinación *f.* inclination
inclinar(se) to bend down
incluir (y) to include
inclusive including
incluso *adv.* even
incomible inedible
incómodo/a uncomfortable
incompatibilidad *f.* incompatibility
incomprensible incomprehensible
inconsciente unconscious
inconveniente *n. m.* difficulty
incorporado/a incorporated
incorporarse (a) to incorporate; to join
incorrecto/a incorrect
increíble incredible
incumplimiento breach (*of contract*)
incursión *f.* raid
indefenso/a defenseless
indefinido/a indefinite

indemnización *f.* compensation
independencia independence; **Día** (*m.*) **de la Independencia** Independence Day
independiente independent
independentista *adj. m., f.* pro-independence
independizarse (c) to become independent
indicado/a appropriate
indicar (qu) to indicate, point out
indicativo (*gram.*) indicative
índice *m.* rate
indiferencia indifference
indiferente indifferent
indígena *n. m., f.* native; *adj.* indigenous, native
indio/a Indian
indirecta *n.* insinuation
indirecto/a *adj.* indirect
individual: habitación (*f.*) **individual** single room
individuo *n.* individual
industria industry
industrial *n. m.* industrialist, manufacturer
industrialista *adj. m., f. pertaining to or in favor of industrialism*
industrializado/a industrialized
inesperado/a unexpected
inestable unstable
inexperto/a inexperienced
infancia childhood
infección *f.* infection
infinidad *f.* infinity
infinitivo (*gram.*) infinitive
inflación *f.* inflation
influencia influence
influenciado/a influenced
influir (y) (en) to influence
influjo influence
información *f.* information
informal informal
informar to inform; **informarse** to inquire, find out
informática data processing
ingeniería engineering
ingeniero/a engineer
ingenio de azúcar sugar mill
ingenuo/a naive, ingenuous
Inglaterra England
inglés *m.* English (*language*)
inglés, inglesa *n.* Englishman, Englishwoman; *adj.* English
ingrediente *m.* ingredient
ingresar to enter
ingresos *pl.* income, earnings
iniciar to initiate; to start
injusticia injustice
injusto/a unjust, unfair
inmediatamente immediately, right away
inmediatez *f.* immediacy; closeness
inmediato/a immediate; close
inmenso/a immense
inmigración *f.* immigration
inmigrante *n. m., f.; adj.* immigrant
inmigrar to immigrate
inocente innocent
inolvidable unforgettable
inquieto/a restless

inscripción *f.* inscription
inseguro/a insecure
insinuar to insinuate, hint at;
  insinuarse to ingratiate
insistir (en) to insist (on)
inspeccionar to inspect
inspector(a) inspector
inspiración *f.* inspiration
inspirar to inspire
inspirarse (en) to be inspired (by)
instalarse to establish oneself, settle in
instantáneamente instantaneously
instante *m.* instant
instinto instinct
institución *f.* institution
institucional institutional
instituto institute
instrucciones *f.* directions, instructions
instructor(a) instructor
instrumento instrument
insultar to insult
integrar to integrate
íntegro/a integral
intelectual intellectual
inteligencia intelligence
inteligente intelligent
intención *f.* intention
intenso/a intense
intentar to try, attempt
intento intention; attempt
interacción *f.* interaction
intercambio *n.* exchange
interés *m.* interest
interesante *adj.* interesting
interesar to interest, be of
  interest; **interesarse (en)** to be
  interested (in)
interior *n. m.* interior
internacional international
internar to check into (*a hospital*)
interpretación *f.* interpretation
interpretar to interpret; to act a part
interrogativas: palabras interrogativas
  (*gram.*) interrogative words
interrumpido/a interrupted
intervenir (*like* **venir**) to intervene; to
  interfere
íntimo/a intimate; close; **amigo/a**
  íntimo/a close friend
intransigente intransigent,
  uncompromising
intriga intrigue
introducir (*irreg.*) to introduce, bring in
intuir (y) to sense
invadir to invade
invasión *f.* invasion
invasor(a) invader
invención *f.* invention
inventar to invent
invento invention
inventor(a) inventor
inversión *f.* investment
invertir (ie, i) to invest
investigación *f.* investigation
investigador(a) investigator
investigar (gu) to investigate
invierno winter
invitación *f.* invitation
invitar to invite (*with the intention of*
  paying)
involucrar to involve, implicate

inyección *f.* shot, injection; **ponerle**
  (*irreg.*) **una inyección** to give
  (someone) a shot, injection
ir (*irreg.*) to go; **ir a +** *inf.* to be going
  to (*do something*); **ir al cine** to go to
  the movies; **ir a una función de**
  teatro to go to a show at the theater;
  ir a un parque to go to a park; **ir de**
  compras to go shopping; **irse** to go
  away, leave (*for a place*); **va a haber**
  there's going to be; **¿vamos?** shall we
  go?; **¡vamos!** *interj.* let's go!
irlandés, irlandesa *n.* Irishman,
  Irishwoman; *adj.* Irish
ironía irony
irónico/a ironic
irregularidad *f.* irregularity
irresponsable irresponsible
isla island; **la Isla** Puerto Rico; **Islas**
  Canarias Canary Islands; **Islas**
  Filipinas Philippine Islands
Islam *m.* Islam
Italia Italy
italiano/a *n., adj.* Italian
izquierdo/a left (*direction*); **a la**
  izquierda to the left; **a mano**
  izquierda on the left(-hand) side

J
jamás never
jamón *m.* ham; **jamón serrano** cured
  Spanish ham
Japón *m.* Japan
japonés, japonesa, *n., adj.* Japanese
jarabe (*m.*) **tapatío** *popular Mexican*
  dance known as Mexican hat dance in
  U.S.
jardín *m.* garden; **jardín botánico**
  botanical garden; **jardín zoológico**
  zoo
jefe/a boss
jarro pitcher
jengibre *m.* ginger
jerarquía hierarchy
jerez *m.* sherry
jersey *m.* sweater (*Sp.*)
Jesucristo Jesus Christ
jesuita *n. m.* Jesuit; *adj. m., f.* Jesuit
jinete *m.* horseman
jornada laboral day's work
joven *n. m., f.* young person; *adj.*
  young; **de joven** as a young person
joya jewel
joyería jewelry store
jubilado/a *n.* retired person; *adj.* retired
jubilarse to retire (*from the work force*)
judía verde string bean
judicial judicial, legal; **orden** (*f.*)
  judicial legal procedure
judío/a *n.* Jew; *adj.* Jewish
juego game; gambling; **juego de salón**
  parlor game (*cards, chess, poker, etc.*);
  Juegos Olímpicos Olympic Games
jueves *m. s.* Thursday
jugador(a) player; gambler
jugar (ue) (gu) (a) to play (*a game or*
  sport); **jugar a las cartas** to play
  cards; **jugar (por dinero)** to gamble;
  jugar al póquer to play poker
jugo juice
juguete *m.* toy

julio July
junio June
juntarse to meet
junto a next to; **junto con** together with
juntos/as together
jurar to swear (*as in a court*)
jurídico/a legal
jurisdicción *f.* jurisdiction
justificar (qu) to justify
justo *adv.* just, exactly; **justo ahora**
  right now, just now
juventud *f.* youth; **fuente** (*f.*) **de la**
  juventud fountain of youth
juzgar (gu) to judge

K
karate *m.* karate
kerosén *m.* kerosene
kilo(gramo) kilogram (*approx. 2.2*
  pounds)
kilómetro kilometer (*approx. .62 miles*)

L
la the (*f. def. art.*); **a la(s) ...** at (*hour*)
la *d.o.* you (*form. s.*), her, it (*f.*)
laboral work, having to do with the
  working world; **jornada laboral**
  day's work
laboratorio laboratory
lado side; **al lado de** beside, next to; **de**
  al lado next door; **por un (otro)**
  lado on the one (other) hand
lagarto lizard
lago lake
lágrima tear
lamentablemente regrettably
lamentar to lament
langosta lobster
langostino prawn
lanza spear
lápiz *m.* (*pl.* **lápices**) pencil
largamente at length, for a long time
largo/a long; **llamada de larga**
  distancia long-distance call; **a lo**
  largo de during; **a lo largo del**
  camino along the way
las the (*pl. f. def. art.*); you (*pl. f. form.*
  pers. pron.), them (*pl. f. pers. pron.*);
  pron. **las demás** the rest, the
  others, others, other people
lástima *n.* pity; **es (una) lástima** it's
  a shame
lastimado/a hurt
lata: ¡qué lata! what a pain!
latino/a Latin; **América Latina** Latin
  America
Latinoamérica Latin America
latinoamericano/a *n., adj.* Latin
  American
lavado *n.* wash
lavadora clothes washer
lavandería laundry, laundromat
lavaplatos *m. s.* dishwasher
lavar to wash
lazo lasso
le *i.o.* to/for you (*form. s.*), him, her, it
leche *f.* milk; **café** (*m.*) **con leche**
  strong coffee served with warm or hot
  milk; **dulce** (*m.*) **de leche** *spread*
  made from sweetened condensed milk
lechuga lettuce

lección *f.* lesson
lectura *n.* reading
leer (y) to read
legal legal
legitimidad *f.* legitimacy
legítimo/a legitimate
legumbre *f.* vegetable
lejos far away; **lejos de** *prep.* far from
lema *m.* slogan, motto
lencería linen goods
lengua language; tongue; **lengua extranjera** foreign language; **sacar (qu) la lengua** to stick out one's tongue
lenguado sole (*fish*)
lenguaje *m.* language
lentitud *f.* slowness, sluggishness
leña firewood
león *m.* lion
les *i.o.* to/for you (*form. pl.*), them
lesión *f.* injury, wound, lesion
letra letter (*of alphabet*); lyrics; *pl.* liberal arts; **filosofía y letras** liberal arts
levantar to lift, raise; **levantarse** to get up; to rise up, rebel
ley *f.* law
leyenda legend
liberación *f.* liberation
liberal: artes (*f.*) **liberales** liberal arts
libertad *f.* liberty; freedom
libertador(a) liberator
libre free; **estar** (*irreg.*) **al aire libre** to be outdoors; **ratos libres** free time, spare time; **tiempo libre** free time, spare time
librería bookstore
libro book; **libro de texto** textbook
líder *m.* leader
ligar (gu) con to pick (*someone*) up
ligero/a *adj.* light
limitado/a limited
limitar con to be bounded by
límite *m.* boundary; limit
limón *m.* lemon
limonada lemonade
limpiar to clean
lindo/a pretty
línea line; **líneas curvas** curved lines
lingüístico/a linguistic
lío problem, trouble
líquido liquid
lírico/a lyric, lyrical
lista list
listo/a: estar (*irreg.*) **listo/a** to be ready, prepared; **ser** (*irreg.*) **listo/a** to be bright, smart
literario/a literary; **obras literarias** literary works
literatura literature
litoral *m.* seaboard, coast
llama: se llama (he/she) is called, named
llamada *n.* call; **llamada de larga distancia** long-distance call; **llamada telefónica** telephone call
llamado/a named; so-called
llamar to call (out); to call (*by phone*); **llamar la atención** to attract attention; **llamarse** to be called, named
llano *n.* plain
llano/a *adj.* flat, level

llanura *n.* plain
llave *f.* key
llegada arrival
llegar (gu) to arrive; **llegar a ser** to become
llenar to fill (up)
lleno/a full, filled
llevar to take; to carry; to wear; to have spent (*time*); **llevar (las) cuentas** to keep the books; **llevar una vida ...** to lead a ... life; **llevarse bien/mal (con)** to get along well/badly (with)
llorar to cry, weep
llover (ue) to rain
llovizna drizzle
lluvia rain
lo *d.o.* you (*form. s.*), him, it (*m.*); **lo antes posible** as soon as possible; **lo cual** which; **lo más posible** as much as possible; **lo más pronto posible** as soon as possible; **lo que** what, that which; **lo siento** I'm sorry
localizado/a located
locamente madly
loco/a: volverse (ue) loco/a to go crazy
lógico/a logical
lograr to manage to, be able
Londres London
loro parrot
los the (*pl. m. def. art.*); *d.o.* you (*form. pl.*), them (*m.*); *pron.* those; **los demás** the rest, the others, others, other people
lotería lottery
lucha fight
luchador(a) fighter
luchar to fight
luego then, next; later; **desde luego** of course; **hasta luego** until later, see you later
lugar *n. m.* place; **en primer lugar** in the first place, firstly; **tener** (*irreg.*) **lugar** to take place
lujo luxury
lujoso/a luxurious
luna moon; **luna de miel** honeymoon
lunes *m. s.* Monday
luz *f.* (*pl.* **luces**) light

M

macho male, manly, macho
madera wood
madrastra stepmother
madre *f.* mother; **Día** (*m.*) **de la Madre** Mother's Day
madrileño/a *n.* person from Madrid; *adj.* from Madrid
madrina: hada madrina fairy godmother
maduro/a mature
maestro/a teacher; master; **obra maestra** master work
mágico/a magical
magnífico/a magnificent
mago: Reyes (*m.*) **Magos** Magi, Wise Men
maíz *m.* corn
majestuoso/a majestic
mal, malo/a *adj.* bad; *adv.* badly;

andar (*irreg.*) **mal** to be going badly; **caerle** (*irreg.*) **mal (a alguien)** to not like, make a bad impression on (someone); **de mal humor** in a bad mood; **estar** (*irreg.*) **mal** to be ill; **llevarse mal (con)** to get along badly (with); **mala suerte** bad luck; **manejar mal** to manage (*something*) badly; **pasarlo mal** to have a bad time; **por bien o por mal** for better or worse; **sentirse (ie, i) mal** to feel bad, ill
malabarista *m., f.* juggler
maleta suitcase; **hacer** (*irreg.*) **la maleta** to pack one's suitcase
maltratar to maltreat, abuse
mamá mom
mamacita mom
mami *f.* mom
mamut *f.* mammoth
mandar to send; to order
mandato order
¿mande? pardon me?, what did you say? (*Mex.*)
mando command; **ponerse** (*irreg.*) **a mando** to take command
mandón, mandona bossy
manejar to drive; **manejar (bien/mal)** to manage (*something*) (well/badly)
manera manner, way
manía mania
manifestación *f.* manifestation; demonstration
maniobra maneuver
mano *f.* hand; **a mano** close by, at hand; **a mano derecha/izquierda** on the right/left(-hand) side; **darse** (*irreg.*) **la mano** to shake hands; **escribir a mano** to write by hand; **huella de mano** handprint
manta blanket
manteca fat, lard; butter (*Arg.*)
mantener (*like* **tener**) to maintain, keep up; to support (*a family*)
mantequilla butter
manufactura *n.* manufacture
manzana apple; city block (*Sp.*)
mañana *adj.* morning; *adv.* tomorrow; **pasado mañana** the day after tomorrow; **por la mañana** in the morning
mapa *m.* map
máquina machine; **máquina de escribir** typewriter; **máquina tragamonedas** slot machine
mar *m., f.* sea; **Mar** (*m.*) **Cantábrico** Bay of Biscay
maravilla marvel
maravilloso/a marvelous
marcado/a (*p.p. of* **marcar**) marked, pronounced
marcar (qu) to mark
marchar to march
marco frame
margarita daisy; drink made with tequila
marido husband
marinero/a sailor
marino/a *adj.* marine; **elefante** (*m.*) **marino** elephant seal
marisco shellfish; *pl.* seafood

marítimo/a maritime
mármol *m.* marble
marrón brown
martes *m. s.* Tuesday
marxismo Marxism
marzo March
más more; most; plus; **a más tardar** at the latest; **cada vez más** more and more; **lo más posible** as much as possible; **lo más pronto posible** as soon as possible; **más allá de** *prep.* beyond; **más de** more than; **más o menos** more or less; **más tarde** later
masas *pl.* the masses, the people
máscara mask
masculino/a masculine
matemáticas mathematics
mateo carriage; **andar** (*irreg.*) **en mateo** to take a carriage ride
materia subject; **materia prima** raw material; *pl.* courses
materialista *n. m., f.* materialist; *adj.* materialistic
materno/a maternal
matrícula tuition
matricularse to matriculate; enroll
matrimonial marital; **cama matrimonial** double bed
matrimonio marriage; married couple
máxima maxim, saying
máximo *n.* maximum
máximo/a *adj.* maximum; greatest
maya *n. m., f.* Mayan; *adj.* Mayan
mayo May
mayonesa mayonnaise
mayor bigger; biggest; older; oldest; greater; main
mayoría majority
mayoritario/a pertaining to the majority
mazapán *m.* marzipan
me *d.o.* me; *i.o.* to/for me; *refl. pron.* myself; **¿me permite … ?** could you give me . . . ?
mecánico mechanic
media thirty (half past) (*with time*)
mediados *pl.* middle; **a mediados de** halfway through
mediano/a average; middle; **de estatura mediana** of average height; **edad** (*f.*) **mediana** middle age
mediante by means of
medias stockings
medicina medicine
medicinal medicinal, curative
médico/a *n. m., f.* doctor; *adj.* medical
medida measure, step
medieval medieval
medio *n.* middle; means; medium; environment; culture; **medio ambiente** environment; **medios** (*pl.*) **de comunicación** means of communication, media; **medios** (*pl.*) **de transporte/ transportación** means of transportation; **por medio de** by means of
medio/a *adj.* half; average; **clase** (*f.*) **media** middle class; **medio/a hermano/a** half brother, half sister; **Oriente** (*m.*) **Medio** Middle East
mediocre mediocre

medioeste Midwest
medir (i, i) to measure
Mediterráneo Mediterranean
mejillón *m.* mussel
mejor better; best; **a lo mejor** maybe; **mejor amigo/a** best friend
mejorar to improve; to raise; **mejorarse** to get better, improve
melocotón *m.* peach
melódico/a melodic; "easy listening"
melón *m.* melon
memoria memory; **de memoria** by heart
mencionar to mention
menino/a *young page of the royal family; young lady-in-waiting*
menor younger; youngest; least
menos less; least; minus; except; **a menos que** unless; **al menos** at least; **echar de menos** to miss, long for; **más o menos** more or less; **por lo menos** at least
mensaje *m.* message
mentir (ie, i) to lie
mentiroso/a *adj.* lying
menú *m.* menu
menudo: a menudo often
mercadillo market
mercado market
merluza hake (*fish*)
mermelada marmalade, jam
mes *m.* month; **al mes** per month
mesa table; food; cooking
mesero/a waiter, waitress
meseta plain, plateau
mestizo/a *n., adj.* mestizo
meta goal
metal *m.* metal
metalúrgico/a metallurgical
meterse (en) to get involved (with, in); to meddle (in)
metódico/a methodic
metro meter; subway
metrópoli(s) *f.* metropolis
metropolitano/a metropolitan
mexicano/a *n., adj.* Mexican
México Mexico; **Ciudad** (*f.*) **de México** Mexico City
mexicoamericano/a *n., adj.* Mexican American
mezcal *m.* mescal
mezcla mix
mezclar(se) to mix; to be mixed
mezquita mosque
mi(s) *poss.* my
mí *obj. of prep.* me; myself
microondas: horno de microondas microwave oven
miedo: tener (*irreg.*) **miedo (de)** to be afraid (of)
miedoso/a cowardly
miel *f.* honey; **luna de miel** honeymoon
miembro member
mientras *conj.* while; *adv.* meanwhile; **mientras tanto** meanwhile
miércoles *m. s.* Wednesday
migrar to migrate
mil (one) thousand; **hace un calor de mil demonios** it's a hellishly hot day

milagro miracle
militar *n.* soldier, military man; *adj.* military; **golpe** (*m.*) **militar** military coup
milla mile
millón *m.* million
milpa corn field (*C. Am., Mex.*)
mimado/a spoiled, overindulged
mimar to spoil
mimos *pl.* pampering
minero/a *adj.* mining
mineral mineral; **agua** (*f. but* **el agua**) **agua mineral** mineral water
mínimo/a minimal
ministerio ministry
minoritario/a *adj.* minority
minuto minute
mío/a(s) *poss.* my; mine; of mine; **¡Dios mío!** *interj.* my God!
mirada look, glance
mirar to look (at); to watch; **mirar la televisión** to watch television
misión *f.* mission
mismo/a same; **ahora mismo** right now; **al mismo tiempo** at the same time; **sí mismo/a** himself, herself, itself
misterio mystery
misterioso/a mysterious
mitad *f.* half
mítico/a mythical
mito myth
mixto/a tossed
moda fashion, mode; **de moda** fashionable
modelo *n.* model
modelo *adj. m., f.* model
moderación *f.* moderation
moderar to moderate
modernismo modernism
modernización *f.* modernization
moderno/a modern
modesto/a modest
modificar (qu) to modify
modo way
mojarse to get wet, soaked
moldear to mold
mole (*m.*) **poblano** *casserole dish prepared with meat and chili sauce* (*Mex.*)
molestar to bother, annoy; **molestarse** to get irritated
molestia bother; **siento la molestia** I'm sorry to bother you
molino mill; **molino de viento** windmill
momento moment; **de momento** for the moment; **en este momento, en estos momentos** right now, currently; **por el momento** for the time being
monarca *m., f.* monarch
monarquía monarchy
moneda coin; **la otra cara de la moneda** the other side of the coin
monja nun
mono monkey
monótono/a monotonous
montaje *m.* production
montaña mountain
montañoso/a mountainous

montar to set up; **montar a caballo** to ride horseback

monte *m.* mount, mountain

monumento monument

moño bun (*of hair*)

morado/a purple

morir(se) (ue, u) (*p.p.* **muerto/a**) to die

moro/a *n.* Moor; *adj.* Moorish

morrón: pimiento morrón red pepper

mosaico mosaic

mostaza mustard

mostrar (ue) to show

motivo motif; motive; **el motivo por el cual** the reason why

motor *m.* motor

mover(se) (ue) to move

movimiento movement

mozo/a waiter/waitress; *f.* young lady

muchacho/a young boy/girl

mucho *adv.* much, a lot of

mucho/a *adj.* a lot of; *pl. many;* **muchas gracias** thank you very much; **muchas veces** often; **mucho gusto** pleased to meet you

mudarse to move (*from one residence or city to another*)

mudéjar Mudejar (*Mohammedan living under a Christian king in Spain*)

muerte *f.* death; **dar** (*irreg.*) **la muerte a** to put to death

muerto/a (*p. p. of morir*) dead; **naturaleza muerta** still life (*painting*)

muestra proof

mujer *f.* woman; wife; **mujer de negocios** businesswoman; **tienda de ropa para mujeres** women's clothing store

mujeriego/a womanizer

multinacional multinational

mundial world(wide); **guerra mundial** world war

mundo world; **mundo de habla española** Spanish-speaking world; **Nuevo Mundo** New World; **todo el mundo** the whole world; everybody

muñeco/a doll

muralista *m., f.* muralist

muralla wall

murmurar to murmur, whisper

museo museum; **visitar un museo** to visit a museum

música music

musical musical

músico/a musician; **músicos ambulantes** strolling musicians

musulmán, musulmana Moslem

mutilar to mutilate

mutuo/a mutual

muy very; **muy bien** very well

N

nacer (zc) to be born

nacimiento birth; **certificado de nacimiento** birth certificate; **de nacimiento** by birth

nación *f.* nation

nacional national; **himno nacional** national anthem

nacionalidad *f.* nationality

nacionalización *f.* nationalization

nada *pron.* nothing, not anything; *adv.* not at all; **de nada** you're welcome; **no me gusta(n) nada ...** I don't like . . . at all

nadar to swim

nadie no one

napolitano/a Neapolitan

naranja *n.* orange (*fruit*)

nariz *f.* nose

narración *f.* narration

narrador(a) narrator

narrar to narrate

natación *f.* swimming

natal natal, native

nativo/a native

natural natural; **ciencias naturales** natural sciences; **recurso natural** natural resource

naturaleza nature; **naturaleza muerta** still life

náutico/a nautical

navegación *f.* sailing

navegar (gu) (en barco) to sail

Navidad *f.* Christmas

necesario/a necessary

necesidad *f.* necessity, need

necesitar to need

necio/a foolish

negar (ie) (gu) to refuse

negativa *n.* refusal

negativo/a *adj.* negative

negocio(s) business; shop; **dueño/a de negocios** shop owner; **hombre** (*m.*) **de negocios** businessman; **mujer** (*f.*) **de negocios** businesswoman

negro/a black

nene, nena baby

neoclásico/a neoclassic(al)

nervioso/a nervous

nevar (ie) to snow

nevera refrigerator

ni neither, nor; **ni ... ni ...** neither . . . nor . . . ; **ni siquiera** not even

nieto/a grandson, granddaughter; *m. pl.* grandchildren

nieve *f.* snow

ningún, ninguno/a *adj.* no, none, not any; **en ninguna parte** not anywhere, nowhere

ninguno/a *pron.* not one, not any

niñez *f.* childhood

niño/a young boy, young girl; young child; *m. pl.* young children; **de niño/a** as a child

nivel *m.* level

no no; not; **¿no?** right?, don't they (you, etc.)?; **no hay** there is not/are not; **ya no** no longer

noche *f.* night, evening; **buenas noches** good evening/night; **camisa de noche** night shirt; **de la noche** in the evening, at night; **de noche** at night, by night; **esta noche** tonight; **por la noche** in the evening

nocturno/a *adj.* night, nocturnal

nómada *m., f.* nomad

nombrar to name; to appoint

nombre *m.* (first) name; **a nombre de** in the name of

nopal *m.* cactus

nórdico/a Nordic; **esquí** (*m.*) **nórdico** cross-country skiing

noreste *m.* northeast

normalidad *f.* normality

noroeste *m.* northwest

norte *m.* north

Norteamérica North America

norteamericano/a *n., adj.* North American; *adj.* from the United States; **fútbol** (*m.*) **norteamericano** football

norteño/a *adj.* northern

nos *d.o.* us; *i.o.* to/for us; *refl. pron.* ourselves

nosotros/as *sub. pron.* we; *obj. of prep.* us

nostalgia nostalgia

nota note; grade, mark (*in schoolwork*); **nota al pie** footnote; **sacar (qu) buenas/malas notas** to get good/bad grades

notar to note, notice; **notarse** to be noted

noticia piece of news; *pl.* news; **últimas noticias** latest news

noticiero news (program)

notorio/a notorious

novecientos/as nine hundred

novela novel; **leer (y) novelas** to read novels; **novela policíaca** detective novel, mystery

novelista *m., f.* novelist

noveno/a ninth

noventa ninety

noviazgo engagement, courtship

noviembre *m.* November

novio/a boyfriend, girlfriend; fiancé(e)

nube *f.* cloud

nublado/a cloudy, overcast; **está nublado** it's cloudy, overcast

nuclear: familia nuclear nuclear family

núcleo nucleus

nudo knot

nuera daughter-in-law

nuestro/a(s) *poss.* our

nueve nine

nuevo/a new; **de nuevo** again

Nuevo Mundo New World

nuevomexicano/a New Mexican

número number; **número de la suerte** lucky number

numeroso/a numerous

nunca never, not ever

O

o or

obedecer (zc) to obey

obelisco obelisk

obispo bishop

objetivo *n.* objective

objeto object

obligado/a obliged, obligated

obligar (gu) to oblige, force

obra work (*of art, literature, etc.*); play; **obra de teatro** play, dramatic work; **obra literaria** literary work; **obra maestra** master work

obrero/a *n.* (manual) worker; laborer; *adj.* working; **clase obrera** working class

observar to observe; watch
observatorio observatory
obsesión *f.* obsession
obsesionarse to be(come) obsessed
obstáculo obstacle
obtener (*like* **tener**) to obtain, get
obvio/a obvious
ocasión *f.* occasion
occidental western
océano ocean; **Océano Atlántico** Atlantic Ocean; **Océano Pacífico** Pacific Ocean
ochenta eighty
ocho eight
ochocientos/as eight hundred
octavo/a eighth
octubre *m.* October
ocultado/a (*p.p. of* **ocultar**) hidden
ocultar to hide
ocupado/a busy
ocupar to occupy; **ocuparse** to occupy oneself
ocurrir to happen, occur; **ocurrirse** to come to mind
odiar to hate
odio hatred
oeste *m.* west
ofender to offend
ofensa offense, affront
ofensivo/a offensive
oferta offer; **aceptar la oferta** to accept the offer; **hacer** (*irreg.*) **una oferta** to make an offer; **oferta de trabajo** job offer; **rechazar (c) la oferta** to reject the offer
oficial *adj.* official
oficina office
oficio occupation, job
ofrecer (zc) to offer
oído ear
oír to hear; to listen
ojalá (que) God willing; I hope
ojo eye; **¡ojo!** *interj.* watch out!, be careful!, pay close attention!; **ojos claros** light-colored eyes; **ojos expresivos** expressive eyes
ola wave
olímpico/a Olympic; **Juegos Olímpicos** Olympic Games
olivar *m.* olive grove
olmeca *n. m., f.; adj.* Olmec
olvidar(se) (de) to forget (about)
olvido *n.* forgetting; oblivion
omitir to omit, leave out
once eleven
opción *f.* option
ópera opera
operador(a) operator
opinar to think, have an opinion
opinión *f.* opinion
oponer(se) (*like* **poner**) to oppose; to be opposed
oportunidad *f.* opportunity
oportuno/a opportune
oposición *f.* opposition
opresión *f.* oppression
oprimir to oppress
optimista *m., f.* optimist; *adj.* optimistic
opuesto/a (*p.p. of* **oponer**) opposed
oración *f.* sentence

orden *m.* order (*chronological*); *f.* order (*command*); **a sus órdenes** at your service; **en orden** (*m.*) **cronológico** in chronological order; **orden** (*f.*) **judicial** legal procedure
ordenado/a orderly; ordained
ordenador *m.* computer (*Sp.*)
ordenar *m.* to put in order; to ordain; to order (*a meal*) (*Mex.*)
oreja ear
orfanato orphanage
organismo organism
organista *m., f.* organist
organización *f.* organization
organizar (c) to organize
orgullo pride
orgulloso/a proud
oriental oriental; eastern
oriente *m.* east; Orient; **Oriente Medio** Middle East
origen *m.* origin
originario/a *adj.* originating
orilla bank (*of a river*); **a orillas de** on the banks of
ornamentación *f.* ornamentation
oro gold
orquesta orchestra
ortografía spelling
os *d.o.* you (*fam. pl. Sp.*); *i.o.* to, for you (*fam. pl. Sp.*); *refl. pron.* yourselves (*fam. pl. Sp.*)
oscuro/a dark
ostra oyster
otoño autumn
otro/a other, another; **la otra cara de la moneda** the other side of the coin; **otra vez** again; **por otro lado** on the other hand
oxígeno oxygen

P

paciencia patience
paciente *n. m., f.* patient; *adj.* patient
pacífico/a peaceful; **Océano Pacífico** Pacific Ocean
padrastro stepfather
padre *m.* father; priest; *pl.* parents; **Día** (*m.*) **del Padre** Father's Day
paella *Spanish dish of rice, shellfish, chicken, and meat*
pagar (gu) to pay (for)
página page
país *m.* country, nation
País (*m.*) **Vasco** Basque region (*of Spain*)
paisaje *m.* countryside; landscape
pájaro bird
palabra word; **palabras interrogativas** (*gram.*) interrogative words
palacio palace
palmas applause
palo stick
paloma pigeon
palomitas popcorn
pampa pampa, grassland
pan *m.* bread; **pan tostado** toast
panadería bakery; pastry shop
panadero/a baker
panceta bacon (*Arg.*)

panorámico/a panoramic
pantalón, pantalones *m.* pants; **pantalón corto, pantalones cortos** shorts
pañuelo handkerchief, kerchief
papa potato (*L.A.*); **papas fritas** French fries
papá *m.* dad, father
papel *m.* paper; role; **hacer** (*irreg.*) **el papel (de)** to play the role (of)
papelería stationery store
paquete *m.* package
par *m.* pair; **un par de** a pair of; **un par de (días)** a few (days)
para *prep.* for, in order to; **no es para tanto** it's not that big of a deal; **para pensar** something to think about; **para que** *conj.* so that, in order that (for); **¿para quién?** for whom?; **para saber qué pasó** to find out what happened
parada *n.* stop; **parada de taxis** taxi stand
paradero whereabouts, location
parador *m.* inn
parar to stop
parcela plot, parcel (*of ground*)
parcha passion fruit
parcial partial
pardo/a brown
parecer (zc) *v.* to seem, appear; **parecerse a** to be similar to; to resemble; **al parecer** apparently
parecer *n. m.* appearance
parecido *n.* resemblance
parecido/a *adj.* (*p.p. of* **parecer**) similar
pared *f.* wall; **entre la espada y la pared** between a rock and a hard place
pareja couple
parentesco relationship, kinship
paréntesis *m. s., pl.* parenthesis, parentheses; **entre paréntesis** in parentheses
pariente *m.* relative, family member; **visitar a los parientes** to visit relatives
parlamentaria parliamentary
parque *m.* park; **parque zoológico** zoo
párrafo paragraph
parrilla grill
parrillada barbecue
parte *f.* part; **en ninguna parte** not anywhere, nowhere; **formar parte de** to be or form a part of; **por parte (de alguien)** on behalf of (someone); **por todas partes** all over; everywhere
participar to participate
participio (*gram.*) participle
particular *adj.* particular; private; *n.* matter
partido game, match; (political) party; side
partir: a partir de starting from
parto childbirth
pasado *n.* past
pasado/a *adj.* past, last (*in time*); **huevos pasados por agua** soft-boiled

eggs; **pasado mañana** the day after tomorrow

pasaje *m.* passage, fare; ticket; **pasaje de ida y vuelta** round-trip fare

pasajero/a *adj.* passing; *n.* passenger

pasaporte *m.* passport

pasar to happen; to pass (*someone*); to come by; to pass, spend (*time*); **pasar por** to come by to pick up (*someone, something*); **pasar por agua** to boil (*eggs*); **pasarlo bien/mal** to have a good/bad time; **para saber qué pasó** to find out what happened

pasatiempo hobby

pasear to stroll, take a walk

paseo walk; drive; avenue; **dar** (*irreg.*) **un paseo** to take a walk

pasillo corridor

pasión *f.* passion

paso step; float (*in parade*); passing, passage; **al paso que** at the same time as

pastel *m.* pastel (*color, drawing*); pie

pastelería pastry shop; bakery

pastilla pill

pasto pasture; grazing

patata potato (*Sp.*); **patatas fritas** French fries

paterno/a paternal

patio patio; yard

patito duckling

pato duck

patria fatherland

patriarca *m.* patriarch (*male head of the family*)

Patricio: Día (*m.*) **de San Patricio** St. Patrick's Day

patriótico/a patriotic

patriotismo patriotism

patrocinador(a) sponsor; backer

patrón, patrona patron, patron saint

pavo turkey

paz *f.* peace; **que en paz descanse** may he/she rest in peace

peaje *m.* toll; tollbooth

peatonal *adj.* pedestrian; **calle** (*f.*) **peatonal** pedestrial mall

pecar (**qu**) to sin

pecho chest; breast

peculiar peculiar; characteristic

pedido *n.* order

pedir (**i, i**) to ask for, order; **pedir prestado/a** to borrow

pelea fight

pelear(se) (**con**) to fight (with)

película movie, film

peligro danger

peligroso/a dangerous

pelo hair; **pelo canoso/rubio** gray/blond hair; **tomarle el pelo (a alguien)** to tease someone

pelota ball

peluquería barber shop; hairdresser shop

peluquero/a barber; hairdresser

pena punishment; sorrow; **es una pena** it's a pity; **me da pena** I'm sorry; **(no) vale la pena** it's (not) worth the trouble; **¡qué pena!** *interj.* what a pity!

península peninsula; **Península Ibérica** Iberian Peninsula

pensar (**ie**) to think; to intend to (*do something*); **para pensar** something to think about; **pensar en** to think about

pensativo/a thoughtful, pensive

peor *adv.* worse; worst

pequeño/a small; **desde pequeño/a** since he/she was small

pera pear

percusión *f.* percussion

perder (**ie**) to lose; to miss; **perderse** (**ie**) to get lost

pérdida loss

perdidamente madly

perdón *m.* pardon; *interj.* pardon me, excuse me

perdonar to pardon; **perdone** *interj.* pardon me, excuse me

peregrino/a pilgrim

perezoso/a lazy

perfecto/a perfect

perfume *m.* perfume

periódico newspaper

periodismo journalism

periodista *m., f.* journalist

período period (*of time*)

perla pearl

permanente permanent

permiso permission; **con permiso** may I pass by?

permitir to permit, allow; **¿me permite ... ?** could you give me . . . ?

pero *conj.* but

perplejo/a perplexed

perro/a dog

perro caliente hot dog

persecución *f.* persecution

pérsico/a *n., adj.* Persian

persistente persistent

persistir to persist

persona person

personaje *m.* character

personal *n. m.* personnel; *adj.* personal

personalidad *f.* personality

perspectiva perspective

pertenecer (**zc**) to belong

pesadilla nightmare

pesado/a boring, tedious

pesar to weigh

pesar: a pesar de in spite of

pesca *n.* fishing

pescadería fish market

pescadero/a fishmonger; fishwife

pescado (*caught*) fish

pescador(a) fisherman; fisherwoman

pescar: caña de pescar fishing pole

peseta *monetary unit of Spain;* **peseta puertorriqueña** quarter (*U.S. coin used as monetary unit of Puerto Rico*)

pesimismo pessimism

pesimista *n. m., f.* pessimist; *adj.* pessimistic

peso *monetary unit of Mexico;* weight; **bajar de peso** to lose weight

pesquero/a *adj.* fishing (*industry*)

petróleo petroleum

petrolífero/a *adj.* oil

petroquímico/a *adj.* petrochemical

pez *m.* (*pl.* **peces**) (*live*) fish

picada: carne (*f.*) **picada** ground meat

picante spicy, hot; **salsa picante** hot sauce

picnic *m.* picnic; **hacer** (*irreg.*) **un picnic** to have a picnic

pico point; peak

pie *m.* foot; **al pie de** at the bottom of; **nota al pie** footnote

piedra stone

pierna leg

pieza play, piece

pijama *m.* pajamas

pilón *m. frozen dessert similar to a Popsicle*

piloto/a pilot

pimentero pepper shaker/grinder

pimiento pepper; **pimiento morrón** red pepper

pincel *m.* paintbrush

pintar to paint

pintor(a) painter

pintoresco/a picturesque

pintura painting

piña pineapple

piragua *SnoCone*

pirámide *f.* pyramid

pirata *adj. m., f.* pirate

Pirineos Pyrenees

pirulí *m. frozen dessert similar to a Popsicle*

piscina swimming pool, pool

piso floor

pista track; trail

pistola gun

placer *m.* pleasure

plan *m.* plan; **hacer** (*irreg.*) **planes** to make plans

planchar to iron

planear to plan

planeta *m.* planet

plano (turístico) map (*of a city*)

plano/a flat

planta plant; **planta baja** ground floor

plantación *f.* plantation

plástico plastic

plata silver

plátano banana

platicar (**qu**) to talk, chat

plato plate; dish; **plato principal** entrée, main course; **plato apetitoso** appetizing dish

platónico/a platonic

playa beach

plaza plaza, square; place

plenamente fully

plomero *m., f.* plumber

plomo lead

población *f.* population

poblano: mole (*m.*) **poblano** *casserole dish prepared with meat and chili sauce (Mex.)*

pobre *n. m., f.* poor person; *adj.* poor

pobrecito/a poor little thing

pobreza poverty

poco *n.* **un poco de** a little; **dentro de poco** very soon

poco *adv.* little; **poco a poco** little by little; **por poco** almost, nearly

poco/a *adj.* little; *pl.* few, a few; **al poco tiempo** shortly after; **pocas veces** seldom

poder *v.* (*irreg.*) to be able, can; *n. m.* power

poderoso/a powerful

¿podría + *inf.*? could I (*do something*)?; is it possible for me to (*do something*)?

poema *m.* poem

poesía poetry

poeta *m., f.* poet

polaco/a *n.* Pole; *adj.* Polish

policía police

policíaco/a *pertaining to police*; **novela policíaca** detective novel, mystery

poliéster *m.* polyester

política *s.* politics

político/a *n.* politician; *adj.* political

pollería poultry shop

pollo chicken

polo polo; pole; **polo sur** South Pole

pomelo grapefruit (*Arg.*)

ponceño/a *person from Ponce (P.R.)*

poner (*irreg.*) to put, place; to put on; **poner (a alguien) a cargo (de)** to put (someone) in charge (of); **ponerle una inyección (a alguien)** to give (someone) a shot, injection; **ponerse** + *adj.* to become + *adj.*; **ponerse a mando** to take command

popularidad *f.* popularity

popularizar (c) to popularize

póquer *m.* poker; **jugar (ue) (gu) al póquer** to play poker

por *prep.* by; in (*the morning, evening, etc.*); through; along; for; because of; per; **estar** (*irreg.*) **por** (+ *inf.*) to be about to (*do something*); to be ready to (*do something*); **pasar por** to come by to pick up (*someone, something*); **pasar por agua** to boil (*eggs*); **por bien o por mal** for better or worse; **por casualidad** by chance; **por cierto** by the way; certainly; **por completo** completely; **por delante** ahead of one; **por desgracia** unfortunately; **por Dios** *interj.* for heaven's sake; **por ejemplo** for example; **por eso** for that reason, that's why; **por excelencia** par excellence; **por favor** please; **por fin** at last, finally; **por un lado** on the one hand; **por lo general** generally, in general; **por la mañana** in the morning; **por lo menos** at least; **por medio de** by means of; **por el momento** for the time being; **por otro lado** on the other hand; **por parte (de alguien)** on behalf of (someone); **por poco** almost, nearly; **por primera vez** for the first time; **por semana** in a week's (time); **por su propia cuenta** on his/her/its/your/ their own account; **por suerte** fortunately, luckily; **por supuesto** of course; **por la tarde/noche** in the afternoon (evening); **por teléfono** by telephone; **por todas partes** all over; everywhere; **por última vez** for the last time; **por lo visto** evidently; **terminar por** + *inf.* to finish or end up by (*doing something*)

porción *f.* portion

¿por qué? why?

porque because

portarse to behave; **portarse** + *adj.* to act + *adv.*

porteño/a *inhabitant of Buenos Aires*

portugués *n. m.* Portuguese (*language*)

portugués, portuguesa *n., adj.* Portuguese

poseer (y) to possess

posesión *f.* possession

posesivo: adjetivos posesivos (*gram.*) possessive adjectives

posibilidad *f.* possibility

posible possible; **lo antes posible** as soon as possible; **lo más posible** as much as possible; **lo más pronto posible** as soon as possible

posición *f.* position

positivo/a positive

postal *f.* postcard; **tarjeta postal** postcard

postguerra postwar period

postre *m.* dessert

postular to stand as a candidate for

práctica practice

practicar (qu) to practice; to carry out; to perform; **practicar un deporte** to play a sport

pragmático/a pragmatic

preceder to precede

precio price

precioso/a precious; beautiful, lovely

precipitado/a hasty, hurried

precisamente precisely, exactly

preciso/a necessary

precolombino/a pre-Columbian

precursor(a) precursor

predecir (*like* **decir**) to predict

predicción *f.* prediction

predilecto/a favorite

predominar to predominate

preferencia preference

preferible preferable

preferido/a favorite

preferir (ie, i) to prefer

pregunta question; **hacerle** (*irreg.*) **preguntas (a alguien)** to ask (someone) questions

preguntar to ask (*a question*); **preguntarse** to wonder; to ask oneself

prehispánico/a *n., adj.* pre-Hispanic

prehistórico/a prehistoric

prejuicio prejudice

premio prize

prensa press (*newspapers*)

preocupación *f.* preoccupation, worry

preocupar(se) to worry

preparación *f.* preparation

preparar to prepare

preparativos preparations

preposición *f.* preposition

preposicional: pronombre (*m.*) **preposicional** (*gram.*) prepositional pronoun

presencia presence

presentación *f.* presentation; introduction

presentar to present; to introduce; **presentarse** to appear

presente *n. m., adj.* present

presentimiento presentiment, premonition

presentir (ie, i) to have a presentiment of

presidencia presidency

presidencial presidential

presidente *m., f.* president

presidido/a (por) presided (over)

presidir to preside over

presión *f.* pressure

prestado: pedir (i, i) prestado/a to borrow

préstamo loan

prestar atención (a) to pay attention (to)

prestigio prestige

prestigioso/a prestigious

presupuesto budget

pretérito (*gram.*) past; preterite (tense)

pretexto pretext, excuse

prevenir (*like* **venir**) to prevent

previo/a previous

primo/a: materia prima raw material

primaria: (escuela) primaria elementary school

primariamente primarily

primavera spring

primer, primero/a first; **amor** (*m.*) **a primera vista** love at first sight; **de primer año** *adj.* freshman; **en primer lugar** in the first place, firstly; **(por) primera vez** (for the) first time

primo/a cousin

primordial primordial, fundamental

princesa princess

principal main, principal; **plato principal** entrée, main course

príncipe *m.* prince

principio beginning; **al principio** at first; at the beginning

prisa haste; **darse** (*irreg.*) **prisa** to hurry; **de prisa** quickly, in a hurry; **tener** (*irreg.*) **prisa (por** + *inf.*) to be in a hurry (*to do something*)

prisión *f.* prison

prisionero/a prisoner

privacidad *f.* privacy

privado/a private, personal; **baño privado (con ducha)** private bath (with shower); **vida privada** personal life

privatización *f.* privatization

privatizar (c) privatize

privilegiado/a privileged

probabilidad *f.* probability; likelihood

probable probable

probar (ue) to try (on); to taste (*food*); to prove

problema *m.* problem

problemático/a problematic

proceder to originate

procesión *f.* procession

proclamar to proclaim

producción *f.* production

producir (zc) to produce

productivo/a productive

producto product

productor(a) producer

profecía prophecy

profesión *f.* profession

profesional *adj.* professional; **secreto profesional** confidentiality

profesor(a) teacher, professor

profundo/a profound
programa *m.* program
programación (*f.*) **de computadoras** computer programming
programador(a) programmer; **programador(a) de computadoras** computer programmer (*L.A.*)
progresar to advance, improve
prohibir to prohibit, forbid
promedio/a *adj.* average
promesa promise
prometer to promise
promulgación *f.* promulgation
pronombre *m.* (*gram.*) pronoun; **pronombre preposicional** (*gram.*) prepositional pronoun
pronto soon; **hasta pronto** see you soon; **lo más pronto posible** as soon as possible; **tan pronto** como as soon as
pronunciación *f.* pronunciation
propiedad *f.* property
propietario/a proprietor, owner
propina tip
propio/a *adj.* own, one's own; **por su propia cuenta** on his/her/its/your/their own account
proponente *m., f.* proponent
proponer (*like* **poner**) to propose
propósito intention
prosperar to prosper
próspero/a prosperous
protagonista *m., f.* protagonist
proteger (j) to protect
protesta *n.* protest
protestar (por) to protest (about)
provincia province
provinciano/a provincial
provocar (qu) to provoke
próximo/a near; next
proyecto project
prueba(s) proof; test
psicología psychology
psicológico/a psychological
psiquiatra *m., f.* psychiatrist
psiquiatría psychiatry
publicar (qu) to publish
publicitario/a *adj.* advertising
público/a *n. m., adj.* public
pueblecito village, small town
pueblo people; town
puente *m.* bridge
puerta door; **tocar (qu) la puerta** to knock on the door
puerto port
puertorriqueño/a *n., adj.* Puerto Rican; **peseta puertorriqueña** quarter (*U.S. coin used as monetary unit of Puerto Rico*)
pues *interj.* well
puesto *n.* position, job
puesto/a (*p.p. of* **poner**) put, placed
pulso pulse; **tomar el pulso** to feel the pulse
punto point; (**estar** [*irreg.*]) **a punto de** (to be) at the point of; about to; **a tal punto que** to the point that; **en punto** on the dot (*with time*); **¿hasta qué punto?** up to what point?; **punto de vista** point of view

puntual punctual
puntualidad *f.* punctuality
puré *m.* purée

Q

que that, who; **lo que** what, that which; **para que** so that, in order that (for); **que en paz descanse** may he/she rest in peace; (**el mes, el año ...**) **que viene** the coming, next (month, year...); **ya que** since
¿qué? what?; which?; **¡qué + *noun/adj. / adverb*! *interj.*** what a . . . !; how . . . !; **¡qué barbaridad!** how awful!; **¿qué diablos?** what the devil?; **¡qué pena!** what a pity!; **¿qué tal?** how are you (doing)?; how about . . . ?; **¿qué tal si ... ?** what if . . . . ? **¡qué va!** don't put me on!; **¡qué vergüenza!** how embarrassing!; **¿y qué?** so what?; what do you want me to do?
quedar to be situated; **quedar + *adj.*** to be + *adj.*; **quedar bien impresionado/a** to be left with a good impression; **quedarse** to stay, remain; to be left; **quedarse + *adj.*** to become + *adj.*
quehacer *m.* chore
queja complaint
quejarse (de) to complain (about)
querer (*irreg.*) to wish, want; to love
querido/a (*p.p. of* **querer**) (**de**) *adj.* dear; loved (by)
queso cheese
quien who
¿quién(es)? who?, whom?; **¿a quién?** to whom?; **¿con quién?** with whom?; **¿de quién?** whose?; **¿para quién?** for whom?
química chemistry
quince fifteen
quinientos/as five hundred
quinto/a fifth
quiosco kiosk
quisiera + *inf.* I would like to (*do something*); **quisiera cambiar ...** I would like to change . . .
quizá(s) maybe, perhaps

R

racismo racism
radicar (qu) to live; to be located
radio *m.* radio (set); *f.* radio (broadcasting medium)
raíz (*pl.* **raíces**) root; (**agente** [*m., f.*] **de**) **bienes** (*m. pl.*) **raíces** real estate (agent)
rana frog
rapidez *f.* rapidity
rápido/a rapid, fast; express, fast (*train*); **comida rápida** fast food
raqueta racket (*sports*)
raro/a rare, uncommon; odd, peculiar
rascacielos *m. s.* skyscraper
rasgo trait, feature
ratificado/a ratified, confirmed
rato while, short time; period of time; **a ratos** at times; **ratos libres** *pl.* spare time, free time
rayo ray; **rayos X** X rays; **sacar (qu) rayos X** to take X rays

raza race (*of human beings*)
razón *f.* reason, cause; reason, faculty of reasoning; **con razón** understandably so; **la razón por la cual** the reason why; **tener** (*irreg.*) **(toda la) razón** to be (absolutely) right
razonable reasonable
reacción *f.* reaction
reaccionar to react
real royal; real
realidad *f.* reality; **en realidad** actually, really
realista *n. m., f.* realist; *adj.* realistic
realización *f.* fulfillment
realizar (c) to carry out; to fulfill, accomplish
realmente really, truly; actually
rebelarse to rebel
rebelión *f.* rebellion
recámara bedroom (*Mex.*)
recepción *f.* front desk (*in a hotel*); reception
recepcionista *m., f.* receptionist
receta prescription; recipe
rechazar (c) to reject; **rechazar la oferta** to reject the offer
rechazo rejection
recibir to get, receive; to receive (*visitors*)
recibo receipt
recién casado/a recently married, newly wed
reciente recent; fresh
recitar to recite (*poem*)
recoger (j) to pick up; to go for
recomendable commendable; recommendable
recomendación *f.* recommendation
recomendar (ie) to recommend
recompensa reward
reconciliarse (con) to be reconciled, come together; to make up (with)
reconocer (zc) to recognize; to acknowledge
reconocido/a (*p.p of* **reconocer**) acknowledged
Reconquista Reconquest (*struggle to end Moorish rule in Spain*)
reconstrucción *f.* reconstruction
reconstruir (y) to reconstruct
recordar (ue) to remember, recall; to recollect; **recordarle (algo) (a alguien)** to remind (someone) of (something)
recrear to recreate
recto/a straight; **seguir (i, i) (g) recto** to continue straight ahead
recuerdo memory; memento, souvenir
recuperar to recover, retrieve
recurrir (a) to resort (to)
recurso natural natural resource
redactar to write; to draw up
reemplazar (c) to replace
referirse (ie, e) (a) to refer (to)
refinado/a refined, polished
refinamiento class; refinement
reflejar to reflect; to show, reveal; **reflejarse** to be reflected
reflexión *f.* reflection
reflexionar (sobre) to reflect (on)
reflexivo/a reflective, thoughtful

reforma agraria land reform
refrescarse (qu) to refresh oneself
refresco soft drink
refugiado/a refugee
regalar to give (*as a gift*)
regalo gift, present; **regalo de despedida** going-away present
regañar to scold, reprimand
regatear to bargain
regateo *n.* bargaining
régimen *m.* regime
regimiento (*military*) regimen
región *f.* region
registrar to register
regla rule
reglamento regulation; rules
regresar to return, come or go back
regreso *n.* return; **de regreso** *adj.* return (flight); **de regreso a** on returning to
regular fair, average; common, ordinary
rehacer (*like* **hacer**) to remake, make over
reina queen
reinar to reign
reino kingdom
reír(se) (i, i) (de) to laugh (at); to laugh (over)
relación *f.* relation, relationship; **relación estrecha** close, intimate relationship
relacionar to relate; to associate
relajarse to relax
relativo/a *adj.* relative
religión *f.* religion
religiosidad *f.* religiousness
religioso/a religious
relleno/a stuffed, filled
reloj *m.* watch
remar to row
remolcar (qu) to tow
remontarse to go back (*to some date in the past*)
renacer (zc) to be reborn
rendir (i, i) culto (a) to worship; **rendirse** to surrender; to conquer
renunciar to renounce, give up (*right, claim*); to resign (*post, position*)
reparaciones *f.* repairs; **taller** (*m.*) **de reparaciones** repair shop
reparar to repair
repartición *f.* distribution
repasar to review
repaso *n.* review
repente: de repente suddenly
repentino/a sudden
repetir (i, i) to repeat
réplica replica, copy
reponerse (*like* **poner**) to recover (*from an illness*); to get better
reportaje *m.* article, report; special feature
reporte *m.* report
reportero/a reporter
reposo rest
representación *f.* representation; performance
representante *m., f.* representative
representar to represent; to act, perform; to show, express

reprochar to reproach
repugnar to disgust
requerir (ie, i) to require
requisito requirement
res: carne (*f.*) **de res** beef (*Mex.*)
rescatar to save, rescue
rescate *m.* rescue
resentido/a resentful; annoyed
resentimiento resentment
resentir (ie, e) to resent
reserva reservation (*Sp.*)
reservación *f.* reservation (*L.A.*); **hacer** (*irreg.*) **una reservación** to make a reservation
reservado/a reserved; reticent
resfriado *n.* cold
resfriarse to catch a cold
residencia dormitory; residence
residir to reside
resistencia resistance
resistir to resist, oppose
resolver (ue) (*p.p.* **resuelto/a**) to resolve; to solve
resonar (ue) to resound; to resonate
respaldo support, backing
respectivo/a respective
respecto: con respecto a with respect to
respetar to respect
respeto respect
respirar to breathe
responder to respond
responsabilidad *f.* responsibility
respuesta answer
restablecer (zc) to reestablish, reinstate
restaurante *m.* restaurant
restaurar to restore
resto *n.* rest
restricción *f.* restriction
resuelto/a (*p.p of* **resolver**) resolved
resultado result
resultar to result; to turn out to be
resumen *m.* summary
resumir to sum up, summarize
retrato portrait
reunión *f.* meeting, gathering
reunirse (con) to get (back) together (with); to be reunited (with)
revelación *f.* revelation; unveiling
revelar to reveal
revisar to check, inspect; **revisar las cuentas** to audit accounts
revista magazine
revolución *f.* revolution
revolucionario/a revolutionary
revuelto/a (*p.p. of* **revolver**) scrambled; **huevos revueltos** scrambled eggs
rey *m.* king; **Reyes Magos** Magi, Wise Men
rezar (c) to pray
rezongón, rezongona *n.* grouch, grumbler; *adj.* grouchy
ribera shore, bank
rico/a *n. m., f.* rich person; *adj.* rich; wealthy; tasty, delicious (*food*); abundant (*crops*)
ridículo/a ridiculous
riesgo: correr riesgo to run a risk
riguroso/a rigorous
riñón *m.* kidney

río river
riqueza richness; *pl.* riches
risueño/a smiling
ritmo rhythm
rivalidad *f.* rivalry
robar to steal
robot *m.* robot
roca rock
rock *m.* rock (*music*)
rocoso/a rocky
rodeado/a surrounded
rogar (ue) (gu) to beg
rojo/a red
romántico/a romantic
romper (*p.p.* **roto/a**) to break; **romper con** to break up with (*someone*)
ron *m.* rum
ropa clothing; **cambiarse de ropa** to change one's clothes; **tienda de ropa para hombres/mujeres** men's/women's clothing store
rosa rose; rose color
rosado/a pink
rosal *m.* rosebush or plant
rostro face
rubio/a blond(e); **pelo rubio** blond hair
ruido noise
ruina ruin
ruleta roulette
rumba rumba (*Cuban dance*)
ruso/a *n., adj.* Russian
ruta route, way
rutina routine

S

S.A. (sociedad anónima) Inc. (incorporated; stock company)
sábado Saturday
saber (*irreg.*) to know (*information*); **saber + inf.** to know how (*to do something*)
sabio/a *n.* wise person; *adj.* wise
sabor *m.* flavor
saborear to savor, taste
sabroso/a tasty
sacar (qu) to get out; to take out; to take out, withdraw (*from an account*); to get, receive (*grades*); **sacar buenas/ malas notas** to get good/bad grades; **sacar una foto** to take a picture, photograph; **sacar la lengua** to stick out one's tongue; **sacar rayos X (equis)** to take X rays; **sacar vídeos** to take videos
sacerdote *m.* priest, clergyman
sacrificar (qu) to sacrifice
sagrado/a sacred
sal *f.* salt
sala living room; **sala de cine/teatro** theater
salchicha sausage
salero salt shaker
salida departure
salir (*irreg.*) to leave (*a place*), go out; to turn out; **salir con los amigos** to go out with friends; **salir de la ciudad** to get out of the city; **salirse con lo suyo** to get one's own way
salmón *m.* salmon; **de color salmón** salmon-colored

salón *m.* lobby; **juegos de salón** parlor games (*cards, chess, poker, etc.*); **salón de clase** classroom
salsa sauce, dressing; salsa (*style of music*); **salsa de tomate** ketchup; **salsa picante** hot sauce
saltar to jump; to fly off
salto waterfall
salud *f.* health; **¡salud!** *interj.* to your health!
saludar to greet
saludo greeting
salvar to save; to rescue
san, santo/a saint; holy; **Semana Santa** Easter (Holy) Week
sandía watermelon
sándwich *m.* sandwich
sangriento/a bloody
sano/a healthy; wholesome; sound
sátira satire
satisfacción *f.* satisfaction
satisfacer (*like* **hacer**) (*p.p.* **satisfecho/a**) to satisfy
se (*impersonal*) one; *refl. pron.* yourself (*form.*), himself, herself, yourselves (*form.*), themselves
secadora clothes dryer
sección *f.* section; **sección de (no) fumar** (non)smoking section
seco/a dry
secretario/a secretary
secreto secret; **secreto profesional** confidentiality
secuencia sequence
secundaria secondary; **(escuela) secundaria** high school
sed *f.* thirst; **tener** (*irreg.*) **(mucha) sed** to be (very) thirsty
seda silk
sede *f.* headquarters
sedentario/a sedentary
seductor(a) seducer; charmer
seguida: en seguida right away, immediately
seguido/a followed; in a row, running
seguir (i, i) (g) to follow; to continue; to keep on; **seguir (todo) derecho/recto** to continue straight (ahead); **seguir vigente** to continue to be viable
según according to
segundo *n.* second (*time*)
segundo/a *adj.* second
seguridad *f.* security; **seguridad social** social security
seguro *n.* insurance; **seguro social** social security
seguro/a *adj.* sure, certain; safe; **(no) estar** (*irreg.*) **seguro/a** (not) to be sure; **seguro que** of course, certainly
seis six
seiscientos/as six hundred
sello stamp (*Mex.*)
selva jungle
semáforo traffic light
semana week; **día** (*m.*) **de la semana** day of the week; **fin** (*m.*) **de semana** weekend; **por semana** in a week ('s time); **Semana Santa** Easter (Holy) Week

semejante *adj.* similar
semejanza similarity
semestre *m.* semester
seminario seminary
senado senate
senador(a) senator
sencillo/a simple
sendero path
sensación *f.* sensation
sensible sensitive
sentar (ie) to seat, lead to a seat; **sentarse** to sit, sit down
sentido sense; **sentido común** common sense; **(no) tener** (*irreg.*) **sentido** (not) to make sense; **sentido de culpabilidad** sense of guilt or responsibility
sentimiento feeling
sentir (ie, i) to feel; to regret; to feel sorry about; **lo siento** I'm sorry; **sentirse** to feel; **sentirse bien/mal** to feel well/bad (*ill*); **sentirse solo/a** to feel lonely; **siento la molestia** I'm sorry to bother you
seña sign; signal, gesture
señal *f.* signal, sign
señor (Sr.) *m.* Mr., sir; gentleman, man
señora (Sra.) *f.* Mrs., lady, woman
señores (Sres.) *m. pl.* Mr. and Mrs.; gentlemen
señorial noble, majestic
señorita (Srta.) Miss; young lady, woman
separación *f.* separation
separar(se) to separate
septiembre *m.* September
séptimo/a seventh
ser (*irreg.*) to be; **es cierto** it's certain; **es decir** that is to say; **es una pena** it's a pity; **lograr ser** to manage to become; **llegar (gu) a ser** to become; **ser listo/a** to be bright, smart; **ser unido/a** to be united, close-knit, close
ser *n. m.* being; life; **ser humano** human being
serenata *n.* serenade
serenidad *f.* serenity
sereno/a calm, serene
serie *f.* series; TV series
serio/a serious; **¿en serio?** seriously?; **tomar en serio** to take seriously
serpiente *f.* snake, serpent
serrano: jamón (*m.*) **serrano** cured Spanish ham
servicio service
servilleta napkin
servir (i, i) to serve; to be suitable, useful; **servir de** to serve as, act as
sesenta sixty
sesión *f.* session; sitting
setecientos/as seven hundred
setenta seventy
severo/a severe
sevillano/a Sevillian (*of or from Seville*)
sexto/a sixth
si if
sí yes; **claro que sí**, *interj.* of course
sí mismo/a himself, herself, oneself, itself
sicología psychology

sicólogo/a psychologist
siempre always
siesta siesta, nap; **dormir (ue, u) la siesta** to take a siesta, nap; **tomar una siesta** to take a siesta, nap
siete seven
siglo century
significado meaning; significance
significar (qu) to mean
siguiente next, following; **al día siguiente** the next day
silenciar to silence
silencio silence
simbólico/a symbolic
simbolizar (c) to symbolize; to typify, represent
símbolo symbol
simio ape
simpático/a nice, pleasant
simpatizar (c) to get along will together
simplificado/a simplified
simultáneo/a simultaneous
sin *prep.* without; **sin chistar** without saying a word; **sin duda** no doubt, without a doubt; **sin embargo** nevertheless; **sin que** *conj.* without
sinagoga synagogue
sincero/a sincere
sino but (rather)
sinónimo synonym
sintético/a synthetic
siquiera: ni siquiera not even
sirviente/a servant
sistema *m.* system; **sistema solar** solar system
sitio site, place
situación *f.* situation
situar to situate; **situarse** to be located
sobre *n. m.* envelope; *prep.* about; on; **sobre todo** above all
sobresalir (*like* **salir**) to stand out, excel
sobrevivir to survive
sobrino/a nephew, niece; *pl.* nieces and nephews
social: ciencias sociales social sciences; **clase** (*f.*) **social** social class; **seguridad** (*f.*) **social** social security; **seguro social** social security
sociedad *f.* society; **sociedad anónima (S.A.)** incorporated; stock company (Inc.)
socio/a member; partner
socioeconómico/a socioeconomic
sociología sociology
sofá *m.* sofa
sofisticado/a sophisticated
soga rope
sol *m.* sun; **hace (mucho) sol** it's (very) sunny (*weather*); **tomar el sol** to sunbathe
solamente only
solar solar; **sistema** (*m.*) **solar** solar system
solas: a solas alone; in private
soldado soldier
soleado/a sunny
soler (ue) + *inf.* to tend to be, be in the habit of (*doing something*)
solicitar to ask for
solidario/a sympathetic (to a cause)
solista *m., f.* soloist

solitario/a solitary; lonely
sólo *adv.* only
solo/a *adj.* alone; sole; **café** (*m.*) **solo** black coffee; **sentirse (ie, i) solo/a** to feel lonely
soltar (ue) to let go, set free
soltero/a single
solterón *m.* bachelor
solución *f.* solution
solucionar to solve
sombrero hat
sombrío/a somber
someter to subject
sonar (ue) to sound; to ring
sonido sound
sonrisa smile
soñador(a) dreamy
soñar (ue) (con) to dream (about)
sopa soup
sopaipilla *fritter dipped in honey* (*Mex.*)
soportar to bear, put up with
sor *f.* sister (*used before the name of a nun*)
sorprendente surprising
sorprender to surprise; **sorprenderse** to be surprised
sorpresa surprise
sospechar to suspect
sospechoso/a suspicious
soviético/a *n.* Soviet, *adj.* Soviet (*of or from the Soviet Union*); **Unión** (*f.*) **Soviética** Soviet Union
su(s) *poss.* his, her, its, your (*form. s., pl.*), their
suave smooth, soft
súbdito/a citizen; subject
subir (a) to go up
subjuntivo (*gram.*) subjunctive
subrayar to underline
suceder to happen
sucesivamente successively
suceso event
sucesor(a) successor
sucio/a dirty
sucursal *f.* branch office
sudadera sweatshirt
Sudamérica South America
sudar to sweat
suegro/a father-in-law, mother-in-law; *m. pl.* in-laws
sueldo salary, pay
suelo floor, ground
sueño dream; sleep; **tener** (*irreg.*) **(mucho) sueño** to be (very) sleepy
suerte *f.* luck; **buena/mala suerte** good (bad) luck; **número de la suerte** lucky number; **por suerte** fortunately, luckily; **tener** (*irreg.*) **(buena) suerte** to be lucky, in luck; **tener** (*irreg.*) **mala suerte** to be unlucky
suéter *m.* sweater
suficiente enough, sufficient
suficientemente sufficiently, enough
sufrimiento suffering
sufrir to suffer
sugerencia suggestion
sugerir (ie, i) to suggest
suite *f.* suite
Suiza Switzerland
sumamente extremely
superar to get through; to overcome

superficie *f.* surface
superior: escuela superior high school
superlativo (*gram.*) superlative
supermercado supermarket
suplicar (qu) to implore, pray
supuesto: por supuesto of course
sur *m.* south; **polo sur** South Pole
sureste *m.* southeast
surgir (j) to present itself
surf *m.* surfing
suroeste *m.* southwest
surtido assortment
sustantivo (*gram.*) noun
sustituir (y) to substitute
sustituto/a *n., adj.* substitute
susto scare, fright
sutil subtle
sutileza subtlety
suyo/a(s) *poss.* your, of yours (*form. s., pl.*), his, of his; her, (of) hers; its; their, of theirs; **salirse con lo suyo** to get one's own way

T

tabaco tobacco
tabla table, list (*of figures, etc.*); board
tablavela windsurfing
taco taco (*tortilla filled with cheese, chicken, roast pork, etc.*) (*Mex.*)
taino/a *n. m., f.* Taino (*member of an extinct Indian people of the West Indies*); *adj.* Tainan
tajo cut; slash, gash
tal such (a); a certain (fellow) called; **como tal** as such; **con tal (de) que** so that; **¿qué tal?** how are you (doing)?; how about . . . ?; **¿qué tal si... ?** what if . . . ?; **tal como** just as, exactly the same as; **tal vez** perhaps, maybe
talento talent
taller *m.* shop (*for manufacturing or repair*); repair shop (*automobiles*); **taller de reparaciones** repair shop
tamal *m.* tamale (*dish made of corn meal, chicken or meat and chili wrapped in banana leaves or corn husk*)
tamarindo tamarind (*tropical fruit used to make juice*)
también also, too
tampoco neither, not either
tan as, so; **tan ... como** as . . . as; **tan pronto as como** as soon as
tanque *m.* (gas) tank
tanto *adv.* so much; **estar** (*irreg.*) **al tanto** to be informed, up to date; **mientras tanto** meanwhile; **no es para tanto** it's not that serious; **tanto como** as much as
tanto/a/os/as *adj.* as much/many; so much/many; **tanto/a/os/as ... como** as much . . . as
tapas hors d'oeuvres (*Sp.*)
tapatío: jarabe (*m.*) **tapatío** *popular Mexican dance known as Mexican hat dance in U.S.*
taquería taco stand
tardanza delay, tardiness
tardar to be long; to be or take a long time; **tardar (en)** + *inf.* to be or take a long time (to) (*do something*); **a**

más tardar at the latest
tarde *n. f.* afternoon, evening; **buenas tardes** good afternoon; **de (la) tarde** P.M., in the afternoon; **por la tarde** in the afternoon
tarde *adv.* late; **hacerse** (*irreg.*) **tarde** to be getting late; **llegar (gu) tarde** to arrive late; **más tarde** later; **se me hace tarde** it's getting late
tarea task; (*school*) assignment
tarifa rate, price
tarjeta de crédito credit card
tarjeta postal postcard
tasa rate; **tasa de desempleo** unemployment rate
taxi *m.* taxicab; **parada de taxis** taxi stand
taxista *m., f.* taxicab driver
taza cup
te *d.o.* you (*fam. s.*); *i.o.* to, for you (*fam. s.*); *refl. pron.* yourself (*fam. s.*)
té *m.* tea
teatral theatrical
teatro theater; **ir** (*irreg.*) **a una función de teatro** to go to a show at the theater; **obra de teatro** play, dramatic work; **sala de teatro** theater; **teatro campesino** farm workers' theater
telefonear to telephone
telefónico/a *adj.* telephone; **llamada telefónica** telephone call
teléfono telephone; **por teléfono** by telephone
telegrama *m.* telegram
telenovela soap opera
tele(visión) *f.* television (*broadcasting medium*); **hacer** (*irreg.*) **televisión** to work in television; **mirar (la) televisión** to watch television
televisor *m.* television set
telón *m.* (*theater*) curtain
tema *m.* theme, topic
temática collection of themes
temer to fear, be afraid of
temor *m.* fear
temperatura temperature; **¿a cuánto estaba la temperatura?** how high was the temperature?; **la temperatura está a ... grados** the temperature is . . . degrees; **tomarle (a alguien) la temperatura** to take (someone's) temperature
tempestuoso/a tempestuous
templado/a temperate, moderate
templo temple
temporada period (*of time*)
temprano early
tender (ie) to tend, have a tendency
tenedor *m.* fork
tener (*irreg.*) to have; **(no) tener sentido** (not) to make sense; **que tenga (un) buen viaje** have a nice trip; **tener ... años** to be . . . years old; **tener un aire ...** to be like, resemble . . . ; **tener (buena) suerte** to be lucky, in luck; **tener celos (de)** to be jealous (of); **tener como fin** to have as a goal; **tener cuidado** to be careful; **tener la culpa (de)** to be to blame (for); to be guilty (of); **tener en cuenta** to keep in mind; **tenerle**

envidia (a alguien) to envy (someone); **tener éxito** to be successful; **tener una fiebre** to have a fever; **tener ganas de** + *inf.* to feel like (*doing something*); **tener hambre** to be hungry; **tener lugar** to take place; **tener mala suerte** to be unlucky; **tener miedo** to be afraid; **tener (mucha) sed** to be (very) thirsty; **tener (mucho) calor/frío** to be (very) hot/cold; **tener (mucho) sueño** to be (very) sleepy; **tener prisa (por** + *inf.)* to be in a hurry (*to do something*); **tener que** + *inf.* to have to (*do something*); **tener que ver con** to have to do with, be related to (*a topic*); **tener (toda la) razón** to be (absolutely) right

tenis *m.* tennis; **cancha de tenis** tennis court; **zapatos de tenis** tennis shoes

tensión *f.* tension

tenso/a tense

tentar (ie) to tempt

teñir (i, i) to dye, tint

teoría theory; **en teoría** in theory

terapia therapy

tercer, tercero/a *n., adj.* third

terco/a stubborn

termal *adj.* thermal

terminación *f.* end; ending

terminar to end, be over; **al terminar ...** when . . . is/was over; **terminar con** to finish (*something*); **terminar por** + *inf.* to finish or end up by (*doing something*)

termómetro thermometer

ternera veal

ternura tenderness

terraza terrace

terremoto earthquake

terreno terrain

terrible: ¡qué terrible! how terrible!

territorio territory

testamento will, testament

testigo *m., f.* witness

texano/a Texan

texto text; **libro de texto** textbook

ti *obj. of prep.* you (*fam. s.*); **contigo** with you

tiempo time; weather; (*gram.*) tense; **al mismo tiempo** at the same time; **al poco tiempo** shortly after; **¿cuánto tiempo hace que ... ?** how long has it been that . . . ?; **hace buen/mal tiempo** it's good (bad) weather; **¿qué tiempo hace?** what's the weather like?; **tiempo libre** free time, spare time; **todo el tiempo** all the time, the whole time, all along

tienda store, shop; **tienda de antigüedades** antique store; **tienda de comestibles** food store; **tienda de ropa para hombres/mujeres** men's/women's clothing store

tierra land, earth

tigre *m.* tiger

timbre *m.* stamp (*Mex.*)

tímido/a timid

tinto: vino tinto red wine

tío/a uncle, aunt; *m. pl.* uncles and aunts

típico/a typical

tipo type, kind; guy

tiranía tyranny

tirano tyrant

tirar to throw out; **tirarse** to throw, cast oneself

tiro: al tiro immediately

titi *fam. form of* **tía**

título title; diploma, degree; **título universitario** university degree

tocar (qu) to touch; to play (*musical instrument*); **tocar la puerta** to knock on the door; **tocarle (a alguien)** to be someone's turn; to be coming (to someone)

tocino bacon

todavía still, yet

todo *n.* whole; all, everything; **ante todo** above all; **sobre todo** above all

todo/a *adj.* all, every; **de todas formas** in any case; **por todas partes** all over, everywhere; **todo el tiempo** all the time, the whole time, all along; **todo el mundo** the whole world; everybody; **todos los días** every day

tolerancia tolerance

tolerante tolerant

tolerar to tolerate

tomar to take; to have something to eat or drink; **tomar el aire** to get some fresh air, go for a walk; **tomar un autobús (barco, avión, taxi, tren)** to take a bus (ship, plane, taxi, train); **tomar decisiones** to make decisions; **tomar en serio** to take seriously; **tomar una foto(grafía)** to take a picture, photograph; **tomar el pulso** to feel the pulse; **tomar una siesta** to take a siesta, nap; **tomar el sol** to sunbathe; **tomarle (a alguien) la temperatura** to take (someone's) temperature; **tomarle cariño (a alguien)** to start to have affection for (someone); **tomarle el pelo (a alguien)** to tease (someone)

tomate *m.* tomato; **salsa de tomate** ketchup

tono tone

tontería foolishness; *pl.* nonsense

tonto/a *n.* fool; *adj.* stupid, dumb; **hacerse** (*irreg.*) **el tonto** to play dumb

toque *m.* touch

tormenta tempest, storm

toro bull

toronja grapefruit

torre *f.* tower

tortilla *thin unleavened cornmeal or flour pancake* (*Mex.*); *egg and potato omelette* (*Sp.*); **tortilla arrollada** rolled tortilla

tortillería tortilla shop

tortuga turtle; tortoise

torturar to torture

tos *f.* cough

tostada slice of toast

tostado/a toasted; **pan** (*m.*) **tostado** toast

totalitario/a totalitarian

trabajador(a) *n.* worker; *adj.* hardworking; **clase** (*f.*) **trabajadora** working class

trabajar to work; **trabajar de** to work as; **trabajar de noche** to work at night

trabajo work; school paper, report; job; **costarle (ue) trabajo** to be hard, take a lot of effort; **Día** (*m.*) **del Trabajo** Labor Day; **oferta de trabajo** job offer

trabalenguas *m. s.* tongue twister

tradición *f.* tradition

tradicional traditional

traer (*irreg.*) to bring

tráfico traffic

tragamonedas: máquina tragamonedas slot machine

tragedia tragedy

trágico/a tragic

trago drink

traje *m.* suit; dress, costume; **traje de baño** bathing suit

tranquilidad *f.* tranquility

tranquilo/a calm, peaceful; quiet

transbordador (*m.*) **espacial** space ship; space shuttle

transcripción *f.* transcription

transformarse to be or become transformed

transición *f.* transition

transportación: medios (*pl.*) **de transportación** means of transportation

transporte: medio de transporte means of transportation

tras *prep.* after

trasatlántico/a transatlantic

trasladar(se) to move

trastorno upheaval; disturbance; disruption

tratamiento treatment

tratar to treat; to deal with; **tratar de** + *inf.* to try to (*do something*); **tratar de tú** to use informal address (**tú**) in conversation; **tratarse de** to be a question of

traumático/a traumatic

través: a través de through, across

travieso/a mischievous, naughty

trazar (c) to trace; to plan, design; to create, form

trece thirteen

treinta thirty

tremendo/a tremendous

tren *m.* train; **estación** (*f.*) **del tren** train station

tres three

trescientos/as three hundred

triángulo triangle

tribu *f.* tribe

trimestre *m.* (*school*) quarter

triste sad; **¡qué triste!** how sad!

tristeza sadness

triunfar to triumph

triunfo triumph

trono throne

tropas troops

tropical: bosque (*m.*) **tropical** tropical forest

Trópico de Capricornio Tropic of Capricorn

tu(s) *poss.* your (*fam. s.*)

tú *sub. pron.* you (*fam. s.*); **tratar de tú** to use informal address (**tú**) in conversation

tubo tube, pipe
tumba tomb
tumultuoso/a tumultuous
tuna *group of student serenaders*
túnel *m.* tunnel
tungsteno tungsten
turismo tourism
turista *n. m., f.* tourist
turístico/a *adj.* tourist; **atracción** (*f.*) **turística** tourist attraction; **clase** (*f.*) **turística** tourist class; **guía** (*m., f.*) **turístico/a** tourist guide; **plano turístico** map (*of a city*)
tutear to use the informal address (**tú**) in conversation
tuteo use of the familiar form (*tú*) of address
tuyo/a(s) *poss.* your, of yours

U

u or (*used instead of* **o** *before words beginning with* **o** *or* **ho**)
últimamente lately
último/a last, final, ultimate; latest; **por primera vez** for the first time; **por última vez** for the last time; **última vez** last time; **últimas noticias** latest news
ultrafeminista ultrafeminist
un, uno/a one; a, an (*indefinite article*); *pl.* some, a few, several
UNAM Universidad Nacional Autónoma de México
unicelular *adj.* unicellular
único/a unique; only; **hijo/a único/a** only child
unidad *f.* unity; unit
unido/a united; close-knit, close; **ser unido/a** to be united, close-knit, close; **Estados Unidos** United States
Unión (*f.*) **Soviética** Soviet Union
unir(se) to unite; to join
universidad *f.* university
universitario/a *adj.* university; **título universitario** university degree; **zona universitaria** university campus, grounds
urbano/a urban; urbane
urgencia: de urgencia emergency; **hospital** (*m.*) **de urgencia** emergency hospital
urgente urgent
urna ballot box
usar *v.* to use
uso *n.* use
usted (Ud., Vd.) *sub. pron.* you (*form. s.*); *obj. of prep.* you (*form. s.*)
ustedes (Uds., Vds.) *sub. pron.* you (*form. pl.*); *obj. of prep.* you (*form. pl.*)
útil *adj.* useful
utilizar (c) to utilize, use, make use of
uva grape

V

va: ¡qué va! *interj.* don't put me on!
vaca cow; **carne** (*f.*) **de vaca** beef
vacaciones *f. pl.* vacation
vacilar to vacillate
vacío emptiness
vacuna vaccine
vago/a vague

vagón *m.* wagon
valenciano/a *n., adj.* Valencian
valentía bravery
Valentín: Día (*m.*) **de San Valentín** St. Valentine's Day
valer (*irreg.*) to be worth; **(no) vale la pena** it's (not) worth the trouble; **vale** great, OK
válido/a valid
valiente brave
valioso/a valuable, highly esteemed
valle *m.* valley
valor *m.* worth, value; *pl.* values
valorar to value
¿vamos? shall we go; **¡vamos!** *interj.* let's go!
vanguardia: de vanguardia avant-garde
vanidoso/a vain, conceited
variación *f.* variation, change
variado/a varied, diverse
variar to vary, change
variedad *f.* variety
varios/as various; several
vasco: País (*m.*) **Vasco** Basque region (*of Spain*)
vascuense *m.* Basque language
vaso (*drinking*) glass
vasto/a vast
vecino/a *n.* neighbor; *adj.* neighboring
vegetación *f.* vegetation
vegetariano/a *n.* vegetarian
veinte twenty
veintún, veintiuno twenty-one
vela sail
velada evening
vellón *m.* five-cent piece (*P.R.*); nickel (*U.S.*)
velorio wake, vigil
vendedor(a) salesclerk
vender to sell; **se vende(n)** for sale
venerar to venerate
venida arrival; return
venidero/a *adj.* coming, future
venir (*irreg.*) to come; **que viene** coming, next
venta sale; **en venta** for sale
ventaja advantage
ventana window
ver (*irreg.*) to see; **a ver** let's see, let's have a look; **tener** (*irreg.*) **que ver con** to have to do with; be related to (*a topic*)
verano summer
verbo verb
verdad *f.* truth; **¿de verdad?** really?; **decir** (*irreg.*) **la verdad** to tell the truth; **¿verdad?** right?
verdadero/a true, real
verde green; **judía verde** string bean (*Sp.*); **zona verde** open space; public park
verduras greens, vegetables
vergüenza shame; **¡qué vergüenza!** *interj.* how embarrassing! **tener** (*irreg.*) **vergüenza** to be embarrassed
verificar (qu) to verify; to check
versión *f.* version
verso verse
vértigo vertigo
vestido dress; suit
vestir(se) (i, i) to get dressed, to dress

veterinario/a veterinarian
vez *f.* (*pl.* **veces**) time, occasion; **a la vez** at the same time; **a veces** at times, sometimes; **alguna vez** ever; **cada vez más** more and more; **de una vez** now, right away; **de vez en cuando** sometimes; **en vez de** instead of; **érase una vez** once upon a time; **muchas veces** often; **otra vez** again; **pocas veces** seldom; **(por) primera vez** (for the) first time; **por última vez** for the last time; **tal vez** perhaps, maybe; **última vez** last time; **una vez** once; **una vez al año** once a year; **una vez más** one more time
viajar to travel
viaje *m.* trip; **hacer** (*irreg.*) **un viaje** to take a trip; **que tenga (un) buen viaje** have a nice trip
viajero/a traveler; **cheque** (*m.*) **de viajero** traveler's check
viajes: agencia de viajes travel agency; **agente** (*m., f.*) **de viajes** travel agent
vicepresidente/a vice-president
vicio bad habit, vice
vicioso/a vicious
víctima victim
victoria victory
vida life; **llevar una vida ...** to lead a . . . life; **vida diaria** daily life; **vida privada** personal life
vídeo: sacar (qu) vídeos to take videos
videocasetera VCR
videograbadora VCR
viejo/a *n.* old woman, old man; *adj.* old; **llegar (gu) a viejo/a** to get to be old
viene: que viene coming, next
viento wind; **hace (mucho) viento** it's (very) windy; **molino de viento** windmill
viernes *m. s.* Friday
vietnamés, vietnamesa *n. adj.* Vietnamese
vigencia force, effect
vigente in force; in vogue; **seguir (i, i) (g) vigente** to continue to be viable
vigilar to watch; to keep an eye on
vino wine; **vino blanco** white wine; **vino tinto** red wine
viña vineyard
viñador(a) grape grower
violación *f.* violation; rape
violado/a violated
violar to violate; to rape
violencia violence
violento/a violent
violincelista *m., f.* cellist
violinista *m., f.* violinist
virar to turn (*P.R.*)
virgen *f.* virgin; **Virgen María** Virgin Mary
visión *f.* vision
visita *f.* visit; visitor
visitante *m., f.* visitor
visitar to visit
víspera the night before
vista view (of); sight; **amor** (*m.*) **a primera vista** love at first sight; **punto de vista** point of view

vistazo glance
visto: por lo visto evidently
vitalidad *f.* vitality
vitamina vitamin
viudo/a widower/widow
vivido/a lived; experienced
vivienda dwelling, house; housing
vivir to live; **vivir de** to live off of, support oneself by
vivo/a alive, live, living
vocabulario vocabulary
vocación *f.* vocation
volar (ue) to fly
volcán *m.* volcano
vólibol *m.* volleyball
volumen *m.* volume
voluntad *f.* will, willingness
volver (ue) (*p.p.* **vuelto/a**) to return; **volver a** + *inf.* to do (*something*) again; **volverse** to become, turn into; **volverse loco/a** to go crazy
vos *sub. pron. s. and pl.* you (*substitute for* **tú**) (*Arg.*)
vosotros/as *sub. pron.* you (*fam. pl. Sp.*); *obj. of prep.* you (*fam. pl. Sp.*)
votar to vote
voto vote

voz (*pl.* **voces**) *f.* voice; **en voz alta** out loud
vuelo flight
vuelta return; **a la vuelta** around the corner; **billete** (*m.*) **/pasaje** (*m.*) **de ida y vuelta** round trip ticket (fare); **estar** (*irreg.*) **de vuelta** to be back; to have returned; **pasaje** (*m.*) **de ida y vuelta** round trip fare
vuestro/a(s) *poss.* your (*fam. pl. Sp.*); of yours (*fam. pl. Sp.*)

X

X: rayos X X rays; **sacar (qu) rayos X** to take X rays
xenofobia xenophobia
xerografía xerography (*system for copying printed material*)
xilófono xylophone

Y

y and; **¿y qué?** so what?; what do you want me to do?
ya already; now; later, later on; right away, at once; at last; **ya lo creo** of course; **ya no** no longer; **ya que** since
yema yolk

yerba grass
yerno son-in-law
yo *sub. pron.* I
yucateco/a *from the Yucatan peninsula*

Z

zanahoria carrot
zapatería shoe store
zapatero/a shoemaker
zapato shoe; **zapatos de tenis** tennis shoes
zar *m.* czar
zarina czarina
zarzuela *Spanish musical comedy or operetta*
zona zone; neighborhood; **zona universitaria** university campus, grounds; **zona verde** open space; public park
zoológico: jardín (*m.*) **zoológico** zoo; **parque** (*m.*) **zoológico** zoo
zumo juice (*Sp.*)
zurdo/a left-handed

INDEX OF CHARACTERS

This index includes the names of most of the characters who appear in *Destinos*, alphabetized by their first name in most cases. Photographs are included for many characters as well, along with a brief description of them and a city in which they live.

Alfredo Sánchez, Madrid, España. A reporter who meets Raquel.

Ángel Castillo del Valle, Buenos Aires, Argentina. Son of Fernando Castillo Saavedra and Rosario del Valle.

Ángela Castillo Soto, San Juan, Puerto Rico. Daughter of Ángel Castillo and María Luisa Soto.

el Dr. Arturo Iglesias, Buenos Aires, Argentina. A psychiatrist and the son of Rosario and Martín Iglesias.

Blanca Núñez, San Juan, Puerto Rico. A real estate agent.

Carlitos Castillo, Miami, Florida. Son of Carlos and Gloria and grandson of don Fernando.

Carlos Castillo Márquez, Miami, Florida. One of don Fernando's sons and director of the Miami office of the family company.

Carlos Soto Contreras, San Juan, Puerto Rico. One of Ángela's uncles.

Carmen Contreras de Soto, San Germán, Puerto Rico. Ángela and Roberto's grandmother.

Carmen Márquez de Castillo, La Gavia, México. Second wife of don Fernando and mother of their four children, Ramón, Carlos, Mercedes, and Juan.

Carmen Soto, San Juan, Puerto Rico. One of Ángela's aunts.

el ciego, Sevilla, España. He sells lottery tickets.

Cirilo, Estancia Santa Susana, Argentina. A gaucho and ex-employee of Rosario.

Consuelo Castillo, La Gavia, México. Don Fernando's daughter-in-law, she lives at La Gavia with her husband Ramón and daughter Maricarmen.

Dolores Acevedo, San Germán, Puerto Rico. A longtime household employee of doña Carmen and her family.

Elena Ramírez de Ruiz, Sevilla, España. Daughter-in-law of Teresa Suárez and mother of Miguel and Jaime. Her husband is Miguel Ruiz.

Federico Ruiz Suárez, Madrid, España. Son of Teresa Suárez, Federico is a guitar maker.

Fernando Castillo Saavedra, La Gavia, México. Patriarch of the Castillo family, don Fernando initiates the investigation that is carried out by Raquel Rodríguez.

Flora, Buenos Aires, Argentina. Wife of José, a sailor.

Francisco (Pancho) Rodríguez Trujillo. *See* Pancho Rodríguez Trujillo.

Gloria Castillo, Miami, Florida. Carlos's wife and mother of Juanita and Carlitos.

Guillermo, New York, New York. Pati's assistant director at the university theater.

Héctor Condotti, Buenos Aires, Argentina. An experienced sailor and friend of Ángel.

Isabel Santiago, San Juan, Puerto Rico. A bank executive.

Jaime Ruiz Ramírez, Sevilla, España. Grandson of Teresa Suárez and son of Miguel Ruiz.

Jaime Soto Contreras, San Juan, Puerto Rico. One of Ángela's uncles.

Jorge Alonso, San Juan, Puerto Rico. Ángela's boyfriend and a professor of theater at the University of Puerto Rico.

José, Buenos Aires, Argentina. A sailor and friend of Héctor.

Juan Castillo Márquez, New York, New York. The youngest child of don Fernando and a professor of literature at New York University; married to Pati.

Juanita Castillo, Miami, Florida. Daughter of Carlos and Gloria.

el Dr. Julio Morelos, Toluca, México. The Castillo family physician.

Laura Soto, San Juan, Puerto Rico. One of Ángela's cousins and the daughter of tío Jaime.

Luis Villarreal, Los Angeles, California. The former boyfriend of Raquel.

Lupe, La Gavia, México. A household employee of the Castillo family at La Gavia.

Manuel Díaz, Sevilla/Madrid, España. A schoolteacher who meets Raquel.

Manuel Domínguez, New York, New York. The producer of Pati's current play.

María, Madrid, España. Federico's girlfriend, who teaches flamenco dancing.

María Luisa Soto de Castillo, San Juan, Puerto Rico. Daughter of doña Carmen and wife of Ángel Castillo.

María Orozco de Rodríguez, Los Angeles, California. Raquel's mother.

la Hermana María Teresa, un pueblo, México. A nun who gives Ángela and Raquel a place to rest and bathe.

Maricarmen Castillo, La Gavia, México. Daughter of Ramón and Consuelo.

Mario, Buenos Aires, Argentina. A storekeeper in the La Boca district.

Martín Iglesias, Buenos Aires, Argentina. Second husband of Rosario, stepfather of Ángel Castillo, and father of Arturo Iglesias.

Mercedes Castillo de Martínez, La Gavia, México. Don Fernando's only daughter, who lives at La Gavia with her father.

Miguel Ruiz Ramírez, Sevilla, España. Grandson of Teresa Suárez and son of Miguel Ruiz.

Miguel Ruiz Suárez, Sevilla, España. Son of Teresa Suárez and father of Miguel and Jaime.

Ofelia, Miami, Florida. Carlos's Cuban-born secretary.

Olga Soto Contreras, San Juan, Puerto Rico. One of Ángela's aunts.

Osito, Sevilla, España. A dog purchased by Miguel and Elena Ruiz for their sons, Miguel and Jaime.

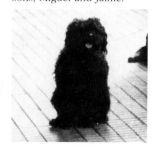

Pancho Rodríguez Trujillo, Los Angeles, California. Raquel's father.

Ramón Castillo Márquez, La Gavia, México. The oldest son of don Fernando. He runs Castillo Saavedra, S.A.

Roberto García, Sevilla, España. A taxi driver from the Triana district.

el Dr. Salazar, Guadalajara, México. A specialist who examines don Fernando.

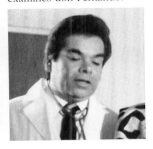

Pati Castillo, New York, New York. The wife of Juan and professor of theater at New York University, as well as a writer/director.

Raquel Rodríguez Orozco, Los Angeles, California. A lawyer contracted by Pedro Castillo to conduct the investigation.

el Padre Rodrigo, un pueblo, México. A priest who offers comfort to Raquel and Ángela.

Teresa Suárez, Madrid, España. Friend of Rosario who writes the letter to don Fernando that initiates the investigation.

Pedro Castillo Saavedra, México, D.F., México. Law professor at the National University of México and brother of don Fernando.

Roberto Castillo Soto, San Juan, Puerto Rico. Son of Ángel Castillo and María Luisa Soto.

Rosario del Valle de Iglesias, Buenos Aires, Argentina. First wife of don Fernando Castillo.

Virginia López Estrada, México, D.F., México. A real estate agent.

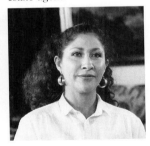

Pepe, Sevilla, España. A barber in Sevilla.

Index

About the Authors

Bill VanPatten is Professor of Spanish and Second Language Acquisition at the University of Illinois at Chicago. He has held a variety of administrative positions and is currently the Director of Spanish Basic Language. He received his Ph.D. in Hispanic Linguistics from the University of Texas at Austin in 1983. His areas of research are input and input processing in second language acquisition and the acquisition of Spanish syntax and morphology. He has published widely in the fields of second language acquisition and second language teaching and is a frequent conference speaker and presenter. He is the lead author of *Vistazos* (2002, McGraw-Hill) and *¿Sabías que... ?* (2000, McGraw-Hill). He is also the lead author and designer of *Destinos*, a television series for PBS, is the co-author with James F. Lee of *Making Communicative Language Teaching Happen* (1995, McGraw-Hill), and is the author of *Input Processing and Grammar Instruction: Theory and Research* (1996, Ablex). In addition to his involvement in a variety of research projects, Dr. VanPatten is currently working on a book called *Theories in Second Language Acquisition*.

Martha Alford Marks received her Ph.D. in Spanish Literature from Northwestern University in 1978. She subsequently served on the faculties of Kalamazoo College and Northwestern University, where she coordinated the first- and second-year Spanish programs, supervised teaching assistants, appeared consistently on the Faculty Honor Roll, and won an Outstanding Teaching Award. Nationally known for her work as an ACTFL Oral Proficiency tester and trainer, Dr. Marks is also the co-author of several other McGraw-Hill Spanish textbooks for the college level, including *¿Qué tal?* and *Al corriente*.

Richard V. Teschner has been a professor of Language and Linguistics at the University of Texas-El Paso since 1976. His 1972 Ph.D. in Spanish Linguistics is from the University of Wisconsin-Madison. He has published over 50 articles and a dozen monographs, most recently *CUBRE: Curso breve de gramática española* (McGraw-Hill College Custom) and *El triple diccionario de la lengua española (TRIDIC)*, a CD-ROM (Star-Byte, Inc.). In 1988 he was President of the American Association of Teachers of Spanish and Portuguese and the Linguistic Association of the Southwest.